Con

MW00462532

SECOND EDITION

Also available from Bloomsbury Academic:

International Conflict Resolution, Charles Hauss
A Handbook of Conflict Resolution, Chris Mitchell and Michael Banks
*Capturing the Complexity of Conflict: Dealing with Violent Ethnic
    Conflicts of the Post-Cold War Era*, Dennis J. D. Sandole
Conflict Resolved, Alan Tidwell

CONFLICT

From Analysis to Intervention

SECOND EDITION

Sandra Cheldelin, Daniel Druckman,
and Larissa Fast (editors)

B L O O M S B U R Y

LONDON · NEW DELHI · NEW YORK · SYDNEY

Bloomsbury Academic
An imprint of Bloomsbury Publishing Plc

50 Bedford Square   175 Fifth Avenue
London   New York
WC1B 3DP   NY 10010
UK   USA

www.bloomsbury.com

First published in 2003 by the Continuum International Publishing Group Ltd
Updated and revised edition first published 2008
Reprinted by Bloomsbury Academic 2012

British Library Cataloguing-in-Publication Data
A catalogue record for this book is available from the British Library.

ISBN: HB: 978-0-8264-9570-9
PB: 978-0-8264-9571-6

Library of Congress Cataloging-in-Publication Data
A catalog record for this book is available from the Library of Congress.

Printed and bound in the United States of America

Contents

Foreword

Herbert C. Kelman

Fourteen years ago, faculty members and associates of the Institute for Conflict Analysis and Resolution (ICAR) at George Mason University pooled their efforts to produce a book on the theory and practice of conflict resolution, which presented the state of the art as of that time.[1] The present volume is an entirely new venture, with a different structure and thematic emphasis, but it shares many of the characteristics of the earlier book. It too takes advantage of the rich human resources that ICAR represents; indeed, half of the authors in this book also appeared in the 1993 volume. Expanding on the earlier book's goal of integrating theory and practice, the present volume strives for the integration of theory, research, and practice – what the editors describe as the three "legs" of the field. Like the earlier volume, this book took shape in the context of a graduate seminar in which the authors presented the ideas that were ultimately transformed into their chapters. And finally, like the earlier volume, the present book presents the state of the art in this field as of the time of publication.

Much has happened in the decade between the publication of the two volumes. The easiest way to capture the substantive developments in theory and practice in recent years is to note that the concepts of peace-building, conflict transformation, and reconciliation – which are discussed extensively in the present book – do not even appear in the index of the 1993 volume. Organizationally, too, there have been many new

[1] D. J. D. Sandole and H. van der Merwe (eds), *Conflict Resolution, Theory and Practice: Integration and Application*. Manchester and New York: Manchester University Press, 1993.

developments, with the growth of academic programs, practice organizations, networks, and professional associations in conflict resolution.

George Mason University was one of the earliest institutions to establish (in 1981) a graduate training program in conflict resolution, which eventually took on the name of ICAR. It was the first university in the world to offer a Ph.D. in the field. For the past two decades, I have been directing students who consulted me about advanced training in conflict resolution to GMU. In fact, even when students came to inquire about working with me at Harvard, I would lay out the following options for them: If they wanted to work for a Ph.D. in social psychology with a specialization in conflict resolution, then they should apply to my department and I would do my best to provide them with relevant training and to guide them to other valuable resources – especially in the field of negotiation – available at Harvard and elsewhere in the Boston area. If, however, they wanted to be part of a program explicitly dedicated to training in conflict analysis and resolution, then they should apply to George Mason! When students come to consult me now, I am in the fortunate position of being able to list a number of high-quality, dedicated programs in conflict resolution, but ICAR still tops my list as the pre-eminent program in the field.

The book reflects what I see as the hallmark of ICAR's contribution to the field: an active awareness of the *multiplicity* of tasks to which theory, research, and practice must be addressed, and of the *diversity* of approaches toward addressing these tasks. There are, to be sure, many common threads that run though most of the book. The authors seem to be committed, by and large, to conflict resolution as a non-adversarial, analytical, problem-solving process that involves direct participation by the parties with the help of professionally trained practitioners and that focuses on both identity and structure as key issues to be addressed in analysis and resolution of conflict. The influence of John Burton and others who focus on deep-rooted conflict, human-needs theory, and efforts to eliminate the systemic causes of violent conflict remains evident in this volume. Still, the book does not espouse a single point of view. Mindful of the different levels of conflict, the different phases of a given conflict, and the different functions of intervention, the authors collectively recognize the need for multiple approaches to conflict analysis and resolution. And, indeed, the chapters of the book – like the ICAR faculty members who wrote them – represent a diversity of approaches, based in different disciplinary backgrounds, different theoretical models, different research styles, and different forms of practice.

The multiplicity of tasks and diversity of approaches that are inevitable – and indeed healthy – features of the landscape we work in make it difficult to integrate theory, research, and practice. This integration is a central goal for ICAR, as it is for others of us in the field who are committed to the scholar–practitioner model. The hope is that the work of theorists and researchers in the field will increasingly be informed by the experiences of practice and be able, in turn, to inform the practice of conflict resolution. Similarly, the hope is that practitioners will be able to utilize theory and research in their practice and in the evaluation and further development of that practice. The primary purpose of this book is to contribute to the integration of theory, research, and practice. The editors are fully aware of the fact that this integration is an ongoing process and cannot be achieved in a single volume published at a finite point in time. Their purpose has been to narrow the gap between the three activities, to point to the possibilities of integration, and to experiment with ways of promoting this integration, as discussed in the final chapter prepared by Daniel Druckman. In this purpose, they and their authors have succeeded admirably.

Editors' Biographies

Sandra Cheldelin is the Vernon M. and Minnie I. Lynch Professor of Conflict Resolution at the Institute for Conflict Analysis and Resolution at George Mason University. She was the former Director of the Institute and has held faculty and administrative appointments at several colleges and universities including Provost at the McGregor School of Antioch University, Academic Dean at the California School of Professional Psychology (Berkeley campus), and Director of Educational Development at Ohio University College of Osteopathic Medicine. She is an active reflective practitioner, psychologist, and expert in organizational conflict. She has worked with more than 150 organizations, and is often keynote speaker and invited lecturer on workplace issues of violence, change, race, gender, and conflict. She has facilitated large-scale interethnic and interfaith community dialogues on topics of fear, terrorism, violence, and suspicion, and has convened large and small groups to build community resilience. In addition to authoring chapters and journal articles, she is coauthor (with Ann Lucas) of *Conflict Resolution* (Jossey Bass, 2004). She has served on a variety of conflict resolution-related boards.

Daniel Druckman is Professor in the Department of Public and International Affairs at George Mason University and at the Australian Centre for Peace and Conflict Studies, University of Queensland (Brisbane, Australia). He has been the Vernon M. and Minnie I. Lynch Professor of Conflict Resolution and coordinator of the doctoral program at ICAR. Previously he directed programs at the U.S. National Research Council and held senior positions at Mathematica Inc. and at Booz.Allen and Hamilton. He has published widely on such topics as negotiating behavior, nationalism and group identity, nonverbal communication, peacekeeping, political stability, human performance, and research methodologies. He received the 1995 Otto Klineberg Award for Intercultural and International Relations from the Society for the Psychological Study of Social Issues, a Teaching Excellence award in 1998 from George Mason, and best article (2001) and best book (2004–2005 for *Doing Research: Methods of Inquiry for Conflict Analysis*) awards from the International Association for Conflict Management (IACM). He currently sits on the boards of eight journals and is an Associate Editor of *Simulation & Gaming*, the *Negotiation Journal*, and *Group Decision and Negotiation*. He is the recipient of the 2003 Lifetime Achievement Award from the IACM.

Larissa Fast earned her Ph.D. (2002) from the Institute for Conflict Analysis and Resolution (ICAR) at George Mason University in Fairfax, Virginia. She is Assistant Professor of Conflict Resolution at the Kroc Institute for International Peace Studies, University of Notre Dame. Her current research focuses on humanitarian security, humanitarian politics, development and conflict, and peace-building. She has worked for several international development NGOs, both in the United States and in Africa, as a project manager, consultant, and conflict analyst. In addition, she has trained individuals and organizations in conflict analysis and resolution. She has received support for her research on humanitarian security from the United States Institute of Peace, and is currently working on a book manuscript on this topic. Her publications include articles in *Disasters*, the *Journal of Peacebuilding and Development*, *Peace and Change*, and *International Negotiation*.

Notes on Contributors

Kevin Avruch is Professor of Conflict Resolution and Anthropology and Associate Director of ICAR. He is also senior fellow in the Conflict Resolution and Peace Operations Policy Program in the School of Public Policy at George Mason University. His most recent books include *Culture and Conflict Resolution* (1998) and *Information Campaigns for Peace Operations* (2000).

Alex J. Bellamy is Senior Lecturer in Peace and Conflict Studies at the University of Queensland, UK. He is co-author of *Understanding Peacekeeping* (Polity, 2004) and co-editor of *Peace Operations and Global Order* (Routledge, 2005).

Peter W. Black is Emeritus Professor of Anthropology at George Mason University, and earned his undergraduate degree in government from Columbia University and his M.A. and Ph.D. in anthropology from the University of California at San Diego. He was a member of the group which founded ICAR and teaches an occasional course in the Institute. A specialist in the cultures of the Pacific Islands, his most recent project involves the repatriation of cultural knowledge to the Republic of Palau via the Internet.

Johannes "Jannie" Botes is Associate Professor and Director of the Program on Negotiation and Conflict Management at the University of Baltimore (UB). He has published articles on communication and conflict (focusing on the role of the media in national and international conflict and conflict resolution), conflict transformation, informal third party roles, and conflict resolution in Africa. He holds a Ph.D. from the Institute for Conflict Analysis and Resolution (ICAR) where he was teaching as a visiting professor when this book was conceived.

Dr. Sara Cobb is Director of the Institute for Conflict Analysis and Resolution (ICAR) at George Mason University. Dr. Cobb has a Ph.D. in communication from the University of Massachusetts, Amherst. She has published widely in communication studies and legal studies, supported by grants from the Ford Foundation and the U.N. High Commission on Refugees. She has held either administrative or academic positions at a variety of research institutions, including the Harvard Law School, the University of California, Santa Barbara, and the University of Connecticut. She has consulted to a host of family-owned businesses in North and South America, as well as to public and private organizations, including the U.N. High Commission on Refugees, La Caxia Bank, and Exxon, to name a few.

Tamra Pearson d'Estrée is Henry R. Luce Professor of Conflict Resolution at the University of Denver, and received her Ph.D. in social psychology from Harvard University. Dr. d'Estrée's research interests include social identity, intergroup relations, and conflict resolution process, as well as evaluation research. Her forthcoming book (with Bonnie Colby) is entitled *Braving the Currents: Lessons in Environmental Conflict Resolution from the River Basins of the American West*. She has facilitated interactive problem-solving workshops in various intercommunal contexts, and has led conflict resolution trainings in Europe, the Middle East, and countries of the former Soviet Union.

Ho-Won Jeong is Associate Professor of Conflict Resolution, George Mason University. He has published several books, including *Peace and Conflict Studies: An Introduction* (2000), *Conflict Resolution: Dynamics, Process and Structure* (1999) and the *New Agenda for Peace Research* (1999), *Global Environmental Policies* (2001), and *Approaches to Peace Building* (2002). He is also a senior editor of the *International Journal of Peace Studies*.

Terrence Lyons is Associate Professor at the Institute for Conflict Analysis and Resolution (ICAR), George Mason University, Fairfax, Virginia. He received his Ph.D. from the Johns Hopkins University School of Advanced International Studies in 1993 and worked at the Brookings Institution and the International Peace Research Institute,

Oslo, prior to joining the ICAR faculty. Among Lyons's publications are *Voting for Peace: Postconflict Elections in Liberia* (Brookings, 1999) and *Sovereignty as Responsibility: Conflict Management in Africa* (co-author, Brookings, 1996).

Christopher Mitchell is the Drucie French Cumbie Professor of Conflict Analysis at the Institute for Conflict Analysis and Resolution (ICAR), George Mason University, and has undertaken practical intervention work in Cyprus, the Middle East, Liberia, Moldova and the Horn of Africa. Most recently he is the author of *Gestures of Conciliation* (London/New York: Macmillan/St. Martin's Press, 2000).

Susan Allen Nan is Assistant Professor at the Institute for Conflict Analysis and Resolution at George Mason University. Her current research focuses on intermediary roles, coordination, networks, and holistic peace processes. Prior to taking on her current faculty position, she engaged in conflict resolution practice at the Alliance for Conflict Transformation and at The Carter Center, and taught conflict resolution at American University. In 2000 she received her Ph.D. in Conflict Analysis and Resolution from George Mason University.

Agnieszka Paczynska is Assistant Professor at the Institute for Conflict Analysis and Resolution and associate faculty at the Center for Global Studies. Her research interests include the relationship between economic and political change and conflict, distributive conflicts, and the relationship between globalization processes and local conflicts, in particular in the Middle East and eastern and central Europe. She is the author of a forthcoming book, *Confronting Change: Labor, State, and the Transition to a Market Economy* (Penn State University Press, 2008). She is currently working on her second book, *Rebuilding Society, Downsizing the State: Post-Conflict Economic Reconstruction Policies*, which examines the relationship between peace-building and economic policies after civil wars. She holds a Ph.D. in political science from the University of Virginia.

Richard E. Rubenstein is University Professor of Conflict Resolution and Public Affairs at George Mason University. He is the author of seven books on violent social conflicts and methods of resolving them, and teaches courses at ICAR on conflict theory, religion and conflict, and conflict and empire. His most recent book is *Thus Saith the Lord: The Revolutionary Moral Vision of Isaiah and Jeremiah* (2006). He is currently at work on a book entitled *Why People Fight: Stories of War and Peace*.

Dennis J. D. Sandole received his Ph.D. in politics from the University of Strathclyde in Glasgow, Scotland, in 1979. Arriving at George Mason University from Britain in 1981, he remains the only founder-member of the Institute for Conflict Analysis and Resolution (ICAR), where he has been active in teaching, research, and practice. Among his publications are: *Peace and Security in the Postmodern World: The OSCE and Conflict Resolution* (2007); *Capturing the Complexity of Conflict: Dealing with Violent Ethnic Conflicts of the Post-Cold War* (1999); *Conflict Resolution Theory and Practice: Integration and Application* (1993); and *Conflict Management and Problem Solving: Interpersonal to International Applications* (1987).

Paul D. Williams is Associate Professor in the Department of Politics and International Studies at the University of Warwick, UK, and a Visiting Associate Professor in the Elliott School of International Affairs, George Washington University. He is co-author of *Understanding Peacekeeping* (Polity, 2004) and coeditor of *Peace Operations and Global Order* (Routledge, 2005).

Preface

Almost a decade ago the faculty of the Institute for Conflict Analysis and Resolution (ICAR) struggled to design and implement significant curricular revisions of both the Masters and Doctoral programs. Concurrently, retreats and lengthy discussions at faculty board meetings reflected our passions and concerns about the scope, growth, and development of the field at that time. For a number of reasons – frustrations of identifying good textbooks for introductory graduate-level courses, demonstrating better linkages between theory, research, and practice, forcing ourselves to continue our scholarly enterprise as a Hewlett Theory Center and grant recipient as a Commonwealth of Virginia Center of Excellence, to name a few – we decided to write a book. We hoped we would be successful and agreed that all royalties would be placed in an ICAR scholarship fund to recruit and support future students.

Surely this would be an intriguing and relatively easy challenge, as our faculty had grown in numbers and diversity to reflect the depth and breadth of conflict analysis and conflict resolution. We had theoreticians, practitioners, and researchers. We had area specialists. We had some of the first- and second-generation thinkers. So, if each wrote a chapter based on her or his area(s) of expertise, we would have the book well underway within the year. We developed a framework (introduced in Chapter 1) reflecting three components of the book: diagnosing conflict, influences, and contexts of conflict, and intervening in conflict (Parts I, II, and III, respectively). We asked various faculty members to write chapters that reflected the state of the art in their own field and, with their agreement, we officially launched our project.

The experiment worked, but it took longer than we expected. There were a number of interruptions, busy academic lives notwithstanding. Kevin Clements, ICAR's director, left for a leadership position at International Alert. Sandra Cheldelin became the next director of ICAR. With an unusual and tenacious shepherding from Dan Druckman, then doctoral program coordinator, and Larissa Fast, then the doctoral research assistant, it still took three years before the project finally came to fruition. Now it is four years later and busy lives notwithstanding we offer a second edition. Since the book was first published, the editors have moved on in their careers and several new faculty have joined the Institute (see notes on contributors). The authorships now extend beyond the boundaries of ICAR. As with the first edition, the amounts and kinds of editorial work performed were evenly distributed among us. Thus, once again we list the editors in alphabetical order.

This project continues to be a work in progress for the field. Since the first edition we have updated the topics originally included and we have added four new chapters – on narrative analysis, globalization, development, and peace operations. We ponder what changes will occur that reflect our colleagues' interests, the growth of the discipline, and the needs of society a decade from now. We suspect the framework may still be applicable, but are hopeful that new theories and conceptual frameworks will have emerged, new models of practice will be common, and both will be informed by the considerable growth of research. Whether or not we will undertake a ten-years-later updating of this second edition is not yet part of any community discussion. What is certain, however, is that if this book is successful, we will have influenced many new students who will ultimately graduate from conflict resolution programs and actively contribute to the building of the field.

We welcome you on our journey.

Sandra Cheldelin, Daniel Druckman, and Larissa Fast

CHAPTER 1

Introduction

The Editors

The field of conflict resolution is an experiment in theory, research, and practice, much as this book is an experiment in combining diverse perspectives on the field. Conflict resolution, as an academic discipline and professional field of practice, has come into being over the past few decades. The proliferation of academic programs at the graduate and undergraduate levels, the growth of organizations dedicated to conflict resolution, and the diffusion of conflict resolution ideas and practices within a multitude of diverse organizations and agencies are a testament to its popularity and maturation. At the Institute for Conflict Analysis and Resolution (ICAR), we have been thinking, teaching, practicing, and researching about conflict analysis and resolution for the past twenty-five years. This book reflects where we are in the "experiment," and where we think we are headed in the future. Although the verdict is not yet in about whether the experiment has been a success, we continue to generate knowledge about conflict and its resolution.

The experiment to which we refer concerns whether it is possible to think generically about conflict. This book reflects the belief that it is possible, and the following chapters provide our "evidence." The book cuts across the traditional distinctions scholars make between domains (domestic vs. international) and levels of analysis (intrapersonal, interpersonal, intragroup, intergroup, and international), and presents perspectives from a variety of academic disciplines in order to advance toward a general theoretical perspective on conflict. We have combined these distinctions while retaining them as diagnostic tools to present a purview and a vision of the emerging and maturing field of conflict resolution.

Generic knowledge is best understood in relation to theory development. We accept the definition of theory that Stern and Druckman (2000) propose:

> By theory we mean a conceptual model that defines a set of actors and conditions (such as intervention strategies, outcome conditions, and factors other than the intervention that affects the outcome) and postulates associations and causal relationships among them. To the extent that evidence is consistent with a theory and inconsistent with alternatives, confidence is increased that the postulated associations and causal relationships constitute *generic* knowledge about the actors or conditions. (p. 84; italics added)

But we are also concerned with theories that have practical implications. On this matter Stern and Druckman add that

> theory is practical to the extent that it produces reliable *generic* knowledge that can be used, along with case-specific knowledge, to enable a practitioner to identify the intervention most likely to yield a desired outcome in a particular situation. (p.84; italics added)

By considering in this book perspectives on sources, influences, and contexts for conflict as well as the kinds of intervention that have been used to address, settle, and resolve them, we contribute to the development of practical theory, which may also be considered as generic or widely applicable knowledge.

We have chosen a somewhat eclectic route to theory development. Rather than craft our own synthesis of the field, we organize the approaches of our colleagues according to a general framework, as presented later in the chapter as Figure 1.1. An advantage of this approach is that it builds on the specialized topic expertise of our colleagues who come from many social science disciplines. A disadvantage is that the product is less integrated than it might have been had we relied on a smaller team of writers. But the smaller team is in evidence throughout the book, as developers of the framework, authors of the next chapter on theory, research, and practice (with Kevin Clements), as editors of all the chapters, and by one of the editors (Daniel Druckman) as generator of lessons learned in the final chapter. What emerges from this small (the editors) and large (the authors) collaboration is a kind of "hybrid vigor" that moves the experiment forward a few steps. In the remainder of this Introduction, we tell you who we are, why there is a need for this book, and what it is about.

Who Are We?

ICAR began as the "Center for Conflict Resolution" (CCR) in 1981, an institution designed with teaching, research, and outreach as its goals. The primary emphasis, however, was on establishing a Master of Science in Conflict Management, now called an MS in Conflict Analysis and Resolution. Bryant Wedge and Henry Barringer served, respectively, as founding director and associate director of the CCR, while Dennis Sandole joined as the first faculty member, a joint appointment between the CCR and the Department of Public Affairs at George Mason University (now the School of Public Policy). CCR was housed within the Department of Sociology and Anthropology until it became a Hewlett Foundation theory center (1987) and a Commonwealth of Virginia Institute (1987). John Burton arrived during the 1986 academic year, and provided an explicit theoretical base for the analysis and resolution of deep-rooted conflict ("Basic Human Needs" theory; see Burton, 1990a), with which ICAR became associated. Burton was instrumental in obtaining additional funding that enabled ICAR to flourish. The program grew from approximately twenty MS students in the early 1980s to over 160 students in both programs today.

CCR became the Center for Conflict Analysis and Resolution (CCAR), and then the Institute for Conflict Analysis and Resolution (ICAR) in the late 1980s, after establishing the first Ph.D. program in conflict analysis and resolution in the world in 1988. The Hewlett Foundation and Commonwealth of Virginia funding enabled ICAR to hire additional senior faculty members. A number of related organizations became affiliates of ICAR – the National Conference on Peacemaking and Conflict Resolution (NCPCR, now the Network of Communities on Peacemaking and Conflict Resolution), the Consortium on Peace Research and Education (COPRED), and the Northern Virginia Mediation Service (NVMS) – and maintain or maintained offices on ICAR's premises. To date, ICAR has awarded approximately twenty-five Ph.D. degrees.

The current curriculum is an integrative one. The MS degree is geared toward encouraging and developing reflective practitioners – practitioners with a theoretical foundation who are able to more effectively design, implement, and evaluate interventions. The Ph.D. degree program cultivates practical theorists – individuals who do theory and research with practical consequences. This implies developing an understanding of a broad range of theoretical approaches to conflict at both the micro and macro levels, and of complex philosophies ranging from positivism to postmodernism, as well as cultivating research skills across a spectrum of methodologies that will be useful for designing and evaluating conflict resolution approaches.

The collective theoretical perspectives, practices, and research experiences of our faculty, students, and alumni, and the dearth of literature that integrates the theory, research, and practice related to conflict and its resolution led us to write this book.

Why This Book?

A number of textbooks and surveys about the field of conflict resolution already exist. A few examples include *Contemporary Conflict Resolution* by Miall *et al.* (1999), *Constructive Conflicts* by Kriesberg (1998), *The Handbook of Conflict Resolution* by Deutsch and Coleman (2000), *The Structure of International Conflict* by Mitchell (1981), *Interpersonal Conflict* by Hocker and Wilmot (1995), *The Functions of Social Conflict* by Coser (1956), *Conflict Resolution* by Schellenberg (1996), and *Building Peace* by Lederach (1997). So why another book? Most of these texts reflect the disciplinary home of their authors. Schellenberg, Kriesberg, and Coser, for example, focus on the social nature of conflict, while Hocker and Wilmot emphasize communication's role in conflict. Mitchell develops the international dimensions of conflict, grounded in his disciplinary training in political science and international relations. Miall *et al.* present an interdisciplinary perspective, but focus only on one type of conflict – violent intergroup or international conflicts. Lederach, in contrast, proposes new thinking about conflict transformation as a broader concept than what most term *conflict resolution*.

Each of the above authors, and others not mentioned here, contributes to the advancement of our field as a whole, but they reflect to varying degrees the interdisciplinary nature of the field. The parent disciplines of sociology, anthropology, political science, law, social psychology, psychology, and international relations simultaneously give direction, but also constrain thinking and research within disciplinary boundaries. This is not to imply that we cannot continue to learn and borrow from these parent disciplines, but the object of inquiry in the field of conflict resolution – conflict – differs from that of its parents. This book brings together various perspectives on conflict and its resolution in order to make progress toward developing generic theory.

The various chapters in this volume offer different perspectives on the emerging field of conflict resolution. The cross-disciplinary nature of the book is a strength, but its corresponding weakness is the lack of boundaries this implies. This paradox mirrors the field in its struggle to define not only its terminology (e.g., differences between conflict settlement, management, resolution, or transformation), but also what it is and what it is not. Grappling with the intricacies and difficulties of integrating these practitioner and academic perspectives is by no means unique to our field. This book demonstrates the strength in the eclectic nature of the field and the struggle to integrate theory, research, and practice that presently plagues the field of conflict resolution.

Just as the various disciplines upon which the field draws cannot remain isolated, neither can the three "legs" of theory, research, and practice. Addressing the gaping disconnect between theory, research, and practice about conflict and its resolution is the primary goal of this text. We elucidate what we consider to be the connections between these three in Chapter 2, "Theory, Research, and Practice," but this theme recurs throughout the text. The respective bodies of literature on each of these – conflict theory, the practice of conflict analysis and resolution, and research on conflict and conflict resolution – are growing. To advance the field as a whole, the three legs cannot remain separate from each other.

We began the book project with the goal of integration, both in terms of theory, research, and practice, and in terms of disciplines. We have only begun to scratch the surface. The chapters in this book reflect, at least to some extent, the disciplinary home of their authors, and make only preliminary connections between theory, research, and practice. The contributors are usually well grounded in one or two of our metaphorical legs, but not always in all three. Their writing emulates their disciplinary heritage, its emphasis on theory, research, or practice, and the corresponding conventions of each leg. Nevertheless, the chapters of the book form a whole, unified by the overarching framework (see Figure 1.1), Chapter 2 that proposes the connections between theory, research, and practice, Chapter 22 that provides an integrative function and summarizes the insights from previous chapters, and the introductions to each of the three parts of the book. These all provide avenues for integrating disciplines and the three legs to which we refer throughout the book.

Integration is the primary task of the second generation of conflict resolution – those who have studied in interdisciplinary programs and learned from those trained in a variety of academic (and practice) disciplines. Several of our recent graduates have begun the task of integration through their own dissertation or thesis projects, on such topics as: coordination among intervenors; a theory of the South African Truth and Reconciliation Commission (TRC) process; interagency conflict and intervention processes; ecological conflict in multilateral negotiation privacy conflicts between online industries and consumers; and mediators' conceptions of power, causes of genocide, and the way that negotiating processes influence outcomes. These dissertation and thesis projects, and others, are available through ICAR.

Obviously, the field is simultaneously growing and struggling to define its boundaries and areas of inquiry. We have tried to make the book as comprehensive as possible, but have not adequately covered some topics (e.g., ethics or evaluation of conflict resolution practice) and have left out others almost entirely (e.g., monitoring regimes, the economics of conflict, technology, human rights, and criminal tribunals or truth commissions). Many of these have growing or substantial literatures in their own right, while others remain fruitful topics for further analysis. Unfortunately, we cannot cover all of these topics in depth in a book of this size. However, we have updated most of the chapters that appeared in the first edition and added four new chapters. This recognition leads us forward to a description of what the book is about.

What Is the Book About?

This book is primarily about developing a broadly applicable and eclectic purview of conflict. Our goal is not to advocate a particular way of analyzing conflict, but instead to provide an overview of the various scholarly pieces composing analysis of, as well as intervention in, conflict. A generic framework is supposed to defy traditional parameters of disciplines and levels of analysis in order to assist us in analyzing and resolving conflict. However, using such a model does not imply that we should ignore the importance of contextual and specialized knowledge. Indeed, our model presents context as a crucial part of any analysis. One way of envisioning the relationships between the composite parts of a generic model is shown in Figure 1.1.

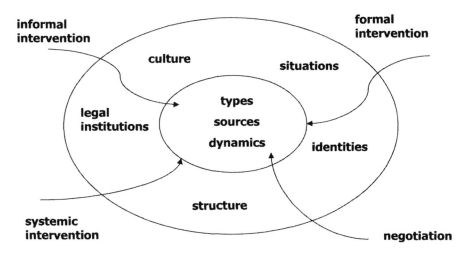

Figure 1.1 A framework for conflict: from analysis to intervention

Figure 1.1 depicts the three sections of this book as a series of concentric circles, with wavy lines penetrating the circles. The inner circle represents the core of the analysis – typologies, sources, and dynamics of conflict. Part I, "Diagnosing Conflict," asks the questions: What is conflict? Where does it come from? How does it unfold or change over time? The chapters on a typology of conflict, sources of conflict, and dynamics of conflict propose various responses to these key questions. The chapter on narrative provides another approach to diagnosing conflict. Diagnosis is about peeling away the layers of the conflict to reveal the heart of the matter, the phenomenon itself, and the innermost circle.

Situations, identities, culture, structure, and institutions all influence the core elements. Part II, "Influences and Context" – the second circle – proposes questions about the conditions that affect choices about how to engage in conflict, whether it becomes constructive or destructive, and the context within which conflict develops. The influences on conflict change rapidly and over time, and represent immediate or proximate causes of conflict. Yet conflict is also situated in a particular context that includes culture, structure, and legal institutions, the distal causes. The topics within the second circle reflect this notion that context and influences are pervasive, and encompass the core concepts of types, sources, and dynamics. These chapters ask questions about how culture affects conflict and its resolution, about the global and local structures within which conflict and resolution take place, and the legal institutions through which conflict and its resolution are mediated. The chapter on development contributes further to our understanding of the context for conflict.

Diagnosing the sources, types, and dynamics of conflict, identifying the influences on the unfolding conflict, and analyzing the context all inform the choice between and effectiveness of various possible interventions to resolve conflict – the wavy lines that permeate the two circles. Because intervention is never linear and often changes midcourse, we have presented each of the four broad types of intervention (negotiation and informal, formal, and systemic intervention) as wavy lines. Negotiation is separated from the other three because it is an unassisted process, meaning the parties in conflict reach an agreement on their own and without assistance from third parties. Each of the other three types refers either to the level of formality in the process (from informal to formal, including facilitation, consultation, mediation, arbitration, problem-solving, and peacekeeping) or to the systemic nature of interventions (chapters on systemic transformation and peacebuilding). Each of these analytical circles affects the choices we make as parties and as third parties in terms of intervention in conflict. A central element of effective intervention is an informed and thorough analysis of the conflict. How can we decide what might work or not work if we do not have a complete picture of the influences and context of conflict, or if we cannot identify the type of conflict, its sources, or its dynamics? Good analysis – analysis that diagnoses conflict and its influences and context – is the key to resolution.

Part III, "Intervening in Conflict," presents literature reviews or commentaries on the state of the field as it currently exists, while Parts I and II, "Diagnosing Conflict" and "Influences and Context", tend to reflect the values and theoretical emphases of the contributing authors. Each chapter ends with a series of study questions to stimulate further thinking about the ideas raised in the chapter. The final chapter presents some of the key insights from the previous chapters and suggests where the critical gaps lie for future theorizing, research, and practice. In doing so, it summarizes some of the lessons we have learned about conflict and its resolution, and sets out the areas about which we know very little. The bibliography combines references from all the chapters, collecting key articles and books in the field of conflict resolution. It is a wealth of sources for further study.

You should read this book for a variety of reasons. First, because a practical and urgent need exists to improve our ability to deal with the variety of conflicts that occur in the world. Second, conceptual approaches help us improve the way we think about (and therefore act upon) conflict. This book presents one conceptual approach that begins to integrate disciplines and the tripod of theory, research, and practice. Again, the book does not present any "answers" about conflict and its resolution (we don't have them), but instead prompts you to look for complexity and clues about analysis and intervention that inhabit this complexity. Third, you do not want to be "left behind" in the marketplace of ideas. Fourth, it's fun to glimpse an experiment in progress. Being a participant in an experiment like this one allows you to agree, disagree, challenge, and improve the lessons and thinking presented here in this book. Finally, you want to get a good grade in the course that uses it!

CHAPTER 2

Theory, Research, and Practice

The Editors with Kevin Clements

As we reflect upon the human conflict of the twentieth century, we know it to have been the bloodiest epoch of all human civilization. The barbarism that characterized that century was greater than any that afflicted earlier times. Two major world wars decimated millions, and over 150 smaller wars fought in more than seventy-five countries resulted in even more deaths and destruction. A glimmer of hope emerged from the data in *The Human Security Report* (2005) (http:// www.humansecurityreport.info/) documenting trends from the 1990s to 2003 finding a significant decline in the number of wars, genocides, and human rights abuses, but noted that this decline – partially in response to the "upsurge of international activism" – has witnessed a shift to internal conflicts. It does not, however, include the conflicts post 2003 – Darfur, Afghanistan, and Iraq.

These gloomy statistics may be set alongside more optimistic recent trends in terms of medical and technological advances, expanding levels of wealth and affluence (though accompanied by growing internal and external gaps between rich and poor), and modern transport and communication systems that generate extremely high levels of global knowledge and interdependence. The challenge at the beginning of this millennium, therefore, was the same that existed at the end of the last: namely, how to ensure that we learn from past mistakes and solve our problems creatively and nonviolently. How can we advance human community and civil society and prevent avoidable local and global catastrophes?

This book presents the emergent role of conflict analysis and resolution. We believe that a conceptual analysis – the tripod of theory, research, and practice – helps to improve the way we think about human conflict. The kinds of questions we continuously struggle with are: What can this interdisciplinary field contribute to our understanding of, solutions to, or transformations of some of the most pressing conflicts confronting human societies? What are the prospects for developing new social technologies, or inter- and intra-active processes that will enhance social and political life, and ensure that we solve our problems in ways that do justice to all? How do we ensure that most social action is benign and does not result in harm to others? Is there a seamless web between such trivial disputes as neighbors in conflict over a barking dog and the much more complex issues of inter- or intra-state wars or the most common violent conflict of the past few years, namely large-scale internal conflicts between diverse ethnic and cultural groupings? What can we say about the origins and dynamics of different conflicts? What theories and processes are available to laypeople and professionals alike to identify escalating conflicts and de-escalate them? What techniques exist to control, manage, and transform such conflicts?

In this chapter we focus on the distinctive contributions of theory, research, and practice to this enterprise. We begin by asking what role theory plays in our understanding of the sources and dynamics of conflict. We then look at what we know from research, what are the best practices in the field, and how we can promote interdependence among these three.

The Role of Theory

The *Oxford English Dictionary* (1979, p. 3284) defines theory as:

> contemplation, a speculation, a mental view; a conception or mental scheme of something to be done, or the method of doing it; a systematic statement of rules and principles to be followed.

In another section theory is defined as:

> a scheme or system of ideas or statements held as an explanation or account of a group of facts or phenomena; a hypothesis that has been confirmed or established by observation or experiment and is propounded or accepted as accounting for the known facts: a statement of what are held to be the general laws, principles or causes of something known or observed.

What are the theoretical principles, explanations, hypotheses, propositions, and mental views underlying our understanding of the causes and dynamics of human conflict? How well do they help us think about processes for their evolution, management, or resolution? Are we anywhere near developing what may be called a theory or theories of conflict and conflict resolution, or are we still at that pre-theoretical stage of developing a taxonomy of ideas and concepts that help us describe different types of conflict?

While academic conflict analysts and intervenors draw on a variety of social science disciplines in our research, thinking, and practice, those who work in the field as researchers or practitioners wish to focus specific and exclusive attention on the complex origins, dynamics, and resolution of conflict. This is because conflict and cooperation lie at the heart of all communities. All communities juggle both of these processes and we need to understand how each contributes to the continuity and persistence of societies through time. Conflict and cooperation are not neutral processes, good or bad in themselves. Both can have destructive as well as creative consequences. Cooperation, when harnessed to malign ends, can result in totalitarian and repressive outcomes. Conflict, when harnessed to benign ends and occurring within agreed rules and frameworks, is capable of generating high levels of creativity and positive change.

One of the central tasks facing conflict theory, therefore, is to understand the ambivalent nature of conflict, its capacity to generate creative change and high levels of personal and collective integration, as well as its more malign consequences when conflict becomes vicious and violent. After identifying the sources of conflict (see Chapter 4), it is possible to design intervention strategies capable of addressing the structural sources of conflict, specific triggers, and accelerants (see Part III). Without this diagnostic facility, however, much of what passes for conflict resolution is simply good neighborliness or enlightened friendship extended to others in time of need. Awareness of some of the underlying sources of conflict is critical to its effective resolution in terms of designing partnerships and intervention strategies that will enable a wide variety of social and political actors to increase the positive and diminish the negative features of conflict. Different theories of conflict will determine what sorts of processes are designed to deal with its management, resolution, or transformation. This book builds on the assumption that successful interventions are dependent upon thoughtful and accurate analyses of conflict.

In designing intervention strategies, some of the most important current debates revolve around which theories can deliver viable alternatives to those proposed by exponents of a "realist" persuasion emphasizing power, coercion, and political dominance. What is becoming clearer is that imposed political solutions by those in political authority are less likely to yield short- or long-term survivable solutions to problems than those responses that enhance relationship, community, and integrative solutions, a point noted by some of the early explorers of conflict management such as Mary Parker Follett (1942, p. 32).

Generating conflict theory

The emergent field of conflict resolution aspires to be both analytic and normative. It is both because it is oriented toward research and practice. Some practitioners are indifferent about final outcomes as long as the processes used to secure these outcomes have been substantively, processually, and psychologically satisfactory. While there is general agreement within the field that solutions lie with the parties themselves and a generalized indifference about what solutions are agreed, there is, at the same time, a strong commitment to ensuring a reduction in overall levels of violence, and to the emergence of societies that are more cooperative than conflictual, more ordered than disordered, more communal than atomized, and more oriented toward the generation of institutional processes aimed at solving problems than the concentration and consolidation of power. In this sense conflict theory is radical political philosophy (see e.g., Burton, 1993). Its mission is not to maintain the status quo but to devise processes that will generate both positive orientations to change, and the institutional and processual mechanisms for doing this nonviolently. In these ways conflict resolution theory has both diagnostic and prescriptive dimensions. Its evolution stands very clearly in that reformist tradition of American sociology, which articulates an ethic of change and reform. These traditions are ably described by Coser (1964) in his classic book *Sociological Theory*.

The reformist impulse generates both supporters and critics. Radical critics complain that conflict resolution focused on changing attitudes and perceptions can be seen as a sophisticated set of "soft" social-psychological techniques for making people feel "good" about the conflicts in which they are involved rather than helping them focus on the deeper structural sources. They argue that conflict resolution, by stressing perceptions, misperceptions, attitudes, and emotions, obscures some of the deeper more structural and intractable dimensions of conflict. Interestingly, these criticisms come from both liberals and conservatives. Liberals believe that far too little of conflict resolution addresses the sources of structural inequality or class-based conflict. Conservatives believe that concentration on the therapeutic obscures awareness of some of the more malign political forces at work in the world, forces which demand strong state and military solutions.

All the critics believe the field is no more successful than sociology at understanding the deeper relationships between individuals and society.

In particular, it is not making much sense of the relationships between micro psychological and social-psychological theories and the macro sociological and political explanations of both the sources of conflict and their resolution. Whether or not cooperation and integration is best achieved through processes of compliance with culturally determined rules of social order – norms, customs, laws – or the pursuit of enlightened self-interest, remains a largely unanswered question.

Given the subject matter of conflict analysis, the question is whether we should be aspiring to a positivist agenda in which the logic of the natural sciences is applied or whether the content of the field is so "subjective" and conflict processes so idiosyncratically constructed, that we should abandon any aspiration to developing scientific theory using natural science analogies. If we abandon the positivist project, what is its replacement? The critics charge that conflict resolution is simply another way of applying a liberal political agenda (packaged as science) to social and political processes. Insofar as this is true, it is highly probable that the field will lack social scientific substance. Insofar as it is not true, it should be possible to identify some theoretical principles, explanations, hypotheses, and propositions underlying our understanding of the causes and dynamics of conflict and how we can manage, resolve, or transform them.

We need to know whether conflict resolution theory – as opposed to the sociological, psychological, or political theories associated with it – is developing any widely agreed axioms (some would even ask for laws), which might enable us to explain conflictual and cooperative behavior. If they do, the next test is to determine if these same theories help construct creative solutions to problems. We believe conflict resolution theory is now at exactly the point at which applied social theory was in the 1960s. As Zetterburg (1966, p. 190) described it:

> The gap between theoretical knowledge and practical action remains wide. When a client approaches an academic scientist with the phrase "I have a problem … " he usually gets the answer "let's do research about it" … (p. 16). Applied social theory thus holds out prospects for improvement in the quality of theoretical sociology. One can only hope that these improvements will be of the same magnitude as those that applied social research in recent decades has brought to basic research techniques and methods.

Conflict resolution theory holds out prospects for a similar development. When a client approaches a conflict resolution expert with the phrase "I have a problem … ," we don't first think of doing research about it. Instead, the conflict resolution specialist will say "tell me about it." Depending on the answer, the expert may propose a variety of possible intervention strategies. In almost all of them, the underlying theoretical rationale, its research underpinnings, or the systematic practice are unclear. In this way, therefore, we are somewhat behind where Zetterburg thought applied social theory was four decades ago.

This book is, in part, an effort to respond to the person, group, or party with a problem, with more sophisticated theory, research, and practice than is currently available. If we can identify some of the core and agreed upon assumptions of applied conflict theory we can enhance both our diagnostic and practice capacities.

Structures or individuals?

Perhaps the first theoretical issue to address is whether most conflict theorists apply what Rhoads (1991) calls "methodological structuralism" or "methodological individualism" to their evolution of axioms and theories of conflictual behavior. As he puts it,

> One line of thought takes the position that social structures have an independent existence that is not reducible to the characteristics of individuals. Consequently, societies and their structures are to be studied on their own terms. Another line of thought holds that collectivities are constituted solely by individuals and their relationships. Consequently, the study of societies can be reduced to the study of their members. (76)

This is not simply an academic question. If one adopts the first strategy of methodological structuralism, attention is focused primarily on the ontological status of social structures and how these generate both conflict and holistic solutions to conflict. In this instance, most social systems are construed in terms of the levels of organization generated below the individual and which extend beyond them. Social, political, and economic systems and their interrelationships are the primary focus of attention and the source of most explanations about conflict. These theories tend to establish a causal priority of the social over the individual, but also acknowledge that individuals make society possible, and without them social systems are unable to achieve their goals.

Methodological individualism, on the other hand, assumes that social systems consist entirely of their members and that they (individually) are the appropriate units of analysis. In this perspective, societies – social, economic, and political systems – are reduced to characteristics abstracted from individual citizens. This results in propositions such as that of Homans (1974) that "sociology is reducible to psychology" or more nuanced constructivist approaches which argue that individual persons determine for themselves how they connect with and relate to others, and that this is where we must identify the underlying sources of conflict and its management. These highly individualized interactions with others determine whether or not "associative" or "communal" relationships prevail, what conflicts are likely to emerge, and how they can be managed.

Both of these perspectives are at the heart of discussions about the theory, research, and practice of conflict resolution. Those who believe that most conflicts are caused in people's minds and flow from particular kinds of attitudinal and behavioral dispositions will be inclined toward methodological individualism. Those who believe most conflicts are generated in response to complex processes of inclusion or exclusion from political, economic, social, or cultural resources are inclined to adopt a structural orientation toward conflict theory and practice. An intermediate position exists which suggests that most conflicts are an outcome of a very delicate interplay between social and psychological disposition, structural location, and critical precipitants. Or, as our colleague Mitchell (1981b) describes it, the structural analysis of conflict involves attending to the interplay between situations, behavior, and attitudes.

The question about the relationship between individual and social agency and which is theoretically and politically most important lies at the heart of political and social philosophy. It was the key debate in relation to nineteenth-century sociology and psychology as theorists such as Marx, Weber, and Durkheim argued about ways in which individuals acquired their consciousness of language, culture, and society, and were willing to comply with the dominant norms and folkways of the societies of which they were a part. It is particularly important to conflict resolution specialists because the answers will, to a large extent, determine what sorts of intervention we design and what sorts of intervention are likely to result in creative problem-solving, or the management, resolution, or transformation of the conflict. In particular, our task as conflict theorists is to unravel the complex dynamics of interactive processes in order to understand how and why systems persist through time and why most people engage in collaborative rather than conflictual processes most of the time.

Georg Simmel (1955), a classical predecessor of modern conflict theory, was preoccupied with the relationship between the individual and the society and whether or not society "alone" was "real" or individuals "alone" were "real" and how these two "realities" were connected. He focused on the ways in which humans constituted societies – the ontology of social forms – and he was also concerned with how we understand this constitution, the epistemology of social relationships. Perhaps the first theorist to begin grappling with the thorny questions of methodological structuralism and individualism, his analysis and its subsequent elaboration in Coser's (1964) classic work set the stage for most modern sociological theorizing about conflict, and the relationship between individual dispositions and group formation. Perhaps also the first to focus on ways in which conflicts assisted boundary formation in groups, he identified ways in which conflicts varied in intensity depending on how close the parties were and how internal cohesion flowed from conflicts with outgroups. He grappled with questions about what made conflict realistic or non-realistic and why conflicts turned hostile and violent. Although Simmel and Coser presented a number of insightful and testable propositions (see Druckman and Zechmeister (1973) for examples), it cannot be said that they developed a general theory of conflict. On the contrary, like most theories of conflict, the propositions put forth by Coser are middle range, having the advantage of being stated in the form of hypotheses that can be evaluated empirically.

Similarly, Marx's (1964) powerful and insightful analyses of the sources of conflict as flowing from the structural inequalities generated by the dominant mode of production, its division of labor, and the political systems associated with this, suffer from a certain degree of partiality as well. The work of Weber (1956) on class, status, and power, and the conflicts that flow from the interplay between these variables also is not sufficiently sensitive to social-psychological dynamics, although he did draw attention to the critical role of values in conflict.

In all of this we need to identify ways in which different theories of conflict – classical and contemporary – understand human behavior and different root causes or origins of conflict. Second, we need to identify how different explanations of conflict result in the development of specific mechanisms for addressing and solving or transforming conflict, and what sorts of intervention and practice flow from different theoretical assumptions.

Our uncertainty about whether or how to synthesize micro-macro explanations of conflict relates to whether or not there is any desire to develop something approximating natural science models and theories in relation to conflict resolution processes. In particular, is there any desire to develop a search for causal relationships and generalizations in the field, or is there a general contentment with a series of discrete theoretical propositions that may or may not yield systematic theory and change practice in some fundamental ways? Some justification exists for thinking that many practitioners in the field do not want grand theory; they want recipe knowledge that will help inform their practice in a very direct and pragmatic fashion. Somewhere between the Scylla of grand theory and the Charybdis of abstracted empiricism, however, lie opportunities for synthesis and the evolution of middle-range theories. This may eventually result in the evolution of single theoretic themes that connect the seemingly disconnected.

Our constant ethical dilemma is the extent to which all of the existing theories – and any integrated theory that may emerge from this text – will improve communication and understanding, promote tolerance and diversity, yield positive sum agreements, acknowledge core identity needs of all antagonists, overcome negative stereotyping, promote clear communication, and achieve justice, peace, and reconciliation between peoples and between state systems. This is no small order but one that determines whether or not human beings win the race between civilization and catastrophe.

The integrative theoretical task cannot be achieved without a solid grounding in both research and practice. It is in the interplay between theory, research, and practice where ethically sound applied theory will emerge to guide all that seek to pre-empt, manage, resolve, or transform conflict.

The Role of Research

What is research? *Funk and Wagnells Standard Dictionary* (1965) defines research as "diligent, protracted investigation; studious inquiry; ... a systematic investigation of some phenomenon." *Webster's New Collegiate Dictionary* (1961) adds: "Studious and critical inquiry and examination aimed at the discovery and interpretation of new knowledge." These definitions depict a goal-driven activity aimed at discovering new knowledge through a serious, organized, and strategic plan. The goal of discovery is intended to contribute to theory (our understanding of a phenomenon) or practice (our use of knowledge to improve conditions). The strategic plan is the method designed to produce the knowledge. In this section, we discuss how research is done, different paradigms of research, and what we have learned about conflict resolution through research. The discussion is framed by considerations of the human dimensions of research, first, with regard to researchers' motivations, and, later, with regard to ethics.

Researchers' motivations

At one time it was fashionable to describe one's profession as either a basic or applied researcher. Social scientists did not "march to the same drummer." Some scholars wanted to understand the world. They were the basic researchers who measured their accomplishments in terms of contributions to the science or discipline. Other researchers wanted to solve practical problems. These applied researchers measured their accomplishments in terms of problems solved or practices improved. In the past it was easy to distinguish between these researchers: basic research was done mostly in universities; applied research in public or private "think-tanks" or consulting firms. Today the distinction is blurred. Most researchers in social science – whether inside or outside the academy – construe their work in both basic and applied terms. A discernible trend toward a merging of theory, practice, and research is evident, particularly in the field of conflict resolution.

Yet, differences in emphasis exist among researchers. Those who are closer to the basic research "wing" prefer the slower pace of design, data collection, analysis, and peer review publication. For them, professional rewards derive from publications in prestigious research journals. Those closer to the applied research "wing" engage in the faster paced enterprise of solving problems for clients. They, too, derive rewards from publications but also strive to maintain relationships with clients, and are more focused on the practical applications of their research. The standards of systematic inquiry, as defined by the philosophical traditions that inform their research, guide both of these types of researchers. They differ, however, with regard to the way their research is used: to contribute primarily to theory or to practice.

Researcher motivation can influence the quality of the research. In his textbook on methods, Robson (1993) distinguishes between features that produce successful or unsuccessful research. Important contributions are more likely to result from a genuine curiosity, excitement about doing research, being part of a network of researchers with similar interests, theoretical understanding, seeing clearly the next steps in a progression of findings on a topic, or understanding the real-world value of the project. They are less likely to occur if a researcher is motivated by expedience, the promise of publication or funding, using a particular method for its own sake, or a lack of concern for and/or understanding of theory. A key difference between these features is a long-term career commitment to research and a desire to attain short-term gains from taking on assignments.

Systematic inquiry: how research is done

In some disciplines, and for many investigators, scientific research is synonymous with experimentation and a positivist philosophical approach to research. Both the *Funk and Wagnells* (1965) definition used above, and an elaboration from that same dictionary – "to search again or anew" – imply a particular method of discovery (experiments) that can be used repeatedly for replication (repeated investigations of the same variables) or cumulation (building on previous findings). The attractiveness and popularity of the experimental method is due to its ability to discover causal relations among a few variables. By creating control groups, experimentalists can confidently infer that, for example, constituency pressures (the independent variable) caused an impasse in negotiation (the dependent variable). To the extent that they can be confident in making such inferences, the result is regarded as being valid, referred to as internal validity.

Experimental methods thrive in disciplines where theory is highly developed. By theory, here, we mean a framework that distinguishes between relatively important and unimportant variables. Such guidance helps identify the particular variables to manipulate and assess in experiments. Experiments are not fishing expeditions; their purpose is to provide evidence for hypothesized relations between certain variables defined in theoretical frameworks. Even complex multivariate experiments accommodate only a few variables we choose on the basis of theoretical rationale. For good reason: effective controls depend on examining the effects of only a few variables at a time; and results from experiments that manipulate more than three variables are difficult to interpret, especially if there are interactions among the variables.

A rich tradition of experimentation exists in conflict resolution. Extending back four decades, experiments contribute important insights about conflict processes and outcomes. Several of these insights are illustrated in the following section. However, the method is not without its critics. A number of researchers in the field criticize the artificial nature of the experiments: they are too far removed from the settings in which conflict – and particularly deep-rooted conflict – occurs. Can experiments be designed to capture the important dimensions of real-world conflicts? Another – and more fundamental – criticism is that theories of conflict are not sufficiently developed to identify the critical variables to be manipulated in experiments. What then are appropriate research strategies for developing theory?

Three research strategies are being used to increase the realism – referred to as external validity – of experiments. Each strategy is designed to increase generality while preserving the rigor of the experimental method. One consists of embedding experiments in simulated contexts. Simulations are designed to reproduce features of a particular real-world setting. Designers are primarily concerned with the fidelity of the construction and devise procedures for ascertaining the "fit." For them, the interesting issue is the extent to which experimental findings apply to the situation being simulated – the external validity question (Guetzkow and Valadez, 1981; Druckman, 1993).

Another strategy is referred to as quasi-experimentation. This is an attempt to conduct a field experiment. Missing in most quasi-experiments are opportunities to assign "subjects" to conditions on a random basis and, often, to create control groups. The gains in realism (external validity) are achieved at some cost to confidence of interpretations (internal validity). However, we have sophisticated procedures to improve the quality of inferences even when random assignment is impossible (see Cook and Campbell, 1979).

A third strategy is referred to as controlled comparisons. This is an attempt to impose experimental logic on case analyses. Based on John Stuart Mill's methods of similarities and differences, controlled comparisons are intended to allow an investigator to infer causality by selecting cases (usually a small number) that are similar on all but certain key independent variables. An excellent example is Putnam's (1993) comparison of northern and southern Italian legislative systems. He identifies economic and political explanations for the differences. The increasing popularity of this approach is based on recent improvements in the methodology of comparison, especially in political science (see George, 1979; Faure, 1994). A recent study used this method to test hypotheses about coordination among multiple third parties in three former Soviet republics (Allen Nan, 1999).

Regarding theory development, various non-experimental research strategies are useful for sorting variables in an exploratory mode. One consists of using data on events accumulated over long periods of time. Fluctuations in conflictual and cooperative interactions are used to explore the impact of mediation and damaging stalemates in the conflict between Armenia and Azerbaijan (Mooradian and Druckman, 1999), and to develop models of reciprocity in the Sino–American relationship (Lepgold and Shambaugh, 1998). Surveys are also used to develop theories. One study surveyed the membership of a professional mediation association to learn about mediators' assumptions about power and implications of these assumptions for their approach to mediation (Birkhoff, 2000). A third strategy uses information provided by case ethnographies written by anthropologists. Each ethnography is "a thick" description (see Geertz, 1983) of cultural practices for a particular group. A large sample of these cases may be used for comparative research. For example, using the cases deposited in the Human Relations Area Files, Ember and Ember (1992) coded such variables as resource scarcity (independent variable) and the frequency of warfare (dependent variable). The codes were then used to explore relationships between these variables, providing a basis for models of the causes of war in non-industrialized societies. An advantage of this approach is that it preserves the richness of case studies without forfeiting the wide sampling of cases characteristic of survey and comparative research.

An additional growing vein of inquiry is evaluation research. Evaluation research, whether summative (focus on outcome) or formative (focus on the process), links the research and practice elements of our tripod. Both focus on an assessment of what happened, but at different points in a program. Summative, or outcome, evaluation usually occurs at the end of a program. Formative, or process, evaluation usually occurs during program implementation. Summative evaluation aims to assess program achievements as compared to program goals, whereas formative evaluation looks at the approaches of the program, what worked or did not work, and what other factors may have influenced the success of the program. Scholars like Patton (1997) emphasize the importance of developing utilization-focused evaluation, or techniques and strategies that invite input from the intended users of the evaluation and that make evaluation an integral part of all programs or interventions from the very beginning. Within the field of conflict resolution, researchers have developed frameworks to evaluate Interactive Conflict Resolution (ICR) processes (Rouhana, 2000; d'Estrée et al., 2001), environmental dispute resolution processes (d'Estree and Colby, 2000), and general intervention processes (Stern and Druckman, 2000). Evaluation research combines the research and practice dimensions of our field. (For a discussion of each of these methodologies in the context of a multi-method approach to conflict research, see Druckman, 2005.)

Alternative research paradigms
Other researchers and theorists who fall outside a positivist approach use a variety of methods that reflect their own assumptions about research and ways of knowing. Constructivist and constructionist (see Gergen, 1985) research paradigms have emerged out of critiques to the positivist tradition of research over the past four decades. Although each of these traditions and the differences between them are the topic of much analysis and writing (e.g., Hollis, 1994; Denzin and Lincoln, 1998), theorists and researchers from these traditions often differ on four key aspects. First, constructivist and constructionist researchers emphasize how ideas and thinking evolve over time. They argue that positivist researchers do not include the same kind of temporal analysis. Second, for many (but not all) researchers working in a positivist tradition, the unit of analysis is an individual entity (individual, a state) whereas those within the constructivist and constructionist tradition analyze the *interaction* between entities (e.g., individuals or states). Third, positivist researchers often emphasize causality and the need for internal validity in research. Constructivist and constructionist researchers acknowledge the presence of multiple realities, and instead emphasize the interpretive frames of individuals and the interdependence of researchers and the subjects of the research. The fourth difference lies in the importance researchers attach to language.

Positivists tend to assess a particular meaning of a concept, whereas constructivists and constructionists search for how individuals or groups interpret or give meaning to concepts. Depending on the type of methodology a researcher chooses, these four differences increase or decrease in salience. For example, a positivist researcher who uses a time series methodology attempts to account for the way in which a phenomenon changes over time.

Three methods within the constructivist or constructionist traditions – grounded theory, participant observation, and narrative analysis – are gaining popularity within the field of conflict resolution. Other methodologies and traditions include ethnographies (Clifford and Marcus, 1986; Agar, 1996), phenomenology (Husserl, 1931; Bentz and Shapiro, 1998; Creswell, 1998), and symbolic interactionism (Meade, 1934; Denzin, 1992; Pearce and Littlejohn, 1997). A partial list of scholars using these methodologies to study conflict or conflict resolution include Nordstrom (1997) on people's coping mechanisms in times of war, Roy (1994) on conflict in India, Valley *et al.* (1995) on the effects of relationships on negotiation, Watson-Gegeo and White (1990) on conflict discourse in Pacific societies, and Mahmood (1996) on the intersection between religion and conflict.

Although researchers generally fall within a particular philosophical tradition, which guides their choice of qualitative or quantitative research methods, it is important to note that many of the methodologies explored in this and the previous section may be used within both philosophical traditions (see Guba and Lincoln, 1998). In addition, researchers who use qualitative methodologies have developed their own standards of rigor and quality (see Lincoln and Guba, 1985; Marshall and Rossman, 1999). These researchers often use inductive approaches to inquiry.

An inductive way of generating theory from experience is grounded theory. Glaser and Strauss (1967), and later Strauss and Corbin (1990), describe the process of doing grounded theory. Researchers collect data primarily using in-depth interviews, focus group discussions, and participant observation, then code the data to create a visual model of the phenomenon under study (Creswell, 1998). In this way, the theory is derived from lived experience. Several upcoming dissertation projects at ICAR are using this methodology to develop theory about elicitive training and mergers and acquisitions in organizations. One dissertation explores scholarly and practitioner descriptions of their views of elicitive training to develop a broad description of the practice and a theory that accounts for what guides practitioner decisions. Another explores the merger of two corporate cultures in order to determine what issues are most important in merging organizations.

In participant observation, and in the broader family of methodologies referred to as action research, researchers spend significant amounts of time living in and becoming part of the societies or cultures they are studying. For example, Nordstrom and Martin gather a series of ethnographic studies of sociopolitical violence in their book in order to discover what "social and cultural dynamics foment, perpetuate, and resolve conflict" (1992, p. 9). Action research seeks to integrate the subjects of the research into the research process and to present the research from participants' point of view. It is thus a methodology well suited to integrating practice with research, with the goal of improving practice (see Jorgensen, 1989; Atkinson and Hammersley, 1998; Marshall and Rossman, 1999).

Narrative analysis seeks to describe meaning in the stories of individuals. The focus of narrative analysis is frequently on the narratives of oppressed or marginalized individuals whose voices are often silenced or unheard. Narrative analysis is often used with historical texts, such as autobiographies, life histories, and biographies, as well as with personal interviews (see Mishler, 1986). A study by Cobb and Rifkin (1991) examined the way mediators practice neutrality, both in terms of their own accounts and in the discourse of neutrality during the mediation session. They found the practice differed from the theory and rhetoric about neutrality in mediation.

What have we learned from research on conflict?

As research topics compete for attention within the disciplines, conflict resolution has offered almost irresistible challenges to researchers both with regard to conceptualization and applied issues. The pay-offs in terms of interesting findings are considerable. Here is a sampling of what we have learned to date:

- From experiments on mediation in field settings, we know about some consequences of taking a problem-solving approach (with information search) compared with a settlement orientation (emphasizing moving towards compromises) to disputes. The former usually produces better outcomes (Kressel *et al.*, 1994).
- From laboratory simulations of international conflict, we have found mediation functions (diagnosis, analysis, advice) delivered by computer results in more agreements than when the same functions are performed by live mediators. However, disputants showed a preference for the live mediators (Druckman *et al.*, 2004).
- From a meta-analysis of twenty-five years of experimental research

on bargaining processes, we know that such variables as negotiator orientation, pre-negotiation experience, and time pressure have considerably stronger effects on outcomes than representation, accountability, and visibility of the bargaining process (Druckman, 1994a).

- From content analyses of negotiation transcripts, we know that when delegates engage in sustained problem-solving behavior through the middle phases of the talks, the outcomes are more likely to be integrative (all benefit) than compromise (all sustain some losses) or impasse (Wagner, 1998).
- From complex simulations, we know that when representatives choose between courses of action that favor their interests or their ideologies, their interests prevail (Druckman et al., 1977).
- From events analyses of interactions between nations (including negotiations), we know that actors adjust their moves toward each other's previous move (or concession) in order to achieve synchrony and reduce any perceived unfair advantage. This behavior can produce impasses (Patchen and Bogumil, 1995).
- From both comparative case studies and simulations, we know that bilateral negotiating structures lead to better outcomes than do multilateral structures, especially when the bilateral interactions occur between relatively weak parties whose power is roughly equal (Beriker and Druckman, 1996; Druckman, 1997).
- From a simulation of the dispute in Cyprus, we know that cooperative negotiation processes result from confronting and discussing differences in values prior to negotiation (referred to as facilitation) as compared with ignoring those differences both before and during the negotiations (referred to as fractionating the issues) (Druckman et al., 1988).
- From a score of laboratory experiments, we see the ease with which subjects develop ingroup–outgroup perceptions and biases (even in temporary groups formed on the basis of trivial issues). We also know the difficulty of changing these perceptions and biases (Brewer and Kramer, 1985).
- From time series analyses of violent conflicts between former republics of the Soviet Union, we know that timing of mediation efforts is critical. They are more likely to work following a series of military campaigns that produce a damaging stalemate (Mooradian and Druckman, 1999).
- From survey research in former Soviet Republics, we have learned that traditional clan identities can buffer the insecure feelings that are aroused during periods of rapid social change. The secure feelings provided by the clans enabled citizens to cope with the

disruptions without jeopardizing the needed social and political societal changes (Burn, 2006).

- From field experiments of community conflict resolution centers, we know that the anticipation of arbitration can either chill or hasten movement toward reaching agreements. Chilling effects occur when bargainers fear looking weak by making concessions, when they expect a split-the-difference solution, and when they have had favorable experiences with (or actually choose) the arbitrator (Pruitt, 1981).

- Studies within organizations show that team-building exercises reduce conflict within units but can increase inter-unit conflict throughout the organization (Buller and Bell, 1986; Insko *et al.*, 1988).

- Based on results from simulated environmental conflicts, we know some conditions that lead parties down a path toward agreements and other conditions that traject them toward impasses (Druckman, 1993, 1995).

- From ethnographic descriptions, we have a richer but context-specific understanding of people's coping mechanisms in times of war. One researcher observed the ways in which people living in the midst of brutal conflict creatively resist violence through their personal stories, songs, poetry, and dance. These acts, she argues, when taken together, constitute "politics in the making" that counter violence and build the foundation for the restoration of peace (Nordstrom, 1997).

- Using narrative and discourse theory, one researcher analyzed the stories of individuals involved in the tobacco conflict, paying particular attention to power. She examined and conceptualized types of discourse in conflict (generalized, specialized, dominant, and demotic) in order to understand the stories of those in the conflict. She found, however, that these categories were not static, and individuals could choose to move among the categories, exercising influence over the course and dynamics of the conflict in the form of power or knowledge (Johnston, 2000).

- From the application of process-tracing techniques in the context of the Northern Ireland school integration movement, we have learned that social change depends on the development of a critical mass of change agents. This occurs as a consequence of fostering networks that knit together members within the same and across different community lines. These networks facilitate the education of future leaders and help them to be successful in achieving their aspirations for macro-level change (Dougherty, 2006).

- Using multiple methods (aggregate case studies, focused comparisons, and process tracing), we discovered that discussions during the process of negotiating peace agreements (as being primarily distributive or integrative) strongly influence whether a comprehensive or only partial outcome will be achieved. This relationship is causal and can be explained by the building of trust during the course of the talks (Irmer, 2003).

From findings such as these, using a wide range of methodological approaches, we can draw implications for both theory and practice. Some contributions to theory include the prevalence of equilibrium-seeking behavior, trajectories toward escalatory or de-escalatory paths, and structure (macro-level) behavior (micro-level) linkages. With regard to practice, the findings suggest ways for third parties and negotiators to arrange situations, construe issues, and encourage certain behaviors or postures that are more likely to produce beneficial agreements or improve relationships.

Improving the human condition or invading privacy?
Whether our goals reflect basic or applied purposes, research is not immune to ethical issues. We often ask subjects and respondents to provide private information or to engage in unfamiliar and sometimes uncomfortable activities, or sometimes we do not completely inform subjects about the purpose of the study. Subjects may even receive inaccurate information about themselves or others. At issue is the trade-off between the benefits of the data gathered and the potential human costs of gathering them. This issue is addressed by human subjects' review boards mandated to monitor research conducted within their institutions.

Typical examples of issues that confront the review boards include the following risks to participants:

- Control groups may miss efficacious treatments administered only to experimental (treatment) groups.
- Experimental subjects may receive information with implications for their self-images as, for example, feedback that creates low self-esteem.
- Giving subjects false information about the purpose of the study, about themselves, or about the other subjects.
- Unintended consequences of an intervention such as the shock effects of watching a simulated accident in order to study bystander behavior or strained relationships between subjects created by competitive tasks.
- Sharing data with other investigators or students without obtaining permission from the subjects or respondents.

- Devising situations that suggest to subjects that they are being "controlled" or are manipulated in an asymmetrical power relationship.
- Protecting already marginalized or manipulated populations, such as those enmeshed in deep-rooted conflict, from further harm or trauma.

In response to these and other egregious violations of subjects' rights by researchers (e.g., Milgram, 1963), some social scientists called for institutionalized procedures to protect individuals who participate in research studies (e.g., Kelman, 1968). By placing a burden on investigators to prove that subjects are fully informed about the purpose of each procedure administered and each question asked, the process adds an ethical dimension to research. Investigators are challenged to design studies that produce valuable information without harming the individuals who provide it. Researchers in many scientific fields, including conflict resolution, are rising to the challenge. They create a normative climate that encourages openness and cooperation with "no strings attached." This trend is unlikely to be reversed in the future.

This discussion of research signals some of the ways in which findings should prompt an evaluation of some of our taken-for-granted assumptions about conflict and related aspects of human behavior. Research seeks to challenge old orthodoxies and create knowledge that forms a basis for new theories. It seeks also to generate diagnoses so that practitioners might develop prescriptions in partnership with parties in conflict. Whether this is done in the framework of contingency models (e.g., Fisher and Keashly, 1991) or in terms of escalatory and de-escalatory strategies linked to some conception of when interventions are most likely to work (see Pruitt and Rubin, 1986; Kriesberg, 1992), what is now clear is that more explicit discussions need to occur between the theorists (grand, middle range and pragmatic), the researchers (from all methodological traditions), and the practitioners. It is this tripartite coalition that is most likely to result in solid theory and improved practice.

We need to classify, compare, and contextualize different types of conflict and develop higher levels of awareness about what sorts of intervention processes might yield durable solutions to some of the most complex problems confronting the world. Simultaneously, it is important to try and unravel some of the ethical and normative values underlying the field so that we are clear about why we are intervening in different conflicts and what the likely outcomes may be.

The Role of Practice

We do not need to make a case for the importance of practice when we write about human conflict and its structures, processes, and resolution. We embrace its importance and the field is burgeoning with new practitioners. We are interested in exploring, rather, what it means to be a professional practitioner and, more specifically, how effective practitioners do their work. We begin this section with a brief account of what we mean by practice, its current scope, and levels of analysis. We look at the historical connection and then separation from theory and research. We conclude with a model of reflective practice that is one attempt to reconnect the three.

What is practice?

Simply put, when we talk about practice we refer to the work that professionals do – lawyers, doctors, engineers, college professors, and, specific to our field, negotiators, mediators, consultants, conflict resolvers, and peace-builders – that involve their clients, the range of cases they are called upon to help, and their performance in professional situations. Professional practice requires a specialist who encounters certain types of situations again and again, whereby their *knowing-in-practice*, as Schön (1983) describes it, becomes tacit, spontaneous, and nearly automatic. Over time professional practitioners gain an extraordinary knowledge base that we like to believe has at its roots both theories derived from scientific research and the wisdom of practical experience. What we know is that at the heart of what it means to be a professional practitioner is the service provided to clients (patients, students, cases, projects, or other "parties" which make up their practice).

Traditional professional–client relationships are linked to a practice that may be described in a contract. These have shared norms that influence the behavior of each party. Most of the well-established professions have some codification of standards of professional and ethical behavior (e.g., the American Psychological Association's code for psychologist–patient relationships, the American Bar Association's code for attorney–client relationships, the (former) Society for Practitioners in Dispute Resolution's (SPIDR)[1] code for mediator–disputant relationships, or the International Alert Code of Conduct for NGOs). The standards are one way whereby professionals maintain quality and distinguish their work from one another.

---

[1] SPIDR is now one of the consortia associations that formed the Association for Conflict Resolution (ACR).

Types of practice

Defining the scope and limits of our practice as conflict resolvers is not easy. The interdisciplinary nature of the field tends to blur the boundaries with more traditional practitioners. The most obvious and well-known practitioners in our field are "third-party intervenors" who are not part of the dispute, and are as neutral to the outcome as possible. Examples of prominent types of practice involving third-party interventions are fully developed in Part III.

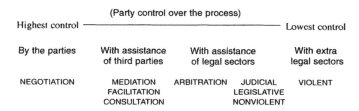

Figure 2.1 Conflict management and resolution practices
Source: adapted from Stutzman (1994, p. 131)

One distinguishing categorization of practice deals with the amount of control parties have over an intervention process. Figure 2.1 presents conflict management and resolution approaches from the perspective of the amount of control parties have over the process. The figure illustrates that disputants have the greatest degree of control over the intervention when they are in *negotiation* – private decision-making by the parties. They have lesser amounts of control over the process when third-party intervenors enter the picture: *mediation, facilitation, consultation,* and *arbitration.* The *judicial, legislative, nonviolent,* and *violent* strategies of the legal and extra-legal sectors provide disputants with the least amount of control. Similarly, intervenors who engage in practices of negotiation, facilitation, consultation, and mediation tend to be more neutral to the outcome and have less "power over" the process than when parties enter the judicial, legal, and extra-legal sectors.

The largest group of all practitioners is engaged in the middle section of this continuum: negotiation, mediation, facilitation, and arbitration, and other third-party roles. These roles are more fully developed in Part III.

Levels of conflict intervention

Practitioners provide interventions at multiple levels. They work one-to-one in informal or formal negotiations, or as third-party mediators, facilitators, or consultants, depending on the level of entry. Conflicts primarily occur within one of the following four levels:

1 *Intrapersonal* conflicts involve the dynamics that develop within individuals including their predispositions, thoughts, ideas, drives, and emotions that come in conflict with each other. Conflict resolution practitioners do not focus on the intrapsychic dynamics (this work is left to other practitioners such as therapists), but understand the implications of these internal processes when the behavior is manifested in the social setting. Examples would be unwarranted anger, hostility, aggression, fear, and depression.

2 *Interpersonal* conflicts occur between individuals. Examples include domestic disputes, sibling hostility, boss and subordinate relationships, and neighbor disputes. These are common problems for negotiators, mediators, and community or village conflict resolution practitioners.

3 *Intragroup* conflicts occur within a group such as members of a work team, departmental colleagues, clubs, associations, and political parties. These practitioners must have special expertise in the understanding of the development, processes, and dynamics of group behavior.

4 *Intergroup* conflicts occur between groups. The largest group of conflict resolvers do their work with such clients as union and management leaders, feuding neighborhood groups, competing gang members, citizens and police, and citizens and leaders of warring nations.

Practitioners usually specialize in one arena, (e.g., organizational, environmental, societal, national, and international conflicts), even though similarities exist across arenas. This type of focus, study, and practice increases conflict resolvers' ability to provide expertise in a particular area.

Implications of the history of practice

We know what we mean by practice and where practitioners do their work. But what is the relationship between theory, research, and practice? How do theories and research findings inform the work of professionals in the field?

A historical perspective is useful here. One of the earliest studies from the Carnegie Foundation for the Advancement of Teaching resulted in the famous Flexner Report on medical education (1910) which profoundly influenced the education and training of all professional practitioners in North America. Flexner was responsible for moving medical education into research universities, greatly increasing its prestige, but even more importantly, providing a new science-based component for medical practice. In the decades that followed nearly all of the professions did the same. As a result, "professionalism" meant the replacement of the artistry of their work – informed by tutorial apprenticeships – to a highly valued technical, scientific and systematic understanding of the field. This technical, research-based connection received a second boost around the time of World War II when the U.S. government began an unparalleled rate of funding research institutions with the belief that promoting the generation of new knowledge would serve to better humankind.

Governmental support continued through the Sputnik era (1957) and the Cold War, and the education and training of professionals became solidly grounded in the universities. What emerged was a disturbing tendency for research and practice to follow divergent paths as professionals made commitments to specialize and thereby pursued different enterprises. In addition to the divergent paths, a hierarchy of prestige developed with theory "on the top" and practice "on the bottom." (A classic disconnect today is what we know from research and theory in cognitive psychology about how people learn, and what actually happens in most classrooms with children and youth.) It is clear that a better balance is needed, as the separation of knowledge from practice becomes greater and the fields of specialization grow farther apart.

Reconnecting Theory, Research, and Practice

For decades, social scientists have tried to articulate how the particular processes involved as theory, research, and practice join together, but struggle to find a useful language. Originally published in 1938, Chester Banard made an important distinction between *thinking* processes from *non-logical processes*, referring the latter to those processes we are not capable of expressing into words and which are only made known by some manifestation of our behavior. Michael Polanyi (1967) invented the phrase *tacit knowing* to explain this phenomenon. (An example is our ability to recognize someone whom we know in a crowd, but not being able to describe how we do that.) Can the tacit knowledge that senior practitioners bring to their work be made more explicit if we explore fully the nexus of theory, research, and practice?

Most curricula of traditional professional programs begin with a solid grounding in the relevant basic and applied sciences, then move to skill-building and the application of this knowledge to simulated or real cases. Some attention is given to attitudes, values, and ethics in this application process. Interestingly, medical education has again taken the lead: originally there was a clear distinction between the first two years – the basic sciences – from the next few years – clinical applications. Innovative schools have since adopted problem-oriented approaches that require first-year medical students to analyze complex case-based problems that integrate the scientific, biological hard data, and the expressed symptoms and concerns of the real patient. Yet most professional programs still begin with the basics as "foundations" for practice that follows.

The Reflective Practitioner

Schön (1983) spent much of his professional life at the Massachusetts Institute of Technology (MIT) trying to understand the components of theory, research and practice, how they relate, and what impedes greater integration. Following his extensive research of practitioners in multiple fields – architecture, psychology, medicine, and engineering – he rejected outright the unnecessary and artificial separation of the three. In fact, he believed they are essential to one another. These insights emerged from his research:

> Research is an activity of practitioners. It is triggered by features of the practice situation, undertaken on the spot, and immediately linked to action. There is no question of an "exchange" between research and practice or of the "implementation of research results," when the frame – or theory testing experiments – of the practitioner at the same time transforms the practice situation. Here the exchange between research, theory, and practice is immediate, and reflection-in-action is its own implementation. (Schön, 1983, pp. 308–9)

Schön provides valuable insights into what it takes to be an effective practitioner, and a new language to describe the process. Good practitioners developed the ability to think about what they are doing while they are doing it: an on-their-feet reflection-in-action.

Since the 1960s a rebirth of interest has emerged in the ancient topics of mythology, intuition, craft, and artistry. Writers on the epistemology of practice acknowledge that good practitioners do something beyond what we can explain (Banard's non-logical processes, Polanyi's tacit knowing, Schön's reflection-in-action). Deborah Kolb and her associates (1994) offer the concept of "frame." Based on their extensive analysis of how mediators actually do their work in the mediation process, and their attempt to understand the structured patterns of science and the more ad-hoc qualities of artists at work, she offers:

> Frames are interpretive schemes that mediators use to make sense of and organize their activities while at work on a dispute. What a mediator does in a case is a blend of intentional and explicit technique, the tacit and taken-for-granted ways each has developed

of dealing with the typical cases in the practice, and more general beliefs about the causes of conflict and the possibilities for its resolution. We see frames as a way to capture some of the implicit but nonetheless powerful orientations mediators have toward their role. (Kolb, 1994, p. 469)

Experiential Learning Theory

Particularly helpful in developing a frame for understanding how practitioners do their work are the efforts of David Kolb (1984) and his colleagues at Case Western Reserve. He presents an experiential learning theory based on decades of research. He focuses on the basic dimensions of learning, how knowledge is perceived, and how it is processed. Figure 2.2 highlights Kolb's learning cycle of how experience is translated into concepts that, in turn, are used as guides in the choices of new experiences, and how this relates to practice. Learning is conceived of as a four-stage cycle. Immediate concrete experience (top of the circle) is the basis for observation and reflection (moving clockwise around the circle). These observations are assimilated into a "theory" (bottom of the circle) in which new implications for action may be deduced (the "active practice" component). These hypotheses then serve as guides in acting to create new experiences.

Rice (1996) articulated the connection between the practitioner-scholar and Kolb's learning cycle. Practitioners grapple with the basic tensions between different approaches to knowing and their own development in the process. The first tension (the vertical axis) deals with how knowledge is *perceived*. At the bottom pole of the tension is the abstract, analytical approach to the acquisition of knowledge usually associated with theory and research. What is valued here is objectivity, distance, hard quantitative evidence, and experimental rigor. At the top end is an orientation that begins with concrete experience, or what is learned from contexts, relationships, and communities. This is a very different approach to learning, building on connections and relationships, where values reveal rather than mask what is worth knowing. The practitioner attends to context and relationships to understand and make meaning of what is happening (in our case, the conflict).

The second basic dimension of learning (horizontal in Figure 2.2) deals with how knowledge is *processed* with the tension between intellectual reflection (right side) and active practice (left side). This allows us to think of theory and practice not standing in a hierarchical relationship, but rather the two mutually reinforcing and enriching each other (Rice, 1996). The study of conflict resolution is solidly embedded in the universities, and we offer this as a viable way of thinking about the

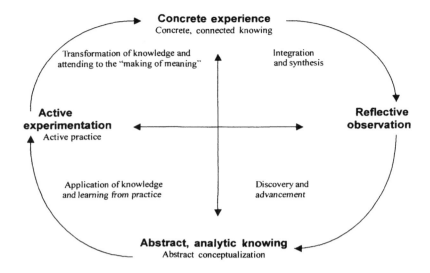

Figure 2.2 Experiential learning cycle

practitioner-scholars' connection of theory, research, and practice of conflict resolution.

What Have We Learned?

The jury is out as to whether or not we are adequately integrating theory, research, and practice. We clearly need greater insights about practice, including an understanding of the sustainability of our myths about practice, in spite of research that demonstrates the contrary. The rapid growth of the field calls us to special attention about both an understanding of this nexus of theory, research, and practice, and the ways they disconnect. Schön provides a viable model that needs further research. All of this can significantly influence the education and training of new professionals in our field.

We hope we have highlighted the critical interdependence of these three aspects to conflict analysis and resolution, and the importance of making explicit the ethical frames within which these processes are being articulated. There is, within the field, a strong analytic tradition that is connected to reformist processes of amelioration, transformation, and change. There is also a strong research tradition that has, in the past, tended to be fragmented, and has yielded often disconnected research results. It is clear that a strong practice tradition exists that challenges both theory and research. This text is aimed at exploring how these three fields connect, whether we can develop some middle-range testable theories that will result in changed diagnostic ability and practice effectiveness, and whether we can do all this in ways that will result in more effective peace-building, peacekeeping, peacemaking, and the construction of lively human communities where all peoples, all identity groups, all cultures can realize their full potentialities free from avoidable violence, death, or paralyzing dysfunctional conflict. This is a difficult charge, and, as readers will see, the authors of the various chapters are grounded in one or two of these three areas – theory and research, research and practice, or theory and practice – but not often in all three. We need to do this at all levels of action: intrapersonal, interpersonal, intragroup, and intergroup. It is to this task that we now turn.

Part I

Diagnosing Conflict

Introduction to Part I

The diagram in Chapter 1 (Figure 1.1, p. 6) has at its core – the inner circle – components necessary for *diagnosing* conflict. It provokes such questions as: What is conflict? Where does it come from? How does it unfold? Does it change over time? Part I of this book focuses on these questions. Three important variables to consider in the process of diagnosis are the types, sources, and dynamics of conflicts.

When we create a typology for analysis, we are creating a framework. Chapter 3 on types of conflict presents a comprehensive mapping of conflict and conflict resolution including the well-established "three-pillar" model of conflict. The first pillar is a discussion of the various elements – parties, issues, objectives, means, conflict orientations, and environmental contexts. The second pillar addresses the conflict causes and conditions. Here, the distinction is made between more or less complex conflicts, and emphasis is given to the importance of the complexities of the situation. These complexities must relate to the third pillar, the design of an appropriate intervention. Other typologies in the field are reviewed, such as those introduced by Boutros-Ghali when he talks of preventive diplomacy, peacemaking, peacekeeping, and peace-building; Galtung who distinguishes between positive and negative peace; and Davidson and Montville who introduced track 1 and track 2 actors and processes. The chapter provides relevant examples from around the globe, demonstrating the application of these conflicts to the three-pillar framework.

A second strategy for diagnosing conflicts involves understanding the *sources* of the conflict. Conflict sources relate to the needs, interests, values, and ideologies of the parties, institutions, or organizations. Chapter 4 focuses, in particular, on sources of destructive conflict. An archetypal conflict – the crime of Cain – is provided as an introduction to this discussion to illustrate the personal and situational sources. Building on this story throughout the chapter helps us to consider the role of social change in generating destructive and intergroup conflicts that include class, identity, and differing worldviews. A level of complexity is added by introducing the debate in the field associated with rapid social change: that destructive conflicts cannot be easily distinguished by these categories. Rather, there are multiple sources at play. The chapter concludes with a discussion of these sources – especially as they relate to the processes of modernization – for conflict resolvers. Because this chapter introduces several major theorists struggling with such concepts as Moore's social transformation and modernization, Gurr's relative deprivation, and Burton's basic human needs, it concludes with the idea that the newer theories allow us to explore the nexus between social systems and personal needs, offering a more complex understanding of deep-rooted conflicts. Challenges for the student and the conflict resolver alike include the broader political and cultural interventions that go beyond needs and situations. Current, familiar, and international conflicts are presented to illustrate the complexity of the issues.

Chapter 5 looks at the *dynamics* of conflict. The chapter begins by acknowledging that intergroup conflict requires the "three legs of a stool" presented by Brown: real differences in interests, resources, and power; stereotypes; and perceived injustices. To Brown's three legs is offered a fourth element: the interaction between the parties. It is this interaction, or *dynamics*, that moves predisposing conditions to actual conflicts. An engaging review of models of escalation (Rubin, Pruitt, and Kim; Deutsch; Tajfel; and Pruitt and Gahagan) is followed by a discussion distinguishing these deterministic models with the probabilistic nature of conflict dynamics. It introduces the influence of cognitive frameworks such as schemas, and the cumulative and generative nature of interaction. This chapter assists conflict resolvers in understanding forces for stability and change, and strategies for altering conflict dynamics.

Chapter 6 introduces a relatively new methodology for diagnosing conflict by attending to meaning-making processes based on the language the parties use in a specific conflict context. It begins with a case illustrating a complex set of circumstances in the northern region of Guatemala that has resulted in a serious conflict over ecological and cultural resources and concerns of environmental preservation. It then describes three approaches to narrative analysis – thematic content analysis (Level I), structural and functional analysis (Level II), and critical and positional analysis (Level III). At Level III the diagnosis attends to the narrative in context and the struggles that exist between the parties around power, inclusion, and marginality. The chapter concludes by revisiting the Mirador Basic case in northern Guatemala using a Level III narrative analysis. Like the others, the chapter illustrations of real-world conflicts engage the reader and provoke us to make connections between the theories of conflict and conflict resolution, and actual situations around the world. These four chapters begin our struggle to better connect theory, research, and practice as we diagnose the types, sources, and dynamics of human conflict utilizing ways the parties make meaning of their situation.

CHAPTER 3

Typology

Dennis J. D. Sandole

The purpose of this chapter is to identify and discuss *typologies of conflict*. A typology facilitates analysis and a typology of conflict could facilitate resolving as well as analyzing conflicts. Arguably, the more distinct, or even overlapping the types of conflict the better, as one would then have different, albeit interrelated insights into a given conflict situation. Such insights could enable an analyst and potential third-party intervenor to see a conflict from various angles, thereby enhancing the likelihood of a more effective response.

This chapter outlines an overarching framework in terms of which a number of different typologies may be interrelated. The underlying assumption is that the analytical potency of any one of the typologies is enhanced by its relationships with all of the others.

A Comprehensive Mapping of Conflict and Conflict Resolution

Sandole (1998a, 1998b) advanced a *three-pillar framework* (3PF) for analyzing and resolving conflicts at any level. This framework locates any particular conflict including its distinguishing characteristics under *pillar 1*, the causes and conditions of the conflict under *pillar 2*, and conflict intervention design and implementation under *pillar 3*. Schematically, the three-pillar framework is represented in Figure 3.1.

The subject matter: conflict
Before proceeding further with the framework, we should be clear about its referent, *conflict*: a process characterized by stages of initiation,

Pillar 2	Pillar 1	Pillar 3
Conflict causes and conditions	**Conflict [Latent (pre-MCP) MCP/AMCP]**	**Conflict intervention Third-party objectives**
Individual level	Parties	[*Violent*] Conflict *prevention*
Societal level	Issues	Conflict *management*
International level	Objectives	Conflict *settlement*
Global/ecological level	Means	Conflict *resolution*
	Conflict-handling	Conflict *transformation*
	Orientations	[Conflict *provention*]
	Conflict	**Third-party approaches**
	Environment	Competitive and/or cooperative processes
		Negative and/or positive peace orientations
		Track-1 and/or Multi-Track actors and processes

Figure 3.1 A comprehensive mapping of conflict and conflict resolution: a three-pillar approach

escalation, controlled maintenance, de-escalation and some kind of termination (e.g., settlement, resolution). We can distinguish between *latent conflicts* (pre-MCPs), *manifest conflict processes* (MCPs) and *aggressive manifest conflict processes* (AMCPs).

Latent conflicts are conflicts that are developing, but have not yet expressed themselves in an observable manner, even for the parties themselves. MCPs are conflicts that have developed to the extent that they are observable, but have not been expressed in a violent manner. AMCPs are conflicts that have escalated from MCPs to a violent level of expression: they are not merely capable of being noticed and experienced, but are also destructive to parties, resources, and others as well (Sandole, 1993, p. 6; Sandole, 1999b, pp. 16–17).

A practical as well as theoretical problem, then, is how to prevent latent conflicts (pre-MCPs) and MCPs from escalating to AMCPs (Sandole, 1999b, p. 1). Implicit here are different stages of conflict development and, according to Ronald Fisher and Loraleigh Keashly's *contingency theory* (see Fisher and Keashly, 1991; Fisher, 1997a, ch. 8), different types of intervention at different stages as well. As part of a comprehensive design, third parties might, for instance, use one set of intervention tools to reduce the intensity of a conflict and, once that has been accomplished, introduce other types of intervention to achieve other goals.

Also implicit here is *timing* of intervention (Kriesberg, 1987; Kleiboer, 1994; Mitchell and Banks, 1996; Mitchell, 2000b). Clearly, it would be less costly in terms of lives and other resources to prevent a violent conflict from developing while at the latent stage, rather than try to deal with it later on as an AMCP. But this is often not the case. Consider, for example, the case of Kosovo. From the time that Serb leader Slobodan Milosevic abrogated Kosovo's autonomy in 1989 until NATO's air war against Serbia to prevent further ethnic cleansing of the Kosovar Albanians during March to June 1999, eleven years had passed. During that time, thousands of Kosovar Albanians were thrown out of work and were compelled to either emigrate or create parallel structures for health care, education, and so on. This *structural violence* was often accompanied by physical violence, leading to the emergence of the Kosovo Liberation Army (KLA) and their attacks on Serbian police and other targets in the late 1990s, which led to a concerted Serb policy of ethnic cleansing of Kosovar Albanians. Hence, the comments made by heads of delegation to the Organization for Security and Cooperation in Europe (OSCE) in Vienna, following the NATO air war – that "We all saw Kosovo coming!" – indicate that violent conflict prevention certainly did not occur in this case.

Assuming that actors have the *political will* – the determination, even in the face of initial resistance from constituents and opposition parties – to do what it takes to act effectively at the right time, this is the point where an integrated set of conflict typologies could be useful in facilitating a *proactive* instead of the traditional *reactive* response. To use a metaphor well known to diplomats, some appropriate typologies could help to prevent a "house from catching on fire" (Sandole, 1999c).

Pillar 1 types: elements of conflict
Starting with pillar 1 of the three-pillar framework (3PF), *conflict* itself (latent, MCP, AMCP) – the phenomena we want to understand, predict, and somehow influence – we can distinguish between parties, issues, objectives, means, conflict-handling orientations, and the conflict environments within which conflicts occur.

Parties
Under *parties*, we can distinguish between individuals, groups, organizations, societies, states, and regions. Correspondingly, as indicated in Figure 3.2, we can also distinguish between personal, family, labor-management, environmental, identity (ethnic, racial, religious, gender), and international/"civilizational" conflicts.

While these types of conflict are analytically distinct, operationally they may overlap. Groups may be fairly small, such as the family; or

Types of conflict	Levels of conflict	Units
Personal	Intrapsychic	
	Interpersonal	Individuals
Family	Interpersonal [intragroup]	Individuals
	Intergroup	Groups
Labor management	Interorganizational/	Organizations
Environmental	Group-organizational/ interorganizational	Groups
	[intrasocietal/intrastate]	Organizations
	Intersocietal/intrastate, interstate	Societies States
Identity [class, ethnic, gender, racial, religious]	Intergroup/interorganizational [intrasocietal/intersocietal]	Groups Organizations Societies
	Intra-/interstate	States
International/ "civilizational"	Interstate/transnational	States Civilizations

Figure 3.2 A party typology of conflict

large, such as ethnic, racial, and religious *identity* groups. Organizations may be local, national, regional, or international as well as governmental or nongovernmental.

Another useful distinction under parties is between *intrapsychic* and *inter-actor* conflicts. In many cases, such as those involving the genocidal ethnic cleansing associated with the recent Balkan wars of the 1990s, a potential third party (pillar 3) may have to deal first with *chosen traumas* (Volkan, 1997) at the intrapsychic level (pillar 2) – for example, the impact of the fall of Kosovo on June 28, 1389 to the Ottoman Turks, on the identities of Serbs and their perceptions of Turks and Muslims in general – as a necessary (but not sufficient) condition for dealing with later conflicts at the inter-actor level between Serbs and Albanian or Bosnian Muslims (pillar 1) (Parkinson, 1977, pp. 202–3; Sandole, 1987, p. 296; Sandole, 2002).

A typology developed by Kenneth Boulding (1956, 1959) in his work on cognitive, evaluative, and affective images is useful here. The *cognitive* level deals with beliefs; the *evaluative* with the values we assign to beliefs; and the *affective* with the emotional energy mobilized to defend highly valued beliefs under threat.

For example, a woman abused by her parents at a preverbal stage of life may be carrying around a lot of repressed emotional energy from her traumatic childhood, and spend the greater part of her life, with or without therapeutic assistance, trying to "attribute" the right meaning (cognition) to the affect. In Boulding's system, the woman's affective image may overwhelm and dominate her cognitive image.

When there is such a gap between the affective and cognitive interpretations of the same event, the challenge for a prospective third party is to assist the individuals involved to achieve consonance between the two so that the cognitive is an accurate reflection of the affective. Otherwise, the individual may spend her entire life engaging in inter-actor conflicts through spillover (*transference*) from the intrapsychic level, displacing feelings originally aroused by a situation earlier in her life on to individuals in later situations which may be similar, as part of her effort to make sense of and perhaps eliminate acutely uncomfortable feelings.

Cognitive dissonance – Leon Festinger's (1962) concept which captures the experience of such acutely uncomfortable feelings – may be viewed as a breakdown between cognitive and affective images, where highly valued needs for predictability, regularity, and stability (the "PRS" needs; Sandole, 1984, 1987) may have been violated. The less an actor's expectations are fulfilled, the less *predictability* she or he experiences; the less predictability, the less *regularity*; and the less regularity, the less *stability* (and overall emotional security). The PRS needs – a subset of Maslow's (1987) *safety and security* needs – are deeply rooted, possessing the status of what Boulding (1962) calls *inner-core values* (in contrast to the more negotiable *outer-shell values*). This leads to yet another, but overlapping, distinction by Burton (1990b) between *conflicts*, which are about non-negotiable (inner-core) values, and *disputes*, which concern negotiable (outer-shell) values.

Examples of intrapsychic conflict, which may or may not spill over to the inter-actor level, include role-set conflict and multiple-position conflict. *Role-set* conflict deals with two conflicting parts of the same role, e.g., the wife vs. mother components of the married woman role, where a married woman finds that the more she tries to perform her role as a mother, the more she does so at the expense of her spousal role, and vice versa. *Multiple-position* conflict, on the other hand, deals with conflict between two or more different roles, e.g., married woman vs. working woman (Thompson and Van Houten, 1970). Multiple-position conflict may also apply to a member of a third-party team intervening in, for instance, the conflict between Israelis and Palestinians, where the person is a Palestinian or an Israeli Jew concerned for the safety and rights of his or her "own" people as well as a specialist in conflict resolution concerned with third-party-facilitated processes leading to fair, durable outcomes.

There are also *motivational* conflicts, one characteristic of which is that, due to countervailing forces, they tend to lead to decision-making impasses. The most benign of these is the *approach–approach* conflict between two equally attractive options, such as might be experienced by parties to a conflict negotiating their way between two equally attractive settlement packages. Probably the most painful type of motivational conflict is the *avoidance–avoidance* conflict between two equally unattractive options; for instance, the Holocaust-era nightmare faced by the Jewish mother in *Sophie's Choice* (Styron, 1979). A more recent example is the emotional crisis in Britain caused by the dilemma about whether to separate conjoined twins. To separate the twins, as sanctioned by the Court of Appeal, would lead to the death of one twin, "Mary," so that the other, "Jodie," could live. To leave the twins attached – the parents' choice, supported by the Roman Catholic Church – would probably lead to the death of both (Barr, 2000; O'Callaghan, 2000; Raspberry, 2000).

Then there are the more "complex" motivational conflicts. For example, *approach–avoidance* conflict can occur between the equally compelling negative and positive elements of a given option, such as might be experienced by parties to a conflict confronted by one peace plan characterized by negative *and* positive elements. *Double approach–avoidance* conflict can occur between two options, each characterized by equally weighted negative and positive elements, such as might be experienced by parties to a conflict confronted by two settlement packages, each characterized by negative and positive features (Brown, 1957).

At the inter-actor level, the classic distinction is between *balanced (symmetrical)* and *unbalanced (asymmetrical)* conflicts. Here the key question for intervenors is whether the parties are the same (balanced or symmetrical) or different (unbalanced or asymmetrical) in terms of access to resources (Curle, 1971). If, as is often the case, one party is observed to have the upper hand, a potential third party adhering to a strict notion of *neutrality* may experience a decision-making quandary. If he facilitates the parties arriving at an agreement that leaves intact the original iniquitous relational system that helped bring about the conflict in the first place, then the settlement may not be a durable one. If, on the other hand, he steps temporarily outside of the neutral role to help empower the originally disempowered party (e.g., by providing a workshop in negotiation skills for residents of a contaminated area in an environmental conflict), perhaps initially compromising his neutrality in the eyes of the originally more powerful party, he may nevertheless, over time, help the parties reach a durable agreement.

Hence strict neutrality, which leaves in place "structural violence," may be a less important norm for a third party than working within an overarching, flexible framework focusing on durable (and therefore, *impartial*) solutions: if conflicts are indeed complex, as the author has argued elsewhere (Sandole, 1999b), then efforts to deal with them must capture that complexity.

The various units and levels of analysis listed in Figure 3.2, and the possibility for conflicts to spill over from one level to another, are a useful reminder that theorists/researchers and practitioners should be clear about what units and levels they are focusing on at any point in time. Otherwise, they may inadvertently "vertically drift" across units and levels (Singer, 1961). This includes generalizing inappropriately from macro to micro levels (*ecological fallacies*), and generalizing inappropriately from micro to macro levels (*individualistic fallacies*). Apart from genuine cases of spillover or appropriate generalizability, one may start out talking about actors at one level and end up making fallacious conclusions about the same or other actors at other levels (Frankfort-Nachmias and Nachmias, 1996, pp. 54–5).

Issues
A plethora of typologies exists under the second component of pillar 1, *issues*: the reasons parties claim they are waging conflict with each other. For instance, conflicts may be *structural* or *nonstructural* (Moore, 1986). If structural, conflicts may be concerned with change in, or maintenance of existing political, economic, social or other systems (e.g., during the Cold War, the West's defense of democracy and capitalism against the perceived threats posed by Marxism/communism, and vice versa). Nonstructural conflicts, on the other hand, may be concerned with means to ends in existing systems; for instance, enhancing the rights of minorities in order to conform to an existing state constitution and, subsequently, to the norms and values of entities in which the state seeks membership, such as the European Union.

Issues may also be *realistic* or *nonrealistic* (Coser, 1956): really about something, such as territory (Vasquez, 1993), or "merely" the manifestation of a need to let off steam. Apropos the complexity of many conflicts, sometimes, through transference of responses associated with earlier conflicts, the need for emotional release (*catharsis*) may translate into a realistic conflict. In such a case, a potential third party may have to deal first with the earlier conflict, and the associated unresolved need to release pent-up energy, as a necessary (but not sufficient) condition of dealing with the more recent conflict. This highlights further the importance of the intrapsychic level and the necessity of bringing the affective and cognitive definitions of the situation into a harmonious relationship, one of many challenges facing the third party (Sandole, 2002).

Issues may also be, according to Morton Deutsch (1973), *displaced*, in which case we may have the right parties, but the wrong issues. For example, the passion may have gone out of a relationship between a husband and wife, and rather than deal with the threatening dissonance in the valued relationship, they may argue about other, "safer" issues, for example, where to spend their vacations, or what to watch on television. Thus the "real" problem remains unresolved, always ready to break out again.

Further, issues may be suggestive of *misattributed* conflicts (*ibid.*), where, for instance, political leaders – consciously or otherwise reflecting the propositions of Simmel (1955) and Coser (1956) – may even go so far as to invent enemies if none already exist in order to project/displace conflicts (affect) within the ingroup on to some outgroup, as a way to stave off internal dissent and remain in power. This is what Burton (1979) calls *role defense*, one of the most salient examples of which was Serb leader Slobodan Milosevic's manipulation of the legacy of Kosovo for many Serbs in the late 1980s – culminating in the genocidal ethnic cleansing of Albanians in Kosovo during 1998 to 1999 – as a way to hold on to power when, during and after the ending of the Cold War, other communist leaders were collapsing all around him (Sandole, 1999b).

Objectives

The *objectives* component of pillar 1 includes *status-quo-changing* and *status-quo-maintaining* options (Lerche and Said, 1970). For instance, if the husband and wife referred to above start to face their real conflict directly, the wife may want to terminate the marriage (structural/status-quo-changing) while the husband may want to hold on to it (status-quo-maintaining). The question here, of course, is how should a potential third party deal with a clash between two apparently irreconcilable opposites? This has become a major challenge for third parties attempting to deal with a defining characteristic of the post-Cold War world: situations involving clashes between the contradictory preferences within existing states for self-determination on the part of status-quo-changing minorities and for territorial integrity on the part of status-quo-maintaining majorities (Mikeladze, 2000).

Means

The *means* that parties employ to achieve their objectives include violent and nonviolent forms of conflict. In this regard, one of the classics in the field, Anatol Rapoport's *Fights, Games, and Debates* (1960), is suggestive of a useful typology. In *fights*, the parties view each other as enemies and attempt to destroy each other (AMCPs). In *games*, the parties view each other as opponents and attempt to outwit each other (MCPs). And in *debates*, parties view each other as opponents and attempt to persuade each other (and/or some neutral third party) that each's position is valid (MCPs). In contingency theory fashion (Fisher, 1997), if an intermediary finds that a conflict is at the AMCP level, his or her priorities would include exploring how to extinguish the fire and then how to transform the "fight" into a "debate."

While many in the diplomatic and other fields talk about conflict *prevention*, we in the field of conflict analysis and resolution (CAR) do not endeavor to prevent conflict as such, as conflict (an MCP) may be an early warning sign that something has gone wrong in an otherwise valued relationship, which should be addressed. Conflict in this "functional" sense would not be a bad thing. Instead, as indicated above, we are advocates for the prevention of MCPs (debates, games) escalating into AMCPs (fights), because then conflicts become more costly and difficult to deal with. We are, therefore, concerned with *violent conflict prevention* (a third-party option to which we will return in our discussion of pillar 3).

Conflict-handling orientations
Next under pillar 1 are the parties' approaches to *conflict handling*. Along a competitive–cooperative gradient (Deutsch, 1973), parties may be characterized by *avoidance, accommodation, confrontation, compromise*, and/or *collaboration* (Thomas, 1975). Implicit here is the question of the parties' underlying worldviews, their philosophies, and views of human nature. Competitive parties may be associated with a *Realpolitik* approach to life, characterized by a dim, Hobbesian view of the human condition and a Machiavellian philosophy that says, "anything goes!" Cooperative parties, on the other hand, may be associated with an *Idealpolitik* approach, characterized by a sanguine view of human nature and a philosophy that seeks to advance social justice for all concerned (Sandole, 1993, 1999b). The value of this for potential third parties is that, although they may initially find that a conflict is at the AMCP level, they may also find that the parties are fundamentally characterized by cooperative orientations to conflict handling, which could make their task of helping to transform the AMCP (fight) into an MCP (debate) considerably easier (Abu-Nimer, 2003).

Conflict environments
Finally under pillar 1, we have *conflict environments*, where, again, Rapoport (1974) has been helpful, in this case distinguishing between endogenous and exogenous environments. *Endogenous* conflict settings are those where there are mechanisms available for controlling or resolving conflict, in contrast to *exogenous* environments where there are

few, if any, mechanisms of this kind, as in the *Realpolitik* conception of the international system (Waltz, 1959).

Given that the "space" within which a conflict unfolds may comprise multiple environments – cultural, religious, economic, political, institutional, each with its own possible presence or absence of appropriate mechanisms – the third-party assessment here may not be an either/or one, but an exploration of the *extent* to which a conflict environment *is* endogenous and then to *coordinate* with those who administer the corresponding mechanisms to help the parties reach a cooperative, durable outcome.

Since the end of the Cold War, the Organization for Security and Cooperation in Europe (OSCE) has been endeavoring to transform the OSCE area, covering fifty-six participating states "from Vancouver to Vladivostok," into more of an endogenous conflict resolution system. The system currently includes mechanisms for violent conflict prevention, crisis management, and post-violent conflict rehabilitation, such as the Office for Democratic Institutions and Human Rights (ODIHR) in Warsaw; the High Commissioner on National Minorities (HCNM) in The Hague; the Conflict Prevention Centre (CPC) in Vienna; various field missions in member states; and most recently, "REACT": the Rapid Expert Assistance and Cooperation Teams (see Zaagman and Thorburn, 1997; Hopmann, 1999, 2000, 2005; Kemp *et al.*, 1999; *OSCE Newsletter*, 2000).

It is quite possible that not all the parties to conflicts within the OSCE area are aware of what the OSCE (and other international organizations such as the European Union, NATO, and Council of Europe) have to offer, or that OSCE and other "early warners" themselves may not always be aware of what each has to offer or of latent conflicts developing in the region. Potential third parties, therefore, could help to identify those mechanisms and conflicts, and facilitate coordination between the mechanisms and the parties concerned as all seek to avoid "future Yugoslavias" (see Sandole, 2007).

It is by now evident that pillar 1 is rich in typological possibilities, comprising a variety of different approaches to, and insights into different conflict situations. Again, in identifying various perspectives on conflict – *which are not necessarily mutually exclusive* – we are able to learn more about any given conflict, thus enhancing our efforts to respond effectively to it.

Pillars 2 and 3 are less bountiful than pillar 1 in this respect, but, further enhancing our efforts to understand *and* deal effectively with conflict, they nevertheless are suggestive of some typologies.

Pillar 2 types: conflict causes and conditions

Under pillar 2, *conflict causes and conditions*, we can distinguish between relatively more or less *complex* conflicts. The more dimensions surrounding – or *variables* involved in – a conflict, the more complex it is and, by implication, the more difficult it would be to deal with. In a conflict involving two children fighting over a toy, for example, the conflict might be successfully dealt with by producing another toy of equal value. This clearly contrasts with the genocidal ethnic conflict in the Balkans during the 1990s, where it could take one or more generations for the parties – Serbs and Croats, Serbs and Bosniac Muslims, Croats and Bosniac Muslims, Serbs and Kosovar Albanians – to live together again (Lederach, 1997).

It is important to be aware of the complexity of many conflict situations. It is also important to be aware of possible connections (for instance, through spillover) between types/levels (Kriesberg, 1980; Sandole, 1999b). Further, it is important to be aware of the possibility of cross-type/cross-level commonalities, such that a *generic theory* of (1) conflict causes and conditions, and (2) conflict intervention may be developed.

The premise here is that a generic theory would be useful, not just for explaining, but for responding to, conflict at *all* levels, including the violent ethnic conflict and warfare of the post-Cold War era (Mitchell and Banks, 1996; Lederach, 1997). Although, as indicated in Figure 3.2, conflict may be expressed at different levels (pillar 1) – and in that sense, conflicts are truly different – their etiology may nevertheless reflect variables operating in terms of the same set of levels (pillar 2). This has been suggested by, among others, Kenneth Waltz (1959) and Robert North (1990) in international relations, and by John Paul Scott (1958) in his work on the biological sources of human aggression. Hence conflicts may be very similar in terms of their causes, conditions, and dynamics, involving, for example, *structural* and *cultural violence* (Galtung, 1969, 1996), *relative deprivation* (Gurr, 1970), *rank disequilibrium* (Galtung, 1964), *frustration-aggression* (Dollard *et al.*, 1939), and *basic human needs* (Burton, 1979, 1990, 1997). Further, if conflicts (pillar 1) are caused by factors at different levels (pillar 2), then efforts to deal with them (pillar 3) must "capture that complexity" as well (Sandole, 1999b).

Pillar 3 types: conflict intervention

This takes us into pillar 3, *conflict intervention*, where a potential third party can attempt to facilitate processes leading to quite different, albeit potentially interrelated outcomes (see Part III of this volume). Again using the metaphor of a burning house, a potential third party could aim to prevent the house from catching fire in the first place: *violent conflict prevention*, as was accomplished by the first-ever UN preventive deployment mission (UNPREDEP), in Macedonia (Ackermann, 1999; Sokalski, 2003; Williams, 2000).

If that fails, which it often does, the intervenors have a number of other options available to them. They can attempt to prevent the fire from spreading: conflict *management*, as was attempted by the UN Protection Force (UNPROFOR) in Bosnia-Hercegovina. Failing that, as UNPROFOR in fact did, they can attempt to put the fire out, forcefully if necessary: conflict *settlement*, as was done by NATO following the shameful débâcle of the fall of the first UN-protected "safe area" in Bosnia-Hercegovina, Srebrenica, in July 1995 (see Honig and Both, 1996; Rohde, 1997). The third party may then enforce the settlement, as NATO had been doing in Bosnia-Hercegovina, first with the Implementation Force (IFOR) and then the Stabilization Force (SFOR) before it was replaced by the European Union's EUFOR in December 2004. NATO is still involved in Kosovo (KFOR).

Having put the fire out, intervenors may (or, as is often the case, may not) decide to go further and deal with the underlying combustible, causes and conditions of the fire at hand: conflict *resolution*. (*Resolution* is still lagging behind military-based *management* efforts in Bosnia and Kosovo (Smith, 2000; Washington Post, 2002).) Having achieved that, they may decide to work on the long-term relationships among the survivors of the "burned house" and their neighbors so that, next time they have a conflict, they do not have to burn down the house, the neighborhood, and the "commons" (as Israelis and Palestinians have been doing for years). This is conflict *transformation*, leading to, in John Burton's (1990b, 1997a) scheme, conflict *provention*: the prevention of deep-rooted conflict by eliminating structural violence and other underlying causes and conditions of deep-rooted conflict (Mitchell and Banks, 1996; Lederach, 1997).

The typology advanced by former UN Secretary General Boutros Boutros-Ghali in his *An Agenda for Peace* (1992) – as part of his effort to make the UN more relevant to the conflicts of the post-Cold War world – comes to mind here. For example, his

- *preventive diplomacy* = violent conflict prevention;
- *peacemaking* = (coercive) conflict settlement and (noncoercive) conflict resolution;
- *peacekeeping* = conflict management;
- *peace-building* = conflict transformation [provention].

Implicit here is another set of types: negative vs. positive peace (Galtung, 1969). There is nothing inherently wrong with *negative peace*. Negative in this context merely means the *absence* of something: the absence of hostilities, achieved either through the prevention of potential, or the cessation of actual hostilities, usually by competitive means such as the threat or actual use of force by police or military forces. Negative peace is what most people mean by peace.

Positive peace, on the other hand, may assume negative peace, but, in any case, moves beyond it to deal with the underlying conflict causes and conditions (pillar 2), through the use of cooperative and/or competitive means, to aim for Burton's provention by eliminating structural violence: situations where members of certain racial, religious, ethnic, gender, and/or other minority *outgroups* are denied access to political, economic, social, and other resources typically enjoyed and controlled by the majority *ingroup*, primarily because of the former's involuntary status as minorities.

Combining some of the above categories together, the common objectives of preventive diplomacy (= violent conflict prevention), *coercive* peacemaking (= conflict settlement), and peacekeeping (= conflict management), are to achieve and maintain *negative peace*. By contrast, the common objectives of *noncoercive* peacemaking (= conflict resolution), and peace-building (= conflict transformation), are achieving and maintaining *positive peace*.

Negative peace measures, therefore, are concerned with preventing a house from catching fire at the latent or MCP stage. Or, if the fire is occurring, transforming MCP into AMCP, then putting the fire out entirely. However, negative peace measures do not necessarily deal with the underlying causes and conditions. Positive peace measures, on the other hand, are designed to deal with underlying causes and conditions.

The difficulty of achieving and maintaining long-term durable peace demonstrates the need for a variety of actors working to achieve peace through different means at different levels. Thus another set of pillar 3 types is useful here: track 1 and multi-track actors and processes (Davidson and Montville, 1981/1982; McDonald and Bendahmane, 1987; Diamond and McDonald, 1996). While *track 1* refers to governmental/international governmental actors (i.e., states and interstate governmental organizations [IGOs], such as the UN, OSCE, NATO, European Union, Council of Europe), multi-track refers to local, national, and international conflict resolution NGOs and other nongovernmental actors (for example, individuals, religious groups, multinational corporations, philanthropic and other grant-giving institutions, trainers, the media).

Traditionally track 1 has aimed for negative peace, often through competitive means, while multi-tracks (2–9) actually came into existence to fill the void, picking up where track 1 has tended to leave off, attempting to achieve positive peace through cooperative means. Clearly, to achieve and maintain positive as well as negative peace, track 1 and tracks 2–9 must work together in a *coordinated* fashion, as Michael Lund (1996) has argued in his book, *Preventing Violent Conflicts* (also see Nan, 2004). This is the objective of the Platform for Cooperative Security of the OSCE's Charter on European Security (*OSCE Istanbul Summit*, 1999), and of the Stability Pact for South Eastern Europe: an EU and American initiative for a coordinated *regional* approach to the problems of the Balkans (see Pierre, 1999; Soros, 1999; SP, 1999; AIIS, 2000; Busek, 2006). The author's own design for an integrated, coordinated post-Cold War peace and security system – the *new European peace and security system* (NEPSS) – reflects these sentiments as well (Sandole, 1998c, 1999a, 1999b, 2007).

Conclusion

The regional focus of the Stability Pact for South Eastern Europe is one example of potential, significant movement toward capturing the complexity of the identity-based conflicts of the post-Cold War world. The savage wars in Croatia and especially Bosnia were apparently not sufficient for the international community to recognize the utility of a regional approach to violent conflict prevention, management, settlement, resolution, and transformation. Reflecting a major principle of complexity theory – that everything is connected to everything else (Waldrop, 1992) – it took the further brutality of Kosovo to encourage policy-makers and laypersons alike to realize that any strategy for dealing with *any* conflict in the Balkans must deal with *all* of them, if not at the same time, then certainly in sequence. The same applies to conflicts in other regions as well, for example, in Africa (Crocker, 1999) and the Middle East (Callan and Sevastopulo 2006). In this regard, the three-pillar mapping of the field used to structure this discussion could be a useful point of departure for capturing the complexity of conflict at any level, anywhere, anytime, as a necessary (but not sufficient) condition for doing something about it (Sandole, 2007)!

Again, this demonstrates the utility of types of conflict. The more types – the more angles or perspectives we have on conflict – the more likely it is that we are capturing the whole beast and not just any one part of the proverbial elephant as defined by any of the three blind men (or women). The problem with the fragmentation of knowledge associated with the traditional disciplines and our academic degrees is that we tend to have only one of those perspectives at a time (Burton, 1997a).

With the return to Europe of genocide and its persistence in Africa (e.g., Rwanda, Darfur) and elsewhere (Gurr, 1993, 2000; Marshall and Gurr, 2005), the time has surely come to resurrect Renaissance Man *and* Woman; to put "Humpty Dumpty back together again" (Burton, 1997a; Wilson, 1998a, 1998b; Sandole, 1999b), and recapture the complexity of conflicts. Otherwise, our well-intentioned but nevertheless one-dimensional, simplistic efforts to do something about them may only make matters worse. In that event, we become complicit, part of the problem instead of the solution, enhancing the reactive tendency of policy-makers to perpetuate the often structurally violent status quo (e.g., Iraq).

Discussion Questions

1 What is the analytical value of the three-pillar framework (3PF)?
2 Discuss some of the aspects of each of the elements of *pillar 1*: actors, issues, objectives, means, conflict-handling orientations, and conflict environments.
3 Why is it important to deal with the intrapsychic level in deep-rooted, protracted conflict?
4 Why is it important to achieve congruence between the affective and cognitive levels?
5 What is the point, under *pillar 2*, of identifying potential causes and conditions operative at multiple levels (e.g., the individual, societal, international, and global/ecological levels)?
6 Using the metaphor of the "burning house," indicate, under *pillar 3*, the options available to a potential third party who is interested in responding to any complex, identity-based conflict.
7 What is "structural violence" and how can it be dealt with?
8 How might a third party's strict emphasis on neutrality lead to counterproductive outcomes?
9 Discuss how the three-pillar framework (3PF) might be useful to better understand and deal with the conflicts that seem to lead to school and workplace violence in the USA.
10 How might third parties deal with the often zero-sum clash between self-determination and territorial integrity: a distinguishing feature of the post-Cold War world?

Key Words

Affective level
Aggressive manifest conflict processes (AMCPs)
Basic needs
Chosen trauma

Cognitive dissonance
Cognitive level
Complexity
Comprehensive mapping
Conflict typologies
Cultural violence
Ecological fallacies
Evaluative level
Generic theory
Idealpolitik
Individualistic fallacies
Inter-actor level
Intrapsychic level
Latent conflict (pre-MCPs)
Manifest conflict processes (MCPs)
New European peace and security systems (NEPSS)
Organization for Security and Cooperation in Europe (OSCE)
Realpolitik
Structural violence
Three-pillar framework (3PF)

CHAPTER 4

Sources

Richard E. Rubenstein

Human conflict is omnipresent and ubiquitous. The potential for conflict exists whenever individuals or groups pursue goals that they perceive to be incompatible. In this sense, conflict is an inescapable feature of our social life, an activity whose effects are often beneficial either because they help to clarify differences, let off steam, or generate needed change (Coser, 1964). But *destructive* conflict – conflict that destroys or injures valued lives, psyches, institutions, and possessions – is another story. Although highly probable under certain circumstances, it is by no means inevitable. Identifying and understanding the sources of destructive social conflict is a key to reducing its frequency and intensity, and, in time, to making massive violence a rare occurrence in human affairs.

Generations of storytellers, commentators, and analysts have proposed two general sources of destructive conflict: human nature and social situations or structures. Clearly, since humans are social beings, these categories cannot be neatly separated. Suppose that one is trying to understand the rise of German Nazism, for example. Should the conflict in that nation be attributed to *personal* factors, like the vengefulness of Western leaders toward Germany after World War I, Hitler's aggressive and charismatic personality, the mass neuroses and prejudices of his German followers, or a masculine love of warfare? Or should primary emphasis be placed on *situational* factors, like the authoritarian strain in German culture, class divisions exacerbated by the collapse of the German economy, the weakness of the Weimar Republic, and intensified competition between the Great Powers?

Since each of these causes or conditions seems to have played some role in bringing the Nazis to power, one is tempted to answer, "All of the above." But good theory about the sources of conflict ought to tell us (among other things) which factors are more important and which are less so, which are underlying conditions of the conflict and which are active causes, which are limited to a specific conflict environment or likely to cause destruction in other environments. Daniel Druckman (1999) has argued persuasively that, in most cases, the situation is of primary importance in political explanation. Still, scholarly debate continues over which general source is more potent in explaining how destructive conflict is generated, escalated, and resolved. An interesting example is the dispute over Adolph Hitler's role between the historian A.J.P. Taylor, who viewed the German dictator as a nationalist leader responding to Great Power competition (situational explanation), and other historians, who saw him as the embodiment of ideological fanaticism and power-lust (personal explanation). (For further discussion, see Martel, edn, 1999.)

At the same time, combining the two perspectives often yields a richer understanding of complex conflicts than relying on either one alone. The point can be illustrated by considering one of the narratives most influential in shaping Jewish, Christian and Islamic views on the sources of conflict: the biblical tale of Cain and Abel.

Personal and Situational Sources of Conflict: The Crime of Cain

In the story told in the Bible (Genesis, 4:1–16), Adam and Eve's younger son, Abel, offers a gift to God in the form of the firstborn of his flock of sheep, and God accepts it. But when Cain, the elder son, makes a sacrifice of farm produce, God spurns his offering. In consequence, Cain hates Abel. God upbraids him for being angry and warns him against the sin that "couches at the door," but Cain disregards the warning and kills Abel in the field. When God asks him, "Where is your brother?" Cain replies with a surly denial reflecting on Abel's shepherding occupation: "I do not know; am I my brother's keeper?" God punishes the killer by driving him from the soil and condemning him to wander the earth as a fugitive, but he protects him against vengeful men by marking him with a sign. Cain settles in the "land of Nod, east of Eden," where he becomes a founder of cities, and Adam and Eve conceive another son to replace Abel: Seth, the ancestor of Noah.

At first glance, the sources of this archetypal conflict seem purely personal. Cain is jealous of his brother. The murderous rage generated by this jealousy is clearly one source of his destructive violence against

Abel. But it is a necessary, not a sufficient cause, since the storyteller assumes that Cain's fratricidal impulse is resistible. The sin that "couches at the door," which God warns him against, is the temptation to turn aggressive feelings into aggressive action, and so to move from potential to actual destructiveness. In yielding to temptation, Cain misuses his freedom, and it is this act (rather than jealousy *per se*) that justifies God's punishment of him. (See the discussion in Bill Moyers *et al.*, 1996.)

The overt sources of the conflict, therefore, are portrayed as doubly personal: first Cain experiences aggressive impulses directed toward his brother, then he ignores God's warning (i.e., he acts aggressively towards God) by acting on these impulses. These two ideas – the propensity of human beings to want to injure others and to sin against God – are fundamental to certain pessimistic (or, as their advocates like to say, "realistic") approaches to conflict. Some theorists believe that aggressiveness is a fundamental instinct for which we have been genetically programmed as a result of evolutionary pressure (Lorenz, 1974). Others, like the storyteller of Genesis, emphasize people's incurable tendency to break moral rules out of sheer rebelliousness (Augustine, 1963, pp. 40–51) or because they want to be God (Niebuhr, 1996). The implication, in either case, is that there is not much one can do about these feelings and behaviors except to try to control them both externally, through threats of punishment by parents or public authorities, and internally, through the self-punishment of guilt.

But suppose that we consider the same conflict situationally. Cain does not become jealous of Abel for no reason at all; his jealousy is a *response* to God's preference for the younger brother's sacrifice – a divine "put-down" that the story does not explain. Biblical commentators have long supplied speculative reasons for this preference: for example, that Abel's sacrifice was given with a pure heart (see Moyers *et al.*, 1996, p. 76 *et seq.*). But there is nothing in the text to justify this sort of addition. Some modern social psychologists would explain things this way: rather than being a basic instinct that strives always to express itself, like boiling water giving off steam, aggressiveness is a behavioral *capacity* that becomes manifest only in response to certain situations that the individual finds extremely threatening or frustrating (Dollard, 1980). In this view, when the level of threat or frustration gets high enough, anti-social behavior will occur. Those strongly motivated to control their aggression (in the Genesis story, to heed God's warning) may resist acting aggressively for a time or direct their rage against some other target. But if the level of provocation continues to rise, all but the rarest individuals will give way eventually to aggressive or self-destructive behavior.

We would still like to know, however, *which* situations (which types of threat or frustration) are most likely to produce destructive conflicts among human beings. Here, two approaches – psychoanalytic theory and human needs theory – may have something more to tell us about Cain, Abel, and ourselves.

Psychoanalytic theory would suggest that the situation portrayed in Genesis is one of sibling rivalry, with God "standing in" for the parent for whose attention and approval the children compete (see, e.g., Akhtar and Kramer, eds. 1999). The less-favored child is hurt and angered when the parent seems to reject him (God asks Cain, "Why are you so downcast?"), but hating one's parent is taboo. The forbidden anger is therefore "repressed," or denied entry into consciousness. But repressed emotions do not simply disappear; after a time, they return to consciousness detached from their original object and directed against some more "acceptable" and vulnerable target (Freud, 1915/1957; see also the more recent research summarized in Druckman and Bjork, eds. 1994, pp. 277–93). The rejected child substitutes the favored sibling for the parent and directs his anger against that sib, who serves the role of scapegoat. The scapegoat in this story is Abel, but the real target of Cain's anger is God.

Certainly, one might reply, sibling rivalry is a normal part of family life, but most children work out their displaced anger without killing each other! What accounts in this case for Cain's lethal response? One answer is provided by the theory of basic human needs, which holds that people have certain fundamental, imperative, and irrepressible needs that *must* be satisfied if destructive feelings and behaviors are to be avoided (Maslow, 1987). Among these are basic needs for identity and recognition that prove, if unsatisfied, to be more productive of violence than material needs or desires. People will not necessarily revolt if they lose their jobs or their homes, but threaten to deprive them of their individual or group identities, and rebellion is predictable (Burton, 1997). Thus, ordinary sibling rivalry may be tolerable, but acts by a parent that withdraw recognition from a disfavored child are like the acts of a state or an ethnic majority refusing to honor the identity of a despised ethnic minority. They are quite likely to provoke a violent explosion.

Note that the perspectives of depth psychology and basic human needs, like the more general theories of threat-aggression and frustration-aggression, attribute the Cain-Abel conflict to interactions taking place in the context of a social structure. In this case, the *structure* is a family triangle composed of two siblings and a parent (or parent-substitute), and the *situation* that generates the conflict is the parent's refusal to satisfy one sibling's need for recognition. Unlike earlier approaches to aggression and sin, these theories locate individual capacities to harm others in a social context that largely determines whether and how those capacities will be unleashed. The tendency of these theories is to distribute the responsibility for anti-social behavior, to some extent, among all the parties who participate in a conflict-generating system. Furthermore, they relieve the pessimism of the earlier theories by implying that, if it is a definable social situation that generates the destructive conflict, it may be possible to alter the situation so as to reduce or prevent that type of conflict in the future.

This does not relieve the Cains of the world from moral responsibility for their actions. But it does expose the complicity of other parties and institutions that function either as active causes or necessary conditions for outbreaks of violence. And it may call attention to concrete steps that would move the parties toward resolution of their conflict. In the story of Cain and Abel, God practices the first recorded act of conflict resolution: even while exiling Cain and sentencing him to a life of hardship, he marks the killer in order to prevent others from taking revenge on him. Foreseeing continued strife in the future, God interrupts the cycle of vengeance, and makes it possible for Cain to become a founder of cities. In the same forward-looking spirit, one may also ask, why not alter the situation in which what one child (or group) has to offer is recognized, while the other's offering (or identity) is refused recognition? The great biblical narrative may also teach us something about the unintended consequences of inequality, in this case with regard to recognition.

The Social Sources of Destructive Conflict

The story of Cain and Abel leads us directly to consider the role of social change in generating destructive intergroup conflicts. The context for Cain's sin, of course, is God's acceptance of Abel's sacrifice of the firstlings of his flock, and his rejection of Cain's offering of the "fruits of the earth." What explains this apparently arbitrary favoritism? Some commentators have suggested that the family dispute pictured in Genesis actually symbolizes and reflects a much larger historical conflict. The Cain and Abel story recapitulates the ancient social struggle between nomadic herdsman and settled farmers – a long battle won on a global scale from 5,000 to 10,000 years ago by the farmers and their urban allies (Finkelstein and Na'Aman, 1994). The Cain of Genesis begins as a farmer, one recalls, but ends as the founder of cities.

In this analysis, God's preference for Abel's sacrifice reflects the attempt by later Jewish leaders to sanctify certain virtues associated with their community's nomadic prehistory, and so to legitimize rulers who had moved far from that original social base. For example, the book of Kings makes much of the fact that King David, Israel's first imperialist ruler, was once an innocent shepherd boy. It is not unusual for the winners of a historic social struggle to seek in this way to clothe themselves in the values of their predecessors. Much later, American historians would do the same sort of thing by picturing Abraham Lincoln, the sophisticated politician and corporate lawyer, as "Honest Abe," the prairie farmer and rail-splitter (see Hofstadter, 1948, pp. 93–136).

The Lincoln *mythos*, in fact, points to the vast social transformation that has for centuries generated enormous advantages for some groups and deep frustration or despair for others: the historic shift from an agrarian to an urban-industrial society (Polyani, 1980). Ever since the Industrial Revolution altered the European social landscape out of all recognition, theorists have noted that the economic, political, and cultural changes associated with shifts of this magnitude frequently outrun the ability of traditional conflict-managing institutions to contain them. By challenging long-established patterns of thought and behavior, the process sometimes called "modernization" and more recently known as "globalization" (Martel, edn, 1999) provides the context in which conflicts based on threats, frustration, repressed hostility, or unsatisfied human needs often occur. Analysts differ over how this transformation takes place, but many subscribe to the following propositions (which, of course, remain subject to debate):

(1) Socioeconomic transformation generates class conflicts
The method of producing goods and services shifts from subsistence agriculture to commercial agriculture, and thence to capitalist industry. This thoroughgoing transformation undermines the old landowning and peasant classes, driving people en masse from the countryside to the cities. It creates new classes of rural and urban wageworkers, and vests preponderant economic power in another new class defined by its ownership and control of capital (Marx, 1848/1988; Thompson, 1966). Economic development in rapidly changing societies is uneven, advancing the interests of some groups while subjecting others to new forms of poverty and indignity. The business class itself struggles to maintain its hegemony against the challenges posed by endemic economic crises, foreign competition, and workers' demands. Class conflicts multiply and intensify.

Writing in the mid-nineteenth century, Karl Marx prophesied that the outcome of these conflicts would be increased violence and political instability, culminating in a series of revolutionary explosions that would bring the working class to power, first in the highly industrialized regions, then in the rest of the world (Draper, 1989). To an extent, these expectations were realized. Industrial development brought in its wake a series of economic crises, social revolutions, and world wars – the latter, at least in part, a product of competition over global resources between capitalist ruling classes (Lenin, 1917/1969). But in the West, business enterprises supported by governments demonstrated their ability to survive downturns in the business cycle, develop new technologies, and expand their operations globally. When the revolutionary movements predicted by Marx did appear, Western regimes either crushed them (see, e.g., Christiansen, 1996) or moderated them by introducing welfare state reforms and opening their governance systems to more inclusive participation. As a result, "evolution" replaced "revolution" on the agendas of most working-class organizations and parties (Steger, 1997).

Class struggles persisted in advanced industrial societies, but at least in the absence of serious economic crises, they tended to take the form of negotiable disputes between recognized parties and "interest groups," i.e. trade unions and corporations (Dahrendorf, 1959). Social revolutions, on the other hand, were more likely to occur in impoverished, semi-industrialized states like Russia and China, which produced, as a result, bureaucratically deformed regimes very far from Marx's vision (Skocpol, 1979; Trotsky, 1980). In nations subject to economic domination or exploitation by the industrial giants, class conflict continues to produce violent confrontations both at the workplace and in struggles for national liberation (Wolf, 1999). In addition, both modern and modernizing societies experience intense conflicts between ethnic, racial, or religious "identity groups" whose economic status often coincides with their membership in particular cultural communities (Horowitz, 1987). Around the world, threatened or frustrated classes often mobilize for conflict behind the banners of ethnicity, race, nationality, or religion. Whether self-conscious class struggle is still a possibility in the advanced industrial nations remains a contentious topic, particularly in Europe (see, e.g., Mandel, 1999).

(2) Political transformation generates identity-group conflicts

As modernization continues, large groups formerly excluded from politics begin to participate, making old political organizations and relationships obsolete, creating new institutions, and forcing a reorganization of the state (Rosenau, 1990). The right of rulers to exercise authority, formerly legitimized by local custom and divided among numerous sub-authorities, is now based on legal norms and administered by a central government. The "religion" of nationalism, often promoted by new political and economic elites, replaces prior local loyalties, setting the stage for intensified international conflict. Political institutions, once autocratic and personalist, become more democratic ... but also more bureaucratic. As the pioneer sociologist, Max Weber, contended, bureaucracy – a hierarchy of offices defined and governed by legal norms – is a central characteristic of the modern state, whether politics is organized along democratic lines or not (Weber, 1977).

What Weber did not foresee, however, was the extent to which political modernization would generate new forms of destructive conflict. To begin with, the struggle for democracy often proved a tumultuous process (Moore et al., 1993), and continues even now to generate violent political conflicts (Snyder, 2000). Moreover, violent political conflicts may continue to erupt long after democratic institutions are established, pitting majorities of various sorts against minorities asserting their needs for identity, recognition, and security. The centralization of authority generated provincial rebellions like the American Civil War and the wars of German and Italian unification. Majority rule has sometimes led dominant groups to threaten the interests, identity, and even the very existence of ethnic, racial, and religious minorities. And bureaucratization spawns both the cold violence of mechanized interstate warfare and the passionate violence of anti-bureaucratic and anti-state terrorism (Arendt, 1990).

The notion that the modern state would be inherently peaceful was shattered, first, by the intense violence associated with Europe's colonization of Africa and Asia, then by Germany's descent into barbarism in the 1930s and 1940s, and, later, by tendencies even in democratic societies like the USA to engage in violent attacks on foreign regimes declared "rogues" or "enemies," as well as massive imprisonment of domestic lawbreakers.

Some analysts have argued that modernization actually increases the capacity and willingness of states to employ violence in the pursuit of their policy goals (Aron, 1981). Whether operating in a formally democratic or autocratic manner, the modern state subjects its citizenry to unprecedented media influence and legal control, and uses rewards, as well as punishments, to eliminate pockets of unsupervised dissent. Violence against real or fancied enemies is therefore justified by appeals to law, order, and peace – a linguistic twist anticipated by George Orwell in his dystopian novel, *1984* (Orwell, 1990).

(3) Cultural transformation generates worldview conflicts

Perhaps the most profound of the changes connected with modernization are those involving the transformation of cultural norms – the ensemble of conscious and unconscious images, philosophical assumptions and ethical ideas, habitual behaviors and emotional experiences that determines, to a large extent, how people view themselves and each other. Since relationships based on "deep culture" (Geertz, 2000) do not change as quickly or universally as economic and political relationships do, the gap between older and newer worldviews generates conflict between nations, between groups within nations, and within individual minds.

An example is the surprising global revival of religious conflict, which not only intensifies ethnic and interstate struggles, but also takes the form of intense disputes within religions over issues of doctrine, church organization, church-state relations, and ethics. For a long time, modernization theorists believed that religious zeal would abate, and religious struggles become obsolete, in the brave new world of secular states and bourgeois social values. They did not reckon with the potential of religious ideas and leaders to serve as rallying points for conservative opponents of cultural change (Hunter, 1992), or, especially after the collapse of Soviet Communism, as sources of alternative visions of social transformation (Juergensmeyer, 2000).

Viewing this resurgence of culture-based conflict from a Western perspective, Samuel F. Huntington (1998) reaches the conclusion that destructive conflicts in the current era will largely be between "civilizations": pan-national units committed to incompatible worldviews, most of them based on religious beliefs and values. Other theorists disagree on the grounds that worldview conflicts are more likely to divide pan-national blocs than unite them, and that they will moderate, in any case, if the socioeconomic and political inequalities that fuel them are reduced (Rubenstein and Crocker, 1993).

This debate suggests that conflicts associated with rapid social change cannot easily be distinguished by assigning them to separate categories like "class," "identity," and "worldview." One might think that the ferocious civil conflict in Algeria, for example, which has taken close to 100,000 lives since 1992, is basically a doctrinal struggle between radical Islamists and their more moderate Muslim or secular opponents. But this would be to reckon without the economic troubles that have caused skyrocketing unemployment among young Algerian men (i.e., social class and gender issues), the corruption and inefficiency of the prior moderate nationalist regime (political and ethical issues), and the confusion about national identity that continues to divide the nation into pro- and anti-Western groupings (cultural issues). The most destructive social conflicts, in fact, seem to occur when multiple sources are in play: oppressive class relationships, threatened group identities, *and* clashing worldviews.

From Conflict Analysis to Conflict Resolution

The processes of modernization that we have been discussing describe the situational factors, operating on a global basis, that provide the social context for many types of conflict. But modernization alone does not tell us why, in some cases, the clashes that social transformation produces become intensely violent, while in others the parties pursue their conflicting interests by relatively peaceful means. (For discussion of the various paths to modernization, see Moore, 1993.) Some analysts have attempted to answer this question by linking situational with personal factors in order to discover when social change is likely to trigger mass violence.

"Relative deprivation" theorists, for example, combine an appreciation of the modernizing situation with psychological concepts of frustration-aggression and threat-aggression. The basic idea is that trouble is likely to occur when people feel seriously frustrated or threatened because of their inability to make the gains they believe they deserve or to hold on to cherished values. Rapid social change frequently raises expectations that are not satisfied, either because the modernization process falters, or because some groups experience the burdens of change without corresponding benefits. Alternatively, the same processes of change may threaten traditional identities, beliefs, and ways of life with apparent extinction. According to relative deprivation theorists, the probability that conflict will turn violent rises when group members experience *increasing* divergence between their reasonably expected entitlements and the system's ability to satisfy them (Gurr, 1970). If the gap continues to widen, a social explosion is predictable, especially at the point that there is some dramatic increase in group expectations or decrease in satisfactions (Davies, 1997).

Human needs theorists approach the same problem from a slightly different angle. They argue that certain needs – for example, the needs for identity, recognition, and security – are both universal and non-negotiable. People demand their satisfaction and will not hesitate to put their own lives and the lives of others at risk in order to achieve it. Rapid social change often eliminates traditional methods of satisfying these needs without creating effective new satisfiers (Burton, 1990a). From the point of view of this theory, the most explosive source of conflict in the modern era is the desperate need experienced by members of socially and politically disempowered groups for, a recognized and defensible group identity.

Rulers who believe that demands for identity and recognition can be ignored with impunity, or that subject populations can be deterred by force from asserting them, soon discover that they are mistaken. Unfortunately, this discovery often leads ruling classes to escalate official violence to the level of state terror – and even this escalation may prove ineffective. During the Vietnam War, the terror unleashed against insurgents by the U.S. programs of assassination (the "Phoenix Program'') and massive air strikes did not blunt, and may even have encouraged, the Communist-led drive for independence from foreign domination (Fitzgerald 1972, esp. pp. 548–84). The same lesson was taught by the Soviet leaders in the case of the Afghan insurgency, and their Russian successors in the case of Chechnya. Where basic needs are concerned, deterrence does not deter (Burton, 1997). Hence the need for more peaceful *and* effective methods of conflict resolution.

We noted at the beginning of this chapter that older conceptions of human nature as incurably aggressive or sinful had pessimistic implications for conflict resolution. Situational approaches, on the other hand, suggested that destructive conflicts might be prevented or resolved by altering the social environments that generated them. We can see now that matters are not quite so simple.

Theories like relative deprivation and basic human needs create both new possibilities and new problems for conflict resolvers. Their great advantage is that, by exploring the nexus between social systems and personal needs, drives, or expectations, they offer a more complex understanding of what motivates people to engage in violent collective action. In theory, this should produce a wider range of options for conflict resolution – and so it does. But since basic human needs and other psychic structures are part of our "deep culture," which changes very slowly over time (Rubenstein, 1990, p. 241), most of these options turn out to be situational. That is, they point to changes in social, political, and cultural behaviors, systems, or institutions that are necessary if violent conflict is to be prevented or resolved.

Why is this a problem? The answer is implicit in another question: How can conflicting parties gain sufficient control of a rapidly changing social environment to alter or eliminate the conflict-generating situation? Of course, if such situations are temporary and local, their alteration will not require heroic measures. But what if they are features of long-range, deep-rooted, society-wide processes like modernization/globalization? If the needs of unrecognized ethnic groups, say, cannot be satisfied without transforming well established political and cultural institutions, or if the vital interests of oppressed social classes require equally significant economic and legal changes, assisting the parties to alter *these* situations will be no easy or short-term task.

For conflict resolvers, recognizing the systemic sources of conflict poses not just a problem, but a challenge. How can dysfunctional, conflict-generating systems be transformed consensually and deliberately, without dictation or massive violence? This is a question that must concern us increasingly as communities around the globe become ever more closely interconnected. The Princeton University conflict specialist, Richard A. Falk, has described globalization as a process involving two related tendencies: "unification at the top, fragmentation at the bottom" (Falk, 1993). While great business corporations and their political allies create cooperative institutions of unprecedented scope and influence on a global level, frustrated or threatened ethnic, national, religious, and occupational groups demand recognition of their local identities and interests. As a result, the traditional nation-state is attacked both from above and below. Social disorder intensifies, and conflicts of a sort once believed to be obsolete threaten to become endemic (Van Creveld, 1991).

Faced with these developments, conflict resolvers are challenged to design strategic plans capable of identifying and mitigating the causes of destructive conflict both at the "top" and at the "bottom" of the global system. This suggests, in turn, that while facilitating negotiations between conflicting parties will remain an important activity for peacemakers, other efforts aimed at "proventing" violence by eliminating its systemic causes are of equal or, perhaps, greater importance (Burton, 1990b).

One need is scholarly: conflict resolution requires more thorough, insightful, and useful analyses of the relationship between globalization and conflict. Mid-level theories that can convincingly explain the interplay between situational and personal factors are in particular demand. Another need is political. System-altering changes often require a broad base of active support of the kind that can best be mobilized by political leaders and organizations. Some escalation of non-violent conflict at the political level, in other words, may be a pre-requisite to preventing future outbreaks of destructive violence. Finally, a third need is processual. How can the confidential processes of dialog and negotiation currently used by many conflict resolvers be linked with renewed analytical and political efforts to produce new forms of con-sensual decision-making? Answering this question successfully could open up new possibilities of preventing and resolving the globe's most troubling and destructive conflicts.

Discussion Questions

1 Give examples of personal and situational factors in conflict. In your view, are the primary sources of serious social conflict personal, situational, or both? Please explain, using as an example a conflict with which you are familiar.

2 Select a violent social conflict with which you are familiar as a result of your reading or experience. Which theory discussed in this chapter best explains the sources of this conflict? In what respects does this theory fail to explain the conflict?

3 Imagine a conversation between three theorists, one advocating psychoanalytic theory, one relative deprivation theory, and one the theory of basic needs. On which points would the three theorists agree? On which points would they disagree?

4 What do conflict analysts mean when they talk about the structural sources of conflict? What can conflict resolvers do to help resolve conflicts rooted in social systems?

Key Words

Aggressiveness
Basic human needs theory
Class conflict
Conflict-generating system
Deep culture
Frustration-aggression theory
Globalization
Identity–group conflicts
Modernization theory
Personal factors in conflict
Psychoanalytic theory
Relative deprivation theory
Religious conflict
Situational factors in conflict
Structural factors in conflict
Worldview conflicts

CHAPTER 5

Dynamics

Tamra Pearson d'Estrée

Introduction

It has been argued that people's identities are both multiple and changeable. If this is the case, then how can they influence conflict? Isn't conflict really determined by something larger and "deeper" ... like imbalances in social structures? Do actions by individuals matter?

In order to answer these questions, we have to look more closely at the mechanisms by which identity, and other factors, might exert influence on the shape of conflict. Identities, like resource discrepancies or power differentials, in and of themselves do not "produce" conflict. Rather, they set the conditions for the everyday rubbing up against each other that we as independent agents may do to "spark" something more serious.

Consider this example: In a more modern retelling of Shakespeare's *Romeo and Juliet* that has itself become a classic, the film *West Side Story* realistically conveys the suspicion and mistrust between neighboring ethnic communities. When two rival gangs, divided along ethnic lines, are brought together simultaneously by love and by aggressive defensiveness, the result is tragedy. In both the original Shakespeare and in the movie remake, we watch individuals and groups make tragic misinterpretations that move their actions down paths toward mutual destruction, all the while knowing that at any point the story could have been turned toward a different ending.

The climax of the movie occurs when the two story themes of love and aggression converge. The two gangs have agreed, suspiciously, to a "fair fight" (fistfight) to determine control of their small piece of territory. The hero, in a valiant demonstration of his new love for the heroine and his rejection of his former gang behavior, attempts to prevent the fight from occurring at all. But suspicions, mistrust, and negative expectations prevent the parties from considering new options, or even believing them when they see them. As the fight escalates from fistfights to switchblades to killing, each deadlier step occurs when confusing behavior is interpreted negatively. As the dust settles, the survivors lament, "No one meant for this to happen." "No one thought it would go this far ... "

Predisposing and Precipitating Conditions

In the above example the precipitating event was one which, while significant in and of itself, would not have escalated into major violence between groups unless other factors had been present first. Roger Brown (1986) proposes that intergroup conflict requires "three legs of a stool": (1) real differences in interests, resources, power, and so on between the two parties, (2) stereotypes, or more general negative schemas or expectations, and (3) perceived injustice. Let us add an essential fourth element to this: interaction between the parties. It is the interaction between the parties, the dynamics of the conflict, that takes predisposing conditions and turns them into actual conflicts.

Interaction serves to build on pre-existing conditions and change them, usually for either better or worse, but sometimes reinforcing the status quo. Regardless of the direction of change, focusing on interaction and change directs us toward a fourth dimension for the study of conflict, that of the *time* trajectory. Conflicts are dynamic; they are always changing. How does a conflict move from festering animosity to open hostilities? How does it move toward a state that may lend itself to resolution? What explains how conflicted systems *change*? In this chapter we consider these dynamics of conflict.

Models of Escalation

In any given conflict, parties attempt to influence each other. Several models have been developed to help us to understand how a conflict between two parties might change, either toward a state of heightened tension and hostilities and more contentious tactics, or toward a state where this is reduced. The former process, *escalation*, will be discussed in this section. We will return to processes of *de-escalation* toward the end of the chapter.

Rubin *et al.* (1994) define escalation as an increase in intensity. They offer a helpful summary of the characteristic changes that take place during conflict escalation. First, conflict tactics may transform from *light to heavy*, from persuasion to threats to violence. Second, the number of issues increases, from *small to large* numbers, redirecting more of each party's resources toward the conflict. Third, issues also transform from *specific*, concrete concerns to *general*, global policies and orientations. Fourth, goals transform from achieving specific changes and *doing well* for oneself, to *winning* or outdoing the other party, and finally to *hurting Other* – preventing the other party from gaining at all costs and making sure the other party suffers more. Finally, the number of participants involved in the conflict grows from *few to many*, as both parties strive to increase their influence by drawing in others.

Deutsch (1973) proposed that a competitive conflict process leads parties to perceive the situation as one where one party will win and the other will lose. Characteristics of a competitive conflict process include: (1) Biased expectations, reinforced by misinformation and error resulting from poor communication. Such biased expectations make it unlikely that any shifts *away* from competitiveness by the other party will be noticed or addressed. (2) A focus on power, since it is perceived that the solution must be imposed through force or strategy. Maintaining a power differential supersedes a focus on the conflict issues. (This focus on maintaining the differential at the expense of absolute benefits has been corroborated through many laboratory studies done in the tradition of Tajfel's (1970, 1981) Minimal Group Paradigm.) (3) Increased sensitivity to differences and threats and minimized sense of similarities, produced by suspicious and hostile attitudes. Since similarities are minimized, traditional norms of conduct and morality are deemed less applicable.

Deutsch's work (1973, 1980, 1982) has shown the self-reinforcing nature of competitive (and cooperative) interaction dynamics. The processes and effects of competition in turn induce further competition, as communication becomes further restricted or deceptive, tactics become more coercive, similarities are minimized and differences highlighted, and attempts are made to reduce the other's power. By comparison, the processes and effects of cooperation in turn induce further cooperation, as communication becomes more open, similarities and common interests are highlighted, and attempts are made to mutually empower.

Models may be conceived of as "flowcharts" that help us to understand the order of events and the influence of variables. Several models have been developed to help us understand how parties attempt to influence each other during conflicts, and how these influence links create a dynamic system.

Probably the simplest model, because it is from the perspective of only one party, is the "Aggressor–Defender" Model. Pruitt and colleagues (Pruitt and Gahagan, 1974; Rubin *et al.*, 1994) identify it as one of three primary models of escalation. One party (the Aggressor) tries to create change that puts it into conflict with the other party (the Defender). As the Aggressor increases the contentiousness of its tactics toward the Defender, the Defender responds in kind. However, in this model the Defender is merely "reacting" to the Aggressor's level of escalation. It is the Aggressor that controls the dynamic, in that it initiates each new increase in escalation until winning or finally giving up.

Rubin *et al.* (1994) note that this model is probably overused in everyday explanation, as it satisfies a natural human tendency to want to assign blame. It may be useful, however, in analyzing a limited frame in a given conflict. It proposes that causes flow in one direction.

A related model that reflects the strategy of decision-makers in various international conflicts in history is the "Deterrence Model" (Schelling, 1963, 1966; Kahn, 1969). The logic of this model is that unless a party shows resolve against a potential or actual Aggressor, that Aggressor will persist and in fact escalate (Jervis, 1976). This strategy is captured by the old aphorism, "Give him an inch, and he will take a mile." Grounded in assumptions resembling those of behaviorist theories of reinforcement and punishment, a party must show the other that it "has resolve," and will not yield on even the smallest issues. This model assumes that the Aggressor is simply that, and has no Defender motives which might call for a different response to counter-threats or other contentious tactics.

Those acting within a conflict may be more likely to apply this model than those observing the conflict from the outside. For example, in *West Side Story*, each gang in the brewing tension declares that the other gang "started it," that their own actions are merely defensive and justified, and that resolve must be shown to "settle it once and for all," and to deter future aggression. The audience, however, is blessed and cursed with the ability to see how such aggression will further escalate the conflict.

Thus, for most conflict analysis, a circular process is a more useful and enlightening metaphor. "Conflict Spiral" models (North *et al.*, 1964; Osgood, 1962, 1966; Richardson, 1967; Jervis, 1976; Smoke, 1977; Rubin *et al.*, 1994) recognize that causes flow in both directions. Each party's actions influence the other party's responses; yet these responses themselves are actions provoking yet another round of response. Looking for initial causes in such a system often has a "chicken-or-egg" quality about it, in that each behavior seems to have been initiated as a response to a prior behavior of the other party. With each cycle, parties increase the contentiousness of their tactics and the competitiveness of their orientation. Using the framework of Rubin *et al.* (1994) outlined above, tactics move from light to heavy, issues proliferate, and parties become absorbed and polarized. In Deutsch's (1973) framework, communication breaks down, suspicions heighten, misperceptions increase, tactics become more coercive, perceived similarities and common interests disappear, and the focus shifts to power.

Jervis (1976) argues that escalation in a conflict spiral comes from two sources: the nature of the larger system or social situation, and psychological limitations that prevent realistic and omniscient appraisal of the intentions of both parties. First, recalling early political philosophy arguments made by Hobbes and Rousseau, he notes that if the system is one of anarchy where there is no "sovereign" (single powerful ruler), each party must protect itself, often through means that menace others. The international system is one such system of anarchy, where each nation cannot assume international protection and thus must protect its own interests. However, such actions themselves often threaten the interests of other nations, contributing to a conflict spiral.

Jervis also argues for the role of psychological limitations in conflict spirals. In the midst of a complex decision-making environment, he highlights that parties can only see their own intentions and must *infer* the intentions of the other. One's own intentions are perceived as not aggressive, yet threatening actions by the other are perceived as stemming from aggressive intentions. A party assumes that the other party will interpret its behavior *as it was intended*, though this is seldom the case. (A party may itself be divided internally on what it intends.) Although a party may acknowledge the difficulty of making credible threats, it paradoxically sees no similar problem in making credible neutral or positive assurances.

Many historical examples exist of the spiral model of conflict escalation, including World War I, the USA and China during the Korean War, and much of the Cold War. In each of these cases we find the characteristic inability to recognize one's own actions as menacing and the related belief that the hostility of the other party or parties could only be due to aggressiveness. Jervis acknowledges, however, that misperceptions alone are not sufficient to induce fundamental insecurity leading to deadly conflict spirals, but must occur in a context of no larger shared system of order; that is, anarchy. In addition to the international system, this anarchy may occur within states where central authority and/or societal consensus has broken down. To broaden this notion further to any conflict domain, the essence is one of a context where both ambiguity and the costs of mistakes are high.

Rubin *et al.* (1994) go a step further in understanding the underlying psychological forces in conflict spirals. Their "augmented" conflict spiral model (Figure 5.1) highlights the role played by motives and

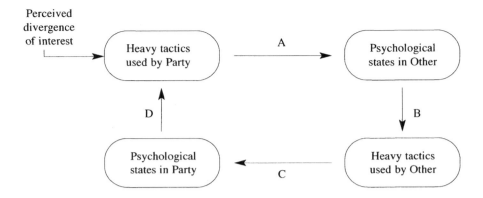

Figure 5.1 Augmented conflict spiral model (from Rubin *et al.*, 1994)

perceptions. Heavy tactics used by one party (Party) produce certain psychological states in the other party (Other), such as blame, anger, fear, and threats to image. These psychological states encourage the other party to respond harshly, through even heavier tactics, which in turn produce these same psychological states in the first party, leading to another harsh response.

Drawing on the work of Burton (1962), Coleman (1957), and Schumpeter (1955/1919), Rubin *et al.* (1994) outline a final model of escalation that sheds light on its persistence, and helps to explain why de-escalation is so difficult. They argue that in addition to more temporary psychological states, contentious tactics by one party also produce *structural changes* in the receiving party, encouraging contentious tactics in response. The "Structural Change" Model proposes that more enduring psychological states, changes in group structure and function, and community polarization carry a conflict past thresholds that make it difficult to return.

Enduring psychological states they outline that reinforce heightened levels of escalation include negative attitudes and perceptions, stereotypes, deindividuation, and dehumanization. These states do not disappear as easily as blame, anger, or fear. Negative feelings and beliefs about the other party lead to negative interpretations of the other party's behavior, reduce contact, make retaliation more acceptable, and result in reduced empathy for the other party. Those in the other party may be seen only as group members and not as individuals, deindividuating them so that aggression is more acceptable. Deindividuation within one's own group also has the same effect: reducing controls on aggression (Zimbardo, 1970). These psychological changes may go so far as to dehumanize the other – reduce or deny the other's humanity so that violence is justified (Kelman and Hamilton, 1989).

In one scene in *West Side Story* that shows the insidious influence of negative attitudes and stereotypes on conflict escalation, the heroine asks a friend to "cross lines" and help the hero by conveying information to him in hiding. However, the mutually negative stereotypes of the heroine's friend and the hero's buddies prevent them from trusting each other enough to even allow communication to pass. As a result, negative expectations are reinforced, miscommunication is used tactically, and the seeds for further tragedy and escalation are sown.

As a result of being engaged in a conflict with increasing tensions, parties may themselves change internally in structure and function. Subgroups may be appointed with special roles *vis-à-vis* the continuing conflict, and more militant leadership may emerge. Perceptions toward the other party may take on the force of group norms, making them difficult to challenge. Groups often become more internally cohesive when facing an external enemy (Simmel, 1955; Coser, 1956), and the attractiveness of this dynamic alone may make *rapprochement* with the other party costly. Such structural changes are difficult to reverse, given their self-perpetuating quality.

Structural changes may include changes to policies or laws. As this chapter was being written, the conflict between Palestinians and Israelis, often called the *Al-Aqsa intifada*, was escalating. One structural change in progress was the move for legislation within Israel that would ban Arab political parties, even though Israeli Arabs are a significant portion of the Israeli population and have traditionally held representation in the Parliament. As another example, laws restricting association between groups, such as those that occurred in the past in both Israel and South Africa, further reinforce the increasing polarization and make de-escalation and cooperative processes difficult to set in motion.

As two parties face off in a conflict, other community members find it hard to remain neutral. In effect, relationships in a community are restructured so that one must interact as part of two opposing poles, called *community polarization*. This dynamic adds to escalation in that each pole continues to strengthen at the expense of those on neutral ground. The swelling of ranks increases confidence that one's group's position is justified, and provides rationale for the use of heavier tactics (Rubin *et al.*, 1994). The bonds within one's group are strengthened, while the bonds across groups are neglected and deteriorate (Coleman, 1957).

The many structural changes induced by such conflicts result in a transformation both of the parties and their relationship. Such transformations are difficult to reverse, and in fact may require wholly new approaches in order to de-escalate. We will return to this topic later in the chapter.

The Role of Probability, Schemas, and Interpretation

Most models of escalation appear inherently *deterministic:* parties are caught in inevitable changes that build upon each other, moving inexorably toward further catastrophe. Unfortunately such models obscure the true *probabilistic* nature of conflict dynamics, where choices are made that open or close further options. The many possible realities mean that predicting the course of a particular conflict is almost impossible, yet this multiplicity also implies that small changes in the course of a conflict can result in large differences in outcomes. A complexity model of conflict is explored further in Sandole (1999b).

At any given "choice point," when a behavior is chosen or elicited, multiple options usually exist. At infinite points in history, there are possibilities for going either one way or another, with multiple and infinite possible futures as a result. One can graph these paths as a tree, continuing to branch and rebranch as it extends forward in time. This shape is sometimes referred to as the "cone of history," as one can start from any point in history and find increasing options as one spreads forward in time. However, certain factors act to constrain the range of choice and possibility, and it is to these factors that we now turn.

In human decision-making, we are faced continually with an enormous wealth of stimuli from the environment of which we must make sense. Being of limited cognitive capacities, we must be selective. In order to process this big, buzzing confusion of sensory information, we must use some of our own cognitive "filters" to select what is relevant to us and make meaning from it. These filters are shaped by our personal, family, and cultural histories. Although in principle we may have multiple options and multiple possible futures, we constrain our perceived options through the meaning-making process and thus direct history down particular paths. Understanding how choices of paths are influenced is key to grasping the dynamics of conflict.

Schemas and their influence

Psychologists posit that information stored in memory is organized according to semantic networks (Collins and Quillian, 1972; Anderson and Bower, 1973; Anderson, 1983). Associated concepts are linked together. This information is structured both vertically, hierarchically, and also horizontally in terms of prototypicality (Rosch *et al.*, 1976; Rosch, 1978). These larger networks of related information are often called *schemas*. We have schemas, not only for objects, but also for people, events, and procedures (Bartlett, 1932; for review, see Fiske and Taylor, 1991). Schemas act as templates or filters to help us to organize information, to make sense of new information, and to make predictions and take action.

Schemas have many sources. Some schemas appear to be "hard-wired," such as those for language-learning (cf. Chomsky, 1959). Other schemas are learned through experience, such as schemas for "good food" or for successfully riding a bike. Many schemas are learned from others, embedded in cultures and learned through socialization. Examples include status hierarchies, biological taxonomies, professional categories, or rituals such as marriage or graduation. We have schemas about behavior in negotiations and in conflict.

Schemas influence perception, memory, and inference. First, because the large amount of stimuli in our environments could be overwhelming, schemas act as filters that help us select the most salient and relevant information. They help to direct our attention to the information most important for our own cognitive and motivational priorities. If someone is threatening us, our attention will be focused on this other party, rather than on the flickering lamp or the car door slamming outside. If the car door slamming outside does not fit our schema of relevant information, we will not notice it. If, however, the slammed car door represents help on the way, we will attend to it. It is not the stimuli themselves that matter, but what meaning we attach to them via our pre-existing schemas.

Schemas also influence what and how information is stored in and recalled from memory. If we have applied a particular schema to a set of stimuli, the information we recall will be consistent with that schema. Events of an unexpected order will tend to be reordered in memory to be consistent with the schema (Bower *et al.*, 1979). Uncharacteristic traits or objects will not be recalled as easily if at all, while characteristic or "stereotypic" traits or associated items will be added to the memory (Anderson and Pichert, 1978; Hastie, 1981). Following the example of the threatening person above, we may neglect to remember the queries of concern he raised, and may add that we were sure he had a bulge in his jacket concealing a weapon. We interpret that his smile was one of deception rather than warmth.

Finally, schemas influence the inferences we make. Expectations depend on what prior information is considered relevant and applicable, or may simply depend on what information (schema) is most recently or consistently active. The invitation to a "clean fight" (i.e., no weapons) in *West Side Story* could be seen as a de-escalatory gesture or as a trap, depending on which schema was held for the other side or for conflict in general.

Social schemas

Schemas exist for most objects and events in our world; however, schemas that involve other people are unique in several ways (Fiske and Taylor, 1991). Schemas for social information incorporate values, valences, and emotions. This is because most other people have implications for one's *self*. Our most complex, highly developed, overarching schema is our *self-schema*. Things that positively impact on the self are coded as positive, while things negatively impacting on the self are coded as negative. Social information by its very nature must be classified in terms of implications for the self, and thus is always tinged as positive or negative. Any new information added to a schema will also be tinged by the pre-existing value or valence (+ or −) of that schema. For example, if I learn that my new neighbor is "tight with money," I will code my new neighbor as "thrifty" if I already had a favorable impression, while if I already had an unfavorable impression I will code the same information as evidence that she is "miserly" (for a fascinating discussion of such language coding, see Brown, 1986).

Because they are such powerful aids to memory and inference, schemas particularly come into play when one is faced with interpreting ambiguous or incomplete information and/or is under stress. Most social information is ambiguous, meaning that much social meaning-making is left up to interpretation. Do I interpret the late paper as due to unfortunate circumstances, due to procrastination, or due to a rebelliousness toward authority and deadlines?

Implications for conflict

These basic human cognitive processes have implications for conflict information-processing. They can result in worst-case thinking and self-fulfilling prophecies. They also reduce one's choices for interpretation and narrow one's perceived options for subsequent behavior. They represent mechanisms within the structural change model that lead to conflict escalation.

Worst-case thinking/scenarios. As noted above, social information is inherently ambiguous, and therefore it is likely to be interpreted in light of pre-existing positive or negative expectations (schemas) about the other. *Worst-case thinking* captures the phenomenon whereby each action or statement by the other is interpreted in its worst possible light. Negative actions such as threats are not perceived as justified, but rather as confirmation of the negative "character" of the other party. Neutral actions such as questions, and even positive actions such as conciliatory gestures, are considered to be attempts to mislead, undermine, or entrap. One famous analysis of such worst-case thinking is that of John Foster Dulles in his interpretations of the behavior of the Soviet Union.

Such negative interpretations, especially when held on both sides of a conflict, virtually preclude all options for behavior that might lead parties out of an escalatory spiral.

Self-fulfilling prophecies. In George Bernard Shaw's play *Pygmalion* and the subsequent movie *My Fair Lady*, a Cockney flower girl becomes a refined lady because others perceive her to be so. This play illustrates the notion from folk wisdom that people often act in accordance with prophecies or predictions in ways that actually have the result of making those prophecies or predictions come true. If we expect another party to behave belligerently, we may take defensive action and relate negatively to them, which ends up producing the very behavior we have expected and sought to avoid. Anyone who has worked with children can see this dynamic operating frequently: those children deemed the trouble-makers will receive less positive attention and more negative attention, leading them to continue to produce behaviors that confirm the initial stereotypic expectations. In their classic study of expectancy effects, Rosenthal and Jacobson (1968) demonstrated that randomly assigned high expectations of children "produced" subsequent achievement levels that confirmed the initial expectation.

We have seen how natural cognitive processes reduce our choices for interpretation and narrow our perceived options for subsequent behavior. We now turn to the additional dynamic introduced when the other party is perceived to be from a group that threatens our own group identity.

The Role of Identities

While the term *identity* may be defined in many ways, one way in which psychologists think about identity is in terms of cognitive frameworks, such as schemas, and the type of processing and subsequent actions that stem from them. As mentioned above, the most elaborate and developed schema each person holds is probably the one for his or her self (*self-schema*). A schema provides one way to think of a person's identity that includes both a personal component (personal history, experiences, and so on) and a social component (parts of the self connected to or derived from one's membership in various groups), often called one's *social identity* (Tajfel, 1981). We also have schemas for other people and other groups of people, as well as for our relationships between ourselves and others. These clusters of schema are called *relational schema* (Baldwin, 1992).

One of the interesting propositions of the classic social comparison theory (Festinger, 1954) is that the self is defined *relatively*, through comparison with others. This notion is mirrored in several other theories, including Cooley's classic notion of the "looking glass self." Subsequent theorists have argued along similar lines that the self is "socially constructed" (Gergen, 1977; Gergen and Gergen, 1988). Because the self is defined relatively, any cognitive construct for the self must also contain information about the other with whom one is comparing oneself (the *comparison other*), and, as with all social information, the relative value of each. Thus new or revised information about a comparison other will have implications for the self, and possibly for one's self-esteem.

Work on *ethnocentrism* has a long history within several social sciences. Originally dubbed by Sumner (1906), ethnocentrism is used to describe the almost universal tendency to positively evaluate one's own group, often coupled with a tendency to negatively evaluate a comparison other group (an *outgroup*) (LeVine and Campbell, 1972; Brewer, 1968, 1979; Brewer and Campbell, 1976).

In attempting to explain ethnocentrism, Tajfel (1978) drew on the postulates of Festinger's (1954) social comparison theory about comparison with others, and proposed that *social identity*, like personal identity, is formed through comparison – this time between one's own group and other groups. Research has shown that people will go to great lengths to preserve their own group's relative advantage over another group, even at the expense of increased absolute benefits for all (Billig and Tajfel, 1973; Locksley *et al.*, 1980). The explanation goes back to the potential threat to social identity and self-esteem represented by any actual or implied comparison between one's own group and another group. This threat's importance is highlighted whenever there are scarce resources to be divided up according to each group's deservedness.

Because self-definition and definition of the other are so intimately linked, categorizing the other has implications for the self. Stereotypes function not only to simplify a complex world, but also to justify discrimination against another group as well as our own group's deservedness, social dominance, or "moral high ground" (Tajfel and Forgas, 1981; Potter and Wetherell, 1987; Sidanius and Pratto, 1999). Groups may go so far as to elevate minor differences (the "narcissism of minor differences") in order to emphasize their group boundaries (Volkan, 1985, 1997) and increased relative value.

When identity issues in a conflict activate self-schemas, they become the overarching, all-penetrating lens through which the world and all behaviors are construed. Even positive behaviors (e.g., gestures) by the other can be interpreted negatively. While many choices for behavior may remain open, interpretations of others' behavior and intentions filtered through negative, identity-implicating schema direct conflict responses toward increasingly disastrous expressions.

The Cumulative and Generative Nature of Interaction

In teaching about conflict dynamics, I like to begin the second session with an "alka seltzer" demonstration. I hold up the innocuous and inert white tablet and a glass of water. One quick flip drops the tablet into the water, and what first begins as a few bubbles quickly becomes a foaming, rising, dramatic chemical reaction. It is difficult to fail to see analogies between the escalating chemical reaction, and conflict's own escalation.

Sometimes people will say, "the conflict took on a life of its own." This statement reflects the awesome fact, seen in the natural sciences as well, that when elements are combined in certain ways, they can start a process that catalyzes its own successive stages of development. Like an embryo splitting and differentiating and taking on its life, a conflict as a dynamic system will manufacture its own momentum. Only by understanding such dynamics may we hope to understand the process of reversing or reorienting such momentum for constructive results.

Structural change model revisited

The Structural Change Model described above is one of the few models that captures this "autocatalytic" dimension of conflict systems. (For more on the dynamics of autocatalytic systems, consult Jantsch (1980).) Complexity theory (Waldrop, 1992) builds on these same notions. Changes within both parties, such as polarized attitudes, conflict-oriented subgroups and leadership, and shifts in parties' ways of operating (e.g., focus on armaments production), themselves become catalysts for responses from the other party. In addition to counter-responses, it is likely that the other party will undergo similar structural changes, catalyzing counter-responses from the first party.

This model also helps to illuminate why de-escalation and resolution of conflict requires more than just improvements in understanding and interaction: structural changes that have escalated and perpetuated violence of many possible sorts need to be disassembled or radically restructured. War machinery, personnel, and other parts of the economy need to be retired or redirected. Hierarchical, often discriminatory social structures which are often codified in law may have been attempted to be justified as necessary to mobilize for conflict (Sharoni, 1995) – and also need to be disassembled or modified to truly de-escalate conflict systems.

Forces for Stability and Change

Kurt Lewin, considered by many to be the father of social psychology and group dynamics, chose to use a physics metaphor to understand dynamics both within and between individuals and groups (1936). He argued that each party exists in a field of social forces that compel certain actions and their opposites *at the same time*. What actually happens (e.g., which action a party might take) is not the result of events clearly adding up in linear fashion, but rather depends on the relative balance of forces for or against each action at any given moment. For example, whether or not we have one more coffee with our friends or go on to the library to study depends on forces pushing for and against another coffee, as well as forces pushing for and against going to the library. Lewin argued and successfully demonstrated that a more successful strategy for inducing a behavior was not to increase the forces toward that behavior, but rather to reduce the forces of resistance preventing the behavior. In this same example, it may mean meeting friends for that coffee very near to the library, so that going to work at the library is easier.

Lewin's framework gives us new ways to conceive of how conflict systems stabilize or change. In this view, conflicts escalate not only because certain factors are "pushing" the parties, but also because resistance to escalation is not sufficient. Conflicts stabilize when these become more equal in pressure. Conflicts de-escalate when de-escalation-promoting activities increase but also as a result of escalation efforts running into increasing resistance. For example, parties may run short of the resources (funds, time) that allow them to engage in open hostilities.

Rubin *et al.* (1994) propose five possible reasons why conflicts stop escalating. One party may simply overwhelm the other party and subdue it, or they may take advantage of a situation, in effect tricking the other without needing to overwhelm it. One party may capitulate. One or both parties may choose to withdraw from and avoid the conflict, simply

Table 5.1 Conflict spiral model

Points of entry into system
- Reduce predisposing stereotypes and negative expectations
- Increase information flow/increase possible interpretations
- Increase behavioral choices
- Restructure situational incentives
- Address barriers to basic human needs

Resolution approaches
- Contact
- Superordinate goals
- Problem-solving
- Expanding the pie/creating value

---

turning its energy and focus elsewhere. Finally, parties may reach a *stalemate*, where both regard proceeding with the conflict as less desirable than ending it. They may still engage in contentious tactics and may not yet know how to proceed to de-escalate, but they recognize that "winning" and defeating the other is not possible.

Such a situation has been called by some a "hurting stalemate" (Zartman, 1989). Rubin *et al.* propose four reasons for the emergence of a stalemate. First, a stalemate may come about because contentious tactics used earlier in the conflict may have lost their effectiveness. Second, a stalemate may occur because parties have exhausted their resources for continuing the highly escalated level of fighting. Third, parties may lose outside support upon which they have depended. This may be social support, as in public image, or resource support, as in outside shipments of arms. Finally, the costs associated with continuing the struggle may be deemed unacceptable. Notice that change in this factor may be primarily psychological or political, rather than a change in something "tangible." It is just this sort of change in appraisal of options which provides entries for conflict resolution efforts.

De-escalation begins when parties have grown tired of escalation, when they have recognized that their fates are intertwined, and they begin searching for ways of settling the conflict (Rubin *et al.*, 1994). Zartman (1989) considers a conflict "ripe" for resolution when the costs of continuing a conflict are perceived to be greater than the costs of settling it. Face considerations, and issues of image and resolve, so important in escalation, continue to dog efforts at de-escalation. Structural changes remain to be undone: "enemy images," negative norms for relating to the other, subgroups and leadership oriented toward conflict rather than toward resolution. Fortunately, several strategies and processes exist for addressing face and image considerations, for reinforcing perceptions of interdependence and common ground, for jointly tackling conflict issues, and for moving parties toward remedial structural changes. It is to these strategies and processes that we now turn.

Altering Conflict Dynamics

One theme throughout this chapter has been the probabilistic nature of behavior. Choices always exist among options for behavior, though perceptions may seemingly limit one's choice of certain options. Given our preceding discussion about the factors shaping choices that produce escalation, we can now return to these factors to deduce points of influence to shape choices that produce de-escalation. These strategies are outlined in Table 5.1.

One strategy is to reduce predisposing stereotypes and negative expectations that tend to produce worst-case thinking and self-fulfilling prophecies. Stereotypes also justify inequities and harsh tactics by dehumanizing the other. By creating conditions which rehumanize the other, these stereotypes and negative expectations begin to break down.

One approach for bringing people together to reduce stereotypes and build common ground comes from a body of work known as "the contact hypothesis" (Allport, 1955) or sometimes just "contact theory." The contact hypothesis states that intergroup prejudice can be reduced through contact between members of the groups under certain conditions: equal status, cooperative interdependence among the groups, opportunities to interact with members of the other group as individuals, and support from authority (Stephan and Brigham, 1985). This hypothesis grew out of foundational theoretical work by Allport (1954), Williams (1947), and Watson (1945) and others into a form most known for its influence on the U.S. Supreme Court's decision to desegregate public schools (*Brown vs. Board of Education*, 1954).

Another strategy comes from the realization that schema-driven interpretations and lack of information constrain what parties believe to be their behavioral options. To counter these characteristics, we can engage in activities which increase information flowing to parties from each other and from outside the system. For example, the standard mediation process is set up to allow the mediator and the mediation context to provide the conduit for information to flow between parties so that assumptions may be challenged and new solutions envisaged. Mediators play an important role in reframing information from each party so that the other parties can hear it. Similarly, the media have sometimes played an important role in altering conflict dynamics by airing a variety of perspectives.

We can also increase opportunities for schema-challenging information to be encountered (this information needs to be significant to overcome the tendency to simply reinterpret the new information within the existing schema (Rothbart, 1981). For further information on schema use and change, see Fiske and Taylor, 1991). One can be made aware of the insidiousness of self-reinforcing schemas, and their potential for blocking out useful information and new options. To guard against this tendency for groups to engage in such information distortion or avoidance as part of the dynamics of "groupthink," Janis (1982) proposed the inclusion of the role of "devil's advocate." Similarly, within each party in conflict, people can be given permission (within certain safe forums) to consider alternative scenarios, and therefore alternative options.

Problem-solving workshops (Kelman, 1996) and other structured interactions (Fisher, 1990, 1997a; Saunders, 1999) allow people from opposing sides of a conflict to share their motivations and concerns driving their positions and actions. Parties to such efforts may discover, for example, that the other group may have been operating out of fear rather than aggression, or that actions that appeared calculated and with negative intent had arisen from internal group dynamics or even by accident. They may learn more about the other party's operating constraints and internal divisions, and discover a shared desire for resolution (Babbitt and d'Estrée, 1996).

Much of the dynamics leading to increased escalation seem to constrain and determine one's behavioral options and choices. The natural evolution of systems may reveal new choices; however, direct interventions also exist for increasing parties' perceived choices. Infusions of new resources from the outside linked to peaceful activities may provoke a reordering of parties' priorities. Examples include aid linked to peace treaties, as in the large packages of U.S. aid tied to the Northern Ireland and Wye River (Israeli–Palestinian) accords, and promises of increased economic activity as a result of conflict de-escalation (sometimes called a "peace dividend," as in that produced by the end of the U.S.–Soviet Cold War).

We frame our behavioral choices, and then choose to behave in a certain way, based on what we perceive to be the goals of the situation and our best interests. As Deutsch (1973) enlightened, if a context is framed cooperatively, people engage in behaviors that reinforce cooperation, while if the context is framed competitively, they will engage in behaviors that reinforce competition. Therefore, another strategy for entering into and de-escalating a conflict system is to restructure the situational incentives (*incentive structure*) (Schelling, 1963; Axelrod, 1984; Axelrod and Dion, 1988). If people perceive that new incentives have been added for reducing harsh tactics, or if they perceive that the goal has been changed from dominating the other to working with that other to achieve a common goal, behaviors will shift accordingly. An important tradition of research has focused on the usefulness of creating a *superordinate goal* to reduce intergroup conflict (Sherif *et al.*, 1961).

Finally, a deeper analysis of the sources of conflict suggests a strategy that focuses on addressing basic human needs (Burton, 1962, 1990a), such as security and identity. As pointed out earlier in the discussion of conflict spirals, parties are much more likely to engage in hostile acts for defensive purposes rather than out of aggressiveness. This is why deterrence strategies so often turn into conflict spirals: each defensive reaction by one party is perceived as a threat by the other party, eliciting their own defensive reaction which in turn threatens the first party, and so on. The primary way to counter this dynamic is to engage in actions that *increase*, rather than decrease, the other side's security (Etzioni,

1962; Osgood, 1986). As Deutsch (1983, 1986) has pointed out in his analysis of and prescriptions for the U.S.–Soviet Cold War, rather than engaging in actions that threaten the other's security (which ultimately threaten one's own as well, particularly in a nuclear conflict spiral), parties should engage only in actions that increase *both* parties' security simultaneously. This does not mean giving concessions or capitulating. Each party should safeguard its own security, but in ways that reduce the threat to the other party as well (which, in a true spiral, should ultimately benefit oneself).

Much has also been made in this chapter of the role of identity in directing interpretations and framing behavioral options that can lead to conflict escalation. Merely invoking social identities sets up a dynamic of social comparison and competition between the groups. This in turn provides justification for competitive, aggressive, and even hostile actions directed toward preserving an advantage over the other party. In extreme cases, the conflict relationship may be construed such that the other party's very *existence* is threatening to one's own party's identity. Identity concerns become intertwined with security concerns, providing deeply powerful incentives for perpetuating a highly escalated state of conflict. Such conflicts may be "settled," in a short-term sense, but they will reappear in the next decade or the next generation if the identity concerns are not addressed.

In many ways, addressing identity concerns needs to follow the same strategy used to address security concerns – parties must find ways to *validate*, rather than threaten, the other party's identity. Ideally, parties learn that the other's existence as a recognized group is not a threat to their own group identity. Parties can search for actions that will mutually validate both identities. Working to reduce or reframe markers in the situational context that seem to imply that one party must dominate (e.g., scarce resources, a single "prize") may also reduce the need to devalue the other party.

Validating the other's identity can take many forms. It may be a willingness to "hear" the other party's view of history without denying it. It may include recognizing the other party's language and/or traditions as an essential expression of their relationship to the world. It may involve acknowledging the aspects of one's own history or culture or structure that may (even unintentionally) invalidate the other's value or contribution or right to exist.

Addressing both parties' identity concerns may not by itself resolve the conflict. Typically it provides the shift in the conflictual relationship so that de-escalatory behaviors can be risked, leading ultimately to a state where negotiations can begin to settle issues.

Approaches for the Resolution Process

At some point in the conflict resolution process, issues must be addressed and settled. Multiple processes exist for this sort of conflict management: negotiation, arbitration, formal court processes. However, as discussed in this chapter, disputed issues are not themselves the source of escalation; therefore merely addressing issues typically will not de-escalate conflict nor be sufficient to provide lasting resolution and constructive relationships.

Approaches have been developed to de-escalate hostile relationships, and to restore parties to a relationship where they can negotiate differences peacefully and constructively. They incorporate many of the strategies discussed above: reducing predisposing stereotypes and negative expectations, increasing information flow, increasing alternative interpretations, increasing behavioral choices, restructuring situational incentives, and addressing barriers to basic human needs. These ap-proaches include superordinate goals, contact, problem-solving, and expanding the pie or creating value. These are discussed further in Part III.

In sum, conflicts arise and escalate through a dynamic process involving interaction between the parties. Each step in escalation may be traced to changes in perceptions, in patterns of behavior, and in structures. Conflicts also de-escalate through changes in perceptions, patterns of behavior, and structures, and these changes can be consciously directed using various intervention strategies.

Discussion Questions

1 What are some of the resources that allow parties to engage in open hostilities? How might these be restructured so as to slow down or stop conflict escalation?

2 How might actions by individuals matter in the development of an intergroup conflict? In its resolution?

3 Describe an example when a group you are a part of engaged in a conflict. How did this conflict escalate? What escalation characteristic did you observe? What sorts of structural changes occurred in one or both groups?

4 Why are escalated conflicts so difficult to de-escalate?

5 Watch the film *West Side Story*. Identify points at which escalation increases, and why? What could have been done at each of these points to counter or guard against escalation? Which model of escalation is most appropriate?

6 Models imply that conflicts are predictable. Are they? Why or why not? (What elements may be more predictable?)

7 Discuss how meaning is made within a group during a conflict.

Key Words

Aggressor–Defender Model
Augmented Conflict Spiral Model
Balance of forces
Basic needs
Choice point
Cognitive filters
Community polarization
Competitive conflict process (and characteristics of)
Competitive interaction dynamics
Conflict escalation (and characteristics of)
Conflict spiral
Contact approach
Cooperative interaction dynamics
Dehumanization
Deindividuation
Deterministic
Deterrence Model
"Devil's advocate"
Expanding the pie
Functional change
"Hurting stalemate"
Identity
Incentive structure
Mediation process
Negative attitudes
Precipitating event
Probabilistic
Probabilistic vs. deterministic
Problem-solving
Relational schema
Schemas: definition, examples of, sources of, effects of
Self-fulfilling prophecies
Self-schema
Social comparison theory
Social identity
Social schema
Stereotypes
Structural change
Structural Change Model
Superordinate goal
Worst-case thinking

Part II

Influences and Context

Introduction to Part II

A conflict does not unfold according to an inherent, if not unique, pattern or rhythm. It is embedded within a context and is thus influenced by that context. The chapters in this section attempt to define or conceptualize the contexts for conflict and resolution. Context refers to the larger setting that frames or defines a conflict and drives it in various directions through time. Situations, social identities, cultures, social structures, and institutions are aspects of contexts for conflict that influence the way they unfold, sometimes toward increasing escalation or toward de-escalation.

The role of situational influences on conflict is discussed in Chapter 7. In this chapter, the situation is defined as those features of the immediate environment in which disputing parties interact. The features are proximal in the sense of being close to the parties, and include such factors as incentive structures, framing of issues, opportunities to communicate, presence of audiences or constituencies, third parties, and time pressure. A long history of experimentation has demonstrated that these factors have major impacts on the course of conflicts. The findings challenge assertions that conflicts are strongly influenced by personal characteristics of individuals. They also support the premise that provides a foundation for research in such fields as experimental social psychology, behavioral ecology, role theory, game theory, and simulation.

Nor do conflicts arise *de novo*. Similar situations are likely to produce similar patterns of conflict behavior. For this reason, taxonomies of types and forms of conflict, negotiations, and third-party roles are quite useful. These taxonomies emphasize the variation that occurs among a wide sampling of cases in a domain. The results of the empirical research discussed in Chapter 7 attest to their usefulness.

Conflict also influences the social identities of the parties concerned. The roles played by identities in conflict dynamics and resolution are discussed in Chapter 8. The idea of a total social identity is developed in this chapter. This refers to an all-encompassing identity that renders a group a powerful source of influence. While this kind of identity can be a root of conflict, it can also generate or reinforce it. Opportunities for escalation arise as group boundaries become reified and enemies are defined. The result can be quite pernicious. However, for most group members, identities are not total, but are sensitive to changed circumstances and are amenable to the kinds of third-party interventions discussed in Part III of this volume. The practical challenges set out in this chapter are to learn about the conditions and practices which can liberate members from those identities that create or reinforce stereotypes that support conflict, and to learn to use shared identities as resources for constructive conflict resolution or to bolster support for the implementation of negotiated agreements.

Attempts made to define culture raise more questions than agreed definitions. Focusing attention on culture and conflict, in Chapter 9 we discuss the issues and the several contributions of cultural analyses to the study of conflict and conflict resolution. Culture is viewed less as a cause of conflict than as part of the context in which it occurs. The chapter emphasizes, in particular, the images, embodiments, schemas, and metaphors parties bring to a conflict. Shared images which group members hold may be reflected in stereotypes that often highlight the virtues of one's own group while denigrating members of other groups considered to be adversaries in a conflict. These images fuel conflict by linking ingroup amity to outgroup enmity, but it is also the case that these interpretations are subject to change during the interaction process as noted also in the earlier chapters on social identity and situations. It is the pull of cultural interpretations brought to the conflict and the push of the interactions and situations faced by parties that influence the unfolding conflict and its resolution. Above all, culture is dynamic and multifaceted in practice, and in analyses of both individual and collective actors.

Another source of conflict, discussed in Chapter 10, emanates from social structures. By structures we mean the organization and norms of the political, economic, and social systems within a society. These structures are believed to be separate from the intentions expressed and behaviors exhibited by individuals. Like culture, structure is thought to be part of the context in which conflict occurs. To the extent that they are viewed by citizens as being legitimate, structures strongly influence the way groups define their interests and values, and the ways in which they relate to one another in terms of relative power. To the extent that the interests of different groups overlap (a lack of shared group identifications), intergroup conflict is likely to be more intense. This is similar to the concept of a total social identity discussed in Chapter 8. When the interests of different groups are cross-cutting (a sharing of group identifications), intergroup conflict is likely to be less intense. Cross-cutting identities reduce the lines of cleavage between socioeconomic, religious, and political groups. Relations among cross-cutting groups, although not always harmonious, are less likely to be framed invidiously in terms of differences in authority or other structural inequalities. Whether overlapping or cross-cutting, the pattern of interests among groups is not fixed. In this chapter, we call attention to the dynamic aspects of social structures and the role played by relative deprivation (and related social-psychological factors) in instigating social change. Some implications of this conception of structures for practice are also discussed.

The focus of Chapter 11 is on alternative sources of legitimacy for social, economic, and political systems. An important distinction is made between consensual and dissensual conflicts. The former usually covers conflicts between parties that make competing claims for resources and is referred to as conflicts of interest. The parties typically negotiate their differences within an accepted or legitimate social order. The latter refers to conflicts that call into question the legitimacy of the prevailing social order. Parties contest each other's moral values and regard the source of their differences to be deep-rooted, and thus not subject to settlement by negotiation. Often one or more parties question the legitimate authority of the legal and political institutions in a society, seeking social change. Widespread dissensus (defenders versus challengers of the social order) may reflect or presage the breakdown of the prevailing conflict-resolving institutions. It is these conflicts, in particular, that require the sort of deep analysis rarely engaged in by legal professionals or mediators who practice alternative dispute resolution. An increase in the frequency and intensity of these conflicts worldwide raises questions about the legitimacy of extant methods of adjudication and suggests the plausibility of different kinds of conflict resolution processes. As discussed in Chapter 10, these processes consist of the sort of deep analysis that requires vigorous and imaginative problem-solving linked to forms of transformative politics. We have only just begun to address the large questions posed at the end of this chapter. They are challenges for conflict analysts and resolvers that are explored also in the other chapters in this section, as well as in Part I on sources of conflict, and in Part III on processes of conflict resolution.

The next chapter examines the relationship between globalization processes and conflict dynamics. It argues that although globalization may intensify various social conflicts in the short term, long-term influences on conflicts are less clear. The chapter explores contending theoretical approaches about long-term effects by examining how each views the relationship between globalization and distributive conflicts, between globalization and intra- and inter-state war, and between globalization and the emergence of various new non-state actors, whether social movements or human traffickers. What emerges from these studies is that globalization processes have multiple and often contradictory effects on social dynamics, sometimes promoting more peaceful relations between state and social actors while at other times aggravating old conflicts and creating new ones.

The final chapter in this section explores the evolution of theoretical approaches to understanding the relationship between development and conflict. It argues that the different approaches of the last five decades have profoundly shaped the types of policies governments, international donors, and NGOs have advocated and implemented in the developing world. Although there is a broad agreement among scholars, policy-makers, and practitioners that lack of development contributes to conflicts, how to generate sustainable and equitable development remains controversial and deeply contested. The debates about the relationship between development and conflict and development and peace-building have taken on a new urgency as the international community has expanded the scope of its involvement in post-conflict reconstruction and reconciliation work in countries emerging from protracted civil conflicts.

CHAPTER 6

Narrative Analysis

Sara Cobb

Introduction

In the northern region of Guatemala, in the Mirador Basin, lies a rainforest. In that rainforest there are approximately 400 families living on the proceeds of forest concessions. They harvest timber under the supervision of local leaders, and are members of an organization called *Asociación de Comunidades Forestales de Peten* (ACOFOP). Forest concessions have been heavily subsidized by the United States Agency for International Development (USAID); these concessions are supervised, and "harvesting" is regulated by a group of international nongovernmental organizations (NGOs), in turn under the supervision of a national agency in Guatemala, *Consejo National de Areas Protegidas* (CONAP). ACOFOP is vehemently opposed to any action that would stop, block, or reduce forest concessions and they have the support of USAID, as well as a legal contract with the Guatemalan government that gave the locals rights to these forest concessions, as part of the 1996 Peace Accord that ended the 30-year civil war.

However, buried in this region lies the oldest and largest Mayan ruins known to civilization. And the "plot" thickens. The *Global Heritage Fund* (GHF), a U.S.-based NGO, in collaboration with Richard Hansen, a U.S. archeologist who "discovered" this site, have sought to develop an eco-tourism project in the Mirador Basin, as part of an effort to preserve the archeological site and the cultural resources of Guatemala. Their plan, supported by an agency within Guatemala, *Instituto Antropologia e Historia* (IDAEH), called for a hotel to be built in this rainforest, so that tourists could come to witness the Mayan ruins. Those in favor of this development aspired to get tourists into the rain forest without cutting new roads which greatly increase the risk of fires, and the destruction of the forest – farmers and poor people would use the road to get into the forest, where they could create land for grazing cattle by burning the forest. So the pro-development group proposed access to the ruins via either a monorail or helicopter. The proposal also advocated the creation of a Board who would regulate the profits from tourism (hotel); none of the proposed members of this Board were from ACOFOP or the local communities.

The plot now goes beyond "thick" to "viscous." The members of ACOFOP were indigenous people, victimized by the government for over 30 years. When the civil war ended, the local people finally received rights to their local resource, the timber, and they had the powerful support of U.S. and Guatemalan federal agencies. They were also backed by *Centro de Accion Legal-Ambiental y Social* (CALAS), a legal defense team that were experienced, tenacious, and media savvy. This is a conflict over ecological and cultural resources that belong to the locals, the Guatemalan government, and as Jeff Morgan, President of a U.S.-based NGO called Global Heritage Fund, would argue, to the entire world. It is a conflict between indigenous people and the colonial families that are embedded within Guatemalan business and politics, between local poor people and international NGOs with huge capital to invest and global networks of influence. It is a conflict with deep historical roots anchored in immediate concerns of cultural preservation and environmental protection.

Approaches to Conflict Diagnosis

The field of conflict resolution offers a variety of approaches for a diagnosis of this conflict. For example, interest-based analysis, which underlies negotiation practice, would focus on "moves" between parties, in an effort to illuminate (or infer) the interests that underlie the positions that parties adopt in the conflict process (Axelrod, 1990). The goal of this analysis would be to move parties towards a focus on interests, on the assumption that creative problem-solving and sustainable agreements occur when people "separate the people from the problem" (Fisher, Ury, and Patton, 1983). However, this analysis is not equipped to address the experience of parties relative to their sense of self, their identity, nor can this approach address (much less manage) the way parties' experience of *Other* restricts and constrains the "options" parties can create. So while decision analysis and the associated methods for research may provide adequate tools for diagnosing conflicts which can be broken down into "utility functions" and ranked preferences, this conflict over rights and culture, entitlements born from a history of civil war, in the context of global networks of power and money, resists this method, as there are issues which cannot be ranked, or even framed as a "preference." And indeed the utilitarian perspective behind game theory would not resonate with either the locals, who have rights to the forest concessions, or with the cultural conservationists for whom "culture" could never be framed as an item in a ranked preference. Additionally, game theory and associated research practices were not designed to make sense of the role of emotion or history. And both of these dimensions are crucial to the understanding of, and intervention in, this conflict.

Social identity theory (Tajfel and Turner, 1986) does offer a perspective that attempts to describe and explain the role of identity via analysis of affiliation and group membership. This line of research has yielded very interesting findings that show that people set up systems of inclusion and exclusion, and once created, these membership systems become the foundation for action and reaction. However, most of the research that draws on this theory has drawn on experimental methods, precisely because the level of complexity of social relationships is so high that only experimental methods can isolate the factors to account for the variance or change. In the Mirador Basin conflict, while it may be helpful to query parties about their experience of their affiliations and group memberships, what we know at the end of that query is where the deepest and hottest social divisions lie. However, Likert-based questionnaires, a common survey tool used in social psychological studies, miss the historical roots which ground this conflict in Mirador; yet it is precisely this foundation that must be illuminated and drawn into the analysis in order for social identities, group memberships, to be taken seriously – much less transformed. The experimental methods and Likert-based questionnaires associated with social identity theory have done much to call attention to the role of identity, but do little to address the conflict itself. Knowing *that* identities exist does not lead necessarily to the design of interventions that would support the evolution of these identities in the context of a given, very complex conflict where power must be addressed as part of the diagnosis of the conflict.

Human needs theory (Burton, 1997) does provide a framework for analysis of the power, via the description of unmet needs. The diagnostic assumption is that these needs can be understood by interviews with parties, as to their assessment of their own needs. However, given its critical theoretical roots, human needs theory also harbors the possibility that persons may not know their (real) needs, or they may have been oppressed for so long that they are not able to imagine their needs.

Needs theory can thus require, methodologically, a paternalistic analysis of what parties need, absent their own participation, drawing on a hierarchy of needs in the abstract, rather than drawing on the local knowledge of real-time actors. For this reason, the research in the human needs tradition can fail to address the cultural particularities, or the historical conditions of real people, engaged in real conflict (Avruch, 1998). Case study research that draws on aggregate data about a region or a people can infer the presence of particular needs; intersecting this data with interviews that detail how real people experience their lives, in the context of a conflict, would fill in the holes in researchers' understanding of the case, reducing paternalism while addressing the cultural critique that has been made of human needs theory. This requires attention to the sense-making, to the meanings that persons in conflict ascribe to self, to their Others, and to the issues, as *they* see them. In fact, it is only via attention to meaning and its production that researchers can deliver either explanations or descriptions that are both valid and reliable (Cobb, 2006; Czarniawska, 2004; Pearce and Littlejohn, 1997).

World view analysis (Nudler, 1993), frame analysis (Gray, 1989; Putnam and Holmer, 1992; Schön and Rein, 1994), discourse analysis (Clegg, 1989; Fairclough, 1995; Hajer, 1995), and narrative analysis (Bamberg and Andrews, 2004; Cobb, 1994a, 2001; Mishler, 1986), are all research methods which seek to *describe* the meaning-making structures or processes which create, maintain, or evolve conflicts. All of these methods generate findings about the meaning systems-in-use in the context of a given conflict. Within these approaches, some kinds of studies yield static descriptions of meaning systems, focused on, for instance, the structure of the world view system (Nudler, 1993) or the structure of narrative (Chapman, 1978), or the structure of conversations (Sacks, Schegloff, and Jefferson, 1974), or the nature or categories of frames (Putnam and Holmer, 1992). These structural approaches contribute to the analysis of the content of meaning systems, and their organization, but they are less able to account for the dynamics of interaction between meaning systems, or the evolution of meaning either *within or across* systems.

However, given the nature of conflict cycles and conflict transformation, it is critically important that research focused on meaning systems contribute to the description of not only structures of meaning, but the *dynamics* of these structures as well. Additionally, given that *power* is always core to the conflict dynamics (Clegg, 1989; Mumby, 1993), the analysis of meaning must also not just list the core meanings, but account for the struggle over meaning, the agentic way in which language is mobilized by parties *to do* something, as an action within a conflict (Harré and Slocum, 2003). Further, understanding the dynamics of interaction and power in conflict process involves "standing under" (von Foerster, 1984) the language *use* of parties in conflict, which requires not just the analysis of transcripts, but interviews with parties, in context. Using these criteria, narrative analysis emerges as an important research method for attending to meaning-making processes, power dynamics, and parties' language-in-use, in a specific conflict context. Narrative analysis provides a *diagnostic* framework for understanding conflict that has direct import for conflict intervention. This approach to diagnosis is discussed in the sections to follow.

Narrative Diagnosis of Conflict Processes: A Critical Approach

There is a tremendous literature on narrative analysis, across a large array of social science disciplines. Mishler has offered a classificatory system of narrative analysis that focuses on three levels: meaning, structure, and interaction (Mishler, 1995). As Elliott (2005) notes, the focus on narrative meaning, or *content*, can yield descriptions of events and experiences (Elliott, 2005). This approach to narrative analysis is often used in the field of conflict resolution, as researchers focus on the events, as they are relayed by the storytellers, and the meaning those events have for the storytellers. This is a form of narrative analysis that often seeks to distill the "themes" that are dominant in parties' stories, such as Johnston's analysis of the tobacco conflict (Johnston, 2000). Attention to narrative content may also include a focus on the meaning that actors themselves impute to the events within the narrative which requires a focus on the moral force of the story (Pearce and Littlejohn, 1997). However, the focus on narrative content tends to yield an *acritical* analysis of conflicts precisely because it does not address the functionality of the narrative itself, closing the door to critical analysis of the narrative and its production. Stone *et al.*'s approach to narrative in their book *Difficult Conversations* is a good example of a content approach to narrative (Stone, Patton, and Heen, 1999). They provide a method for the analysis of the storyline, as well as what meaning (evaluation) the teller assigns to those events. Applied to conflict analysis, the focus on narrative content can be framed as a "Level One" analysis; it is useful to attend to the content of the narrative, but content or thematic analysis alone cannot address either the dynamics of process or the issues of power related to the production of the narrative itself.

Following Mishler (1995), the second kind of narrative analysis calls attention to the structure of the narrative *and* enables researchers to describe the functions of the different features or elements of the narrative, in relation to the whole. This approach allows for the description of patterns in the functionality of narratives. For example, the research in this tradition has examined how narratives create internal coherence (Winslade and Monk, 2000), as well as how they generate closure (Spence, 1986), or the functional features of a given genre such as a "narrative of resistance" (Scott, 1990) or "regression narratives" (Gergen and Gergen, 1986). In some instances, depending on the nature of the research question, this approach to narrative analysis can require close analysis of transcripts of conversation, as well as videos documenting the considerable detail that is involved in the enactment of a given narrative. This approach to narrative analysis can be called "Level Two" analysis. It is clearly more complicated than thematic analysis, as it addresses processes of narrative production, meaning production, and the functionality of narrative components, in relation to the meaning of the narrative.

The third category of narrative analysis offered by Mishler (1995) focuses attention on the "performance of narratives – the international and institutional context in which narratives are produced, recounted and consumed" (Elliott 2005, p. 38). Narrative research in this tradition examines the narrative in context, in relation to the dynamics of the social context in which it is elaborated, maintained, and evolved. The role of social interactions, the relation between narrative and institutions becomes the object of analysis. This attention to narrative-in-context enables attention to the *struggle* over meaning and the processes by which some narratives become dominant, and some are marginalized. This can be called a "Level Three" approach to narrative analysis and it is characterized by attention to the politics of narrative processes. These politics can be seen as a function of the "positions" in narrative. Davis and Harré (1990) have defined positions in the following manner:

> Positioning ... is the discursive process whereby selves are located in conversations as observably and subjectively coherent participants in jointly produced story lines. There can be interactive positioning in which what one person says positions another. And there can be reflexive positioning in which one positions oneself. However it would be a mistake to assume that, in either case, positioning is necessarily intentional. (Davies and Harré, 1990)

Critical analysis of narrative processes calls attention to the way in which speakers are positioned in discourse, as well as how they struggle as agents in the narratives they enact, to re-position self and Other (Bamberg & Andrews, 2004). As "positions" are moral locations in a narrative, they can be seen as the *architecture of identity*; persons who are positioned as "caring," "victim," "intelligent," "productive," etc., end up with *access* to resources, because of their socially constructed legitimacy, while persons who are positioned as "stupid," "victimizing," "lazy," or "mean," have reduced access to resources coincident to the way they are socially constructed as delegitimate. Marginalization is the consequence of delegitimization in narrative.

Once negatively positioned, persons struggle to re-position self in the narrative under development (Cobb, 2006). However, once negatively positioned, the narrative works to close off alternative, more positive positions, unless Others collaborate to open the narrative to new plot lines, character roles, and moral themes (Cobb, 2003). The stability of positions is, from a structural perspective, a function of narrative closure – the more coherent the narrative, the less open it is (Cobb, 1994b); it is very difficult to alter one's own position, from within a given narrative, as the evolution of positions requires the participation of others as co-elaborators, and "storytellers" of the new and improved legitimate or positive position in narrative. This is extremely problematic in the context of a conflict because the positive position of one party is *dependent* on a narrative of the Other as having bad intentions or bad character traits. Thus parties who are negatively positioned will not be able to re-position self, as their Others will not only *not* elaborate any new positions for them, the Others will actively continue to maintain or increase the delegitimacy for those persons on whom their own legitimacy rests.

This attention to the formation, evolution, and struggle over positions calls attention to the performance of narrative, as a political process, in the context of existing dominant narratives, which are, in turn, "regulated" by institutions and large-scale hegemonic processes. For example, one could diagnose the World Bank's narrative about development as illuminating the way that narrative positions recipients of aid/loans as "incompetent," which of course requires that a set of restrictions, guidelines, etc. be imposed. Efforts by the World Bank to engage recipients of aid/loans in the assessment of needs, prior to setting up the projects or the terms of the aid/loan, initiates a process of "consultation" that all too often reproduces the existing power structures and contributes to maintain marginalization in the local context. "Development," from this perspective, is enacted out of a narrative that disqualifies the recipients, and maintains the inequities on the ground, which will, in turn, ripen the social fractures which are at the foundation of violent conflict. All policies are narratives that position persons as legitimate and/or delegitimate. Understanding the narrative positions within policy would be a critical component of creating policies that promote social justice.

Positions matter. Positions are material. They have immediate, serious, and long-term implications for access to resources, legal sanctions, moral legitimacy, and social relations. The economic sanctions threatening Iran are only possible if they are positioned as "willfully" and "flagrantly" disregarding the requests of the international community. If they were being positioned as unintentionally continuing their nuclear program, they would not be at risk for sanctions or the West's scorn. British Petroleum is under investigation not for causing an oil spill in Alaska, but because they may have intentionally ignored the data that indicated the pipeline needed repair. "Callous disregard" and "greed" are the characterizations that could anchor the BP position in the emerging narrative about the spill. What is at stake is far more important than money – positions are "ground zero" for the struggle over meaning, for legitimacy and all that accompanies it.

The more negative the position (and the most negative is the social construction of a person as "evil"), the more dangerous it is for those positioned that way – they are at risk of bearing the consequences of this position; if indeed it is accepted and elaborated by others in that social context. This struggle is further complicated by the hegemonic force of large-scale cultural narratives, anchored by social, political, and economic institutions. Persons/groups/nations that are negatively positioned often cannot re-story their positions as these positions are reinforced by the narratives spun from dominant institutions (Foucault, 1972). Once a discourse or narrative is launched and adopted, it jealously restricts the participation of those that would seek to alter it, marginalizing counter-narratives (Bamberg & Andrews, 2004). All too often, those that are negatively positioned resort to violence, not because they are violent groups, or even "terrorists," but because their narrative, and the legitimacy it provides them, slips continually off the interactional (and often international) stages where these conflicts are enacted and contested. Positions, from this perspective, are not just "talk" as opposed to action (to reproduce a familiar Cartesian distinction between mind/body, talk/action); positions are material enactments of narrative process. They are life and death matters.

The struggle is a struggle not just for survival, but for legitimacy, moral legitimacy. While the field of conflict resolution has argued, persuasively, that "identity" is core to the production of violent conflict, the field has focused less on the role of "legitimacy." We could define "legitimacy" as the positive positions we provide ourselves, *adopted and elaborated by our Others*. Our own elaboration of our legitimacy does not, in and of itself, constitute our legitimacy; this is because legitimacy is a *relational* phenomenon and exists in a relational system: our relationship not to ourselves, although this is certainly important, but rather to our Others. This accents the idea that morality is not absolute, it is conditional on the narratives that are in play, within a given context. And while morality may vary from one context to another, there are likely narrative patterns involved in the production of morality that occur across conflict contexts. Such a cross-cultural analysis of positioning processes would afford analysts an opportunity to examine the way moral positions are anchored, by each narrative, for Self and Other (Us and Them).

Despite this potential diversity of positions and moral anchors for them, narrative logic itself limits the number of anchors for moral legitimacy. While, to date, there is no study of the set of these anchors, across conflicts, we can see some patterns. First, historical victimization is clearly an important narrative logic, used to anchor legitimate positions; in the Mirador conflict, the indigenous people anchor the legitimacy of themselves, as well as their claim to the forest concessions, on the history of the civil war, and their victimization. Second, legitimacy can be anchored on a pragmatist's or utilitarian set of values (efficiency, effectiveness). This is clearly the foundation for the legitimacy for those telling the "pro-development" narrative in this conflict. Third, legitimacy can be anchored on legal rights, or law; however, rights or law may or may not be moral (there may be no moral imperative associated), so it can be seen as a relatively unstable foundation for legitimacy. Of these three kinds of narrative logic, "historical victimization" and "legal rights" are the ones on which calls for "justice" are founded. Note that legal rights may or may not be as solid a basis for stabilizing a claim of legitimacy (positive position) within a narrative of historical victimization: one can argue which legal code is in effect, but one cannot contest the historical fact of a civil war which left a detailed record of victimization.

"Justice narratives" are essentially stories that elaborate a history of victimization, often at the hands of the Others. These narratives have also been described as "humiliation narratives" in which the Others harm with impunity and disregard for the humanity of those they victimize (Lindner, 2006). However, interactionally, these narratives are almost *never* elaborated by the Others, precisely because they carry, from a functional perspective, the legitimacy of the parties that narrate historical victimization. In fact, if any group elaborates a narrative about the historical victimization of their Others, not only do they legitimize their Others, but they delegitimize themselves, for the narrative often leaves them no way to discuss the victimization without acknowledging responsibility for that victimization. So these justice narratives are denied, elided, erased, ignored, by the Others. Further, the tragedy is that the Others are most often the *only* ones that can legitimize the speakers of the historical victimization narrative. And, ironically, they are the *only* ones that cannot, without risking delegitimization themselves.

As we know all too well, we live in a era where it is ever more clear that people are willing to die to "tell their story" as a way of inscribing the world with their narrative, on the faceless and nameless bodies of Others. The consequences of having a "justice narrative" go unelaborated by the Others, or even, at times, *anyone* else, ensures that the speakers, those that attempt to found their legitimacy on historical victimization, will surely continually be unable to establish their legitimacy. Blocked from becoming legitimate, from a narrative perspective, violence is often the only recourse that seems available. As Scarry (1985) has noted, violence appears where words no longer work. Addressing social justice is a narrative process; it involves designing processes and interventions which would enable parties to a conflict to elaborate the narratives of historical victimization.

Narrative diagnosis of conflicts itself promotes social justice, for it materializes and exposes marginality; while some theorists may argue that "narrative interventions" are not material, and perhaps could function as just one more way to avoid the material re-distribution of resources, I would counter this argument by noting that narratives are *material*, and this elaboration of the history of victimization would be the only way to set up the "positions" which could both reflect and construct real changes in roles, in moral themes, and anticipated scenarios, such that marginalization is reduced. Without narrative intervention, efforts to redress marginalization operate on the basis of accusations that do little to build new relationships, and on the contrary, deepen relational fractures. The diagnosis of conflicts, via the analysis of positions in narratives, can illuminate these political processes, this struggle over meaning, and offer strategies by which speakers can reposition self and Other, so as to address and redress marginalization and promote social justice. Thus, positioning analysis, as a subset of narrative analysis, provides a lens with which to both account for, *and alter*, the politics of narrative process, for it is this process that is at the heart of conflict.

In summary, while there are multiple approaches to narrative analysis, only those that address narrative interaction, in context, can begin to make sense of the power dynamics within narratives, and within the social context, where that struggle over meaning, which I have argued *is* a struggle over position, takes place. In the section that follows, I illustrate the use of positioning analysis in the case study of the conflict in the Mirador Basin. This case study will exemplify a "Level Three" approach to narrative analysis.

Data for this narrative analysis was collected using a form of "snowball sampling" (Patton, 2002); over 60 in-depth interviews, across 37 organizations were conducted. Researchers were directed by the funders, *The Nature Conservancy* and *Conservation International*, to key actors, for initial interviews with persons who, in turn, were subsequently asked a circular question (Tomm, 1987): "Who do you think we should speak with to deepen our knowledge of the perspective you hold, and whom do you think we should speak with that would help us understand those that would see things very differently?" These questions require the interviewee to construct the set of persons who agree and disagree with them. In some cases, we followed this question with: "Of these persons you mentioned, who would be the one that would most strongly disagree with your perspective" which would enable us to prioritize and sequence the interviews.

Within the interviews themselves, the research team worked to understand the plot line in each narrative, as well as the characters involved, and the moral themes, tracking positive and negative positions. We explored dimensions of these narratives relative to a set of meanings related to natural and cultural conservation, effective development, and the role of international organizations, archeology, and the nature of tourism. Following this structural (content) analysis, in an effort to understand dynamics related to narrative processes, we analyzed the dynamics related to positioning, across the narratives; from this we were able to assess a narrative's dominance or its marginalization, in a given domain or context. This research thus set the stage for the design of a participatory planning process in which issues could be addressed, and a strategy for conserving natural and cultural resources designed. Implications of narrative diagnosis for conflict resolution practice will be addressed in the concluding comments of this chapter.

Narratives of Conservation and Development: Stories from the Living and the Dead

The conflict in the Mirador Basin in Guatemala has two basic narratives in opposition to each other, and parties to the conflict are polarized along these narrative divisions. However, differences between the narratives are not the problem, from a conflict resolution standpoint; for example, while it may be problematic, from a policy standpoint, if some people "story" global warming as caused by sun spots and others story it as caused by carbon gases, these differences could, theoretically, be addressed and resolved via science alone. However, we know from debates such as these, that each story *also* negatively positions the Other by denigrating their science, which in turn is the foundation for a negative position as a "incompetent scientist." Indeed, conflicts are perpetuated not by narrative differences alone, but by the ways in which each narrative locates the problem in the *actions* (intentions) or *traits* of the Other (Cobb, 1994b). This is functionally accomplished through the inter-relationships between the formal structural features of the plot: antecedent conditions, complicating action, reactions, crisis, and strategic responses. Altogether, these components of the plot provide the logic which, in turn, constructs the characters as legitimate or illegitimate.

The "antecedent condition" in the narrative refers to the situation or conditions that were in place prior to the complications generated by the Others (Cobb, 2006). Usually, parties portray themselves as "in process" dealing with those conditions, before the Others complicate matters. The "complicating action" in the narrative is what the Others do that creates more problems. In a conflictual context, this complicating action is NOT an accident, or a fluke of nature. It is intentional action by the Others and it functionally anchors the negative positions which are core to the "complicating action," without which, the conflict would dissolve into an interaction about "miscommunications" and "unintentional mistakes." As Bateson noted, it is differences which make a difference that constitute information; in narratives, the *difference which makes a difference* is the information about positions (Bateson, 1972).

The narrative "response" that people make to the "complicating actions" is precisely an effort to re-position Self more positively, and solidify negative positions for the Other. It is an effort to build a dominant narrative, and marginalize the Other's story. "Crisis" comes when parties have not been able to totally marginalize their Others, and their narrative efforts to delegitimize their Others have not been adopted in the broader social context. The crisis is always a *crisis of legitimacy*, generated by negative positions created for speakers, by their Others. Parties, however, continue to plot and plan, from a narrative perspective, how they can triumph in relation to their Others; this requires the consolidation of positive positions for Self and, if possible, delegitimacy, disgrace, and perhaps even death for their Others.

In the case of the Mirador conflict, there are two central and competing narratives. The narrative, told by the indigenous people and anchored by a variety of groups/institutions that have supported the forest concessions, financially and politically, has the following plot line:

Pro Forest Concessions Narrators	Antecedent Conditions	Complicating Actions by Others	Reaction	Crisis	Strategic Response
ACOFOP CONAP USAID CALLAS Elected leaders at local, regional and national levels in Guatemala	Civil War; victimization of indigenous people; severe poverty; forest concessions granted as part of the 1996 Peace Accord; Forest concessions reduce or altogether block fires, as local supervision of the forest keeps people from burning to clear trees for cattle grazing; it also protects the region from drug lords, as the area is supervised by locals, who keep an eye peeled for nefarious actors who are not from the region. The largest Mayan ruins in the world are in the region.	U.S.-based Archeologist, Hanson, with U.S.-based NGOs (Global Heritage Fund) develop and circulate a plan for a large eco-tourist project in the Mirador Basin, which would block forest concessions AND set up a corporation that would enrich (greedy) shareholders, without including or consulting locals. Hanson and other Gringo supporters claim concessions are ineffective at blocking fires, archeological smuggling, or drug trafficking. Hanson and supporters worked, via lies and political connections, to try and have the forest concessions cancelled legally.	ACOFOP filed lawsuit to ensure forest concessions were retained. ACOFOP developed a PR campaign against the eco-tourist project. USAID significantly reduced funding to ACOFOP, coincident to this crisis.	Courts ruled in favor of ACOFOP and retained the concessions. However, Hanson and GHF continue to promote the eco-tourist project and denigrate ACOFOP in national and international settings.	Legal vigilance; outreach to national and international groups defending the legitimacy of forest concessions.

The other central narrative is the "pro-development narrative, which has the following plot line:

Pro-Development Narrators	Antecedent Condition	Complicating Action (by Others)	Reaction	Crisis	Strategic Response
Hanson	Looting of a very valuable archeological site in rainforest which was being destroyed by fires and populated by drug runners.	Lawsuit that blocked the cancellation of the forest concessions awarded to the Mirador region; continued looting of the Mayan archeological site in Mirador; increased fires in the rainforest in Mirador; increased insecurity from drug trafficking in Mirador. ACOFOP lies about fires, smuggling, and drugs in the region.	Media events in the U.S., supporting the eco-tourism project, and denigrating the concessions re: looting, fires, and drugs in the area. Destruction of the Mayan ruins becomes the focus of events at Guatemalan Embassy in the U.S.	Guatemalan political support (national level) for ACOFOP, and local leadership in Mirador; World Bank funding sought to fund participatory process in Mirador, for addressing the overlapping needs of both conservation (concessions) and conservation of archeological sites (ecotourism). Publication and wide circulation of ICAR "Stakeholder Analysis for the Mirador Basin" legitimizing the moral need to include the Mirador indigenous people in any development planning.	Continued lobbying in DC, by Hanson and Morgan. Outreach to ICAR (lobbying). Continued publicity of Hanson's discoveries, with publication of "data" on fires, drug trafficking, and smuggling.
Morgan, Preservationist, Global Heritage Fund					
INGUAT (Instituto Gualtemalteco de Turismo)	A plan for an ecotourism project was created; this plan provided a rationale, as well as logistical suggestions for development of a way to improve the local economy.				
National Geographic Society					

In each of these stories, the plot structure – antecedent conditions, complication action, reaction, crisis, and strategic response – functions to set up the narrative logic for the positions for each narrative group:

	Negative Positions	Positive Positions
Within Pro-concession ("us")	*None*	**Impoverished victims of the State* **Hardworking* **Environmentally responsible stewards* **Indigenous people with rights* **Local leaders foster democratic participation and decision-making*
Within Pro-concession ("them")	**Liars* **Greedy transnationals* **Colonizers from the North* **Rich politicians trying to stay in power* **"Consumers" rather than stewards of the environment*	*None*
Within Pro-development ("us")	None	*Discoverer and protector of cultural resources *Educated, cultivated, sophisticated *Experienced in governance that supports, develops AND protects environment *Global perspective *Financially savvy/ dealmakers *Politically savvy *Committed to preservation of environmental and cultural resources, for the world's people
Within Pro-development ("them")	*Liars *Incompetents *Pretenders *Dependent (on USAID/ Government) *"Sheep" *Ignorant/unworldly	None

There are four important observations to be made about these positions: First, neither side constructs the other side with any positive positions, and both narratives function, dichotomously, to anchor positive positions for "us." Second, both narratives anchor negative positions in two ways: with negative intentions, as well as negative traits. Third, negative positions for Other, in each narrative, resonate to the positive positions for self; in other words, the negative and positive positions in each narrative are discursive opposites and thus interdependent. Finally, the combination of positions, positive and negative, comprises the moral system in operation in the conflict. Elaboration of these observations, relative to the dynamics of the narratives, follows.

Positive positions for "us": Perhaps the severity and intractability of a conflict can be assessed on the basis of the relative presence or absence of *any* positive positions for Other, within a narrative, as well as the nature of the negative position of the Other. In the case of the Mirador conflict, both sides create positive positions for Self. The pro-concession narrators anchor their legitimacy on their historical victimization during the Civil War, which in turn is the foundation to their rights-based legal claim to the forest concessions. The pro-development narrative anchors their legitimacy on the need to preserve cultural resources for the world, the need to stop the burning of the rainforest, as well as on the need for economic development in the Mirador Basin. Using their positive positions for Self, each side creates an "us" – the set of characters that elaborate, with us, these positive positions for self. Thus, these positive positions establish the communities of both in-group/out-group relations. This is a narrative-based re-definition of social identity processes.

Anchoring negative positions for "them": The negative positions that both narratives establish for their Others vary in intensity. Generally, negative positions are established via the attribution of negative traits and/or negative intentions (Cobb, 2003). In the pro-concession narrative, the Others are *intending* to harm in order to stay in power, or because of their desire for power. These Others also have negative traits assigned – they are "liars" and "greedy." However, for the pro-development, there are no negative intentions attributed, but there are negative traits – they are "ignorant" and "incompetent liars." It could be argued that the former narrative is more toxic, in that the attribution of negative intention is more globally damning – once intentions are framed as negative, there is no act that is not suspect. It is also the case that negative traits "contaminate" action, but it is easier, in theory, to destabilize a negative trait, as the storyteller would only need to provide a counter-narrative where they were something other than that negative trait, or a reduction of negativity of that trait (e.g., from "lazy" to "day-dreamer").

"Counter-narratives" (Bamberg and Andrews, 2004) can be understood as the stories told by Others in an effort to redress how they are negatively positioned. In the Mirador conflict, the concessionaires were forced to tell a counter narrative, in response to being negatively positioned by the "development narrative." The concessionaires had been marginalized on the international stage, as North American NGOs held public events in Washington, DC, heralding the discovery of the Mayan cultural site, erasing the historical presence of the civil war, the victimization of the indigenous people, and the legitimacy of their claim to the forest concessions. These public events were widely publicized with articles in major newspapers. A documentary was created and circulated about the archeology treasures in the Mirador region, creating pressure to build tourism in that area.

However, research indicates that once positioned negatively, parties ironically are forced to elaborate a counter-narrative on the grounds of the existing narrative in which they are delegitimized; often this inadvertently strengthens the very narrative that the counter-narrative seeks to undermine or alter (Cobb and Rifkin, 1991). The concessionaires struggled to create themselves as legitimate caretakers of the natural and cultural resources in their region, but this struggle was complicated by the fact that the "development" actors had tremendous financial resources with which they could elaborate their narrative. The narrative playing field, in this case, was not symmetrical.

Narrative interdependence: In the Mirador conflict, the positive positions each elaborated for self are the foundation for the negative positions elaborated for their Others; the legitimacy of each group is founded on the delegitimacy of their Other. Thus the work for storytellers in both narrative camps is to ensure that the delegitimacy for the Others is not reduced, as that would destabilize the legitimacy for Self. For example, within the "pro-development" narrative, the concessionaires are delegitimized because they are dependent on USAID funding – the concessions actually cost more to maintain organizationally than the revenue from the sale of the trees. Any attempt to formulate a narrative about how the concessionaries are increasing revenue, or decreasing dependence on USAID, will destabilize the legitimacy of the "pro-development" storytellers. However, this analysis predicts that this will precisely be the location of struggle, the place where "pro-concessionaires" will build a counter-narrative. This struggle over meaning is thus quite predicable, from the analysis of positions within the narrative.

In the Mirador conflict, the counter-narrative which elaborated the ways that concessionaires were utilizing the forest, not just the trees, to build a revenue base was not yet widely circulated across the set of stakeholders; however, the "pro-development" storytellers had already launched a narrative campaign countering this counter-narrative, proof of its importance to the legitimacy of their narrative. Again, given the asymmetry in terms of access to media, the "pro-development" narrators could effectively protect themselves against the counter-narrative launched by the "pro-concession" story. In sum, the dependence of each party's legitimacy on their Other's delegitimacy both reveals the interdependence of positions, as well as predicts the location over the struggle over meaning: the content of the counter-narratives, and the narrative work deployed to counter those counter-narratives.

It also predicts that the "pro-concession" actors would seek to establish and stabilize their legitimacy in legal settings, and they did; as they were not able to launch counter-narratives that would be elaborated by others, and they therefore could do little to challenge the legitimacy the "pro-development" storytellers claimed for themselves, they had little choice but to try and formally anchor their legitimacy via the law. To the extent that there are real asymmetries in access to media and financial resources, "power" can be defined in terms of the capacity of one party to avoid destabilization of its legitimacy, as well as its capacity to have the delegitimacy of their Others widely elaborated.

Positions and the moral field: Across both the positive and negative positions elaborated by parties, for Self and Other, the moral system for evaluating action is constructed. In the Mirador case, the morality had to do with both conservation of natural and cultural resources, and with modernizing the region (electricity, schools) while making it economically independent. The "pro-development" people argued that concessionaires would be "better off" if they would accept development of the tourism project, and then be employed as guides, janitors, and caretakers for that project. The "pro-concession" parties countered in a discourse of "self-determination" which was, in turn, undermined by the narrative about their dependence on USAID. Morally, the heart of this conflict was about the issues surrounding autonomy, with one side arguing the "good" in terms of "self-determination" and the other side defining "good" as "economic independence." The research showed that both stories valued cultural and natural conservation; they just had different means to that end. Even so, this does not imply that there is "common ground." While both narratives advance "conservation" as a value, there are two very different narrative logics at work, and within those disparate logics, "conservation" plays very different roles. As long as "conservation" is linked to the politics of the narratives (the construction of legitimacy and delegitimacy), it cannot provide "common ground" without also "uploading" the struggle over meaning; the struggle against loss of legitimacy and marginalization.

However, this analysis cannot predict which narratives will become dominant; narrative dominance is a function of both the access to resources which could be mobilized to foster elaboration of one narrative, as well as a function of the dominance of the morality that is advanced in the narrative. For example, in this conflict, "economic independence" has tremendous resonance, particularly within the U.S., so the "pro-development" narrative from within the Mirador conflict has been widely elaborated by NGOs, U.S. agencies, and U.S. business. These can be understood as "affinity networks" precisely because they share moral values. The "pro-development" story about Mirador is easily "downloaded" into these networks.

On the other hand, the moral claims within the "pro-concession" narrative have resonance within Guatemala – they are much more regionally pertinent; the exception here is the morality of human rights, which is also at the core of the "pro-concession" narrative. However, this discourse does not mobilize the media or the financial networks of the "economic independence" narrative (within the context of the Mirador stakeholder set). Consequently, the moral resonance of the "pro-concession" and "pro-development" narrative is not symmetrical and portends that the "pro-concession" narrative and counter-narrative(s) will not be able to dominate the "pro-development" narrative, even though the "pro-concession" narrative may win legal battles within Guatemala that block the development of the Mirador Basin and preserve the forest concession. This however, cannot be confused with "winning" or "dominance." To date, legal decisions that favor the concessions do not necessarily provide the moral grounds for the legitimacy for the concessions. And, as long as that remains the case, we can assume that the concessions are threatened by the "pro-development."

The conflict will persist, as it is a struggle for the legitimacy of two competing narratives, and legal decisions do little to reconcile competing moralities. We can assume that asymmetries will continue. "Pro-development" will continue to resonate in international networks of business and politics. If the Guatemalan government succumbs to international pressure (if there is any) and cedes control over the Mirador planning process, by allowing the "pro-development" storytellers to introduce data, call meetings, or "facilitate," we can anticipate heightened intensity in the struggle over meaning, increased polarization, reduction of dialogue, and potential violence. The way to prevent this devolution is not to promote dialogue; it is to ensure that the planning process itself is managed by the Guatemalan leaders. Only in this way will "pro-concessions" be able to have their narrative elaborated and their legitimacy affirmed. Once this is underway, dialogue would indeed be a useful strategy for building a collaborative process where all perspectives can be valued and integrated.

In this case study, the diagnosis of the conflict narratives highlights the structure and the processes of the meaning system that locks parties into interaction that contributes to the emergence of conflict, as well as its escalation, re-affirming parties' narrative of Self/Other. Further, because narrative analysis examines the power relationships engendered in and through positioning processes, it also yields prescriptions for action and intervention: conflict intervention is the process of generating legitimacy for all parties, in the narratives they tell about Self and Other.

Conclusion

The narrative analysis of conflict, as presented in this chapter, is intended to provide a framework for the critical diagnosis of conflict processes, illuminating the struggle over meaning, as a struggle over legitimacy in narrative. This framework relies on "positions" and the "positioning" process to track how legitimacy and delegitimacy are constructed and contested. However, this diagnostic is not just a tool for analysis; it is also extremely relevant for the design of interventions and conflict resolution processes. Conflict resolution practice should be anchored in a description of how the domain for the struggle over meaning is organized/structured, how parties navigate the moral value system they launch via positions in narratives, and how the field of stakeholders, as storytellers, are arrayed in the context of the competing narratives and counter-narratives.

From this perspective, the goal of conflict resolution practice, as a practice of social justice, should be the design of processes to support the evolution of narratives that position parties as legitimate, identify the narrative(s) that are marginalized, and contribute to the centralization and adoption of those narratives, in ways that legitimize the Others in that narrative. Legal legitimacy is insufficient; what is needed in Guatemala, and elsewhere, are processes that provide for the legitimacy of all parties to be advanced, and elaborated. On an asymmetric narrative field, this is of course complicated.

In the spring of 2006, long after the legal decisions were made, re-affirming the "pro-concession" narrative, I was invited to attend a reception at the Guatemalan Embassy in Washington, DC, where the archeology of the Mirador Basin was discussed as one of the most important cultural sites in the world and development was advocated as means to that end. The "pro-concession" narrative was, of course, absent. It did not even appear as a counter-narrative. Instead, data (which are highly contested within Guatemala) on the number of fires in the Mirador region were presented, providing the narrative logic for immediate intervention in the area, so cultural and natural conservation can take place. After the presentation, during the question/answer period, I raised my hand, and asked the presenters if there were any people/perspectives within Guatemala who had a different strategy for "conserving" natural and cultural resources. They then noted the existence of an alternative narrative, but disqualified it as soon as they described the "pro-concession" story. It was clear that this narrative was, and would remain, marginal within the international community.

Simply stating the alternative narrative is not sufficient. Engagement and collective narration of the past, the present, and the future is required. Narrative analysis can provide the foundation for the practical decisions about who engages, with whom, in what process, for what purpose. It can also provide a set of parameters for assessing the effectiveness of any conflict resolution process, which should contribute to the elaboration of narratives in which all parties participate in the construction of a narrative that provides legitimacy for all. Social justice is not just about protecting the marginal. It is about ensuring that legitimacy is afforded to all participants, *on the grounds they advance for themselves*. From this perspective, the diagnosis of conflict narratives provides the foundation for the practice of social justice, focused on advancing legitimacy and reducing marginality for all parties.

Narrative analysis, as a mode of conflict diagnosis, provides a framework for assessing not only the meaning systems of the parties, but the power dynamics that surround the enactment of conflict narratives. While other approaches to diagnosis rely either on inference (of interests, needs, or psychological motivations), the narrative approach provides an empirical foundation on which to assess the conflict and design interventions. This empirical foundation, the narrative structures and processes, contains the data for assessing the meaning system that is at once the cause and the outcome of the conflict process. While making sense of sense making will always be a function of interpretative processes, the only attribution that needs consistently to be done, as a conflict analyst, is the attribution of positive intention for all parties, across all narratives. The analysis of narrative *as if* parties are doing the best they can, in circumstances they did not make (by themselves) and cannot control, begins to create the analyst as a legitimizing resource, and the analysis itself, an intervention that reduces the delegitimacy for the parties, in the narrative of their Others. The attribution of positive intention, at the core of narrative analysis, constitutes this approach as a political act, one that names and alters the marginal positions of delegitimized parties. This is a core dimension which marks a difference between this approach to diagnosis and others based on the analysis of interests or needs, or social identity. While these approaches to diagnosis yield interesting perspectives on the causes of conflicts, and they may even be political in the way they advocate for the needs of the marginal to be addressed, they do not advocate the evolution of the content of the narratives that parties tell about Self and Other. So narrative diagnosis, a la Level Three, is political in two senses: first, it provides a framework for identifying marginality, and second, it advocates for all parties, via the attribution of positive intention.

While I would argue that the politics of narrative analysis is one of its strengths, those that approach conflict analysis from an epistemology of "discovery" rather than one of "invention" would likely assume that the analyst should be neutral and refrain from alteration of the content of parties' narratives. In this case, narrative analysis would be at odds with the assumption that the analyst just *discovers* the deep-rooted causes of the conflict; rather, the Level Three approach to narrative analysis presumes that the analyst is politically involved in the social construction of meaning. The presence of this reflexive role for the analysis can be seen as a limitation of the model, if the goal of the analysis is simply understanding. However, the goal of Level Three approach to narrative diagnosis extends beyond understanding to intervention, and forecasts a reflexive and political role for the analyst as engaged in the making of the story about the conflict stories; one that reduces marginalization of any and all parties, and promotes their legitimacy, in the narrative of their Others.

Discussion Questions

1 What role does history play in the core narratives of the conflict in the Mirador Basin?
2 In the struggle for legitimacy, how does each "side" work to create themselves as legitimate?
3 What role does the international community play in creating dominant or marginal narratives in this case?
4 How is the narrative approach to "diagnosis" resonant or consonant with those efforts to address the role of culture and history?
5 How are the "positions" in this conflict similar to, or different from, those in other conflicts? Are there generic positions? Are they distinctive to each case?
6 What is the nature of "power" that is operating in this case?

Key Words
Character
Delegitimacy

Domination
Elaboration
Legitimacy
Narrative
Plot
Positioning
Power
Themes

CHAPTER 7

Situations

Daniel Druckman

The United States delegation was looking forward to a routine negotiation with Spain to update an earlier agreement on the leasing of military bases. They were prepared to offer an enhanced compensation package including research and development grants. Much to their surprise, the Spanish negotiators shifted the discussion away from the base-rights issues and toward their geopolitical concerns in the larger European context. The Spanish delegation made the bases contingent upon NATO membership, prodding the U.S. negotiators to make the case for inclusion in Brussels. Their unrelenting demands and tough rhetoric led to impasses, including several suspensions of the talks. Faced with an expiration of the leasing agreement, Spain began to reevaluate its position. The prospect of another veto of its application for NATO membership (despite the efforts of U.S. representatives) coupled with a loss of revenues from a closing of the bases served to soften Spain's demands and posturing. The impending death of Franco early in 1976 accelerated the talks as the Spanish negotiators made several major concessions both before and after he died. The final agreement favored the U.S. who actually received a more favorable package than was expected when the talks commenced a year and a half earlier.

This example illustrates the influence of the situation on negotiating behavior and decisions. Three aspects of the situation had strong effects on the process: the linking of smaller to larger political issues, time pressure, and an external event. Negotiators in both delegations reacted to changes in the situation as they occurred through the course of the discussions. The process may be understood in terms of these events irrespective of the particular individuals on the delegations. It is unlikely that the process would have unfolded differently if other individuals had been chosen to represent their countries. This observation is consistent with the results of numerous studies that document the impacts of *situational effects* on conflict-related behavior. In this chapter, we discuss various ways in which disputants are responsive to, and the resolution of disputes are contingent on, changing situations. We begin the discussion by defining a situational approach, which is understood in relation to approaches that focus primarily on individuals or social structures. The chapter continues with a review of the empirical evidence for situational effects, the major research traditions that emphasize the importance of the situation, taxonomies or frameworks of aspects of situations, and implications of the approach for theory, research, and practice.

Situating the Analysis of the Situation

Explanations for behavior may be found by looking inside or outside the person and, if outside, in the immediate situation or in the broader structural or cultural contexts. We choose to focus on the role of the immediate situation in conflict behavior. A situational perspective may be located in the middle of a spectrum of approaches that range from psychodynamics at one end to social systems at the other. The analysis of situational effects on behavior is an alternative to both looking "deep" inside a person as in psychoanalytic perspectives and looking beyond people as in analyses of social structures. The legacy for this approach may be found in behavioral social psychology (e.g., Thibaut and Kelley, 1959; Homans, 1961). In Figure 6.1, we show a spectrum of approaches ranging from psychoanalytic (Freudian) to social systems (Marxist) perspectives. For each perspective we name the key historical theorists, including those that straddle the fence between approaches (e.g., Vallacher and Nowak's (2005) dynamical systems approach). The spectrum ranges from perspectives that focus attention inside the person to those that emphasize factors outside the person. Within this range are two dimensions – one goes from central (underlying) to peripheral (the observable surface) for the "inside" approaches and the other from proximal (close) to distal (far away) for the "outside" approaches.

The situational perspective discussed in this chapter is understood most clearly in relation to perspectives that highlight the person, which are referred to in Figure 6.1 as "inside" perspectives. In the next section we turn to a discussion of this comparison.

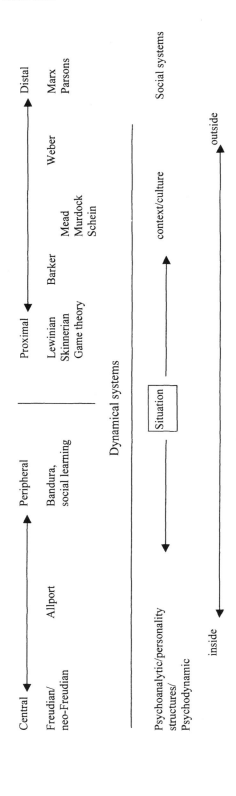

Figure 7.1 Situating the situation

Person- vs. Situation-Centered Analyses

Theorizing in social science focuses attention primarily on processes, events, cultures, situations, structures, and institutions. For the most part, the role of the person or individual is minimized in these frameworks. In contrast, psychology – which has been historically ambivalent about its relationship with the social sciences – places the person at the center of theory and analysis. For many psychologists, the analytical quest is directed at discovering how personalities develop and are manifest in behavior. Such person-centered approaches have also been emphasized in the more applied branches of psychology such as educational, industrial, community, military, peace, and political psychology.

A smaller number of psychologists in each of these specialties has focused on theoretical or applied issues that have brought them into contact or collaboration with other social scientists: for example, with industrial and labor relations, educational or military sociology, peace studies, and international relations. Such contact has highlighted the tension between person- and situation- or structure-centered approaches to analysis. An example of this tension is the debate between the leadership or decision-making analyses that some political psychologists have performed and the systemic-macro analyses (such as the projects on correlates of war or on enduring rivalries between nation-states) that many international relations theorists have conducted. Focusing attention primarily on political psychology, I will raise some issues about the relevance of person-centered approaches in the analysis of international conflict.

The inside and outside perspectives shown in Figure 6.1 differ in terms of the assumed locus of causation. They also differ in terms of the way research is designed. The difference between my approach and that of Margaret Hermann, a political psychologist at Syracuse University, in analyzing conflict illustrates the contrast. Hermann (1995) analyzes policy decisions from the standpoint of leader characteristics (locus of causation). Her typology consists of making distinctions between strategists, advocates, and cue-takers. She then shows how each of these types makes decisions, deals with constituents, and otherwise maneuvers through negotiation or mediation to deal with or resolve conflicts. The cue-taker is the most sensitive to the situation, making his or her behavior more flexible in the sense of adjusting to situational changes. Strategists also adjust to the situation but interpret it in terms of their positions on issues. They use contextual cues to determine when the time is right to make a move. Advocates are the least adaptive in the sense of being driven primarily by relatively unchanging principles, values, or ideologies. Using content analysis techniques, Hermann places a variety of leaders (in her sample) into one or another of these categories. She then interprets their decisions, usually gathered from the same or similar documents, in terms of the hypothesized behavior associated with the category assigned to them. Hermann (1995) relies mostly on anecdotes to illustrate the way each of the three types operate.

In contrast, I take as my point of departure the situation itself, regarded as the locus of causation (Druckman, 1995). I depict or manipulate such characteristics of the situation as role obligations and accountability, visibility or media coverage, available alternatives to negotiating proposals, time pressure, and issue importance. I then show through experiments how these variables influence negotiating flexibility, perceptions of the situation, and tactics such as hanging tough or vacillating. When negotiators are accountable to constituents, have attractive alternatives, or negotiate in private, they are usually more flexible. Rather than analyzing flexibility in terms of individual styles or acquired propensities, I analyze it in terms of those aspects of the situation that influence behavior for most negotiators. They take the form of trajectories proceeding through stages toward or away from a negotiated agreement: for example, friendly relations in stage 1 (pre-negotiation planning) → peripheral locations in stage 2 (setting the stage) → limited media coverage in stage 3 (the give-and-take) → limited media coverage in stage 4 (the endgame).

While Hermann's approach is based on a typology of individual characteristics, I base my approach on a typology of situational variables. Both approaches aim to understand decision-making and behavior in conflict settings, but are rooted in different traditions of psychology: personality versus social psychology. The two traditions even construe the idea of person–situation interactions differently. For Hermann, the person or leader remains at the center, as he or she deals with the various situations presented. She contrasts two types of leaders as follows:

Responsiveness to political constraints (*situation*) suggests how open and sensitive a leader is likely to be to constituents, institutional interests and norms, and discrepant information from the environment (*personality characteristic*). Less responsive leaders are more principled and generally are driven by a cause, an ideology, or problem they want to solve (*personality characteristic*). They are advocates for a particular position. As such, these leaders usually engage in selective perception, seeing what they want to see in the environment. More responsive leaders are more pragmatic, using situational cues to determine what kinds of behavior are appropriate. (Hermann, 1995, pp. 151–2)

She goes on to contrast two types of responsive (to the situation) leaders: strategists who manipulate situations and cue-takers who let the situation shape their behavior (see 1995, p. 152). Note that although the situation influences cue-takers, the focus of the analysis is on the personality that lets the situations influence them rather than the situation that does the influencing.

For me, on the other hand, the situation is the locus of causation, accounting for most of the variation in negotiating (or related) behavior, even though differences exist between individuals in the way they react to the same situation. I summarized the results of several simulation experiments as follows:

> Taken together, the various analyses suggest some conclusions about the conditions (*situation*) that may produce intransigence in negotiation. For example, intransigence is particularly likely when negotiators prepare strategies in cohesive groups (*refers to an experimental condition*), for talks in which only a few issues are being contested; when they perform before an audience that creates strong face-saving pressures; when they are accountable to constituents and do not expect future interactions with their opponents ... and when they are faced with a tough or exploitative opponent whose intentions are easy to discern. These are the aspects of the situation that can be altered as part of a tactical approach to negotiating beneficial agreements. (Druckman, 1995, pp. 72–3)

I go on to show how these findings about situational effects may be used to diagnose negotiating flexibility. Although not all negotiators are likely to be equally flexible or inflexible under the same conditions, those conditions have sufficient impact on the process and outcomes to discourage analysts from seeking explanations in terms of individual characteristics. I contend that there is little if any value added to the analysis by assessments of leader types.

The approaches also differ with regard to the unit of sampling. For Hermann, it is the people who behave in various situations; for me, it is the situations in which people behave or act. Both approaches develop typologies that can then be sorted into broader theoretical categories – as attributes of people or of situations – with the help of statistical scaling procedures. Further, the relevance of the categories for the behaviors of interest must be ascertained with experiments designed to assess relative effects of different independent variables, as in my research. In addition, the way in which the various aspects interact with each other (including person–situation interactions) may be discovered through meta-analyses of the results of numerous experiments that examine the effects of those variables in the typology (see Druckman (1994a) for an example of a meta-analysis).

Another implication of these approaches concerns the generality of findings. A focus on the situation shifts the locus of generality from the person (to a population of persons) to the setting (to a population of settings). Thus we are interested in the extent to which a particular experimental or field situation represents a larger class of situations. We are less interested in whether the particular individuals in the study represent a wider category of people. The empirical issue is the extent to which any situation is similar to or matches a class of situations as specified by a taxonomy. If the primary source of behavioral variation is due to situational variation, then generality or relevance depends on similarity of situations rather than on persons. (See the section below on taxonomies for more about this issue.)

Assessing Personalities

Some may argue that the reason for the poor predictive validity of many personality measures is due to inadequate measurement and/or conceptualization of those characteristics. Perhaps; but psychologists have been developing inventories of numerous "traits" and conducting validity studies for almost a century, and continue to provide little evidence for cross-situational trait-like behavior. However, it is also the case that many of these measures seem to be seriously flawed. An example is the Myers-Briggs type indicator. Respondents must answer each question as either-or (Do you or don't you like going to parties?) and the analyst infers from the answers whether a person is extraverted or introverted, analytical or intuitive, and so on. It would seem that a person could simply be asked to self-report whether he or she is usually (or generally) outgoing or shy (with behavioral definitions attached) and then ask other observers to answer the same questions about the respondent. Why not ask in which situations are you usually shy and when are you outgoing? Why work so strenuously at developing numerous questions to get at the matter so indirectly? Answers to these direct questions would probably show that people's behavior is contingent or dependent on the situation in which they act. If this is so, then knowing about the situation is more valuable than knowing the person for diagnosing conflict behavior.

Further, it is difficult to separate a presumed personality characteristic, such as authoritarianism, from ideological orientations, worldviews, or role-prescribed behavior. For example, commitment to a cause (ideology) or constituency pressures (role-situation) to maintain a particular stand could be interpreted as a "rigid personality."

Empirical Bases for a Situational Approach

In this section, I discuss research findings that document the role of situations as influences on individual, interpersonal, and intergroup conflict behavior.

Empirical evidence

A long history of empirical research exists on the issue of response consistency or variability across situations. Early findings from studies in the 1920s and 1930s by Hartshorne *et al.* (1930) reported that the average intercorrelation of the twenty-three "tests" (designed to measure the same "trait") used to construct a "total character score" was 0.30. Even more dramatic were Newcomb's (1929) findings showing the average correlations among behaviors within a given trait to be 0.14. These findings foreshadowed the results obtained from hundreds of studies on numerous personality traits. This research led Mischel (along with many other investigators) to conclude "that the predictive utility of a trait-based approach to personality still remains undemonstrated and that situational specificity of behavior appears to be the rule rather than the exception" (cited in Bem and Allen, 1974, p. 507). In other words, many (perhaps most) people's behavior can be predicted from situational variables.

These results are also consistent with findings obtained in studies of conflict or negotiating behavior. For example, Druckman's (1967) finding of a relationship between dogmatic attitudes and negotiating flexibility was difficult to replicate in his later studies. The finding was reinterpreted as a subject's definition of the situation rather than as a personality characteristic (Druckman, 1971). Both Terhune (1970) and Hermann and Kogan (1977) showed that personality influenced behavior only early on in the interactions, later to be overtaken by the situation and the mix of participants in the groups. Similarly, Plous (1987) reported that the only significant correlations between personality and simulated arming behavior were for responses made early on in the interactions: overall only six out of ninety-six correlations between personality or attitudes and behavior were significant, a finding that could occur by chance. Further, Druckman's (1994a) meta-analysis of compromising behavior showed that when orientations were manipulated through instructions that defined the bargaining task as either competitive or cooperative (problem-solving), they had a stronger impact on bargaining behavior than when the orientations were assessed prior to the interactions.

Bem and Allen (1974) offered a rather intriguing argument for person–situation interactions. While agreeing that the situation is a powerful influence on behavior, they were reluctant to dismiss personality influences. They argued that construing people as unique combinations of traits or orientations – in an ideographic or clinical tradition – permits the observation (and documentation) of cross-situational regularities. For example, a particular person may be friendly only in certain situations but consistently so, or she may be conscientious in school but not at home. They argued against the approach, used in most studies, that compares people on a linear scale from high to low friendliness or conscientiousness. When shifting to an ideographic (focus on the person) approach, we can distinguish between, for example, high-variability (sensitive to situations) and low-variability (relatively insensitive to situations) people. This distinction is similar to Hermann's (1995) distinction between cue-takers (high variability) and advocates (low variability) discussed above.

More recently, Mischel and Shoda (1995) provided evidence for a different conceptualization of person–situation interactions. They showed that personality may be reflected in patterns of behavioral variation across situations. For example, person A's behavior varies from one situation to the next in a different way from person B's behavior. Thus people may behave consistently *within* rather than *between* situations. According to their model, situational features activate mediating units – particular cognitions and affect – which elicit situation-specific behavior. A stable network of relations among mediating units characterizes an individual's personality system. According to Mischel and Shoda: "The behaviors ultimately generated depend both on the situational features and on the organization of the network of cognitions and affects that become activated" (1995, p. 255). Further, the elicited behaviors may change the situations themselves by altering the interpersonal or group environment to which individuals react in subsequent transactions. Although this is an intriguing model, it has little to say about the effect of learning or development on the way persons perceive particular situations or on the configuration of relations among the mediating (cognitive and affective) units. Neither does it address the difference between role and personality, suggesting the following questions: Could a similar model be used to characterize consistent situation-linked role behavior? If so, how can unique individual behavior patterns be distinguished from unique role patterns?

Viewed from another direction, person and situation effects may be thought about in terms of being prepared to discern differences between situations. Ericsson's (1999) research on deliberate practice suggests that people who are trained to perform as experts in a domain learn to make fine discriminations among the situations in which they perform. He shows that "expert performers have acquired refined mental representations that maintain access to relevant information about the situation and support more extensive flexible reasoning to determine the appropriate actions demanded by the encountered situations" (1999, p. 331). An implication of this finding is that deliberate practice, designed to produce expertise, increases sensitivity to situations, leading to stronger situational effects for those who benefit from such activities. For non-experts, on the other hand, a reduced discrimination among situations may produce more consistent responses, leading observers to describe them in terms of personality traits.

Illustrative situational effects

Research findings on many topics illustrate the way situational variables influence conflict or negotiating behavior. The summaries to follow are intended to give the reader an appreciation for the variety of findings obtained in experiments.

Gaming experiments: By using game matrices with different configurations of pay-offs and varying equilibria (the choice that minimizes losses), investigators have studied relationships between incentive structures and choices. In addition to the structure of pay-offs, a number of variables have been shown to influence choice behavior: number of plays as the difference between single and multiple trials, number of games, communication opportunities, feedback on the other's choice, sequential or simultaneous moves, size of pay-offs, extent of accountability to teammates, prior experience with similar games, the type of relationship between players, and the instructed orientation toward the game. (See Brams (1994) for real-world applications.)

Role obligations: A large number of studies investigated the behavior of group representatives. The question of interest is whether representatives are less flexible in negotiations than non-representatives. The answer to this question is that it depends mostly on the extent to which representatives are accountable for their performance and the latitude they have to develop positions and strategies. Of particular interest is the way representatives maneuver to resolve the competing demands constituents and opponents make, emphasizing the value of tacit bargaining (Walton and McKersie, 1965).

Audience/media effects: Bargaining in front of an audience has only weak effects on process and outcome measures, although the effects may be larger for females than for males. The effects are, however, larger when face-saving pressures are strong. Similarly, media exposure strongly influences the flexibility of international bargainers (Druckman and Druckman, 1996).

Framing: When losses rather than gains are emphasized in the experiment's task instructions, bargainers are more likely to take risks that result in better outcomes. When gains are emphasized they become risk-averse and fare less well. Note that this is an effect of the situation rather than a personality characteristic of risk proneness vs. risk aversion. However, the framing effects in the bargaining studies are not very strong, as shown in a meta-analysis (Druckman, 1994a).

Alternatives: Developing alternatives is a source of power in negotiations. However, spending too much time developing them often leads to attributing even stronger alternatives to the bargaining opponent and to a self-gains (competitive) rather than a joint-gains (integrative) approach to bargaining (Pinkley *et al.*, 1994).

Salient or fair solutions: When fair solutions are salient, they provide a way of reaching an agreement despite pressures to win. Several studies showed that negotiators are sensitive to fairness in process (exchanges) and outcomes (equal or equitable benefits). Especially interesting is the tendency of international bargainers to seek synchrony (equal concession exchanges) during the process of exchanging moves (Druckman and Harris, 1990).

Values and interests: When interests or positions are derived from contrasting values or ideologies, agreements are difficult to attain. Several studies have shown that pre-negotiation facilitation where opponents discuss their different values is more effective than delinking the values from the interests in reducing competitive orientations and achieving agreements (Druckman *et al.*, 1988).

Perceptions of the situation: Actors' perceptions mediate the impact of the situation on negotiating and mediating behavior (Druckman, 1971). Perceptions, construed as being aroused by the situation rather than as reflections of personality dynamics, play a central part in models of conflict resolution, taking the form of situation → perceptions → process → outcome. They are central in the Lewinian tradition, and in research on definitions of the situation (to be discussed in the next section).

The sampling of variables in this section may be extended to include such aspects of the conflict situation as time pressure (hinders integrative bargaining), tactics (tough posturing precedes softer behavior), size of issues (fractionating issues can produce early agreements but leave the larger issues unresolved), and type of conflict (cognitive and ideological conflicts can be more difficult to resolve than conflicts over interests).

Attribution biases and the "psychodynamic fallacy"

Research on attribution theory has demonstrated that people tend to overestimate the degree to which behavior is caused by traits of the individual and underestimate the degree to which it is caused by external factors (Nisbett and Ross, 1980). People are therefore willing to generalize about a person's behavior, extrapolating it to other, unobserved settings in which situational forces may be quite different. We are more apt to attribute another's behavior to his or her dispositions while explaining our own behavior in terms of the situation. Further, we are often unaware of the extent to which our own presence (the situation) influenced the other's behavior, reducing the extent to which that behavior may be generalized to other settings. Moreover, as Bem and Allen (1974) note, our English vocabulary is richer with trait-like terms than with terms that label situations, making them more accessible as descriptors or explanatory concepts.

More recently, Morris *et al.* (1999) identified several processes that contribute to the misperceptions documented in their bargaining experiments. First, in keeping with the evidence summarized in this chapter and other research reviewed by these authors, they conclude that situations are the primary influences on bargaining behavior. Second, following the research on attribution errors, they underscore the primacy of personality traits in attributions. Third, since bargainers do not have sufficient information about the other's situation, it encourages them to make personality attributions. Fourth, and finally, personality attributions persist because they are self-confirming. The self-confirming feature of personality attributions is based on research showing that beliefs support actions that constrain the other's behavior and evoke behavior by the other person that confirms the beliefs. An example of this research is Kelley and Stahelski's (1970) repeated prisoner's dilemma game experiment. They found a competitive game-player's attribution of competitiveness to the other player supported the competitive player's behavior of defecting. The expectation of competitiveness was then confirmed when the defection induced defection from the other player. In interactive situations, one party's actions shape the other's actions, leading the other to behave in expected ways, as though these behaviors emanate from his or her "personality" rather than from the interaction.

Blake's (1959) idea of a psychodynamic fallacy reduces the importance of personality factors in group settings. He claimed that group (including negotiation) behavior should not be explained in terms of the personalities of members of the group. Like Sherif and Sherif (1956) and other social psychologists, he argued for separate levels of analysis, claiming that groups should be analyzed in terms of properties that were not the sum (or other combinations) of their members. However, he did not suggest that groups had personalities or "minds"; rather, they consist of roles that coordinate their actions in response to environmental conditions. Coordination can also be regarded as an emergent group process, understood in terms of rules of influence among the elements of a system (Nowak, 2004). Many theories of conflict resolution describe the various roles played and functions served by resolvers and mediators as well as the challenges of coordination among different roles. These approaches are discussed in the following sections.

On plasticity

Researchers have now amassed considerable evidence for plasticity, from the neurological (brain tissue) to the developmental and behavioral levels of analysis (e.g., Lerner, 1984). More recent neurological research shows that experience plays a role in altering brain anatomy and physiology – nurture can affect nature. Ericsson and his colleagues (1993) present the most compelling evidence for the role of practice on performance. The best performers adhered to a regimen of deliberate practice with precautions taken to avoid burn-out. Performance in early years did not predict later performance, and performance in the early stages of a practice task does not predict performance in later stages. A variety of experiences, including the development of self-confidence, contribute strongly to performance at all ages. Fewer constraints from early childhood experiences exist than many think. (For more on this and on the "innate ability" fallacy, see Druckman and Bjork, 1994, Epilogue; Ericsson, 1998.) The message from this research is that people change; they are not bundles of relatively immutable traits. (See also Cook-Deegan (2001) for an interpretation of biological evidence supporting this assertion.) This conclusion is supported by the correlational evidence reviewed above in the section on empirical evidence.

The situation and intergroup conflict

According to LeVine and Campbell (1972), widespread agreement exists among different theorists with regard to the following four situational aspects of conflict and ethnocentric imagery:

1 Competition over scarce resources is a source of conflict and hostility between groups, a condition independent of psychological factors. The greater the conflict of interests, the stronger the ethnocentrism.
2 Groups return hostile behavior with hostile behavior and corresponding attitudes. Conflict between groups spirals because of the tendency to reciprocate the other's behavior. This is a reaction to the immediate situation and to the other's most recent behavior.
3 Group differences are reflected in stereotypes but they are exaggerated, especially when the relationship between the groups is negative. To the extent that the images reflect actual differences, they are influenced by the situation; to the extent that they are

exaggerated, they are influenced by projections based on ingroup needs and motives.

4 More complex societies are more warlike and ethnocentric than less complex societies. Societies with higher levels of political or administrative complexity have a longer history of intergroup warfare (Ember and Ember, 1992). The source of conflict here is in social structures.

The following are examples drawn from LeVine and Campbell's (1972) treatment of intergroup relations, of questions that compare psychodynamic with situational explanations. The stark contrasts are intended to clarify the issues.

- Do stereotyped images of outgroups reflect actual information about them (based on opportunities for contact) or are they projections of ingroup needs (unrealistic constructions)?
- Is ingroup solidarity produced by external threat (situational) or does the frustration of ingroup solidarity generate hostility that is displaced on to outgroups (psychodynamic)?
- Do ethnocentric attitudes develop from internal group/societal practices or norms such as severe restrictions placed on behavior (a frustration-aggression theory assumption), or from rewards for being aggressive (a social learning theory assumption)? Or are the attitudes reactions to a threatening and hostile environment which includes competition with neighboring groups (a realistic group conflict theory assumption)?
- Is ethnocentrism a dispositional lens through which other groups are perceived, or is it an attitude elicited by circumstances that increase tension?
- More generally, is intergroup conflict better explained in terms of such situational factors as proximity, similarity, intergroup contact experiences, and the characteristics of outgroups such as size, strength, wealth, and demographic diversity, or is it better explained by such internal group factors as socialization and child-rearing practices, economic development (relative deprivation), cultural and religious traditions, and educational opportunities (for cognitive complexity)? The former may be construed as a reaction to outside forces, the latter as a projection of inside forces.

Relevant Research Traditions

At least ten major research traditions or literatures emphasize the influence of the situation with regard to a variety of behaviors. These include behavior in groups or organizations, strategic decision-making, negotiating decisions, performance in the workplace, and various forms of problem-solving. The key concepts from each of these traditions are summarized briefly.

Lewinian field forces and group dynamics

A key idea in Lewin's field theory is the "principle of contemporaneity." By this he meant that "any behavior or any other change in the psychological field depends only upon the psychological field *at that time*" (1951, p. 45). His primary interest was to diagnose behavior in the present, not from the standpoint of past experiences or future expectations. For Lewin, the situation is defined or interpreted by the actor, not by the properties defined or created by the investigator. He pioneered the creation of laboratory situations to test hypotheses, a notable example being the comparison between authoritarian and democratic leader environments. He does not exclude the past, however. For him, a situation is dynamic, not considered as a moment in time but as a time period that allows for development. The settings that intrigued him the most were group situations, and his students initiated the research tradition of group dynamics, including Deutsch's (1949) study comparing cooperative with competitive interdependence among group members, and Festinger *et al.*'s (1950) study on impacts of group cohesiveness. The tradition of research also includes studies of conformity or pressures toward uniformity of opinion in groups, the perception of deviates, behavioral contagion, and communication networks. Of all Lewin's students, the work of Deutsch extended many of these concepts in developing empirically-based theories of conflict resolution (e.g., Deutsch, 1973).

Experimental social psychology

Stimulated by the work of Lewin and his students, many social psychologists turned to laboratory experimentation as a preferred methodology for evaluating hypotheses derived from theoretical frameworks. Emphasizing the importance of the operational definition, studies in this tradition have provided the most precise matching of clearly defined aspects of the situation and behaviors. The theory-relevant knowledge produced is simply breathtaking: studies of social norm formation and perpetuation, opinion formation, attitude and belief change, cognitive dissonance, impression management, risk-taking decisions, interplay between cognition and affect, and group structures and networks. More directly relevant to conflict resolution are the experiments on the situational influences on negotiation and mediation behavior. Although questions about relevance to the real world – referred to as external validity – are important challenges to this tradition, there is little doubt about its usefulness for arbitrating between competing theoretical predictions and discovering mechanisms that explain causal relationships. For conflict theorists interested in micro-level processes, Pruitt's (1981; Pruitt and Carnevale, 1993) experimental work on integrative bargaining uncovers processes that can produce better agreements than compromise. Druckman's (1993, 1995) research on situational levers (see below) shows how experiments may be used to distinguish between important and unimportant variables in a complex framework.

Behavioral ecology

This work focuses attention on aspects of the physical and social environment which are usually not part of a subject's subjective awareness. Referred to as settings, these aspects are the constructed environment surrounding the immediate situations emphasized by Lewin. Barker, one of Lewin's students, has developed typologies of settings, showing how they influence behavior (e.g., Barker, 1968). These studies were also a foundation for the research on proxemics (spatial distance) as a form of nonverbal behavior (see Sommer, 1967, 1968), on influences of the designed environment referred to by Rapoport (1982) as behavioral architecture, and the more recent research on the human dimensions of global environmental change reviewed in Stern et al. (1992). The global environmental research has called attention to the importance of recursive or two-way influences – from humans to (physical) environments and the effects of those environments on humans. In their recent book, Homer-Dixon and Blitt (1998) emphasize connections between ecological destruction and conflict. The case studies presented in this book illuminate the link between destruction, scarcity, and conflict. This link is especially evident in conflicts over water supplies, which, in some regions, may be a more direct cause of war than conflicts over land or identity.

Contextual analysis

The settings that behavioral ecologists study may be regarded as context. More typically, however, the term refers to organizations. According to Sundstrom et al. (1990), organizational context includes organizational cultures, the physical and technological environment, and the integration and differentiation aspects of group–organization (and organization to other organizations) boundaries. Gladstein's (1984) study illuminates the importance of context. The results showed that organization members attributed sales performance to internal team processes when actual performance was largely a function of market growth (a contextual variable). Similarly, research has shown that factors or events operating outside the negotiations, often in the larger international system, exert a greater influence on the outcomes of international negotiations than internal negotiating processes (Hopmann and Smith, 1977; Druckman, 1986). Although these variables are part of the larger situation facing actors, they are more distant (referred to in Figure 6.1 above as distal) than the aspects of the more immediate situation studied in the laboratory. Because it is difficult to represent contexts in laboratory settings, they are rarely included in experimental studies.

Role theory

Developed mostly by sociologists, analyses of social processes in terms of roles contrast with the psychological investigation of personality (e.g., Biddle and Thomas, 1966; Sarbin and Allen, 1969). Roles are defined in organizational or institutional contexts. Their impact on perceptions was clearly demonstrated in an early study of ethnocentric perceptions among simulated role-players: perceptions of own versus other groups varied with (randomly determined) role assignments; the foreign minister was least ethnocentric while the aspiring (out of power) head of state was most ethnocentric (Druckman, 1968). Research on boundary roles – those who negotiate with other organizations – has led to an interesting literature on two-level games, elucidating the dilemmas of representing (and negotiating with) constituencies while negotiating with adversaries (Walton and McKersie, 1965; Druckman, 1977b; Putnam, 1988). In international relations, structural theories claim that states will adjust their identities and their actions to be congruent with the roles attributed to them by other states (Wendt, 1999). This claim contrasts with agent-oriented theories that suggest states will alter the roles other states attribute to them in order to be congruent with their own identities (see Walker, 2000).

Several role taxonomies have been proposed for intermediaries and intervenors in conflict. Perhaps the first distinctions were made by Laue and Cormick (1978) who proposed five roles: advocates, activists, mediators, researchers, and enforcers. More recently, Mitchell (1993b) distinguished among thirteen roles in terms of their tasks and functions: the explorer, convener, decoupler (disengager), unifier (coordinator), enskiller (empowerer), envisioner (fact-finder), guarantor, facilitator, legitimizer (endorser), enhancer, monitor (verifier), enforcer (implementer), and reconciler (see also Kriesberg, 1998). Further, Ury (1999) differentiated between prevention roles (provider, teacher, bridge-builder), resolution roles (mediator, arbitrator, equalizer, and healer), and containment roles (witness, referee, and peacekeeper). With regard to consulting functions, Druckman (2000) defined seven roles: advisors, technicians, applied theoreticians, study directors, bridge-builders, facilitators, and trainers or teachers. These roles are not regarded by the authors as being pure types, even though some may preclude playing others. Intermediaries and consultants often perform several of these functions, sometimes simultaneously. Nonetheless, it is useful to distinguish among the roles to appreciate the diversity and complexity of third parties as well as the flexibility needed to be effective. Yet to be investigated is the relevance of role analysis for functioning in relatively unstructured situations such as the intense and protracted conflicts that reflect or lead to breakdowns in social order.

Definition of the situation
In an early review of the experimental-game literature, Scheff (1967) concluded that "to understand a player's moves, we need to understand his (her) definition of the situation" (p. 219). The components of a player's definition of the situation are *value*, the extent to which his or her subjective utilities for pay-offs correspond to those of the experimenter, and *intent*, including attempts by players to arrive at a common definition of the situation with respect to each other's intentions. Attempts to define an experimental situation raise the issue of whose definition, the investigator's or the subject's? Several approaches exist on this issue. The situations that experimenters create are evaluated in terms of impacts on both perceptions and behavior. Experimental subjects' perceptions have been assessed before, during, and after their participation in a task. Assessments conducted before are usually attempts to evaluate the effects of attitudes prior to experimental manipulations and are closer to the tradition of personality assessment. Those administered during the task are often attempts to check the effects of the manipulated conditions, especially with regard to judging whether subjects understand the condition in which they are placed. Assessments made later are often self-report post-negotiation questions designed to elicit the way subjects viewed the tasks, opponents, and issues. These questions are often regarded as variables that intervene between the situation and behavior or outcomes (e.g., Druckman *et al.*, 1988). They have been found to have strong impacts on bargaining behavior, especially when they reflect the way the task is defined by the experimenter as, for example, competitive or problem-solving (Druckman, 1994a).

In less controlled field situations, investigators often attempt to elicit respondents' views of events or processes through survey questions, or through extended narrative descriptions that become part of an ethnographic study of a culture. Another approach emphasizes the way actors manage impressions in different types of situations or actually create the situations in which they perform. (Note also in this regard the feedback from behavior to situations in Mischel and Shoda's (1995) model.) In sociology, this approach has been referred to as symbolic interaction; it is similar to the phenomenological or constructivist school in philosophy. Goffman's (1959, 1971) interesting work contrasting public and private enactments – referred to by him as front- and backstage behavior – falls within this tradition.

Situated learning
This is a rather extreme version of the situational perspective with practical implications. Theorists in this tradition emphasize the importance of learning in context (e.g., Greeno *et al.*, 1993). By this they mean developing skills relevant to performance in specific vocational domains. The theoretical rationale for this suggestion is based on the assumption that behavior (and performance) is contingent on or closely linked to very specific situations, and thus does not transfer to other situations. These theorists have vocally indicated that abstract subjects, such as mathematics, are largely irrelevant in the real world of work, an important practical implication of this approach. The idea of understanding behavior within its context is widely shared and is the basis for contingent models of conflict interventions (Fisher, 1997a) as well as for the development of situation taxonomies or profiles (discussed below). However, investigators of approaches that emphasize situational effects do not share the assumption of lack of transfer or generality of behavior between similar situations, an assumption made by situated learning theorists. While emphasizing the situated features of behavior, most conflict theorists recognize that different situations or cases share many features as well. The similarities among diverse cases provide a basis for the development of conflict theories (Stern and Druckman, 2000).

Game modeling and simulations
These approaches emphasize constructing representative situations. Focusing primarily on issues of external validity, these researchers attempt to design laboratory environments that represent classes of situations. In the game-theoretic tradition, the environments consist of choice dilemmas illustrated by various configurations of pay-off matrices such as the popular Prisoner's Dilemma, but also such games as Chicken, Deadlock, Bully, Battle of the Sexes, and Coordination. Snyder and Diesing (1977) and Brams (1994) illustrate how a number of these matrix configurations reflect real-world dilemmas in foreign policy and international relations (e.g., the Cuban missile crisis as a game of Chicken, the Iran hostage crisis as a Prisoner's Dilemma, the Berlin crisis as a game of Deadlock). In the simulation tradition, the constructed environments are usually more complex. They often include

many of the aspects of corresponding real-world environments compressed in time. Regarded as operating models, these simulations are used both for research and teaching: simulation researchers often embed experiments within the simulations and compare results with corresponding field studies; teachers often use simulations to provide students with real-world training experiences. A simulation with close correspondence to a real-world environment, referred to as high fidelity, indicates that the designer understands the processes or situations being simulated, referred to as construct validity. Guetzkow and Valadez (1981) provide impressive evidence for the validity of simulations of international relations. Crookall and Arai (1995) present a wide variety of applications, and Druckman (1994b) shows how simulations can be used as vehicles for conducting theoretical research.

Situational levers

Applied to research on negotiation, this approach examines how a variety of aspects of the situation affect decisions, perceptions, and choice of tactics. The idea of "levers" suggests that the situation can be controlled or manipulated for impact. In this way, the approach derives from the behaviorist tradition in psychology, also referred to as stimulus – response. It is an attempt to evaluate frameworks of situations with experimental methodologies. The frameworks identify many aspects of the situation hypothesized to influence negotiating processes and outcomes. The experiments are designed to evaluate the relative importance of these variables at each of several stages in the negotiation process. One result from a simulation of a multilateral environmental conference, conducted with professional scientists and with diplomats, indicated the presence of trajectories toward agreement or stalemate, namely the key aspect of the situation that influenced decisions participants made at each of four stages in the negotiation (see Druckman, 1993, 1995). The practical value of this approach is its focus on aspects that can be controlled by the negotiators themselves or by third parties. Relatively simple alterations, such as whether negotiators sit in a circle of chairs or behind tables, can increase or decrease their chances of obtaining an agreement.

Person–situation interactions

The heated debates over the relative importance of the person and situation as influences on behavior or attitudes captured much attention in social and personality psychology during the decades of the 1960s and 1970s. Mischel (1969), Bem and Allen (1974), and more recently, Mischel and Shoda (1995) review much of this literature. As discussed in some detail above, this debate revolves around the question about the relevance of personality traits, or whether behavior is situationally specific or intrapsychically consistent. The above discussion provides a number of compelling reasons for situational variation. But does this mean that there are simply no unique aspects of individuals? Are people infinitely molded and malleable? Intuitively, it would seem that individuals are distinguishable in ways other than (or in addition to) the situations they are in at any point in time. Of course no two individuals, even siblings close in age, have had the same experiences. The issue remains how to account for these differences. Bem and Allen's (1974) proposal to shift the research strategy from comparing different people on the same scales – in a nomothetic tradition – to regarding their behavior, however inconsistent, in their own unique terms – in an ideographic tradition – is intriguing. It retains a place for individual expression without comparing it to the expressions of others. It also avoids the either/or form of the question, person vs. situation, by retaining a strong place for the influence of situations *and* persons. Mischel and Shoda's (1995) model depicts personality as consistent behavior occurring within rather than between situations. The differences between persons observed within a particular situation are not duplicated when the situation changes. A person may be consistently trustworthy at school (or in formal institutionalized situations) but consistently untrustworthy at home (or in informal interactions in his or her village). Thus, the situation provides important information about when to trust and when not to trust this person; he or she is neither trustworthy nor untrustworthy across situations.

Continuing along these lines, recent theorizing has reframed the issue of person versus situation. In their effort to introduce a dynamical perspective to social psychology, Vallacher and Nowak construe personality as "patterns of thought, emotion, and action in the context of goals, opportunities, and other situational parameters" (2007, 736). Situational factors are not considered as direct influences on behavior, as in a stimulus-response conception. Rather, they shape thought and behavior by influencing a person's internal states. The key is the configuration of external influences and internal dynamics: By configuration, they mean the way that strong or weak situations interact with relatively coherent or incoherent definitions of the self. By emphasizing dynamics, this perspective highlights moments when situational (or external) influences are strong and when they may fade in favor of intrinsic properties. These "properties" can be conceived as mediators of change or resistance as discussed in the next section.

Dynamical systems

A dynamical systems perspective has been gaining popularity in a variety of scientific fields, including social psychology. Generally it is a framework for linking micro with macro features of a system. It is also a methodology adapted from the study of nonlinear relationships of elements or variables within a system (Nowak, 2004). More specifically, it is a perspective on the power of the situation (Vallacher and Nowak, 2007). Its relevance to the issues discussed in this chapter derives from the way that external factors drive thoughts and behavior. Of particular interest is the idea of transient and lasting effects of these factors.

A hallmark of the approach is an elaborate description of internal dynamics that mediate the connection between situations and cognitive, affective, and behavioral effects. Although characterized by a rather unique lexicon, the approach does provide several insights on situational effects. These effects are thought to be strongly influenced by a person's "attractor landscape." Features of that landscape are used to capture a person's motivation to bring about, maintain, or change various psychological states. Research on the self concept illustrates the interplay between the landscape and situations. Conflicting self-relevant information was resisted when presented in small packets separated by time. The same information produced changes in self-evaluation when presented as one packet over a short period of time (Nowak et al., 2000). This result illustrates the way a landscape or system can resist the impact of small changes but embrace the new information when a single large change is experienced. More generally, the approach is used to reinterpret findings from a variety of studies on social influence, showing how strong and weak situations interact with internal dynamics to shape responses (e.g., Story, 2004). It is also shown to provide an interpretation of findings at the societal level, including those from studies of public opinion, norm formation, and change in political and economic ideologies.

Taxonomies and Frameworks

A number of dimensions or themes may be used to depict the situation. These have been the basis for taxonomies that emphasize particular domains of activities. For example, a typology of ecological characteristics emphasizes the physical aspects of situations. An attempt to depict characteristics of organizations emphasizes structures, functions, and reporting requirements. An attempt to capture tasks or jobs would emphasize information, resources, preparation, time available, and support. An interest in depicting professional roles may list such activities as preservation of assets, work supervision, and long-range planning.

With regard to social behavior setting, Krause (1970) distinguished among joint working, trading, fighting, sponsored teaching, serving, self-disclosure, and playing. A better-known typology of conflict situations is Rapoport's (1960) distinction between fights, games, and debates. Less clear in all these typologies is whether the categories refer to behaviors/activities or the situations/settings within which these acts take place. For example, what is it about the social setting that produces fighting or trading activities? A start along these lines was made by Frederiksen (1971). He proposed an empirical taxonomy of situations based on their similarity with regard to the behaviors they elicit.

In an attempt to compare different social systems, Sells (1966) proposed a typology that combined the features of more specialized lists: he organized his fifty-six characteristics in terms of objectives, value systems, personnel composition, organization, technology, physical environment, and temporal characteristics. My own preference in creating a general typology is to list categories that are independent of the behavior that occurs within those settings. An example of such a typology is as follows:

- Physical environments, public and private (e.g., space available);
- Institutional characteristics (e.g., size, voting rules);
- Organizational structures (e.g., hierarchical or flat);
- Roles and accountability norms (e.g., managers and scientists);
- Task demands (e.g., amount of time pressure);
- Technologies available (e.g., computerized accounting systems);
- Cultural traditions, shared values (e.g., mission as conflict resolution rather than management of conflict);
- Relationship networks, individuals, and groups (e.g., extent of fluidity in team membership and participation).

Other proposed typologies have been developed for particular conflict resolution domains such as negotiation and mediation. For example, ten variables were used to organize a review of gaming studies from 1965 to 1970 consisting of the following: task instructions, type and magnitude of pay-off incentives, opponent's intent and goals, opponent's concession-making strategy, type of communication opportunity, prior experience, role, range of possible outcomes, type of difference in initial positions, and time pressure. This typology served to capture the state of the art at that time and revealed gaps in knowledge calling for further research (Druckman, 1971).

By addressing many of these gaps, a body of experimental literature accumulated over the years was summarized and evaluated in a meta-analysis (Druckman, 1994a). The analysis combined results obtained from experiments in each of ten categories. Ranked in order of impact (size of effects), the analysis divided the variables into three clusters: the top four variables included orientation toward bargaining, type of pre-negotiation preparation for bargaining, time pressure, and initial position distance; the middle three were the type of strategy used by the opponent, group representation, and extent of accountability to constituents; and the weakest effects were obtained for framing, large vs. small issues, and bargaining process visibility. Further probes of these effects uncovered reasons for them; for example, visibility effects were strong only when bargainers risked losing face in front of an audience.

Turning to international negotiation, several researchers have attempted to develop taxonomies. Sawyer and Guetzkow (1965) constructed the most popular framework. Others have used this framework to organize literature reviews, design simulations, and analyze complex cases. Randolph (1966) developed a similar, though less popular, framework. More recently, I attempted to connect categories of situational influences to negotiating stages and activities. Monitoring and coordinating activities that occur during early stages influence such variables as team composition and channels of communication. Persuasive debate, occurring during the middle stages, is affected by issue priorities and cultural or ideological differences. In addition, the bargaining that takes place in the endgame of a negotiation is influenced primarily by relative power, audiences, and external events. (See Druckman (1983) for the framework and Druckman (1986) for an application to a case.) Further refinements of the list of variables were reported in Druckman (1993). I identified sixteen aspects of the situation divided into five categories: issues, background factors, context, structure of conference and teams, and the immediate situation. By connecting the variables to negotiation stages, I was able to evaluate their relative impacts at each period of time. One result was the trajectories toward agreement or stalemate noted above.

Other applications of negotiation taxonomies have been in the areas of computer diagnosis and comparative case studies. By describing particular cases in terms of the variables in each of the five categories listed above, a negotiator provides information that is used to ascertain the relative flexibility of the parties and to project possible outcomes (see Druckman (1995) for examples of case applications). Along similar lines, by coding a variety of cases in terms of the same categories, we were able to test Iklé's (1964) well-known typology of international negotiation. The results showed that practically all of the thirty cases were accurately placed in the correct category, as either redistribution, extension, normalization, innovation, or a side-effects negotiation: for example, a redistribution case had a profile of situational characteristics more similar to other redistribution cases than to extension or normalization cases (see Druckman *et al.*, 1999b).

A number of taxonomies of third-party roles have been proposed, and several of these are summarized in the section above on role theory. The most useful taxonomies are those that connect roles with functions and activities. For example, the explorer role sketches a range of possible alternative solutions, the decoupler enlists external patrons to fulfill reassuring, endorsing, or enhancing functions, and the unifier repairs intraparty divisions so that all factions can agree on interests, values, and acceptable solutions (Mitchell, 1993b). Activities that correspond to these roles include selecting issues and parties, communicating each side's views, reframing the conflict as a joint problem to be solved, suggesting new options, adding resources, legitimizing and helping to implement the proposed agreement, and so on (Kriesberg, 1995). These categories provide a lexicon for thinking about the complexity and variety of third-party roles and functions. They are regarded not as pure types but as overlapping functions often performed in sequence or simultaneously by the same actor. Still to be developed are the connections between the roles or practices and stages of conflict resolution processes, or between the roles and functions on the one hand and aspects of conflict situations (as described in the negotiation taxonomies) on the other.

Conclusion

The research reviewed in this chapter has implications for the development of theories, further empirical research, and the practice of intervening in conflict situations. Each type of implication is discussed in turn.

On theory: Theoretical work has consisted of constructing taxonomic frameworks, developing and refining the definitions of concepts, and deriving testable hypotheses for research. Since all of this has been done within the purview of a situational perspective, that perspective qualifies as a class of theories of behavior. This type of theorizing differs from psychodynamic and personality theories, on the one hand, and from social structural theories on the other (see Figure 6.1). The vast amount of empirical evidence accumulated to date encourages theorists to continue developing these concepts, but also to place them in a larger framework that links situations, issues, and contexts to perceptions, processes, and outcomes.

On research: If it is not a richly textured theory (or theories), the situational perspective has been extraordinarily productive of empirical research. The research has elucidated many matches between particular situations and particular behaviors or perceptions. Of interest to conflict theorists is the way situations shape perceptions which affect processes and outcomes. Although this sequence is based largely on experimental evidence (e.g., Druckman et al., 1988), it would seem to provide a framework for analyzing and comparing complex cases of interpersonal and intergroup conflict as well. Applying this framework to the comparative analysis of complex cases is a research priority.

On practice: Two implications for conflict resolution practice are in the areas of diagnosis and intervention. Situational taxonomies provide indicators for monitoring the development of a conflict-resolving process. Our work on negotiation illustrates how the indicators may be used to infer flexibility from which outcomes are projected. Many aspects of situations can be changed. The challenges for intervenors are twofold: (1) distinguishing between those aspects over which they have more or less control, and (2) estimating the likely impact of making changes. By identifying relevant situations, varying those situations, and comparing their effects on conflict-resolving processes, theory and research may be joined with practice to meet these challenges.

Discussion Questions

1 Give examples of factors in the situation that may be (or have been) shown to influence the way disputants behave during the course of a conflict episode.

2 How does an understanding of conflict behavior based on situational factors differ from understandings based on either the disputants' personalities or on the social structure in which the conflict episodes take place?

3 The evidence obtained from studies dating back to the 1920s shows little consistency in observed behavior from one situation to another. What does this evidence suggest for the relative plausibility of personality versus situational interpretations of behavior? Does evidence from more recent studies support or contradict the earlier findings?

4 What are attribution biases? How might attributions made (or stereotypes held) about the sources of another's behavior influence the behavior observed?

5 Discuss the various research traditions that have focused primary attention on situational influences. Which traditions have stimulated large bodies of empirical research? What are some conceptual differences among these research traditions?

6 How might the debate about person–situation interactions be resolved? How may empirical evidence be used to develop a useful conceptualization of these issues?

7 How might the issue of micro (situational)–macro (social structures) influences be addressed? Give examples of particular conflicts that illustrate connections between the roles played by factors at micro and macro levels of analysis.

8 Why are taxonomies or frameworks that depict conflict behavior useful? What are some of the conflict activities and intervention roles that have been identified by the taxonomies? What other activities or roles might be added to the frameworks?

9 What are some of the gaps in understanding, research, and practice that still need to be filled with regard to the impact of situational factors on conflict behavior and conflict resolution activities?

Key Words

Attribution biases
Experimental social psychology
Frameworks
Lewinian perspectives
Role theory
Situational influences
Taxonomies

CHAPTER 8

Identities

Peter W. Black

What do we mean by social identity? As we define it here, the concept refers to the social use of cultural markers to claim, achieve, or ascribe group membership. Note that each of the verbs in that rough definition (claim, achieve, ascribe) points toward a different dimension of what is sometimes known as identity politics. Groups formed on the basis of social identity, which we may reasonably call identity groups, are always and everywhere the main constituents of political struggle. On occasion that struggle escalates (perhaps degenerates is a better word) into a mutually destructive conflict. Loyalty to the identity group in these circumstances can become the highest value; parties increasingly compete in the denial of each other's humanity, as minds on all sides turn, in William Butler Yeats's powerful metaphor, to stone (Foster, 1997, p. 420). The following passage by the travel writer and essayist Jan Morris nicely sets our scene:

> It's hard for citizens of ampler and more fortunate countries to realize how addictive is the nationalist passion among the minority of Welsh people who are subject to it. It is like a love affair, patriotism of a degree and intensity experienced by English people, say, only at times of extreme national danger. Your active Welsh patriot, one who consciously works for the Welshness of Wales, lives and dreams his country and his culture. It is his hobby, his profession, his ecstasy. Every aspect of life is affected by his obsession, every event is measured by its significance to Wales,

> every public figure by his attitude to Wales, every work of art by its
> Welshness, every rise in the price of gold, or drop in the inflation
> rate, or arms agreement, or trade dispute, is judged by its effect on
> Cymru and Cymreictod. (Morris, 1984, p. 417)

Morris here says nationalist passion but she could with equal justice have
said ethnic pride. A moment's reflection will reveal other categories
besides nation or ethnicity, each equally capable of eliciting the same
passionate and obsessive interest she describes so well. For Morris's
Wales, substitute one or another race for racists and race-men; just
about any religion for some of its believers; class for others; gender for
some; caste for many in South Asia; lineage or clan in Somalia and
elsewhere. The list goes on: region (as in the American South); urban
district (as in the Italian city of Siena (Dundes and Falassi, 1975));
sexual orientation; even, for some, a particular sports team, and for
others, perhaps, their generational cohort.

With all the differences among them (and the list is far from complete), each of these loyalties is an instance of a more general
phenomenon – every one of them can form the basis for social identity.
And the social identity so formed can be so compelling and all-
consuming that it becomes what can only be called a total social identity,
displacing or subsuming other aspects of an individual's identity.

When membership in an identity group attains the level of subjective
power which Morris points to, we are justified in calling the identity so
claimed, or achieved, or ascribed, a total identity. Such an identity is
analogous in its all-encompassing extent to such personally overwhelming social settings as prisons or asylums, brilliantly described by
Erving Goffman who calls them total institutions (1970). Finally, in
some circumstances, identity groups can, in fact, become total groups or
even total institutions, moving from analogy with Goffman's concept to
inclusion within it.

Of course, all identities, all selves, are multifaceted – being constituted of some mix of the various attributes indicated above as well as
those that are more strictly idiosyncratic. These attributes are drawn on
both by the individual and by others to understand just who she or he is.
In this chapter, the focus is on social identity, those public dimensions
of the self that are important for group membership, the construction of
social ties, and collective action. Of special interest are the processes by
which specific public dimensions can come more or less to engulf the
self, swamping all other dimensions and thereby becoming a total social
identity.

Social Identity and Conflict

The perspective advanced here requires that cultural categories, classifications denoted by socially significant attributes, be distinguished from social groups formed on the basis of those categories. Height is an attribute, tall people a potential cultural category, the Alliance of Seven Footers a social group. Given the political dynamics involved, a great deal of care is required to avoid confusing these terms. One needs only to reflect on the frequent use of the term "community" to implicitly advance the claim that some category or other is, in fact, an actual social group ("the tall community is tired of banging their heads in low doorways") to recognize the slippery nature of vocabulary in this area (see Baumann, 1996).

It is widely recognized that some of the most recalcitrant of deep-rooted, fundamental conflicts are those between identity groups. Much wisdom, both folk and scholarly, is organized around this truism; such terms as ethnocentrism, outgroup, prejudice, stereotype, xenophobia, racism, othering, and scapegoating, which appear in both scholarly and ordinary discourse on this topic, suggest a highly developed descriptive apparatus for talking about the role of social identity in conflict. Further, it is widely assumed that differences in ethnicity, race, gender, nationalism, class, and so on somehow cause conflict. A casual glance at press coverage of dramatic conflict reveals the explanatory power the mass media frequently assign to such identity-related phenomena. Indeed, so potent is the identity factor that, once invoked, it often simply shuts down further analysis, or even curiosity. This is true whether ethnicity, nationalism, religion, or any of the others mentioned here is made the explanation.

Less widely recognized, though, is the fact that conflict can play an important role in generating and sustaining social identity. In other words, deep-rooted social identity may be a product of conflict at least as much as deep-rooted conflict is a product of clashing social identities. The widespread blindness to this reverse process is due largely to the assumption that social identities are primordial, an assumption coded in biological metaphors of blood and essence. Such essentialism is a prime example of the contamination of "objective" journalism (and social science) by folk biology and folk sociology.

News accounts of events in the former Soviet lands, for example, often reflect a more mythic than historic understanding of the political struggles of various peoples in those regions, seeing them as "simply a revival of 'traditional' enmities from the interwar years – as if the intervening half century were inconsequential" (Verdery, 1991, p. 433). Activists there have proven quick to feed this media tendency, speaking of the newly recovered ancient hostilities as being so inherently natural that they are the same as those between dogs and cats, for example.

Metaphors of blood, as deployed by the press, the folk, and the academy, permeate the ideology of social identity, especially that of race, nation, ethnicity, language, and place (see Strong and van Winkle, 1996). These metaphors do their work of masking the culturally contingent basis of identity groups beneath a gloss of naturalism precisely because their status as metaphors goes largely unnoticed. A good specimen of this mode of thinking may be found in the remarks of Mohammad Khatami, President of the Islamic Republic of Iran. "Nationalism is not a piece of land," he said, "it's in your blood" (Sciolino, 1998). He made this remark to a gathering of over 800 Iranian residents of the USA One can speculate about the political agenda served by this statement; here it is sufficient simply to point out the "naturalness" of the blood metaphor.

Regardless of the direction of the causal arrow, many (if not most) deep-rooted conflicts seem to involve parties organized around competing social identities. In the short term, these disputes appear highly intractable because of oppositional features in the very identities of the parties, even if these different heritages are themselves, in part at least, an expression of a more enduring process of conflict. Very often the challenge facing analysts, policy-makers, and would-be third parties alike is how to deal with the absolute detestation which parties to a conflict have for one another; a loathing they insist is grounded in primordial difference (see e.g., Holbrooke, 1998).

In the sections that follow we discuss several of the most important bases for social identity and identity group formation. We begin with an extended discussion of ethnicity, using it to illustrate some general features of our topic. Building on that discussion, we then turn to progressively abbreviated sketches of race, gender, religion, class, kinship, nationalism, and caste, taking advantage of the opportunity this offers to introduce other important general points and to raise important questions. We conclude with a consideration of conflict between identity groups and its possible resolution. One further preliminary piece of business needs to be taken care of before we continue, however. It has to do with words and their definitions.

Conflict resolution rests, inescapably, on conflict analysis, either explicit or implicit. Analysis, in turn, requires concepts and vocabulary. The question therefore arises: How should we understand the words used to name different forms of social identity? All the social identity terms discussed in this chapter are subject to this question. Where should their meaning for us come from? Substantial issues are involved:

witness the well-known argument between Hutu and Tutsi apologists over precisely what term (ethnic conflict? class struggle?) to apply to the violent conflicts in the Great Lakes region of Africa (Lamarchand, 1994).

Rather than attempt a definitive taxonomy of terms and concepts (probably a hopeless task in this very sensitive and highly contested area), we focus on the ways the terms tend to be used. The anthropologist George Marcus pointed in the direction we should look. He was speaking about the study of law, but could as well have been referring to the analysis of conflict:

> We should probably not look to social theory, as the work of a privileged, detached level of holistic theory building, to provide such new vocabularies. Rather, one might look first to the hesitations, misrecognitions, and anxieties articulated in the discourses of problem-solving institutions and their nurturing professional disciplines that are bent on the technical control of an always unruly world. These are the frontline discourses, so to speak, of institutional practices ... in which one or another version of social theory is evolved and applied to the world. They register even more sensitively than the detached debates of academic social theory the inadequacy of current modes of thinking about society. (1995, p. 238)

Let us now turn to ethnicity, the first of the forms of social identity we wish to explore.

Ethnicity

The standard usage of the term "ethnicity" in the field of conflict resolution seems quite inadequate for the analysis and resolution of deep-seated conflict. In James Clifford's phrase, it remains merely "a weak conception of culture suitable for organizing diversity within the pluralistic state" (1988, p. 339; see Banks (1996) or Jenkins (1997) for excellent summaries of the concept of ethnicity). The inadequacy of that standard usage arises, paradoxically enough, from its ethnocentrism, grounded as it is in the social life of the American nation. That is to say, as compelling as they are, New York City electoral politics (the home of the "balanced ticket") do not provide an adequate model for encompassing all of the world's societies. Furthermore, the weakness of this usage is dangerous, not least because of a global dynamic at work in recent years.

The increasing dominance of American culture has meant the rapid diffusion of American notions of ethnicity, sometimes to situations in which they are perilously inappropriate. How badly, for example, did unexamined ideas about ethnicity drawn on by American policy-makers and implementers distort U.S. intervention in both former Yugoslavia and Somalia? Furthermore, people in these two remarkably different places have had to come to grips with American power and thus American culture, if only to communicate with the world's only remaining superpower. As these people formulate responses to the American juggernaut, will the local understandings of difference that lie at the heart of so much of their recent pasts prove recalcitrant or malleable? What are the consequences of adopting American ideas about ethnicity, even if only to address the so-called "International Community"? It is not just ethnicity that is at issue here; so too may be other forms of social identity. An important cross-cultural question to bear in mind is: Who is enfranchised and who disenfranchised when the politics of difference are forced into an American mold?

The widespread replacement of the word "tribe" with the term "ethnic group," especially in the postcolonial world, has increased confusion around the standard usage of ethnicity. Many newly liberated peoples in Africa and elsewhere rejected tribe as a label for themselves or their fellow citizens because of its associations with primitive backwardness. Yet the kin-based sociopolitical systems characteristic of, for example, many African peoples (including some encapsulated within a single state and others divided by international boundaries), to which the term "tribe" was once applied, are markedly different from ethnic groups as that term is commonly used elsewhere (see e.g., Keyes, 1984). A further complication is the use of the term "tribe" in American jurisprudence, where it refers to Native American groups that may or may not have standing in law (Baca, 1988). Hence the replacement of the word "tribe" with the term "ethnic group" can lead to a real lack of clarity.

In historical perspective, it is apparent that ethnicity, at least in its contemporary form, is a consequence of the creation of nation-states (Anderson, 1991; Skocpol, 1985; Tilly, 1985; Kapferer 1988; but see, Hastings, 1998). Briefly, as previously autonomous cultural groups are brought into the orbit of the state, symbolic markers of difference, often drawn from tradition, real or invented (Hobsbawm and Ranger, 1983), are incorporated into understandings of the self and the other. The resulting reification of boundaries endows these markers with powerful political potency (Baumann, 1999, p. 63). By thinking and then acting as though ethnic groups were the result of natural processes instead of being the products of human activity, the boundaries between them are constituted as permanent features of the natural world instead of the social order, and thus become reified. Furthermore, cultural ideologies of ethnicity (as well as other forms of social identity) often represent a response to threat. It is in part for these reasons, then, that deep-rooted ethnicity may be as much an outcome of conflict as its cause. (For a useful treatment of the politics of ethnicity see Horowitz, 1985.)

Subjectively primordial at the same time that it is historically contingent, ethnicity emerges in a dynamic relationship to the state. This ethnogenesis, as it is called, is often a consequence of the ideological activities of elites. People and groups in, or seeking, power in the context of the state can mobilize society or segments of society by appealing to culturally powerful symbolic markers of difference. Such appropriated markers can become, again in the context of the state, highly potent emblems of group identity, invested with the self, and defended passionately. When groups formed around such cultural symbols are drawn into conflict, or emerge in the course of a conflict, then conflict resolution requires a cultural analysis. (The elements of such a cultural analysis are developed further by Avruch in Chapter 8, this volume.)

It is important to note that a cultural analysis intended to be useful in conflict analysis and resolution should not depend on the public deconstruction of the ethnicity (or any other feature of social identity) of the parties. This is a procedure almost guaranteed to alienate and irritate its targets. Rather, it should involve self-conscious reflection about identity issues on the part of the analyst. Such reflection most usefully takes the form of a sharp alertness to local nuances in the identity categories at play in the dispute, with particular attention to the discrepancies between those categories and those included in the intellectual/cultural baggage carried by the analyst.

Cultural understandings about the self differ from one tradition to another. These differing understandings may lead to local understanding and practice of ethnicity (or other social identities) that differ markedly from those characteristic of Euro-American societies. The possibility of cultural variation in the framing of ethnicity requires the conflict analyst to be sensitive to the relationship between ethnicity (and other forms of social identity) and culture (especially cultural conceptions of the self).

Consider ethnicity (or what passes for ethnicity) in many traditional Pacific island societies. Until recently, and even today in more remote areas, the boundaries between different islander populations (ethnic boundaries in common parlance) were remarkably fluid (from the Euro-American point of view at least). People and families passed in and out of group identities with remarkable rapidity. Traditional conceptions of the self in many Pacific island societies account for this phenomenon (White and Kirkpatrick, 1985). In those societies, people's cultural knowledge stressed the very important role that food played in constituting the self. Not surprisingly then, food and the land from which it was derived were far more important in the acquisition and transmission of group membership than "blood-based" common descent. People who together ate food produced from a particular piece of land were known to share a common essence, a common being. This is what made the people of a given place (district or valley or island) "the same." Several interesting consequences follow from this. One was the absolute value placed on land in these societies. Another was the permeability of identity group boundaries; new members came to share in the common identity over time by taking part in the group's activities, especially those involving food. In the Pacific the form of social identity that seems best captured by the notion ethnicity was acquired, not inherited. It was here that ethnicity in the Pacific differed most strikingly from standard European and American notions of ethnicity (and race). That important feature of Pacific islander ethnicity emerged from common sense knowledge, everyday ideas about the acquisition and sharing of identity and selfhood. This common sense and this acquired ethnicity are part of the cultural heritage of island societies. (See Brison, (2002) for a discussion of ethnicity in the Pacific.)

Changes in cultural concepts of social identity arising out of political and historical processes can have profound political implications. In many of the urban environments in the "new Pacific" and under the influence of the world media and the culture of former colonial rulers, people seem to be adopting more conventional (by Western standards, of course) ideas about the self. These ideas in turn are having a strong impact on local understandings of ethnicity and thus on group relations (see Black (2000, pp. 4–5) for an example of this process).

This last point illustrates the instability of both sides of the equation (forms of social identity and cultural understandings of the self) and their vulnerability to history. A good example comes from the Netherlands where a people known as Ambonese have come to play an important role in Dutch society. Their current ethnic identity emerged in barracks where, as former Dutch colonial troops in "temporary" exile from newly independent Indonesia, they lived for years (Amersfoort, 1982). Over the decades and the generations, and under very energetic political leadership, those soldiers and their families have become a distinct ethnic group. Their cultural roots may lie in the eastern islands of Indonesia, but the formative experience in their emergence into Dutch society has been those years as exiles, living encapsulated within those camps. Any attempt to understand their recent history – and the political positions and conflicts to which they have been party – that ignores this fact is bound to fail.

Social identities are vulnerable to history, especially to the social enactment over time of important cultural propositions about selves, groups, and the relations between them; what might be called "deep politics." This may be the case even when the identity in question has little if any "ethnographic reality." In the USA, WASP (white, Anglo-Saxon, Protestant) ethnicity was apparently invented to round out the cultural landscape (filled with named identity groups of one sort or another) and thus to erase a "default American" identity largely occupied by elites. Many (the majority?) of those so labeled are, in fact, neither Anglo-Saxon in descent nor Protestant in religion. And a substantial percentage is made up of people whose families (Irish, Italian, Eastern European) became "white" not so many generations ago (Ignatiev, 1995; Brodkin, 1998).

Race

Race, perhaps especially in North America, is also subject to deep politics and social construction. For example, when one considers the 1998 American Anthropological Association statement on race, one is immediately struck by the quotation marks around the word "race" in its title (American Anthropological Association, 1998). Given the involvement over the years of that organization in refining the race concept, investigating its empirical correlates, and combating the use of anthropological and other scientific data to support racism, those quotation marks are very strong evidence of the questionable status of race as a scientifically useful concept. Having spent the better part of a century struggling to correct the misuse of data about race, anthropology has now realized that the very concept underlying those data is questionable. This is really no surprise. Strong justification exists for the position that as an intellectual tool for thinking about biological variation in the species *Homo sapiens*, race is irretrievably flawed, at least as it is commonly understood in North America.

The history of human evolution tells us that the separation into ancestral populations happened much too recently and the resulting populations have been much too interconnected for any significant biologically based differences in behavior or neurological capacities between human populations to have emerged. Measurement of those human traits that do differ from person to person reveals, time and again, that more variation exists within than between the so-called races. That is, research has demonstrated that any two people chosen at random from the same racial group (no matter how defined) are no more likely to be similar in their overall genetic makeup than any two people similarly chosen from different racial groups. This is part of the reason the American Anthropological Association, in another statement, urged the U.S. government to phase out the term "race" in the collection of federal data, including future census data (1997).

Cognitive research has demonstrated that enormous confusion remains among the American public about the concepts of race, ethnicity, and ancestry (Gerber and de la Puente, 1996). Nevertheless, a general public understanding does exist that there are fixed, separate divisions of humanity, that is races, which are biologically different from one another in significant ways and revealed by differences in skin color. This factually inaccurate notion arose out of particular historical circumstances, especially the Atlantic slave trade and the expansion of European settlements in North America, Southern Africa, and Australia. Such a flawed understanding lends itself easily to racism, the use of ideas about race in the oppression of one group by another. Imputed racial differences become the basis for invidious distinctions, predicated on supposed differences in moral and mental capacity, and thus in virtue. It is no secret that groups in power use such ideas to justify the social order, especially the maintenance of hierarchy and their own privilege. It is for this reason that studies of socially constructed whiteness have the potential for bringing about either significant social liberation or significant entrenchment of already existing inequality (Delgado and Stefancic, 1997).

Race, in its North American sense a flat earth idea that just does not work as a description of the reality to which it refers, has enormous social and cultural importance (e.g., Dominguez, 1986). Certainty that the earth was flat kept European sailors close to shore for centuries; American certainty that humans are divided into separate races continues to shape the social and political life of North America. Thus, American racial conflicts tend to bring into play a whole set of shared assumptions and predictable disagreements about race, about conflict, and about how conflicts between racial groups play out (Gadlin, 1994). This is ethnocentric knowledge, however; for other cultural traditions and other histories have produced other knowledge about human difference – other places, other races. As with ethnicity, then, American ideas about race are increasingly powerful in the world. For this reason it is important to keep in mind that these ideas are limited when dealing with cross-cultural racial conflict.

Like other forms of social identity, race may well map actual social and cultural differences between groups. But inasmuch as there are differences between the groups so constituted, those differences reside at the group or aggregate level. In other words, there is no reason to assume that each and every member of a group shares all the attributes assigned, claimed, or achieved by that group. Confusing the two levels (individual and group) is an extremely common error. It may be especially pernicious when thinking about gender.

Gender

In many animal species males and females appear almost physically indistinguishable, apart from differing reproductive structures. This is not the case with men and women, though. Sharp differences also exist in social roles, behavior, and psychology between the human sexes. Importantly, these latter differences are neither universal nor inevitable and differ markedly in detail from society to society. Thus it makes sense to use the term "gender differences" instead of sex differences when referring to psychological, behavioral, and social differences between women and men. The point here is that male/female differences in behavior and role and in their psychology are due more to culture than to biology. Gender roles and gender role expectations, which differ from culture to culture, are the crucial determinants of gender difference. Here we describe a few of these differences across cultures. We could equally well have chosen any of the other social identities, because vast research literatures exist for each, in which are recorded the results of innumerable studies of difference. It is important to remember, however, that as we pointed out in the discussion of race, confusion of levels between statements about characteristics of groups and statements about attributes of individuals is both very common and very misleading. One must be wary of converting statements about probabilities (which is all that descriptions of group attributes can be when applied to individuals) to expectations of individual difference.

When discussing gender, questions about the underlying cause of difference seem quite pressing. Evolutionary psychology, whose paradigm holds that psychological phenomena arose in evolutionary response to the demands of the small group hunting and gathering existence of early humans, proclaims the bankruptcy of blank slate models of the human mind. This is an argument with an impressive ancestry, and it is far from clear if any end to it is in sight; yet from the point of view of conflict analysis and resolution it may be largely irrelevant. Broad psychological predispositions, whatever their genesis, are shaped by experience, and experience is socially structured according to the immediate environment, not the imagined circumstances of ancient humanity. Among the most important features of that immediate environment are the particular cultural traditions of the group in question. It is the content of these understandings about men and women and the relations between them that are important.

A survey of the world's societies reveals relatively consistent differences in gender behavior and psychology (Ember, 1995). As in any such survey, the existence of societies that do not conform with the majority is strong evidence that the causes and the sources of the particularities of gender differences are to be found in the realm of culture and not genetics, since the societies in question are drawn from populations between which there are no significant biological differences. Some of those reported gender differences seem particularly relevant to conflict analysis and resolution.

The social roles men and women play differ from each other within and between societies. Warfare, especially combat, and the public dimensions of politics tend to be primarily male realms in all but a few societies. It is especially rare for women to occupy the warrior status. Childcare is more often a female than male task. In the economic realm, all societies have worked out a gender-based division of labor, although the details of the roles men and women occupy in the production, distribution, and consumption of goods and services vary markedly across societies and are subject to change as circumstances change.

Cross-cultural studies of behavior reveal that boys tend to exhibit more aggression (attempts to hurt or injure others), while girls are more nurturing, cooperative, and responsible (but, contrary to popular stereotypes, not dependent). These differences, while impressive, are not universal, and in fact there are societies in which the reverse seems to be the case. Similarly, in societies in which there seems to be marked gender difference in the organization of the self, men's selves tend to be thought of as autonomous, while women's selves tend to be viewed as more interdependent. Related to this, perhaps, is the greater empathy and concern for the feelings of others which women tend to report in a variety of cultures, as well as the greater skill women seem to exhibit in using and understanding non verbal communication. Again, this is far from true of all humans or all human societies, and as noted above, it is important always to remember the dangers in conflating the two levels – group and individual (see Ember, 1996, for a review and survey of cross-cultural material on gender).

Human sexual dimorphism is converted by social processes to human gender dimorphism that can serve as the basis for identity group formation and oppositional politics and even the famous war of the sexes. It is important to bear in mind in any conflict analysis that gender relations (like race relations and ethnic relations) are often also power relations. As Susan F. Hirsch points out when discussing the conflicts of Muslim Swahili speakers on the Kenyan Coast:

> Given, for example, that women are situated in positions of multiple subordination, their oppositional practices might differ from those of men, might be directed against men, or if pursued in concert with men (e.g., against the state), might have gender-specific outcomes.

Understanding the gendered nature of oppositional practice requires careful consideration of how men and women are positioned in the sites where resistance occurs and how they utilize different strategies and goals within them. (1994, p. 210)

The cultural component of sexual dimorphism (called gender here) is frequently lost to sight, especially to the sight of those embedded within a particular culture. For the conflict analyst and/or would-be third party, gender identity can seem so basic and so natural that it easily becomes one of the most determinative elements in a destructive ethnocentrism. As with ethnicity, race, and other forms of social identity, reflecting on and even deconstructing one's own understanding of gender has great utility for the third party. This process allows one to see more clearly just how the gender assumptions held by the parties may be implicated in their dispute, and that insight, in turn, may offer possibilities for useful suggestions or interventions. Of course, cultural analysis should take place in the background, as it were, of the attempted resolution of the conflict.

Religion

As we noted earlier, pointing out the culturally contingent features of a social identity to parties in a dispute in which that identity plays a major role tends to elicit less than useful responses; this can be particularly important to remember when dealing with religion-based identity groups. Religion is notoriously Janus-faced with respect to conflict. All the great world religions contain significant resources for peacemakers (Johnson and Sampson, 1994; Gopin, 2000). These resources include sacred texts extolling peace and forgiveness as well as adherents inspired by those texts to become active participants in peacemaking and conflict resolution. At the same time it is undeniable that religion has been and continues to be deeply implicated in many of humanity's cruelest struggles. This impressive paradox raises several very important questions for conflict analysis and resolution. When does religion become the basis for total social identity? What leads to political action based on that identity? When does that action become oppositional? The record is quite clear: conflict between or within religious communities almost always leads at least some people to adopt membership within such a community as a total social identity, leading to the enactment of the conflict as the kind of ultimate struggle between good and evil that makes resolution so difficult. Furthermore, because religion so often claims for itself a special status as the domain of ultimate truth and morality, religious teachings are very likely to be mobilized as offensive or defensive weapons in other kinds of conflicts.

Religion lends itself to identity formation even when what one might call its theological aspects are heavily muffled. In other words, people proclaiming themselves defenders of one faith or another may in fact have a very weak grasp of the signature spiritual, intellectual, and historical details of that religious identity. Dealing, as they must, with ultimate truths, religious thinkers and functionaries tend to view such adherents with some skepticism – especially when those adherents are members of someone else's congregation. But the widespread propensity of members of amazingly different confessions to mobilize for political action around the symbols of their faith, no matter how little such individuals understand the finer points of their interpretations, leads one to conclude that religion, at least in its political manifestation, may be too important to be left only to the theologians.

Our goal in this brief discussion of religion has been to amplify understandings established in the more extended discussions of ethnicity, race, and gender, without repeating points already made. This also holds true in what we have to say about the remaining bases for social identity covered in this chapter – class, kinship, nationalism, and caste.

Class

Marx taught that social classes, defined by differential relations to the production of wealth, are objectively real and determinative of social relations, especially in the form of class conflict. The question for us here is: When does class become the basis for that form of subjective reality known as social identity? There are several possibilities. Class membership may itself be a self-conscious social identity; people who are members of a culturally recognized social class act as such in their relations with other members of that class and also *vis-à-vis* those who belong to other classes. One thinks here of classic left-wing politics in pre-Blairite Britain.

Class may be fundamental to other social identities such as ethnicity, which may in whole or in part be derived from position in an occupational structure and thus, of course, in the class system. The category of "West African" street merchants in American cities is an example of this phenomenon. Alternatively, location in the occupational structure may derive from ethnic heritage (e.g., Jewish academics pre-adapted to university life by a cultural tradition of Talmudic study or Mohawk high steel workers emerging out of the Mohawk warrior tradition). Class may also be seen as the fundamental reality, underlying and disguised by other forms of social identity, as in Noel Ignatiev's provocative assertion that the white race exists only as a function of capitalism (1996). As with class, none of the possible bases for social identity discussed in this chapter exists in isolation; the empirical challenge for conflict analysis and resolution is to specify in particular situations just how they are mutually intertwined.

Kinship

While often relegated to the arcane reaches of anthropological minutiae in advanced industrial countries, kinship is a highly charged cultural category in many communities and often becomes the basis for total social identity. Here the point is not the technical differences between groups formed on the basis of clanship, and those called kindreds, lineages, or even extended families; rather it is to note the powerful and frequently exclusionary hold of bonds which are believed to be based on the most intimate details of birth and marriage. Furthermore, family and kinship often serve as the ground from which springs a rich harvest of deeply felt metaphors for other social identities. Expressing social identity in terms of motherlands, fatherlands, brotherhoods and sisterhoods, birthrights, and founding fathers is testimony to the evocative force of kinship. How much of Somalia's recent state-deconstructive violence may be understood by reference to the operation of principles of clanship in Somali society is a matter of some dispute (see Besteman, 1996, 1998; Lewis, 1998). What is not in dispute is that those principles played and continue to play a significant role in the lethal politics of that unfortunate land, just as kinship continues to do in many of the world's societies.

Nationalism

The human world is now a world of nation-states, real and potential, and the cultural system that sustains that reality and those dreams has increasingly achieved the status of a human universal. No other principle of social identity is more widely acknowledged and few surpass it in the ordinary hierarchy of loyalties. Nationalism is also impressive because of the speed (at least in historical perspective) with which it has gained such powerful dominance.

Most scholarship on nationalism has been profoundly if implicitly nationalistic itself. Historical narrative, especially, has more often than not been both the creator and the tool of one nationalist project or another. Nationalism is always deeply implicated with the state and its organs of persuasion and coercion – its media, its schools, its courts, and its armed forces. As Oplinger (1990) points out, in even the weakest of states such organs lend themselves to the discovery and suppression of anti-state conspiracies, either real or imagined. When elites in direct or indirect control of the state, whose interests the state directly or indirectly serves, come to feel their social and economic position under threat, the temptation to launch a crusade to stamp out culturally defined deviance can prove irresistible. In such circumstances, negative social identity may be imposed on a category of internal or external enemies from which there is no escape. (See Druckman 2001a for a discussion of nationalism and war.)

Caste

A remarkable feature of the social life of Hindu India and many other South Asian societies, castes are identity groups which are differentially ranked within a sharply stratified social system. They are named and associated with particular territories, occupations, rituals, rights, and obligations. They are ascriptive, meaning that one's membership is fixed at birth and is unchangeable during one's life span. Marriage outside the caste is forbidden. An ideology of purity and pollution and intrinsic worth, combined with a set of rules for intergroup interaction, scaffold this system. Early European intellectual grappling with this phenomenon led to attempts to racialize castes, to little avail. Interestingly, the reverse argument has been made that "races" in the USA are caste-like, a point we return to below.

There is no South Asian equivalent to the English word "caste," which itself probably derives from the Portuguese. "Varna," a term used in India, refers to one of four cultural categories into which society is divided: priests, warriors, merchants and landowners, and servants and artisans, in that order. At the other end of the social scale, villages are composed of local corporate kin groups. These groups form the building blocks for larger dispersed, ranked endogamous units made up of sets of lineages and clans of a particular region – "jati" systems. It is important to note, though, that there is no all-India-wide network of jati.

As with each of the social identities considered in this chapter, a perspective that views caste as socially constructed from cultural materials raises issues about the conditions under which the identity emerges and conditions under which change may occur. We illustrate those issues with a set of questions about caste. Analogous questions could be asked about all forms of social identity.

Is the practice of arranged marriage essential to the continuation of the caste system? Is it shifting to a class system as South Asia urbanizes and industrializes? The answer to both questions is "perhaps." Other societies (including Japan, Rwanda, and South Africa) exhibit elements of similar systems – are these caste systems or only caste-like systems?

Was the segregated USA a caste system? Both race there and caste in India were systems of birth-ascribed inequality that had rules of group separation based on beliefs in intrinsic worth (i.e., purity-pollution).

Both tried to control intermarriage by "safeguarding" higher status women. Both systems involved economic exploitation of lower status groups by higher status groups. One major difference between the two is in the subjectivity of the lower status group; lower castes in the Indian system subscribed to an ideology that justified their subjugation. The racially oppressed in the USA did not. (See Raheja, (1998) and Seymour, (1996) for discussions of caste and its issues.)

Social Identities and Conflict Revisited

The distinction between "we" and "they" is a human universal, present in every language, a feature of every social order. All distinctions are potentially invidious distinctions; this is why social identity, especially total social identity, plays a variety of roles in conflict situations.

Differing social identities may account for differing perceptions, understandings, and behaviors including those relevant to conflict and its management. Since it can provide the symbolic currency for expressing inter- and even intragroup relations, social identity often plays an important role in organizing a dispute. An environmental struggle, for example, may play out along ethnic, or racial, or religious, or gender lines – lines that for the parties involved demarcate separate and fundamentally different types of humanity.

It may be the case that the fundamental cleavage which divides the parties to a dispute is, in fact, social identity. Here one thinks of those destructive processes of mutual demonization, in which each for the other symbolizes deeply devalued moral qualities, qualities that are often secretly feared aspects of the self. These processes of demonization rest on the use of the other as a yardstick of moral benchmarks against which the self may be measured and on to which may be projected unwanted or feared self-attributes, as the following passage demonstrates:

> What we read about the wickedness of Sodom is still strong in the sons of Sodom. Their pride and wealth drag them into wicked ways, they do what is not proper, abusing their own bodies. They should not by right be called human beings, for their sin shows that they have degenerated from human nature into bestial, or rather demonic, insanity.

So wrote a twelfth-century English monk, speaking of the special hell reserved, so he believed, for those guilty of sexual practices which he and his church viewed as perverse (quoted in Bartlett, 2000, pp. 570–1).

Social identity can also provide contending leaders with the basis for the mobilization of mass support. As mentioned above in the discussion of nationalism, the identification and elimination of threats to social order often involve the classification of some social type as enemy, against which collective action must be taken (Druckman, 2001a). In situations such as these, highly effective appeals for support are often heard from leaders and would-be leaders, some more cynical, or at least manipulative, than others. These appeals to group loyalty and self-sacrifice for the greater good can tap some of the deepest springs of human motivation and have led in the past, as they will no doubt lead in the future, to some of the noblest as well as the most shameful pages in human history.

An important challenge is to identify the social matrix from which leaders and followers emerge, especially in rapidly changing social landscapes. Here the work of Derluguian (2005) is particularly instructive. Drawing on the ideas of Bourdieu (1990), he offers a vivid analysis of the unfolding of the process by which unlikely opportunists leapt into identity politics in newly autonomous parts of the former Soviet Union.

Not all changes in the politics of social identity are as extravagantly spectacular as in the former U.S.S.R., just as not all changes in the politics of social identity necessarily lead to conflict. Changes in social identity can equally emerge quietly and slowly. For example, Merry's (1994) account of the operation of the family court in Hilo, Hawaii illustrates a relatively benign venue for the expression of the various bases for social identity, as well as the role elites and state structures can play in producing and manipulating changes in social identity, and thus in the political life of the community.

As Merry points out, courts can play a very important role in the production of social reality by the messages they convey. When the message is that certain attributes of personhood are newly salient, and others are no longer salient at all, then the ritualized decision-making of the court and the penalties it imposes may change the way people understand themselves and their rights and obligations. Although this is a more orderly and peaceful process than that analyzed by Derluguian, the result can be no less transformational.

Social Identities and Conflict Resolution

To speak about social identity on the one hand and conflict resolution on the other is to speak about the relationship of a very poorly conceptualized set of variables (ethnicity, race, and the others) and a very tightly defined agenda, especially if we accept resolution and not just management as the desired outcome for deep-rooted, intractable disputes (Burton, 1987). In Part III of this volume we specify a variety of modes of analysis and resolution. In this chapter we considered why analysis needs to attend to social identity and some of what constitutes social identity.

Analysis begins with reflection and questions. An always appropriate question asks, "What kinds of people do the disputants consider themselves to be? What local meanings adhere to the categories of personhood mobilized by the parties?" For, as Lawrence Rosen says, cultural analysis "requires at its base an understanding of the categories of meaning by which participants themselves comprehend their experience and orient themselves toward one another in their everyday lives" (1988, p. xiv). What is the local knowledge about human difference at play in this social field? What are the salient social identities and how are they defined?

Productive analysis also requires considerable self-awareness. With regard to the subject matter of this chapter, reflective analysis involves attending to one's own ideas and assumptions about the different forms of social identity at issue (including that of the analyst) and remaining alert to how these ideas and assumptions may be inadequate to grasp the reality of the parties (Lederach, 1986). The point here is that the disconfirmation of unconscious predictions, frequently signaled by an experience of surprise, can lead the analyst to potentially productive insights (Black, 1998).

Struggles over social identity and between social identity groups can be an extremely difficult venue for the neutral and collaborative analysis characteristic of problem-solving workshops. In this connection, the interested reader should refer to Burton (1997) for an important statement by a practitioner-scholar with wide experience of such workshops. Here may be found a very clear statement of a perspective in which the parties' frustration with their underlying and unmet identity needs is taken to be one of the major variables driving deep-rooted conflict.

The relationship between total social identity and conflict is best seen in processual terms, as a mutually constitutive cycle. Once that process is in play, deep-rooted conflict and total social identity may easily cause each other to intensify. But their relationship may also work in the reverse fashion so that they lessen one another's intensity. Social identity and awareness of its existence, origins, and content can play an important role in attempts at conflict resolution in a number of ways. Perhaps, like Jordanian organizational managers, the parties handle their conflicts by drawing on shared cultural traditions (Kozan, 1998). Or perhaps a group's symbol system structures and gives content to desired outcomes. Fundamental identity and security needs may be expressed primarily in social identity terms. And social identity itself may provide the basis for resolving a dispute by, for example, validating an appeal to shared heritage to legitimize a settlement.

Ethnicity, race, gender, religion, class, kinship, nationalism, caste: all are possible bases for total social identity. Each offers the opportunity for boundaries to be reified and enemies generated. Each may also hold within it possible resources to be used in the resolution of conflict. Total social identities may be the root of conflict and total social identities may be generated through conflict. Early intervention may have the consequence of leading parties away from the production of the kind of all-consuming total social identity so often associated with deep-rooted conflict. The fact that such identities are social productions, not inherent in "human nature," helps us to understand how this might be the case. On the other hand, just because such identities are socially constructed from cultural material does not mean they are flimsy creations – far from it.

The challenge in every case is to learn to specify which conditions and which practices can lead to liberation from:

> [the] prisons of the spirit that men create for themselves and for others – so overpowering, so much part of the way things appear to have to be, and then, abruptly, with a little shift, so insubstantial. (Naipaul, 1988, p. 105)

Discussion Questions

1 Discuss the process of social identity formation in relationship to conflict.
2 How, if at all, does the concept of total social identity advance the analysis of a conflict with which you are familiar?
3 In what ways are social identities based on gender and on nationalism alike, and in what ways are they different as possible bases for conflict?
4 What are some of the ways in which an attention to social identity is important to conflict resolution?

Key Words

Caste
Class
Ethnicity
Gender
Kinship
Nationalism
Race
Religion
Social identity

CHAPTER 9

Culture

Kevin Avruch

Chou En-lai, the story goes, was asked by a Western diplomat whether he thought the French Revolution was a good or bad thing. "Too soon to tell," the Chinese premier replied.

Understanding the concept of *culture* is a crucial prerequisite for effective conflict analysis and resolution. That said, "Culture," the literary critic and theorist Raymond Williams points out, "is one of the two or three most complicated words in the English language" (1983, p. 87). The problem is not one of "coming up with" a definition. On the contrary, anthropologists and others have come up with literally hundreds of them (Kroeber and Kluckhohn, 1952)! The problem, rather, lies in recognizing that the term comes to us from the nineteenth century with different meanings, and that these meanings came attached to political agendas of one sort or another (Avruch, 1998, pp. 6–9). The same thing is true today. Think of how some regimes resist criticism of their human rights record by saying in effect, "Our culture's notion of 'human rights' is different than yours (in the West), and to criticize us is therefore neocolonial and unjust." Finally, even leaving aside the heavy political baggage carried by the term, it is the case that *culture* is used differently (and sometimes deficiently) in the various social science disciplines that have contributed to the study of conflict and conflict resolution. Noting these problems, some have tried to do away with using the term entirely, substituting for it such concepts as *discourse* (from Foucault (1978)), *practice* (from Bourdieu (1977); see Abu-Lughod, 1991), or *worldview* (Nudler, 1990; Docherty, 1998).

Nevertheless, the concept of culture has been around long enough, is so widely used, accepted, and broadly understood that it makes sense to retain it and direct our energies into making it more useful and less

042113–1

deficient. That is the purpose of this chapter: to define *culture* in a way that helps theoreticians and practitioners to sharpen their thinking and practice, to review some of the ways the idea has been used already in conflict analysis and resolution, and to point to work that needs to be done in the future.

Defining Culture

One of the things that all contemporary social science definitions have in common is that for none of them is culture connected primarily – as Raymond Williams (1983, p. 92) put it – to "culcha": "high" art, superior knowledge, refinement, or "taste" (opera, classical music, Shakespeare, Rodin, or Racine). (This, indeed, is one of the main nineteenth-century meanings of the term that has so confused contemporary, colloquial usages.) For no anthropologist, certainly, is "culture" something possessed only by the educated, aesthetic – and upper – classes. Everyone "has" culture. In fact, everyone "has" potentially *several* cultures – this is partly why (as we shall see) using the concept becomes complicated. At a minimum and very generally, it is possible to think of culture as something widely *shared* by individuals in a society, namely, "the socially learned ways of living found in human societies" (Harris, 1999, p. 19), or perhaps the "socially inherited solutions to life's problems" (D'Andrade, 1995, p. 249). Notice that both of these definitions stress the idea that culture is learned and that it is passed down (reproduced or "inherited") in the context of social groups. Beyond this agreement, however, many questions are raised. For example, is culture *only* learned – is no part of it innate? Does culture refer *only* to how people think about the world, or must it refer also to how people actually behave? How widely "shared" are these things in any event? With regard to the second definition: are the "solutions" proffered by culture always the best ones possible? If solutions differ from society to society, can we – or ought we to – judge some of them better than others? And can it be that "culture" sometimes creates new problems in the course of presenting solutions to old ones? If it does, how can these new problems be dealt with?

Even these few questions may indicate why, pushed beyond the barest minimum, definitions of culture tend to proliferate and contend with one another. In addition, neither of these definitions address some of the oft-found deficiencies that the culture concept is prone to, for example, connotations of *homogeneity* (culture is all one thing – there is a single thing called "Mexican culture," for instance); *stability* (culture is timeless or changeless); *singularity* (culture "maps" on to society in a singular way – so that "Japanese society" is characterized unproblematically by a single "Japanese culture," for instance); or *entityness* (the idea that culture is a *thing* that can act independently of the persons who "carry it"; see Avruch and Black, 1991; Avruch, 1998, pp. 12–16).

For the purposes of this chapter, a fuller and more complex definition of culture is needed. "Culture," writes Schwartz,

> consists of the derivatives of experience, more or less organized, learned or created by individuals of a population, including those images or encodements and their interpretations (meanings) transmitted from past generations, from contemporaries, or formed by individuals themselves. (Schwartz, 1992, p. 324)

In this definition culture retains some of the "traditional" or "customary" force often associated with it – since it is transmitted from past generations – while at the same time the dynamism of contemporary influences and individual agency is recognized. This definition stresses cognitive aspects of culture, such as images, encodements, and also schemas or cognitive representations (D'Andrade, 1992; Romney and Moore, 1998), as well as its interpretive dimension (Geertz, 1973). (A schema is a networked cognitive structure that makes possible the identification of objects or situations along with variably "canned" procedures for behaving with respect to them.) But while culture in this sense exists "in the minds" of individuals, as it provides "solutions to life problems," it is also in no way disconnected from collective behavior and social practice.

Schwartz's definition needs to be supplemented by three other observations. First, because individuals in societies are "distributed" across many different sorts of social grouping – regional, ethnic, religious, class, occupational, and so on – and because each of these groupings is a potential "container" for culture, any complex society is very likely "multicultural." Thus, *culture is socially distributed across a population.* Second, even members of the same social grouping do not internalize cultural representations or schemas equally. Some schemas are internalized very superficially and are the equivalent of cultural clichés. Others are deeply internalized and invested with emotion or affect. The more deeply internalized and affectively loaded, the more certain cultural representations are able to motivate action (Spiro, 1987). In other words, in addition to being socially distributed in a population, *culture is psychologically distributed within individuals across a population.*

Finally, because culture is the derivative of experience it is closely connected to ongoing or past social practice. Therefore, despite its "traditional" or "customary" base, culture is to some extent always situational, flexible, and responsive to the exigencies of the worlds that individuals confront. And because human social experience is often rife with conflict, culture, far from being always identified with "shared values" or consensus, is often contested as well (Martin, 1992).

Culture and Conflict Analysis

Given this definition, how does culture help us to understand social conflict? First of all, notice that for any given individual "culture" always comes in the plural; individuals "carry" multiple cultures, from ethnic, racial, national, or religious ones, to those "contained in" – or derived from experience in the practices associated with – occupational, professional, or class social categories. This point will be especially important when we turn to such conflict resolution practices as negotiation in "intercultural" contexts. For now, it means that a statement such as "Juan is a Mexican" tells us quite a lot less than some culturalists think it does. Is he Zapotecan or mestizo? From the South or the North? A Catholic or a Protestant? A peasant or a university graduate? A military veteran or a victim? It also means – even if we knew the answer to all of these questions – that we should be wary of such simple causal statements as, "Juan behaved in this or that way *because* he is a Mexican." This is so because even a more or less complete listing of all the relevant *categories* would still constitute a rather blunt instrument for getting at the *specific* images, encodements, schemas, metaphors, and interpretations that Juan brings to a *particular* social encounter.

Second – notwithstanding the plural nature of culture discussed above – note that culture is no longer *simply* a label – a name for persons aggregated in some social, often national or ethnic, grouping. Nor is it simply a synonym for attitudes, norms, or values – the "soft" side of the harder (and putatively "more real") materialities of social life. Instead, culture is conceived more deeply and comprehensively, as an evolved constituent of human cognition and social action. It constitutes social worlds for individuals, as it is in turn constituted *by* those actors in those worlds. The dialectical nature of culture means that except in the narrow sense of a "failure to communicate" across cultural boundaries – not an unimportant concern to be sure! – culture is rarely by itself *the* cause of conflict. The mere existence of cultural differences is usually not the primary cause of conflict between groups (cf. Huntington, 1996). However, culture is always the lens through which differences are refracted, and conflict pursued (Avruch and Black, 1991, 1993).

This is so because culture frames the context in which conflict occurs. It does so partly by indicating what factors are subjects for competition or objects of dispute, often by postulating their high value and relative (or absolute) scarcity: honor here, purity there, capital and profits somewhere else. It does so also by stipulating rules, sometimes precise, usually less so, for how contests should be pursued, including when they begin and how to end them. And it does so – to return to our earlier definition of culture – by providing individuals with cognitive and affective frameworks, including images, encodements, metaphors, and schemas, for interpreting the behavior and motives of others (cf. Ross, 1997, pp. 46, 49).

In terms of the above, the important point for analysts of conflict to consider is this. When contestants (and analysts) mostly share frameworks for interpretation – share culture – then the cultural factor "disappears" into the background and the actual conflict may appear (to cultural insiders, anyway) to be entirely over scarce resources or divergent interests. However, in this case culture's disappearance is only an illusion to which cultural insiders are susceptible. Outsiders, who do not share the interpretive frameworks of the contestants, may "see" culture at work when and if they do not understand what the conflict is about or how it is being socially processed – which often means not sharing with contestants the cultural calculus by which certain resources or interests are valued or counted: "You beat your daughter severely to protect your family's ... *honor?*" Note that such cultural non-apprehension is usually experienced and expressed ethnocentrically by outsiders in a moralizing way.

Thus culture (re)appears – literally in sharp relief – when contestants from significantly different cultural backgrounds come into contact, and thus share few frameworks for interpretation. In that case, whatever conflict there is between them over resources or interests is potentially complicated, in part by intercultural interference or impedance to the actual processing of the conflict – what are we really fighting over; do we share the same interests and notions of valued resources; how do we fight? – as well as to communication among contestants about the conflict – how do we negotiate?

Of course, recalling the heterogeneous nature of culture, it should be clear that usually contestants "even from the same culture" may share some, but not all, interpretive frameworks. Individuals in complex, differentiated social systems are in effect "multicultural." This means that even within the same society, "intercultural" encounters abound, and affect the processing of social conflict. In the USA, for example, African-Americans and whites approach conflict differently (Kochman, 1981); members of different social classes do when they interact in such institutions as courts (Merry, 1990; Yngvesson, 1993); workers in different occupations do (Trice and Beyer, 1993); as do middle-class women and men, even within the microsociality of the family or workplace (Tannen, 1994).

Culture, Ethnic Conflict, and Social Identity

Another way to clarify further culture's role in conflict is to distinguish as clearly as possible between culture and ethnicity. (Insofar as they are also socially constructed categories, what holds for "ethnicity" also holds for "race" and "nationality" in the discussion that follows.) This is not so simple, however, since usually ethnicity, race, or nationality are conflated with culture. This means that "ethnic conflict," for example, is thought of as primarily a cultural conflict, and solutions are sought in the cultural realm. Indeed, in the preceding section we briefly mentioned African-American and white interaction as an example of an "intercultural" encounter (cf. Gadlin, 1994). It is the case that ethnicity, or race and nationality, are always constituted by some measure of "cultural content," though often (from an outside observer's perspective), exaggeratedly or even spuriously so. For instance, Hobsbawm has demonstrated that many ethnic or national "traditions which appear or claim to be old are often quite recent in origin and sometimes invented" (Hobsbawm and Ranger, 1983, p. 1).

The key point here is that social categories such as ethnicity, race, or nationality have a peculiar relationship to culture. They are culture "objectified," projected publicly, and then resourcefully deployed by actors for political purposes (Avruch, 2003). To complicate matters, ethnicity, for example, is also a component of an individual's social identity. Social identity, as is made clear in Chapter 7 in this book, "refers to the social *uses* of cultural markers to claim, achieve, or ascribe group identity" (emphasis added). Group identity, in turn, functions not only as a source of psychosocial support for individuals (Erikson, 1959; Isaacs, 1975), but equally as a sociocultural resource and *site* for mobilizing groups (sometimes ranged against other ethnic groups, but often against a state) in their efforts in one political arena or another (Cohen, 1974; Horowitz, 1985). This is so because the "cultural markers" referred to in the chapter on social identity often function to set out the social boundaries by which groups distinguish themselves from others (Barth, 1969).

One way to vividly see the *uses* to which culture is put, as well as its role in conflict, is to consider the large literature on the "invention of tradition" (Hobsbawm and Ranger, 1983), "imagined" national communities (Anderson, 1991), the social construction of ethnic (Cohen, 1969), racial (Dominguez, 1986), or national (Malkki, 1995) identities, as well as the fierce political contests among elites surrounding the "production of national cultures" for ideological control of a state (Gramsci, 1985; see also Handler, 1988; Aronoff, 1989; Fox, 1990; Avruch, 1992; Verdery, 1995). In each of these instances cultural content – most often linguistic, racial, or religious – is infused in the making of social groups, and thereby enlisted in agonistic, sometimes lethal, pursuits.

Yet for all the peculiarity of culture's connection to ethnicity, including the instrumental uses ethnic actors make of cultural content, what makes disentangling culture and ethnicity so difficult in conflict analysis is that when conceived of as a component of a total *social identity*, ethnicity is also invested by individuals with affect, and can thus motivate social action. Like culture, therefore, it serves to link individual and collective identities (Ross, 1997, p. 47), psychodynami- cally by anchoring the former in the latter (Avruch, 1982). In this event a rather small and specific part of "cultural content" can serve as a powerful symbol of group identity while at the same time functioning as a "true" piece of culture – that is, a schema for cognizing the world and motivating social action toward it. Among the most powerful examples of this, and among the most relevant for understanding conflict, is what Volkan (1988) has called "chosen traumas." These are experiences that come "to symbolize a group's deepest threats and fears through feelings of hopelessness and victimization" (Ross, 1997, p. 70). The Nazi Holocaust for Jews, New World slavery and the Middle Passage for African-Americans, the Armenian massacre by Turks, mutual massacres by Hutus and Tutsis, the fourteenth-century Turkish defeat of Serbs in Kosovo (updated in our own time by NATO), the 1948 Calamity for Palestinians, the Cherokee Trail of Tears – the list is depressingly long. For analysts of conflict, the key is that such traumas serve double-duty. They symbolize group distinctiveness in emotionally compelling ways, and therefore provide a site for political mobilization, *and* they provide for individual members of the group, and for elite decision-makers sensitive to history and public opinion, cognitive and emotional maps of the nature of the world that surrounds them. That world, needless to say, is usually perceived as hostile, uncaring, or evil – and dangerous. To take just two examples among many: Who can understand the Israelis' obsessive concerns about their national security without also under- standing the searing role of the Holocaust in the Jewish experience of the twentieth century? Furthermore, who can begin to understand Serbian claims of victimization by the West in 1999 – even as some Serbs themselves victimized Albanian Kosovars – without also under- standing how many Serbs seemed able to experience *in their own generation* what happened to "them" in Kosovo in 1389?

Intercultural Encounters

As our discussion of culture ought to have made clear, many more encounters even in our everyday lives are "intercultural" than we might at first perceive. However, insofar as these are casual or, more to the point, do not involve competition over valued resources or engage us in forms of dispute, we are likely to pass lightly over potential cultural divides. And – recognizing that culture is not homogeneous, but inheres in many different sorts of social categories – we understand that in practice "intercultural" is always a matter of degree. Sometimes, though, the nature of the cultural divide is a great one, typically involving linguistic, religious or, in Huntington's (1996) sense, "civilizational" dimensions. Sometimes we do find ourselves in intercultural encounters in a competitive or otherwise conflictual context. In these latter cases the cultural factor can loom large, and conflict analysts and especially conflict resolution practitioners must be knowledgable and attuned to it.

Avruch and Black (1993, pp. 133–6) set out the rudiments of cultural analysis in intercultural encounters. Following a long ethnographic tradition, they encourage analysts to treat cultural analysis as "thick description" (Geertz, 1973), always sensitive to social context and to seeing the world "from the native's point of view." What they aim for is the collection of schemas, metaphors, and so on that characterize the "natives's" local common sense about the root causes and consequences of conflict, what Avruch and Black call *ethnoconflict theory*; as well as the indigenous techniques or practices used to manage or resolve conflicts, *ethnopraxes* (Avruch and Black, 1991, pp. 31–4). Examples from different cultural settings of different ethno-theories and related ethnopraxes may be found in the case studies reported in Avruch *et al.* (1998).

Culture and Rationality

Ross (1997), in his discussion of how culture provides actors with a framework for interpreting the actions and motives of others, points out that "motives," which link cognition to behavior, serve the same explanatory role as do "interests" in rational choice theory. Indeed, in shared cultural contexts interests and motives appear to be the same thing. But the difference between them – and thus between rational choice and interpretive cultural theories – is a crucial one. For rational choice theorists, interests, conceived of as "utilities" in a cost–benefit mode, are "assumed to be more less transparent," "given," and universal, while "motives are knowable only through empirical analysis of particular cultural contexts" (Ross, 1997, p. 50). In fact, it is precisely in intercultural encounters – especially when the cultural divide is a large one – that the difference between interests and motives becomes important. This is so because what Ross called the presumed universal, "imperialistic," and "dominating" character of interests in rational choice accounts of action can lead to serious intercultural misunderstandings when the *culturally constituted* motivations of one party do not match the assumed universality of interests posited by the other (or by the analyst; see Avruch, 1998, pp. 74–6).

A compelling example of this mismatching is offered by Cohen (1990) in his study of Egyptian–Israeli diplomatic and political mis-communication. Cohen considers why, throughout the 1950s and 1960s, Israeli deterrence, based on massive use of force as reprisals against Egypt for terrorist attacks emanating out of Egypt against Israel, failed to actually deter. As part of a cultural analysis he investigates the broad understandings relating to violence, vengeance, and vendetta in each society. He concludes that Israel's use of massive force violated Egyptian ethno-conflict theories relating to vengeance and retribution; in particular, Israelis misunderstood Egyptian conventions of "pro-portionality" in these matters. The cultural logic of Israeli deterrence was that the "more disproportionate the punishment, the greater the victim's compliance." Unfortunately, Cohen continues, "Egyptian rationality refused to conform to the Western, utilitarian model designed by Israeli strategists" (1990, p. 97). What Egyptians regarded as highly disproportionate vengeance on the Israelis' part had the effect of shaming and humiliating them – a serious loss of honor in a culture where honor is deeply valued, and its loss has great motivational force. To erase the shame and regain lost honor, Egypt supported further attacks against Israel. Continuing Israeli reprisals thus had the effect of ensuring continuing Egyptian support. This positive feedback loop of mounting violence was ultimately predicated, as Cohen put it, on Israel's mistaken assumption that the Egyptians (and Arab confronta-tional states in general) "shared the same Israeli calculus of cost and benefit" (1990, p. 99; see also Avruch, 1998, pp. 48–55). Israelis mis-takenly projected their own understandings of interests, including the avoidance of mounting retaliatory punishment, and expected ways to satisfy them – by preventing terrorist provocations from Egyptian soil – on to their Egyptian adversaries. These interests, however, turned out to be neither as universal, transparent, nor "dominating" as the Israelis thought. Other "interests," culturally constituted in Arab culture, were held by the Egyptians, and they served as strong motives for Egyptian responses to mounting Israeli violence that were unexpected and unsought by the Israelis – and ultimately, of course, costly in lives to both sides.

Culture and Conflict Resolution

If the emergent field of conflict resolution has a fundamental principle – one reflected throughout this book, in fact – it is that effective conflict resolution depends upon conflict analysis. The purpose of this chapter was to propose that effective conflict analysis, in turn, requires cultural analysis. This requirement is especially keen in cases of intercultural conflict, where one can expect that the greater the cultural divide the more acute the requirement. However, as our discussion of the nature of culture has indicated, many more conflicts – ethnic, class, religious, occupational, gender – are "intercultural" than may be initially apparent.

Most of the research and analysis of intercultural conflict resolution thus far has dealt with negotiation, rather than third-party processes such as mediation, or more specialized forms such as the problem-solving workshop. Some of this work aims to get at "national negotiating styles" (e.g., Binnendijk, 1987; McDonald, 1996), or focuses by way of case study on the purported styles of particular countries – Japan (Blaker, 1977), Russia (Schecter, 1998), or China (Solomon, 1999), for example. For the most part these studies concentrate on diplomats and treat culture monodimensionally, only at the level of "national culture." They have been criticized for this, among other, reasons (Zartman, 1993; Druckman, 1996).

Another genre of intercultural negotiation work has tried to be more explicitly comparative by identifying several transcultural dimensions according to which all cultures may be commensurably evaluated. The work of Hall (1976) on "high-context" vs. "low-context" communica-tional styles is foundational here. It has been extended by Cohen (1997), who added to the basic sociolinguistic distinction (high-context language use is expressive and group oriented; low-context language is instrumental and status/individual oriented) other dimensions of cul-tural difference that include orientations toward time ("polychronic" vs. "monochronic"); individual vs. interdependent/communal ethos; and a concern with negotiating mainly for "results" (a prototypical American's "bottom line"), vs. mainly for the maintenance of valued social relationships.

Another influential researcher in intercultural communication is Hofstede (1980), who investigated corporate (transnational IBM) cul-ture and found that values across all "cultures" sampled (again: *national* culture) clustered into four underlying dimensions: power distance (the degree of inequality in a social system, from small to large); collectivism vs. individualism; "masculinity" vs. "femininity" (similar to assertive-ness vs. compliance); and uncertainty avoidance (weak to strong). Later on, work in Asian societies prompted him to add a fifth dimension: temporal orientation (long-term vs. short-term). Building on this and other work (e.g., Weiss, 1994a, 1994b), Salacuse (1998) has proposed ten basic ways in which culture affects negotiating style or behavior: (1) negotiating goals (for contract [outcome] or relationship?); (2) attitudes toward negotiating process (win/win or win/lose?); (3) personal styles of negotiators (formal or informal?); (4) communication styles (direct [low-context] vs. indirect [high-context]; (5) time sensitivity (high or low?); (6) emotionalism (high or low?); (7) agreement form (specific or general?); (8) agreement-building process (bottom up or top down?); (9) negotiating team organization (one leader or consensus?); (10) propensity toward risk-taking (high or low?). (For another perspective on how culture affects negotiating behavior, see Druckman and Hoppmann, 1989.)

The overlap of dimensions for most of these schemes should be apparent. The assumption underlying all of them is that when negotiators from polar-opposite cultures (say, risk-takers vs. risk-avoiders) interact, the effects of the differences are powerful enough to create communicational dissonance and misunderstanding. Cohen (1990) subtitled his earlier study of Israeli–Egyptian negotiations "a dialogue of the deaf."

These studies are useful, and signal a welcome change from the days when cultural factors were ignored more or less completely in the study of negotiation and conflict resolution. They serve well to remind us that even successful and widely accepted prescriptive models for negotiation – that proposed by Fisher and Ury, for instance – should be deployed cautiously in other cultural settings (Fisher *et al.*, 1991; cf. Avruch, 1998, pp. 77–80). Nevertheless, their reliance on transcultural dimensions – say, individualism vs. collectivism – puts us in danger of losing much of the rich context that actor-oriented, ethnographically based "thick description" provides. This context should not be regarded as superfluous: it is not the case, for example, that "individualism" means the same thing for "individualist" Muslim city-dwellers in central Morocco (e.g., Rosen, 1984), and "individualist" Southern Baptists in central Georgia (Greenhouse, 1986). In much the same way, Cohen (1997, p. 108), paying careful attention to context, tells us that even such key negotiating terms as "compromise" may be emotionally valenced entirely differently in American English (where a problem-solving, rationalist, and legalist culture gives it a neutral or even positive gloss), and Arabic (where in fact the word for "it" does not exist; and cognate words negatively connote concession, retreat, and abandonment).

Coming back to the conceptualization of culture outlined in this chapter, and given enough time and resources, we would argue that culturally sensitive conflict resolution would pay attention to elucidating the relevant cognitive representations and their accompanying affect – the images, encodements, schemas, and metaphors – the "psychocultural interpretations," as Ross (1993) has put it, that contestants bring with them to the conflict. Such resolution would aim first to get at the relevant ethno-theories of conflict, and would then try to utilize relevant ethno-praxes as far as possible – the resources of conflict resolution that the parties themselves "bring to the table." This orientation to culturally attuned conflict resolution is expressed most strongly by Lederach (1995b), who compares the "prescriptive models" of resolution that many Western third parties bring with them and try to impose on the parties, with the "elicitive model" – essentially a kind of ethnographic practice (Lederach, 1995b, pp. 29–31) – that uses indigenous techniques and resources as a foundation for resolution work. In this mode, the role of third parties in conflict resolution is to help the contestants modify their psychocultural interpretations of one another and thus of part of the world: to change metaphors and schemas (see Ross, 1993). This does not mean that material interests no longer matter or can be safely ignored. But it does mean that in deep-rooted conflicts (often ethnic, racial, or nationalistic), the parties may never be able to get to the point of negotiating interests until they recognize each other as fully human, if not yet wholly legitimate, interlocutors. Israelis and Palestinians still have water rights to argue over, and water is scarce in the Middle East. But first they had to recognize each other's mutual existential right to exist, before moving on to negotiating nationalist rights to a state. Here we are in the domain of affect, language, and metaphor – of interpretation, of *culture*.

Some Concluding Remarks: Notes for Practitioners

Near the beginning of their *Handbook* for running problem-solving workshops for conflict resolution, Mitchell and Banks point to a key requirement of sound practice for third parties: professionalism. This "involves, as a first step, making oneself aware of one's own goals and values in undertaking any problem-solving exercise" (Mitchell and Banks, 1996, p. 6). A major part of this involves a cultural analysis of oneself: one's own metaphors and schemas, images and encodements. Such auto-ethnography is possible, though not easy, and the reflexivity it demands and brings forth is central to an effective, engaged, and ethical practice. Indeed, one of the key issues for intercultural conflict resolution is the extent to which our very conceptions of effective and ethical practice – negotiation, mediation, facilitation, and so on – are determined by our culturally constituted assumptions and presuppositions about the world. And since so much of conflict resolution "theory" has arisen from the crucible of reflective practice, as we more closely examine our practice, in the end we are also led to examine the cultural underpinnings of these theories.

There is a final and fundamental lesson for students, analysts, and practitioners: *You* have a culture too – several, in fact. Culture is not just something "they," the "others" – the parties – possess, while you have "natural and self-evident," "Western" rationality, goodwill, problem-solving skills, common sense, virtuous intentions, and the

English language. Culturally sensitive conflict analysis and resolution begins with this insight – though it hardly ends there.

Discussion Questions

1 Why is it not sufficient to think of "culture" solely in terms of "high" art, music, literature, and so on? What is a better or more useful way to define culture?
2 Name and discuss some "inadequate" ways for conceptualizing culture. Why are they inadequate?
3 What's a "schema?"
4 Discuss the relationship between culture and the individual: (1) How is a "socially distributed" culture related to individual cognitive schemas? (2) Why is it necessary to say than any individual is a "carrier" of many different cultures?
5 How is culture related to the analysis of conflicts or disputes?
6 How can an awareness of cultural dynamics be used by practitioners in the resolution of conflicts and disputes?
7 What is the relationship between culture and ethnicity or ethnic identity?
8 Discuss how cultural differences affect intercultural communication, with special attention to negotiation.

Key Words

African-Americans
Attitudes
"Chosen traumas"
Conflict resolution
Culture (Note: *The* key word in this chapter – many citations)
Discourse
Egypt
Ethnic groups
Ethnicity
High context
Holocaust (Nazi)
Homogeneity (of culture)
Gender
Individualism
Intercultural encounters
Interests
Israel
Kinship
Kosovo

Low context
Metaphors (as cultural representations)
Middle Passage (New World slavery)
Motives
Nationality
Norms
Palestinians
Practitioners
Race
Rationality (and culture)
Schemas (as cultural representations)
Social identity
Subculture(s)
"Thick description"
Utilities
Values

CHAPTER 10

Structure

Ho-Won Jeong

Conflict arises from various social circumstances, often independently of individual intentions and behavior. While misperceptions, emotions, and a lack of communication are important factors in any type of conflict, structural forces need to be analyzed in understanding the generation, escalation, and outcome of a deep-rooted conflict. An incompatible social relationship stems from structural conditions which produce competitive interests, value differences, and repression of basic needs.

In developing conflict resolution theories, many questions may be raised regarding a social structure that can accommodate different needs and interests of adversaries, and promote social harmony. If structural constraints prohibit achieving an equitable outcome of negotiations, how can conflict be transformed? This chapter illustrates various social theories relevant to analysis of structural sources, and explains how structural issues may be understood in the analysis and resolution of conflict.

Why Does Structure Matter?

Understanding the basis of social injustice is essential in looking for transformative possibilities in a large-scale social conflict involving multiple issues and complex causes. It has been widely suggested by several experts that structural transformation derives from exploring fully the root causes of problems rather than control of defiant behavior (Burton, 1990c, 1996a; Dukes, 1996; Rubenstein, 1999).

Group conflict can find a fertile ground especially in societies where traditional cultural institutions and values disintegrate rapidly with economic deterioration. The collapse of a multi-nation state is driven by competition among the ethnic elite for power. As we have seen in former Yugoslavia, however, political disintegration and group hostilities become more serious with economic and social instability. In many poor countries, long-term ecological degradation has also been a contributing factor in group competition for resources.

There are different theoretical interpretations in understanding structural sources of conflict. The dissatisfaction of basic needs may be attributed to malfunctioning institutions and oppressive social structures (Burton, 1997a). Oppression represents an exploitative situation where one party's advantage over another is maintained by coercion. Feelings of exclusion and powerlessness are produced by an oppressive system. Power is sustained by certain social-economic systems and cultural norms while a psychological element may inevitably influence power relations.

Psychological aspects of conflict may be linked to structural conditions to the extent that the parties are unwilling to recognize a malfunctioning system and fail to accept the necessity for its reform. In relative deprivation theory, frustration is attributed to a social situation that widens a gap between what people have and what they believe they deserve. Perceptional gaps are felt, as sudden economic decline leads to more competition, and consequent marginalization of some groups.

Conflict arises along different axes such as race, class, gender, and sexual orientation. Identity boundaries are established by group differences with the institutionalization of norms and values. Conflictual relationships derive from political, economic, and social divisions which serve as the basis of power differentials. The ethics of caring and empathetic relationships are ignored in a competitive pursuit of interests. Institutions of modernity supported by capitalism, liberal democratic norms, industrialization, and scientific advances have contributed to the creation of homogeneous patterns of life, but have not reduced cultural and economic heterogeneity (Dukes, 1996).

A particular group's positions and interests differ along the allocation of power resources in various social settings. The control of one group over others is sustained either through coercive means or is based on consensual acceptance of institutional order. Marginalization is an outcome of a power-imbalanced structure which benefits only a few at the expense of many others. The analysis of ethnic conflict would be inadequate if we ignore the impact of century-old external domination and the desire of a marginalized ethnic group for self-determination (reflected in their aspiration for autonomy). The following sections discuss how social relations may be institutionalized and transformed in various settings.

Dynamics of Human Action and Structure

Whereas structure is characterized by the nature of relations between major social actors, it is more than an aggregate sum of intergroup relations. Although they may be negotiated or accepted by coercion, rules and normative elements of structure affect behavior of individual actors. Actors are accorded certain rights and status according to authority, and their behavior has to be compatible with the value expectations of the system. Motivations behind social action can vary, ranging from tradition and affection to absolute value (Weber, 1964). The roles of actors can change under various circumstances, and conflict may emerge from changes in the perceptions of these roles.

It is true that structure has been seen conventionally as external to the individuals and constraints on their options and choices. However, structure does not need to be regarded as a fixed and permanent feature of a social system. Even though the rules and resources of the structure are drawn upon in the production and reproduction of social action, the intention to achieve a social purpose is a critical factor in understanding the role of agency (Giddens, 1986). In addition to the will to influence the event, the agency has to possess the ability to redefine the responsibilities associated with its activities.

As certain values and interests are promoted in the pursuit of desired outcomes, social action involves intentionality and struggle (e.g., consumer boycott waged as a means of changing a stronger adversary's behavior). Mutual orientation between actors tends to be competitive in a conflict situation where some actors attempt to carry out their will against the resistance of other actors. Social action directed toward changing others' behavior often entails coercive elements.

Social Functions and Conflict

A modern rational system is different from a traditional communal society where education, social, and cultural functions are supported by family and kinship structures. In modern societies, divided subsystems of polity, religion, and economy replace moral authority and symbolic power by tribal chiefs and religious figures. In the Weberian tradition, social coherence derives from the legitimacy of political institutions and acceptance of authority relationships.

In the secular values of modernity, new social divisions are created along institutional lines, legitimized in rational/legal authority. Conflict can be managed by the mobilization of both symbolic and material resources needed for coordinating and supporting various social functions. Changes have to take place within the existing boundaries of relationships. In an industrial society where rules arise from the need to regulate contract relationships, conflict management is based on motivations oriented toward efficiency and utility.

Maintenance of stable social relations may best be illustrated in the theoretical framework of functionalism which explains how institutions and segments of a society form a relatively unified whole through coordination and accommodation (Parsons, 1971). Interdependent relationships exist among groups performing complementary functions. Stability requires the continuity of existing social functions and cultural patterns. Thus the interactions among actors need to be regulated by given social norms and rules. The main assumption of functionalism is that component actors are motivated to act in accordance with their role requirements to maintain the integration of the system.

Conflict and disharmony may arise when incompatibility exists in functions of different components. Tension may be created by a sudden or radical change in any major segment of these patterns. Changes in an external environment may also weaken support for the system. Therefore, the maintenance of a system requires constant adjustment to both internal and external challenges.

In response to challenges, a social system has to find a new equilibrium between different components through adaptation to new situations. In order to satisfy different demands, more differentiation of social functions may emerge. At the same time, if the coordination between different functions is difficult, some functions can be reintegrated to increase the overall efficiency of the system. As illustrated by periodic government intervention in a market system, the boundaries of subsystems are redrawn during a crisis.

In functionalist perspectives, conflict may be managed through adjustment of the entire system to any malfunction of its components. The active management of conflict can result from reforming the components of a system. As the major concern has been how conflict is stabilized or controlled in an orderly manner, functionalism is oriented toward maintaining the status quo.

The Impact of Conflict on Organizational Structures

Depending on its nature, conflict can play either a positive or negative role in group maintenance (Coser, 1956). The consequences of social conflict are considered to be positive when it increases the adaptation of particular social relationships to new situations. By responding to the concerns of dissatisfied groups, conflict may serve as an opportunity to improve communication. The existing system can even be strengthened by an opportunity to confirm consensus on shared norms, values, and beliefs. A positive aspect of conflict lies in re-establishing unity with stabilizing functions.

In functional approaches, a conflict management strategy would be to prevent disintegration along one primary line of cleavage such as class, race, or ethnicity. Acceptance of legitimate conflicts helps prevent resort to violent methods used for the destruction of society. In order for conflicts to be functional, however, goals and values of the parties should not contradict the basic assumptions upon which the relation is founded (Coser, 1956). The organization of groups can contribute to conflict resolution as long as they agree on certain formal rules of the game that provide the framework of their relationship (Dahrendorf, 1959). To that extent, mediation, arbitration, and other conflict regulation measures can be helpful in reducing the intensity of conflict.

The function of conflict with an outgroup has an impact on maintaining an organizational structure. Group boundaries are maintained by reaffirmation of or search for common values against the outside enemy. Thus an external conflict serves as a catalyst for group cohesion. In preserving group unity, "safety-valve institutions serve to divert hostilities onto substitutive objects or function as channels for cathartic release" (Coser, 1956, p. 41). The need for increased internal cohesion can lead to the suppression of intragroup tension and dissent (see Druckman and Zechmeister, 1973). Groups involved in intense struggle may develop a hierarchical structure for their survival.

Structural Configurations of Post-industrial Society

Compared with functionalist interpretation of conflict, Marxist views stress that conflict is the product of a highly stratified political and economic structure maintained by coercion to serve one group's interests. A hierarchical power structure is maintained to protect the economic interests of a dominant class. Antagonism between classes defined by the ownership of the means of production entails inherent contradictions which may be resolved only through establishing egalitarian class relations. In contrast with traditional Marxist analysis, industrial disputes in advanced capitalist countries have lost class dimensions. Conflict is generated by the authority relationship in control of production rather than patterns of property ownership. The replacement of capitalists with managers changed the basis of modern industrial conflict. The power elite of post-capitalist society comprises those who have specialized expert knowledge, and they have a relatively uniform interest in expanding a free market economy and private sectors.

Class conflict has become institutionalized with the development of industrial democracy. Meeting material aspirations with the increased production of goods for mass consumption has reduced incentives for challenges to the ruling elite. State intervention in the economy and cultural domains has been used for functional management of conflict in capitalist society. The ownership patterns are diverse with the expansion of stock options and other corporate schemes to provide material incentives for the employees. The criteria for the values of work are set up by "market" mechanisms, while contract relationships are protected by a legal and political infrastructure.

Class relations are no longer rigidly polarized since social boundaries have become more fluid with the ascendance of a managerial class which has developed the carriers of industrial authority. Class conflict has been managed by providing increased upward mobility through education and affirmative actions for the employment of minority racial or ethnic groups. Trade union leaders are part of the managerial system, with the bureaucratization of union movements. Changes in the nature of class relations allow interest-based negotiations which avoid value issues, making them less significant (see Druckman and Zechmeister, 1973).

Different social divisions have been formed within the structure of a post-industrial welfare state, as a class has become a relatively less distinct grouping. With complexities in social configurations, people have multiple identities and cross-cutting interests which mitigate against divisions along one line of cleavage. A marginalized position in one arena may be compensated by leadership roles in other arenas. For instance, a factory worker may also be a church leader, civic activist, or volunteer sports coach. Most importantly, intense social conflict is averted by the emergence of multiple issues and the diffuse nature of struggle (Dahrendorf, 1959).

A Dominant Structure and Hegemony

Given that power is located from within a society, its effects would be somehow spread around the social structure as a whole (Laclau and Zac, 1994). The rationalization of the existing systems is supported by legal institutions and administrative structures with the creation of new identities at both individual and state level. The bureaucratic and corporate control of a modern society limits the influence of the popular masses.

In neo-Marxist perspectives (Gramsci, 1971; Poulantzas, 1973), hegemony has become an important concept in explaining the institutionalized forms of power relations based on either physical or mental control. Legitimizing power differentials and institutions of authority derives from the manufacturing of consent through manipulation. The interests of the ruling class are presented as universal through a dominant discourse process which promotes institutional values. Critical theorists suggest that in advanced capitalist societies, legal order is respected with spontaneous assent, and is manipulated not to be seen as external imposition; its necessity is proposed as freedom rather than coercion (Horkheimer and Adorno, 1979).

Hegemony is embedded in a complex web of social and material arrangements producing the very fabric of everyday life (Deetz, 1994). For instance, hegemony in the workplace is enforced by contract and reward systems which influence the behavior and values of the employees. Feminists argue that women are encouraged to voluntarily conform to dominant masculine roles and values in order to advance in a military and administrative hierarchy (Gardiner, 1995).

Hegemony based on persuasive power relies on discourse referred to a set of rules for making authoritative statements (Gramsci, 1971). As power is embodied in knowledge, social reality is defined by discursive practice. Modes of communication are determined by the rules that dictate the status of social knowledge. Beliefs of groups and their social practice have to be compatible with dominant cultural values. Power derives from control of a discourse process and ideology defined in terms of normative value frameworks in which dominant political practices are constituted (Cooper, 1995, p. 21).

In neo-Marxist views, subordinate groups are induced to believe that their interests are satisfied by the existing social and economic structure. The process to form public knowledge and views is justified by moral and rational superiority of the ideology of modern industrial society. As diverse political practices shape subject positions, there is no singular universal oppressive structure. Individual experiences and identity are constructed within social practices embedded in institutionalized discourse (Bourdieu, 1991).

Struggle for Structural Transformation

The complete elimination of conflict is not feasible, and may not even be desirable in the presence of power asymmetry. There will always be a struggle between the groups which want to change the status quo and those which want to maintain it (Darendorf, 1959). Conflict may need to be developed fully to allow the expression of marginalized interests. Then the question remains how to identify and explore strategies to transform the central structure which produces antagonistic relations among different social forces.

In the thesis on a permanent revolution by Leon Trotsky (1969), constant struggle is suggested as a means to social progress. Organic movements reflecting social criticism reveal the contradictions of the relationships between the state and civil society (Gramsci, 1987). The role of an agent for change may exist in any kind of organized movement which challenges the institutions of power. Gramscian perspectives suggest that despite various attempts of cooptation by the state, each class has its own consciousness and intelligentsia to help organize a network of beliefs and challenge ideologies of institutional hierarchies.

The principal crisis of capitalist development is not only economic but also culturally and politically hegemonic; only when the consensus underlying/supporting the accepted social order begins to crumble can society truly transform itself (Habermas, 1987). If consent is withdrawn by the oppressed, the status quo is challenged more easily by new norms and behavior. In critical theory perspectives (McLellan, 1988), social movements represent struggle for historical transformation of political and economic systems associated with class relations.

Consciousness of one's oppressed position is important to any kind of conflict for social change (Freire, 1998). People can be free only when they believe in the possibilities for change (Guevara, 1988). Social action is organized by groups with the ability to recognize their own power. The consciousness of the marginalized class stems from the morality of its culture and hope engendered by that morality.

Oppressive structure itself does not lead to manifest conflict. The perception of inequitable relations has to precede the demand for change. As the sources of conflict are not always visible or obvious, they often remain latent unless one of the parties begins to perceive that the given situation is no more tolerant. Following the perception of the existing conditions, conflict groups demanding changes need to be politically mobilized. Group power refers to human ability to act in concert with others (Arendt, 1986). The success of a movement requires, in part, the quality of the leader, often with stoic principles and guided by strong feelings of love and humanity (Guevara, 1988). Whereas charismatic leadership may be needed to organize and lead the struggle, democratic control of social movements permits constant input from the mass.

Social Change and Conflict Resolution

There are different theoretical approaches to social change. Structural changes can focus on strategies to eliminate unequal power relations and social status. From feminist perspectives, patriarchy, ascribed as the main source of violence and conflict, can be eliminated by guaranteeing gender equality (French, 1994). In social ecology, the essential resolution of environmental conflict would be achieved by the removal of hierarchies in a human world which is responsible for both economic exploitation and destruction of nature. A subsistence economy may mitigate competition for scarce resources resulting from environmental degradation (Jeong and Kakonen, 1999).

It can be easily conceived that the formation of consensual society without a hierarchy alleviates conflict since the need for self-actualization and esteem cannot be met in an authoritarian political relationship. Post-modern approaches propose that decentralized political structures may emerge from a new cultural order which avoids the creation of rigid social boundaries (Seidman, 1994). Through the process to deconstruct a myth created by the dominant discourse, diverse voices can find the expression of differences with a claim to a social space that favors autonomy.

Linkages between different social struggles can be created within "a democratic project based on an egalitarian notion of citizenship" (Cooper, 1995). Gender, race, and class relations located in a specific social space provide a basis of specific forms of identity (e.g., father, worker, church member, neighborhood). We may argue that conflict resolution is designed to uncover the historically contingent origin of the dominant discursive practice whose functions are to perpetuate social and political hierarchies.

Conflict and Structural Transformation

With challenges to opposing values, interests, and identities, conflict has been intentionally pursued either nonviolently or violently (e.g., terrorism, war) by national or subnational actors in achieving their objectives. There are many differences in the ways groups are organized and the means of struggle to be chosen. Changes in power asymmetries have an impact on dynamics for conflict escalation and transformation. The outcome of conflict may reinforce or confirm old relations or establish a new balance of power between groups.

When forces representing a conservative power structure are balanced with forces challenging the status quo, continuing conflict produces a status quo in power dynamics. Reactionary intervention aims to help preserve the system as it exists while progressive interventions advocate changes either in the entire system or its components. With intervention of a more neutral third party, on the other hand, certain compromises may be sought. A reformed structure with some personnel changes may emerge in response to both internal and external challenges.

Transformation of the parties and their particular conflicts may not be possible with rearrangements within a given system. In struggles for the preservation of the rainforests, for instance, certain principles and values have to be respected for durable conflict resolution. The possibility for negotiated settlement is hampered in a situation where a dominant party is unwilling to make changes in the status quo. In overcoming asymmetric relationships, it may well be argued that conflict needs to be further escalated before its resolution (see Kriesberg, 1998; Jeong and Vayrynen, 1999; Mitchell, 1999, 2000b). Nonviolent struggle may be used by a marginalized party and its advocates in order to bring about ripe conditions for negotiated settlement.

Structural transformation can be made possible by either revolution or negotiated settlement. The outcome of conflict has different implications for future relationships between former adversaries. Revolution is characterized by the intensity of conflict, its violent nature, the suddenness of changes, and their radical nature. However, merely overturning one dominant system for another would prepare the seeds for future conflict. The deconstruction of dominant power relations through transformation of values and institutions may be considered as the ultimate form of removing adversarial relationships (Jeong, 1999). Given that conflict situations originate in diverse social settings, their resolution has to reflect different historical circumstances.

Conflict Dynamics

The roles of conflict analysis and intervention may be re-examined for different stages of conflict dynamics. Whereas the demand of social movements during the escalation stage includes radical elements for more dramatic changes, the de-escalation stage involves moderation in their demands, and tends to move toward compromised positions in negotiation with the established forces. Although more activist roles are sought in the transformation of power relations, a neutral third-party role increases during the de-escalation process.

The efforts to change conflict dynamics can be aimed at transforming an existing system. The pursuit of social justice in conflict situations provides an opportunity for structural transformation through nonviolent struggle. Parties may need to become aware that socioeconomic structures not based on consensual support may be altered; nonviolent struggle may be adopted as a strategy for bringing about conditions to be met for negotiated settlement.

Examining core social divisions may lead to an opportunity to transform a structure that is a source of recurrent discontent. Reduction in hostilities has to include such dimensions as autonomy and equity. If power relations are inevitably involved in conflict dynamics, power imbalance between groups has to be redressed. Structural obstacles to a balanced conflict outcome may be overcome by empowerment which enhances the ability of individuals and social groups who are in disadvantageous positions.

In order to achieve the goal of structural transformation, conflict intervention may be geared toward promoting a dialogue and education process to change positions of those entrenched in maintaining dominant interests. For example, conflict resolution in South Africa has entailed a change in the structure of the system; negotiation had to focus on how to re-establish the relationship in a more acceptable manner to both parties. On the other hand, it is important to note that structural changes may not be easily or immediately achieved (Jeong, 2000a). As we have seen in the Palestinian/Israeli peace process, efforts for the settlement of new terms may mean the beginning of long, serious negotiations about establishing new political relationships.

Conflict Resolution Practice

In a dispute attributed to communication problems, changes in institutionalized order may not be required. Many resolution methods concentrate on the particular circumstances of a conflict while ignoring sociopolitical and economic causes. Transformation often means changes in interpersonal psychological relations with improved communication (Bush and Folger, 1994). The concept of harmony is interpreted in terms of improving relations by clearing misperceptions and communication of intentions. Disputes can also be settled by dealing with misinterpretation of agreements or rules in a contract relationship. Structural issues are less important if the goal is simply to maintain or restore harmony at an individual level and inadequate applications of rules within a given system.

From transformative perspectives, alternative dispute resolution (ADR) addresses issues in the outer parameters of deep social divisions but leaves the inner core intact. ADR is seen largely as being akin to a band-aid treatment for modern social problems (Scimecca, 1991). Much of ADR practice suggests the trend toward the privatization of a public decision-making process. In certain circumstances (e.g., slave–master relationships), however, certain structural characteristics can have a direct impact on interpersonal relationships through power or status differentials. Obviously conflict with broad social implications cannot be treated only as a matter of misunderstanding or miscommunication.

Structural issues raise serious questions about the role of the conflict resolution profession in social change. There are different implications resulting from the debate over whether the practice has to be limited to seeking a resolution within the given power framework or somehow has to be supportive of progressive social change. Some have warned that by ignoring social causes, conflict professionals become an agent for the power elite which has a stake in ensuring the continuation of the existing structure (Rubenstein, 1999).

In many societies, conflict is regulated by dominant social norms, political ideology, and/or coercive force. Conflict management may be seen as a means to induce consent of the subordinate group without the necessity of physical coercion by serving as an effective control mechanism in support of the existing social order. The regulation or management of conflict is less concerned with the continued existence of antagonistic interest or values and their causes. Therefore, effective conflict resolution has to encompass the fundamental justice of the causes of the parties and their value premises as well as the justice of each side's interests. The analysis of power reality includes the acceptance of the opponent's rights to make a case for the conflict as an outgrowth of the authority structure.

Conflict resolution efforts may favor existing power structures by virtue of their "false" neutrality and emphasis on individual circumstances rather than systemic conditions (Dukes, 1999). Latent interests are implicated in the social structure of roles and positions, while manifest interests entail specific claims related to given structures of authority (Dahrendorf, 1959). Macro-structural causes are rendered invisible or insignificant by treating deep social conflicts as private (Rubenstein, 1999). It may, in fact, be reiterated that all individual conflicts should be examined to determine if they are embedded in structural variables such as power asymmetry, incompatibilities among different roles, adversarial forms of identity, and group organizations (Dukes, 1999).

Conclusion

One of the past achievements in the field of conflict resolution has been application of various psychological approaches to eliminating misperceptions and enemy images which hamper serious negotiations between adversaries. On the other hand, the field lacks social theories about conflict resolution, more specifically, discussion about what types of structural changes are desirable for a more sustainable relationship and how to achieve them. In particular, the analysis of deep-rooted conflicts should reflect the structural concerns and causes.

Structural approaches to conflict resolution may entail both normative and analytical dimensions. Normatively, respect for human dignity, inclusion, and nonviolence may be advocated as ethical foundations to achieve a just outcome of conflict resolution (Ronen, 1998). An analytical dimension illustrates ways in which different types of relationships are attributed to alienation, frustration, and resentment and how the sources of discontent may be addressed at a structural level.

The focus on structural layers is thus designed to illuminate structural conditions that produce or reduce conflict behavior. Various concepts (such as social action and function, power asymmetry between groups, organizational dynamics) introduced in this chapter may be helpful in broadening the scope of conflict resolution analysis and practice.

Discussion Questions

1 What kinds of social conditions are likely to cause conflict?
2 How can we understand the role of agency for structural changes?
3 Does conflict have a positive impact on social cohesion?
4 How are dominant relationships established among groups?
5 Why has a post-industrial society not experienced intensive class conflict?
6 What types of society may be suggested for reduction of social conflict based on disparities and inequity?
7 How do different theoretical perspectives explain structural transformation?
8 Can conflict resolution contribute to social change?
9 Is conflict desirable for structural transformation?
10 Do structural issues require us to design different processes of conflict resolution?

Key Words

Agency
Alternative dispute resolution (ADR)
Basic needs
Capitalism
Causes of conflict
Class conflict
Class relations
Communication
Conflict dynamics
Conflict management
Conflict resolution
Conflict transformation
Domination
Emancipation
Functionalism
Group conflict
Harmony
Hegemony
Human action
Interests
Marxism
Oppressive structure
Organizational structures
Post-industrial society
Practice

Psychological aspects of conflict
Rationality
Reform
Revolution
Social change
Social functions
Social systems
Structural transformation
Struggle
Subordinate groups
Types of conflict
Values

CHAPTER 11

Institutions

Richard E. Rubenstein

Some Basic Definitions and Distinctions

Every social system rests on a foundation consisting of both force and consent. Even the most democratic and popular systems require some compulsion to maintain their authority, while the most totalitarian and terroristic systems require some consent. In general, there seems to be an inverse relationship between force and consent. An increase in the use of force by the authorities against groups subject to their power often indicates a decrease in the extent to which such groups consent to their exercise of power, while a decrease in force often signals an increase in popular support (see Arendt, 1970). When the degree of consent is sufficiently high, people say that the system and its leadership are "legitimate," whereas when consent is substantially replaced by force, the constitution or the leadership may be termed "illegitimate." In societies seriously divided along racial, ethnic, religious, class, or ideological lines, the leadership may have strong support among favored groups but virtually no support among disfavored groups. In such cases, whether or not people consider their rulers and the governing system to be legitimate often depends upon whether they are favored "insiders" or disfavored "outsiders."

The sort of consent that legitimizes authority in any system over the long term is not just approval of the exercise of authority by particular individuals or groups, but agreement with the *norms* of the system: the basic principles, values, and rules upon which authority is founded and in accordance with which it is exercised (Weber, 1977, pp. 124f.). This form of consent is also known as normative consensus. Ordinarily, if a normative consensus exists, it includes agreement about how disputes between individuals or groups within the system should be defined and handled. *Dispute resolution*, whether through legislatures, administrative agencies, and courts, or through the means of "alternative dispute resolution" (i.e., alternatives to formal legal procedures), is a feature of systems that enjoy a working normative consensus. On the other hand, there are times and places in which this consensus breaks down, and people no longer agree on the basic principles that legitimize authority and the methods of dispute resolution. When dissensus replaces consensus and legitimacy breaks down (or where it has never existed), *conflict resolution* enters the picture (Burton, 1988, 1990c). The purpose of conflict resolution, in other words, is not just to help resolve disputes by using alternatives to accepted legal or political procedures, but to help conflicting parties repair, reconstruct, or create new normative systems.

Note that these distinctions (legitimacy/illegitimacy, normative consensus/dissensus, dispute resolution/conflict resolution) may be used to clarify the relationship between conflicts and methods of dealing with them regardless of the location or ambit of the system being considered. For example, a family is a system in which relations of authority and mutual obligation may be considered either legitimate or illegitimate, as are an organization, a neighborhood, a nation, and a global political or economic order. Whatever the system under consideration, the key point is that processes useful in resolving disputes when a normative consensus exists are not likely to be useful where there is normative dissensus, and vice versa. Where there is normative consensus, the parties to disputes ordinarily frame their differences in terms of competing *interests*. In cases of "consensual conflict" (Coser, 1964), dispute resolution processes feature *interest-based negotiation and problem-solving* within the limits set by the rules, values, and vision of social reality accepted by the parties. Because of this underlying agreement, once misunderstandings have been clarified and passions cooled, the parties may often move quickly to deal with technical matters. Where the conflict is dissensual, technical matters cannot usually be negotiated until the parties have dealt with more fundamental differences. Conflict resolution thus requires processes designed to help the parties *analyze* the reasons for the breakdown of their relationship, *envision* methods of creating or re-creating a legitimate system, and *evaluate* the potential of alternative courses of action to restore normative consensus.

Consensual vs. Dissensual Disputes

What sometimes makes things confusing is that the same name may be given to processes that function quite differently, depending upon whether or not the conflict is consensual. For example, consider the multiple meanings of "mediation." Looked at strictly formally, mediation means the use of a non-authoritative, impartial "third party" to help disputing parties settle their differences. But different social contexts – in particular, the presence or absence of a normative consensus – make an enormous difference in how the process is conceived and how it works. If parties A and B have a dispute about the ownership of a piece of land, and there is normative consensus – i.e., the parties consider the system of landownership legitimate – they may decide to use one of the methods of alternative dispute resolution (ADR) to settle their dispute rather than take it to court. Many methods of ADR, such as arbitration (decision by an authoritative third party), mediation/arbitration (a hybrid process), a mock trial with or without a jury, the use of an impartial fact-finder, or direct negotiations without the aid of a third party may be available, but in the case at hand, let us assume that A and B decide on mediation.

What will the goals of the mediation be? First, the process will probably be designed to permit a facilitated discussion of the legal issues in which A and B (and/or their lawyers), with the mediator's aid, try to ascertain the likely outcome of a lawsuit. If the parties can reach some shared understanding of their relative strength as potential litigators, this will establish a rough range within which they can continue to negotiate. In such cases, the normal baseline calculation goes something like this: If the chances of A winning a lawsuit against B are 60 percent to 80 percent, and if the maximum amount A can expect to recover from B under the best possible circumstances is $500,000, then A and B should settle their case at a figure between $300,000 and $400,000 (minus legal expenses) (see Raiffa, 1982, pp. 33–49). Second, having narrowed the range of negotiation outcomes, the mediator will facilitate a negotiation in which A and B attempt to resolve their disagreement in a way that satisfies each party's interests as far as possible within the general framework of the law, while avoiding lengthy, costly, personally painful, and precedent-bound legal proceedings. Because mediation is generally more informal, flexible, and potentially creative than formal litigation, it may be possible to help the parties fashion a result that they could not have achieved in court. For example, if A has the stronger legal case, but B, who is short of ready cash, has something else of value to A, like a promising opportunity to invest in another industry, A may agree to lower his or her claim substantially or drop the land case altogether in exchange for an agreement by B to allow A to participate in the investment opportunity.

Two further comments are in order before we continue. First, the case presented above is very simple. Suppose that the parties' chances of winning a lawsuit are about fifty-fifty – or that they are basically incalculable (as they may be in a "case of first instance")? Or suppose that A and B are corporations whose boards had been discussing a possible merger before this dispute arose? Because of such complicating factors, negotiation "in the shadow of the law" often involves strategies and calculations far more complex than the simple formula described above – so much so as to give rise to a rich, sophisticated literature on the art and science of negotiation. Second, our example involves only two parties with exclusively economic interests. One of the virtues of mediation is its usefulness in cases where litigation is problematic either because there are too many parties and interests to be dealt with justly and efficiently by a court, because there are confidential matters that the parties wish to avoid publicizing, or because there are personal factors involved, such as a relationship between friends or relatives that might be damaged by a highly adversarial court case (see e.g., Bush and Folger, 1994). Nevertheless, the key to ADR's usefulness, in this case and others, is the existence of a normative consensus which permits the disputants to frame their disagreement in terms of interests and to negotiate or do problem-solving within the context of a system that they accept as legitimate.

A very different situation is presented when such a consensus is lacking. For example: what if the dispute about landownership had taken place in the USA when the West was being settled, and there were ferocious disagreements between cattle ranchers, sheep ranchers, and farmers about how to use the newly acquired land? Or what if the dispute takes place today in a nation such as Brazil or Zimbabwe, where mass movements of impoverished peasant farmers are challenging the right of landowners to maintain their traditional ownership rights and to use the land as they wish? In both cases, rather than the legal system being accepted as one framework, among others, for resolving the dispute, it becomes a weapon in the hands of one party whose use may be violently resisted by the other. In America's nineteenth-century "Cattle Wars," ranchers and farmers fought pitched battles; lawmakers and judges were bribed, intimidated, and assassinated; and prisoners were lynched or broken out of jail. To those on the receiving end of "justice," the legal system seemed little more than partisan violence, while to those in control of the legal system, those who resisted were criminals and terrorists. Much the same may be said of present-day disputes involving landless peasants and absentee landowners (as in Brazil) or black peasants and white landowners (as in Zimbabwe and South Africa). Obviously, to "mediate" dissensual disputes such as these will involve assumptions and processes quite different from those involved in mediating consensual disputes.

How do these processes differ? In a consensual mediation or other ADR process, the disputing parties, their lawyers (if any), and the "third-party" intervenor or facilitator may assume that, unless there is some severe imbalance of knowledge, resources, or negotiating skill between the parties, each party is conscious of his or her rights and interests. Of course, in the heat of struggle, the parties may not have defined their interests adequately or explored a sufficiently wide range of options for satisfying them – this sort of rethinking is part of the purpose of the mediation. But the focus of the process is likely to be on *negotiation* based on some combination of bargaining power and creative problem-solving. If the mediation is successful, the parties will keep their case out of court and arrive at an agreement that satisfies each one's interests to the extent possible. If it is highly successful, they may also restore the personal, business, or political relationship that had been damaged by their disagreement.

On the other hand, where the context of the dispute is normative dissensus, the process, at least initially, will focus more on *analysis* than on negotiation. In such cases, the mediator or facilitator cannot assume that the parties understand the deeper sources of their conflict or the steps that may be necessary to restore consensus. Very often, the sources of serious dissensual conflicts are basic needs or deeply held values of the parties that feel dissatisfied or threatened because of some structural flaw or breakdown in the socioeconomic, political, or cultural system. Exposing these sources therefore requires social and psychological depth analysis of a sort that is unnecessary in most consensual disputes. Moreover, developing adequate options for resolving these conflicts means helping the parties generate options that will permit a *restructuring* of the failed system. In the case of the dissensual land disputes referred to above, for example, this may mean reforming or altering the existing system of land tenure and the legal and social institutions that support it. If analysis successfully identifies the roots of the conflict and the parties are able to envision options for system change, the next step will be negotiation over which option best satisfied the needs of all parties. Note, however, that the process will probably not stop even if an agreement is reached. Implementing a plan to reform a dysfunctional land tenure system will very likely require that large groups outside the immediate negotiation be consulted or mobilized and drawn into the process of conflict resolution.

The Sources of Legitimacy

How do systems become illegitimate, and how can legitimacy be restored? The pioneer sociologist, Max Weber, wrote that there were three types of authority considered legitimate in various social systems, depending upon their state of development and other factors: the authority of custom or tradition, the authority of charisma, and the authority of law (Weber, 1977, pp. 124f.). Weber did not discuss the need for conflict resolution because he did not foresee a *general* crisis of legitimacy – a situation in which no type of authority would seem legitimate. To him (and even more so to his successors, the "modernization" theorists), the history of types of authority, at least in the West, suggested the following pattern: from custom through charisma to legal rationality. What this means will become clearer if we look briefly at each form of authority.

In the beginning, authority was customary or traditional, meaning that the basic norm of the social system was: *"Find the custom and follow it."* What legitimized a command or other act of a person in authority, in other words, was that time and repetition sanctified that person's identity, role, and act. In traditional systems, important customs originate in mythic time, not historical time; they are thus said to exist "from time immemorial." And their observance often has a ritual quality, since the essence of ritual is formality, communality, and repetition. In such systems, to say that the act of some person in authority is "innovative" is a harsh criticism, since innovation is by definition a breach of custom. This is exactly what the English barons said when they forced the Magna Carta upon King John. In refusing to recognize their traditional rights, they charged, the King had altered the custom – an innovation, therefore an illegitimate act. This story has a further implication as well: it suggests that a customary system need not be static. In order to "find" the custom relevant to a particular dispute, the elders must be consulted, and they may disagree about which custom to apply or how to apply it under particular circumstances, since although customs (theoretically) do not change, particular situations do. Therefore, when many situations are changing rapidly and at the same time – that is, when the pace of social change in a society accelerates – customary systems find themselves in trouble.

In many societies, people still rely heavily on customary methods of resolving disputes. For example, in many parts of the world, there are still certain figures in the community (often village elders or religious leaders) to whom people traditionally turn to help them deal with personal, family, or neighborhood conflicts. Modern conflict resolvers can often find inspiration, and sometimes practical assistance, by discovering which traditional methods of dispute resolution still exist in a particular society and trying to adapt them to help conflicting parties deal with their disputes. The problem is that, for the reasons discussed above, processes of rapid social change – what some theorists (e.g., Black, 1969) call "modernization" – tend to undermine the legitimacy and integrity of these traditional methods. Auerbach (1983) has described how immigrant groups coming to the USA often arrived with their communal dispute resolution mechanisms intact, but found that, after a while, they had become useless. And Diamond (1970) suggests that the traditional methods work only so long as there are no serious social divisions in the community. When this traditional consensus disappears (for example, because of the division of the community into conflicting social classes), people abandon customary forms of dispute resolution and turn to other methods. An example from U.S. history is the way Roman Catholic priests, who once played a very important dispute resolution role in communities of immigrant Irish, Italian, or Eastern European Catholics, found their role greatly limited when militant labor unions and companies opposed to unionism began to fight it out in American cities.

According to Weber, the form of authority that first emerges when the legitimacy of custom is challenged is *charisma* – a Greek word meaning "grace" that may be defined as authority based on the personal say-so of a particularly convincing person. For Weber, the model of a charismatic authority figure is Jesus Christ, a Jewish teacher who challenged certain traditional customs of his people in the name of a higher authority: God the Father. Note that charismatic, in this sense, does not mean that the authority figure needs to be a spellbinding orator or a person with what we might call "star" quality. A charismatic leader may be quite soft-spoken, such as the present Dalai Lama, or a poor public speaker, such as Joseph Stalin. Charisma means simply that people believe a particular person represents a higher authority than tradition – that when he or she says, "This is the norm; you should obey," people accept that statement as binding.

Does charismatic authority resolve conflicts? The answer is highly ambiguous. Many charismatic figures are war-makers who use their authority to lead violent attacks against real or fancied enemies. Others are peacemakers who inspire people with a desire to overcome traditional hatreds and enmities, and who often establish a connection between inner peace or spiritual wholeness and harmony between conflicting groups or nations. But even the peacemakers often believe that the road to peace lies through some form of escalated conflict. Jesus preached peace to the point of advocating non-resistance to violence, but he also said, "Do not think that I have come to bring peace on earth;

I have not come to bring peace, but a sword" (Matthew 10:34), meaning that his message was meant to divide the righteous from the unrighteous even among the members of the same family. The Revd Martin Luther King, Jr. also combined peacemaking goals with exhortations to struggle (nonviolently) against injustice. Some scholars (e.g., Huntington, 1969) attribute the connection between charisma and conflict to the fact that charismatic figures appear usually when a traditional system is in crisis, but a modern system capable of organizing dissent and settling disputes systematically has not yet been stabilized. Other commentators, such as Weber, note that whether or not the charismatic leader is a peacemaker, charisma seldom outlasts his or her life.

In some cases, however, personal authority is passed on to an institution and becomes the basis for a far more impersonal form of authority based on legal norms. Again using the history of Christianity as an example, Weber (1977, pp. 363–73) calls this process "the routinization of charisma." Others believe that legal systems originate in other ways, for example, by reinstitutionalizing traditional customs (Bohannon, 1970) or as the result of a power grab by a new ruling class (Engels, 1968). However one explains the origins of modern legal systems, they all share ten common characteristics.

First, the legal system's claim to be authoritative is based on its *usefulness and reasonableness* rather than on custom or personal charisma. The system as a whole justifies its existence by the extent to which it satisfies people's need for security, freedom, and other social goods. Specific decisions are justified by their conformity to certain minimum standards of reasonableness. Judges' decisions, for example, must be accompanied by opinions demonstrating that they are not simply arbitrary manifestations of personal whim, interest, or prejudice. For this reason, Weber (1977, pp. 57ff.) calls modern legal systems "rational-legal."

Second, legal authority inheres in *offices*, not in personalities. The president of the USA has the right to command obedience only when he is acting within the scope of his legal authority. If he acts outside his authority as president, his orders have no legal effect whatsoever. An important implication of this principle is that modern legal systems require the existence of some form of government or state, however undeveloped that state may be.

Third, the characteristic form of legal expression is a *general rule* or *norm*, not a particular command or suggestion. The rule prescribes behavior – it is a statement of legal obligation, saying what people ought to do. And, since a legal system consists of thousands upon thousands of rules, it immediately produces the necessity for interpretation to decide which rule should apply to which situation and how to reconcile apparently conflicting rules.

Fourth, rules may be identified as legal (as opposed to customary or simply moral) because violating them carries with it *legal consequences: sometimes a reward, but more usually a punishment or "sanction."* Rules that are unenforceable or seldom enforced may remain laws in theory but become "dead letters" in practice. As a result, it is necessary to distinguish between the law "on the books" and the law in practice.

Fifth, public offices are defined in terms of legal rules or norms, some of which may be unwritten. This means that they constitute a *bureaucratic hierarchy* in which authority is passed down from higher ranking (e.g., the U.S. presidency) to lower ranking offices (e.g., departments of the president's cabinet). In some systems, the highest level of legal authority is expressed by norms contained in a document – a fundamental legal code or constitution.

Sixth, in modern legal systems, public agencies, private citizens, and certain private organizations are *legal persons.* This means that they have rights, duties, powers, privileges, immunities, and disabilities that are enforceable (at least in theory) by courts or other agencies of the state. The law itself defines who is or who is not a legal person, as well as the attributes and legal consequences of legal personality.

Seventh, the rules that define the exercise of authority by government officers and private individuals must be *publicly promulgated and formally stated.* Private legal rules may be grounded in contracts or other private documents (e.g., deeds and wills), but they also must comply with certain standards of formality and publicity if there is a dispute requiring their enforcement by the state. Some thinkers (e.g., Fuller, 1958) believe that a rule must also conform to certain minimum standards of justice to have legal effect, but others (Hart, 1958) deny that this is the case.

Eighth, these same rules, whether publicly or privately generated, are interpreted and applied by a *cadre of specialized professionals* (lawyers, in our society) who are trained to interpret them in accordance with certain *canons of interpretation and methods of legal reasoning.* As a result, the legal rules and decisions currently in force in any modern legal system form a coherent body of law or *corpus juris* that changes organically over time (see Berman, 1983).

Ninth, certain disputes among individuals or organizations subject to a legal system are resolved through *legal instrumentalities of dispute resolution:* a body of procedural and substantive principles expressed or implied by rules of law, and declared, enforced, and interpreted by state agencies or agencies subject to state supervision. Although most serious disputes are handled legally, the law itself defines which cases and controversies will be subject to its jurisdiction, as well as how those disputes are to be handled.

Tenth, implicit in what has been stated above is that legal methods of dispute resolution are ordinarily not resorted to in the first instance. They are *processes of last resort* that are used by disputing parties when systems based on custom or charisma become ineffective, or when the informal social mechanisms used in every community to resolve disputes fail to produce a satisfactory agreement. If neighbors cannot agree on how to deal with barking dogs, if businesspeople cannot agree on the meaning of some term in their contract, if the police and citizens cannot agree on what constitutes probable cause for making an arrest, dissatisfied parties have the right to "go to law." Often this means going to court (or threatening to do so), but it may also mean going to a legislative or administrative agency in search of the justice and order that less coercive and formal methods have failed to provide.

Since the legitimacy of a legal system depends to a large extent on its capacity to maintain social peace, we must ask whether and how well these systems resolve conflicts both inside and outside their boundaries. This may seem an odd question to ask, since in most modern societies, where legal processes provide the primary means of resolving disputes that informal methods fail to handle satisfactorily, the legitimacy of the law seems beyond question. Indeed, even in societies whose legal institutions are not supported strongly by state power or public opinion, people who break the law or who refuse to use legally prescribed methods to resolve their differences are often branded criminals, vigilantes, or terrorists (Rubenstein, 1985). Still, our inquiry is not so odd, since experience shows that the legitimacy of legal systems can vanish despite their apparent solidity and permanence. We need to examine how legal systems work and how they can lose legitimacy before asking whether there are legitimate forms of authority other than custom, charisma, and law.

How Do Legal Systems Work?

When people become embroiled in disputes that they cannot settle informally, they often have recourse to the mechanisms of law. How does this work? First, they must frame their claim in such a way that a court or other legal institution will recognize it as "justiciable," or capable of being decided by a judge or other legally authorized decision-maker. For example, if one child grabs another child's toy and the second child sues the first, no court will hear the case, since this is a matter that the law considers too trivial on which to expend the state's resources, and since there are other institutions (the children's parents, the school, and so on) authorized to handle such disputes. On the other hand, if one child shoots the other in the course of the fight, legal institutions, from the police to the juvenile courts (and possibly also the legislature) will take jurisdiction of the matter, since it is not trivial and no other institution is authorized to handle it.

But what if the case is not trivial – what if some people consider it desperately serious – and for some reason the legal authorities still refuse to consider it justiciable? This situation, which is not as uncommon as one may think, can produce escalated conflict of the sort that threatens the legal system's legitimacy. For example, suppose that the supreme legal authority is a legislature – a parliament – dominated by one racial, ethnic, religious, or socioeconomic group that refuses to recognize the claims or grievances of other groups. In a number of nations majority groups in control of the legislature do not recognize minority groups as having any legal rights, and are not at all interested in altering that situation. For members of a minority subjected to this treatment, what the majority calls "law" appears as sheer oppressive power. They may try to frame a legal claim cognizable in some other forum – for example, a "human rights" case under international law – but such claims are notoriously difficult to vindicate because of the weaknesses of international legal institutions and their general lack of enforcement power. Assuming that a "human rights" claim will not be effective, the group may well decide to rebel against the state's legal authorities on the ground that they have forfeited their right to the citizenry's obedience (i.e., that they are illegitimate). To the authorities' accusation that they are committing illegal acts of violence, the rebels will reply, "It is you who began using violence, although you called it 'law'."

Even where the supreme legal authority in a state is a constitution interpreted by a supreme court, people's claims may be held to be non-justiciable for various reasons: for example, that the constitution consigns them to the political branches of government rather than to the courts, or that they represent a new sort of claim that has never before been recognized in law. In the USA, attempts to question the legality of the U.S. war in Indochina were turned aside by the courts on the ground that only the U.S. Congress has the power to decide such an issue. For decades, American courts refused to recognize the justiciability of workers' claims to have the right to form labor unions. And thousands of claims currently go unheard because they are considered too novel to be legally cognizable. In this sense, legal systems are inherently conservative. Unless legislatures are willing to make new laws "legalizing" new claims, the courts will generally not perform this function for them. Since legislatures are political by nature, this often means that individuals or groups lacking political power must go without legal remedies for perceived injustices – a necessity that, if prolonged, tends to undermine the legitimacy of any legal system. This is another example of the principle discussed earlier: in systems lacking *normative consensus*, normal methods of dispute resolution ordinarily fail, and more analytical and thoroughgoing methods of conflict resolution may be necessary.

Now, supposing that a claim *is* considered justiciable, how will the dispute be resolved? The claim will be based either on a statute – a rule enacted by a legislature or administrative agency – or on "common law" – a rule developed previously by the courts. Each disputing party, either acting *pro se* or through a lawyer, will present its claim and the evidence required to support it before a judge, jury, or other legal authority authorized to make findings of fact and rulings of law. The presentation of evidence, including the examination and cross-examination of witnesses, rules of evidence, and roles of the judge and jury, is governed by formal procedural rules that may themselves give rise to disputes and litigation. The judge and/or jury will then decide who prevails, the plaintiff or defendant. In non-criminal cases other than small claims, and in appeals of any sort, the court will give detailed reasons for its decision. (The decision in criminal cases is either "Guilty" or "Not Guilty" – or, in Scotland, "Not Proved.") The losing party may appeal the decision to a higher court if the system permits such appeals, but when the last appeal has been exhausted, the loser must either conform to the legal authority's judgment or face the prospect of punishment (for example, a fine or imprisonment for contempt of court).

Through this combination of recognizing justiciable claims, formal procedures for presenting evidence, authoritative decision-making, the issuance of opinions giving reasons for decisions, and enforcement of decisions, if necessary, by state power, the legal system attempts to fulfill certain purposes essential to its legitimacy. These are:

1 providing an available public method of resolving most serious disputes;
2 protecting the rights and interests of disadvantaged parties who may need the protection of formal court processes;
3 settling disputes according to rules of law and applications that are reasonable, or, at least, not grossly arbitrary or whimsical;
4 developing rules of law and applications that make the legal consequences of people's behavior fairly predictable;
5 making decisions to resolve disputes that are final and enforceable.

A more general way of expressing these aims is to say that legal systems intend to guarantee their participants a minimum necessary degree of *procedural and substantive justice*. Procedural justice means fairness and rationality in the treatment of the disputing parties and those affected by their dispute. Substantive justice may be summarized as follows: "Give each party what he [she] deserves," and "Treat all parties as equal before the law." The philosopher John Rawls (1999) has recently added a third principle: "Make decisions whose effect, over time, is to reduce social inequality."

To what extent do legal systems, specifically or in general, fulfill these goals? There are two ways of answering this question, depending upon how one defines "conflict" and "resolution." If resolution means terminating the conflict by identifying and eliminating its underlying causes, and if these underlying causes are deeply rooted in the parties' psyches or in dysfunctional social institutions, legal methods are usually *not* well adapted to resolving conflicts. In fact, the law's inability to deal effectively with deep-rooted, dissensual social conflicts often brings legal systems into disrepute and undermines their legitimacy. If, on the other hand, the conflicts or disputes that parties take to law are consensual conflicts (i.e., "conflicts of interest") capable of being negotiated to a successful settlement, then the law may accomplish for the parties what, for some reason, they have been unable to accomplish for themselves. Under these circumstances legal methods may work very well to settle disputes. However, one must add the following caveat: There are certain types of consensual disputes that conventional win/lose legal methods do not handle well, with the result that methods of alternative dispute resolution are called for.

How Do Legal Systems Lose Legitimacy?

We begin by taking a closer look at the law's relationship to *dissensual disputes*. In theory, legislatures or powerful executive officials are better able than courts to deal with deep-rooted social conflicts, and there are a few notable examples of successful management of dissensual disputes by the political authorities (for example, the labor–management codes enacted by Franklin D. Roosevelt's "New Deal" administration during the 1930s). More often than not, however, conflicts requiring fundamental changes in sociopolitical systems or in public attitudes escape resolution by normal legislative processes, since political processes are insufficiently analytical to expose the conflicts' hidden causes, and since vested interests can usually block systemic reforms. Judicial processes are even less capable, under normal circumstances, of coping with serious dissensual conflicts. Effective legal systems rest on an underlying normative consensus or "social contract" that makes it possible to assume that parties, in general, will not have to be compelled by force to conform to the results of legal processes. They assume, in other words, that even if one party loses its legal case, the loss will not represent an intolerable threat to its vital interests, core values, or basic human needs, and that it will therefore accept the court's decision. Where this is not the case (for example, in the American South following the U.S. Supreme Court's decisions to end racial segregation in the schools and other public facilities), legal rulings can intensify social conflicts rather than resolve them.

This same example – the Supreme Court's reinterpretation of the law to protect the civil rights of racial minorities in the 1950s and 1960s – has other important implications for understanding the law's relationship to deep-rooted social conflict. In that case, the federal legal system played a complex and ambiguous role in resolving the dispute over legally protected racial segregation. For more than a decade, the Supreme Court's decisions provoked massive popular resistance, both violent and nonviolent, throughout the white South. The result of this resistance, after a period of years, was to trigger a counter-mobilization led by figures such as Martin Luther King, Jr., Ralph Abernathy, and John Lewis that produced an intense, region-wide social struggle between segregationist and anti-segregationist forces. By threatening the social peace and challenging the federal government's ability to govern the southern states, this struggle compelled the federal executive and legislative authorities to intervene in support of the judiciary. This result was not inevitable; in other cases, the political branches of the government have refused to support the courts. Here, however, the federal courts gained the political support needed to enforce their decisions when northern officials and popular organizations mobilized strongly to defend the cause represented by Dr. King and the civil rights workers.

In this unusual case, the legitimacy of the legal system, threatened by a local rebellion, was restored on a national basis when the national majority rallied in support of its decisions. But the limitations of this approach were revealed in later decades, when African-Americans attempted to mount legal challenges to *de facto* racial segregation in the areas of public education, housing, and employment, and when the locus of struggle shifted from legally protected to socioeconomically generated discrimination, and from the South to the North. Symbolic of the shift was King's march on Chicago in support of an end to *de facto* housing segregation. Dr. King and his followers were mobbed and (in essence) run out of the city – a defeat that was *not* followed by any massive mobilization among whites in support of the African-American position. In a number of legal cases, the federal courts attempted to deal with problems of *de facto* segregation by prescribing remedies such as the mandatory busing of white students into segregated school districts and "affirmative action" in hiring, but popular resistance to these decisions eventually forced a judicial retreat. The white majority's domination of the political process deprived the courts of the national support they had received in the southern desegregation cases. Forced to choose between a serious threat to their legitimacy and continuing the "civil rights revolution," the courts abandoned efforts to alter discriminatory practices rooted in socioeconomic conditions rather than in racist local laws.

This case suggests that attempts to resolve dissensual conflicts by legal means can succeed only when legal decisions are part of a process that maintains or re-creates a normative, system-wide consensus. Otherwise, courts and other legal institutions become a party to a conflict whose continuation over a prolonged period will almost certainly threaten their legitimacy even if their side "wins" a temporary victory. This is because the legal system's legitimacy as a conflict or dispute resolver depends strongly on the popular perception that legal institutions are neutral as between conflicting parties, or at least that they are fair and reasonably objective. (Recall our earlier discussion about "reasonableness" being the first criterion of a legal system's legitimacy.) Since people will *not* sacrifice the defense of their vital interests, cherished values, and basic needs for the sake of an abstract legalism, their perception of the legal authority's partisanship or unfairness, where these basic requirements are threatened, will lead them to commit acts of vigilantism or rebellion rather than comply with "a law that is no law." This is the great danger to legal legitimacy in an age of dissensual ethnic, racial, religious, and class conflicts.

In consensual dispute cases, on the other hand, threats to the law's legitimacy are more indirect and – up to a point, at least – handled more easily by making adaptations that move in the direction of alternative dispute resolution (ADR). The growth of ADR has been in response to two sorts of problems: undue delays and costs of litigation, and the limitations of formal judicial processes in certain types of cases.

First, in societies such as the USA, the court system (including quasi-judicial administrative agencies) has become so crowded with cases, and legal assistance has become so costly, that many potential litigants are denied in practice their right to have recourse to the courts. This is not merely because these societies are unusually litigious, but because the rapid pace of social and technological change constantly creates new forms of property (for example, computer software and engineered genes) that generate new legal claims and defenses (Reich, 1995). New forms of property increase the opportunities and temptations to engage in disputes and give rise to new government regulations requiring legal interpretation. Furthermore, higher levels of demand for social order generate new criminal laws and stricter enforcement of these laws, with the result that court dockets become jammed with criminal cases (especially petty property crimes and drug cases). Given this pressure

on court dockets and litigants' pocket-books, there has been an understandable turn toward processes of mediation, arbitration, med-arb,
victim–offender reconciliation, and other alternative dispute resolution
procedures that offer to be more informal and efficient, less costly, and
more satisfactory in their results than formal court or administrative
proceedings. The extent to which these claims are   justified has given
rise to some controversy, but the growth of ADR suggests that many
parties believe they are preferable to court procedures.

Second, even where recourse to the courts is not blocked, the nature
of judicial decision-making is such that certain kinds of case may not be
decided to the satisfaction of the parties involved. The law has long
recognized that some cases (denominated "equity" cases in Anglo-
American law) require decision-making that is not based on legal precedent so much as the court's sense of fairness and a practical
commitment to providing the parties with what they need. To put this
somewhat differently, normal judicial proceedings in which arguments
are based on precedent are governed by the principle of equal justice:
"Treat like parties and situations alike." But equity proceedings – for
example, proceedings to establish the appropriate custodian for the
children of divorcing parents – are governed by the principle, "Give each
party what he or she deserves." Now, in many societies there has been a
large increase in cases that are more appropriate for equitable than for
conventional legal decision-making. An example is the sort of case that
calls for what Fuller (1978) has termed "polycentric decision-making":
decisions in which the court must use its practical judgment to adju-
dicate claims made by multiple parties, when each decision made affects
all other decisions that must be made. (A classic case is a dispute
between heirs over which pieces of property left by the deceased should
go to which claimants, when the will only provides that the estate
should be divided in some proportion between them.) Fuller argued that
court proceedings are not well designed to make such decisions equitably, whereas mediation and other processes of ADR may produce far
more satisfactory results.

It may be argued that the increase in demand for ADR is due, above
all, to the increase in demand for forms of dispute resolution tailored to
the particular interests and needs of the parties. Of course, judicial
decision-making is not as rigid as it is sometimes said to be. Courts have
often found ways to induce the parties to arrive at negotiated settlements, or have devised innovative remedies that represent outcomes
that a negotiated settlement might produce. Even so, the search by
disputing parties for forms of resolution that will not impoverish them,
saddle them with unacceptable legal results, publicize confidential
matters, or destroy personal relationships has generated increasing

interest even among large companies in ADR processes. In this connection, it is important to recognize that while these processes *are* often capable of producing satisfactory results, they function not so much as an "alternative" as an *adjunct* to more formal and public legal procedures. Negotiation in ADR processes still takes place in the "shadow of the law," with the parties generally reserving their rights to have recourse to the courts. Furthermore, in most ADR cases, the assumptions about the conflict and its causes made by the parties and practitioners are similar, if not identical, to the assumptions made by the parties to judicial proceedings. To the extent that ADR (which many courts now order as part of their own dispute settlement process) is successful, therefore, the effect is to help maintain the legitimacy of the legal system as a whole. However, in general, ADR processes are no more capable than legal procedures of achieving a satisfactory resolution of serious *dissensual* disputes.

Conclusion: The Need for New Forms of Legitimacy

To resolve serious dissensual disputes satisfactorily requires creating a new normative consensus: that is, a new basis for the exercise of legitimate authority. If this cannot be accomplished by legal methods or by adjunctive ADR processes, how is it to be done? The answer, explored in other chapters of this book, requires processes of conflict resolution that are deeply analytical, highly imaginative, strongly evaluative, and, in the end, linked to forms of transformative politics. Deep analysis, often requiring expert non-partisan facilitation, is necessary to identify the basic human needs, core values, and vital interests that the parties feel are unsatisfied or threatened, as well as the systemic sources of these failures and threats. A high level of imagination is required to help the parties envision options for resolution capable of restoring the decayed or vanished consensus that they had not previously considered or taken seriously. Strong, tough-minded evaluation is called for in order to weigh the costs and benefits of each option, and to consider methods of implementing an agreement, if there should be one. And politics returns, in the end, as a necessary method of providing popular input and gaining popular support for a process aimed at constructing or reconstructing consensus. Processes of conflict resolution cannot guarantee success in this difficult endeavor, but conflict resolvers have the advantage of letting the endeavor define their goals and methods instead of seeking to defend some prior form of legitimacy, whether customary, charismatic, or legal.

For conflict resolvers the great challenge of the future is to develop further the theoretical insights and practical methods that will enable those locked in destructive dissensual conflicts to rebuild consensus and restore legitimate authority to systems that presently lack it. This will mean focusing their attention precisely on those aspects of social life in which legal authority is most controverted and has become most ineffective. *Crime*, for example, has become endemic even in many industrially advanced societies with highly developed legal systems. Clearly, multiplying criminal laws and prosecutions and filling the prisons has not proved to be an effective method of resolving the conflict between lawbreakers and law enforcers (and the social institutions that employ them). But multifaceted, analytical, imaginative conflict resolution processes linked to movements for political change may be able to restore legitimacy by dealing, at long last, with the root causes of crime rather than remaining on the level of symptomology and short-term responses. Again, *religious conflicts* around the world have increased and intensified to a level that few Western analysts and policy-makers predicted. Legal authority seems singularly ineffective when confronted by conflicts featuring intense ideological dissensus and clashing moral values. Conflict resolvers, on the other hand, are struggling to analyze the issues in greater depth, and to develop new forms of dialog that will permit parties with differing worldviews to communicate with each other in a humane way about the deeper causes of their struggle (Gopin, 2000).

Finally, escalating contemporary conflicts over the *effects of socio-economic globalization* escape legal resolution, not least because they take place across national boundaries. At present, no legal or political authority seems able to provide the combination of analytical, imaginative, evaluative, and political skills needed to expose the root causes of these conflicts and to develop effective methods of resolving them. Conflict analysts and resolvers may have a better chance to succeed if they focus their energies as independent researchers and peacemakers on exploring the real processes and less obvious effects of globalization, as well as the claims and counter-claims presented by the defenders and detractors of institutions such as the World Bank and World Trade Organization. The questions that no party to this conflict has yet faced seriously are: Assuming that the current system is dysfunctional in some respects, what feasible alternatives to the present structure of global socioeconomic power exist? Would any alternative or combination of alternatives resolve the conflict by dealing with its underlying causes? If so, how might a workable alternative be constructed and implemented? By assisting the parties to answer questions such as these, conflict resolution processes themselves might claim a legitimacy that legal processes (as well as custom and charisma) seem to have lost. In the same way that modern legal systems re-legitimized certain traditional customs by transcending and, in effect, replacing them, the doctrines and practices of conflict resolution may one day re-legitimize law.

Discussion Questions

1 What are the major strengths and weaknesses of legal systems as mechanisms for resolving disputes? Does your answer depend upon the type of dispute requiring resolution?
2 What are the major types of legitimate authority? Can you find examples of each type still existing in modern Western societies? Are some types more prevalent or important than others?
3 "Justice" can be defined in several different ways, which sometimes produce conflicting definitions. Choose a social conflict that interests you and describe how each party to the conflict defines it.

Key Words

Alternative dispute resolution (ADR)
Arbitration
Charismatic authority
Conflict resolution
Consensual conflict
Corpus juris
Customary (traditional) authority
Dispute resolution
Dissensual conflict
Equity
Legal norm
Legal system (characteristics of)
Legitimate authority
Mediation
Modernization
Negotiation "in the shadow of the law"
Normative consensus
Normative dissensus
Polycentric decision-making
Procedural justice
Rational-legal authority
Substantive justice

Part III

Intervening in Conflict

Introduction to Part III

Part III, as depicted by the wavy arrows in the diagram (Figure 1.1) in Chapter 1, is about intervention. We have designated four types of intervention in our framework: negotiation, informal intervention, formal intervention, and systemic intervention. Negotiation (Chapter 14), which does not involve any third parties, refers to the parties' attempts to resolve their own differences without the assistance of others. The other three types entail a variety of roles for third parties. These roles may be informal (Chapter 15), meaning that those intervening may be family members, friends, neighbors, police, or social workers. Although many individuals in those roles practice conflict resolution every day, it is not part of a formal process of resolving conflict. Those involved in formal processes include mediators and arbitrators (Chapter 16), third parties involved in problem-solving activities (Chapter 17), conciliators and facilitators (Chapter 18), and peacekeepers (Chapter 19). The last type of intervention is systemic, involving attempts to change the structures and systems within which conflict occurs. We describe structural transformation (Chapter 20) and delineate a variety of roles for those involved in peace-building activities (Chapter 21).

Despite our brief explanation of this typology of intervention, Figure 1.1 does not show or explain for us what intervention actually is. Intervention is a topic of much debate within scholarly literature. James Laue, an ICAR faculty member at the time of his death in 1993, defines it as follows: "Conflict 'intervention' occurs when an outside or semi-outside party self-consciously enters into a conflict situation with the objective of influencing the conflict in a direction the intervenor defines as desirable" (Laue, 1987, p. 20). Laue's definition contains two essential elements – that intervention requires a deliberate action by an outside or a partial intervenor, and that it alters the conflict in some way. Although his definition is subject to criticism (such as Mitchell's critique that the definition does not take into account the unintended effects of intervention), it provides a starting point for Part III. Laue's emphasis on the purposeful nature of intervention implies the need for analysis in order to determine what a desirable action might involve. Parts I and II precede this final section in order to lay the foundation for an analysis of conflict. Part I proposes a typology of conflict as well as its sources and dynamics, while Part II provides clues about the influences and contextual elements that may be especially salient in any particular conflict. This section of the textbook captures the range of possible interventions that conflict scholars study and write about and conflict resolution practitioners most commonly use. The revised edition addresses a lacuna from the previous version and includes a chapter on peace operations.

Part III begins with negotiation. While negotiation, by definition, does not include a third-party intervenor, it does represent the parties' own attempts to resolve, and thereby influence, the direction in which their conflict is headed. Chapter 11 presents both general and specific research findings related to negotiation, with a particular concentration on social psychological research. These findings address the influence of emotion, culture, and the processes and conditions of negotiation upon the eventual result. The summary of game and decision-making research highlights the importance of trust in negotiation, while the social psychological research emphasizes the interactive nature of negotiation. The focus of this chapter, a presentation of the research about negotiation, reflects the long history of research and theorizing about negotiation, something lacking as the chapters turn to newer topics of study.

One of these newer topics of study is "Informal Roles," the subject of Chapter 15. Not all conflict interventions have formalized third-party roles, as this chapter suggests. In the public domain, police officers, parents, clergy members, and others play informal roles as third parties, attempting to intervene in a way they deem desirable. For police officers, the law influences the parameters of their intervention and their manner of intervening, while parents or clergy have other concerns such as the welfare of their children or religious teachings at the forefront. We point out that these roles, although extremely important in everyday conflict resolution, have received little theoretical or research attention.

In contrast, mediation and arbitration, the subject of Chapter 16, have long histories and a wealth of research to support the practice and theory. The chapter traces the lengthy history of mediation and arbitration, both in North American and non-Western contexts. The history includes many of the advances in theory and research, as well as details about the practice of mediation and arbitration. The chapter differentiates between several models of mediation and summarizes how mediation has become institutionalized in the USA and beyond. It contains discussions of power, neutrality, and impact, all of which impact on perceptions of the advantages and disadvantages of mediation.

Chapter 17 on problem-solving workshops marks a further turn toward conflict interventions with relatively newer histories. In this chapter, drawing extensively from practical experience, we present the principles underlying problem-solving interventions, most notably what Fisher (1997a) refers to as "interactive conflict resolution." These principles include redefining the problem, correcting negative misperceptions, the search for causal complexity and unrecognized options, identifying unrecognized entrapment, and adopting an analytical versus an adversarial posture. This chapter focuses largely on the practice of problem-solving, with space devoted to the theoretical logic behind each of the principles. The final section about the role of facilitators in problem-solving provides a neat segue to the following chapter on facilitation and consultation.

Chapter 18, in contrast to many of the other chapters in Part III, discusses interventions at multiple levels. Facilitation is usually confined to the interpersonal and intra- and intergroup levels, while consultation has evolved to refer to interventions at the international level. We discuss facilitation and consultation in broad terms, focusing specifically on process and its relationship to content and the roles of facilitators and consultants. This discussion spans the similarities between problem-solving and "appreciative inquiry," an emerging corollary intervention that appreciates what is and envisions what might be. It also discusses the increasing use of dialogue. The chapter concludes with a summary of the theory, practice, and research, and a call for more evaluation of these intervention processes.

Another form of third-party intervention is discussed in Chapter 19 on peace operations. In contrast to many of the other interventions covered in this part, peace operations involve large numbers of people, are usually conducted by military units, and are intended primarily to manage violent conflicts. These interventions often occur following negotiated cease-fire agreements. The authors of this chapter write about the multiple purposes or types of peace operations, the kinds of actors involved in them, and the many challenges that confront peacekeepers and peacekeeping policies. Of particular interest are the expanded mandates for many contemporary operations. Peacekeepers are increasingly performing functions associated with conflict resolution, including many of the third-party roles discussed in other chapters of this part. The inclusion of these practices encourages the development of a broadened, more complex framework of peace operations. The chapter authors make progress toward this goal.

The next chapter, on structural transformation, continues the focus on macro-level interventions. It reminds us that all conflicts, and indeed all interventions, have structural dimensions. The study and practice of how to transform structures, however, is relatively new. As a result, the field still struggles with the theory and practice of structural transformation. Conflict transformation, peace-building, and "post-conflict reconstruction" are the subject of much recent debate and writing, and the field has a long way to go before reaching any kind of consensus about how to address structural conflict.

The final chapter on the subject of third-party roles in peace-building provides a neat complement to our previous discussions of the structural elements of conflict transformation. It describes, in particular, the various practical and theoretical roles for third-party intervenors in designing and implementing peace agreements, illustrating the accompanying challenges and factors affecting the nature and type of intervention with examples from recent international experience. These roles include conflict resolution training and practice, rehabilitation and development, and democratization and support for new political structures. Because the practice and theory of peace-building intervention is so new, little systematic research exists on these topics.

This section proves we have advanced the theory, research, and practice of conflict resolution processes at very different rates. Interventions with a longer history, such as negotiation and mediation, have received more research attention, while newer interventions, such as conflict transformation, still have a long way to catch up. Further evaluation, a bridge between research and practice, has much to contribute to all forms of intervention and remains a topic for future generations of conflict resolution theorists, practitioners, and researchers.

CHAPTER 12

Globalization

Agnieszka Paczynska

Introduction

We live in a world that has over the last few decades become much more integrated. The volume of trade, foreign direct investment, and capital movements have rapidly expanded. New communications technologies and cheaper travel have made us not only more aware of distant cultures and places but have made it possible for us to experience events differently than we have in the past. This perhaps became especially clear when the events of September 11, 2001 unfolded on TV screens across the world in real time. In other words, peoples and societies that may not have even been aware of each other's existence only a few years ago, now encounter one another in multiple venues and in multiple forms, leading to the compression of time and space. As Giddens argues,

> Globalization ... can be defined as the intensification of worldwide social relations which link distant localities in such a way that local happenings are shaped by events occurring many miles away and vice versa. (Giddens, 1990, p. 64)

Globalization processes have, in profound ways, transformed and reshaped the economic, political, cultural, and technological environment in which human interactions take place. Furthermore, the pace of change has accelerated significantly, thus leaving less time for individuals, societies, and states to adjust and respond to the new contexts in which they must now exist. The accelerated pace of change is dislodging old values and ways of organizing political life, undermining traditional norms, and demanding greater flexibility from both governments and people. Thus, many analysts anticipate that at least in the short term globalization processes, like other periods of rapid change, are likely to generate more tensions and conflicts. There is, however, much less unanimity among scholars as to the long-term influence of globalization on conflict processes.

The debate in social sciences concerning the impact of globalization on conflict processes has been contentious and deeply divisive. Although conflict is an inevitable component of social change and is often a creative force, it can also be destructive and violent. For some analysts, globalization processes, by challenging local cultural, religious, and moral codes, and imposing Western, secular, and materialist values alien to indigenous ways of organizing social life, are contributing to the emergence of new cultural and religious conflicts. The imposition of these alien cultural norms along with economic dominance and exploitation is, according to these global chaos theorists, reviving primordial ethnic identities and eliciting local resistance that is often expressed through the construction of an idealized past and in a violent reaction against forces that are perceived as threatening that idealized past (Huntington, 1992; Barber, 1993; Kaplan, 1994). For others, the link between globalization processes and ethnic and cultural conflict is at best indirect or simply non-existent. These analysts point to the numerous studies that show that the degree of economic openness and integration into the global markets correlates with less, not more, ethnic and cultural conflicts (Ishiyama, 2004; Sadowski, 1998; Bhagwati, 2005). These profound differences in how globalization is viewed and its influence on conflict dynamics is reflected in other areas of investigation as well. Whether exploring the relationship between globalization processes and distributive conflicts, inter-state war, civil war, or human rights, there is little agreement among scholars as to what this relationship is.

This disagreement is not surprising. Globalization is a complex set of processes that have profoundly reshaped how people, societies, and states interact with one another. For some, these changes have been beneficial. For others they have been detrimental. But few have been unaffected by these transformations. In other words, both views of globalization are to some extent correct, for globalization is not experienced in the same way by all social groups or world regions. In Milanovic's apt words,

> Globalization being such a huge and multifaceted process presents different faces to different people. Depending on where we live, whether we are rich or poor, where we stand ideologically, we are

bound to see the process differently . . . globalization has two faces: the benign one, based on voluntary exchanges and free circulation of people, capital, goods and ideas; and the other face, based on coercion and brute force. (Milanovic, 2003, p. 668)

We are only beginning to understanding the complex relationship between globalization and conflict processes. A growing number of studies on globalization are shedding light on the often contradictory effects of this phenomenon. A particularly fruitful body of work seeks to disaggregate globalization into discrete components and investigate its influence on different types of conflict dynamics while recognizing and acknowledging that globalization is in fact multi-dimensional. What emerges from these studies suggests that depending on the facet of globalization that we are exploring and the type of conflict we are analyzing, the relationships between them can vary significantly. What also seems to matter greatly is the region of the world that we are focusing on in our investigation. While globalization has affected most parts of the globe, it has not affected all parts in the same way or to the same degree. Hence the relationship between it and conflict dynamics is not always straightforward. Furthermore, in the same locales globalization processes often have contradictory effects, and although they may become a source of new grievances and perceive injustices, they may also provide new opportunities for expression of group values and interests. In the rest of this chapter, we will explore just some of the complex ways in which globalization processes affect conflict dynamics. This will not be an exhaustive treatment of the field. Rather, the chapter will highlight how existing scholarship is seeking to understand how this new international environment is affecting patterns of social interaction.

Economic Integration and Conflict Between States

For some students of globalization, economic integration is the best means of ensuring that a more socially just and peaceful world can be created. Bhagwati (2005), for example, acknowledges that the contemporary world suffers from numerous problems, inequalities, injustices, and inequities. He argues, however, that these problems largely predate the contemporary globalization era. It is by integrating and embracing globalization processes, rather than rejecting them, that societies can best address both the structural and the manifest conflicts that plague them.

A large body of literature also argues that growing economic integration is creating conditions that facilitate the peaceful resolution of international conflicts. It does so by fundamentally changing the way states evaluate their interests and how they pursue those interests. Most significantly, the more economically interdependent countries are, peace becomes more beneficial and war more costly to states. This is because economic integration creates conditions of mutual dependence that make severing such ties very difficult and painful. For some analysts in fact, the greater the degree of mutual dependence, the less likelihood of armed conflict (Polachek, 1980). Furthermore, dense economic relationships mean that there are more points of contact between states and thus, as Duetsch for instance argues, "trade and other forms of intercultural exchange ... help foster development of a sense of community which makes the resort to violent forms of conflict resolution increasingly unlikely" (Deutsch, 1954). Growing integration also has spill-over effects manifested primarily in the emergence of shared norms and complex institutions that link societies together, thus facilitating mutual understanding and providing new channels through which tensions and conflicts between states and societies can be resolved peacefully (Oneal and Russett, 1999). According to these studies, because states benefit from increased trade, they come to care more about absolute gains rather than relative gains. At the same time, the multiple points of contact between economically integrated states create interest groups within such societies which benefit from these relationships, and therefore will pressure their governments to ensure that these relationships remain peaceful. When such deep economic integration is combined with pluralistic political systems, war between states becomes highly unlikely (Oneal and Russetts, 1999; Hegre, 2002).

Additionally, in this view, in the contemporary era new forms of economic organization and production mean that how states pursue their interests have changed dramatically. Because production in today's world is so dispersed, it is virtually impossible for a state to acquire the wealth generated through such production through territorial conquest. Territorial conquest becomes even less attractive to states looking to augment their power because so much of the value-added in today's economy comes not from extraction of natural resources, oil being an exception, but from knowledge-based industries, and thus occupying a particular territory will not guarantee the control of the wealth generated within its borders. Furthermore, in a world where domestic economies rely so heavily on transnational financial transactions and capital movements, territorial invasion may cut off the occupier from important sources of international revenue thus making conquest less attractive (Rosencrance, 1996; Brooks, 2005). Recent data, in fact, point to a dramatic decrease in the number of interstate wars (Human Security Report, 2005).

Economic Integration and Internal Violent Conflict

Other scholars note, however, that the focus on war between states ignores the relationship between globalization and internal conflicts. As the number of international conflicts decline, civil wars have become a more common form of strife in the contemporary era. In this view, globalization processes are creating an environment that is conflict-generating both in the short and in the long term (Mittelman, 2000). These analyses point to inequalities and inequities that have emerged within societies as well as between states. These have grown as a consequence of the economic changes associated with opening up of domestic markets to international competition, the weakening and often withdrawal of the state from providing social services such as education, health care, and consumer subsidies, and the growing foreign debt burden. These changes are creating conditions that are socially unjust and increase the probability of violent conflict.

These critics charge that much of the evidence marshaled by those who, like Bhagwati, argue that neoliberal economic globalization has benefited the world's poor, comes from data that are often of suspect quality and that rely too heavily on economic dynamics in two countries, China and India. But if these two are excluded, the picture looks far grimmer. Growth has been anemic in most parts of the world, including advanced industrialized countries, and inequalities have been growing internationally. Moreover, globalization processes have made it easier for transnational drug cartels, criminal mafias, and terrorist networks, as well as other non-state actors who challenge the state's monopoly on the control of violence to expand their activities and function with greater ease.

The complexity of globalization processes leads us to suspect that both views of how globalization has affected violent conflict are to some extent true. Although in parts of the globe these changes have encouraged "a virtuous cycle of growth, prosperity and stability," the same processes have also brought about "durable forms of disparity, instability, and complexity" (Duffield, 2000, p. 70). Thus, while the democratic and highly industrialized countries of the "Global North" have been experiencing less civil strife, countries of the "Global South," where economies are still largely based on the production and extraction of primary commodities and where authoritarian political systems continue to dominate, have continued to witness conflict and war. In these poor states we are more likely to see the emergence of what Paul Collier and his collaborators have termed the conflict trap. Poor societies tend to experience more violent political conflict, including civil wars, than wealthier societies. Civil wars leave in their wake a devastated society, economy, and infrastructure. In other words, a post-conflict society is likely to be even poorer than when the conflict started, and thus at greater risk of seeing the conflict re-ignite (Collier, 2003).

Although in recent decades civil wars have become the dominant form of mass political violence, the relationship between civil wars and globalization is far from clear. As Woodward notes, while the number of civil wars has been fluctuating and in fact their numbers have recently declined, global economic integration has been accelerating (Woodward, 2005). In other words, economic integration by itself does not seem to affect the incidence of civil wars. Furthermore, most violence occurs in countries that are the least integrated into the global economy as measured by almost any standard indictor, for instance, volume of trade and foreign direct investment.

Do globalization processes affect the incidence internal of violent conflict, and if so through what mechanisms? A number of recent studies suggest that the relationship is quite complex. Different aspects of globalization appear to have differing influence on internal conflict. Likewise, globalization processes seem to have varied influence on different types of internal conflict.

Gessinger and Gleditsch (1999), for instance, find that trade and foreign direct investment shape internal conflict in distinct ways. While foreign direct investment tends to generate political instability, trade has a more pacifying effect. However, it also matters what is being traded. In particular, they point out that countries that rely primarily on exports of agricultural commodities tend to experience more strife than those where manufacturing exports predominate. This is because societies with agriculture-based economies tend to be poorer and more unequal. Le Billon (2001) comes to a similar conclusion and notes that, "most empirical evidence suggests that countries economically dependent on the export of primary commodities are at a higher risk of political instability and armed conflict"(pp. 562-63). The devastating war in the Congo is one instance where the existence of a highly valuable natural resource (coltan) allowed warring factions to continue the fight by tapping into global markets.

Others find that economic interdependence between states reduces the likelihood of internal conflict (Hegre, Gissinger, and Gleditsch, 2003). Gleditsch finds that especially significant for establishing internal peace are highly integrated regional economic systems. In such areas, neighbors are dependent on each other for their economic well-being and will therefore seek to ensure peaceful relations with their neighbors and will avoid sponsoring rebel movements in neighboring countries since such rebellions would have negative regional repercussions. Hence, those regions that are more economically integrated will experience fewer conflicts (Gledistch, 2007).

Globalization processes can, in some circumstances, create conditions that facilitate the emergence of violent conflict as a consequence of the changes in state structures and state capabilities, as well as the emergence of new international actors. One of the consequences of economic globalization has been the weakening of the state at least in some regions. Especially in poorer countries, saddled with foreign debt and required to implement structural adjustment policies which entail limiting the state's role in the country's economic life, the shrinking state has created a window of opportunity for various criminal organizations to move in. This has proven to have especially negative consequences where violent conflict was already brewing or had already erupted since the parties to the conflict now had greater ability to tap into international markets to sustain their campaigns. As Duffield notes, although "globalization and liberalization have not caused these new forms of instability, they have made it easier for warring parties to establish the parallel and transborder economic linkages necessary for survival" (Duffield, 2000, p. 74).

At the same time, states, even wealthy states, find it increasingly difficult to effectively confront these new criminal networks. For one, the sheer volume of international financial transactions and the numbers of people moving across international borders means that monitoring of illicit activities is extremely difficult, if not impossible. Furthermore, traffickers in arms, drugs, and people, as well as money launderers are more flexible than the states that confront them. In states that are poor and lack effective state institutions, these criminal networks can move in all the more easily and once established, prove even more difficult to confront, contributing to internal violence. As Naim (2003) points out,

> It pits governments against agile, stateless and resourceful networks empowered by globalization. . . . Globalization has not only expanded illegal markets and boosted the size and resources of criminal networks, it has also imposed more burdens on the governments: tighter public budgets, decentralization, privatization, deregulation, and a more open environment for international trade and investment all make the task of fighting global criminal networks more difficult. Global crime has not just soared in volume but, thanks to its ability to amass colossal profits has also become a powerful political force. (pp. 29-30)

Neoliberal Economic Reforms

Many poor countries have been experiencing globalization not through direct integration into global production or financial networks, but rather through the implementation of structural adjustment programs.

Designed by the International Financial Institutions (the International Monetary Fund and the World Bank), these programs have commonly included cutting public expenditures, including various social services, the privatization of the public sector, and the opening up of the economy to international competition. By implementing these neoliberal reforms, supporters argue, poor countries can jump start economic development. In this view, integration into the global economy and the implementation of economic restructuring may in the short term increase social tensions. However, over the long term, because these policies are likely to result in improved economic performance and growth in per capita incomes, they are likely to reduce distributive conflicts within society.

Regardless of the long-term consequences of these policy changes, they clearly alter the political, economic, and social environment in which people encounter the state and one another. Although some social groups have benefited from these economic changes, others have struggled to survive and have become increasingly marginalized and impoverished. Not surprisingly, groups whose previous socio-economic status and security are threatened or undermined by these changes have often resisted these restructuring policies. In other words, for many the economic policies associated with globalization and structural adjustment have been a source of new grievances.

Among groups most negatively affected by the changes were often the urban workers, especially those employed in state-owned enterprises. Many of the new policies had an immediate and often devastating impact on this population. Especially painful were the cuts in many subsidies on consumer goods, reduction of various social services available at reduced cost, and the privatization of the public sector. Sale of state firms to private owners almost always entailed reductions in levels of employment. At the same time, privatization was often also accompanied by changes in laws governing labor markets with the overall result of making jobs less secure than they had been prior to the initiation of structural adjustment policies. Women have also tended to bear most of the reform costs. Although new opportunities for employment outside the home often became available, the reduction in social services and in particular health, education, and social security, meant that women had to shoulder additional burdens of caring for sick and elderly relatives as well as taking on additional child caring responsibilities. Simultaneously, the reduction in consumer subsidies means that women in many parts of the world took on growing food on their own in order to supplement their families' diets (Moghadam, 2005).

Furthermore, new communications technologies have made people much more aware of not only how those better off in their societies live, but also how those in other world regions' live, thus often deepening the sense of relative deprivation (Birdsall, Graham, and Pettinato, 2000). Depending on the resources available to particular groups and the specific institutional and political context in which they exist, they can and often do engage in protest actions, be they in the form of demonstrations, strikes, or at the ballot box. One study found that such conflicts were especially likely to occur in highly urbanized countries that also had high levels of International Monetary Fund involvement (Walton and Ragin, 1990). Social conflict is also more likely to intensify if there is a perception that the costs of reforms are not equitably distributed and that some groups, be they classes or ethnic or religious minorities, are shouldering most of the burden.

In addition to generating distributive conflicts locally in countries undertaking structural adjustment reforms, tensions have been mounting in many countries because of the widespread perception that the rules that govern the international economy have been designed by the dominant states of the "Global North" and in particular the United States, and thus benefit those states at the expense of countries of the "Global South." In other words, there is a widespread perception that the way the international economy has been constructed and how it functions is deeply flawed and socially unjust. Numerous public opinion surveys and focus groups have found that although people do not reject globalization wholesale and in fact see a lot of benefits flowing from the growing global integration, nonetheless they are deeply dissatisfied and often angered by many changes associated with globalization processes. Scholte, in his in-depth interviews with civil society leaders, found that there was a prevailing sense of powerlessness and a perception that ordinary people have little ability to influence and shape policies that affect their daily lives. Rather than participating in and benefiting from growing global integration, there was a sense that most social groups were being left behind. Among those Scholte interviewed, "less than a dozen had a positive assessment of the state of democracy in the current regulation of global trade, global investment, global finance, global communications, and global migration [and that] most judgments were harshly negative" (Scholte, 2000, p. 18).

A similar picture emerges out of a survey conducted in 2003 by the Pew Research Center for the People and the Press (38,000 people in 44 countries participated in the study). Most people see globalization as a force that has, over the last few decades, become a routine part of their lives and is experienced through travel, trade, financial transactions, communications, and culture. Yet, despite its central presence in their lives, most reported concerns about the social problems, deteriorating financial conditions, and the growing gap between the rich and the poor that were part the changes associated with globalization processes. Equally important were concerns about the loss of traditional ways of life (Pew Research Center, 2003).

A recent report by the International Labor Organization comes to a similar conclusion. The study finds "that people see deep-seated and persistent imbalances in the current working of the global economy and find it ethically unacceptable and politically unsustainable since there is a perception of a growing polarization between winners and losers" of changes associated with globalization (ILO, 2004, p. 3). There is also a widespread perception that the rules governing the global economy are unfair and that they tend to reinforce and further solidify the inequalities and inequities. Singled out for criticism were the structural adjustment programs promoted by the International Financial Institutions, which were widely seen as further marginalizing and making more insecure the most vulnerable groups in societies and in particular, workers, women, the indigenous, and the poor. At the same time, most thought that the processes of globalization have raised expectations without actually creating new opportunities, thus deepening a sense of injustice and resentment (ILO, 2004, p. 4). Overall, although the report finds that people largely favor openness to the global economy and interconnections between societies, they are also concerned about their livelihoods and want to see better social protection, income security, and fairer rules for governing the global economy than those that exist today.

Mobilizing Transnationally

The growing concerns about the consequences of economic globalization and the pervasive sense of insecurity and resentment help us understand the reasons for the recent emergence of a transnational social justice movement, often referred to in the media as the anti-globalization movement. Although protests against neoliberal economic policies are not new and have been frequent since the 1980s when many developing countries began to implement structural adjustment policies, what is distinctive about the new wave of protests is that participants have made an explicit and concerted effort to both form transnational alliances and linkages, and frame the movement's goals in transnationally meaningful ways. Thus, changes associated with economic globalization have generated new grievances while at this same time provided new opportunities for mobilizing and organizing to address those grievances.

The social justice movement has been a diverse coalition and has included groups promoting labor rights, human rights, and environmental causes, among others. Although these groups have multiple agendas that are often in tension with one another, what they do have in common is their view that neoliberal economic policies promoted by the International Financial Institutions have deepened inequalities both within and between states; that they have favored multinational corporations at the expense of working people and the environment; that rather than ensuring sustainable development, they have led to the deterioration of education, health, and living standards of poor people; and more fundamentally, that they have been designed by and benefit only the rich and powerful. As Ayers notes, "critical to its [protest movement's] development has been the crystallization of a broadly interpretive, increasingly transnationally shared diagnostic frame that attributes a variety of social ills of the past 15-20 years span of neoliberal ascendancy. The record of neoliberalism has given a wealth of shared experiences from which to fashion a meaningful and increasingly transnationally shared understanding of the perceived negative effects of such policies" (Ayers, 2004, p. 13).

Reflecting the complex nature of the phenomenon, while many changes associated with globalization have negatively affected the socioeconomic status of many social groups, other changes have afforded these often marginalized groups new opportunities to more effectively press their claims and make their voices heard in the public arena. In particular, changes in communications technologies, new human rights norms, and the growth of transnational non-governmental organizations, transnational social networks, and transnational social movements, have allowed those who otherwise had few opportunities and means to shape policy debates to form alliances across borders, thereby strengthening their local bargaining position (Brysk, 1996). By facilitating access to new resources, expertise, and international media outlets, transnational organizations, networks, and movements help marginalized groups to engage governments more effectively. They also draw international attention to local problems and conflicts that otherwise may have gone unnoticed, thus providing local groups with new sources of leverage. Such transnational connections have proven especially important in cases where the local political landscape is highly repressive and opportunities for organizing and mobilizing are few. In such cases, local groups' international supporters can bring pressure to bear on governments to change unjust and oppressive policies. As Sikkink and Keck point out, this boomerang effect can serve to push through significant changes at the local level (Sikkink and Keck, 1998) and allow local groups to frame their grievances that resonate with international audiences which in turn facilitates gaining access to new resources and assistance (Guidry, Kennedy, and Zald, 2000, p. 3).

Transnational non-governmental organizations, networks, and social movements have also brought various issues to international attention and have thus been able to often significantly shape and influence international policies toward conflict issues. For example, the international campaign to ban landmines succeeded in pushing states to sign the Mine Ban Treaty in December 1997. The Treaty became binding under international law in March 1999 when the fortieth of the 122 signatory governments ratified the Treaty. Similarly, various civil society organizations were instrumental in putting in place the Kimberly Process that seeks to control the export of diamonds from conflict areas. Transnational non-governmental actors have also sometimes succeeded in shaping state and corporate behavior indirectly through changing norms that govern our everyday life, by making some issues more salient and making certain behaviors less acceptable than they had been in the past. It is largely thanks to transnational organizing that the problem of sweatshops in the developing world has become part of the political discourse in Western Europe and the United States. Although much progress still needs to be made to ensure decent wages and working conditions in such enterprises, nonetheless the pressure from civil society groups on multinational corporations such as Nike and Gap have forced them to be more attentive to the labor issues as they outsource their production. Through such activities, furthermore, as Keck and Sikkink note, by blurring the boundaries between a state's relations with its own nationals and the recourse both citizens and states have to the international system, advocacy networks are helping to transform the practice of national sovereignty (Keck and Sikkink, 1998, pp. 1-2).

Conclusion

Globalization processes have pushed the world toward ever greater integration and have accelerated the pace of change. By expanding the interactions between peoples, societies, and states, these processes have profound influence on conflict dynamics. However, as this chapter has underscored, the relationship between various transformations associated with globalization and different conflict processes are very complex and are not yet fully understood. In some circumstances some changes brought on by globalization seem to be facilitating the establishment of more cooperative and peaceful relations between states. In other cases, the opposite trend appears to dominate, with globalization processes contributing to the aggravation of old conflicts as well as the creation of new ones. The challenge before conflict analysts now is to better understand these diverse and often contradictory dynamics.

Addressing and resolving many of the conflicts that globalization processes have deepened will be a difficult challenge. For instance, stemming the flow of illicit goods and arms that have helped fuel much violence and civil wars is difficult not only because of the volume of trade involved but also because such trade crossed international state boundaries. Crafting effective ways of stopping such trade requires not only tremendous resources but also coordination between various state and non-state actors who may often be hostile toward one another. However, as the Kimberly Process indicates, transnational civil society which has grown thanks to many of the changes brought on by globalization can play a constructive role in shaping responses to such illicit trade. Clearly, in and of itself, making funding for rebel groups and state actors more difficult to secure is only the first step toward resolving protracted civil conflicts. But often this is an important first step.

Rethinking the organization of international economy which most people see as deeply unjust and unfairly favoring the dominant world powers, and especially the United States, will not be easy. At least two very basic challenges must be met. First, alternative arrangements which would address the underlying causes behind the distributive conflicts in and between societies would have to be proposed. This in itself is likely to prove difficult. As the global justice movement has demonstrated, even when there is a common diagnosis of a problem, crafting a common alternative is very contentious. If an alternative way of organizing the international economy can be formulated and win broad acceptance, the second challenge will be to convince and compel those who benefit from current arrangements to support change. Acknowledging the difficulties, however, should not imply that inaction. Some of the recent proposals for the World Bank and the International Monetary Fund to make their management more transparent, more accountable, and more responsive to all their member states and not just those who form the largest voting block in both (the G-8 countries and especially the United States) point to the potential alternatives.

Discussion Questions

1 What is globalization?
2 Do processes associated with globalization affect all parts of the globe in the same way, and if not what are some of the important differences?
3 In what ways might globalization processes be facilitating the resolution of conflicts?
4 In what ways might globalization processes be contributing to conflicts?
5 What role does transnational civil society play in addressing conflicts generated by globalization processes?

Key Words

Globalization
Compression of time and space
Neoliberal economics
Social classes
Distributive conflicts
Global North
Global South
International Financial Institutions
Transnational civil society
Transnational criminal networks

CHAPTER 13

Conflict and Development

Agnieszka Paczynska

The end of World War II, the devastation it had brought to numerous regions, and the fall of colonial empires that followed brought issues of development and reconstruction firmly onto the international agenda. Already during the war the dominant world powers came together in Bretton Woods, New Hampshire to design new international institutions that would, they hoped, create conditions that would prevent the outbreak of such destructive violence in the future. Those attending located the root causes of the conflict in the economic environment that existed prior to the outbreak of open hostilities in 1939. Specifically they placed blame on the international financial instability and world-wide depression as well as the onerous reparations imposed on Germany during the Versailles conference at the end of World War I. Consequently, the world powers sought to design institutions that would ensure international financial liquidity and provide adequate financing to rebuild economies devastated by war. It was at this time that the International Bank for Reconstruction and Development, more commonly referred to as the World Bank, and the International Monetary Fund were set up. Over time, the institutions' roles have significantly evolved, but their influence in setting the international development agenda has not.

From the beginning the development models that these International Financial Institutions (IFIs) and the great powers promoted generated deep controversies and opposition in many quarters. These controversies revolved around the fundamental nature of development, the international relations of power and exploitation, the relationship between the state and society, and between society and economy. There exists a broad agreement among scholars and practitioners that poverty, inequality, and lack of development contribute to conflict, including violent conflict. The adoption of the Millennium Development Goals in 2000 by the United Nations underscored how widespread this agreement is:

> More than one billion people – one-sixth of the world's population – live in extreme poverty, lacking the safe water, proper nutrition, basic health care and social services needed to survive. The consequences of this poverty reach far beyond the afflicted societies. Poverty, inequality and disease are chief causes of violent conflict, civil war and state failures. A world with extreme poverty is a world of insecurity. (http://www.unmillenniumproject.org/who/index.htm)

However, how to reduce poverty and ensure a more sustainable and just development remains deeply contested among scholars and practitioners. At the heart of these debates are profoundly different understandings of the relationship between development and conflict. Some view development as the most effective means of ensuring that over the long term the severity of social conflicts declines and more effective mechanisms for managing conflicts peacefully are created. For others, the process of development itself is inherently conflictual. Even more important, the way development has been promoted and experienced has often exacerbated social conflicts and devastated indigenous economic, political, and cultural institutions. The different causal linkages between development and conflict that underpin these theoretical frameworks also shape the types of policies advocated to enhance development and peace-building prospects.

In this chapter we will explore some of the main theories that have sought to understand the relationship between development and conflict, and focus particular attention on how these theories have informed early post-World War II development strategies, structural adjustment policies that many developing countries have been pursuing during the last two decades, and the particular challenges of development in conflict and post-conflict environments.

Approaches to Development

During the 1950s modernization theory emerged as the dominant model explaining patterns of development. Although scholars working within this tradition produced a diverse body of work, their analyses had a number of common features (So, 2005). Most important, modernization theory, taking the nation-state as the main unit of analysis, proposed that all countries evolved along a similar trajectory although at different rates. All societies, in this view, develop from traditional to modern modes of social, political, and economic organization. The changes tend to be gradual until a 'take-off' stage is reached and the country breaks decisively with traditional past (Rostow, 1960).

There are a number of underlying assumptions common to studies produced within this theoretical framework. Traditional societies are characterized by pre-Newtonian attitudes toward the physical world, agricultural production dominates, and there is little vertical or spatial mobility. Families and clans are the primary institutions governing political life and there is a rigid social hierarchy in place. These conditions are viewed by modernization theorists as deeply inimical to social and political progress and economic development.

Modernity, on the other hand, is characterized by diffusion and widespread appreciation of science and rationality, the high value placed on personal achievement, and a decline in people's reliance on the family and clan. Modern societies are also characterized by social and spatial mobility, complexity of economic activities, and organization and differentiated political institutions. In this view the traditional patterns of social relations, the value system, and the institutions together form a formidable obstacle to development and have to be discarded if modernization is to take place. As Valenzuela and Valenzuela note, "To enter the modern world, underdeveloped societies have to overcome traditional norms and structures opening the way for social, economic, and political transformations ... since in the process of modernization all societies will undergo by and large similar changes, the history of the presently modern nations is taken as the source of universally useful conceptualization" (Valenzuela and Valenzuela, 1978, p. 538). Hence, for modernization projects to be launched in the developing world, some form of external intervention on the part of Western societies was necessary.

Modernization theory's understanding of development and change processes came to inform international development assistance during the early post-World War II decades. With decolonization accelerating in the 1960s, more new independent states faced the task of constructing political, economic, and social institutions. The language adopted by the international community during this time reflected ideas embedded within the modernization framework. Terminology first adopted by the United Nations that classified countries as highly developed, less developed, and least developed soon became part of public discourse. The highly developed states were those of Western Europe and North America indicating the development path for the newly independent states. To be developed and modern was to emulate Western economies and societies.

Although the World Bank was initially created to facilitate European post-conflict reconstruction, in fact most of its attention quickly turned to the new states of what came to be known as the Third World. Likewise, former colonial powers focused on development promotion in their former territories. The lending and policy recommendations placed emphasis on promoting construction of local industries and large infrastructure projects in order to create modern societies. Initially, policies advocated by the international donor community saw the state as the main promoter of development and emphasized state capitalism as the most effective strategy for ensuring economic growth in poor countries. As we shall see, the perception of the state's role in the economy within the donor community changed dramatically in the 1980s, leading to a fundamental revision in the policies pursued by the donor community vis-à-vis the developing world.

Although in some modernization theory accounts, the processes of social and economic change can produce conflict (Lipset, 1959; Deutsch, 1961), in others it is surprisingly conflict-free. Groups that had previously held power in a society often appear to relinquish that power without much resistance. Traditions disintegrate without creating social dislocation, insecurity, or resentment. In Lerner's classic study of changes in the Middle East, those who exercised authority before the advent of modernization seem sometimes surprised by the changes, perhaps resigned, but never hostile (Lerner, 1958). The march of progress is inevitable and beneficial, and therefore accepted by societies and individuals experiencing these changes.

Just as the process of change seems relatively conflict-free, the transformations ushered in by modernization processes, in the view of modernization theorists, also create conditions that are likely to facilitate the emergence of more effective mechanisms for managing social conflicts than was the case in traditional societies. As the economy becomes more complex, important political and social changes also take place. These in turn have profound influence on conflict dynamics in modernizing societies. With modernization comes increased urbanization and expanding literacy rates, and thus more people are able to acquire knowledge and access information previously unavailable to them. As the economy grows, the middle class expands creating the basis for the emergence of a vibrant civil society which in turn places ever greater pressure on the state to establish more participatory forms of governance. Lipset, for instance, points out that, "Democracy is related to the state of economic development. The more well to do a nation, the greater the chance that it will sustain democracy. A society divided between a large impoverished mass and a small favored elite would result either in oligarchy or tyranny" (Lipset, 1959). Thus mechanisms for peacefully resolving social conflicts emerged as societies became more modern.

Two broad critiques of modernization theory emerged in the 1960s and 1970s. One questioned the fundamental assumption that all nation-states moved along the same development path. These dependency, neo-Marxist, and World Systems analyses argued that on the contrary, the advanced industrialized countries and developing countries evolved very differently and that these processes of change have been deeply exploitative and violent (Gunder Frank, 1966; Wallerstein, 1979). These theorists were also critical of the assumption that the traditional and indigenous modes of political, social, and economic organization were inferior to Western models and inhibited countries' ability to change. Because these analyses viewed the integration of the global periphery into the global economy as the root cause of their poverty, they promoted indigenous development and advocated making it more difficult for global capital to penetrate local markets.

Other scholars (Huntington, 1968; Schmitter, 1971; O'Donnell, 1979) were critical of the modernization theory assumption that 'all good things go together'. They noted that the processes of economic and political development in the developing world were often not mutually supportive and reinforcing, and in fact were frequently deeply con-flictual and even violent. Hence these critics argued countries have often been forced to make what one analyst called a 'cruel choice' between economic growth and pluralistic political systems.

Dependency theorists reject the modernization assumption that the nation-state is a meaningful unit of analysis. Rather, they argue it is only by placing the nation-state within the international context that the processes of change can be understood. Dependency and World Systems theorists point out that depending on that international context and the nation-state's position within that international context, the processes of evolution will be very different. In particular they posit that what is of key significance in understanding the patterns of development within the global periphery is the manner of their incorporation into the global economic structures and the underlying power relationships. Because countries of the periphery were incorporated into the global economic and political structures through the expansion of capitalism, imperial-ism, and colonialism, the way they have evolved in no way resembles the evolution of the core states as modernization theory suggests. In fact, in this view the very development of the advanced industrialized or core countries was predicated on the exploitation and conscious under-development of the periphery (Gunder Frank, 1966; Wallerstein,

1979). In other words, development and underdevelopment are mirror images of the same phenomenon of capitalist expansion and are functionally interlinked.

Because of this exploitative relationship, countries of the periphery are unable to chart their own policies. Their economic structures and production profiles have little do to with the needs of the local populations and everything to do with the interests and needs of the core countries and their local allies. The patterns of domination are maintained through an international hierarchy of power between states of the core and the periphery, and perpetuated by those social classes within the periphery who benefit from these exploitative relationships. In other words the exploitative relationships between the core and the periphery are not limited to the international arena but are also reproduced locally (Cardoso and Falleto, 1979). These relationships of domination are further strengthened by the penetration of developing countries by multinational corporations which transfer profits out of the periphery and into the core, and contribute to deepening social cleavages within the periphery. Thus, unlike in the modernization framework, the processes of change as seen by Dependency and World Systems theorists are ridden with conflict, exploitation, and violence. In other words, the social, economic, and political institutions reproduce and perpetuate this violence (Galtung, 1971).

The other set of critiques of modernization theory came from scholars who viewed as erroneous its assumptions about the inherent compatibility between political and economic changes. The re-emergence of authoritarian regimes in much of the developing world during the 1970s further bolstered their arguments. Drawing in particular on the Latin American experience, some scholars argued that authoritarian systems are more capable of undertaking ambitious development projects thanks to their greater insulation from popular pressures. Democratic governments, on the other hand, are constrained by their need to win elections. They are therefore more likely to yield to political pressure from special interest groups and more hesitant to push through policies that may potentially facilitate long-term economic growth, but undermine short-term electoral support. In other words, in this view economic development inherently generates social conflict not only because some groups lose their status, sense of security, and well-being as a consequence of economic changes, but also because new groups become politically mobilized and thus more capable of expressing their views. These social conflicts can create tremendous pressure on the state to satisfy demands of certain groups, especially those that are better organized and dominate in the urban areas. The growing assertiveness of the urban workers, however, eventually triggers a reaction of the old elites and foreign interests threatened by socio-political changes inherent in working class demands. In many countries of the periphery, this intensifying conflict between the old elites and the newly mobilized social groups has often ended with the imposition of military rule and the suppression of popular demands (O'Donnell, 1979).

A related critique saw modernization processes as inherently conflictual, producing not political pluralism but instability. Huntington, for instance, argues that economic and political development often occur at different rates and this rate-differentiation is likely to produce conditions conducive to social conflict (Huntington, 1968). Rapid economic growth tends to raise aspirations and expectations. When these remain unmet, the level of frustration tends to rise (Gurr, 1971). Simultaneously, processes of modernization and economic development tend to increase urbanization rates and literacy and educational levels. These urban, educated strata are more likely to demand greater say in political life than the less educated, rural dwellers. Modernization processes also tend to break down traditional authority patterns, existing values, and behavioral norms, thus making people less constrained by previous patterns of social control. While the demands and aspirations of the public increase, however, the political institutions in most developing societies are too underdeveloped to effectively respond to these demands, mediate these demands, and resolve the social conflicts that these demands generate. Consequently, rather than economic development producing democracy and more effective institutions of social conflict-mediation and resolution, it tends to generate profound political instability, conflict, and violence as evidence in the large number of coups and revolutions in the developing world. The instability that changes associated with modernization is especially likely in states where people are already divided by culture, religion, and language.

Structural Adjustment Policies

The very different ways of understanding the relationship between development and conflict developed during the 1960s and 1970s were recast in a new light during the 1980s when much of the developing world found itself grappling with a growing economic crises and crippling foreign debt. With few resources available domestically to address these crises, countries were forced to turn to the IFIs for assistance. The IMF and the World Bank were willing to offer this assistance only if countries implemented far-reaching structural adjustment programs. The newly dominant neoliberal analysis that the IFIs subscribed to identified state involvement in the economy as the primary reason the developing world faced such profound economic difficulties. Consequently, structural adjustment programs sought to limit that involvement and allow for the unencumbered functioning of markets. Like modernization theory earlier, neoliberal analysis assumed that the ability to jump-start the development process was a matter of putting together the right policy-package. Since such a package was unlikely to emerge without external support, the IFIs concentrated on providing the necessary external pressure and financial incentives to ensure change in policies.

Often dubbed the "Washington Consensus," these policies had a number of common features. The structural adjustment programs emphasized reducing public expenditures, liberalizing the trade regime, encouraging foreign direct investment, and the privatization of state-owned enterprises. Although their proponents conceded that initially the reforms were likely to generate economic hardship, over the long run these restructuring measures were to ensure sustainable growth beneficial to all segments of society (Dollar and Kraay, 2000). Critics of neoliberal policies, however, argue that rather than promoting broad-based economic development, structural adjustment programs are more likely to have negative social, political, and economic consequences both over the long and the short term (Mittelman, 2000). In the short term, these policies have tended to exacerbate social inequalities and undermine people's sense of security, and growing evidence suggests that such inequalities tend to persist over time. These policies, critics charge, are also frequently reducing the ability of states to generate sustainable economic growth by expanding local industry since the opening up to international investment and markets tends to destroy the less competitive indigenous producers. Furthermore, because structural adjustment programs significantly reduce educational and health budgets, countries undertaking such economic restructuring are unable to sustain a productive and internationally competitive workforce. In many developing countries the opening up of the local market to international investors results in the expansion of sweatshops which undermine labor rights in particular and human rights more broadly. At the same time, the neoliberal attack on the state often means that state capacity is severely undermined rendering it less able to perform many basic functions, such as providing citizens with basic security.

The debates about structural adjustment programs, like the earlier debates between modernization theory and its critics, reflect very different ways of understanding the relationship between development and conflict. For supporters of neoliberal policies, the development of advanced industrialized countries serves as a model and a blueprint that can and should be replicated with only few modifications in developing countries. In other words, neoliberal policy supporters make similar assumptions as modernization theorists about the patterns of development. In both views, all states move along the same continuum from developing or traditional societies to developed or modern ones. Similar policies will result in similar outcomes regardless of where they are applied. Like modernization theorists, supporters of neoliberal programs assume that the relevant unit of analysis is the nation-state, and it is here at the national rather than the international level where corrections and policy modification have to be made for economic development to occur. Similarly, both see developing countries needing a nudge from external sources to ensure that this development process begins.

Although the IFIs concern themselves primarily with economic policy reform, they and other proponents of neoliberal programs like modernization theorists also assume that 'all good things go together'. In other words, there is an underlying assumption among supporters of these policies that by launching economic development, market reforms will also contribute to the development and consolidation of political democracy. This is because structural adjustment programs are the most effective mechanisms for ensuring the resumption of economic growth. By restoring economic growth, these reforms will begin to usher in social changes identified by modernization theorists which, over time, produce conditions conducive to the establishment of pluralistic political systems. In other words, the resumption of economic growth, expansion of the private sector, increasing educational opportunities, and improved living standards will contribute to the expansion of the middle class. This will thus provide a greater number of people with the opportunity and the ability to engage in civic activities and to put ever greater demands on the state for increased political participation. Democratic political institutions, in turn, are the most effective institutional mechanisms for ensuring peaceful resolution of conflicts that inevitably arise in any society. Supporters of neoliberalism recognize that at least initially such profound restructuring of the economy and the relationship between the state and society is likely to generate conflicts between those who lose as a consequence of changes and those who benefit. However, these conflicts are not viewed as presenting long-term problems to either the implementation of market capitalism or to liberal democracy nor to undermining social cohesion.

Critics of neoliberal policies are much less sanguine about the possibility of establishing more accountable and responsive political systems simultaneously with the push to restructure the economy along the lines advocated by the IFIs. Although the critiques of the neoliberal project are diverse, many of these echo the earlier arguments of dependency theorists. Most fundamentally, critics point out that the underlying assumptions of the neoliberal project are flawed. In the first place, it makes little sense to treat nation-states as units of analysis without considering how they are incorporated into the global political and economic structures. How states are incorporated into the global political economy matters greatly for the type of development that emerges, for the type of social relations that evolve, and for the types of conflicts that a society experiences. To many critics, the policies promoted by the IMF, the World Bank, and the World Trade Organization are reconfiguring colonial structures of domination and exploitation, where the growth of the core countries is made possible by the prying open of developing country markets. Thus, the neoliberal policies are not proving the basis for the development of market capitalism and democracy on the model of the core countries, but are ushering in a new system of global inequality and underdevelopment of the periphery. For other critics, the assumption that the neoliberal program provides the basis for lunching sustainable development is deeply flawed. Rather, they note the policies advocated by the IFIs result in deepening social inequalities, impoverishing ever larger segments of the population and making the state less capable of performing its most basic functions of ensuring rule of law and security for its population. These critics point to the devastating experience of Latin American countries, hailed until recently by the IMF for their commitment to reforms, as evidence of the failure of neoliberalism. This failure has resulted not just in declining rates of economic growth, but to polarization of societies where these projects were implemented, leading to growing social tensions and outright violence (Barr, 2005; Carranza, 2005).

Critics also note that the very processes of development produce conditions of profound violence as industrialization and urbanization remove people from their traditional surroundings and place them in an alien world. As Kothari and Harcourt, for instance, note, "The grave physiological and psychological impacts that displaced people experience are well documented but little has been done to address this massive social and cultural violence done in the name of development to millions of people every year" (Kothari and Harcourt, 2004, p. 4).

Some analysts also note that the assumption that economic restructuring would be compatible with establishing more pluralistic and accountable forms of governance is equally flawed. While capitalism and democracy may have been mutually supportive in the advanced industrial democracy, conditions prevailing in most developing countries and the policy choices made when economic restructuring programs were designed and implemented have undermined the democratic process. Przeworski, for instance, suggests that the neoliberal program "was a project initiated from above and launched by surprise, independently of public opinion and without the participating of organized political forces. As a result, citizens were taught that they could vote but not choose" (Przeworski, 1993, p. 175). Furthermore, the social inequalities and widespread perception that certain segments of society have disproportionately borne the costs of restructuring has weakened rather than augmented civil society organizations and made the mediation of social conflicts through existing political institutions more difficult (Oxhorn and Ducatenzeiler, 1998).

Post-Conflict Reconstruction and Peace-building

Understanding the relationship between development and conflict has in recent years become a growing concern for both scholars and practitioners. As we have seen the debates about this relationship have underpinned many of the discussions concerning the dynamics and long-term consequences of structural adjustment policies. These debates have increasingly taken center stage as the international community has become more involved in development assistance to conflict areas and in post-conflict reconstruction projects.

Over the last couple decades and in particular during the 1990s, as the number of interstate wars has declined, the number of civil wars has risen. Although during the next decade the number of civil wars went down, internal strife continued to be a more common form of violent conflict than inter-state war. While the root causes of these violent and often very protracted intra-state conflicts vary between cases, in many instances poverty and socioeconomic inequalities have contributed to the emergence of these civil wars. Especially combustible have been contexts where economic exploitation has coincided with ethnic, religious, cultural, and other social divisions (Collier et al., 2003; Kahl, 2006).

Since the end of the Cold War, the international community has become much more actively involved in various interventions designed to bring these hostilities to an end. With the stalemate between the United States and the Soviet Union that paralyzed the United Nations Security Council over, the UN was able to expand its peacekeeping, peace monitoring, and peace enforcing activities. The UN as well as other international organizations and international donors have also pushed for including elections within peace agreements and have devoted significant financial resources to reconstruction programs. At the same time, the spread of modern media technologies made people more aware than in decades past of violence and human rights abuses, making inaction more difficult politically for governments especially in Western Europe and North America.

The end of Cold War, the new communications technologies and cheaper travel, as well as the emergence of neoliberal economic ideology have also contributed to the expansion of the international NGOs. By

2000 there were an estimated 25,000 such NGOs engaged in a variety of activities, including development work, humanitarian assistance, human rights advocacy, and increasingly post-conflict reconstruction (Paul, 2000). As the state institutions across the globe contracted and restructured, governments increasingly came to rely on NGOs to perform these various functions, many of which were previously the purview of the state.

The overwhelming majority of civil wars erupt in very poor countries, and in 44 percent of cases civil war reoccurs within the first five years after cessation of open hostilities (Collier *et al.* 2003, p. 83). There is widespread agreement that ensuring socio-economic development is essential to preventing a renewed civil war. Although economic growth in and of itself is unlikely to be sufficient buffer against resumption of hostilities, as Junne and Verkoren point out, the "lack of economic development can be a guarantee for the resumption of violence" (Junne and Verkoren, 2005, p. 2). However, while there is agreement that development is a key component to reconstruction and peace-building, there is less agreement on how programs should be designed to achieve these goals. Policies advocated by international actors involved in post-conflict reconstruction and peace-building are often based on very different assumptions about the relationship between development and conflict.

Many international donors, including the World Bank, initially assumed that the key to ensuring successful post-conflict reconstruction was not much different from what they argued was essential to a successful exit from deep economic crisis that plagued most developing countries throughout the 1980s and 1990s. As a result, in post-conflict countries multilateral donors also encouraged the establishment of market economies which they saw as the best mechanism for jump-starting sustainable economic growth. In the late 1990s in fact, the World Bank considered some of its post-conflict reconstruction programs, like those in Tajikistan, Algeria, Nicaragua, and Georgia, to be actually programs of transitions to a market economy (World Bank, 1998).

In 1997 the World Bank did create a Post-Conflict Unit (later renamed the Conflict Prevention and Reconstruction Unit), but to many critics of the programs this institution advocated, this has not been sufficient to fundamentally alter the policy prescriptions the Bank promotes in post-conflict settings. Most important, the World Bank did not change its fundamental assumptions about the relationship between the state, economy, and society, and continued to place emphasis on what were essentially structural adjustment programs that emphasized a reduced role of the state in the economy, privatization of the state sector, and the opening of the local economy to international investment and competition (Moore, 2000). Although in the World Bank's view these policies were most likely to ensure the resumption of growth in a post-conflict setting and the country would be able to escape the "conflict trap" of poverty and civil war, critics argued that such policies were particularly ill suited to reconstruction efforts. Especially problematic is the decline in the state's ability to address the needs and grievances of the public as more responsibilities and functions are privatized. This can pose particular problems when the level of dissatisfaction is high, the needs are great, and the public is uncertain about the government's credibility as is often the case in post-conflict settings.

The challenges posed by international intervention in post-conflict environments, however, are not limited to the particular policy pre-scriptions of the World Bank. Among these problems is the unreliability of international financial assistance, the lack of coordination among and often mutually contradictory priorities of international donors, and the lack of understanding of the particular context in which intervention is taking place. International donors are, however, becoming increasingly aware of these challenges and have begun to rethink the policies they pursue in post-conflict settings. As Duffield underscores, "It is now generally accepted that international organizations should be aware of conflict and, where possible, gear their work toward conflict resolution and helping to rebuild war-torn societies in a way that will avert future violence"(Duffield, 2001, p. 1). How this should be done, however, continues to be a matter of debate.

Reconciling development and peace-building activities presents a number of challenges. For one, objectives of the two types of pro-gramming may differ. For instance, in order to solidify a peace agreement, reconstruction should begin quickly so that the public may begin to see tangible benefits of peace. However, the easiest way to achieve such a quick pace of reconstruction may well involve bringing in foreign contractors to do the job. This is likely to conflict with the long-term development objectives which would focus on providing jobs locally and facilitating the establishment of local businesses which would likely involve more time (Junne and Verkoren, 2005, p. 9). Likewise, the differences among international donors concerning goals, objectives, and principles may lead to contradictory programs and projects. Not all these differences are easy to reconcile, and often difficult trade-offs have to be made by donors concerning programming priorities. As Uvin points out in his study of the international community's involvement in post-genocide Rwanda,

> Democracy and governance objectives do conflict as do reconci-liation and formal justice, economic efficiency and political

imperative, short term security and human rights. Everyone pretends that such unsavory choices do not exist and that all good things go together, but the reality is otherwise. (Uvin, 2001, p. 185)

Donors and practitioners thus often have to make difficult decisions concerning project goals and objectives. However, it is often unclear how those decisions are made and who can be held accountable for decisions taken. More often than not, local communities where development and peace-building programs are implemented are not consulted about the project choices and objectives even though they are the ones who have to live with the consequences of these choices. "The new post conflict agenda allows donors to make life and death decisions that are often bound to be wrong; yet those suffering the consequences of these errors are never those making decisions," Uvin argues. He continues, "Foreigners are encouraged to make deeply interventionist life and death decisions for other societies, unbound by outside control, unconstrained by procedure, unaffected by outcomes" (Uvin, 2001, pp. 185, 186-187). Furthermore, international assistance that does not involve local communities in programming decisions also tends to be less effective and less likely to accomplish the designated goals.

Another challenge facing international assistance to conflict and post-conflict areas is how to ensure that the humanitarian, development, and peace-building work does not contribute to conflict. Anderson, for instance, argues that humanitarian organizations working in conflict areas despite good intentions may often make the situation worse. This can happen because warring factions may demand payments from international NGOs in exchange for allowing them to work with populations in the affected areas; because unwittingly humanitarian organizations may channel resources to a particular civilian group thus aggravating inter-group conflicts; because international NGOs interacting with local groups and authorities may strengthen some actors while weakening others thus deepening conflicts; and finally, the public rhetoric of international NGOs can worsen inter-group relations by demonizing or victimizing a particular party to the conflict (Anderson, 2001). As Anderson points out,

International assistance can worsen war when it reinforces inter-group divisions and tensions and when it undermines and weakens inter-group connections; it can promote peace when it reduces inter-group divisions and when it supports and strengthens inter-group connections ... program decisions about whether to provide aid, where to work, when and for how long, who to hire locally, whom to target, the roles of international staff, how to deliver goods – these and other basic management decisions all have effects on inter-group relationships in the areas where aid is provided. (Anderson, 2004, p. 4)

A final challenge to peace-building and development assistance is the volatility of international aid. Such volatility can be especially detrimental in post-conflict settings. Aid tends to move into a country shortly after the signing of a peace agreement to end the violence, peaks within a couple of years, and then begins to decline. Five years after the signing of an agreement when need for assistance tends to increase, international aid usually becomes scarcer as international attention turns to another crisis.

In recent years international donors and international NGOs have become much more aware that engagement of international actors in conflict areas can have far-reaching repercussions on local conflict dynamics. Consequently, donors and international NGOs have come to recognize that in order to improve the quality of their work, they need to sharpen their analytic tools to better understand the particular contexts in which they work as well as to improve their monitoring and evaluation techniques that would allow them to better assess the impact and effectiveness of their work. Until now, many organizations have brought general knowledge of conflict resolution practices and techniques but lacked deep knowledge of the particular conflict area in which they were intervening. They also frequently assumed that their work was contributing to development and peace-building, but did not evaluate those assumptions.

In response to a dearth of techniques and tools for assessing the effectiveness of development and peace-building activities, and growing evidence that all too frequently well-intentioned programs rather than contributing to development and peace were in fact exacerbating conflicts, a number of scholars have been exploring ways of addressing and mitigating these problems. In his study *A Measure of Peace*, Kenneth Bush has proposed the Peace and Conflict Impact Assessment (PCIA) as a means of evaluating programs already in place and as a mechanism for exploring the potential impact of programs still being designed. PICA aims to extend evaluation "beyond the stated outputs, outcomes, goals and objectives of a conventional development projects or programmes. Rather, it attempts to discern a project's impact on the peace and conflict environment – an area it may not have been designed explicitly to affect" (Bush, 1998, p. 7).

In a related effort International Alert, an independent peace-building organization, and other partners have developed tools that allow donors and international NGOs to engage in a "conflict-sensitive approach to development." This approach takes seriously the notion that the linkages between conflict and development are complex and run both ways – development can in some circumstances contribute to violent conflict, and violent conflict can undermine development. By exploring these linkages and taking them into account when designing development programs, NGOs and others will be better able to contribute to both development and peace-building. Donors and NGOs must therefore understand the conflict context in which they operate, understand the complex linkages between development and conflict in the specific context in which they operate, and ensure that conflict-sensitivity is applied to planning, implementing, monitoring, and evaluating programs (International Alert, 2004).

Conclusion

Theories that explore the link between development and conflict have informed both scholarly debates and influenced the types of policies governments, international donors, and NGOs have advocated and implemented. Because this link has been understood very differently by different schools of thought, the programs and policies that these various actors have promoted have diverged. The new wave of studies of peace-building and development work in conflict and post-conflict settings has raised important new questions concerning the relationship between development processes and conflict dynamics. They have challenged many of the assumptions that have guided international donor policy in conflict and post-conflict countries. They have also challenged the assumptions that have guided development programs in non-conflict settings. Modernization theorists following World War II and the neoliberals in the latter part of the twentieth century have suggested a particular relationship between development and conflict. According to some scholars, the processes of change were relatively conflict-free. According to others, they were indeed conflictual, but these conflicts were creative rather then destructive in nature and helped to move a country along the path of modernization. Studies of conflict and post-conflict development have found that these assumptions are overly optimistic. Development programs, often well intentioned, can sometimes exacerbate tensions in such conflict countries. One reason they do is that donors and NGOs have paid insufficient attention to the particular context in which they work. By not understanding the conflict dynamics of these settings, they can inadvertently undermine peacebuilding initiatives.

The insights of studies that have explored the relationship between peace-building and development work in conflict and post-conflict settings raise questions that could be usefully applied in contexts where descent into civil war and violence is unlikely. Development programs by their very nature affect local social processes, dynamics, and institutions. By changing social interactions and altering power relationships, they can often contribute to non-violent conflicts. As Pruitt and Kim remind us, such conflicts may serve a very beneficial and creative role (Pruitt and Kim, 2004). However, understanding the ways in which development assistance affects such non-violent conflicts remains to be more fully explored. Likewise, how economic policies implemented in post-conflict settings, such as privatization of state-owned enterprises, reform of the tax system, and labor market restructuring, affect the long-term peace-building processes still needs to be more fully investigated and better understood.

Discussion Questions

1 What is development according to modernization theory?
2 Why are dependency and world systems theories critical of modernization theory?
3 What are structural adjustment policies?
4 What are some of the challenges international donors and NGOs face when intervening in conflict and post-conflict settings?
5 What are conflict-sensitive approaches to development?

Key Words

Development
Modernization
Dependency
Neoliberalism
Structural adjustment programs
International donors
International non-governmental organizations
Post-conflict reconstruction
Development assistance

CHAPTER 14

Negotiation

Daniel Druckman

Introduction

According to *Webster's New Collegiate Dictionary*, "to negotiate is to hold intercourse with a view to coming to terms; to confer regarding a basis of agreement." An influential text on the subject defined bargaining as "the process whereby two or more parties attempt to settle what each shall give and take, or perform and receive, in a transaction between them" (Rubin and Brown, 1975, p. 2). Both of these definitions highlight a relationship between a process (give and take) and an outcome (settlement, impasse). That relationship has been the basis for a considerable amount of research intended to probe the way various types of processes lead to alternative types of outcomes. The investigators, coming from many disciplines, have examined negotiation in a variety of settings. The knowledge has expanded our understanding both of negotiation in general and negotiating as it occurs in specific settings. In this chapter, we discuss the frameworks that have guided the research, review the key findings, and show some of the ways in which this knowledge may be used. The chapter concludes with some questions that remain for further research.

Negotiation takes many forms. It consists of communications exchanged from a distance or face-to-face. It occurs between two or more parties (or their representatives) in bilateral, trilateral, or multilateral forums. It concerns matters in a wide variety of issue areas that, in addition to the parties themselves, may have consequences for their organizations, their nations, regions, or for the globe. While there are some insights, derived from research, that apply widely to many of these forms, there are also differences of context and scope. For example, the finding that negotiations pass through stages marked by transitions referred to as turning points is a general insight. The specific activities that precipitate a change in process are described and understood in terms of the parties, issues, and history of a particular negotiation. The research accomplished to date has addressed both types of questions. A wealth of experimental studies has explored the *general* aspects of negotiation. An expanding number of case studies has elucidated many of the *context-specific* aspects of negotiating in international and domestic settings. Findings obtained about the general aspects complement those discovered about the specific, and, by pursuing both approaches, we gain appreciation for the applicability of general theories to specific cases or situations. Both are discussed in this chapter.

Conceptual Frameworks

Like many of the topics considered in this book, negotiation may be understood at both a micro and macro level of analysis. It consists of interactions among a small number of parties, but it also occurs within organizational and international contexts. Some analyses focus attention exclusively on the way that a small group of negotiators attempt to settle their differences. Other analyses concentrate on the larger context within which negotiations occur. These alternative foci have resulted in different ways of thinking about negotiation, reflected also in different theoretical frameworks. From a micro perspective, analysts are concerned with moves and preferences as well as communication processes. The two bodies of scholarship from this perspective are the formal approaches of game and decision theory and the empirical approach of social psychology. The macro perspective is defined by its focus on organizations and social (political, economic) systems. Research from this perspective has been done in the fields of organization behavior and international relations. Each of these approaches is summarized briefly in the sections that follow.

Game and decision theory

Game and decision theorists think about negotiation as if it were a puzzle to be solved. Focusing primarily on the parties' preferences for outcomes, they suggest solutions to the puzzle. The key question for game theorists is: How do parties make optimal choices when these choices are contingent on what other people (or players) do? According to the classical theory advanced by Von Neumann and Morgenstern (1944), players choose strategies, or courses of action, that determine an outcome.

The most prominent puzzle for game theorists is the well-known prisoner's dilemma. This game is based on the story of two suspected criminals who face the following consequences: If one confesses and the other remains silent, the confessor goes free and the silent suspect gets a ten-year sentence; if both confess, they each get five-year sentences; if both remain silent, they get one-year sentences. Four possible outcomes are represented in a two-by-two matrix: an optimal compromise outcome (both remain silent), an "equilibrium" conflict outcome (both confess), and a win-lose outcome where one suspect wins at the expense of the other (one confesses while the other remains silent). Typically, both suspects have dominant strategies of confessing, resulting in the conflict outcome (both get five-year sentences). The challenge is to get the players to avoid the temptation of confessing (resulting in both losing) and remain silent in order to attain the best joint outcome. To do this they must trust one another. This challenge has been the basis for research aimed at discovering the conditions for trust (e.g., Deutsch and Krauss, 1962).

Another question asked by game theorists is: What are the consequences of alternative strategies used by players through the course of repeated games or interactions? An answer is given from Axelrod's (1984) studies of the iterated prisoner's dilemma game. He concluded that while no particular strategy was optimal, the "tit-for-tat" approach (strict reciprocity of moves) fared the best over the long term, when the value of future pay-offs is important and when the other players' strategies are not known. Such an approach works, according to Axelrod, because it avoids provocation, makes exploitation impossible, is forgiving, and is simple. The fact that the strategy does not always work suggests that it may be viewed as an attempt to coerce rather than as an effort to stimulate cooperation, and, may lead to downward spirals in relations between the parties. A more effective strategy may be to "follow two tracks: a tough responsive strategy on substantive issues, and an unconditional cooperative policy on process issues" (S. Brown, 1986, p. 381). This approach sends two messages to the other player, namely that we encourage a stable working relationship but will not be exploited. (See also Druckman (1990a) for a review of this literature.)

Not all negotiation problems involve the sorts of interaction captured by game-theory modeling. Many decisions are made under conditions of uncertainty in non-interactive, non-competitive situations such as problem-solving discussions at a distance. These situations are, however, captured by another formal approach referred to as "decision theory." Like game theory, this approach concentrates on players' preferences for alternative outcomes. Unlike game theory, it analyzes decisions one negotiator at a time (i.e., it does not derive from a premise of interdependence among the decision-makers). The approach uses each negotiator's stated preferences for the outcomes on several issues to arrive at acceptable outcomes for all the parties. This type of analysis has been used during the preparation stage to assist negotiators in deciding where to offer a compromise or concession, and where to remain adamant. It has contributed to the processes of a variety of international negotiations including the Panama Canal talks (Raiffa, 1982), the Philippines–U.S. base rights talks (Ulvila, 1990), multilateral negotiations concerning oil tankers (Ulvila and Snyder, 1980), and the United Nations Conference on Environment and Development (Spector, 1993). For step-by-step procedures, see Ulvila (1990). For the theory behind the applications, see Raiffa (1982). Along with game theory, these contributions demonstrate the practical utility of using formal approaches to solve negotiation puzzles.

Social-psychological approaches

The interesting question for social psychologists is how the interactions that define a negotiating process lead to outcomes. Attempts made to answer this question often consist of observing (and coding) the interactions that take place in contrived game-like situations. The early research in this tradition discovered some conditions that lead to beneficial outcomes. For example, in the case of buyer and seller negotiations, Siegel and Fouraker (1960) found that the best outcomes occur when (1) there is a prominent optimal outcome, (2) there is complete information so that the prominent outcome may be identified, (3) each party has veto power, ensuring that the outcome is mutually acceptable, and (4) there are only two parties involved. Later research added the condition of systematic concession-making emphasizing reciprocity (Kelley and Schenitzki, 1972).

What happens, however, when there is no prominent outcome or when it is difficult to find? Who concedes first? Which party makes the larger concession? The bargaining then becomes a contest of wills between tactical adversaries, each trying to pressure the other into conceding first or more frequently. Much of the research has focused on this situation, and the findings have identified tactics that could tilt the contest in favor of one or the other bargainer. Examples are commitment tactics, alternating from initially tough to subsequently soft postures, the tactical use of deadline pressures, and distinguishing between the "good cop" negotiator and the "bad cop" constituents. Tactics such as these could lead to an agreement that favors the more effective tactician. Used effectively by both bargainers, however, the tactics could produce a deadlock.

More recently, social psychologists have recognized the dilemma of competitive or tactical bargaining, namely that one or all parties lose. This understanding has led to the construction of a different paradigm to guide research. Referred to as "integrative bargaining," this paradigm focuses on the conditions that lead to mutually-beneficial agreements or to absolute (no party loses) rather than relative gains (one party benefits from another's losses). It emphasizes the importance of problem-solving through an exchange of information about each party's preferences, interests, and needs during the negotiation process. The research has shown that this sort of process can result in better agreements than competitive bargaining (e.g., Kressel *et al.*, 1994). It has also highlighted some of the conditions that encourage sharing of information and empathic problem-solving (Druckman and Robinson, 1998).

Yet, despite impressive advances in understanding negotiating behavior, the relatively simple game-like situations created by social psychologists are limited to exploring only a few variables at a time. An attempt was made by Sawyer and Guetzkow (1965) to expand the way that the social-psychological aspects of negotiation are conceived. They devised a framework that links pre-conditions to background factors, conditions, processes, and outcomes. This and other, similar frameworks (e.g., Iklé, 1964; Walton and McKersie, 1965; Randolph, 1966) serve useful synthetic functions. They provide the larger context within which the bargaining literature may be organized (Druckman *et al.*, 1977a). In addition, they cover more aspects of complex cases than is possible in an experiment or simulation (e.g., Bonham, 1971; Ramberg, 1977). By capturing the complexity of actual negotiations in a systematic manner, the frameworks provide tools for performing comparative analyses of many cases.

Negotiating in organizations

Many negotiations occur within the context of organizations. These negotiations are more complex than those studied in the game-like situations created for experimentation. They involve attempts to build consensus among diverse constituencies with a stake in the outcome. These attempts highlight the importance of an intraparty negotiation process that may occur at the same time as the negotiations between parties (or organizations). This process renders negotiation a two- (or multi-) tiered activity which has been referred to as a two-level game (Putnam, 1988).

From the standpoint of the negotiator, the two- (or multi-) tiered process creates a dilemma of being caught between the often conflicting expectations of constituents and those of the other negotiating party or parties. This dilemma, referred to as a boundary role conflict, was recognized initially by Walton and McKersie (1965) in the setting of labor–management negotiations. These authors discussed the conditions for conflicting expectations among the constituencies and tactics that can be used by negotiators to resolve the dilemma. The tactics consist of various ways of managing impressions. For example, to increase the negotiator's flexibility, limit constituent participation in the formulation of proposals. To reduce the discrepancy between constituents' expectations and performance, limit the opportunities for surveillance of the process, obscure concessions, and exaggerate the level of achievement. To execute these tactics effectively, it is sometimes necessary to elicit the cooperation of the other party's negotiators. But, of course, the constituents also use various tactics to maintain control over the process. In essence, the dilemma is reflected in a struggle between constituents and negotiators for control over the process and its outcomes.

This approach adds the dimensions of organizational culture and structure to the negotiation process. By culture, we refer to an organization's values and assumptions about "proper" practices or activities. These differences can hinder communication in negotiation. Offsetting these differences, however, are the similar values (or understandings) held by professional negotiators representing different organizations, known also as negotiator subcultures (Modelski, 1970). By structure, we refer to the bureaucracies that create the sorts of constituents' interests discussed above. As the number of bureaucratic actors seeking to control the negotiation process increases, the negotiator finds it more difficult to resolve his or her boundary role dilemma. The challenge is even more daunting in multilateral negotiations where the conference itself becomes bureaucratic. A trend toward increased structural complexity in many negotiating domains encourages analysts to view it as a management process (see Winham, 1979; Lax and Sebenius, 1986).

An expanded framework of organizational negotiation is presented by Burke and Biggart (1997, Figure 5-1). This framework embeds a negotiation process within organization processes and functions. Their lifecycle model includes five stages with feedback loops. The first stage is pre-engagement. Parties identify strategic goals, assess their power, and form bargaining positions. A second stage is negotiation. Resources are allocated, performance measures are clarified, and an agreement is reached. The third stage is referred to as operation and includes coordinated functioning, sharing of resources, and decision making. The process then proceeds to evaluation. Various assessments of progress are made leading to decisions about whether the agreement is working for the organization. The result of these assessments could lead to continued joint operation of the relationship, adjustments, or renegotiation. They could also lead to an exiting of the negotiated arrangement if the parties conclude that the agreement is not working.

Negotiation as diplomatic politics

A fourth approach to the study of negotiation emphasizes the larger system within which negotiations (and other conflict-resolving methods) take place. Negotiations are microcosms of international (or organizational) relations, where parallel interactions or cross-linkages among many types of diplomatic activities occur. Instead of focusing attention on a particular negotiating process – as is done in the other approaches – these analysts are interested in the implications of a variety of negotiations for relations between nations (or organizations). Thus, the decisions made, for example, by Syrian and Israeli negotiators in their recent discussions in West Virginia are evaluated in relation to the broad issues of security and land that define their relationship. These sorts of questions are asked primarily by the policy-maker (or policy analyst) rather than the analyst of negotiation.

By placing negotiations in the context of international (or inter-organizational) relations, the analyst develops an appreciation for the variety of policy objectives that may be served by negotiations, the precedents or predilections that may constrain negotiators, the linkages among different negotiating venues, and the influences of external events on the process. Recently, Druckman and his collaborators (1999b) showed that the type of agreement sought – for example, to redistribute land or to create a new regional regime – influences such aspects of the negotiating process as its form (concession-making or problem-solving), tempo (progression through phases), and frequency of impasses. The way parties negotiate is influenced as well by the legacy of past agreements, especially in negotiations intended to extend those agreements, but also when domestic constituencies emphasize the logic of precedent (Kelleher, 1976). Attempts made by negotiators to link their negotiation to others in the same issue area are often done to either create or break impasses. For example, base-rights negotiators use parallel talks to cite precedents for their demands (Druckman, 1990b). More generally, negotiators are influenced by specific external events, as demonstrated by the research reported by Hopmann and King (1976) and Hopmann and Smith (1978). These studies illuminate the importance of the contexts within which negotiations occur.

Empirical Research

Of all the topics treated in this book, negotiation has benefited the most from empirical research. Our understanding of negotiation processes comes primarily from the findings of research reported in professional social science journals. This includes laboratory experiments conducted mostly by social psychologists and analyses of cases (including comparative case analyses) done mostly by political and management scientists. Empirical work has been carried out in each of the four research traditions described above, although more of it emanates from the social-psychological approach. In this section of the chapter, we introduce the reader to some of the key findings reported in this literature. More detailed reviews of the research may be found in the work of Druckman (1997a) and Weiss (1996).

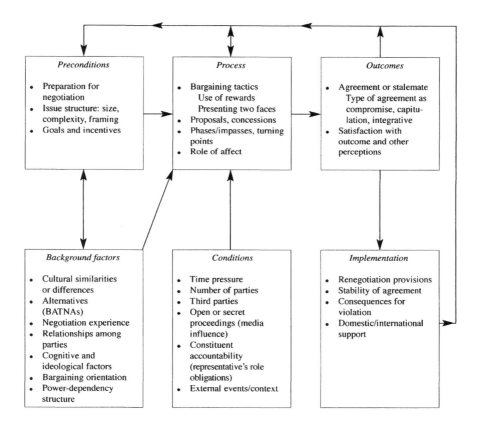

Figure 14.1 A framework of influences and processes of negotiation

The research literature may be organized in terms of a framework of influences and processes. As shown in Figure 11.1, the framework depicts the several aspects of negotiation including pre-conditions, background factors, processes, conditions, outcomes, and implementation by themes. Within each box are the variables or themes that have received attention from the research community. A sampling of key findings obtained on some of these themes follows with an emphasis on results that are less obvious or even counter-intuitive.

Background factors

Relationships: Friends bargain differently with each other than non-friends or strangers. They show less concern for immediate pay-offs, display more trust, and reach agreement more quickly (Halpern, 1994). However, because friends often agree quickly, they are less likely to engage in the sort of information exchange processes needed for integrative agreements. Many outcomes reached in these negotiations are sub-optimal. In addition, impasses are more likely in negotiations between friends if expectations are disappointed (Druckman and Bonoma, 1976; Druckman, 1986).

Experience and orientations: Experienced negotiators are usually more effective negotiators. However, the research shows that the experience may be used either to maximize one's own or the joint outcomes. This depends on whether the negotiator is competitively or cooperatively oriented (Thompson, 1990, 1993). Whether a negotiator views the negotiation as a contest to be won (competitive) or as a problem to be solved (cooperative) may be induced through instructions, by the way a task is structured, or through prior experience such as having been rewarded for cooperating on similar tasks. Induced orientation can be a powerful variable, often making the difference between sub-optimal (such as one side capitulating to the other) and optimal or integrative agreements (Druckman, 1994a). An asymmetrical outcome favoring the more experienced delegation is more likely to occur in international negotiations when the delegations are not matched in terms of experience (Druckman, 1990b). However, experience can also help negotiators deal with novel situations if the experience provides them with analytical tools or frameworks that can be applied to many kinds of situations (Neale and Northcraft, 1986).

Alternatives: Attractive alternatives to the terms on the table often produce better outcomes for the negotiators who have them. They have less need to compromise in the face of deadlines or to rush toward agreements. Thus, they have an opportunity to search for optimal agreements. That opportunity is lost if the negotiators use their alternatives to pressure the opponent to settle on their terms. It is also lost if the negotiator with attractive alternatives takes a self-centered approach or perceives the opponent to have even better alternatives as the research indicates (Pinkley *et al.*, 1994).

Culture: Although national culture has been a popular topic in this literature, its effects on negotiating behavior are not clear. Part of the problem consists of how to think about culture: for example, as a variable compared to other variables or as the context that shapes the way other factors in the negotiating environment operate (Druckman and Hopmann, 1989; Faure and Rubin, 1993). Another part of the problem concerns the unit for cultural expression: for example, the nation as in comparisons between Japanese and American negotiators or the type of culture as in the distinction between collectivist and individualist cultures (Gelfand and Realo, 1999). Further complications arise when we consider that professional negotiators may be influenced primarily by their shared organizational subcultures and that these, rather than their national identifications, exert strong influences on their behavior (Modelski, 1970).

Processes

Emotions in negotiation: Positive emotions and good feelings are beneficial in negotiation. They lead to a reduction in the use of contentious tactics and to a stronger willingness to make concessions (Carnevale and Isen, 1985; Baron, 1990). They are particularly effective when following tough postures, a sequence that has been referred to as a "reformed sinner" strategy (e.g., see Harford and Solomon, 1967; Wilson, 1971). The tougher postures may also include expressions of anger which can actually be quite beneficial if they are directed at the task and convey clearly how strongly a negotiator feels about an issue (Daly, 1991; Jehn, 1994).

Tactics: Although many tactics have been described in the literature on negotiation, only a few have received attention from researchers. One of these consists of presenting two faces: a cooperative and a competitive posture. Consistent cooperation or competition has been shown to be less effective in producing optimal agreements than a strategy that alternates between cooperation (soft postures) and competition (hard postures) (Hilty and Carnevale, 1992). The alternating can be orchestrated by different members of a delegation, by negotiators and their principals, or by the same negotiator over time. Another tactic concerns the use of rewards or giving away concessions without making them contingent on reciprocity. This tactic has been shown to be a useful starting mechanism which can lead to quick but sub-optimal agreements. In asymmetrical power negotiations a reward strategy can lead to exploitation and asymmetrical agreements. In equal power negotiations, it can produce reciprocity and symmetrical agreements. The danger, however, is that rewards encourage concessions rather than the sorts of information exchange processes that lead to optimal agreements (Bateman, 1980; Lindskold and Aronoff, 1980; Buss *et al.*, 1987).

Turning points: Turning points are pivotal to a dynamic conception of negotiation processes. They are usually defined as events or processes that mark the passage from one stage to another, signaling progress from earlier to later phases. They can, however, refer also to downturns in the process where events slow progress or cause impasses. Whether positive or negative, turning points have been shown to be useful as benchmark events for depicting the way a negotiation process unfolds (Tomlin, 1989; Druckman *et al.*, 1991; Chasek, 1997). More detailed case analyses demonstrate that they are usually precipitated by crises that occur as a result of either external (outside the negotiation) or internal (procedural or substantive) events (Druckman, 1986). More recent comparative case analyses distinguish between types of international negotiations: negotiations over security issues, such as arms control, are characterized primarily by external precipitants leading to abrupt departures in process which typically turn the talks in the direction of agreement; the process departures that occur in political or trade talks are usually precipitated by either internal procedural or substantive decisions that also lead toward agreements (Druckman, 2001b). Further work on departures in negotiation has been developed in conjunction with a Processes on Negotiation (PON) project on critical moments (Druckman, 2004). In this work, the author probes for the underlying impetus for departures (turning points). Psychological and social processes that occur before, during, and after departures are identified. Further insight about turning points are found in the articles compiled in a special issue of *Negotiation Journal* (Leary, 2004).

Conditions

Time pressure: This is a two-edged sword. On the one hand, time pressure can be beneficial if it is used to seal agreements tentatively arrived at earlier. On the other hand, it makes self-interested negotiators more competitive and collaborative negotiators more willing to concede even if it favors the other party (Druckman, 1994a). The decision dilemma created by time pressure – to reach an agreement or disband the talks without an agreement – reduces the chances for obtaining optimal agreements (Carnevale and Lawler, 1986). If imposed at the beginning of the talks, negotiators can pace themselves toward an endgame, reducing the dilemma of making sudden decisions; if imposed later in the talks, as a tactic, the decision dilemma can be severe.

Conditions influencing flexibility in negotiation: Many aspects of a negotiating situation affect the extent to which negotiators are flexible in the sense of being willing to adjust their positions or interests to reach an agreement. However, an apparent flexibility by the less powerful bargainer may result from being coerced into agreeing to terms more favorable to the more powerful opponent (Beriker and Druckman, 1996). Other factors that can reduce flexibility include preparing for a negotiation by developing strategies only with members of the same delegation (Druckman, 1968), linking bargaining positions to broader ideologies (Zechmeister and Druckman, 1973), giving control over the process and outcomes to constituents (Benton and Druckman, 1973), and negotiating in public (Brown, 1977; Druckman and Druckman, 1996). Each of these aspects of the situation may be altered in directions that increase flexibility. An example of how this is done in simulated multilateral negotiations is given by Druckman (1993). Referred to also as situational levers, these factors are the keys to diagnosing the relative flexibility of the parties at any point in time (Druckman, 1995).

Third parties: Another source of influence on the negotiation process comes from third parties. Although various types of third parties are discussed in several of the other chapters, here we are concerned specifically with the way negotiators perceive and react to mediators. A mediator's presence can induce flexibility if the mediator is viewed as being trustworthy and competent, especially when the level of hostility between the parties is high (Carnevale and Henry, 1989; Harris and Carnevale, 1990). Suggestions made by mediators are more likely to be taken seriously when the implications for who gives up what are clear and do not favor one party over the other. Thus it has been shown that mediators who suggest compromises (equal concessions by the parties) produce more agreements than those who make suggestions that result in either integrative (favoring both parties but complex) or asymmetrical (favoring one party more than another) outcomes (Conlon *et al.*, 1994). However, once viewed as being fair, the mediator can then suggest that the negotiators avoid the temptation of actually agreeing on a compromise and engage in problem-solving toward an integrative agreement. The research by Conlon and his collaborators (1994) suggests that the mediator's activities can be phased with early suggestions geared toward compromise and later advice oriented more toward attaining agreements that are better than compromise.

Outcomes

Integrative agreements: These are agreements that satisfy all parties' interests. Referred to also as optimal solutions, they are difficult to achieve. One way to increase the chances of getting integrative agreements is to avoid conceding too quickly or not at all (Kressel *et al.*, 1994). Another is to take the time to engage in an exchange of information that reveals each party's interests and needs (Tutzauer, 1990). This kind of process may, however, reveal other incompatibilities that serve to escalate the conflict (Johnson, 1971). For this reason, it should be pursued only under certain conditions, namely when an integrative solution is difficult to identify, when the parties approach the negotiation as a problem to be solved, and when they trust each other.

This sampling of findings makes it evident that we have a considerable body of empirical research on negotiation. An active community of researchers has made possible the establishment of several journals devoted exclusively to this topic. These include *Negotiation Journal, International Negotiation,* and *Group Decision and Negotiation.* As the knowledge continues to accumulate, we ask also about applications for improved analytical support, for negotiating strategy, and for training. We now turn to a brief discussion of the relation between research and practice.

Research and Practice

Although the findings summarized in the previous section came from studies conducted in the tradition of basic research, many of them may be used to inform practice as well. (See Chapter 2 for a distinction between basic and applied research.) Examples of application include giving advice about how to negotiate, contributing to improved case analysis and strategy development, and performing diagnoses of trends in an ongoing negotiation. Each of these applications is described briefly in turn.

Giving advice: The research offers implications for several strategies that may be used to improve the chances of reaching an agreement that satisfies all parties. Some examples include the following suggestions.

- Discourage quick agreements by avoiding rapid concession exchanges. (From research on integrative agreements)
- Avoid exchanging "too much" information if the prospect of an optimal solution looks promising. In-depth probes may reveal incompatibilities that escalate the conflict. (From research on information exchange)
- Time the displays of tough (withholding concessions) and soft (offering concessions or rewards) tactics, sequencing them by presenting firm postures early, softer postures later. (From research on concession-making strategies)
- Use experience or acquired skills in log-rolling and other tactics to secure improved outcomes for all the parties, not just the negotiator's. (From research on experience)
- Avoid approaching a negotiation as if it is a competition, and be wary of the temptation to see settlement itself as the main goal. (From research on orientations)
- Orchestrate the negotiating situation for flexibility by insulating the talks from the media, avoiding ideological debates, and reducing accountability to constituencies or other parties with vested interests in the outcome. (From research on the constraints on negotiator flexibility)
- Avoid embarrassing opponents. Allow them to take risks and be

inventive, and give them room to be flexible. (From research on face-saving)

• In mediation, third parties should suggest compromises early to establish a reputation for fairness, but discourage negotiators from actually making the suggested compromises in favor of an information search process. (From research on third-party effects)

Some of these suggestions involve managing the impressions conveyed from one negotiator to another. Others consist of altering the situation. All are under the control of the negotiators. The chances of any of them working depends to a large extent on whether all the negotiating parties agree that the tactics (or situation changes) are instrumental in achieving their shared goals.

Case analysis and strategy development: Another type of application consists of the use of research findings in the context of complex cases. The findings and the framework shown in Figure 11.1 provide a way of interpreting the process and outcome of a negotiation. For example, students working with the case of the Korean Joggers (a 1977 shoe export agreement) showed that the two nations – South Korea and the USA – reached quick agreements, leaving aside the resolution of issues that would have contributed to a more lasting solution. The combined influences of time pressure with power asymmetry served to limit the amount of time spent exchanging information. Korea's flattery coupled with tough posturing secured it a pretty good deal, as might be expected from the findings on two-face (or "reformed sinner") strategies in negotiation. These and other case analyses benefited considerably from the research.

The research findings help also in the development of strategies for resolving impasses in actual cases. For example, a student team working with the failed 1983 multilateral talks over Lebanon developed a plan to help move the parties toward a favorable agreement. They proposed a format for exchanging information, using rewards in conjunction with sanctions, minimizing the role of time pressure, and tactically using friendship, ingratiation, and secrecy in building and sustaining relationships. Ideas from the research were also useful in developing a strategy for the failed 1989 multilateral FAO governing conference. By relaxing time pressures, appealing to moderate constituencies in the USA, building friendships, and using rewards, this student "consulting" team offered a plan that could provide the flexibility needed for an agreement that eluded the diplomats. In attempting to improve the 1977 Korea–U.S. agreement on shoe exports, the strategy team proposed a two-step process that included a pre-negotiation conference for relationship-building and a negotiation structured for problem-solving. These strategies were based on research findings on the tactical use of anger, rewards, information exchange, and alternatives.

The students who participated in these exercises were given summaries of findings in narrative form corresponding to the themes discussed in the previous section. They then applied this knowledge in their work on analysis and strategy development. They also designed exercises for training that highlighted the themes. For example, using the case of the Korean Joggers, one team built a training exercise to prepare the negotiators to participate in their proposed two-step problem-solving strategy. The exercise incorporated ideas from the findings on relationship in the context of power asymmetry, affect, flexibility, and integrative processes. For more details on these exercises and on an evaluation of their effectiveness, see Druckman and Robinson (1998). An update on the exercises and further evaluations can be found in Druckman (2006). This article is a chapter in a larger work edited by Schneider and Honeyman (2006). In that work the editors present a considerable variety of approaches to negotiating and to developing negotiating skills. They conclude that a canon may be emerging in the form of things that should be included in every negotiation course. The list is long but manageable thanks to the way these editors have organized the 80 chapters of their book.

Diagnosing negotiating flexibility: The research is also useful for diagnosing the state of a negotiation and for projecting future trends. By asking questions, derived from findings, about various aspects of the process and the conditions surrounding that process, analysts can develop estimates of the extent to which each party is flexible at any point in time. Supported by computer software, the estimates may be displayed on a grid indicating where each party stands and what this means for the chances of reaching an agreement. Applications of this approach have shown that it is possible to isolate the source for inflexibility – in the internal delegation processes, in the interparty communications, in the situation, or in the issues themselves. These applications have been quite useful for diagnosing a variety of international cases (see Druckman, 1995; Druckman *et al.*, 2000). For other interesting computer applications for negotiation analysis, see Starkey *et al.* (1999).

More recently, computer-aided methods have been used for addressing complex problems of international conflict resolution and prevention. The complexity of these problems – including those relevant to negotiation – entails more sophisticated analytical methods. These methods include Markov chains, self-organizing maps, decision trees, rule learning by machines, and wavelet analysis. The approaches are shown to provide added value to analyses performed with statistical techniques, both for identifying important variables in negotiation and at the macro level of international (or inter-state) relations on security, trade, and environmental issues.

As noted in Chapter 2, the divide between research and practice is not as wide as it once was. There was a time when basic and applied researchers interacted largely within their own communities and cultures. Now the gap is bridged by the sorts of effort described in this section. Research knowledge becomes applied knowledge when it is translated into skills that contribute to the resolution of conflicts. These skills include the advice given to a practitioner by a consultant, the explanations given by an analyst for why particular processes result in certain outcomes, the strategies devised by third parties for resolving impasses, and the diagnoses developed by analysts with the help of computer aids.

Conclusion

The discussion in this chapter makes evident the progress made to date. The progress has occured in several directions. One direction consists of the crafting of frameworks that guide theory and research. Whether focusing attention on preferences, moves and counter-moves, organizational processes, or systemic relations, frameworks are useful instruments for analysis and synthesis. Another direction is the large amount of empirical research reported in journals over the past thirty years. From ways emotions influence negotiation to the effectiveness of various tactics, research gives us a wide body of knowledge that helps us interpret negotiating behavior. It also provides advice, sometimes counter-intuitive, about what may or may not work during the process of negotiating. The nexus between theory and research on the one hand and practice on the other is the third direction of progress. Whether used to facilitate case analysis and strategy or in the form of computer-aided tools, applications to date have reduced the gulf between theory and practice. Today many researchers are actively engaged with practitioners in diagnosing the course of a negotiation and planning strategies that can resolve impasses and produce optimal results.

Looking ahead, there are some gaps in our understanding that need to be addressed by the research. One area for further exploration is the organizational subcultures of professional negotiators: What are these cultures? How are negotiators socialized to become part of them? What role do they play in resolving conflicts through negotiation? To what extent have these cultures contributed to the gulf between researchers and practitioners? Another area concerns the increased complexity of both domestic and international negotiation. A larger number of actors and relationships among these actors have increased the complexity of analysis and practice. Our conceptual frameworks must now encompass the trend toward multilateralism as well as the burgeoning number of internal conflicts that occur within countries and organizations. We are only beginning to develop frameworks to guide research on multilateral negotiation and the wider web of constituencies that complicate the negotiator's boundary role dilemmas (Zartman, 1994). As we focus on highly charged negotiations among groups seeking new sources of identity in failed states (and organizations) and countries undergoing profound social and economic changes, the role of values and emotions in negotiation will undoubtedly receive more attention. As we encourage comparative case analyses, we must also view negotiation as a larger process that includes pre-negotiation and implementation stages and as part of a larger strategy that includes unilateral initiatives, mediation, and multi-track activities. The study of negotiation will benefit from attempts to connect it to developments in the larger field of conflict resolution as discussed in this volume.

Discussion Questions

1 Discuss some differences between micro- (dyads, small groups) and macro- (organizations, nations) level perspectives on negotiation. How might the different perspectives be combined in analyses of negotiation?

2 Discuss the value of conceptual frameworks for organizing the various parts of negotiation. What aspects of negotiation might you add to those listed in Figure 11.1?

3 What are a few of the conclusions you might reach from the research findings on the role of background factors in negotiation?

4 What are a few of the conclusions suggested from the research on the influence of conditions surrounding a negotiation?

5 Discuss some relationships between negotiation processes and outcomes. What processes are most conducive to reaching integrative agreements?

6 What are some ways in which the research on negotiation has contributed to the practice of negotiating? What kinds of support can researchers or analysts provide to negotiating delegations?

7 What are some gaps in understanding of negotiation that need to be filled by research or analysis?

8 Negotiation is one of several approaches that can be used to resolve conflict between groups. How does it differ from the other forms of intervention discussed in this section? What are some advantages and disadvantages in relation to the other approaches?

Key Words

Conceptual frameworks
Negotiating behavior
Outcomes
Practice
Processes
Research applications
Strategies
Tactics
Theory

CHAPTER 15

Informal Roles

Johannes M. Botes

Most people do not think of themselves as peacemakers, conflict resolvers or third parties that intervene in conflict as part of their everyday lives. Yet, as Kolb and her associates (1994, p. 355) point out:

> People do it all the time. Yet their professional identity is not that of mediator. Rather, they are policemen, employees, mothers, diplomats, judges, social workers, bosses, neighbors, [and] teachers. In ongoing situations of conflict and dispute, people get involved and try to help parties deal with their differences.

Ury (1999, p. 7) has a similar and also very broad understanding of the way that everyone – relatives, neighbors, allies, friends, or onlookers – become "the third side" in the disputes they encounter in their daily lives. On occasion, we all assume roles that prevent, contain, or resolve conflict. Moreover, the countless informal interventions in social conflict that occur in a multitude of cultural contexts every day provide a "kind of *social immune system*" against the negative effects of interpersonal and community conflict.

In spite of the broad consensus that informal conflict intervention is a central part of continuous social interactions, this phenomenon seems understudied. The lack of empirical literature in this regard does not apply to the study of managers as informal third parties (see Walton, 1969; Kolb and Sheppard, 1985; Kolb, 1986; Sheppard *et al.*, 1989; Karambayya and Brett, 1994; Schoorman and Champayne, 1994; Pinkley *et al.*, 1995; Arnold and O'Conner, 1999). It is not possible to provide a comprehensive overview of informal third parties within the scope of this chapter. The aim here is rather more limited. It is to provide some comparisons between formal and informal third-party intervention, to explore different types of informal third-party intervention, and finally to provide some thoughts on how some different avenues for research could add to a more precise description of informal third-party intervention.

Formal Versus Informal Third Parties

Informal intervenors are often described in terms of how their actions or roles differ from those of formal third parties. Individuals who perform informal third-party roles do so outside of the realm of conflict management as a profession. In fact, many of them might not even know that such a formal social role or field of study exists. As Dukes (1996, p.7) observes, as elected officials, civil servants, teachers, attorneys, and citizens from every walk of life, these individuals do not consider themselves part of any field, or movement. In fact, "one does not have to belong to a professional organization, or use the title 'mediator' or 'facilitator', to be doing this work." How then should informal third parties, as opposed to third parties who intervene in conflicts in more formal settings, be defined?

There are a number of ways in which informal interventions differ from more formal mediation or arbitration efforts. Based on the work of Kolb and Sheppard (1985), Sheppard *et al.* (1989, pp. 166–7) note first that informal third parties have a continuing relationship with the disputants, as opposed to the "transient relationship of a neutral [formal] third party whose primary concern is resolution of the conflict." Informal third parties are also often part of the dispute, or at least part of the family, organizational, or community setting within which the conflict occurs. In contrast to formal third parties, such as mediators, judges, and arbitrators, informal third parties have a range of intervention options available to them. They have intervention options that are less dictated by the nature of their societal roles or by any training that prescribes how they should intercede in their work or interpersonal environments. The social context within which informal interventions occur is therefore a determining factor for the behavior and strategies of this kind of third-party intervenor.

Informal third parties are often viewed as individuals with "professional" roles (doctors, parents, and managers) who incorporate mediation techniques into their work, either intentionally or unintentionally. Kriesberg's (1991, p. 23) notion of "quasi-mediators" is helpful in order to illustrate this conception of informal third-party intervention. He refers to the work of Berman and Johnson (1977) and

McDonald and Bendahmane (1987) in noting that "these include church officials, journalists, and academics representing constituencies which are not one of the primary adversaries in the dispute." Leaving aside the international context in which Kriesberg first mentioned this concept, quasi-mediators could be described as individuals who perform a number of overt or behind-the-scenes dispute resolution roles without becoming mediators in any formal sense.

In their capacities as third parties, some informal intervenors are also similar to what Wehr and Lederach (1991, p. 87) call "insider-partial[s]." They become "mediators" from inside the sphere of the conflict whose "acceptability to the conflictants is rooted not in distance from the conflict or objectivity regarding the issues, but rather in connectedness and trusted relationships with the conflict parties." They are therefore neither truly neutral, nor external to the conflict, as one could argue is the case with formal intervenors (Pinkley et al., 1995). Conversely, informal intervenors are sometimes also "outsiders" to many of the conflicts they become involved in because they have no relationship with the parties prior to their intervention encounter. "Outsider-neutrals," according to the Wehr and Lederach (1991, p. 87) model, leave the conflict as soon as it is settled, or, at the very least, addressed. Informal intervenors adhere to both of these models. They can be insider or insider neutrals, depending on the nature of the intervention or the type of intervenor.

Writing about workplace settings, Kolb (1992, p. 65) uses the concept of insider-outsider intervenors in a related but somewhat different manner. She defines outsider mediators as people who intervene as consultants or mediators for organizations or within specific cases. They are conflict resolution experts and are usually paid for their services. She defines insider "peacemakers" as people whose expertise come from their insider status, their understanding of the psychology of the situation, and their knowledge of political realities of the system within which they operate. As examples of the insider-outsider model, Kolb (1989) mentions labor mediators as outsiders and ombudspersons as insiders. Informal peacemaking has become one of the most common forms of conflict management in organizations. It is probably one of the conflict arenas where informal intervention is currently most accepted.

Informal Intervention

Most informal third parties have very little or no training, nor professional rules or descriptions, for their interventions. Broadly speaking, third parties are categorized in terms of the nature of the intervention and the intervenor's mandate (Kaufman and Duncan, 1989). Informal third parties such as parents or police officers decide to intervene on their own or are brought into the dispute by the parties concerned. As insider intervenors they are therefore self-appointed, or become involved in an incident where they will maintain control over the process, and to a degree, also over the outcome of the intervention. In contrast, formal mediators transfer information and inform choices, according to Kaufman and Duncan's model, but they do not make, promote, or implement choices. Parents, in contrast, indeed make and implement choices when they intervene in their children's disputes, as do police officers in dealing with members of the public at times. The mandate (to intervene) that various formal and informal intervenors have clearly differs depending on their professional and societal roles.

A number of typologies have been created to define the informal dispute intervention behaviors that occur in organizations (Sheppard, 1983, 1984; Karambayya and Brett, 1989). Pinkley and his colleagues note that while they differ in their emphasis, the various categorizations of managerial third-party actions essentially consist of a number of strategies that exert both process and outcome control. Intervention strategies are obviously also linked to the goals of the intervenor. In their study of the factors that managers and police officers consider in deciding whether to intervene, Lissak and Sheppard (1983) identified fairness, effectiveness, and efficiency, as well as disputant satisfaction and commitment as significant criteria. Another important issue is which intervention style will be the most effective in achieving specific goals. Lewicki *et al.* (1997, pp. 210–12) note that higher and lower amounts of process or decision control will achieve different results. They refer to Sheppard's (1983) identification of four intervention styles used by managers: inquisitorial, mediational, adversarial, and providing impetus (exerting very little control over the process, but warning the disputants that the solutions can be imposed on them if necessary). According to Lewicki and his colleagues, it is important to note that "mediational intervention" is not a style commonly used by managers because they have a need to exert control over the outcome of the conflict.

> Although managers claim to prefer mediation as a third-party style, it is not clear that managers really understand how to mediate without being trained to do so. When handling a conflict, managers seem prone to assume responsibility for having a major impact on the outcome of the conflict; that is, the specific decision or outcome arrived at by the disputing parties. Therefore, managers may be very uncomfortable using a mediation strategy which requires that they control the process of conflict but leave the situation in the hands of the disputants. (Lewicki *et al.*, 1997, p. 211)

In spite of the questions about whether managers really mediate,

Sheppard's (1984, 1989) research demonstrates that most informal workplace interventions follow a pattern that resembles a very scaled down model of mediation: defining the problem, discussing the relevant information, selecting alternatives and making attempts at reconciling the parties.

In her study of women as peacemakers in organizations, Kolb (1992) observed four types of intervention activities: providing *support* by allowing people to tell their stories, *reframing* people's understanding of a situation, *translating* the parties' perceptions of each other, and *orchestrating* occasions for private conflicts to be made public. Kolb (1986, 1989) also suggests that the way managers frame their third-party roles is highly dependent on their backgrounds and professional training. The frame which informal third parties such as managers impose on their work influence the criteria they use in their interventions (Sheppard *et al.*, 1989). Intervention frames, such as judging which party is right or wrong, or recognizing that there might be legitimacy to the arguments on both sides, or a frame that essentially wants to end the conflict, will each shape the behavior of the third party differently (Sheppard *et al.*, 1991).

Informal Third Parties in Other Than Organizational Settings

Based on their individual and professional contexts, some informal third parties frame what they do very differently from organizational third parties. Police officers, who are expected to "resolve" conflicts at the scene of an interpersonal dispute (between parents and children, neighbors, and others), normally do not have a prior relationship with these parties while the parties in the majority of these cases have an ongoing relationship. DuBow and Currie (1993) argue that police officers rarely solve problems in interpersonal disputes and rarely make efforts at serious mediation. They quote from Black's (1980) study, which concluded that while police officers intervene in conflict they are relatively indifferent to the parties' legal, medical, or interpersonal needs. Black's major finding about dispute settlement by police is that in most cases officers do nothing, or very little, to assist parties in reaching a lasting solution to the conflict.

In an author's note to his study on *Mediation and Arbitration by Patrol Police Officers*, Cooper (1999) "calls attention to the reluctance of police administrations and police officers to welcome non-conventional conflict/dispute resolution training and trainers into police work." Cooper defines non-conventional conflict/dispute resolution (NCDR) as methods and processes that do not involve force, coercion, or arrest. According to him, NCDR is suitable in a number of situations with which patrol police officers are confronted, such as public disputes, barricades, community disputes, domestic conflict, and family disputes. This scaled-down mediation model may be conducted by patrol officers in a multiplicity of places such as basketball courts, parking lots, living rooms, or sidewalks, and the parties can be either sitting down or standing up.

The actual interventions should consist of a number of simplified mediation phases: listening to the disputants, helping them to frame the issues, and keeping the discussion goal-directed in order to assist the disputants to reach their own resolution. Cooper (1999, pp. 8–9) calls this model "formal" mediation versus "informal" mediation, which can occur unbeknownst to the parties because getting their permission to mediate, or to explain the process, might escalate an already intense situation. When this mediation process fails, or in situations where the officer has given the parties ample time to create their own solution, the officer could simply decide on an outcome. In subsequent work, Cooper (2001, p. 285) argued that whether police officers perform "real" mediations or a "variant" of mediation should be answered by whether they adhere to a systemic process of mediation in performing their third-party roles. Furthermore, police officers who have not been trained formally in mediation processes tend not to conduct formal mediations. In Davis's (1991, 2000) studies of stranger intervention into child punishment in public places, as well as stranger intervention into intimate assaults by men against women in public settings, the reasons for intervening are again very distinct. Most intervenors in the child punishment cases (Davis, 1991, p. 232) describe their reasons for intervening as "instinctive," or "a matter of reflexes." Davis (1991) argues that this type of informal intervenor experiences what Adler (1981) refers to as "intervention momentum." Under such circumstances, he or she starts by tolerating the initial hitting before feeling compelled to step in by verbally intervening. Based on the work of Emerson and Messinger (1977), Davis (1991, p. 242) defines members of the public who initiate a face-to-face encounter with wrongdoers as "intervention generalists," intervenors who lack any recognized authority, formal intervention ideologies, or institutional support for their actions. As a result these interventions are normally very brief and they might end, irrespective of the outcome of the hitting incident.

While there are as yet no societal rules for engagement in public intervention cases, Davis (2000, p. 33) holds that such intervenors may have "informal remedial protocols" in mind, especially as public intervention becomes more normative. Such protocols, he argues, "might take the form of ideas about what steps aggravate or mollify the people involved and about the 'tricks' and techniques intervenors might use to distract, placate or reform wrong doers."

Invariably many informal third parties struggle to find an appropriate role and method of intervention for themselves. Consider the self-doubts a Mennonite pastor experienced about how to respond when two members of his congregation requested a meeting to discuss their differences:

> What exactly was my role in such a meeting? Mediator? No, at least not in a traditional sense. Could I be completely objective? No. I had a previous relationship with both of them. Could I provide a safe space? Would I be able to respond in an equally pastoral way to both? Perhaps, I wasn't sure. (Adams, 1998, p. 9)

As this case indicates, many informal intervenors seem to sense that their roles should be less than that of a mediator, but at the same time they have difficulties defining exactly what the process should be. The lessons from one situational or organizational setting do not necessarily translate to other social contexts (because of the informal third party's different goals and intervention needs in diverse settings). Moreover, as Kolb and Sheppard (1985, p. 387) observe: "if arbitration and mediation are alien to managerial settings, what about parents, friends, deans, neighbors, or the clergy?"

Only when these informal intervenors are studied in greater depth will we be able to understand how their interventions (roles, behaviors, and strategies) should be explained and utilized. Our need to have better answers to questions in this regard might arise much faster than we think. As Davis (2000, pp. 33–4) foreshadows: "as people come to see interpersonal violence, racism, and harassment as 'everybody's business,' we can expect more people giving public intervention a try."

Further Defining Informal Third Parties: Intent, Goals, Arenas, and Roles

According to Kolb and her colleagues (1994, p. 355), informal intervention in conflict is important because it probably represents the form of mediation that is used most extensively. If we accept the premise that more and more professionals outside of the conflict resolution profession – police, managers, teachers, and physicians – are "incorporating the techniques of mediation" into their work, then this burgeoning area of the field deserves much more scholarly attention than it is currently receiving. Most of these social actors, as well as their particular type of "mediative" interventions, are very diverse in type and behavior. For example, the notion that informal third parties normally intervene in conflicts where they have an ongoing relationship with the parties involved does not seem to hold up across the various types. While parents, managers, and teachers always have continuous relationships with the parties, the same cannot be said of the police, or bystanders who are mostly uninvited intervenors in random disputes. Some of these interventions transpire as part of an ongoing stream of interaction (Kolb, 1986) between the parties, while others occur between parties who do not work or live together, thereby changing the nature of the dispute.

In spite of the range and prevalence of informal intervention activities in various professional and other settings, it is difficult to study this phenomenon in a systematic manner. In some part this is due to the unpredictability of how and when such interventions occur, and the fact that "on the spot" interventions are rarely documented in any ongoing fashion. Meanwhile informal intervention keeps developing in different milieus. Of late, for example, military officers who are part of peace-keeping operations have reluctantly become informal intervenors as part of larger "nation-building" roles. These conflict situations have turned all levels of command, from soldiers to platoon leaders, as well as company and battalion level commanders, into positions where they have had to assume roles as facilitators and "quasi-mediator [s]" of conflict (Cucolo, 1998, p. 21).

Other than studying the new environments in which informal interventions take place, it may also be beneficial to consider the intervenors' intent and goals. Most formal third parties are either assigned to perform this role, or actively seek it. Most informal third parties are compelled to do so as an auxiliary task based on their professional role (in the case of managers and police officers) or structural position (in the case of teachers and parents). So while most informal intervenors do not have an "intervention intent," some normally have little choice in the matter. Yet others – such as individuals who intervene in public violence – do so out of moral conviction or act based on a set of personal values.

The various conflict arenas where these interventions take place may also assist in defining this phenomenon more precisely. For example, when a pastor intervenes in the dispute of two members of the church – as described in the Adams case above – it is clearly an informal act because it is done as a part of his larger pastoral role within his professional system, the Mennonite Church. However, when the Mennonite Church in America organizes and formalizes its peacemaking roles (see Sampson and Lederach, 2000), in order to perform such activities in other conflict settings and even in other countries, one could argue that these activities constitute purposeful intent and formal intervention roles. Similarly, when scholar practitioners such as Fisher (1991, 1997a) and Kelman (1992) intervene in foreign conflict by providing interactive training workshops, one could again reason that they operate outside of their own academic and professional systems and that they do so with a formal conflict resolution intent. Put differently, when individuals intercede in conflicts that do not form part of their family, work, or community systems, they make an active choice that places them in the sphere of formal intervenors. Therefore, third-party roles performed on anything but an ad hoc basis seem by definition to be done in a formal, organized, and institutionalized manner.

Finally, the concept of "role" is a very underappreciated notion in much of the literature on informal intervenors, and in fact it is often used without any explanation of its meaning or application in this regard. In his seminal study on social roles, Banton (1965) noted that while the role concept may be utilized to formulate problems for investigation, the notion of social roles is defined in a variety of ways which pertain to status, role behavior, and role enactment. According to Banton (1965, pp. 28–9), the original role theorists did agree on the following:

> that behavior can be related to a *position* in a social structure; that actual behavior can be related to an individual's own ideas of what is appropriate (*role cognitions*), and to other people's ideas about what he *will* do (*expectations*), or to the other people's ideas about what he *should* do (*norms*). In this light, a role may be understood as a *set* of *norms and expectations applied to the incumbent of a particular position.*

Current role definitions, such as the one proposed by Johnson (1995), conform to these demarcations. In addition to the notion that "role" is associated with social status, Johnson also defines role performance as linked to self-image, values related to goals, and attitudes toward work. Such role factors all come into play when we define third parties of all stripes, and therefore need closer attention. As Kolb (1986, p. 209) asserts, "third-party interventions are highly variable processes shaped by the institutional contexts in which they occur and by the ideology and role frames of its practitioners."

Discussion Questions

1 How would you define informal third parties as opposed to formal third parties?
2 Can you think of any informal third parties that were not mentioned in this chapter?
3 Should informal third parties be trained in third-party skills, or would they then become formal third parties?
4 Do formal and informal third parties perform different intervention roles?

5 From your personal perspective, are the public intervention actions that Davis refers to in this chapter appropriate third-party roles?
6 Is it possible, or advisable, to create ethical rules or codes of conduct for informal third parties?
7 Can you think of ways of conducting research on informal third parties in action?

Key Words

Formal intervention
Formal third parties
Informal intervention
Informal third parties
Insider neutrals
Outsider neutrals
Quasi-mediators

CHAPTER 16

Mediation and Arbitration

Sandra Cheldelin

Alternatives to litigation – especially mediation and arbitration – for resolving conflicts have a rich and varied history. Moore (1996) documents the practice of mediation over the centuries and across cultures. He cites examples during biblical time in the Jewish communities as well as practices in Islamic, Arabic, Hindu, and Buddhist cultures. There is evidence of centuries of practices in Spain, North Africa, Central and Eastern Europe, the Middle East, China, and Japan. As we know of mediation today in North America, however, the practice became official in 1913 when the U.S. Department of Labor established a panel called the Commissioners of Conciliation. The biggest boom to the movement emerged over the following decades due to struggles between labor and management in the USA. The contemporary (North American) practice of mediation has since received much attention, especially in the past several decades.

Arbitration, though not as old, was evident as early as the 1400s with the English using their own "law merchants" – guided by their merchant culture – as first alternative to English public law. Several colonies, and especially New York, practiced commercial arbitration prior to the American Revolution. Labor arbitration in the USA boomed during the 1940s with the growth of labor unions. Today more than 95 percent of collective bargaining contracts provide for final and binding arbitration (Goldberg *et al.*, 1999).

These two practices today are key components of the fastest growing area of practice of conflict resolution, and fall under the broad category of alternative dispute resolution (ADR). A significant growth spurt occurred following the national conference of the American Bar Association in 1976. There, participants explored causes and solutions to the growing log-jams in the courts and general public dissatisfaction with the legal system. The conference concluded with an agreement that other forms of resolution would reduce costs and help with overcrowded dockets. By the 1980s a number of experiments emerged as alternatives to the traditional legal system, including Neighborhood Justice Centers, Multidoor Court Houses, Mini-trials, and Regulatory Negotiation (Kolb, 1994). Many practitioners took their work to conflict-ridden schools, communities, and organizations. But the largest groups of these ADR practitioners were, and continue to be, mediators and arbitrators. This chapter's primary focus is on the practices of mediation and arbitration today. Other popular forms of third-party intervention and conflict resolution are expanded in subsequent chapters. We begin with mediation – what it is and how it works – followed by a brief survey of the research on its practice. The second part of this chapter introduces arbitration – what it is and how it works – followed by examples of hybrids that exist that combine the two, of which the most common example is "med-arb."

Mediation Defined

Moore's (1996, p. 8) definition of mediation best captures the essential elements of mediation in Western (North American) tradition:

> an extension or elaboration of the negotiation process that involves the intervention of an acceptable third party who has limited or no authoritative decision-making power.

This third party assists the disputants in reaching an acceptable settlement by problem-solving, transforming the relationship, or some combination of the two. We are most familiar with this model of mediation where the mediator is neutral, or at least not directly involved in the dispute, and acceptable to each party in conflict. Mediation models are not universal, however. To understand any model we must look at the assumptions about the process, the roles of the intervenor, and the purposes or goals of the mediation. Processes, roles, and purposes vary considerably across cultural contexts. Different goals are particularly apparent in two types of mediation: the traditional Western model and the newer transformative model.

The Western model of mediation

This is the most commonly used model of mediation in North America. The process is confidential and voluntary and can be stopped at any time by any of the parties, including the mediator. The process helps parties repair relationships, communicate more clearly, understand their own needs and interests, and generate creative solutions to their problems. It usually begins with an initial assessment by interviewing each party. Mediators then convene the session, establish their role, outline the process, set ground rules, and create structures for parties to tell their "stories" about their dispute. Mediators help parties achieve clarity on the issues, assist with collaborative problem-solving, and conclude by drafting written agreements for parties to endorse and implement.

Mediators are impartial – not stakeholders in the conflict – and therefore referred to as third parties or neutrals. Mediators do not impose decisions; rather, they serve as gatekeepers of a process. They vary significantly, however, in the ways they define their role, and especially their involvement in promoting solutions. In contrast, some focus primarily on the process of negotiation, leaving the substantive content to the disputants. This procedural orientation is common among labor-management, environmental, and (many) family mediators. Some believe that they, while staying relatively neutral, should be actively engaged in the substantive issues, especially when the parties have significant power differences. Many child custody mediators take this perspective because of their concern for unrepresented stakeholders (e.g., children).

The transformative model

The goal of the previous model of mediation is to help parties engage in a problem-solving venture in order to seek a formal (contractual) agreement. Proponents of transformative mediation are actively challenging this model (Bush and Folger, 1994; Lederach, 1995a; Kraybill and Price, 1995). The most important goals of transformative mediation are empowerment of both parties and recognition of the value of their relationship. For these practices, the problem-solving approach is limiting because it does not provide adequate opportunities for people to develop new relational connections. The problem-solving model measures success according to whether the parties reach settlement, whereas the transformative model empowers parties, allowing them to fully appreciate each other's situation regardless of any eventual outcome.

Lederach (1995a) identifies four dimensions of transformation: personal, relational, structural, and cultural. The personal dimension involves the emotional, perceptual, and spiritual impact on the individuals involved. The relational dimension involves the communication and interactive patterns of the disputants. The structural dimension includes the underlying causes, patterns, and changes in their social systems including basic human needs and resources. The cultural dimension involves the impact of accumulated shared patterns of interaction. Operationally the two mediation models are very similar – assessment, story-telling, problem-solving, agreement – but embedded in the transformational model is recognition of the need for emotional healing.

The debate about the differences is ongoing. Milner (1996), for example, argues that many of the points proponents such as Bush and Folger espouse remain in the structural and political domain and therefore set up false expectations for mediation to address injustices in the heat of the conflict. This is further explored later in this chapter as some mediators believe structural changes can be addressed in the mediation process. Such concerns are often the topics at national and international ADR conferences.

Institutionalization of Mediation Services

Regardless of the purported goals, the breadth of articles promoting mediation across sectors, the changes in regulations to provide access to the practice of mediation, and the growth in the number of practitioners seeking education, training, and, in some states, licensure, all exemplify the impressive growth of mediation services and what we might call the institutionalization of the practice. Chaney's (1999) "Mediation for the masses" accentuates this expansion of mediation services as she promotes the readily available low-budget conflict resolution services that mediators offer to the public for civil or domestic related disputes.

The Alternative Dispute Resolution Act of 1998 required all federal district courts to adopt local rules creating voluntary dispute resolution procedures and was responsible for creating mediation programs in all federal courts. The same is happening in several state courts. The U.S. Equal Employment Opportunity Commission (EEOC) – which administers and enforces the U.S. antidiscrimination laws – expanded its voluntary mediation program and, in the 1999 fiscal year budget, the U.S. Congress authorized the agency to spend up to $13 million on its ADR program. The American Bar Association's House of Delegates approved the resolution supporting the use of mediation and arbitration to resolve disputes involving private health plans and managed care programs.

Corporations and small businesses, too, are encouraging employees to use ADR – particularly mediation and arbitration – as the first option with conflicts. Trade magazines such as *Business Week* (October 12, 1998) promote the use of mediation in terms of costs, outcomes, and increasing long-term effects of settlements. For example, Lee (1998) explains what ADR is, how to access ADR professionals, and provides case examples of the types of conflict ADR professionals resolve. Hovey (1999) found a significant number of small businesses had joined large corporations pledging to use mediation instead of the court system to settle any Y2K disputes (though as we now know, ultimately unnecessary). Women with legal grievances (e.g., sexual harassment or discrimination) are encouraged to use mediation so that their voices will be both heard and seriously considered. Herrnstein (1996) believes this alternative is less confrontive or adversarial, and likely to be taken seriously at the lowest levels of entry into grievance processes.

The tension is lessening between the traditional legal system and the emergence of alternatives for resolving conflicts. Although ADR systems are generally well received in the world of attorneys, guides are readily available to help attorneys fully understand the concept and process of mediation with particular attention to ways mediators can work with inexperienced negotiators (Craver, 1999).

Examples of mediation are also found in the religious community, such as when former President Jimmy Carter brought together twenty Baptist leaders – feuding conservatives and moderates – that resulted in a signed declaration expressing mutual respect for one another and voicing common concerns about racial reconciliation and religious persecution (*Christian Century*, April 22–29, 1998). The Mennonite Conciliation Service offers mediation services around the world for the prevention and response to conflict and violence (Kraybill, 1995).

Mediation services are not limited to adults. Peer mediation programs are found in schools across the USA where students are trained to mediate problems among their peers. At both the primary and secondary levels, the National Association for Mediation in Education (NAME) facilitates and coordinates dissemination of peer mediation information. Parent–child mediation programs work with families involving truant and runaway children.

The use of mediation with families is also prevalent. Take, for example, child custody disputes. Mediation may be a "fast and cheap" means to pay direct attention to the rights and interests of children, especially when parents are without fear of intimidation when confronting each other (Mason, 1999). For several years some states have even required mediation as a prerequisite to the traditional court system for working out child custody and visitation recommendations (Kelly, 1996).

Mediation with different stakeholders could be a creative way to challenge the dominant model of child protective services. In most of these cases, service providers engage "immediate stakeholders" – children, parents, grandparents – yet the failings of child protection systems have been problematic for years, even though providers continuously explore alternative means of helping children. What if we were to get the community involved in child welfare cases by letting mediators link families to community members who can provide constructive feedback and support mechanisms? Barsky (1999) proposes such a model. He realizes this would, of course, require ongoing community development. Some family members may not want others in the community to become involved in their problems, may have significant concerns about lack of privacy, and the lack of apparent strategies for "saving face." Nevertheless, expanding child protection resources may assist in the family healing process.

The institutionalization of mediation is not limited to North America. In post-World War II Europe (1949) grave concern existed about the protection of human rights and the need for common legal procedures throughout Europe. The Committee of Ministers – the decision-making body of the Council of Europe – adopted a recommendation at its 616th meeting of the Ministers and Deputies to introduce and promote mediation in resolving family disputes (Lavin, 1999). Ten process criteria proposed in their recommendation included some key elements of what is now seen as traditional Western mediation: it should be voluntary, the mediator should be impartial to parties and neutral with respect to the outcome, should respect the points of view of all parties, should preserve the equality of the parties' bargaining positions, and should have no power to impose a solution. Any discussion of the mediation is confidential and a guarantee of privacy must exist. In addition, they recommended that states consider setting up mechanisms for using mediation when there is an international element, especially concerning child custody issues.

The Western model strongly advocates an individualistic approach both in the legal and ADR systems. The importance of community becomes more apparent as we consider the international arena and intercultural settings (Cooks, 1995). What follow are further examples of the institutionalization of mediation practice around the world, and variations on the Western practice model. The literature demonstrates a lively debate, a remarkable endorsement of mediation practice in new arenas, and research on the impact and understanding of the dynamics of the practice.

Mediation across disciplines and cultures

Sunoo (1990) offers practical rules of conduct for intercultural mediation practitioners based on her intercultural work. Along with such typical rules of listening carefully, and working toward win-win solutions, four are especially helpful: expect different expectations; do not assume you are being understood; be patient, humble, and willing to learn; and dare to do things differently.

Ogay (1998) presents the contribution of social psychology to mediation in the new networks of mediators in Europe. These mediators offer their services to the community to resolve minor conflicts through a mediated process. The mediator reconstructs the different perspectives of the dispute – from representatives throughout the community – and then negotiates a new means of interaction acceptable to all parties. These mediators are highly involved in the process, the creation of new stories (narratives), and the outcomes.

Could it be possible that the Japanese model of restorative justice could be adopted in the USA? Haley (1995) considered this model, also communitarian-based, where offender correction and restoration takes place in the community. Formal victim–offender mediation practices of the West do not exist in Japan. Rather, mediation is an integral part of the norms of Japanese culture. For example, law enforcers encourage offenders to confess, demonstrate remorse, and compensate the victim. The offenders are then pardoned. Communities embrace this model, allowing offenders full restoration – opportunities to be contributing members of their communities. This method of dealing with crime is unmatched in the USA. To adopt such a model would require significant community-based reintegration strategies.

Mediation is also being used to solve political conflicts in new social movements. Saretzki et al. (1997) explored an active mediation – vs. removed facilitation – as a popular alternative to other forms of conflict resolution, again, where the mediator takes initiative in the intervention. Potential problems with such an activist model, though, include the possibility of redrawing old lines of the conflict, and difficulties implementing mediation outcomes. The removed facilitation model is more likely to have the parties take responsibility for these initiatives where the disputants generate initial suggestions for resolution. Furthermore, Saretzki (1997) argues that mediation is not a social movement itself, nor is it intended to be one. Rather, mediation should examine how it can alter the opportunity structures of social movements. He is pessimistic that mediation can improve democratic participation and practice in its current form, especially when conflicting values exist (for example, often found in environmental disputes).

Tyler et al. (1998) conducted two studies to determine reactions to conflict resolution interventions depending on whether the conflict was within or across cultural boundaries. The within group were 305 employees and their supervisors in a U.S. public sector organization. The cross-cultural group included 215 English and Japanese teachers on an English-teaching program in Japan. Their research supported their prediction that mediators are judged more favorably if relational concerns are at the heart of the issues, especially in within-group disputes. This is a strong endorsement for the transformational mediation model being promoted in the West, if mediators want to be perceived as helpful.

When comparing family mediation practices within Vietnamese, Malaysian, Pakistani, and Ismaili communities in Canada, Barsky *et al.* (1996) used focus groups and informal interviews. They found that mediators can be successful working with different cultures. Callister and Wall (1997) supported their research when they studied non-Western cultural mediation practices in Japan, Hawaii, Malaysia, and China. Japanese traditions strongly influence Japanese mediation: preferences for harmony, value of hierarchy, and the importance of "saving face." Japanese mediators tend to be nonassertive. They focus on gathering information, listening to disputants, and relaying to each party what they learn from the other (a rephrasing technique). Compared to South Korea and the People's Republic of China, Japanese mediators were significantly less assertive.

A respected elder in the community is at the heart of mediation practiced in the Hawaiian oral-based mediation (ho'oponopono or "disentangling"). First, Wall and Callister (1995) studied this twelve-step process where there are specific tasks at each step. Disputants are brought together by the respected elder. Several religious practices are included and the process concludes with a period of silence, mutual forgiveness, and sharing of food. Wall and Callister (1999) also studied Malaysian community mediation. In Malaysian cities, conflicts are either tolerated, managed, or require police intervention. However, a different model exists in the villages: disputes are reported to the village administrator, a ketua kampung, or to the religious mosque leader, an imam. The imam settles all religious and some family disputes. The ketua kampung also settles family disputes. In their study of 127 ketua kampungs and fifty-two imams, they found that these mediators rely heavily on techniques of meeting with disputants, listening, gathering information, and then calling for concessions. The imams rely more on prayer, moral principles, and third-party advice and call less often for concessions. These mediators – ketua kampung and imams – are unique among Pacific Rim nations.

The practice of mediation is also present in the People's Republic of China. Wall *et al.* (1995) interviewed 125 mediators, asking them to describe two of their cases. One was a community-based dispute and the other a family-based dispute. In the interviews the researchers noted the frequency with which mediators reported use of any of thirty-three possible mediation techniques. They found that mediators in family-based disputes relied heavily on four mediation techniques: separating the parties (caucuses), calling for empathy (compassion), stating the other's point of view (paraphrasing and reframing), and utilizing logic (rationality). They did not find mediators separating the parties in community-based disputes. These same techniques are present in family- and community-based disputes in the West, but probably not with the same level of emphases.

Wall and Callister found China's mediation system to be very formal (unlike Malaysia, Korea, and Japan). The Chinese have a permanent set of mediators who handle disputes in each commune (village), street committee (city units), and work unit (Yin, 1984). The Chinese mediators' goal is to provide harmonious social relations to the community. The mediators in China are trained by the army to be forceful, and they employ force in their resolution processes (Wall and Callister, 1999).

The Study of Mediation Practice

In the past decade not only has the practice of mediation expanded significantly; so too has the study of the practice. Using a variety of research techniques, scholars and practitioners have tried to understand the nature of practice across a number of variables and cultures. A few examples and results of the research on mediation practice follow:

- Using one agency and conducting a historical content analysis, Wells and Liebman (1996) traced the history of the Federal Mediation and Conciliation Service (FMCS), the primary mediation source for labor and management in the USA. They found that the impact of revolutionary changes in the workplace, the global economy, and union–management relationships are significant contributors to the increased use of mediation.
- Milburn (1996) compared international and interpersonal mediation to identify any insights for mediation theory and practice. He looked at the similarities and differences of mediators, mediation processes, mediation subtleties, and enforcement success. He found that these two entry levels – interpersonal and international – can inform each other and should not remain as separated as they are in the field today.
- Hirschsohn (1996) studied the labor law reform in South Africa that created an unintentional rapid growth of a powerful black trade union movement. The Independent Mediation Service of South Africa helped to disseminate information from the broader industrialized use of the practice of negotiated order. As a result of the negotiation transition, a new democratic order emerged that utilized inclusive, consensus-building, and policy-making processes.

- Carter's (1999) research demonstrates a need to improve the mediation processes and outcomes when violence is a significant factor. Studying school-based conflicts, she found mediation with diverse disputants – by ethnicity and gender – often failed to reach "just" solutions for both parties. In seeking justice, further research may help determine whether or not "assertive" negotiation – mediation tactics that advocate or influence – will work better in seeking "just" solutions for disputants when assertiveness is not their normative behavior.

- Kruk (1998) surveyed more than 500 family mediators across Canada focusing on the nature of their practice, including issues, strategies and interventions, theories, and models for their practice. While most research focuses on outcomes of mediation, Kruk assessed the actual process of mediation and the working methods of mediators. Briefly, he found the practice to be extremely diverse – dispute characteristics, client populations served, and methods or options utilized. He found the greatest differences between the lawyer mediators and mental health practitioner mediators. Kruk also found a significant shift over the past decade:

  In its [family mediation field] zeal to establish itself as a viable alternative method of dispute resolution, only a decade ago it focused on the development of a mainstream, highly struc- tured, neutralist approach that would unify a diverse group of professionals working in a range of practice settings. ... Alternative practice models have flourished during the past decade ... mediation will become an attractive alternative for a much larger group of clientele. (Kruk, 1998, pp. 214–15)

- As a final example of research on mediation practice, Lund's (1999) research resulted in a compelling plea for special emphasis in mediation training to be placed on the understanding and management of emotions. She found that to intervene effectively and appropriately, trainee mediators must learn to understand their own emotions as well as ways to cope with emotional reactions of disputants. She presents specific techniques to prepare mediators to deal with high-conflict emotional mediations. Although most mediators believe they control the process but not the content, their control over the process may be limited as some high-conflict cases go back and forth between mediation and litigation. Having emotional stamina is essential for effective mediation, particularly in these difficult cases.

A further review of the literature found a number of research articles that clustered around specific and current topics.

Profiles of practitioners

Deborah Kolb and her associates (1994) presented one of the most influential studies of mediation. They conducted in-depth analyses of the work of twelve highly visible and successful mediators to learn more of the practice of mediation. They found three types of practitioners who fall into the two categories noted above: those who seek a trans-formation of relationships, and those who seek settlement of disputes. The first category of the three types of practitioners includes the *builders of the field* who engage in public advocacy for mediation and its processes. They are strong promoters of mediation to potential users. The second group consists of the *full-time professionals*. They often have pragmatic goals as their livelihood is based on getting clients and finding their niche in the marketplace. The third group is the *outsiders* who, like the first, tend to have transformative goals. These practitioners come from other professional and occupational cultures and have taken ADR to new arenas. Most are ideal-driven and deeply committed to their value-based work.

Kolb and her associates' research raises interesting questions about the commercialization and professionalization of the field, especially by the third group who have taken ADR to new settings. The work of these outsiders generates its own particular problems in relation to theory, research, and practice. Some might argue that the commercialization of others' pain mitigates ethical commitments toward its alleviation; others may think that this commercialization is a very natural evolutionary outcome and a major step toward professionalization of the field.

Kleiboer (1995) reviewed three books on mediation (see Jabri, 1990; Hume, 1994; Princen, 1995). Each of the authors looked at the role and status of mediators in high-stakes conflicts. Their common interest was in the differences between "principals" (indirectly interested bargai-ners) and "neutrals" (uninterested facilitator mediators). He found that one of the authors – Princen, 1995 – advocates the use of multiple forms of mediation depending on the stage of the conflict (situation). Although we have not discussed the role of situation (see Chapter 7) as it relates to mediation, Princen is an advocate of this concept.

Power and empowerment

Central to the work of good mediation, we believe, is attending to imbalances of power between the disputants. Creating conditions for all parties to allow their voices to be heard and their views considered are core mediator tasks and clearly at the heart of any transformative mediation practice. Pinzon (1996) examined the dynamics of power and knowledge in mediations at the micro level of society, reminding us that the imbalances are a mirror image of macro-level issues. (It raises questions about the social justice of any mediation if no corresponding macro-level changes exist.) Take, for example, a culture which implicitly condones sexist practices, such as higher salaries for men performing the same tasks women perform. If the core issue at mediation involves this practice, the "settlement" of the dispute will probably relate only to the disputants, and not tackle the larger organizational, cultural, or societal practices of sexism. Mediation relates to individuals rather than to structures, and little precedent exists for structural intervention (as compared to court-based cases).

Several researchers and practitioners are developing strategies to empower parties. Kelly (1995) presents a framework for mediations to challenge interpersonal kinds of imbalances, especially in divorce and family mediation. Nelson and Sharp (1995) studied a particular project, "The Helping Hand," in Boise, Idaho. Families in the project were at high risk of becoming homeless. The volunteer mediators conducted initial assessments and then provided referral services and pertinent information to families and providers. The result was an impact on the social systems – landlords, utility companies, service providers – resulting in empowering families at risk and minimizing homelessness.

Neutrality

Significant controversy exists around the concept of a neutral third party. The concept of neutrality, itself, is difficult to operationalize. For several years the ongoing debate is whether or not a third party is ever entirely neutral, or should be. Gibson *et al.* (1996), for example, believe there are shortcomings to the concept of neutrality and propose a model that requires mediators to seek agreements only if positive bargaining conditions exist. They encourage mediators to search for fully efficient and pragmatic agreements, and to help parties think through issues of fairness. McCormick (1997) implores mediators to confront social justice – a non-"neutral" position – as an imperative of the practice. He believes that the ethic of impartiality is important but not isolated. It should be joined by other ethical principles such as equality, justice, and relationship-building (toward transformation). Therefore mediators should challenge imbalances of power and encourage cooperative forms of using power and making decisions.

An obvious power imbalance occurs in court-based mediation of domestic violence. Pearson (1997) explored how these mediators (and administrators) responded to the criticism from advocates for victims of domestic violence. To ensure safety, mediators must modify the traditional mediation processes. Many mediators do not believe domestic violence cases should be "settled" and that the legal system is the appropriate recourse of action. Women with other legal grievances (e.g., sexual harassment, discrimination), however, may find that mediation can provide new solutions, short of entering the legal system. Herrnstein (1996) wants women to be educated about mediation as a viable option under such circumstances. Banks (2004) has created a promising "surrogate" mediation model for domestic violence whereby abused women meet with abusive men – not their own abuser – and with facilitated mediation in exploring the dynamics and impact of abuse. Women who have participated reflect significant growth and recovery as well as satisfaction with the model.

In the international arena, Touval (1995a) strongly endorses the importance of ethical considerations (non-neutrality) by peace mediators. Humanitarian concerns require mediators to consider the injustices behind the conflict while attempting to restore order. Cease-fires – often justified to stop the immediate killings – must be followed by mediators who will pursue peace that endorses international norms, even if these norms are more difficult to negotiate than any immediate settlement.

Impact

Beyond the case already made of the institutionalization of mediation, research consistently demonstrates the usefulness and practical outcomes of a mediation process. It is now mandatory in child custody and visitation disputes in nearly a dozen states before other adversarial means are available (Kelly, 1996). Mediation is less costly than court settlements (Pearson and Thoennes, 1984), it takes less time than the courts to resolve conflicts (Mernitz, 1980; Susskind and Weinstein, 1980), it has higher levels of compliance (Kelly, 1993), and lower re-litigation rates (Pearson and Thoennes, 1985). A number of indicators demonstrate that mediation fosters better post-divorce cooperation regarding children than traditional adversarial divorce mechanisms (Dillon and Emery, 1996). Mediation allows parties to express their wants, feelings, and concerns and to discuss and work toward joint post-agreement behavior without the time pressures of courts' calendars and without the financial pressures of high legal fees.

We can even predict the suitability of divorcing couples to successfully mediate child custody. Cohen et al. (1999) have a typology that consists of seven "types" of divorcing couples. They found that the four most likely to benefit from mediation are "semi-separated" couples, couples who are emotionally withdrawn and non-communicative, couples in power struggles, and couples where one wants out of the relationship and the other does not. Two are not helped by mediation: violent couples and couples who are seriously enmeshed. One type –

couples in significant conflict with one another – could "possibly" be helped by mediation.

Problems

Mediation is not without both critics and problems. The use of mediation for resolving environmental disputes has grown rapidly. Evidence exists (Sipe, 1998) that environmentally related mediated cases settle more frequently than traditional methods, but there is little evidence that they result in higher rates of compliance or implementation. Tils (1997) found that activists in the environmental movement believe mediation to be inferior to other forms of conflict resolution. The literature on environmental mediation in Germany identifies its opportunities as procedural transparency and inclusion of experts from several disciplines. Its risks far outweigh the advantages, however: framing the problems in confining ways, erosion of noncooperative movement strategies such as mobilization, exclusion of politically critical viewpoints, and depletion of organizational resources.

Cobb (1997) challenges the use of mediation in domestic violence situations. By inappropriately shifting victims' stories from "rights" they actually have to "needs" they would like, mediation resulted in the "domestication of violence." Eighty percent of the thirty community mediation sessions in New England demonstrated this phenomenon. She argues that the domestication process contributes to erase any morality that competes with the morality of mediation and therefore cries out for a "rights-based" – as opposed to the Western "interests-based" – model under these circumstances.

Zaher (1998) agrees that mediation provides divorcing couples with increased savings in time and money and a faster resolution than the traditional litigation process. However, she is very concerned about the inherent gender-based power differences that are probably not addressed in mediation. An equitable solution is in jeopardy when women come to the table in good faith of a fair process and men take an adversarial position. If mediators are unable to adequately address power imbalances, women are likely to suffer.

Another concern and challenge is the nature of secret meetings on issues of public policy and participation. Often mediators exclude the press and public from sessions, permitting only representatives and invited guests. Kirtley (1999) cites such a case. The Virginia Department of Transportation faced public opposition to their proposal to build highways through several residential areas. By excluding the public, those voices got silenced, enhancing the appearance of corruption and self-interest.

"No more mediation!" was the outcry of the Mexican bishop as reported by Malcolm (1998) in her article of the same title. Following the resignation of Bishop Samuel Ruiz Garcia of San Cristobal de las Casas, in Chiapas, who was head of the National Mediating Commission sponsoring peace talks between the Mexican government and the Zapatista movement, the representatives of the Catholic Church said they did not want a mediating role in the conflict. Rather, they believed all parties should talk directly to each other.

Perhaps one of the most obvious places where mediation could not work best is the landmark civil rights ruling of Brown vs. Board of Education by the Supreme Court of the United States. As Keeva (1999) notes, there is consensus from the Section of Dispute Resolution panel sponsored at the American Bar Association's annual meeting that litigation was the only real option. The racial climate of the times would have inhibited any end to segregation. This kind of change needed the back-up (power) of the courts.

Mediation Training and Research for the Future

The Hewlett Foundation (a foundation especially generous to the emerging field of conflict resolution) funded a project "Training Mediators for the 21st Century." The culmination of the project was a three-day seminar in February 1999 that assembled eighteen international mediation trainers to think about central policy issues facing the field of mediation training. The participants raised eighteen points during the seminar that reflect many of the issues and research cited in this chapter (Mosten, 2000). Their recommendations for mediation training programs were especially insightful. For example, they stated that training must result in mediators who have a deep understanding of conflict and its ramifications. These mediators need to be aware of societal and professional forces outside of the mediation room. They also need to be oriented to the fast-developing technology that affects our work. They must have training in working with issues of diversity. Like all professions, mediation practice is a lifelong process. It requires particular qualities: a sense of perspective; knowledge of adult learning; an ability to move back and forth from abstract to concrete; a desire and skill to coach others; a willingness to share control and be flexible; a commitment to and knowedge about collaboration; and significant insight into the mediator's own attitudes, skills, and talents. This is an excellent summary of skills which effective practitioners must be able to demonstrate.

Similarly, Kelly (1996) reviewed ten years of divorce mediation research and concluded that the focus of research of the future should be to understand the family mediation process and the methodology of mediators. This includes looking at attitudes, beliefs, behaviors, and strategies of these mediators.

We turn now to a practice that moves us one step closer to the legal system yet is still considered an "alternative." What follows is a brief overview of the history of arbitration, ways in which it is used, research considering its effectiveness, and concerns about its scope and viability.

Arbitration Definition and Process

Webster New World Dictionary (1978) defines arbitration as "the settlement of a dispute by a person or persons chosen to hear both sides and come to a decision" (p. 70). This seems to be the broadest and most inclusive way of thinking about arbitration. It always involves the selection of one or more neutrals, experts, or impartial third parties. These people hear the evidence and testimony and then make binding or nonbinding decisions, depending on the conditions of the arbitration. If binding, no follow-up litigation can occur. If nonbinding, the parties may chose to re-enter the legal process.

Like mediation, arbitration is an alternative to litigation. It is typically less formal and less expensive than court proceedings but often as adversarial, and follows similar rules as any litigated court case (Weinhold and Weinhold, 2000). When parties in dispute reach a deadlock without successful resolution of differences, an appointed arbitrator listens to the disputants' perspectives, reviews the evidence, and makes a "ruling." Sometimes called the businessperson's method of resolving disputes, arbitration tends to occupy a space between politics and business. We cannot describe arbitration in a way that explains all types of arbitration systems, but some remarkably common elements exist. First, arbitration is led by a neutral who receives "proofs" or "arguments" about the dispute. Second, the neutral has the power to issue a binding decision. (It differs from court adjudication in that there is no pre-trial discovery unless it is mandated by the arbitrator.) Finally, the hearing is usually less formal than litigation, as are rules of evidence.

Arbitration can be initiated either in accordance with an existing policy or contract (e.g., by request of an employee of an organization with policies that include arbitration agreements) or on an ad hoc basis where both disputants agree to use this process. The Federal and the Uniform Arbitration Acts (FAA and UAA) – adopted in nearly every state – makes such ad hoc agreements enforceable. Parties typically use nonprofit providers of arbitration services such as the American Arbitration Association (AAA) or the Center for Public Resources (CPR). If the government is involved, the Federal Mediation and Conciliation

Services (FMCS) assist in selecting, administering the hearing, and/or providing rules for conducting the hearing.

The AAA makes available to legislators and attorneys copies of the UAA, adopted by the National Conference of Commissioners on Uniform State Laws in 1955, and approved with amendments by the House of Delegates of the American Bar Association in August 1955. The FAA allows many disagreements to be enforceably arbitrated. This is used across the USA to provide ADR clauses in a variety of contracts. The AAA also serves as a clearing-house on proposed arbitration legislation.

The National Arbitration Forum publishes an Arbitration Bill of Rights that includes eleven principles, each with commentaries. Some categorical examples of the eleven entitlements for all parties include: fundamental fairness in process; reasonable access to information about arbitration; background and qualifications of arbitrators; contractual relationship guidelines; anticipated costs; reasonable time limits; hearing processes; and legal restrictions on awards and remedies. Arbitration is governed by state and federal law (Federal Arbitration Act 9 USC, Sec. 2, ff.). Most states have provision in their civil practice rules for arbitration. Many have adopted the Uniform Arbitration Act (UAA).

The use of arbitration in various settings

Because of its success as an arrangement for submitting disputes to an impartial decision-maker chosen by the parties, arbitration is an acceptable method for resolving both domestic and international business disputes (Brown and Rogers, 1997). The largest practice of arbitration occurs here, yet arbitration is not limited to the business sector. Alford (1997) describes the huge success of South Carolina's juvenile arbitration program in Lexington County, modeled after a program in Florida, and unique in that no attorneys are permitted to attend the arbitration hearings, juveniles accepted into the program have to admit their guilt, no fees are required, and arbitrators – volunteers – have to be nonprofessionals. Alford found that along with these conditions, empowerment of the community is a primary aspect of the program's success. Astarita (1997–98) provides an overview of the arbitration process as it applies to the securities industry, citing Shearson vs. MacMahon, 482 U.S. 200 (1987) as the legislation that allowed arbitration to become the most widely used means of resolving disputes in this industry. Finally, Brown and Rogers (1997) highlight the role of arbitration in resolving transnational disputes with their specific focus on the People's Republic of China.

The Study of Arbitration Practice

As with the practice of mediation, not only has arbitration expanded significantly, but so too has the study of the practice. Several studies have focused on the results of arbitration and factors influencing their relative successes. Here are a few examples:

- Simpson and Martocchio (1997) examined how work history factors affected arbitrators' decisions in dismissal cases blamed on absenteeism. They analyzed 179 arbitrators' responses to survey questions about thirty-two hypothetical absence discharge cases. They found that due process by management had the strongest impact, and that rehabilitative themes were dominant in arbitrators' decision-making.
- Olson and Rau (1997) tracked data between 1977 and 1986 from the Wisconsin teacher negotiations to understand the impact and dynamics of previous settlement decisions on cases that followed. When the union's final offer was selected (rather than when the employer's offer was selected) the negotiated settlement following an award was higher.
- After evaluating the current system of adjudicating disputes, Sherwyn and Tracey (1997) present the implications for policy and practice of mandatory arbitration of employment disputes. They found that it favors employees who file false discrimination claims as well as employers who discriminate against employees. They conclude that mandatory arbitration agreements are the most effective strategy for settling employment disputes.
- Arnold and Carnevale (1997) created two studies to investigate preferences for dispute resolution procedures as a function of several situational factors. The first study varied intentionality of the conflict, consequences, and expected future interaction between the parties. Third-party procedures were most preferred when the wrongdoing was intentional and when high consequences existed. The second study varied intentionality, consequences, and the power relationship between the parties. They replicated the relevant effects of the first study and found that arbitration was the first choice when the conflict involved parties of equal power.

Other research clusters around the advantages and problems of selecting arbitration as a means of conflict resolution.

Advantages

Goldberg *et al.* (1999) identified a number of theoretical advantages to the use of arbitration instead of court adjudication. The parties are able to select their own arbitrator (decision-maker) based on their own criteria. Should they so choose, the process can be confidential and therefore no public records will be available for access and scrutiny. The parties decide what procedural rules will be used so the process can be informal and simple. The process is usually less costly. There is no discovery at the beginning, or appeal process at the end. This also makes the process faster as disputants do not need to wait for a trial date or follow-up appeals.

Unfortunately not all people make full use of these advantages. Disputants may take most of their time finding the right "fit" of the background of the arbitrator with the particulars of their conflict. Once the person is identified, they may relinquish opportunities to tailor-make the session to meet their needs.

Problems

As with the practice of mediation, arbitration is not without problems and critics. Only limited court review is permitted, the decisions cannot be appealed if the arbitration is binding, punitive damages cannot be assessed, and, with the exception of labor arbitration, decisions have little or no precedential value (Weinhold and Weinhold, 2000, p. 172).

Two studies highlight problems and are worthy of note. Braun (1998) found that contrary to the conventional wisdom, arbitration is not faster, cheaper, or fairer than a lawsuit. He also found that the safeguards present in the courtroom are not available to parties in arbitration. No recourse exists to appeal an unfavorable decision. Levin (1997) is also concerned that most arbitration statutes do not address the role substantive law plays in decision-making by arbitrators. Arbitrators have a practice that consists of a discretionary combination of law and common sense. Again, there is little recourse for unfavorable rulings.

Pacia (1997) writes about the use of arbitration with uninsured motorist cases. He believes attorneys should view arbitration as a trial, and they should use all their advocacy skills to ensure clients are represented effectively. He advises the use of emotion, creative discovery, preparing arbitration notebooks, preparing clients for both direct and cross-examination, calling lay witnesses and experts to testify, and developing a complete understanding of the medical literature relating to their client's personal injury. These trial activities are usually absent in arbitration.

It is not always clear if the differences between arbitration and mediation are advantages. Neutrals retain control over the outcome. It is quite possible, because of this, that no compromise exists (often the outcome of mediation). What has developed, perhaps because of this lack of clarity, are a number of ADR hybrid options. Settlement conferences, early neutral evaluations, mini-trials, summary jury trials are all examples. The one that seems to receive the most use, however, is med-arb. This is briefly described below.

Med-arb

Med-arb combines mediation and arbitration processes. Typically, disputants select a neutral that will do both, allowing them the benefit of problem-solving but ultimately making a final decision. Mediation is the first process implemented. If unable to come to an agreement, the same person then moves to the role of arbitrator to issue a final decision. Mediation is designed to seek a win-win solution. Adjudication and arbitration ultimately have a win-lose solution. This process is likely to offer a "partial win-partial lose" result (Goldberg *et al.*, 1999).

Obviously the primary advantage to this model is that if the case moves to arbitration, the neutral already knows the details. The combination is more efficient as it saves time and resources. If the parties are candid in the story-telling phase, more information is available to ultimately render a decision than would be likely in a pure arbitration case. The process can serve to get parties to resolve their own disputes. If the parties cannot come to an agreement, they do not need to bring in yet another neutral and begin the process again.

More often than not med-arb neutrals play roles with binding decision-making power. This may prevent parties from fully disclosing their perspectives and instead, trying to persuade the neutrals that their position and situation is the "right" one. Transformative mediation is highly unlikely here; even honest dialog and problem-solving may be limited. If parties know that their candidness may hurt their case, they will be less likely to be forthcoming in disclosure. Med-arb practitioners, then, have less information for consideration than pure mediation practitioners.

Conclusion

There is little question that mediation and arbitration are practices that are here to stay, and every indication that they will continue to grow and prosper in the future. Evidence of the usefulness of third parties is well documented even with the problems we have highlighted.

As practitioners work around the world, we need special sensitivity to both the nuances and obvious differences of the various cultures and populations we will serve. We are not convinced that we are neutral or impartial, nor are we convinced we should be in all cases. We want practitioners to be cognizant of the important variables of identity and culture. Mediators and arbitrators need to be sensitive to the complexities of ethics, power, values, and social justice.

How do we train mediators to be sensitive to these variables? How do we recognize when and if to be neutral and not neutral? How do we get practitioners, theoreticians, and researchers to work hand-in-hand so that their work informs each other? We believe the opportunity for mediator conflict resolvers in the field is wide open. As societies reflect the impact of globalization, what models will need to be developed? Will they be hybrids of existing models, or entirely different? How will the multicultural considerations impact on personal, relational, and structural dimensions of the role of mediators and arbitrators and their respective processes?

Discussion Questions

1 How do we train mediators to be sensitive to the complexities of ethics, power, values, and social justice?
2 How do we recognize when and if to be neutral and not neutral?
3 How do we get practitioners, theoreticians, and researchers to work hand-in-hand so that their work informs each other?
4 We believe the opportunity for mediator conflict resolvers in the field is wide open. As societies reflect the globalization of our world, what models will need to be developed? Will they be hybrids of existing models, or entirely different?
5 How will the multicultural considerations impact on personal, relational, and structural dimensions of the role of mediators and arbitrators and their respective processes?

Key Words

Alternatives
Alternative dispute resolution (ADR)
American Arbitration Association (AAA)
American Bar Association (ABA)
Arbitration
Center for Public Resources (CPR)
Federal Arbitration Acts (FAA)
Federal Mediation and Conciliation Services (FMCS)
Med-arb
Mediation
Neutrality
Neutrals
Non-Western mediation model
Transformation
Uniform Arbitration Acts (UAA)
U.S. Equal Employment Opportunity Commission (EEOC)
Western mediation model

CHAPTER 17

Problem-solving

Christopher Mitchell

Implicit in our later discussion of facilitation and consultation as means of responding to conflict is a philosophy that conflicts can best be approached as shared problems to solve rather than contests or cases to win. It is an over-simplification to argue that, in real life, there is a clear distinction between responses to conflict adopting "problem-solving" processes, as opposed to the "bargaining" or "rule-applying" procedures discussed in Chapters 11 and 13 on negotiation or arbitration. The real world of conflict is too messy for such simplicity, and states, societies, and organizations usually employ a mixture of techniques in responding to social conflicts. However, even in the real world of Cyprus, south-central Los Angeles, Kosovo, Pittston, Sri Lanka, or Belfast, different approaches to managing or resolving conflict emphasize different principles and practices, and occasionally such approaches take the form of workshops, consultations, or facilitated dialogues that adopt a fundamental orientation which is in sharp contrast to bargaining and negotiation, or to the application of legal norms, rules, or sanctions. This chapter summarizes and clarifies the nature of "problem-solving approaches" as a contrast to more familiar responses to social conflict, such as coercion, deterrence, the enforcement of "law and order," or power-based bargaining.

Principles of Problem-solving

As its name suggests, any problem-solving process seeks, at its most fundamental level, to change the views of those involved in some conflictful interaction. Problem-solving workshops, sustained dialogues, or facilitated encounters all attempt to change adversaries' views of their situation from a "conflict to be won" to a "problem to be solved," with attendant "dilemmas" that must be dealt with if they are to tackle the main problem successfully. To state this as a basic principle obviously sounds strange, particularly to parties and leaders locked in a conflictful relationship that has involved coercion, costs, violence, and – frequently – deaths. To adversaries, "the problem" is obviously the other side – its goals (unreasonable and illegitimate), its behavior (violent and immoral), and sometimes its very existence (unlawful and unrecognizable). Changing from that way of framing the situation to another which accepts that a mutually shared problem might exist and that all the parties involved are part of one another's problem is a difficult switch to make. However, until parties can make it, the conception that all the parties' joint efforts are needed to discover or construct a solution remains impossible to envisage.

Parties in conflict find it equally difficult to shift their conceptualizations of and beliefs about other aspects of their situation, and to get them to see that their individual goals and their efforts to achieve those goals result in a series of mutually shared *dilemmas*. For example, one side's search for increased security through the maintenance of large numbers of armed protectors, as in the case of the Turkish Cypriot community, simply reduces the sense of security felt by Greek Cypriots. Moreover, it highlights the existence of a mutual insecurity dilemma for which some mutually satisfactory solution has to be sought if there is to be progress in resolving the overall problem of how two very different communities can live together on a small island.

If one of the key principles underlying problem-solving approaches by third parties involves providing the adversaries with opportunities to reconceptualize their situation, others are almost as important. In addition to what might be termed the principle of *problem redefinition*, we can mention several equally basic principles of problem-solving, the first of which might be termed the principle of *negative misperception*. Simply put, this asserts that, in conflict situations, adversaries almost inevitably become the victims of strong psychological tendencies to view the other side in negative terms, to pay more attention to others' willfully chosen misdeeds, destructiveness, and cruelty while excusing "our" own similar acts – if acknowledged at all – either as reactions to the others' actions ("They did it first") or as behavior forced upon "us" by circumstances ("We had no alternative"). Processes of negative stereotyping, dehumanization, and systematic rejection of information that does not conform to an image of a uniformly malevolent other become increasingly evident the more intense the conflict.

Accepting the almost inevitable existence of such psychological and political processes in any protracted conflict indicates strongly that one of the strategies of any problem-solving approach must involve some examination of these perceptions and the reasons for their being prevalent within adversaries. Given that human beings have a tendency to try to make sense of a complex world by using simplifying processes, and that in situations of conflict this gives rise to Manichean explanations of events and mono-causal reasoning, a problem-solving approach must be based partly upon procedures which complexify the adversaries' view of the situation in which they find themselves. If this can be achieved, simple explanations for events, policies, and statements will no longer suffice and the full difficulties of extricating themselves from a relationship of continuing conflict and mutual coercion can be recognized.

Closely linked with such a principle of *causal complexity* is another which also seems to fly in the face of both common sense and common ethics. This is the principle that protracted conflicts need to be viewed as nobody's fault. If anything sets apart problem-solving approaches from other means of responding to conflict, it might be this aspect of the approach, because the search for responsibility – for who must be labeled as being at fault – seems again to be a central feature of the way in which conflicting events are approached and analyzed, and particularly events that cause damage. Quite apart from the tendency of those in conflict to view the responsibility for there being a conflict – and for the damage and disruption caused by the conflict – as solely (or, at best, largely) the fault of the other side, many forms of conflict settlement involve efforts to assign fault, blame, and responsibility. Most litigation processes, for example, focus on the question of fault or responsibility – who was responsible for the undesired outcome of a medical procedure, which country was guilty of "aggression," or – less frequently in recent years – which party caused the marriage to break down? Similar attitudes may be found in other arenas of conflict. Who was to blame for the outbreak of World War I? Whose fault was the breakdown of the ceasefire in Northern Ireland in 1996? Who was responsible for the 1998–99 blood-letting in Kosovo? The temptation to adopt such a standpoint, such a way of framing analysis of such happenings, is widespread and understandable. Conflicts bring forth horrors, and the natural reaction is to look for those who "brought about" these events and to assign responsibility. Yet one of the principles of problem-solving is largely to abandon such a standpoint and to proceed with efforts to find a way out of the conflict relationship without making any effort to assign fault or pin down responsibility. Apart from the purely pragmatic grounds for such an approach – that no adversary is going to accept sole or even primary responsibility for causing a conflict and its concomitant damage and destruction, so that to attempt such an analysis will doom resolution efforts from the start – there are at least three reasons for adopting this principle of *no-fault*. The first links to the argument that to find fault assumes the validity of mono-causal explanations for complex social phenomena – in this case, protracted conflicts – and most analysis to date (especially that not carried out by partisans in the heat of an ongoing conflict) indicates quite clearly that there are many factors – distant and proximate, central and peripheral – that have "caused" a conflict. Hence, doctrines of "international aggression" or "the last clear chance to avoid" are really not much help in understanding why protracted conflicts come about and what their causes might be. If conflicts are multi-causal, then it becomes difficult to pin down "responsibility" to a single party, or a particular policy or a key event that might have been avoided through alternative behavior.

The second argument for a no-fault approach to protracted conflicts is that much analysis of the dynamics of conflict reveals that those involved often do genuinely perceive that they have little alternative to courses of action that, ultimately, make things "worse." Decision-makers in conflict situations frequently see themselves as being in the grip of forces over which they have no control and become "reactors" rather than "actors." "We had no alternative" is often a justification for failing policies, but equally it is a genuine view of the dilemmas which are involved in conflicts that threaten core values of the rivals and in which few safe alternatives exist.

Moreover, as leaders become more and more committed to a course of action in which they invest resources of time, material, and political reputation, they become less and less able to envisage alternatives or, if they know that some exist, to see how these might be attempted safely without major costs to their people and – more importantly – to themselves. This dynamic may well be viewed as yet another principle influencing and informing a problem-solving approach, and justify the title of the principle of *unrecognized entrapment*. The process can be "unrecognized" in two senses. The first is that decision-makers frequently fail to recognize how they themselves are becoming entangled in an increasingly conflict-exacerbating course of action, of closing off alternatives so that, eventually, there seems to be no escaping the commitment to victory, or to the bitter end. The second is that, while recognition of their own entrapment may eventually dawn on decision-makers, it remains very difficult to see a similar process affecting the decision-makers in their opponent. "There is no alternative" may apply to "us." "They" are seen as having many options, yet perversely choosing the most damaging.

Finally, there is the further pragmatic argument that part of the whole dynamic of protracted conflict consists of attempts by the adversaries to fix the blame on one another, attempts which show an almost admirable degree of ingenuity, sophistication, and determination. Demonstrating that it is the other's fault often becomes part of the whole coercive, win-at-all-costs strategy employed by parties in intense conflict, so that the only way in which a facilitator or consultant can implement a different, problem-solving approach is to avoid the whole issue of blame or fault for either side, and to adopt the *no-fault principle* from the beginning of any problem-solving process. This guideline is a sensible way of avoiding becoming involved in the fault campaign. Adopting a strategy of acknowledging that adversaries – caught up in the dynamics of what Rupesinghe (1995) calls "conflict creation" – inevitably make errors or see no alternative to escalation will help to deal with the problem that, frequently, adversaries do genuinely feel that "It is all the other side's fault." Given the dangers of any procedure that contains an aspect of blaming, anyone adopting a problem-solving approach needs to abandon any narrative of the conflict that defines fault or determines responsibility. One key tactic thus becomes devising a blame-free language for describing past events.

Linked to this conception is another principle focusing on the need to adopt an analytical as opposed to an adversarial posture. Inevitably, whatever problem-solving strategy is adopted, representatives of parties in conflict involved in that process will generally see it as simply another adversarial arena and, initially at least, use it as another opportunity to behave adversarially – making a case, trying to undermine the claims of the other side, appealing to historical events, legal precedents, or ethical principles and attempting to sway the facilitators so that the latter take their part in the process. For obvious reasons, third parties adopting a problem-solving approach need to avoid being drawn into the role of judges or arbiters, however informal, or appearing to approve of one side more than another.

Rather, the approach should be one of involving the adversaries in an analytical rather than an adversarial process, and to get them to undertake a joint search for causes rather than for responsibilities. In the inevitable and valuable recounting of the adversaries' histories of the conflict, this *analytical principle* should dictate that efforts are made to focus on the "why" of underlying events, rather than on how justified actions were, or what judgmental principles should be applied to evaluating the adversaries' strategies, goals, and behaviors. A problem-solving approach involves the analysis of a dynamic process rather than passing judgment on the goals and behavior of one or other side in the conflict.

Two final principles of problem-solving arise from a recognition of the dynamism of parties' goals and even of underlying interests and values. One principle of *evaluative dynamism* has several aspects. The first is the regularly observed phenomenon that, while parties in a protracted conflict come both to pronounce and demonstrate their unswerving commitment to enunciated goals, and to view those goals as non-negotiable representations of basic interests and unchanging values, it is possible for the goals to change over time, and yet remain ways of fulfilling ostensibly unchanging interests. We say "ostensibly" because analysis of many protracted conflicts has shown that even apparently impermeable, long-term interests can alter over time when circumstances change.

This principle resembles Homans's argument (1961) that different people can evaluate exactly the same thing differently, which is one reason he gives for arguing that a fruitful aspect of creative negotiation takes the form of "log-rolling" – exchanging things which one side values highly but the other not at all for things which the first side values little but the second values highly. However, the argument underlying the evaluative dynamism principle is rather that adversaries can actually change their evaluations of goals if alternative ways of fulfilling the interests underlying those goals can be found or created – a key strategy in any problem-solving process. This principle may be linked to a second idea, namely that adversaries' views and evaluations of their current bargaining positions can change through a reference to their "higher order" values and alternative means of fulfilling these values. Add a third set of ideas about "super-ordinate goals" requiring the cooperation of a current adversary (Sherif, 1966), and the opportunities for finding alternative solutions to the conflict/problem are much expanded. Realistic and acceptable alternatives to continuing the current, coercive interactions become much more likely.

All these arguments link to a final principle on which much problem-solving is based: the principle of *unrecognized options*. Again, this principle is based upon a relatively simple idea, namely that one of the bases of a problem-solving approach initially involves accepting that the adversaries' invariable perception will be that there exist only a limited number of possible outcomes from the conflict, and that the only acceptable one fulfills the winner's current goals, usually at the expense of the loser's. The idea that there may be alternative ways of resolving the conflict which enable the parties to achieve all their goals or, more realistically, to fulfill or safeguard their interests is not one that occurs readily to adversaries locked politically and psychologically in a protracted conflict. However, it should be a principle that facilitators, consultants, and others using a problem-solving approach take with them into even the most apparently intractable disputes. At the very least, problem-solving practitioners should themselves be convinced of the potential for positive sum outcomes from most conflict situations. Thus, one basic strategy is to convince the opponents to abandon the zero-sum, winner-loser assumptions which most hold about protracted conflicts, and to entertain the notion that solutions might well be sought that produce winners all round – or, at the very least, successes rather than victories.

Problem-solving Strategies

Enunciating principles that underlie a problem-solving approach to protracted conflict is relatively straightforward, but the practical question of how best to apply these principles in the real world of conflict, coercion, negative communication, and mistrust is hardly without problems. The issue of *process* – how best to bring about a joint reconceptualization of the adversary relationship – can be tackled at both a strategic and tactical level. The former involves more general questions of how best the parties might be brought to engage in some resolutionary process, and the latter involves questions about the detailed nature of such a process once initiated.

In a negative sense, there is one strategic guideline for the successful application of problem-solving techniques, and that is to avoid settings likely to give rise to the use of defensive negotiating tactics, power bargaining or coercive behavior. In other words, avoid settings that inhibit flexible and creative thinking and the open exchange of ideas between adversaries. There is a great deal of evidence that innovative thinking, including the ability to reconceptualize relationships and to tolerate a necessary amount of complexity and cognitive dissonance, is inhibited in certain conditions, especially those that make people angry and defensive, or where they are fearful and suspicious or feel threatened. Unfortunately, being involved in protracted and intense conflicts produces an overall atmosphere characterized by just those conditions. For individuals, meeting an enemy directly often intensifies these feelings, thus exacerbating those very conditions that inhibit being innovative, thinking anew, and exploring alternatives. In the wrong setting, useful problem-solving solutions can often be suppressed through mistrust, never brought up for consideration or rejected for fear of giving the others a bargaining advantage.

A basic need is for problem-solving to take place in an appropriate setting and with appropriate preparations if it is to have any chance of success. Hence, a major part of the strategy of problem-solving is to discover (or to create) a conducive setting in which problem-solving tactics can have their best chance of initiating new visions and new alternatives in the minds of some of the adversaries.

However, this strategic "rule" does highlight the tricky question of when or whether it is morally justifiable to engage in such a process in which adversaries come to review and perhaps alter their view of their situation, their goals, and their relationship with one another. On what moral basis does a third-party attempt to place poor peasants seeking land reform in a process whereby they will reconceptualize their relationship with rich landowners? Or a discriminated ethnic minority "enjoying" the benefits of democratic rule in a country dominated by a large and indifferent majority? The moral implications of problem-solving are still subject to fierce debate, even when theorists and practitioners can agree about the most effective processes to use.

Returning to arguments about appropriate strategies, it seems clear that a problem-solving *strategy* should be based upon the idea of putting key individuals into a frame of mind where alternatives to continued coercion become a possibility. This implies a need to place at least some of them in a setting where, together with participants from other parties and stakeholders, some creative exploration of alternatives can take place – such alternatives to include innovative ideas about sources of the conflict, underlying motives for behavior, mutual fears and possible outcomes if current obstacles can be overcome. In an ideal world, the strategy of problem-solving would involve the following procedures:

1 Make adversaries aware of the possibility (theoretical, at least) of a range of positive sum solutions to their conflict.
2 Persuade adversaries to stop coercion and violence, even if only in a temporary truce, and to de-escalate the intensity of the conflict.
3 Persuade key leaders of the adversaries to send representatives on a problem-solving exercise which also involves opponents customarily viewed as implacably hostile.
4 Provide a safe, insulated setting in which problem-solving discussions can take place, and a procedure which maximizes the chance of genuine discussion, analysis, and exploration so that participants – and indirectly their sponsors and leaders – are: (a) made aware that the problem is not solely of the adversary's making; (b) given the opportunity to explore each other's underlying interests and commitments, together with the likely costs of continuing the conflict via coercion; and (c) enabled to explore those obstacles that confront both sides in achieving acceptable solutions, other than the currently defined version of "victory."

5 Help to initiate a more formal process for removing current obstacles to a changed pattern of less conflictful interaction between the adversaries.

At the heart of a problem-solving approach is the idea that useful innovative thinking can take place if adversaries are placed jointly in a setting that is *insulated* from the pressures of intraparty politicking, *isolated* from the day-to-day needs of consideration and decision, *supportive* of efforts to view the conflict analytically rather than in a partisan fashion, and unusually *stimulating*, in that it avoids being or becoming the standard arena for statement of positions and rebuttal of the other side's case. In such a setting, productive changes of understanding and forecasting can emerge. The problem-solving contention is that if, indeed, adversaries can be brought together in "the right" setting and then follow "the right" process, this will maximize the chance of their finding a solution to the conflict in which they find themselves mutually enmeshed. Both setting and process must maximize the chance that those present will be enabled to *reconceptualize* their situation and past relationship; *re-evaluate* the likely future that will result from the course of action they are currently pursuing; and *re-vision* the future in terms of alternative activities and outcomes that become feasible. At the very least, an effective problem-solving exercise should convince the leaders of adversaries and stakeholders that there is a potential negotiating partner on "the other side."

Problem-solving Timing

Inevitably, one of the strategic dilemmas for anyone seeking to launch a problem-solving initiative is to decide at what stage of a conflict such an intervention is likely to have the best chance of success – always supposing that the intervener has the luxury of choice, which is rarely the case. At present, the only general guidelines to dealing with this "timing dilemma" take the form of a theory, a model, and a rule of thumb. The theory is the one originally advanced by William Zartman twenty years ago (1985) and later elaborated by others such as Stephen Stedman (1991) and Marieke Kleiboer (1994) and by Zartman himself (2000), and centred around the conception of the conflict having reached a stalemate in which the adversaries are suffering major costs with no apparent possibility of success. It is in conditions of a mutually hurting stalemate that peacemaking – and hence problem-solving – processes have the best chance of success, although others such as Jeffrey Rubin (1991) have implied that successful problem-solving exercises can also take place in anticipation of the adversaries reaching a stalemate and as a preparation for discussions and negotiations that will take place once the frustration and hurting are recognized.

The model is the one advanced by Loreleigh Keashley and Ron Fisher (1996), which also makes successful interventions – including problem-solving exercises – contingent upon the stage reached in a conflict. The Fisher-Keashley model is based on the not unreasonable assumption that adversaries will be more or less willing to attempt problem-solving – as opposed to tough bargaining, coercion, or violence – depending on whether the conflict is in one of four stages – discussion, polarization, segregation, or destruction. Problem-solving approaches – the model uses the term "consultation" – are most useful to improve relationships during the segregation stage or to help adversaries analyze the sources of the conflict in the destruction stage, prior to formal mediation or negotiation efforts. The model is also useful in that it emphasizes that problem solving can work best when used in concert with other types of peacemaking activity.

The rule of thumb is more of a negative guideline about when not to attempt problem solving as it is a general answer to the timing dilemma. Inherently plausible, it suggests that problem solving is likely to have little chance of success if employed immediately after the outbreak of "hostilities," which in many cases means the use of massive violence in order to beat the adversary into an appropriate state of submission. Common sense seems to argue for the accuracy of this idea, as decision makers, having committed themselves and their people to the effort and sacrifice involved in organized, coercive violence in pursuit of victory, are unlikely to consider reversing course so promptly – at least until the nature and size of that effort and sacrifice have become all too obvious. This suggestion seems to be born out by the observations of those researching industrial conflict, whose data indicate that strikes or lock-outs that continue beyond the first two or three days usually are those most difficult to bring to an end. Strikes tend to be either very short or very long.

As far as using the empirical record of problem-solving initiatives over the last 25 years to throw some light on this timing dilemma, the evidence is rather confusing. The very first few problem-solving workshops were intended to break log jams in existing, (official) peace processes that were taking place during a lull in violence (Cyprus, 1966), or hopefully to prepare the way for subsequent (official) negotiations that adversaries had been avoiding (Indonesia/Malaysia/Singapore, 1965; Kenya/Somalia/Ethiopia, 1969). These early efforts (Burton, 1969; Doob, 1970) could, therefore, be characterized as taking place during either a pre-negotiation stage or in the midst of a negotiation that had broken down so that some different form of communication and analysis was needed to get formal processes back "on track." Later problem-solving exercises took place in widely different circumstances, however. A series on the Falklands/Malvinas conflict was held in the mid-1980s immediately following the 1982 South Atlantic War and the British Government's declaration of "victory." Part of the peace process in South Africa involved a series of problem-solving meetings held in England as preliminaries to mutual confidence-building measures and subsequent formal negotiations (Lieberfeld, 2005). The Oslo Conversations on a Middle East peace took place while official negotiations were taking place at the same time in Madrid and Washington. Later, extended dialogues took place between the signing of the Oslo Accords and the anticipated – and abortive – final status negotiations at Camp David and Taba. A series of workshops in the Moldovan/TransDniestrian conflict took place in the interstices of official, OSCE-sponsored negotiations and even involved some members of the official delegations to the OSCE talks (Williams, 2005).

Even if we try to produce some "patterns and principles" about timing out of this empirical evidence, and suggest that problem solving has been used in a *preventive* mode, prior to the actual outbreak of violence [in Macedonia]; in a *pre-negotiation* mode [in South Africa]; in a *negotiation* support mode [in the Israel-Palestine case]; and in a *post-agreement* mode [in the former Yugoslavia], this is likely to "paper over" some other important distinctions that need to be recognized. It surely will make a difference to the acceptance and likely success of a problem-solving initiative if it is launched at the height of reactive violence when no negotiations (or even "talks about talks") are contemplated by anybody at all, rather than being launched when the adversaries are still continuing increasingly costly violence, but looking for some face-saving way of renewing previously abortive peace feelers. Yet both would be initiatives undertaken during a pre-negotiation stage while violence continues. Similarly, there would seem to be key differences between problem-solving initiatives launched as an adjunct to on going, formal negotiations [working on detailed-technical issues like proposals for sharing water, for example] compared to those launched when Track 1 processes hit a – hopefully – temporary impasse or those launched to try to salvage a total breakdown at the official level, complete with recriminations, threats, and complaints about bad faith.

In summary, our ideas about the most appropriate timing of problem solving initiatives – the circumstances in which informal, unofficial, and exploratory exchanges of ideas can most usefully contribute to a productive peace process and a durable solution – are sketchy and have to be tentative. There are examples where problem-solving approaches have been used fruitfully as initiatives prior to negotiation and others where they have helped during and after negotiations. Equally, there are cases where such approaches have been used to less or no helpful effect, or where the whole peace process, formal and informal, official and unofficial, confidential and open, has broken down and combat and violence resumed. The record about effective timing is mixed and needs further evidence and closer analysis. It is certainly more mixed than the record about successful problem-solving tactics, where there seems to be some agreement about what "works" and what is to be avoided.

Problem-solving Tactics

Given that a third party has succeeded in arranging a problem-solving exercise in a conducive setting, what tactics are available to ensure a productive exchange based upon problem-solving principles rather than a repeat of intransigent hard bargaining leading to stalemate and frustration? Detailed answers to this question may be found in Chapter 18, which deals with processes of facilitation and consultation, and in the increasing volume of literature on analytical, interactive problem-solving and its uses (e.g., see Burton, 1969; Kelman and Cohen, 1976; Fisher, 1996; Mitchell and Banks, 1996; Rothman, 1997; Saunders, 1999). At this point, we will merely outline some of the typical tactical approaches to conducting an effective problem-solving exercise, approaches which reflect the keynote guidelines of being non-directive and characterized by flexibility, informality, and creativity.

The size of most problem-solving discussion groups (usually known as "workshops") tends to be small (twelve to twenty-five at most), on the grounds that it is only the dynamics of small groups that enables participants to maximize the benefits of a flexible agenda, informal exchange of views and ideas, and the development of minimally trusting personal relations over the duration of each meeting (normally one to two weeks). The structure is frequently triadic, although with more complex, multi-party conflicts, and, bearing in mind the principle of involving all parties and stakeholders simultaneously, this structure inevitably becomes more complex. However, there is usually a clear distinction between those who represent (in an informal and usually unofficial sense) the conflicting parties (the participants), and those from the third party conducting the exchange (the panel of facilitators).

The agenda is usually simple and flexible, consisting of four or five broad headings under which free-flowing discussion can be launched in any direction which participants choose. One pioneer in the use of problem-solving approaches has described this as "creative uncertainty," and argues that its presence helps participants to avoid falling into conventional bargaining behavior, such as accusation and refutation (De Reuck, 1983). On the other hand, such ambiguity frequently causes initial discomfort to participants used to a detailed agenda and a rigid timetable. Often, however, they come to appreciate having the time and opportunity to pursue issues in some detail and in a non-time-bound fashion.

The objectives of most workshops, sustained dialogues, or problem-solving encounters are to help participants (and, hopefully conflicting parties) to reconceptualize their situations from a conflict to be won to a joint problem to be resolved; and their relationship from being one in which one side's gain is axiomatically the other's loss. Hence, the role of the facilitators is crucial, and their tactics key. Again, these are discussed in detail elsewhere (Mitchell, 1981; Kelman, 1992; Rothman, 1997; Saunders, 1999) and later in this work, but here we will highlight five important aspects of the facilitator's role. Facilitators should:

1 Provide a role model for behavior that is non-judgmental, analytical, and questioning but supportive. Successfully fulfilling this function can lead to the development of a "group culture" in which partici-pants switch back and forth between roles as (defensive) "representative" and (enquiring) "analyst," and thus find it easier to shed the perceptual and political burdens of the former role. Being able to assume the role of "fellow problem-solver" often enables participants to take risks and make statements that would be impossible in conventional bargaining roles.

2 Provide a sympathetic audience for participants who invariably find it necessary to "vent" feelings about the wrongs committed by the other side during the course of the conflict, but avoid being put in the position of a judge, awarding praise and blame for past acts or omissions. In addition, facilitators should also provide what some practitioners have described as an "innocent eye," to enable them to ask pertinent questions of the participants and thus force the latter into a deeper self-examination and explanation, so that issues are clarified in an analytical fashion. Others have described this as the function of providing "an eye, an ear and a shoulder," while yet others refer to the task of acting as a safety-valve!

3 Provide a neutral, non-accusatory, and non-offensive language in which the group as a whole can discuss the conflict, past events, and future possibilities. The role is frequently associated with the introduction into the interaction of analytical concepts, and with the gradual shift from the language of fault and responsibility to that of causation, feedback, and reaction. Having this language adopted by participants is often a slow business, but it is another part of a

problem-solving process that assists participants to develop both a capacity and a willingness to reconceptualize.

4 Provide analytical insights, relevant theoretical explanations, and new ideas about the reasons for the conflict developing as it did, as well as possible options for the future and ideas about outcomes that could fulfill parties' underlying interests. Part of this role involves theoretical knowledge, but part of it depends upon familiarity with other conflicts and ways in which others have managed to find or construct acceptable solutions to their particular problems and dilemmas. Inevitably, participants will argue (at one level, quite correctly) that theirs is a unique relationship, so that facilitators need to anticipate the initial rejection of any parallels they draw or useful ideas they adapt from other, familar situations.

5 Finally, and somewhat paradoxically, adopt the function of being an agent of reality for workshop participants. This role becomes particularly important toward the end of any set of discussions, especially, if the participants have neglected the question of the acceptability or saleability of any new ideas, insights, or suggestions to their leaders who have not been involved directly in the discussions. In many cases this role of "reality checker" is an unusual contribution from facilitators who spend much of the rest of their time gently urging participants to be creative and to break out of traditional molds of thought. However, it is a necessary task if the problem-solving process – which, by its nature, is a gradual one – is to have any impact on the formal level of policy-making within adversaries. Ideas that seem unassailable at the end of successful problem-solving discussions will often appear ridiculously utopian in the hard political light of national capitals, or corporate headquarters or party conferences. As one of their major tasks, facilitators should facilitate the return of participants.

Conclusion

Much of this chapter has focused on the principles by which two types of third party – facilitators and consultants – practice their interventions into intractable conflicts. While the precise details of how they go about their work as third parties differ, I would argue that both are very clearly based upon the principles, strategies, and tactics of problem-solving. While these continue to be elaborated and adapted, the fundamentals we have discussed above may be seen as underpinning much of the contemporary third-party work currently being undertaken as a response to intractable conflicts between individuals, groups, communities, and countries. Such problem-solving approaches do differ substantially from those involving mediators, arbitrators, and judges, as may be seen from the content of preceding chapters. At the least, however, they are a useful supplement to the practices of these more traditional third-party figures, a point that should become clearer in Chapter 15, which focuses on the practice of facilitation and consultation in more detail.

Discussion Questions

1 What are the fundamental differences, if any, between problem-solving approaches to coping with conflicts and other approaches discussed in Part IV of this book?

2 Would it really be possible to apply problem-solving principles to resolving really intractable and violent conflicts that have been going on for decades, such as the Israeli–Palestinian conflict, the conflict over Cyprus or the dispute over Ngorno Karabagh?

3 What might be some of the moral dilemmas of applying "no-fault" principles to conflicts between oppressed and oppressors?

4 What are some of the theories about human behavior that underlie problem-solving approaches to conflict resolution?

5 Problem-solving approaches seem to involve mainly small groups of "participants" from adversary parties. How can such exercises have any effect on the mass of rank-and-file followers who have come to believe strongly in the cause for which (they have been told) they are fighting and often dying?

6 Problem-solving approaches – and indeed conflict resolution approaches generally – have been characterized as essentially conservative activities that result in shoring up a status quo. What merits are there in this argument?

7 Problem-solving has been criticized as being an invention of rich, Westernized, industrial societies, and hence inapplicable to other types of society. Are such criticisms justified?

Key Words

Attribution
Bargaining
Blaming
Causal complexity
Coercion
Commitment
Consultation
Dehumanization
Deterrence
Dilemmas

Entrapment
Evaluative dynamism
Facilitated dialogues
Facilitation
Litigation
Manichean explanations
Mistrust
Mutual insecurity dilemma
Negative perceptions
No-fault principle
Positive sum outcome
Problem redefinition
Problem-solving
Reconceptualization
Responsibility
Security
Setting
Stakeholders
Stereotyping
Sustained dialogues
Workshops

CHAPTER 18

Facilitation and Consultation

Sandra Cheldelin and Terrence Lyons

Introduction

Negotiation and mediation are the two third-party practices most commonly studied and used. We now turn to two equally important practices, both borrowed from other disciplines, and now applied to large-group, multi-party, and organizational conflicts: facilitation and consultation. This chapter begins historically with the insights we have learned both domestically and abroad from fifty years of study of small-group behavior. It impressively informs our understanding of the role and tasks of third-party facilitators. We present models which conflict resolution practitioners and researchers can and do use to assist small and large groups engaged in addressing deep-rooted, protracted, and often violent conflicts. The reader will find that we talk about facilitation in a broad context: the relationship between process and content, the importance of identity issues, and models of learning. In the international arena, the process is often referred to as *consultation*. We have developed methods to promote better communication and analysis, more constructive relationships, and a re-examination of perceptions in order to assist in the resolution of large-group, international conflicts. We conclude with a discussion of the nexus of research, theory, and practice and by pointing to the need for more systematic research on evaluation.

History of Facilitation

Much of the early research on, and practice of, facilitation occurred both in England at the Tavistock Institute of Human Relations in London and in the USA at the NTL Institute for Applied Behavioral Science (formally known as the National Training Laboratories) and the Gestalt Institute of Cleveland. Patten (1989) provides an excellent historical perspective, summarized below.

Beginning in London, a significant influence on the study of group behavior began at the Tavistock Institute, founded in 1920 as an outpatient clinic providing therapy based on psychoanalytic theory and insights from the treatment of shell-shocked veterans of World War I. The Tavistock approach, known as "group relations," had its roots in the work of Bion (1959) and Rice (1963). Beginning in the 1940s, Bion's studies of small groups led him to believe that "individuals cannot be understood, nor their behavior changed, outside of the groups in which they live" (Patten, 1989, p. 7). The group behaves as a system with a primary goal of survival. Group functioning, leadership, and authority are connected to Bion's assumptions about basic group issues for survival: dependency and counterdependency, flight and fight, and pairing and oneness. Tavistock staff found that individuals learn about how groups function and behave by examining these basic issues. Important insights into individual behavior in group settings are the foundation of analyzing and understanding conflicts, and are useful in designing third-party interventions.

At the same time but an ocean apart, Kurt Lewin, a German immigrant and professor at MIT, conducted a workshop for the Connecticut Interracial Commission that used discussion groups to achieve changes in "back-home" work situations. One of the earliest to study identity-based conflicts, Lewin focused on issues of majority–minority relations in pluralistic, democratic societies. He found identity issues were a significant contributor to the hostilities between groups.

Lewin's understanding of group dynamics and knowledge of change processes greatly influenced the workshop staff members at the Interracial Commission – Kenneth Benne, Leland Bradford, and Ronald Lippitt – who subsequently became leaders on identity-based conflicts. These individuals learned that "providing feedback at the end of each day to participants about their individual and group behavior – now referred to as 'process' – stimulated higher levels of interest, insights, and learning by the participants than did more traditional lectures and materials on interracial matters – now known as 'content'" (Patten, 1989, p. 4). Benne, Bradford, and Lippitt took their learning and created the National Training Laboratory in Group Development in Bethel, Maine, in 1947, conducting workshops, seminars, and conferences. Their summer programs were (and are) referred to by various names – encounter group, human relations, human interaction, interpersonal skills, T-groups, sensitivity training, or experiential training (Bradford *et al.*, 1964) – with common goals of studying small-group behavior. Lewin died in 1947, but his colleagues Ronald Lippitt, Alvin Zander, and Rensis Likert continued his research in group dynamics, mostly at the University of Michigan.

In 1954 the Gestalt Institute of Cleveland was established by some of the earliest students of Fritz and Laura Perls, Isadore Fromm and Paul Goodman, all pioneers of Gestalt psychology. Gestalt theory is rooted in perceptual psychology and systems theory. (*Gestalt* is a German word meaning a complete pattern or configuration.) In 1966 the Institute introduced training programs that applied Gestalt theory to the work with small and large groups – from families to large corporations – and trained facilitators to conduct this work. Today it is one of the largest institutes teaching facilitation skills that employ complex systems theory including the study of the interactive parts of large and small systems.

The early groups at the Tavistock Institute, the National Training Laboratories, and the Gestalt Institute studied the phenomenon of facilitation as it relates to individual and group behavior. What emerged from their studies are facilitation processes that third-party consultants now use to address group conflict. This chapter, and several that follow, cite models of facilitation and consultation, problem-solving workshops, and other third-party interventions. Only recently – borrowing from fields of organizational development, clinical and social psychology, management and communication – have we directly made research, theory, and practice applications to problems in our field of conflict analysis and resolution.

Facilitation Defined

Most of the academic research and writing about facilitation in the academic community provides a fairly consistent definition, at least regarding the role of the facilitator and the steps involved in the facilitation process to resolve conflicts. The term *facilitation* comes from the verb *facilitate*, which means to make easier or less difficult, or to assist in the progress (*Random House Webster's College Dictionary*, 1997). Facilitation is conducted by a third party – individuals external to a dispute between two or more people – whose task is to help disputants reach an agreement. A commonly used definition is an "assisted negotiation" (Burgess and Burgess, 1977). Most mediation practice involves two parties. In contrast, facilitation is used for multi-party meetings and consensus-building processes. The emphasis is on the negotiation *process* and less on the *substance* of the outcomes. Unlike mediation, facilitation is likely *not* to be a confidential process.

A broader definition is offered by Barsky (2000) describing the task of the facilitator: to assist with *communication* between parties to a conflict. He believes the functions of the facilitation process are to bring parties together, and to provide conditions to enhance discussion, including opportunities to hear one another. Kiser (1998) says that masterful facilitators make their facilitation every bit an art as well as a science, combining their research and planning skills with their intuitive and communication skills when working with groups.

Perhaps the broadest definition of the facilitator is offered by Webne-Behrman: "One who makes the process easy" (1998, p. 1). The facilitator is designated openly by group members to be the caretaker and guide of their process, remaining neutral to solutions, objective regarding the meaning of issues, and ethically committed to a collaborative and democratic process (p. 2).

The Facilitation Process

The literature is fairly consistent in describing the various phases or stages of a facilitation process. It begins at the initial meeting with the client to determine whether or not the facilitator can provide the necessary skills the group needs. This is a rapport- and confidence-building process (Kiser, 1998). If successful, the tasks of the second phase are to clarify the goals, decide how to work together, and establish a contract that defines expected results. In the contracting phase it is important to have all parties agree on expectations, roles, and values. If the parties determine that they can work together, and agree upon a contract, the process moves to a third and perhaps most creative stage, the intervention design. This is then followed by the fourth, implementing the design.

Facilitation designs (stage three) must address immediate concerns as well as the hopes, and long-term goals. Understanding the group's stage of development is also important. Schwarz (1994) makes a distinction between two types of groups: "basic groups" that want some substantive task accomplished, and "developmental groups" that want to improve their own process and members learn to diagnose and intervene on their own problems. Another design consideration is the level of intervention. Micro-level interventions are common with interpersonal or small-group conflicts. These interventions seek changes in communication patterns and agreements as to how members will work together. Large systems and multi-party conflicts require facilitations that usually include structural changes (e.g., laws, policies, procedures, rules). Finally, facilitators must also be concerned about timing and sequencing when there are multiple issues, especially with multi-party conflicts.

The fourth phase of a facilitation process is the facilitation itself.

Implementing the design requires tailoring it as necessary to group dynamics that emerge. After the initial set-up, facilitators review the goals, create ground rules, and present informed reflections on the current situation. The group tasks may vary: to solve problems, create visions, or identify tasks to be accomplished. It concludes with summary remarks and action plans.

The final phase of facilitation, too often short-circuited, is evaluation. Cheldelin (2006) conducted an evaluation of a two-year facilitated dialogue project post 9/11 to rebuild community resilience. She also evaluated the viability and effectiveness of each of four dialogue models. However, the paucity of impact data in the literature suggests that facilitation evaluations are a much needed area of research.

Intervention Models

There are many models for facilitation that conflict resolvers have developed over the past several decades. These include strategies to diagnose group processes, confront and provide individual and group feedback, manage processes, teach requisite skills to members, foster group cohesion, all the while demonstrating (modeling) effective communication skills such as empathy, active listening, clarifying, paraphrasing, and reframing.

Schein (1999) presents four intervention models that are used at the small-group (micro) level. One helps participants develop effective communication skills, giving deliberate feedback. Another focuses on group tasks – e.g., problem-solving and decision-making – and strategies for groups to be intentional about how they will accomplish their tasks. A third intervention model attends to the interpersonal processes of building and maintaining a group, assessing group maturity, and developing structures to enhance interpersonal communication. His fourth model uses dialog for deeper understanding of the conflicts, issues, hopes, and aspirations of the parties involved. Examples of these models of facilitation are expanded in other parts of this section.

At the micro level Webne-Behrman (1998) focuses on conducting effective meetings. New and alternative models to traditional problem-solving are appreciative inquiry (Cooperrider and Srivastva, 1987; Thatchenkery, 1999), narrative and dialogue (Monk *et al.*, 1997; Winslade and Monk, 2000), and conversation (Baker *et al.*, 1997). At the macro level of intervention we have problem-solving workshops, large multilateral meetings, and ad hoc facilitations (Strauss, 1993; Kelman, 1996; Kriesberg, 1998). Fisher (1997a) makes an important distinction between problem-solving and process promotion models. Rubin *et al.* (1994) present contractual and emergent models.

Facilitator Roles

A basic assumption of any facilitated approach to conflict resolution is that people are capable of envisioning or problem-solving, and often need only permission to do so. Within this framework, the facilitator becomes a *guardian* of the process, encouraging and supporting participants in resolving their issues. The role as guardian, however, requires expertise that extends mere "techniques."

Many have studied the guardian role including the requisite repertoire of skills these practitioners have: heightened self-awareness of their strengths, weaknesses, needs, and areas of vulnerability; a level of credibility based on knowledge, experience, and technical competence; and alignment and congruence in verbal and nonverbal behaviors, commonly referred to as "walking the talk." Kiser (1998) stresses excellent communication skills. Webne-Behrman (1998) suggests guardians must be able to ensure that all members have an equal opportunity to speak and to be heard, a capacity to clarify goals and agendas, and an ability to help groups accomplish their tasks while maintaining individual needs of their memberships; to assist all members in exercising leadership opportunities; and to encourage all to learn to facilitate their own group processes (p. 5). Guardians must also have a keen knowledge of group process and an understanding of resistance to change (Cheldelin, 2000), compassion, and empathy (Zimmerman and Coyle, 1991), and a deep commitment to honesty, integrity, and human development (Rogers, 1961, 1977; Gastil, 1993).

Using a modified Delphi technique, Ewert *et al.* (1994) examined the personal qualities and skills of effective intercultural community development facilitators. They found the most important variables of effectiveness to be discernment (wisdom), patience, people-oriented, respectful, culturally sensitive, flexible, and balanced. They also found that intercommunication skills, an ability to gain confidence, listen, be savvy to group process, and understand social processes are essential for effective facilitation.

Problem-solving and Appreciative Inquiry

Most third-party interventions are problem-solving driven, where an obvious "felt need" exists and parties come to settle their differences. The section on the Western model of mediation in Chapter 16 presents problem-solving at length. Increasingly, practitioners are developing alternative models that take into account the use of new metaphors to think about their situation (Cooperrider, 1990), as the focus on problems enable negative, and "fixing it" language.

One growing alternative to problem-solving is *appreciative inquiry*. Cooperrider and Srivastva (1987) present this model as a: "search for knowledge and theory of intentional collective action which are designed to help evolve the normative vision and will of a group, organization, or society as a whole" (p. 159). Appreciative inquiry facilitators ask parties to generate images of their collective future by exploring the best of what is and has been (Thatchenkery, 1999). As Cooperrider and Srivastva (1987, p. 159) put it, the basic rationale of appreciative inquiry is to:

> begin with a grounded observation of the best of what is, help the group to articulate what might be, ensure the consent of those in the system to what should be, and collectively experiment with what can be.

Schein (1999) also endorses this model. He believes facilitators and parties using appreciative inquiry are likely to use more expansive metaphors than those focusing on problems. Their inquiry is about what works well (or at one time worked well), and what common values and goals participants can imagine might work well. Appreciative inquiry helps parties envision a future together. In Table 15.1, Schein (1999, p. 56) presents comparative variables highlighting fundamental differences between fixing an existing problem (problem-solving) and building a capacity to learn so that such problems will not recur (appreciative inquiry).   Problem-solving facilitation operates on a belief that there is a set of problems that need to be solved (or at least managed). Appreciative inquiry facilitation believes that whatever issue is being presented is a "miracle to be embraced and enhanced" (Schein, 1999, p. 56).

Cheldelin and her ICAR colleague, Wallace Warfield, developed a combination of these two models and call it the "zig-zag" model. Reflecting on their experiences in the field, facilitators must begin with the parties'"felt needs" or "problems." Only then do they move to having parties appreciate what has worked or envision a better future. Cheldelin, Jakobsen, and Yuille (2007) provide a case of a stakeholder consensus building facilitation using the zig zag model with significant success.

Table 18.1 Two facilitative intervention models

Problem-solving focus	vs.	Appreciative inquiry
"Felt need"		Appreciating what is
Identification of problem		Valuing what is
Analysis of causes		Envisioning what might be
Analysis of possible solutions		Dialoging what should be
Action planning		Innovating what will be

Source: Schein (1999, p. 56)

Narrative, Dialog, and Conversation

Like facilitation and consultation, the concepts of narrative, dialog, and conversation originated in disciplines other than conflict resolution. Narrative as a therapeutic metaphor came from the work of White and Epston (1991) who were significantly influenced by the anthropologist Gregory Bateson and his concept of "news of difference." The counselor deconstructs a problem, giving an opportunity to explore the situation fully, forming an alliance with the client against the problem and constructing an alternative story (narrative) that could be helpful in rethinking the situation. An excellent explanation of the use of narrative in therapy is found in the work of Monk *et al.* (1997), who later applied the concept to mediation (Winslade and Monk, 2000).

Conflict resolvers are not counselors or therapists. Nevertheless, many of the skill sets are remarkably similar. Counselors use the narrative approach in therapy on a broad range of human difficulties: relational and family dysfunctions, depression and other psychiatric illnesses, and substance abuse. Narrative is used in mediation, counseling, and new ways of conducting community and clinical supervision. In this process (therapy) the clinician invites clients to "begin a journey of coexploration in search of talents and abilities that are hidden or veiled by a life problem" (Monk *et al.*, 1997, p. 3). It has a precious sense of optimism in that counselors become facilitators and allies of the process with particular "roles" that differ from traditional therapeutic techniques. The counselor is not the expert but rather a co-investigator, co-explorer, and co-creator of new narratives. With an underlying belief that "the person is not the problem but rather the problem is the problem" (p. 6), curiosity becomes an essential practice tool. Narrative facilitation borrows these roles and skills from counseling. Beginning with an assumption that all parties at the table have different ways of making meaning out of their situations, and that mutual understanding is probably an illusion, it begins by making tacit all assumptions about participants' understanding (the "news of difference").

In their important work on the use of narrative with mediation, Winslade and Monk (2000) make a critical distinction between traditional and narrative theories. The traditional (Western) mediation model is based on the belief that disputants are motivated primarily to fulfill their own personal interests, and therefore mediators help parties to find common underlying interests to forge a settlement. Narrative mediation does not support the assumption that what people want stems from their inner needs or interests. Rather, people construct conflict from narrative descriptions of the event. Their stories are in the context of their cultural and historical experiences.

This distinction applies well to the use of narrative in facilitation. Narrative strategies change the ways members of a group see themselves in their particular conflict, allowing group members to consider new possibilities for resolution. Thus, the social contexts that influence conflict – often macro-level issues such as culture, race, gender, and class – are important parts of the stories. As White (1989) frames the narrative: "We enter into stories, we are entered into stories by others, and we live our lives through stories" (p. 6). This is more fully explored in the first part of this book, Chapter 6, by Sara Cobb.

Dialogue, narratives, and deep conversations have traditions around the world. As William Isaacs notes, "Whenever one looks throughout history, one can see evidence of tribal gatherings, community events, and councils, where the central glue of human organizing was conversation – often around a fire – usually carried on for days at a time" (p. 77). Internationally, there is a promising increase in the use of dialogue as a counter measure to global violence. In November 1998 the General Assembly of the United Nations proclaimed 2001 as the *United Nations Year of Dialogue among Civilizations*. Each year since then the Islamic Educational, Scientific, and Cultural Organizations (ISESCO) has sponsored regional theme-based dialogues – *Dialogues and Coexistence among Civilization and Cultures, . . . Among Civiliations in a Changing World, . . . Among Civilizations for Coexistence* – as has the United Nations Education, Scientific, and Cultural Organization (UNESCO) supported East-West Intercultural dialogues throughout Central Asia such as the Silk Road Dialogue Project examining historical heritage and identities.

Facilitating dialogue and conversation not only highlights similar perspectives of group members, but also bridges differing perspectives as catalysts for potential new visions. As Baker *et al.* (1997) say this about conversation:

> Conversation is one of the most fundamental forms of connection. As people weave their patterns of relationality and interdependency, their similar and differing ways of perceiving and responding emerge. (p. 7)

Facilitating a conversation begins as any facilitation – clarifying expectations – but then the facilitator prepares the intervention to be hospitable and receptive to good conversations. Baker *et al.* (1997) talk about the important skills and values necessary to guide these conversations: these facilitators must have a profound respect for each participant, they must provide opportunities for all voices to be heard, they must model reflective listening and effective speaking, and, equally important, they must be open to surprise.

Third-party Consultation in Social Conflict

We now move from the various roles and strategies used by facilitators to a more conventional way of thinking about third-party consultation with social and deep-rooted conflicts. Consultation tends to be a specific subset of the broader category of interactive conflict resolution practice. The goal of the third-party consultant is to facilitate problem-solving through improved communication and analysis of the basic relationship between the conflicting parties. This type of consultation differs from mediation in its focus on process rather than on substantive issues or specific settlements. Third-party consultants emphasize the importance of understanding and improving relationships as a means to resolve social conflicts (Walton, 1969; Kelman, 1976; Fisher, 1983; Mitchell, 1993a). It differs from facilitation primarily around issues of scale. Consultation is the language used in the international arena, though the facilitation skills are quite similar.

The assumptions behind third-party consultation derive from social-psychological perspectives that see conflicts at least partly, and at times predominantly, as subjective social processes. If a given conflict is driven by such issues as misperception, mistrust, poor communication, and a lack of constructive diagnosis of the conflict, then a skilled and experienced consultant may work with the parties to improve the relationship and help the parties find mutually satisfying outcomes.

Third-party consultations are generally organized as facilitated small-group discussions in a neutral and informal setting. Such meetings are often compared to academic seminars, and are designed to encourage a secure and creative atmosphere for open discussion. Flexibility is important, as the meeting should follow the needs of the parties. Such meetings are often confidential and private. In such a secure, "off-the-record," and flexible setting, participants are able to focus on basic perceptions, attitudes, and relationship issues relating to the conflict.

Participants to the dialogs are selected on the basis of their connections to important policy-makers and opinion leaders from the parties in conflict. In other words, participants may be selected because they are mid-level but influential members of a ruling party or have the ability to shape opinion by virtue of their positions as community leaders. Lederach (1997) emphasizes the importance of middle-range leadership and what he calls a "middle-out" approach for building peace. The key is for participants to be able to act as channels to translate the new perceptions and ideas, and communicate to authoritative decision-makers involved in the conflict. Participants are often selected on the basis of their positions as "unofficial but influential" representatives who are not bound to rigid positions but who have indirect influence on policy-making.

The consultant's role is predominantly facilitative and diagnostic, and is generally neutral and non-directive with regard to outcomes. Consultants draw on their social scientific knowledge of conflict processes and their human relations and facilitation skills to assist the parties to analyze their conflict. In many instances, a panel of academics collectively facilitate the discussions. Expertise – rather than power, status, or resources – is the main asset third-party consultants bring to the parties. This expertise allows the third-party consultant to contribute to conflict resolution by increasing the parties' motivation for problem-solving and by improving the openness and accuracy of communication. Consultants may regulate the interaction in a number of ways to promote constructive discussions, by assisting in agenda-setting and establishing deadlines, for example. Better understanding of the conflict and improved communication are seen as prerequisites for creative problem-solving. Figure 15.1 illustrates a model of third-party consultation.

Third-party consultations, like problem-solving workshops and conflict resolution training, are based on an assumption that changes in attitudes, perceptions, and skills, and relationship- and trust-building within a small group can translate to the level of policy-makers who have a role in making decisions relating to conflict behavior. In this way, two different processes with relation to conflict resolution are taking place. At the level of the small group – the dozen or so participants in any given consultation or problem-solving workshop – a successful consultation will change perceptions, develop new ideas, improve communications, and build trust and stronger relationships among the participants. Such changes are an important but not the sole goal of the consultants' intervention.

For new social and psychological conditions to contribute to the resolution of a conflict that extends beyond the small group, however, the new ideas and perceptions need to be transferred to constituencies both above and below the participants. This is the second level at which third-party consultation plays a role in conflict resolution. In this way, third-party consultations are externally oriented, with a goal toward affecting the broader context of the conflict. To succeed in transferring new ideas and relationships to the macro-political level, it is critical to pay attention to the selection of participants, identifying the unofficial yet influential individuals who can act as channels to higher levels. It is also important to consider how to facilitate the effective "re-entry" of participants back into their social and political contexts.

Fisher and Keashley (1991) have argued that third-party consultation may be most effective if employed during a specific phase of a conflict cycle. Consultation, with its focus on communication and relationship issues, has important contributions to make in promoting the success of

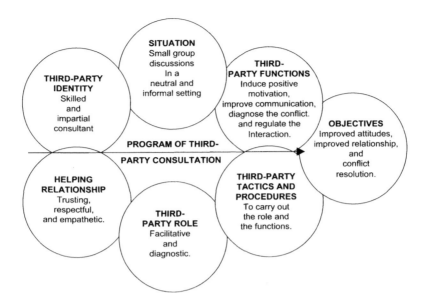

Figure 18.1 A model of third-party consultation
Source: derived from Fisher (1997b, p. 258).

other forms of intervention. Such facilitated dialogs shed light both on the subjective dimensions that hamper mediation, and on issues of miscommunication and lack of trust following a settlement in a particularly protracted or destructive conflict. In particular, consultation may serve as a form of "pre-negotiation" when a conflict has polarized the parties but has not yet reached a destructive phase. Third-party consultation may also be an important component of implementing a settlement following mediation.

Fisher and Keashley (1990) apply their contingency model to the Cyprus conflict. Other scholars (Bloomfield, 1995; Webb *et al.*, 1996) have suggested that the contingency model is too linear and that different phases occur simultaneously, providing scope for third-party consultation throughout a conflict. Saunders (1996) discusses the importance of pre-negotiation in the consultation process.

Applications of Third-party Consultation

Third-party consultation has been used in a wide variety of settings, ranging from business and community to protracted international conflicts. In industrial and business settings, third-party consultants have contributed to shifting competitive, destructive, and hostile relations between labor and management and between units within organizations into more cooperative and collaborative relationships

(Blake *et al.*,1964; Walton, 1969). Others have analyzed the ability of third-party consultants to contribute to conflict resolution within organizations ranging from social service agencies and schools, to mental health systems (Blumberg and Weiner, 1971; Alderfer, 1973; Druckman and Bonoma, 1977). It has been used in a variety of community settings addressing ethnic and racial tensions, and relationship-building between police and citizens (Lippitt, 1949; Bell *et al.*, 1969; Cleveland, 1971).

Third-party consultations have shown promise in international settings as well. Burton (1969) pioneered *controlled communication* as a method of conflict resolution in international conflicts. Using his design, a panel of social scientists create problem-solving workshops with participants from the conflicting states as a means to examine perceptions and explore resolution. Doob (1970) and Doob and Foltz (1974) experimented with the application of human relations and sensitivity training methods drawn from the work done with T-groups at the Tavistock Institute to international conflicts including conflicts in the Horn of Africa, Northern Ireland, and Cyprus. Kelman (1976, 1996), Fisher (1980), and Cohen and Azar (1981) developed an interactional approach to problem-solving workshops in the Middle East and the India–Pakistan conflicts, arguing that international conflicts may be reduced to individual needs and fears that may be addressed in facilitated workshops and then fed back into the political debate. Wedge (1970, 1979) added an additional case study of his work in the 1965 Dominican Republic conflict and argued the value of such consultations as a prelude to direct negotiations.

Research, Theory, and Practice

A number of early proponents of third-party consultancy and problem-solving workshops have developed theory and research agendas along with practice. Mitchell (1981) developed his theory of the subjective dimensions of conflict while working to advance an effective methodology for problem-solving workshops. Kelman (1996) similarly had theoretical goals from the start of his work developing his action research program on the Israeli–Palestinian conflict.

As noted above, problem-solving workshops assume a linkage between the small-group exercise itself and an effect on the larger conflict. Such workshops provide opportunities to assess theory at a micro level, including such questions as: What size of a group works best? What types of panels of facilitators and procedures work best? Social scientists who have studied third-party consultation have examined questions relating to the roles and attributes of the consultant and which types of third parties are likely to be most effective. Kelman and Cohen (1979) argue that specialized knowledge is important, while Burton (1969), Walton (1969), and Fisher (1972) suggest that only a moderate knowledge is necessary. They argue that too much knowledge may create predefined perceptions that could promote rigidities which hamper discussions.

While there is considerable experience in third-party consultation, systematic research on its effectiveness is less well developed. Evaluation is difficult, particularly given the ethical considerations of dealing with actual conflicts where costs are high. Very few follow-up studies on "transfer effects" (Kelman) have been conducted. Babbitt and d'Estrée (1996) used an Israeli–Palestinian women's workshop to investigate what constitutes the "transformation of a relationship," a change that is assumed to be a prerequisite for stable peace. They argue that a willingness to explore the underlying assumptions of the relationship can be demonstrated through the workshop experience but that later stages of changing assumptions and sustaining such changes are more difficult to evaluate in relation to a specific third-party consultancy. D'Estrée and Colby (2004) have developed a set of criteria and methods for assessing environmental conflict resolution cases.

Conclusion

As scholars and practitioners became students of group dynamics and group processes, the field of facilitation and consultation emerged in terms of helping groups accomplish their tasks and goals. We have a number of third-party facilitator roles and models available from which to chose. The practice is moving well beyond the traditional problem-solving facilitation of multi-party disputes. Facilitation is used widely in planning, prevention, envisioning, and healing. Many third-party consultations have been documented in their application to deep-rooted and protracted social conflicts.

As new models of facilitation have emerged, too little has been studied as to their applicability in consultation. Consultation as a part of interactive problem-solving is a large part of "practice" in our field. So is dialogue. We need to be more intentional about introducing and evaluating appreciative inquiry, narrative, and conversation in the small-group components of problem-solving workshops. Can the attitudes, perceptions, values, and skills have sustainable change as an outcome of consultation processes? What else is needed and how can we measure this? Future inquiry and research is clearly open for students interested in the particular practices of conflict analysis and resolution.

Discussion Questions

1 What were the contributions of early research of group dynamics on the phenomenon of facilitation as it relates to group behavior?
2 Of the intervention models discussed, which do you think are the most helpful? Are certain models appropriate for specific situations, or will they work equally well under all circumstances?
3 What does it mean to say that the facilitator is "the guardian of the process?"
4 What is the contribution of narrative to the facilitation process, and why is it important to emphasize narrative and conversation during intervention?
5 How is it possible for facilitators to aid the transfer of new ideas and relationships to the macro-political level?

Key Words

Academic panel of facilitators
Appreciative inquiry
Basic groups versus developmental groups
Connecticut Interracial Commission
Consultation
Contingency model
Controlled communication
Conversation
Evaluation
Facilitation
Facilitator as guardian
Field theory
Gestalt Institute
Gestalt psychology
Group dynamics
Group relations
Identity-based conflict
Institute for Applied Behavioral Science
Metaphor analysis
"Middle–out" approach
Narrative and dialogue
National training laboratories
Problem-solving workshops
Process versus content
Pre-negotiation
"Re-entry" following consultation
Relationship transformation

Sensitivity training
T-Group
Tavistock Institute of Human Relations
Third party, third-party functions, third-party identity, third-party
 tactics
Transfer effects

CHAPTER 19

Peace Operations

Alex J. Bellamy and Paul D. Williams

Peace operations represent one of the most significant forms of third-party involvement in armed conflict. Traditionally, they were seen as mechanisms to manage and contain conflicts but they have played other roles as well. As a result, peace operations have become part of the conflict resolution process in numerous armed conflicts around the world. This led some analysts to argue that conflict resolution should form a core part of the rationale behind peace operations (see Ramsbotham and Woodhouse, 2000, 2005). Fetherston (1994), for instance, suggested that peacekeepers should place less emphasis on the use of military force and devote more attention to developing the skills needed to resolve violent conflicts. Others have endorsed this suggestion but pointed out that, in practice, peacekeepers have been involved in mediation and conflict resolution on a regular basis. Indeed, Wall and Druckman (2003, p. 703) found mediation to be one of the core functions of peace operations. Consequently, analyzing peace operations within a conflict resolution framework should improve our understanding of what roles peacekeepers are actually playing in the world's war zones and how they might contribute to bringing about long-term, stable peace (see Druckman, Wall, and Diehl, 1999).

Peace operations involve the dispatch of expeditionary forces, with or without a United Nations (UN) mandate, to implement an agreement between warring states or factions, which may (or may not) include enforcing that agreement in the face of willful defiance. The UN's Department for Peacekeeping Operations (DPKO) is currently overseeing sixteen peace operations, which by the end of October 2006 involved the deployment of over 80,000 military and police personnel. These figures surpass the UN's previous highpoint in the early 1990s when the organization conducted large, high-profile missions in Cambodia, Somalia, and Bosnia and suffered ignominious failures in the latter two cases and Rwanda.

In addition to the recent surge in UN peace operations, there have been an increasing number of non-UN peace operations launched by a mixture of individual states, coalitions of the willing and regional organizations. Although these missions operate outside of the UN's command and control, they have usually been either authorized and/or welcomed by the Security Council or have operated with the consent of the host government. Increasingly, UN and non-UN components have worked alongside one another in hybrid operations. Significantly, the recent expansion of peace operations cannot be explained as a response to growing levels of violent conflict around the globe because it has occurred alongside a decline in both the number of armed conflicts and their deadliness (Human Security Centre, 2005).

This chapter provides an overview of contemporary peace operations and the challenges they face by addressing three sets of questions. First, what is the purpose of peace operations? We argue that peace operations can be divided into five broad types based on their underlying political purpose. Second, what actors make the most legitimate and effective peacekeepers? In this section we try to make sense of the proliferation of actors conducting peace operations. Finally, we ask what challenges contemporary peace operations confront and what policies they may adopt to overcome them? Here we argue that although an international consensus has emerged around the so-called Brahimi paradigm, significant challenges remain, especially in relation to civilian protection.

What Are Peace Operations For?

The most popular way of thinking conceptually about peace operations is to identify their characteristics, functions, and types. Boutros Boutros-Ghali's *An Agenda for Peace* (1992) sparked widespread debate about the interrelated concepts of peacekeeping, peace-building, peacemaking, and peace enforcement. He defined peacekeeping as, "the deployment of a UN presence in the field, hitherto with the consent of all parties concerned" (Boutros-Ghali, 1992, p. 5). The problem with this approach, however, is that unfortunately, peacekeeping is uncertain, unregulated, and unpredictable (Diehl, 1994, p. 1). What, for instance, are we to make of operations that carry the label of 'peacekeeping' but do not enjoy the consistent consent of all the parties or do not exclusively employ UN personnel?

The approach we adopt is to identify different types of operation according to their underlying political purpose(s). Close scrutiny suggests that there is much less consensus about what peace operations are for than we might be led to believe. For example, if we look at the politics surrounding the deployment of the first fully fledged peacekeeping mission, UNEF I in the Middle East (1956-67), we find at least three very different ideas of what it was for. For the UN Secretary-General at the time, Dag Hammarskjöld, the primary purpose of the mission was to prevent conflict escalation. For Britain and France, whose intervention had helped spark the crisis, its primary purpose was to keep the Suez Canal out of the hands of Egypt's President Nasser and permit them to withdraw their forces without losing face. For most of the region's states – and most post-colonial states – the mission's primary purpose was to put a halt to British and French imperialism and force their withdrawal. The purpose of the taxonomy offered here, therefore, is to identify different types of operation based on what they are supposed to achieve. It is important to note that these are ideal-type distinctions. In practice, individual operations can and do move between the categories.

Traditional peacekeeping operations are intended to promote peaceful relations between states. In practice, this means constructing the political space necessary for belligerent states to reach political agreement. Traditional peacekeeping takes place in the space between a ceasefire agreement between states and the conclusion of a political settlement. Traditional peacekeepers do not propose or enforce particular political solutions. Rather, they try to build confidence between the belligerents in an attempt to facilitate political dialogue and negotiation. Although there is no consensus on what activities constitute traditional peacekeeping, the general principles that underpin it are consent, impartiality, and minimum use of force. *Consent* refers to the idea that peacekeepers are deployed with the consent of the belligerents, normally the rulers of whichever territory peacekeepers are being deployed into. *Impartiality* literally refers to the idea that peacekeepers should treat all belligerents alike, but in the context of traditional peacekeeping – especially during the Cold War – impartiality was often understood as remaining neutral with regard to the political dispute. *Minimum force* was traditionally understood as only using force in self-defence.

Traditional peacekeeping involves non-coercive consent-based techniques, usually in support of interim ceasefires or agreements, to help prevent the resumption or escalation of violence and provide a breathing space in which a settlement can be agreed. It is based on three assumptions: (1) that the belligerents are states; (2) that the combatant units are hierarchical militaries; and (3) that the parties to the dispute wish to end the conflict and search for a political settlement. This means that the success of traditional peacekeeping missions depends upon the cooperation of the disputants.

Typically, traditional peacekeeping activities range from observation and fact-finding, to monitoring compliance with the conditions of ceasefires and physical interposition between disputants. Peacekeepers monitor borders, patrol buffer-zones separating opposing forces, verify the various aspects of demilitarization including weapons decommissioning and troop withdrawals, and attempt to create a political space based on mutual confidence that will facilitate a political resolution of the conflict.

Its conceptual roots are to be found in the Cold War context of its birth and the UN's attempt to maintain international peace and security. Although the architects of the UN Charter envisaged a powerful institution capable of enforcing collective security, the rapid deterioration of relations between its two most influential members, the U.S. and USSR, meant that many of the instruments that were originally envisaged (including a standing army) either failed to materialize or failed to take on their assigned role. Superpower rivalry soured relations in the UN and the lack of consensus in the Security Council, demonstrated by the high number of vetoes cast (113 between 1945-1965), meant that the organization was unable to fulfill the collective security function that was initially envisaged for it.

The organizing principles that underpin traditional peacekeeping were worked out in the context of the Suez Crisis in 1956 and the deployment of UNEF I. Discussion between Hammarskjöld and his advisors concerning the potential nature of UN intervention in the crisis was informed as much by political considerations about what the organization would be allowed to do by the Security Council as by technical thoughts about what the aims and activities of peacekeepers should be (Urquhart, 1994, p. 175-83). Hammarskjöld believed that the UN needed to be pragmatic rather than idealistic in its approach, and this perception contributed to the influential idea that peacekeeping was (and should be) an ad hoc response to particular problems rather than a blueprint for international action.

Around the world today, observer and traditional peacekeeping missions are still visible. These include the long-standing missions in the Middle East (UNTSO and UNIFIL), Kashmir (UNMOGIP), Western Sahara (MINURSO), and Cyprus (UNFICYP), as well as newer missions such as the UN mission on the border between Ethiopia and Eritrea (UNMEE). Although many of these missions have fulfilled important roles – for example, UNMEE has prevented the escalation of border clashes into all-out war by interposing itself between the belligerents – there are also important limits to what traditional peacekeeping can achieve, especially in cases where the core assumptions are not satisfied.

Most obviously, the issue of consent is problematic in complicated conflict environments. Traditional peacekeeping's reliance on the goodwill of the disputants means that it is unable to achieve its goals if the belligerents do not cooperate. All the operations mentioned above have suffered from these problems at some point. In the Middle East, UNIFIL was unable to persuade or enforce Hezbollah's compliance with the Security Council's demands that it be disarmed, sowing the seeds for the 2006 conflict with Israel. Similarly, UNEF I was forced to withdraw after continued animosity between Israel and Egypt saw their relations deteriorate into war in 1967. The problems caused by dependency on consent are magnified in more complex conflicts where consent is variable and where the belligerents are of many different types. In these cases, not only is consent variable, in terms of the appropriate authority changing its mind, it is also multilayered in that there is no guarantee that the entire rank and file of a particular group will grant their consent even if their political leaders do.

In addition, the traditional approaches to impartiality and minimum use of force have also been seen as anachronistic. Extending from the core principle of consent, they only exacerbate the problems peace-keepers face when that consent is not forthcoming. UNTSO, UNEF, UNFICYP, UNIFIL, and numerous other traditional peacekeeping operations were powerless to prevent open breaches of the agreements they were meant to oversee. Their limited military capabilities under-mined their right to act in self-defense as well as their capacity to fulfill their mandates. UN peacekeepers have regularly been killed all around the world: troops from UNEF I were caught in the crossfire of the Six Days War (160 peacekeepers were killed in total in UNEF I and II) and in 2006, four UNIFIL observers were killed by the Israeli air force (a total of 258 peacekeepers have died while deployed with UNIFIL).

Finally, although traditional peacekeeping was intended to provide an environment conducive to resolving the conflict, it has sometimes been accused of entrenching those conflicts by simply freezing them in place (MacGinty and Robinson, 2001, p. 30). This occurs when one or more of the belligerents prefer the status quo to the likely outcome of a political settlement, a phenomenon most apparent in Cyprus.

Managing transition operations aim to facilitate and then help implement a settlement agreed by the conflicting parties but often with outside assistance. They are usually deployed within (rather than between) states after the parties have agreed to a ceasefire and a political settlement. They take place with the consent of the parties, but unlike traditional peacekeeping they are concerned with the implementation of an agreed political settlement. At their most expansive, they take the form of transitional administrations in which the UN assumes both the reigns of government and sovereign authority (see Caplan, 2005).

Managing a transition is qualitatively distinct from traditional peace-keeping because it takes place at a different stage of the conflict cycle and encompasses a significant civilian component. Such operations are multi-dimensional because they deal with the panoply of issues connected with the transformation of states and societies. They are concerned with the implementation of peace accords and usually have important military functions associated with the demilitarization of conflict. These may range from traditional peacekeeping tasks such as patrolling neutral zones, separating combatants, and monitoring troop movements to verification of disarmament, cantonment of opposing military forces, and even temporary responsibility for the provision of security. However, because they are conducted at the behest of the parties to the conflict, they are not technically exercises in enforcement and are predicated on the same principles as traditional peacekeeping (consent, impartiality, and minimum use of force), although transitional administrations enjoy significant enforcement powers. The military component exists alongside multiple civilian components responsible for managing various aspects of transition, including civil administration, policing, democratic institution-building (often including reform of the judiciary and political system), human rights promotion, supervision of electoral processes, as well as a longer-term commitment to facilitate aid and post-conflict rehabilitation.

As noted above, this type of operation can be further distinguished by the degree of authority granted to the UN. In operations such as those in Namibia, El Salvador, and Cambodia, the UN oversaw most aspects of government but without actually assuming sovereign authority. In more recent transitional administrations in Eastern Croatia, Bosnia, Kosovo, and East Timor, however, the UN assumed both the full responsibilities of peacekeeping and sovereign authority over the territory. In effect, therefore, it became both peacekeeper and government – two roles that demand quite different things.

As a broad type, managing transition operations have been the UN's most successful, especially at the 'lighter' end of the spectrum. Transitional administrations have tended to be judged as being less successful, but it is important to note that success in these cases is measured by reference to a wider set of more exacting criteria than other types of peace operations. Their success has typically depended on a range of factors including the legitimacy and support given to the peace process by the former belligerents. Moreover, they have typically required a relatively stable security situation that derived from the deployment of peacekeepers after *both* a ceasefire and a political settlement. This, in turn, contributed towards a clear conception of the operation's goals and timetable. Finally, it is important to note that almost all the operations that fall under this rubric enjoyed a benign and/or supportive international environment.

Despite these factors, managing transition operations have encountered many problems. First, in the 'lighter' types of operation, the military components were often too weak to fulfill their mandates, particularly with regard to the verification of demilitarization commitments. They were also unable to enforce compliance, as shown by the UN's inability to hold the Khmer Rouge to its agreements. On the other hand, transitional administrations have often been accused of being too heavy-handed, creating a 'democratic deficit'. Sensitivity to such criticisms persuaded the UN to withdraw from East Timor earlier than originally envisaged, leaving weak institutions unable to cope with a political crisis that erupted into violence in 2006 which required Australian and Portuguese intervention to halt. Third, some critics argued that the peace settlements that provided the foundations for these operations favored negative peace over justice and long-term stable peace. SFOR in Bosnia, for example, was criticized for not actively seeking out suspected war criminals such as Ratko Mladic, accused of genocide in relation to the 1995 Srebrenica massacre.

Wider peacekeeping operations are intended to fulfill the aims of traditional peacekeeping as well as certain additional tasks within an environment of ongoing conflict. They developed an ad hoc response to the breakdown of ceasefire or political agreements that enabled the deployment of a traditional or managing transition operation combined with a belief on the part of peacekeepers that they should continue to have some sort of role in the conflict area. Wider peacekeeping has many different labels. According to British military doctrine which bears the same name, it refers to "operations carried out with the consent of the belligerent parties in support of efforts to achieve or maintain peace in order to promote security and sustain life in areas of potential or actual conflict" (HMSO, 1995, p. 2-1). The 'wider' of wider peacekeeping refers to "the wider aspects of peacekeeping operations carried out with the consent of the belligerent parties but in an environment that may be volatile" (HMSO, 1995, p. 2-1). Wider peacekeeping is also sometimes referred to as "second generation peacekeeping" (Mackinlay and Chopra, 1992). The 'second generation' was distinct from the first generation of traditional peacekeeping because such operations tended to take place within states rather than between them and in an environment where the interposition of blue helmets between organized belligerents was either not possible or ineffective. Wider peacekeeping is also sometimes referred to as Chapter 6½ peacekeeping. This term was used to highlight the problem that wider peacekeeping fell somewhere between the pacific and consensual provisions of Chapter VI of the UN Charter and the enforcement measures envisaged under Chapter VII. The ambiguous Chapter 6½ nature of wider peacekeeping operations is often claimed to lay at the heart of the failures in Bosnia, Rwanda, and Sierra Leone (O'Shea, 2002, p. 147).

These terms refer to similar practices and in our view, four characteristics of wider peacekeeping operations can be identified. First, they are predicated on the basic assumptions of traditional peacekeeping but involve a wider range of purposes. Second, they occur within a context of ongoing violence. Whereas both traditional and transitional peace operations take place after the belligerents have signed a ceasefire agreement, wider peacekeeping takes place either in the complete absence of such agreement or in situations where agreements are fragile and prone to collapse. In Bosnia, UNPROFOR negotiated literally hundreds of ceasefires, most of which were broken within 24 hours. Similarly, UN missions in both Rwanda and Sierra Leone were plagued by collapsing peace agreements and violence. Third, soldiers engaged in wider peacekeeping are given tasks beyond those of traditional peacekeepers, including the separation of forces, disarming the belligerents, organizing and supervising elections, delivering humanitarian aid, protecting civilian UN personnel and those from other governmental and non-governmental organizations, guaranteeing freedom of movement, host state capacity building, monitoring ceasefires, and enforcing no-fly zones (also see Diehl, Druckman, and Wall, 1998, p. 39-40). Although peacekeepers involved in managing transitions in Namibia, Mozambique, and Cambodia also took on many of these roles, the context of enduring violent conflict dramatically altered their nature and salience. Finally, wider peacekeeping operations have a significant humanitarian component, and in some cases their primary objective may involve securing the delivery of humanitarian aid to civilians in the absence of a workable ceasefire. This requires peacekeepers to cooperate closely with a range of other actors.

Wider peacekeeping tends to be associated with many of the UN's most disastrous missions in the 1990s and is thus generally seen as something to be avoided. Missions in Somalia, Rwanda, and Bosnia were tasked to keep the peace and conduct a range of other activities while operating within the strictures of traditional peacekeeping concepts. As a result, peacekeepers were neither adequately equipped nor mandated to fulfill their wider tasks. Although lessons have been learned, many contemporary operations share these characteristics. A good example of this is the African Union's mission in the Darfur region of Sudan (AMIS). Deployed in 2004, AMIS was tasked with overseeing a variety of ceasefires and, where possible, protecting civilians. However, it had no mandate to use force directly against the perpetrators of mass killings, and with a force of fewer than 7,000 troops who lacked adequate transport and intelligence, it was unable to stem the ongoing violence (see Williams, 2006).

Peace enforcement operations are designed to impose the will of the Security Council upon the parties to a particular conflict. They are the closest manifestation of the collective security role originally envisaged by the UN's architects. Although in practical terms the neat distinctions between peacekeeping and peace enforcement eroded as the UN became involved in more complex operations, in conceptual terms there remain important characteristics that continue to distinguish peace enforcement from other types of operations. In particular, peace enforcement is concerned with those activities that fall under Chapter VII of the UN Charter. Enforcement measures usually refer to the imposition of either economic sanctions (under Article 41) or military sanctions (under Article 42). Between 1946 and 1989 the UN invoked Chapter VII on 24 occasions. In comparison, during the 1990s there were a further 166 Chapter VII resolutions.

The idea of collective security provides the intellectual basis for the UN's conception of peace enforcement. In Chapter VII the UN intended to establish the means to enforce a general system of collective security. The central idea is that the system's participants should work to uphold certain shared values, by peaceful means if possible and through the threat and use of force if necessary. From the outset, the UN's architects realized that constructing a collective security system would require a mixture of military and non-military means. Since 1990, the Security Council has imposed economic sanctions on over a dozen (sometimes non-state) targets with mixed but always controversial results. Much of the controversy stemmed from the widespread recognition that general trade sanctions were a blunt instrument that raised questions about the legitimacy of inflicting suffering on a population as a whole in order to exert an uncertain degree of pressure on political leaders whose primary concern may not be the welfare of their subjects. Partly in recognition of this dilemma, since 1994 all UN sanctions have been targeted, that is, comprising various packages of financial sanctions, travel bans, arms embargoes, and commodity boycotts rather than general trade sanctions. In relation to financial sanctions, these were initially imposed only on government assets, but starting with the case of Haiti in 1994, the Council has also targeted the accounts of designated individuals and groups such as the

Haitian military junta, UNITA leaders in Angola, and the Taliban regime in Afghanistan. In 2001, the UN imposed sanctions upon Liberia because of its continued material and financial support for the Revolutionary United Front in Sierra Leone (Security Council Resolution 1343).

In relation to military measures, Boutros-Ghali made clear in *An Agenda for Peace* that these were "essential to the credibility of the United Nations as a guarantor of international security" (1992, para. 43). Once Article 42 has been invoked, it is up to the member states to make armed forces and facilities available to the Security Council to enable it to carry out its mandate or delegate its powers to an appropriate entity. In practice, it is possible to distinguish two varieties of the UN's use of military force – collective security operations and enforcement operations within a broader peace mission. Collective security operations are those occasions when the UN has authorized the use of force against a particular state in response to an act (or acts) of inter-state aggression. Examples include the UN's authorization of force against North Korea following its invasion of South Korea in June 1950 and against Iraq following its invasion of Kuwait in August 1990. The other variety of peace enforcement refers to those occasions when the UN has authorized the use of force against a state or non-state entity in response acts of violence that may occur within the borders of a particular state but is deemed to represent a threat to, or breach of, international peace and security, such as the massacre of civilians or attacks against UN personnel. Such actors are sometimes referred to as 'spoilers' and may seek to either undermine the whole peace process or to manipulate the process for their own purposes (Stedman, 1997). Examples include the UN's authorization of military force in the Congo in the early 1960s, in Somalia in the early 1990s, in Bosnia during Operation Deliberate Force, in Albania in 1997, in East Timor in 1999, and measures against militia groups in the Democratic Republic of Congo (DRC) since 2003.

In practice, enforcement measures may prove counter-productive to the goal of establishing long-term peace and security. Indeed, as the Somali case shows, apart from the numbers of people suffering from severe malnutrition, the intervening forces left the country in much the same state as they found it, that is, suffering from low-intensity conflict and without an effective central authority (Clapham, 2002, p. 200). In the case of UNOSOM II, the use of force against spoilers contributed to the emergence of other spoilers leading, in turn, to a need for peace-keepers to use ever greater force. In these situations, the peacekeepers themselves might contribute to conflict escalation. In contrast, the East Timor case provides more room for optimism inasmuch as the threat and limited use of force enabled the transition to independence and a democratically elected government. Likewise, in the DRC, the threat and use of force was a necessary precursor to the 2006 elections, and when moderate violence erupted in Kinshasa shortly afterwards, the rapid deployment of European peacekeepers helped prevent any escalation.

Peace support operations are designed to transform war-torn states into stable liberal democracies. That is, they aim to establish liberal democratic societies within states as the most effective means of maintaining peace and security. They combine robust military forces, capable of limited peace enforcement tasks should a ceasefire break-down, with a strong civilian component that includes civil administration, humanitarian elements, and civilian policing. Peace Support Operations (PSO) attempt to enforce a political agreement that usually involved a high level of input from outsiders and which supports the establishment of liberal democracy.

The need for robust military forces was supported and developed by NATO doctrine writers and has become a core rhetorical component of the 'Brahimi paradigm' discussed below. It was developed on the back of recognized failings with earlier approaches to peace operations. In particular, the earlier focus on consent and the rigid distinction between peacekeeping and peace enforcement was viewed as anachronistic. Instead, there was a growing appreciation that force and coercion played important roles in peace support and that there was a need to think precisely about how it should be applied (e.g., Roberts, 1995).

In military terms, the PSO concept insists that it is possible to use force in a peace operation without losing impartiality and hence consent. In order to retain impartiality, any use of force must be directed against a specific breach of the mandate and must be linked to a clearly defined outcome. To achieve this, the military component of a peace operation must be robust and able to move swiftly from traditional peacekeeping to peace enforcement and back again.

PSO doctrine also tried to think more carefully about the nature and role of consent. On one hand the level of consent changes. Parties which give consent at the outset may change their minds and vice versa. On the other hand, consent operates at a number of levels. While a faction leader or government may give their consent, it does not always follow that local fighters will do likewise. This is particularly true in cases where the conflict is not between two disciplined armies. This prompted a further concern for 'consent management', which emphasized the idea that peacekeepers themselves had an important role to play in promoting and maximizing consent, not least through the use of effective public information strategies.

The final important aspect of the PSO concept is the recognition that the military component is only one element of a broader multi-agency engagement aimed at creating a liberal democratic society. The military tasks therefore need to support the broader tasks of the mission. In East Timor and Kosovo, for instance, the military took on wider roles beyond the provision of physical security, including infrastructure development and institutional capacity building.

Like the other types of operation, in practice, PSOs have also encountered problems. Thus, although it stands to reason that clear and recognizable objectives backed up with sufficient forces is desirable, it does not necessarily follow that states will always agree about what is best in a given situation or find the political will to contribute troops and money. Furthermore, the PSO concept is not universally applied. As discussed earlier, some current peace operations still bear the negative hallmarks of wider peacekeeping. What, therefore, is to be done when no Western state wants to take the lead? Or, when there are no means available to secure even the narrowest mandate in the world's most hazardous places? The danger is that by selectively applying the PSO concept, the West risks creating a two-tier system of peace operations. On the one hand there are well-equipped, well-funded operations led by one of the world's richer states trying to secure an achievable mandate. On the other hand, there are peacekeepers, particularly in Africa, whose primary function remains burying the dead.

In this brief survey we have identified five types of peace operations based on the purposes they seek to fulfill and the different stages of the conflict cycle in which they are deployed: traditional peacekeeping theoretically takes place in the period between a ceasefire and a political settlement; wider peacekeeping tends to take place in a context of fragile ceasefires and ongoing violence; and both managing transitions and peace support operations presuppose the existence of comprehensive peace agreements, though the latter type does not assume good faith compliance with its terms. Finally, peace enforcement can take place at any stage of the conflict, though traditionally it has been most effective in cases where there is broad international agreement about the desired end state. In practice, it is important to note that decisions about what type of operation to deploy are framed by the political wishes of key states, but each type has strengths and weaknesses and are more or less suited to different types of context.

Who Conducts Peace Operations?

It is not only the purpose of peace operations that is contested. Since their inception, states have argued about the types of actors that have the authority to mandate and the capacity to conduct peace operations. Although the UN has the most experience in authorizing and conducting peace operations, the organization has never possessed a monopoly on them. This situation has become more obvious in recent years as a wide variety of non-UN actors have conducted peace operations, often without the Security Council's authorization. In Africa, for instance, since 1990 there have been twelve peace operations conducted by regional arrangements: five by the Economic Community of West African States (in Liberia, Sierra Leone, Guinea-Bissau, and Côte d'Ivoire), two under the mantle of the Southern African Development Community (in Lesotho and the DRC), one by the Economic and Monetary Community of Central African States (in Central African Republic), and four by the African Union (in Burundi, the Comoros, Somalia, and Sudan). The continent has also experienced, among others, British operations in Sierra Leone, French operations in Central African Republic and Côte d'Ivoire, a South African Protection Support Detachment deployed to Burundi, and a French-led Emergency Force to the Ituri region of the DRC. In Europe, Italy led a peace operation in Albania in 1997, Russian troops – often under the umbrella of the Commonwealth of Independent States (CIS) – have deployed to Moldova, Georgia, and Tajikistan, and NATO continues to lead a large peace operation in Kosovo and in 2004 handed control of its Bosnia operation over to the European Union (EU). In addition, in 2003, NATO took command of the International Security Assistance Force (ISAF) in Afghanistan. In the same year, and following NATO's departure, the EU conducted Operation *Concordia* in Macedonia and followed it with a police mission, *Proxima*. In the Americas, the U.S. led a multinational force into Haiti after the departure of President Aristide in spring 2004. Finally, in Asia, Australia has led peace operations to East Timor in 1999 and 2006 and the Solomon Islands in 2003.

Whether this proliferation of non-UN peace operations should be welcomed is a question that has divided practitioners and commentators alike. On the one hand, there are those who believe that regional solutions could bridge the gap between means and ends that plagued peace operations in the early 1990s and offer an alternative to the 'corrupt', 'wasteful', 'politicized', and 'overly bureaucratized' practices of the UN (Boulden, 2001, p. 130-2; Fleitz, 2002). On the other hand, there are many former and current senior UN figures that insist regional arrangements do not offer a panacea. Former UN Secretary-General Boutros Boutros-Ghali (1999, p. 306), for example, condemned regionalization as a 'dangerous' idea that threatened to weaken the internationalist basis of the UN. Former head of the UN's Department of Political Affairs, Marrack Goulding (2002, p. 17) also cautioned that most regional arrangements lacked the experience and bureaucratic structures and resources necessary to conduct peace operations effectively. Similarly, the current head of the UN Department of Peacekeeping Operations, Jean-Marie Guéhenno (2003, p. 35-6) has warned that regionalization has encouraged an 'only in my backyard' approach that spells trouble for regions that lack the necessary capacities.

If we are to draw conclusions about the relationship between UN and non-UN peace operations, it is important to have a sound grasp of current trends. The first point to note is that almost all the UN peace operations created since 2000 have enjoyed close relationships with non-UN actors. For example, UNMIK in Kosovo provides only one of the transitional administration's four pillars, the other three being provided by NATO (security), the EU (economy), and OSCE (democratization and human rights); French forces have operated alongside UN forces in Cote d'Ivoire; EU forces have intervened on more than one occasion to assist MONUC in the DRC; UN forces in Liberia (UNMIL) and Burundi (ONUB) took over from non-UN operations conducted by ECOWAS and the AU respectively; and the two international forces in Sudan (UNMIS and AMIS) operated alongside one another. This suggests a significant 'hybridization' of peace operations wherein a number of different organizations operate independently but in cooperation with or alongside one another. The second point is that with the partial exception of Africa, UN peace operations remain absent from many of the world's most troubled areas, including Afghanistan, the Balkans, Chechnya, Colombia, Iraq, Palestine, Sri Lanka, and Somalia. These gaps have been partially filled by non-UN actors. Finally, the trend has not all been in one direction. In Africa especially, non-UN actors such as ECOWAS and the AU have tended to hand operations over to the UN, as ECOWAS did in Liberia and Sierra Leone, the AU did in Burundi, and the AU is attempting to do in Sudan.

Peace operations of the future are therefore more likely to be hybrids. In the post-Cold War era these missions have taken a variety of forms, most notably: (1) 'spear-head/vanguard' operations, where non-UN troops prepare the security environment on the ground in order to hand over to a UN or other international peace operation; (2) 'stabilization' operations, where non-UN troops work alongside UN and/or other international peace operations provide military security; (3) 'fire-fighting' operations, where non-UN troops provide in-theatre support to beleaguered UN or other missions already in the field; and/or (4) 'over-the-horizon' operations, where Western troops are despatched to within striking distance of the theatre in question to perform a deterrent and perhaps later enforcement role in support of a beleaguered operation.

Examples of 'spear-head/vanguard' operations include the IFOR designed to help implement the Dayton Accord in Bosnia (1995), the Australian-led INTERFET force that stabilized East Timor prior to UNTAET (1999), the French *Operation Licorne* that played an inter-position role between the belligerents in Côte d'Ivoire's civil war before the arrival of ECOFORCE and then MINUCI (2002-03), and the Multinational Interim Force deployed to Haiti that paved the way for MINUSTAH (2004). Arguably, this sort of operation gives credence to the British government's claim that Western troops are most suited to these difficult, first-in missions. But contemporary peace operations are usually about more than just suspending the violence, and the West's proclivity for quickly handing over the peacekeeping baton to other actors is hardly indicative of a strong commitment to the job of peace-building.

Once the violence has abated, 'stabilization' operations have been undertaken in a variety of settings including the NATO-led SFOR in Bosnia (1996), the KFOR, which supported UNMIK in Kosovo in the aftermath of Operation Allied Force (1999), and the UK-led ISAF in Kabul and its environs (2001). Unlike ISAF, which has gradually expanded its size, remit, and area of operations, the two Balkan forces have been gradually down-sized as the situation on the ground stabilized. SFOR was replaced by an EU-led mission (EUFOR), authorized by Security Council resolution 1575 on November 22, 2004. Since then, the EU has further down-sized its initial force of 7,000 to 2,000 'theatre troops' and approximately 700 support staff, drawn from more than 20 different states.

'Fire-fighting' operations involving Western personnel would include NATO's *Operation Deliberate Force* in support of UNPROFOR in Bosnia (1995), the French-led *Operation Turquoise* ostensibly in sup-port of UNAMIR in Rwanda (1994), the UK's *Operation Palliser* in support of UNAMSIL in Sierra Leone (2000), and the French-led *Operation Artemis* in support of MONUC in the DRC (2003). These missions aim to address specific challenges confronting already existing UN operations that require the use of force. They are generally short in duration and direct force against specific spoilers, such as the Bosnian Serbs (in the case of *Deliberate Force*) or the Revolutionary United Front and 'West Side Boys' (in the case of *Palliser*), though they run the risk of escalation that we identified earlier. Fire-fighting operations have tended to be explicitly authorized by the UN Security Council and hence represent a form of subcontracting of the UN's enforcement powers. Although 'fire-fighting' clearly speaks to the argument that Western forces are best utilized in circumstances where their superior firepower, support, and training can be brought to bear – such as in limited operations to defeat and deter spoilers – concerns abound about the temporary nature of the West's commitment.

The limits of 'fire-fighting' are perhaps best demonstrated by the experience of *Operation Artemis*. *Artemis* was a French-led operation comprising 1,500 troops drawn from eight states (France, Germany, Belgium, Sweden, UK, South Africa, and Canada) deployed to the town of Bunia in Eastern DRC between early June and September 1, 2003. The mission's aim was to put an end to the periodic killing of civilians in Bunia and to protect the 5,000-8,000 civilians who sought refuge near the UN's compound. The deployment of well-armed Western (mainly French) troops with air support had a rapid impact on the security situation in Bunia, granting international NGOs greater freedom of movement and 'severely weakening' the key spoiler in the region, the so-called Union of Congolese Patriots. However, because the mission was limited temporally (*Artemis* was only a three-month deployment) and geographically (its mandate extended only to the town of Bunia), its contribution to saving lives in the wider Ituri province was 'minimal' (Grignon, 2003, p. 3). The killing of civilians continued in the countryside around Bunia and continued steadily after the operation's withdrawal. In February 2005, for example, Bangladeshi peacekeepers were ambushed in Ituri province and nine were killed and mutilated. Throughout 2005-06, UN forces have been consistently engaged in enforcement operations in Ituri, the most recent being *Operation Ember* conducted alongside DRC government forces. The key points here are that 'fire-fighting' in the short term does not always remove the spoiler problem or create conditions for UN troops to perform peacekeeping duties without the need for force.

The final type of hybrid missions is 'over-the-horizon' operations. To date, these have been rarer than the other types of operations. In 2003, for example, the U.S. deployed a marine ship off the coast of Liberia and despatched a small protection force to the U.S. embassy in Monrovia in support of ECOMIL and later UNMIL forces. A more prominent case, however, is the EU's 'reserve deployment' to assist in the smooth running of the 2006 elections in the DRC.

In April 2006, the Security Council authorized the deployment of a EUFOR 'reserve deployment' (EUFOR RD) to the DRC in order to assist MONUC and the Kinshasa government during the elections. EUFOR RD's mandate, set out in Security Council Resolution 1671, included the protection of civilians "without prejudice to the responsibilities of the Congolese government," the provision of security at Kinshasa's airport, and limited operations aimed at extracting key individuals associated with the elections if their security was threatened. The mission is, to date, unique in that it comprised a modest-sized 'advanced deployment' of approximately 400-500 peacekeepers to Kinshasa and a larger 'battalion size' (around 1,500 troops) deployment on standby outside the DRC ('over-the-horizon') that could be called upon if necessary. When violence broke out in Kinshasa shortly after the 2006 elections, EUFOR peacekeepers were deployed to stabilize the situation, which they did effectively.

This section has discussed the different types of actors that are engaged in peace operations and the developing relationship between them. It is apparent that an increasing number of operations involve two or more different types of organizations. If the future lies in hybrid operations, more attention needs to be given to the relationship between the UN and a range of other organizations. It will also be important to identify the different types of hybrid operation in order to evaluate the contribution that each type makes to third-party intervention. We identified four types of operation: spear-head, stabilization, fire-fighting, and over-the-horizon. Furthermore, we observed that the West's contribution to peace operations is increasingly to be found outside the UN. Although in most cases these operations are not "anti-UN" and have been publicly welcomed by UN officials because they can provide important services such as fire-fighting, their emergence has coincided with an overall reduction in both the size and duration of Western contributions to UN peace operations. The following section addresses the emerging consensus within the UN about the most appropriate manner of conducting peace operations and explores the extent to which it has developed new practices in relation to the protection of imperilled civilians.

Addressing the Challenges to Peace Operations

This section considers how the nature and efficacy of peace operations are shaped by the organizational structures and rules that surround them and recent attempts to improve the UN's ability to meet the challenges posed to peace operations. As a large, politically driven bureaucracy, the UN sometimes lacks the necessary flexibility to mediate effectively. On the other hand, the organization's actions are endowed with "an aura of legitimacy" (Touval, 1995b, p. 208) that enables it to fulfill a variety of roles in relation to conflict resolution. The bureaucratic and political nature of the UN is therefore a double-edged sword: it inhibits flexibility but enables third-party intervention in a variety of forms, including peace operations. The challenge for UN reformers is to minimize the former while maximizing the latter.

The so-called Brahimi Report (2000) was officially launched at the UN's Millennium Summit in September 2000. It focused upon how the

UN Secretariat's staff working on peacekeeping might better manage personnel in the field to produce more effective results. But it also contained important insights into how peace operations them selves should be conducted. Since 2000, a broad consensus has developed around its ethos and main recommendations. To promote better management of peace operations, the Report made four major recommendations:

- The military component of a peace operation should be robust enough to defend itself effectively, "confront the lingering forces of war and violence," and protect civilians under its care.
- There should be greater consultation between the Security Council and troop contributing countries (TCCs).
- The Security Council should not authorize a mission until it has the means to accomplish its goals.
- The planning and management of peace operations should be reorganized to improve coordination, and personnel should be recruited on the basis of expertise.

Although the UN General Assembly welcomed the Report, albeit with some reservations, the Secretariat has had difficulty persuading member states to implement its main recommendations. Shortly after the Report was published, the Secretary-General outlined the steps necessary for its implementation. In particular, Annan (2000) agreed that improving coordination between the Security Council and TCCs was crucial. In addition, new "integrated mission task forces" were envisaged that would coordinate the efforts of the UN's different agencies and enhance the organization's rapid deployment capabilities. To help persuade states to contribute personnel, material, and funds to these new missions, the Secretary-General called for them to participate more fully in the UN's standby forces arrangements. Annan (2000, p. 22) also requested "additional resources for the Secretariat," without which the reforms would have little hope of producing results on the ground.

The Secretary-General's implementation reports highlight two important points (see Durch *et al.* 2003). First, the political, decision-making, and operational aspects of the Brahimi Report have been side-lined from the official agenda. The implementation reports make no mention of proposed reforms to the way that the Security Council mandates operations. Nor has there been significant progress towards institutionalizing coordination between troop contributors, the DPKO, and the Security Council, despite Annan identifying this as a priority. In 2001, the Security Council resolved (in Resolution 1353) to institutionalize consultation. However, two years later, it emerged that Uruguayan peacekeepers deployed in Bunia, northeastern DRC, had been provided with no background briefing by the UN, no special training, and very little indication of how they should interpret and secure their mandate. In addition, the public has little way of knowing the exact nature of the relationship because the substance of discussions between the troop contributing countries and the Security Council is not a matter of public record.

In all likelihood, the lack of progress in the political sphere is a product of sharp disagreements about the future direction of peace operations. For example, several states in the General Assembly argued that peacekeeping operations should not be enlarged in the ways envisaged by Brahimi and that 'basic principles' such as consent, impartiality, and minimum use of force should be maintained (UN, 2002, p. 2). Second, it is also clear from the reports that the process of reform that has been undertaken (which is much less extensive than that called for by Brahimi's panel) is incomplete.

The majority of the Brahimi Report focused on the institutional capacity of the UN Secretariat and the bureaucratic organization of individual missions. Issues such as 'political will', funding, and the responsibility of the Security Council were given relatively scant attention and have been further marginalized during the subsequent implementation process. The preoccupation with technical issues looks even more out-of-place given that the UN-sanctioned reports on Rwanda and Srebrenica clearly demonstrated that it was political factors rather than institutional/bureaucratic factors that were primarily responsible for the respective failures. This is no great revelation. As Boutros Boutros-Ghali (1992, pp. 4 and 7) warned in 1992, among the most serious problems confronting the UN was the danger of its member states assigning the organization more and more onerous tasks without giving it the requisite resources to fulfill them. In his words, "a chasm has developed between the tasks entrusted to the organization and the financial means provided to it . . . nothing is more dangerous for a peacekeeping operation than to ask it to use force when its existing composition, armament, logistic support and deployment deny it the capacity to do so." This issue remains central to the contemporary agenda but apart from suggesting 'draft resolutions' and 'standby forces' (an idea with a much longer history), the Brahimi Report did not make much headway.

Brahimi's reformist agenda has already experienced problems and come under criticism on a variety of different counts. For a start, the idea of having better strategic planning and analysis for peace operations has been sidelined primarily as a result of concerns raised by a number of Southern states that something more sinister and neo-imperial might lie behind the development of such a capability. The post-Brahimi UN is also still having great difficulty obtaining sufficient pledges of reserve contingents of troops. Moreover, even when pledges have been forthcoming, member states have often reneged upon them. To give one example, the entire UN force in the DRC has just one reserve battalion. This problem is indicative of the fact that member states often make declarations of intent but are less likely to commit money and troops. As well as these difficulties, the Report has been criticized for not going into detail about command and control, and the financial aspects of peace operations (White, 2001, p. 136-7). At the operational level, critics have also chided the Report's authors for not devoting enough attention to civil-military relations, or the relationship between UN and local actors in conflict zones (e.g., Bell and Tousignant, 2001, p. 44). In addition, the Report was criticized for being "largely silent on gender issues" and its apparent inability to draw upon work already undertaken on these issues within the UN system (Whitworth, 2004, p. 127).

However, one important issue that sets the Brahimi paradigm apart from earlier perspectives on peace operations is its position on the use of force to protect civilians. These questions have also been the most controversial. John Mackinlay (2000), for example, argued that the Report failed to recognize that even small operations such as Britain's *Operation Palliser* in Sierra Leone (2000) required immense levels of planning, logistical and intelligence support, military expertise, and finances. If the UN is seriously thinking about developing new and comprehensive responses to complex emergencies, he argued, it needs to think about these military issues in far more detail than that found in the Brahimi Report. As we noted earlier, this gap is being filled by non-UN actors that can cobble together the necessary military expertise and resources to supplement UN capacity through hybrid operations. Consequently, the Report's failure to seriously explore the relationship between the UN and regional arrangements constitutes a major limitation.

In relation to what peacekeepers actually do in the field, the Report argued forcefully that once the UN had committed itself to deploying a peace operation, its personnel must be able, if required, to impose order on conflict zones. Specifically, the UN must be capable of projecting "credible force" in order "to confront the lingering forces of war and violence, with the ability and determination to defeat them" (Brahimi, 2000, p. viii). The ability to act as both peacekeepers and peace enforcers was made possible by the Panel's re-conceptualization of impartiality as "adherence to the principles of the Charter: where one party to a peace agreement clearly and incontrovertibly is violating its terms, continued equal treatment of all parties by the United Nations can in the best case result in ineffectiveness and in the worst may amount to complicity with evil" (Brahimi, 2000, p. ix). This stance raises at least two fundamental challenges.

First, the UN would need to overcome its traditional reluctance to distinguish between aggressors and victims, perhaps most tragically illustrated in Bosnia and Rwanda. If the UN wishes to use credible force against spoilers, it must clearly define who they are and how (and whether) they can be turned into willing participants in conflict resolution processes. This is a complex issue and one that cannot be resolved easily at an abstract level – every case will have to be judged separately. At present, UN practice would appear to indicate that it sees spoilers as those actors fundamentally opposed to resolving conflicts without recourse to violence and who are not prepared to participate in the construction of liberal polities, economies, and societies within the state in question.

But while identifying spoilers is one thing, doing something about them is another. For instance, contrary to popular mythology, from 1992 onwards UNPROFOR in Bosnia *did* have a mandate to use force to protect humanitarian supplies, and (later) to deter armed attack on the safe areas under Security Council resolutions 770 (August 13, 1992, authorizing "all necessary measures" to ensure the delivery of humanitarian aid) and 836 (June 4, 1993, authorizing UNPROFOR "to take necessary measures, including the use of force" in reply to bombardment or armed incursions into the safe areas). Similarly, in 1998, the Security Council clearly identified the Serbian government as the spoilers in Kosovo. However, in neither case did the identification of spoilers lead to decisive action against them.

The second challenge, therefore, is to identify what means can be put at the UN's disposal to deal effectively with spoilers, particularly when this requires the use of force. Although most commonly associated with post-Cold War peace operations, the protection of civilians and promotion of human rights formed a core part of several peacekeeping mandates during the Cold War (Månsson, 2005). Given the requisite political will to overcome issues such as command and control, training, and financing, forces operating under the UN flag should be able to deal with most spoilers. In practice, however, states have been reluctant to place their troops under UN command and have instead looked for alternative means of deploying force. The Brahimi Report did not support the creation of a UN standing army to meet these needs, even though the formation of just such a force was the centrepiece of the organization's collective security system until 1948 when Cold War animosities resulted in the idea being dropped. This was in spite of the fact that the U.S. (among others) had begun to plan significant contributions to the force. Instead, Brahimi and the Secretariat pinned their hopes on standby forces agreements between the UN and member states, which have not – to date – proved revolutionary.

In relation to the challenge of civilian protection, Victoria Holt (2006, pp. 55-56) has identified six approaches that envisage a potential role for military forces:

- Protection as an obligation within the conduct of war.
- Protection as a military mission to prevent mass killings.
- Protection as a task within a UN-mandated peace operation.
- Protection as providing area security for humanitarian action.
- Protection through assistance/operational design of relief and humanitarian programs.
- Protection as the use of traditional force to stop enemy actions.

Holt also points out, however, that even well-developed national peace operations doctrines like U.S. and British doctrines lack clear guidelines on how best to protect civilians. Current British doctrine, for instance, does not insist that British peacekeepers ought always to be in the civilian protection business and offers no guidelines for soldiers. Instead, only the protection of civilian members of the mission is specifically dealt with (HMSO, 2004, para. 324). Thus, even among Brahimi's staunchest supporters there has been reluctance to operationalize effective civilian protection. In addition, there remains deep scepticism about the civilian protection role among some members of the General Assembly.

This reluctance to fully embrace civilian protection is also evident in recent mandates handed down by the Security Council. Although most recent mandates have made reference to civilian protection, the Council has demonstrated a preference for limiting its scope by including various caveats. For instance, UNMIS was mandated "to facilitate and coordinate, *within its capabilities and in its areas of deployment*, the voluntary return of refugees and internally displaced persons, and humanitarian assistance, inter alia, by helping to establish the necessary security." Similarly, UNMIL's civilian protection mandate was "to protect civilians under imminent threat of physical violence, *within its capabilities.*" In MONUC's case, it was authorized in 2000 to "take the necessary action, *in the areas of deployment of its infantry battalions and as it deems it within its capabilities*, to protect . . . civilians under imminent threat of physical violence."

These resolutions and others like them exhibit a clear preference for limiting the role of civil protection to regions covered by the mandate and the capabilities of the peacekeepers. Of course, it makes sense to match mandate and means, but as Brahimi's panel put it (2000, p. x), "operations given a broad and explicit mandate for civilian protection must be given the specific resources needed to carry out that mandate." This is not the same as the Security Council devising mandates with caveats that are compatible with under-resourced missions. In practice, therefore, the Security Council has shied away from the recommendation that civil protection should become a core component of peace operations irrespective of other aspects of the mandate. As Ian Johnstone (2006, p. 7) has noted, this preference for geographically limiting the protection of civilians itself creates at least three problems. First, when local expectations that UN forces will protect civilians go unfulfilled, this is likely to generate anger against the peace operation, thus reducing levels of consent and cooperation. Second, such mandates can encourage population displacement as civilians move to find shelter under the protection of peacekeepers. Finally, protecting civilians in one area can produce reprisals against other civilians elsewhere. The corollaries to havens of peace are zones of instability, where civilians are left at the mercy of warlords.

The fact that the civilian protection role has yet to be fully embraced either by supporters of the Brahimi paradigm or its sceptics partly helps to explain why militaries and governments have so far failed to do much serious doctrinal thinking about the precise modalities of civilian protection. Questions as to whether peacekeepers should use force preemptively or only as a last resort have been seldom posed let alone deeply explored. As a result, just as before Brahimi, decisions about civilian protection continue to be taken by field commanders in a relatively ad hoc fashion.

This section has identified the new and preponderant way of thinking about peace operations as outlined in the 2000 Brahimi Report. The Report argued that UN peacekeepers should be equipped and mandated to fulfill a civilian protection role, irrespective of the other duties given to them. Although this recommendation was warmly received at first, doubts have since been raised about the implications for state sovereignty and the potential for robust operations to further inflame already volatile situations. As a result, the Security Council has been reluctant to fully embrace the envisaged transformation. To date, powerful states have been reluctant to do what is necessary to protect civilians in their homes, opting instead for a geographically limited approach that is itself problematic.

Conclusion

Peace operations come in a variety of shapes and sizes, and it is unwise to draw blanket conclusions about their purpose or efficacy. Most recent peace operations, however, have an explicit interest in resolving rather than simply monitoring conflicts and promoting certain outcomes on the ground. As a consequence, it is necessary to think through the strengths and weaknesses of peace operations as instruments of conflict resolution. It is also important to publicize what peace operations can and cannot achieve so that expectations (international and local) remain realistic.

As instruments of conflict resolution, peace operations are being shaped by at least four key trends. First, a consensus is emerging around some of the central recommendations of the Brahimi Report, perhaps most notably in relation to the definition of impartiality and the need to protect civilians. Second, there is a trend towards more PSOs, although Western states remain reluctant to deploy their soldiers in strategically unimportant areas. Third, there has been an increasing number of intensive transitional administrations. This trend, however, may be reaching its limit. On the one hand, the UN sought to limit its involvement in Afghanistan by adopting a 'light footprint' approach designed to encourage local authorities to take the lead and maintain sovereign authority with much reduced levels of international assistance. On the other hand, it is notable that there have been no transitional administrations in Africa despite collapsed states like Somalia. Finally, there are a variety of actors conducting peace operations, with regional organizations playing more prominent roles. However, only a few regional organizations have the resources to conduct complex operations for long periods of time. Consequently, the number of hybrid operations is likely to increase and these may become the norm.

These trends raise serious questions about coordination between numerous actors at both the political and operational levels. At the political level, different actors and organizations need to harmonize their objectives and principles if they are to cooperate effectively. In particular, the nature of the relationship between the UN and regional organizations needs clarification. At the operational level, more work is needed to ensure that agencies do not duplicate work or undermine the mission through inter-agency competition. Tied to this are questions of capacity. The danger connected to the proliferation of actors is that not all regions have institutions capable of conducting complex peace operations, raising the possibility of the emergence of two classes of peace operations: well-funded, well-staffed, multi-agency operations with broad mandates including civilian protection in areas of strategic interest to the great powers; and poorly funded, under-staffed missions with mandates written to accommodate the lack of political will in other regions.

Finally, the Brahimi Report took the laudable step of defining impartiality as protecting the principles of the UN Charter and civilians in danger. However, more thinking is required about how to operationalize this concept and generate the necessary political will. There will be no quick and easy answers, but a reasonable place to start would be in designing appropriate national doctrines.

In recent years, therefore, the scope of peace operations has expanded markedly. Most operations today go well beyond traditional efforts to monitor ceasefire lines in order to help conflicting parties resolve their differences. Instead, peace operations have their own normative goals such as the protection of civilians, contributing to the transformation of war-torn societies by providing security and training the indigenous security sector, and creating conditions that are conducive to completing large multifaceted and multi-agency missions. As such, peace operations today are closely associated with peace-building and the structural transformation of war-torn societies, the theme of the following two chapters.

Discussion Questions

1 To what extent can traditional peacekeeping operations help resolve conflicts?
2 What are the main challenges in conducting peace enforcement operations?
3 What should be the ideal relationship between the civilian and military elements of peace support operations?
4 Are transitional administrations a form of neo-imperialism?
5 To what extent does the so-called "Brahimi agenda" address the problems inherent to peace operations?
6 What are the main challenges associated with civilian protection in volatile regions?

Key Words

Civilian protection
Enforcement
Gender
Peace agreements
Peace operations
Peacekeeping
Security Council
Third-party intervention
Transitional administrations
United Nations

CHAPTER 20

Structural Transformation

Johannes M. Botes

All forms of conflict intervention imply having an understanding of social systems and social contexts, including the social structures they spawn in the form of institutions and organizations. Comprehending (1) to what degree such structures are sources and causes of conflict, or (2) the extent to which changing the system (and the political, economic, and social structures within which the conflict occurs) could end conflict, becomes central to intervention strategies. However, transforming conflict systems structurally into a future state in which the parties can deal productively with their differences is an intricate and time-consuming process.

For the field of conflict resolution, the necessary and important task of mapping any conflict requires the analysis of contextual and systemic factors. Such factors include the parties' positions, interests, issues, relationships, values, and needs, all of which are embedded in a structural context. Wehr's (1979, p. 19) conflict-mapping guide invites us to expand this analysis to include a more macro approach. He defines the structural dimensions of a conflict as "geographical boundaries; political structures, relations, and jurisdictions; communication networks and patterns, [and] decision making methods." This list reflects structures that are both tangible and non-tangible. Moreover, Wehr notes that these notions of structures are applicable to the full range of conflict types from interpersonal to international.

While this chapter will largely address structural issues as they relate to intranational or international conflict settings and focus somewhat more on examples from the African continent, these concerns apply equally to interpersonal as well as community-oriented spheres of conflict. Because all levels of conflict have structural dimensions, the inequities that result from the establishment and maintenance of oppressive structures are indeed plentiful. This includes subsystemic levels of conflict, the levels at which our social institutions and decision-making policies are nested in the larger social system:

> Subsystem level conflicts often mirror conflicts of the broader system, bringing inequities such as racism, sexism, classism, and homophobia to the offices and factories in which we work, the houses of worship in which we pray, the courts and beaches on which we play, the streets on which we meet our neighbors, even the houses in which we live. Subsystem level problems may also exist on their own, not produced by broader societal realities. (Dugan, 1996, p. 16)

Defining the structural context of a conflict may be done deductively or inductively (Cousens, 2001). Former United Nations' (UN) Secretary General, Boutros Boutros-Ghali's policy statement, *An Agenda for Peace*, became a way to deductively analyze and map the need for peaceful structures across the globe. With this important document, the Secretary General advocated new tasks for the UN and the international community, namely to provide "support for the transformation of deficient national structures and capabilities," in order to create and strengthen new democratic institutions (1992, p. 33).

In contrast to the Secretary General's deductive analysis of conflict resolution needs worldwide, conflict intervenors tend to analyze conflict inductively. They do this by gaining information directly from the parties, by personally witnessing the structures within which the conflict occurs, and by attempting to understand the views and perceptions of the parties on these matters. They then factor this knowledge into ways of assisting individuals and communities to construct systems that will provide sustainable peace.

In both domestic and international conflict settings, this process starts with a relatively general form of analysis of the different contexts in which the conflict is occurring. Only after mapping the political landscape can conflict intervenors develop an understanding of their roles in transforming interparty or intergroup conflict into "viable political processes [and indeed structures] that are both lasting and legitimate" (Kumar, 2001, p. 187).

Exploring the concept of structural transformation in theory, as well as how it is operationalized in practice, are the main aims of this chapter. In Chapter 9, Jeong discusses social systems, especially with regard to how they are sources of conflict. Here, however, we will give more specific thought to the social structures that make up larger social systems. This discussion requires the analysis of related concepts such as "social change," "structural violence," and "conflict transformation," terms that are the conceptual building blocks toward an understanding of structural transformation.

Conflict and Structural Change

The elements and relationships among social structures within a larger social system are often hierarchical, marked by social and power differentiation, and resistant to change – all possible causes of conflict. To complicate matters still further, social structures are not always neatly identifiable, observable, or verifiable. They are also not deterministic of social interaction. More simply stated, social structure alone does not decide human behavior. As Abercrombie *et al.* (1994) suggest, it is incorrect to assert that human behavior and interaction are necessarily the direct result of social and political structures. This argument denies the role that human creativity and freedom of choice play in human interactions. Indeed, in uncovering social structures we always find a "human factor" (Berger and Luckmann, 1967, p. 186), which makes social structures the creative work of active human beings. Humans, therefore, have to take responsibility for the sociopolitical and economic structures they establish, and how these either cause conflict or facilitate its resolution. Social structures are ultimately the result of the dialectic, or interplay, between structural entities (their histories and uses), and the human enterprise of producing and shaping new structural realities.

Attempts at resolving conflict without challenging structural inequalities are inevitably open to criticism of supporting the status quo. It is also generally argued that conflict (and its resolution), by definition, has to lead to some form of future social change, away from the previous status quo. As the peace scholar Johan Galtung (2000, p. 51) so aptly observes, "Conflict is a challenge with the problems shouting 'transcend me!' go beyond, a force motrice driving human beings, societies, the whole world forward." The question, of course, is what form this change should take. However it is answered, resolving conflict implies creating or re-creating societal and relational structures. Some conflict theorists go as far as arguing that the only way social change can be analyzed is in relation to specific structures. Coser (1968), for example, observed that conflict prevents social systems from becoming rigid by exerting pressures for innovation and creativity.

If change is the currency of social conflict, then the other side of the coin is the fact that while conflict leads to change, change often creates conflict. Changes that occur within the larger background or setting of a social system, such as drought, environmental changes due to large migrations of people, or power shifts resulting from military takeovers sometimes create structural strain (Gamson, 1996). Under such structural strain, the basic connection among the various institutions of a society become disconnected or collapse, affecting not only the system itself, but also its "public," namely all the members within the social system (Himes, 1980, p. 58). The humanitarian crises in African states, such as Burundi, Rwanda, and the Democratic Republic of the Congo, come to mind. These countries experienced what Rubenstein (1999, p. 180) refers to as "structural crisis," situations where the social and political structures are in ruins. Such examples give credence to Dahrendorf's (1958) observation that the genesis of conflict is to be found in aspects and changes of social structure.

Throughout history, as Rabie (1994) concludes, conflict and change have maintained a mutually reinforcing relationship, each paving the way for the other. He maintains that change often starts as a shift in thinking in the collective mind of a community or society. This, in turn, then transforms social and political perspectives, which subsequently challenges existing systems and institutions. Needless to say, existing structures are nearly always resistant to change, and their defenders will endure as much conflict as possible in order to preserve the status quo. Eventually all social systems are challenged and restructured due to the changing circumstances and needs of the people it either serves or controls. Modernization and democratization can also lead to instability, division, and conflict. In her comparative study of what modernization as opposed to conflict resolution has meant for post-socialist change in Central and Eastern Europe, Shapiro (1997) asserts that modernization translated into the maintenance of the status quo, stability, and order. Conflict resolution efforts in this region, in contrast, were mostly aimed at system change, and structural innovation.

Conflict resolution practitioners are indeed change agents, some of whom conceptualize their work broadly as a form of social intervention. As social scientists, they make implicit and explicit assumptions about the nature and the (structural) outcomes that they deem essential or appropriate. Based on the seminal work of Kelman and Warwick (1978), one could argue that social intervenors are in the business of evaluating institutional structures and their practices. While performing their roles within a form of social intervention, conflict intervenors not only visualize structural outcomes, but also target their interventions toward creating the capacity for a range of structural options that will provide peaceful outcomes. In sum, conflict intervention actions are deliberate in their aim to change the characteristics, relationships, and structures that frame individuals and groups in conflict. Over the past twenty years, conflict resolution practitioners have become not only increasingly skilled, but also professionalized and institutionalized in their roles as change agents – facilitators, conciliators, mediators, and peace-builders, to name a few.

Structural Causes of Social Conflict

Social systems and social structures have been central issues in developing theories of conflict for the past hundred years. The keys to the causes of social conflict were sought in the conditions and changes of the social structure, according to Himes (1980). Himes provides a history of the work of theorists who have applied a structural approach in explaining social conflict. Among them are Marx (1906), who made class structure a central element in his causal model of conflict; Parsons (1951), and other American structural functionalists who defined social conflict as a pathological by-product of ongoing social systems; and Dahrendorf (1959), who advocated a form of conflict analysis that links conflict with specific social structures and structural situations.

Since the advent of "structural violence," one of Galtung's major contributions to the fields of conflict and peace studies, violence has come to mean far more than physically violent behavior. Galtung (1969, p. 168) defined structural violence as "those factors that cause people's actual physical and mental realizations to be below their potential realizations." Structural violence, often referred to as institutional violence, arises from social, political, and economic structures that sanction the unequal distribution of power and resources. Over the past thirty years this term has been widely used to describe and analyze how political systems and social and organizational structures act as sources of social conflict.

Societal structures are major sources of conflict. "Root causes" of conflict, Cousens (2001, p. 8) asserts, are usually "shorthand either for long-standing or structural factors, often found within social, economic, or cultural spheres." Structural tensions in any given society are also early warnings of a high probability for outbreaks of violent conflict. Inequities in the distribution of land, income, social development, or large economic gaps between social groups and regions, are all early warning indicators (Leathermen *et al.*, 1999). In Africa, for example, the causes of violent conflict all point to a variety of structural factors that are embedded in the political, social, and economic systems of a large number of countries on the continent (see Adedeji, 1999). Laurie Nathan (2000, p. 189), the director of the Center for Conflict Resolution in Cape Town, South Africa, summarizes structural causes of crisis and violence in Africa into four conditions which he calls "The Four Horsemen of the Apocalypse." These factors are: authoritarian rule, the exclusion of the minorities from governance, socioeconomic deprivation combined with inequity, and weak states that lack the institutional capacity to manage normal political, and social conflict. Sustainable peace, he argues, will only be possible in Africa when these primary structural causes of large-scale violence are addressed in a meaningful way.

Uvin (1998) observes that structural violence is also described as a combination of inequality, oppression, and racism, as evidenced by living conditions in Brazil, apartheid South Africa, and inner-city America. More pointedly, he draws our attention to structures and processes that, in a Galtungian sense, are "violent" because of the way they limit individuals' physical and psychological capabilities. His case study on Rwanda documented how a large mass of poor Rwandans were excluded from, and were vulnerable to, the country's sociopolitical system.

Galtung's implied challenge to conflict and conflict resolution theorists to examine the societal impact of structural violence has indeed been taken up by a number of scholars in direct and indirect ways. The terms these authors use are not necessarily synonymous with structural violence, but rather provide various dimensions of the term. Spitz (1978, p. 867), for example, broadened the term to include "silent violence" in referring to situations of hunger, poverty, and inequality. In subsequent writings, Galtung (1990) has noted that exploitation is a central feature of the archetypal violent structure. This theme is echoed in Azar's (1990) work on identity-based intractable conflict, which refers to "structural victimization." This kind of victimization consists of a lack of effective political participation for minorities, or the majority population's failure to recognize the identity and culture of minorities.

Similarly, Burton (1997a) connects structural violence directly with social deprivation resulting from social institutions and policies. Structural deprivation and violence, Burton contends, is prevalent throughout a large variety of institutions and social systems. For him, structural violence may be found in policy and administrative decisions, economic sanctions, the workplace, and families (where it can lead to domestic violence, and the sexual abuse of children). When these structural situations and conditions go beyond the human beings' or groups' ability to accommodate what is being done to them, they often lead to physical (behavioral) violence. The cornerstone of Burton's (1997a, p. 32) work is that human beings have

> ontological human needs that will be pursued, that they will provide a power greater than police and military power, that they lead the individual and the identity group to defy compliancy requirements, and that they explain and even justify in some circumstances, anti-social and violent behaviors.

Writing more specifically about community disputes, Laue and Cormick (1978) make similar assumptions about the nature of human beings. Human beings, and the systems within which they live, they contend, have a need for personal freedom, social justice, and self-determination (empowerment). The absence of these core values are therefore, by their very nature, forms of structural violence. "Wherever systems discriminate between groups, communities, and nations to the point of threatening lives and livelihoods," according to Fisher *et al.* (2000, p. 9), "the result is structural and institutional violence."

Conflict Transformation as Structural Transformation

The relatively new and interdisciplinary field of peace and conflict studies is still in the process of building and defining its terminology. In much of the academic literature, terms such as "conflict management," "conflict resolution," and "conflict transformation" are often used indiscriminately and interchangeably. Some theorists have offered definitions in an attempt to provide some clarity. Miall *et al.* (1999), for example, describe conflict management as a generic term, similar to conflict regulation, which covers all forms of conflict intervention processes. They see conflict resolution as a more definitive and comprehensive term, which refers more specifically to how deep-rooted sources of conflict are addressed and resolved. Of late, in what has the makings of a terminological debate, the term *conflict transformation*, which refers to the longer term structural, relational, and cultural changes brought about by conflict resolution, is gaining ground.

Depending on one's conception of the term, conflict transformation is not necessarily a new innovation. Mitchell (2000a, p. 4) reminds us that "in the early days of conflict resolution practice, there was a clear understanding that many 'resolutions' certainly implied the need to bring about major structural changes in social systems, countries, and communities, as well as changes in fundamental relationships." Without such structural changes, "genuinely acceptable, self-supporting and durable 'resolutions' were not sustainable." This weakens the argument of transformationalists who profess that systemic change, in order to "end" conflicts, is what distinguishes transformation from resolution.

As a development out of conflict resolution, the implication is that conflict transformation goes beyond conflict resolution in providing a deeper and more permanent level of change. The preference for the term conflict transformation over conflict resolution, as the core concept to describe intervention practice in anything from interpersonal to international conflicts, has another underlying premise. The premise holds that conflict resolution theory and practice deal more with the dynamics of the conflict itself, than with that of the system (political, social, or economic) within which it is embedded, although not exclusively so. Mitchell (2000a) disagrees. Referring to the works of Burton and Dukes in the 1990s, he maintains that conflict resolution processes not only examine the parties' needs and options, but also produce changes in pre-existing systems and patterns of relationships.

There is no doubt, however, that the proponents of conflict transformation have a strong bias toward systemic change, with the implication that conflict resolution does not provide the necessary end-state:

> Conflict transformation refers to the process of moving from conflict-habituated systems to peace systems. This process is distinguished from the more common term of conflict resolution because of its focus on systems change. Social conflicts that are deep-rooted or intractable get these names because the conflict has created patterns that have become part of the social system. With the social system as the unit of analysis, the term "resolution" becomes less appropriate. Transforming deep-rooted conflicts is only partly about "resolving" the issues of the conflict – the central issue is systemic change or transformation. Systems cannot be "resolved," but they can be transformed, thus we use the term conflict transformation. (*http://www.imtd.org/transform.html*)

As implied in this definition – used by the Institute for Multi-Track Diplomacy (see also Diamond, 1996) – transformationalists see this concept as an improvement over conflict resolution because conflict resolution supposedly "resolves" the conflict but ultimately sets the parties up for failure. The argument, of course, is that it leaves the system within which the conflict occurs, or the underlying causes of the conflict, untouched.

Leaving the terminological differences aside, conflict transformation is now becoming entrenched as the ultimate aim of all conflict resolution undertakings. The term *conflict transformation*, in use for barely a decade, is hence only to be found and defined in very recent literature (e.g., Lederach, 1995a; Rupesinghe, 1995a; Väyrynen, 1991, 1999). While some definitions provide more specificity than do others, conflict transformation is always related to social and systemic change. For example, Fisher *et al.* (2000) maintain that conflict transformation theory has as its underpinnings the idea that conflict is caused by inequality and injustice within social, cultural, and economic frameworks. To them, therefore, the goals of conflict transformation practice are:

- to change structures and frameworks that cause inequality and injustice, including economic redistribution;
- to improve longer-term relationships and attitudes among the conflict parties; and
- to develop processes and systems that promote empowerment, justice, peace, forgiveness, reconciliation, [and] recognition. (Fisher *et al.*, 2000, p. 9)

In his *Thesaurus and Glossary of Early Warning and Conflict Prevention Terms*, Schmid (2000) uses a definition provided by International Alert, a British nongovernmental organization steeped in conflict transformation practice. Conflict transformation is described as an approach that addresses the structural realities of inequality, rights, and justice, and aims to transform violence and destruction into constructive social change. More importantly, the term conflict transformation is intended to communicate multifaceted, ongoing tasks:

- [a] focus on the developmental *process* of a conflict, rather than on its end-point;
- [an] awareness of how conflict *transforms* relationships, communication, perceptions, issues, and social organizations;
- [the] intention to *transform the conflict* from violent expression (in armed conflict and war) to constructive and peaceful expression;
- [a] concentration on the *structural* transformations usually necessarily in or between societies in order for peace to be sustainable;
- intervention in the resolution processes by combatants themselves, local individuals and communities, and external third parties, in an integrated *multi-track framework*. (Schmid, 2000, p. 31)

From this list of transformational tasks, it is clear that conflict transformation is an intervention process that has at its core the aim of transforming existing structural frameworks. Even more broadly defined, as a form of third-party intervention, it is process, structure, and outcome oriented. As such, it aims to overcome direct (behavioral or physical) violence, structural violence, as well as the ways in which violence is culturally legitimized (Reimann, 2001). All of this, of course, implies a long-term peace-building process.

Peace-building as Structural Transformation

Since the end of the Cold War, the international community has turned its attention anew to violent intrastate conflict and humanitarian crises. Such conflict phenomena stretch over various countries, regions, and indeed continents: Africa (Angola, Burundi, the Democratic Republic of the Congo, Mozambique, Rwanda, and Somalia), Asia (Cambodia and

East Timor), Central America (Columbia and Mexico), and Central and Eastern Europe (the former Yugoslavia, Georgia, Azerbaijan, and Armenia). The initial approach to internal wars was to address them via "post-conflict peace-building – action to identify and support structures which will tend to strengthen and solidify peace in order to avoid a relapse into conflict" (Boutros-Ghali, 1995, p. 46). This approach revealed the limitations of "preventive diplomacy" as a way to resolve disputes before violence breaks out, as well as "peacemaking" and "peacekeeping" approaches designed to end conflicts and to preserve the peace afterwards. Since then the United Nations, nongovernmental agencies, and both conflict theorists and practitioners have had to come to terms with the need to address peacemaking in a more holistic manner, by utilizing a multitude of tasks at various stages of a conflict.

In this regard Lund (2001, p. 16) argues that the task of moving a violent conflict toward a durable peace requires devising and implementing "multi-tooled" strategies. His "toolbox" for responding to conflict and building peace ranges from official and unofficial conflict management methodologies to political, economic, judicial, and military measures, as well as communications and educational peace-building measures. While Lund's classification and subcategorization of these tasks are too numerous to list in detail here, a cursory overview of the continuum of tasks can be provided. For example, official diplomacy tasks range from negotiation, conciliation, and mediation to a number of other formal (government to government) activities, such as providing good offices, sending special envoys, diplomatic sanctions, and coercive diplomacy. The scope of nonofficial conflict management is equally large, ranging from nonofficial facilitation, mediation, and problem-solving workshops to the use of civilian peace monitors, nonviolent campaigns, and cultural exchanges. Preventive peacekeeping forces, the creation of demilitarized zones, and peace enforcement are listed as some of the military peacemaking measures, and development assistance, economic sanctions, and humanitarian assistance are mentioned in the list of economic measures. This expansive catalog of procedures to prevent or mitigate a conflict and build peace also gives special attention to political and governance measures (such as building political parties and civil society), as well as judicial and legal measures (which may include constitutional, judicial, legal, and police reforms). Finally the holistic nature of this toolbox of intervention activities is underscored by communications and educational measures which encompass the training of journalists, the professionalization of media systems, peace education, and formal education projects.

Unless conflicts are addressed through such comprehensive and sustained peace-building efforts at all structural levels of affected societies, most intervention efforts will eventually come to naught. One could argue that the international community's intervention attempts in African countries such as Burundi and Rwanda, and especially in Liberia, Sierra Leone, and Sudan, are examples of interventions that lacked the comprehensiveness to affect systemic change. Conflict scholars also disagree about the degree to which preventive intervention can bring structural and overt forms of change in such countries, or whether conflicts should play themselves out in order to affect political (structural) change (see Lund, 1995; Stedman, 1995; Miall et al., 1999).

One can actually make a circular argument about systemic change: that structural tensions cause conflict and that conflict, in turn, will eventually lead to structural and systemic changes. Therefore, constructing and strengthening authoritative, and eventually, legitimate mechanisms to resolve internal conflict without violence, is the ultimate peace-building priority (Cousens, 2001). The notion that peace-building is linked to structural change, and that transformative peace-building is about constructing a vision of change, resonates with transformative practitioners:

> The journey toward transformation and peace building has been a journey toward an understanding that the work of conflict transformation and reconciliation involves both the termination of something undesired – violent conflict – and the building of something desired. It is about change, *and* construction. (Lederach, 2000, p. 55)

The most important peace-building tasks, therefore, are first to visualize (and work with the parties in the conflict) toward a form of "structural peace" and then to obtain that objective via "structural peace-building" (Montiel, 2001). Social systems that are structurally peaceful are distinguished by economic, political, and cultural institutions in which decision-making power is equitably distributed. In addition to the social-psychological process of transforming conflictual relationships, structural peace-building is the task of creating social systems in which all of its population groups, or political factions, have a form of equitable control over political and economic resources.

This, however, begs the question of how and when structural peacemaking will provide "sustainable peace," a situation that is evident by the absence of physical and structural violence, and where the society and its systems are self-sustained because of their internal and external legitimacy and support by all concerned. Such a conceptual framework for sustainable peace, according to Reychler (2001), can be achieved only through the establishment of peace-enhancing structures: a consolidated political democracy, a legitimate and restorative justice system, and a free-market system with built-in education, information, and communications institutions (see also Reychler, 1997, 1999).

The task of creating "peaceableness," Boulding (2000, p. 161) contends, is essentially to examine the "structural bases of violence in today's world, and [to consider] the transformational potential within each of the interrelated sets of structures [locally, regionally, or globally] for movement toward viable cultures of peace." For her, this means analyzing how people and states construct their social systems, and how people create, and are created by their biosocial (rural, urban, technological) environments. Humankind's current extremes of militarism, resource depletion, and economic and social injustice, Boulding argues, do not bode well for its survival. Moreover, without building systems away from dominance and toward cooperation and problem-solving, a much needed diversified and sustainable peace culture will not be attainable.

The theme that runs through the literature on structural peace-building is clear. It is, namely, that peaceful structures, however complex, multidisciplinary, or diversified, are preconditions for the prevention of direct or indirect violence:

> without social development (education, health, housing, work), economic development (growth, employment, productivity), political development (freedom, democracy, respect for human rights, participation), cultural development (national and ethnic identity, respect for the cultural rights of the indigenous peoples, science and technology, fine arts) it is not possible to establish the conditions of a lasting peace. (Padilla, 1994, p. 22)

In the above description, as indeed in much of the literature on peace-building, it is often defined as proactive, creating long-term interventions and changing structural inequalities (Clements, 1997), and also proventive by attempting to remove structural causes of social conflict that have the potential for violence (Burton and Dukes, 1990; Burton 1993, 1995).

At its core, peace-building is about institutional change and community-based solutions, an approach that de-emphasizes extreme individualism and pushes social transformation and empowerment to the fore (Christie et al., 2001). The structural transformation of systems and institutions literally and figuratively give voice to the unfulfilled basic human needs of individuals and groups by providing societal structures and institutions in which grievances can be expressed and disputes addressed (Schmid, 2000). However, peace-building is not merely a one-time task. It is an ongoing political and social process that in a sense is never concluded, as we will see in a later part of this chapter.

Structural Transformation

Legislative, political, family, or any other kind of societal structure is unavoidably reflective of underlying power structures. Elites at the top of decision-making or decision-enforcing structures not only hold, but dispense power, in the way they control the production, allocation, and utilization of the sources that are needed to satisfy basic human needs (Parsons, 1961; Galtung, 1975). Oppressed and exploited individuals and communities within such societies have social power of their own, illustrated by the often violent political uprisings in states such as apartheid South Africa, or the former Soviet-controlled states of Eastern Europe. Another notable example of violent protests against structural political control is the Palestinian uprisings against Israel.

But attempts at promoting structural transitions can also come in the form of peaceful, nonviolent demonstrations in opposition to state-imposed structural violence. The issue in such cases is not so much between war and peace (or conflict and peace), but rather a tension between peace and justice. Nonviolent demonstrations, although peaceful in nature, are nevertheless a forceful way of opposing the way some governments use the state's "legal and political systems to violate fundamental economic, political, and social rights of subordinate groups" (Burgess and Burgess, 1994, p. 7).

The most obvious examples of this phenomenon are Mohandas Gandhi's use of nonviolence against British rule in India and against apartheid in South Africa, and Martin Luther King, Jr.'s use of nonviolent sit-ins, boycotts, and other forms of protest during the civil rights era in the United States in the 1960s. The activities of the Mothers of the Plaza de Mayo are a more recent, but equally pertinent example of nonviolent demonstrations calling for social justice and structural change. In April 1977, after unsuccessful attempts at finding their sons and daughters, in police stations, hospitals, morgues, and army barracks, a small group of Argentinean mothers gathered in front of the presidential palace in Buenos Aires. Since then, these mothers have not only played a role in bringing an end to the state terror of the military regime, but, by wearing white scarves and demonstrating weekly for justice for the so-called "disappeared," they have served as a reminder of what state-sanctioned structures can do to people under their control. These nonviolent demonstrations are examples of transformative people power that are purposefully directed both at removing structural inequalities, and at removing the abusive power behind political institutions to prevent further transgressions (see Abreu Hernandez, 2002).

Transformative structural peace-building is aimed not only at removing structural disparities between conflictual groups, but also at global, structural peace-building (Montiel, 2001). Especially among a younger generation of political activists, discontent is growing with human-based, political and economic processes that do not distribute wealth equally among the different nations and regions of the world. The recent protests at annual meetings of international organizations such as the World Bank, the International Monetary Fund, and the World Trade Organization in North American and European cities (for example, in Seattle in April 1999, in Washington, DC in April 2000, in Prague in September 2000, and in Quebec City in April 2001) are evidence of this displeasure with structural inequities.

Building and transforming structures that give societies the capacity and ability to address and resolve disputes nonviolently is an ongoing peace-building task. Peace, as Cousens (2001) proposes, can be cultivated only by institutionalizing peace-building as everyday politics. Legitimizing social, political, and legal structures as containers of conflict, and as mechanisms through which conflict ought to be resolved, is part of everyday life in peaceful societies. Institutions that direct social conflict into nonviolent channels act as a form of "structural prevention," as opposed to "operational prevention" where the intent is to prevent immediate crises from developing into deadly violence (Stern and Druckman, 2000).

Structural conflict prevention is also a way of conceptualizing a peaceful future. Broadly speaking, conflict management activities are attempts at approaching manifest conflict, and sooner or later this will mean creating peaceful structures to avoid the future recurrence of the same conflicts. It has now indeed become a working assumption within both the theory and practice of the field that conflict management methodologies should not only work preventively, but also do so by transforming underlying structural issues, as exemplified here by the writings of Brand-Jacobsen and Jacobsen (2000, p. 252):

Today's challenge is not only to be able to come up with mechanisms and institutions to *prevent* war, but to develop the creativity and the imagination necessary to come up with creative and viable alternatives. What is needed is to take up that challenge and to search for alternatives that can once again offer the hope of a future in which violence will no longer be seen as a legitimate response to conflict, or as a means for reaching one's goals, and to transform the underlying structures and cultures of violence at the heart of many of today's wars.

For these European peace-scholars, transforming today's wars entails dealing with deeper emotional and psychological structures and cosmologies such as memory and trauma, as well as the values and beliefs that sustain these conflicts. They belong to a school of scholar-practitioners, who have designed the "TRANSCEND" dialogue method for conflict transformation (Galtung and Jacobsen, 2000). Fundamentally, the TRANSCEND method is a form of intervention which has as its main goal to assist the parties to expand the spectrum of acceptable outcomes. Trained "conflict workers," as Galtung defines them, enter into dialog with all the parties, one at a time (Galtung and Tschudi, 2001, p. 212).

It is, however, not within the scope of this chapter to discuss transformation methodologies such as Galtung's TRANSCEND dialog method in depth. Suffice it to say that such methodologies, in some way or another, deal with how people and conflict management processes work toward designing and operationalizing peaceful societal structures. In the context of this discussion, it makes more sense to focus on what happens when structural issues are ignored, or are not given attention in peace agreements or during the implementation stage of ending conflict. Land claims in the ex-settlement colonies of southern Africa, an issue of cardinal importance to both sides of the liberation wars, provide us with such examples.

In Zimbabwe, as is the case in a number of southern African countries, a mostly white minority owns the primary land resources to the detriment of the mostly black population, which has led to violence and instability. As McCandless (2000) observes, the rapid structural and social transformation that President Mugabe envisioned around land reform at the time of independence in 1980 never materialized. Furthermore, the Lancaster House agreement that brought an end to this conflict provided limited resolution of this matter. This peace agreement, she concludes, focused on a process of conflict termination rather than on ensuring justice and a sustainable peace. The longer term result of this process was not real economic justice for Zimbabweans.

The need for an immediate peace agreement in Zimbabwe resulted in a peace that neglected to resolve long-term structural issues. Reconciliation, as indispensable as it might be to creating a sustainable peace, cannot be done at the expense of some form of redistributive or social justice (Pankhurst, 2000). In other words, not dealing with the structural issue of inequities of land ownership in a way that would preclude future conflict has proved to be a potential for and reality of conflict in southern Africa. Whether the peace settlements are ultimately the result of military victory (as was the case of Angola and Mozambique), or a negotiated compromise (as occurred in Zimbabwe, Namibia, and

South Africa) the lack of clear provisions for justice and fairness for competing sets of land rights and systems of land tenure now threatens peace in the region.

The land issue in countries such as Zimbabwe points to a number of factors around structural issues such as land reform. From the ramifications of how this policy problem, and indeed conflict, has played out in the different countries, it is clear that the decisions about structural land reforms in each of these countries will eventually differ based on their histories and their ideological and cultural beliefs around land. The leadership of political figures such as President Mugabe, who has been accused of exploiting land reform issues for personal political gain without taking heed of race relations in the country, will also be a factor in countries with conflicts around land reform.

As these structural issues around land reform in southern Africa have revealed, social and economic structures cannot be neglected in peace-building processes. Moreover, as Pankhurst (2000) concludes, the balance between reconciliation and justice regarding structural issues needs to be factored in over the long term, irrespective of whatever concessions and compromises are made in peace settlements in order to expedite peace and an end to war. Otherwise we end up with what in Galtonian parlance would be a negative peace and a real potential for structural violence that will elicit physical violence. In the long run, the structure of the peace is, therefore, more important than the creation of an immediate, but ultimately flawed, peace.

Post-conflict, Postwar Reconstruction

The physical and social rebuilding of communities or countries that have been devastated by violent conflict is normally discussed in the literature as part of postwar, or post-conflict, reconstruction. Re-creating and reinstating destroyed relationships, infrastructure, and social structures (e.g., governance or education) are all part of a larger peace-building process. Such interventions are intended to construct anew, or to reconstruct, just and durable structures. Within such conflict transformation ventures, building in the capacity for the affected societies to once again resolve their own conflicts peacefully becomes a primary task. Post-conflict reconstruction, therefore, has to prevent renewal of the conflict by restoring social and political structures and institutions. One could, however, argue that without some form of psychological reconstruction of relationships, healing and forgiveness on some broader societal level, as was attempted with the Truth and Reconciliation Commission in South Africa (see De La Rey, 2001; Huyse, 2001), the basis for building, or reconstructing, a peaceful future does not exist.

Moreover, conflict, especially violent conflict, destroys the social capital needed to make societies function. It renders the amount (or probability) of mutually beneficial cooperative behavior between parties in conflict obsolete, because of the absence of the building blocks of social capital: the social, psychological, cultural, cognitive, institutional, and related assets built into human relationships (Uphoff, 2000). The structural social capital built into social organizations in the form of roles, rules, precedence, and procedures, as well as the relational networks that link their members, is therefore an important part of peace-building in a post-conflict phase.

All of this, to say the very least, is far easier said than done. In fact, in her comparative study of peace-building efforts between Latin American countries (El Salvador, Nicaragua, and Peru), and southern African countries (Angola, Mozambique, and South Africa), Eade (1999, p. 6) asks very pertinent and critical questions about post-conflict reconstruction:

- Does reconstruction bring structural change?
- Does peace bring justice, and does justice bring peace?
- What is the role of collective memory in healing and reconciliation?
- How can we recognize and work with the many different levels of transition?
- What is the role of NGOs (nongovernmental organizations)?
- With rising levels of violence in many "post-conflict" societies, can we speak of peace at all?

This friction between theory and practice, between concept and achievement, runs through much of the literature on social conflict, and is without a doubt where the challenges for post-conflict peace-building efforts lie in this century.

The role of various types of NGOs in post-conflict reconstruction, also as it pertains to structural change, has indeed received some academic attention. Since Anderson (1999) cautioned aid agencies that their work could indeed support peace – or war – others have jumped into this broader fray. Based on his study of the development aid system in Rwanda, Uvin (1998, p. 143) maintains that across the continent of Africa, development aid contributes to structural violence in a number of ways:

It does so directly, through its own behavior, whether unintended (as in the case of growing income inequality and land concentration) or intended (as in its condescending attitude towards poor people). It does so indirectly, by strengthening systems of exclusion, and elite building through massive financial transfers, accompanied by self-imposed political and social blindness. Once more, most of what I discuss here applies to all of Africa, and not solely to Rwanda.

Worse, Uvin makes a link between Rwanda as a model developing country, its reality of structural violence, and the eventual genocide that took place in the country. He further argues that the development enterprise underwrote and legitimized the processes that excluded some segments of Rwandan society, and that the development aid processes of exclusion and structural violence are in a symbiotic relationship with each other. The development aid system, he concludes, "becomes part of society's stakes, conflicts, expectations, myths, structures of oppression, and channels of gain" (1998, p. 153).

Development aid projects, as indeed many conflict intervention efforts, irrespective of under what kind of rubric (conflict management, conflict transformation, and so on) they are executed, are normally time, funding, and focus sensitive. According to Uvin, project planners and managers often pay scant attention to the national, international, or political background against which these ventures occur. Hence, such developmental initiatives can serve indirectly to legitimize the political order of the day, or function as a form of distraction away from the (structural) inequality in the host country. Moreover, one can deduce from this that the development task, defined independently from political and social processes, is not necessarily contributing to social change or structural peace.

It is difficult to make distinctions between different kinds of NGOs, as their activities and functions are expansive, ranging from relief and rehabilitation, to human rights monitoring, and conflict resolution activities (Aall, 1996). NGOs which involve themselves more directly with conflict management or peace-building activities, whose resources are essentially skills-based, differ from development NGOs in some important ways. Conflict intervenors rarely bring large financial or economic resources into conflict situations, and therefore are not exposed to the same degree of criticism. They are, however, not immune to accusations that they contribute to the existence and permanence of structural violence. NGOs, as indeed the conflict resolution field at large, are also vulnerable to criticism of contributing more to the status quo than to structural, social change. A related and somewhat similar charge is often leveled against members of the international community. For reasons of political expediency, industrialized nations often have political and economic policies toward Third World countries that are complacent in allowing such countries to maintain abusive government structures. In the name of economic and Cold War interests, for example, the United States supported some of Africa's most notorious leaders, such as Samuel Doe of Liberia and Mobuto Sese Seko of the then Zaire (Berkeley, 2001).

Pre- and Post-conflict Structural Transitions

If we conceptualize the process of peace-building in terms of a social, architectural design, as Lederach (1998) suggests we should, it logically follows that we frame a post-conflict phase as a social, political, and economic system undergoing a process of structural change. The restructuring of the parts of such a system is hardly ever conflict-free, nor does it happen in a smooth or uninterrupted manner. As conflicts and indeed communities undergo dramatic changes in their dynamics and social relationships, transitions from one phase to the next create instabilities and insecurities that endanger the process of transformation itself. How to transition from the end of hostilities, or a peace agreement, to a situation where the total system of the conflict is transformed to the extent that it will provide a sustainable peace, is ultimately a very complex question. The short answer is that conflict can be transformed only by paying attention to an array of personal, relational, and structural transformations.

Among the growing number of conflict theorists who are writing about conflict transformation and "how to achieve it," Lederach (1995c, pp. 202–13) provides the greatest specificity. Lederach (1998, p. 242) advocates a post-conflict phase where the peace-building system is not driven by a hierarchical (top-down) focus, but by an organic political process, which "envisions peace-building as a web of interdependent activities and people." He espouses a process of transformation where, rather than dealing with the narrowness of the official table, peace-building and politics in the post-conflict phase must be seen as an open, accessible system that rests on a broad base of participation from all levels of society. Such multi-level "approaches to conflict transformation" should involve high-level negotiations between top leaderships, problem-solving and peace-building at the level of ethnic, humanitarian, and intellectual leadership figures, as well as grassroots peace activities by community leaders, NGOs, and other local leaders (Lederach, 1998, p. 241).

Lederach's work in this regard makes another crucial point, namely that post-conflict peace-building ought to be more than mere political transitions. In post-apartheid South Africa, and in Eastern European (post-communist) countries, much of the peace-building efforts have indeed occurred as part of political transitions. Lederach's work envisions a move away from hierarchical structural changes to a form of peace-building that is broader based and includes the whole body politic. This will, in time, lead to systemic changes, to new political, military, and cultural structures that will have wider acceptance and legitimacy.

To obtain such forms of sustainable peace presupposes a model of conflict that transcends political transitions and creates larger processes of social reconciliation. As Simpson (1999) contends, political and economic reconstruction is not enough to prevent social conflict. In South Africa, he observes, there is still the incorrect perception that the 1994 elections which provided formal constitutional and other human rights sealed the transition process. In fact economic reconstruction or redress for past inequalities is only the beginning of transitional processes. If structural transitions are not linked to political and human empowerment, they will ultimately fail. Moreover, as Simpson (1999, p. 105) argues, because the sources of social conflict shift over time and take on new forms and manifestations, there is no such thing as "post-conflict."

Conflicts that are at a pre-settlement stage, as was the case in apartheid South Africa, and is still the case in Northern Ireland, and Israel/Palestine, in spite of previously signed agreements, also provide different kinds of attempts at structural change. Ever since the 1960s, internal and external pressures on successive white South African governments built up to the point where these governments were forced into political "reforms" and structural change. These reforms went as far as instituting a tri-cameral parliament for whites, Indians, and (so-called) coloreds in 1984. However, the real system of racial segregation that excluded the largest population group – black South Africans – remained. It was always clear that these structural adjustments were essentially ways of maintaining the system, and were rather awkward and unsuccessful attempts at pacifying black groups in the country who were challenging the status quo through boycotts, violence, and other forms of social resistance.

The question then becomes to what extent can structural sources of conflict be addressed, especially in situations where the state holds a monopoly of coercive (police and military) and economic power? The late Hendrick W. van der Merwe, a pioneer in facilitating negotiations between the African National Congress (ANC) and apartheid governments, concluded that "fundamental structural change [was] essential for constructive accommodation of conflict" (1989, p. 116). In other words, as van der Merwe essentially prophesied a year before President de Klerk officially ended apartheid, the system could not be modified and had to be replaced altogether. Furthermore, from this example, it is evident that postwar, or post-conflict, reconstruction, which equates to systemic collapse, provides more fertile ground for reconstructive conflict resolution than mere system dysfunction or system decay (Rubenstein, 1999).

The Importance of Structural Transformation

There is little doubt that power political systems of governance have led to structural violence and social conflict in many parts of the world. The challenge for the field of conflict resolution, as Burton (1995) envisages, lies in offering alternatives to the kinds of adversarial system that are inherently part of power politics. Conflict resolution scholars agree that the impact of structural issues on conflict and conflict resolution are profound. All disputes are affected by the structures in which they are implanted; thus conflict resolution practitioners need to give serious thought to structural issues. Furthermore, efforts at resolving conflict and peace-building should pay close attention to structural matters. Moreover, some conflict resolution activities should focus on supporting social movements that confront structural problems, with education, training, and organizational assistance (Dukes, 1999).

Not to engage with structural issues is contrary to the kind of deep prevention and lasting settlement that are needed to create positive peace, a peace with justice (Miall *et al.*, 1999). More importantly, not addressing exploitation and structural inequalities at all levels of conflict, be they at a community, state, regional, or global level, may render conflict resolution efforts futile. Conflict resolution practice that fails to recognize the need for structural transformation, as discussed in this chapter, simply perpetuates the status quo, and does not contribute to ameliorating social conflict.

Discussion Questions

1 What is the relationship between social systems and social structures?
2 Define "structural violence" by giving examples of this phenomenon that are not mentioned in this chapter.
3 Is there always a connection to be made between social change and structural change?
4 Is conflict intervention always about structural change?
5 How is conflict transformation different from conflict settlement, conflict management, and conflict resolution?
6 Are the goals and the tasks of conflict transformation, as they are defined in this chapter, different from that of conflict resolution?
7 How are the core concepts in the field of peace and conflict studies, such as peace-building and conflict transformation, related to one another?
8 How is peace-building a form of structural transformation?

9 How would you define "peaceableness" and "structural peace?"
10 Can you give examples of how conflict resolution practices sometimes contribute to structural inequality rather than structural
transformation and justice?

Key Words

Conflict analysis
Conflict transformation goals
Conflict transformation practice
Deductive analysis
Inductive analysis
Peaceableness
Peace-building
Peace-building toolbox
Post-conflict reconstruction
Social intervention
Social systems
Structural causes of conflict
Structural change
Structural crisis
Structural inequality
Structural land reforms
Structural peace
Structural peace-building
Structural prevention
Structural social capital
Structural strain
Structural transformation
Structural transitions
Structural violence
Sustainable peace

CHAPTER 21

Peace-building

Susan Allen Nan and Ho-Won Jeong

Different types of intermediary activity can be performed along the continuum from violence prevention to social reconstruction. Third parties can mediate in crisis situations, help renegotiate a timetable and provide technical expertise, financial and material resources for infrastructure-building. In a post-conflict peace-building context, the most immediate task is short-term management and prevention of renewed violence which often requires the presence of peacekeeping forces. At the same time, third-party functions involve more than restoring order and physical protection of the civilian population. Social situations are monitored by international agencies working in the field of human rights and development.

Since the ultimate goal of peace-building cannot be achieved without improvement in intercommunal relationships, third-party support is necessary in building cooperation and trust. An acceptable framework of rules and institutions, which guide the conduct of former belligerents, emerges from a mutually benefiting sense of interdependence between all the parties. Assistance can be provided in repairing relationships at a psychological level through reconciliation. In addition to psychological healing, structural transformation needs to be encouraged for the elimination of the sources of injustice (Jeong, 2000a). International assistance has to support long-term social change through development and community-building beyond the immediate protection and settlement of refugees. This chapter reviews different types of third-party functions in a peace-building process and the roles of outside intervention in changing the dynamics of conflict situations between former adversaries.

Challenges and Strategies for Intervention

The issues faced in a post-conflict settlement process are different from the challenges found in small-group negotiation or mediation settings as discussed in the previous chapters of Part III. Challenges to a post-conflict settlement process stem from the fact that negotiated solutions do not necessarily guarantee successful implementation (Hampson, 1996). The failure of several attempts to end the long civil war in Angola prior to 2002, in particular, suggests how difficult it is to implement peace agreements and bring about stability. In other situations, high levels of violence may have been controlled, but many unresolved issues continue to regenerate confrontation. In Cambodia, for instance, violence, which erupted over the control of the new government following the 1998 national elections, threatened the disruption of the peace process. While Cambodia has not returned to civil war, Prime Minister Hun Sen's use of intimidation and the threat of violence to maintain power raise questions about long-term stability in Cambodia (Hoddie, 2006).

Intermediaries can change the dynamics of conflict by getting involved in the continued efforts to diffuse tension (Druckman *et al.*, 1999a). The measures for proactive intervention can focus on detecting threats and minimizing the risk of violent escalation. In the absence of trust, an "escalating spiral of alleged violations and counter-recriminations" is likely to happen without third-party intervention. The significance of a third role in preventing the eruption of renewed violence in volatile situations is well illustrated by timely intervention of the international community to stop the withdrawal of rebel forces from the 1994 election process in Mozambique.

Third-party intervention has been inevitable in resolving ambiguity in the design of a peace agreement and reducing uncertainties of a fragile settlement process. A facilitated process is often necessary in the renegotiation of certain aspects of a peace accord that is difficult to implement (including land transfer and a revised schedule of demobilization of forces and reform of the military). Resolving differences at the negotiation table does not necessarily lead to building trust at a societal level, and there is a continuing need for the reconciliation of competing values and interests in achieving sustainable peace (Jeong, 2000b). In building trust and inducing cooperation, third parties help change the perceptions and behavior of the disputing parties.

Overcoming fragmentation and reducing animosities is essential to the successful implementation of peace-building plans and restructuring the adversarial relationship. Intercommunal programs designed for building new relations through social reconstruction and reconciliation bring hostile groups together to heal past wounds and search for a common future. Civil society building cannot proceed without the cooperation of adversarial communities, and technical training programs can provide opportunities for dialog and exchange. Through an inclusive peace-building process, as many stakeholders as possible can be engaged in the projects of social reconstruction and rehabilitation as well as confidence-building. Dynamic NGO networks that connect local civil society actors focused on inter-communal activities, technical training, or any other element of peace-building can serve both to address concrete reconstruction needs immediately and also increase social capital and cross-cutting ties for long-term impact in the post-war environment.

The implementation of the agreement can be discussed through consultative mechanisms of dialog and understanding. Differences arising from ambiguities in interpreting the previous agreement can be resolved by facilitation, mediation, and arbitration. The mutually satisfying formula can also be explored by an informal search for alternative ways and means to ensure the agreement. Confidential negotiation may be conducted at a higher level to break through the impasse especially in the midst of group hostilities against each other. Formal conflict management mechanisms such as ethnic conciliation commissions can be institutionalized for the effective handling of crisis and confrontation. An impartial forum can be created to conduct fact-finding and hold pubic hearings on issues that are a continuing source of intergroup tension.

In the implementation of a peace agreement, third parties can bring both incentives and deterrence power so that the peace process would not derail. External aid may be used not only to prevent a breakdown of a fragile peace process, but also to lend support to new initiatives. Economic aid can be employed as a major carrot to commit former adversaries to abide by the agreement. The commitments will be weak if the parties do not find enough stakes in the peace process, so major donors often promise funds as incentives. Side payments can induce cooperation, especially when former adversaries depend on a third-party's resources for rebuilding their societies.

Appeasement strategies responding to non-compliance are, in general, counterproductive. In Cambodia, faced with Hunsen's refusal to accept the election outcome, concessions were made to help his party share government power, but this policy emboldened him to wipe out his opponents from the cabinet militarily. The external actors' failure to insist on human rights generated grievances among opposition party members and undermined confidence in the resettlement process.

In the event that one of the former opponents returns to violence, an enforcement function may be required to prevent the breakdown of law and order (Pugh, 1997). The warring factions do not suddenly change their behavior after peace agreements, and the prospects for more forceful intervention can be assessed in terms of the degree of the commitments from various parties. The promise of nonviolent problem-solving has to be carefully assessed with the evolution of new situations. The continued intolerance of other groups can be a good indicator of renewed violence, and preventive deployment of forces might be necessary.

Powerful third parties may threaten military sanctions to overcome the resistance of extremist parties to compromised solutions and use force to impose rules (Garver, 1997). Despite the involvement of difficult and costly military operations, peace enforcement functions have often been adopted when political institutions and norms do not exist to regulate behavior of the parties involved. In Bosnia where extreme nationalists and war criminals attempted to obstruct a peace process, the 1995 deployment of a NATO-led multinational force served as an instrument of coercive diplomacy, and it has fulfilled the enforcement function first as Implementation Force (IFOR) and then the 1996 Stabilization Force-Joint Guard (SFOR) and in 2004 the European Union Force in Bosnia and Herzegovina (EUFOR). Forces were also used to bring war criminals in Bosnia to justice through an international judicial system.

Successful coercion can be difficult without greater use of force and the support of the local population. As we have seen in the 1993 failed attempt by the UN to arrest a warlord in Somalia, the effects on the target are not always successful, and enforcement strategies can lead to possible re-escalation of violence. Coercion is a short-term option, and has to be used in the context to convince the parties to honor the agreement. Political compromise needs to be balanced with enforcement functions in implementing rules.

Factors Affecting Third-party Intervention

The nature and degree of third-party intervention can be affected by such factors as the capacities of local populations for resource mobilization as well as social and political dynamics. With the existence of reliable administrative structures supported by community groups, the task of rebuilding a physical infrastructure may simply need outside technical support. When public confidence in the local administrative authorities is low, more intensive support and assistance are needed. In addition to poor local administrative capacity, external groups may also have to be more heavily involved in the event of a low level of trust between adversaries.

In the absence of a reliable political structure, key elements in the settlement can be defined by an intervenor, and external intervention is a key element in managing continuing ethnic tension before the creation of an alternative structure. In Namibia, the UN special representative had extensive review power over the activities of local administrators and helped draft election laws in preparation for the 1989 elections and 1990 transition to independence. In the case of Cambodia, government agencies were not trusted, and the 1998 election process was organized and managed by the UN Transitional Authority in Cambodia (UNTAC). Before the election, UNTAC's civil administration unit took over government functions to ensure normal day-to-day life as well as monitoring human rights conditions.

International assistance is also critical when local organizations do not have the technical capacities and material resources to meet both immediate and long-term community needs. United Nations High Commissions for Refugees (UNHCR) is engaged in short-term emergency relief activities as well as documenting refugees and implementing their settlement programs. Through their country assistant programs, the United Nations Development Programme (UNDP), World Food Programme (WFP), World Health Organization (WHO) and United Nations Children's Fund (UNICEF) offer technical training programs as well as delivering urgently needed services (Ginifer, 1997). UNDP and other United Nations agencies have assisted local councils in Ethiopia and other African countries in improving resource management and food security. Many international NGOs have also been involved in the economic and social rehabilitation of war-torn societies where government services do not exist (Goodhand and Hulme, 1997).

The types of support and degree of intervention have to be appropriate to the desired activities for different levels from local and national to international. Development and reconciliation at a community level (designed to promote the well-being of individuals and groups) focus on capacity-building in support of the implementation of locally initiated programs. Because their outcomes have a high stake for all the parties involved, elections and political reform at a national level would require scrutiny of an international community. On the other hand, the responsibility for the control of violence falls on international peace-keeping forces (Whitman, 2000).

Priorities in intermediary activities can change with the evolution of a peace process. At the early stage of peace-building, preventing a return to violence with the support of coercive diplomacy is necessary for restoring confidence. At the same time, mediation, conciliation, and arbitration can be introduced to diffuse tensions arising from conflicting claims over property and land. Promoting social capital and democratization can be pursued in a long-term perspective (Reychler, 2001).

Conflict Resolution and Training

International communities can help divided local groups develop interpersonal skills to be utilized for reconciliation work. Whereas techniques for conflict resolution may exist in the local culture, the skills to break through the barriers of miscommunication, hatred, and fear have to be reintroduced or nurtured. Some workshops can be designed for short-term problem-solving processes (resolving specific tasks) while a series of seminars can target the middle-level elite who have single or multiple constituencies. Seminars for community leaders attempt to have an impact on intergroup relations through changes in their perceptions.

Small-group seminars can be expanded to bring together participants from a single region or country. Workshops for community-building help people deal with grief and loss, heal grievances, and build new relations across ethnic, class, or racial lines (Fisher, 1999). Participants identify creative roles for reconstruction of destroyed communities through team-building, organization, and neighborhood facilitation programs. Local communities are encouraged to make self-sustaining efforts to develop skills for the reduction of fear and prejudice, strategic questioning, active listening, and trust-building. Training for cross-cultural communication, mediation, and problem-solving can also be added to a series of short-term workshops which teach practical skills such as public administration and business development.

Despite differences among elites at a national level, conflict resolution practice can serve as a vehicle for nonviolent expression of different interests and values (Lumsden, 1999). Local peace commissions and grassroots workshops contribute to gradual changes for political cultures and the construction of a new system. In particular, NGOs have been active in facilitating informal, low-key, non-threatening dialog through their capacities to develop links across ethnic boundaries. Even though they do not have financial or military clout, NGOs can recruit highly motivated people and operate with low costs (Macdonald, 1997).

In carrying out their own programs, local groups that are essential to a peaceful transition have to be supported by foreign agencies which have technical and financial resources. The continuing support of international assistance would help stabilize a society devastated by long-term violent conflicts. On the other hand, the process to find and develop a local NGO can be coopted by external institutions which have different objectives. Mutual support between locals and their international partners has to be based on the integration of different backgrounds and skills.

The relations between international and local facilitators change with the advancement of peace-building missions. While international facilitators play a catalytic and organizing role at the early stage, later their role moves more toward training, education, and mentoring instead of direct involvement in community disputes. No matter how deeply third parties get involved, the participation of local groups is essential due to external experts' unfamiliarity with a local culture, language, social structure, and past political history.

Rehabilitation and Development

Various peace-building projects cannot start easily without initiatives to solve the issues of refugees and displaced peoples. Displaced populations come back to rebuild their community, but many may not settle in their original homes due to destruction and demographic changes. Settlement in one area could have an impact on ethnic balance in other regions. External funding can be used to encourage multi-ethnic groups to work together collectively for their survival. Relief is aimed at reducing the suffering of vulnerable civilian populations subject to famine and malnutrition resulting from civil war. While relief activities have to meet short-term needs, they have to be designed to be compatible with long-term goals of development and capacity-building (Gilles, 1998). Following the 1992 peace settlement in El Salvador, UNDP, Food and Agricultural Organization (FAO), and UNCHR were involved in social, economic reform beyond humanitarian assistance.

Considerable external funding is required to develop an extensive infrastructure such as schools, housing, and bridges. Credit also has to be obtained for various business and household economic activities. Grassroots initiatives need to be assisted by access to external resources. International development agencies financially and technically support local communities to build a water supply system as well as distributing basic grains and livestock. While supplying seed and tool packages for households is important for sustainable agricultural activities, business workshops help the development of local entrepreneurial skills.

Many international NGOs have provided assistance in a large framework of the relationships between development efforts and war prevention. The International Committee of Red Cross (ICRC), Save the Children, Oxfam, the Mennonite Central Committee, and the Brethren Service Committee have been involved in economic and social rehabilitation of war-torn societies where government services do not exist. Some NGOs, such as Oxfam, began to expand their support to demobilization programs in El Salvador and Mozambique.

The management and distribution of relief aid have become central to national and local politics. With the increasing number of female-headed households and feminization of poverty caused by war, women's organizations and other marginalized groups have to play a key role in reconstruction (McKay, 2002). Empowerment of these groups can be supported by grant programs to promote small-scale, labor-intensive projects.

Local initiatives for building roads, renovating houses, and digging wells can be used to foster intercommunal collaboration. For instance, Serbs may help build houses for returning Muslim refugees with materials provided by international donors. Mutual benefit results from joint planning of development projects and management of regional resources such as water. Fighting over water sources between sub-clans in areas of Somalia ceased temporarily through the negotiation of elders when an international agency supported the agreement to dig additional water points with its technical assistance programs.

Cooperation in one sector can spill over to other sectors with an increasing opportunity to understand different perspectives. Transportation and communication buttress community-building by helping the movements of goods and people between local communities. Goods may be purchased from neighboring villages which used to be antagonistic. Such cooperation is not a panacea. For example, since its beginning in 1994, the European Union's Administration in Mostar (EUAM) attempted to bring together the divided communities of the town by promoting small business projects, infrastructure, and utilities. A group of individuals from different ethnic communities seeking credit was allowed to have easy access to UNDP funds by forming a joint business association. However, despite numerous international incentives to reunify, Mostar remains a divided city (International Crisis Group, 2003).

External intervention has not only intended but also unintended consequences. As we have seen in Mozambique and El Salvador, monetary and other macro-economic policies prescribed by international financial institutions contradicted human development agendas. Obviously too much reliance on outside elements and ignorance of local situations undermine long-term economic viability. While foreign relief activities help meet urgent physical needs, aid can reduce incentives for local production and create dependency.

On the other hand, the unprepared withdrawal of foreign aid following a prolonged period of assistance will lead to sudden scarcity of resources. A local community's ability to rehabilitate itself may be hampered by foreign assistance's domination of the local economy. Overall, self-reliant development strategies can enhance local capacity-building, and a community-based cooperation can emerge from the involvement of former adversaries in decision-making and implementation of the project.

Democratization and Support for a New Political Process

Third parties can be engaged in assisting with the establishment of participatory political institutions. Sustainable peace can be maintained by creating political structures and institutional procedures which are acceptable to all the parties and the general population. For democratic institution-building, community groups have to learn how to represent themselves. In the absence of reliable political mechanisms, third-party roles are extended to guarantee fair rules of the game. Outside resources and aid may be used to enhance the capacity and legitimacy of local governments.

Since elections are the only legitimate means for changing positions of power, all members have to be allowed to participate in the process without discrimination (Griffiths, 1998). In an atmosphere of intimidation, external assistance has been critical in helping people trust the process by guaranteeing free and fair elections. A third party provides a safe environment for elections to be held free of violence as well as logistical support. In addition, election monitoring by international observers can help avoid disputes. Even after elections, continued assistance is necessary for strengthening political parties and institutions which are committed to democratic values and grass roots political representation.

Intergovernmental and nongovernmental organizations not only provided logistical support in preparing for elections but also supervised and monitored elections in Nicaragua, for example, four times between 1990 and 2006. Coordination and support for the work of international observers in many elections around the world were given by the UN regional offices. Following a needs assessment mission, the UNDP frequently offers technical assistance to national electoral commissions. Experts in various fields such as electoral systems and election administration are sent to the country. Donor conferences can be organized by the Electoral Assistance Division. Western NGOs and regional organizations such as OSCE have participated actively in voter education as well as building a framework for the political system such as the organization of political parties. In the election process in Bosnia and Herzegovina, multiple international actors (including the NATO Implementation Force, the United Nations International Police Task Force, the United Nations Operations Civil Affairs and Human Rights teams, UNHCR, and the Organization for Security and Cooperation in Europe) have performed security, training of personnel, voter registration, and other critical tasks. In 2006 the International Election Observation Mission (IEOM) observed the first elections to be fully administered by the Bosnia and Herzegovina authorities since the 1992– 1995 war (IEOM, 2006).

The role of NGOs has been well known through their complementary role for UN activities in the areas of voter registration, electoral observation, and monitoring. Training programs have focused on civic education, election administration, and the management of local governments. In addition, some Western NGOs conduct programs which support the development of parliamentary rules and procedures, the organization of political parties and civic organizations, and reforming of legal institutions.

It is a critical issue to make sure that parties abide by election outcomes, because post-election situations are often volatile (Harris and Reilly, 1999). As seen in Angola and Cambodia, election outcomes were not respected fully by the losers. Sanctions were put on the UNITA rebel forces in Angola who refused to accept the 1992 election outcomes. In Cambodia, a third party helped to negotiate for power-sharing arrangements spelled out in the Paris Agreements signed in 1991. Mediation between warring parties before, during, and after elections has to be in place to cover possible disputes. Most importantly, external political support for those committed to nonviolent change is crucial in transforming conflict relationships. The capacity of external actors to promote political change would be curtailed if their focus is narrow and limited to pursuing short-term goals such as the successful completion of elections.

Conclusion

As discussed above, third-party intervention is essential in a situation not only where the trust level between adversaries is low but also where the ability to implement the agreement is hampered by the destruction of ordinary social and political functions. Third-party intervention should be effective in achieving the goal of long-term settlement by supporting the process of building a stable society. Dealing with challenges, arising from adversarial relationships, demands more than passive intermediary roles associated with neutrality. Changing the dynamics of the existing structure is helped by a deeper understanding of post-conflict societies through political economy analysis of ethnic group and class relations. External aid needs to establish cross-party ties by narrowing social distance originating in economic disparities such as income gaps between urban and rural areas as well as cultural differences.

For the effective intervention of an international community in post-conflict societies, some serious limitations need to be overcome. First of all, since various international agencies help to rebuild war-torn societies in many parts of the world simultaneously, there is a limitation in available resources to respond to overwhelming appeals. Not only as related to the issue of limited resources, but also in response to the complexities entailed in the involvement of multiple international organizations with different sector specialties and goals, coordination is critical in achieving both political and humanitarian goals (Jeong, 2005). The Department of Humanitarian Affairs of the UN Secretariat exercises its role as the focal point in the UN system for mine clearance activities, in collaboration with the Department of Peacekeeping Operations, other international agencies, and national governments.

It needs to be stressed that foreign intervention is supposed to be temporary in considering that its eventual disengagement is inevitable. Then the important task would be to identify, nurture, and support elements that make a peace process durable. It is essential not only to recognize and strengthen the peace-building potential, but also to track and weaken the spoilers in the process, if necessary, with enforcement functions. Depending on political and social circumstances, the use of deterrence strategies can be limited. Those who are likely to block implementation can be consulted with or be incorporated into the peace process. Most importantly, in a similar manner to peacemaking and -keeping activities, peace-building is not a therapy to impose on an unwilling patient. Peace-building has to be primarily the task of former adversaries supported by external assistance.

Discussion Questions

1 How should third-party functions be defined for peace-building operations?
2 How are third-party roles in peace-building different from those at other stages of conflict?
3 What are the types of third-party interventions in post-conflict societies?
4 Should the role of intermediaries change at an advanced stage of peace-building?
5 What kinds of strategy are possible when one of the former adversaries refuses to implement the agreement?
6 What would be the limitations of third-party intervention?
7 What kinds of condition are conducive to successful third-party roles in peace-building?

Key Words

Conflict dynamics
Development
Elections
Facilitation
Intermediary roles
Mediation
Peace-building
Peace enforcement
Peacekeeping
Peace operations
Political reform
Problem-solving
Reconciliation
Reconstruction
Social rehabilitation

Part IV

Conclusions

CHAPTER 22

Toward Integrated Knowledge

Daniel Druckman

The chapters in this book are an attempt to convey the state of the art in conflict analysis and resolution. They do this in two ways. By introducing readers to various perspectives, the book highlights the complexity of the field. By providing a framework that organizes the perspectives, we highlight the coherence of the field. The goal of integrated knowledge, discussed in Chapter 2, is achieved by bringing order to the plethora of theories, methods, and practices that have been developed by conflict scholars and practitioners. This concluding chapter attempts to elucidate further the concept of integrated knowledge. We do this by specifying some criteria for integration, and then apply the criteria to a couple of illustrative theories. We also make an attempt to draw some lessons that emerged from the chapters and to show how these lessons contribute to the goal of integrated knowledge.

Integrated Knowledge

According to *Webster's New Collegiate Dictionary* (1961), to integrate is "to form into a whole; to unite or to become united so as to form a complete or perfect whole; unify." Scholars develop frameworks that bring together diverse concepts, processes, and practices. Conflict resolution practitioners and third parties aspire to agreements that satisfy the interests of all disputing parties. Theorists judge the value of theories by the research they have spawned or the practices they have generated. Researchers juxtapose and compare cases in order to reach generalizations about relationships between variables or to achieve more in-depth and specific knowledge about a phenomenon. In addition, many scientists attempt to understand an organism or society as a whole rather than in terms of any of its parts, as noted in a book review that appeared in a recent issue of the *American Scientist*:

> Keller leaves us with a sense of excitement about and feeling of responsibility for a coming age of biological research in which the dynamics of development and evolution will call for an integrated understanding of the organism as a whole and will not be crudely reduced to genetic mechanism. (Rheinberger, 2001, p. 66)

These definitions, approaches, and activities have several common elements. One is that they are holistic rather than piecemeal approaches to knowledge, theory, and research. Another is that they are attempts to assemble parts systematically in order to function as a whole. A third element is that they mix both similar and dissimilar parts, concepts, or processes. Further, the parts are placed in juxtaposition rather than in opposition. They provide multiple-factor explanations or explanatory frameworks and understandings. Furthermore, they emphasize the importance of contingencies or interaction effects, as well as dynamics in operation and development.

In this book, the elements come to life in several ways. These include the organizing framework shown in Chapter 1, moving between micro and macro levels of analysis, crossing disciplines for insights into sources, influences, or processes, developing knowledge from research done in a variety of settings with different methods (triangulation), and articulating the theoretical foundations for practices (see Part III). The experience of this project has increased our collective understanding of integrated knowledge. It has also helped us to articulate criteria that can guide the process of integration and serve as signposts for evaluating theories in terms of the extent to which they are integrative.

Criteria for Integration

The common elements of integration can take the form of questions asked about a theory, a research study, or a practice. For example: Are connections sought between diverse concepts? How many and varied are the studies that provide a foundation for new research? What is the level of abstraction used to explain diverse findings? Running through these and related questions are the criteria of *variety, complexity, quantity, abstraction,* and *harmonization. Variety* in the search for explanation is indicated by flexibility in moving between concepts or methods. *Complexity* refers to combinations in the sense of relationships between concepts or the extent to which a theory elucidates contingencies. *Quantity* refers to the number of concepts considered by a theory or the number of experiments conducted or cases analyzed in a study. *Abstraction* concerns the structure of logic. A more abstract theory is one that specifies principles that generate hypotheses; formal models are more abstract than conceptual frameworks. *Harmonization* refers to complementarity of parts, the way they work together over time. These criteria may be applied to existing conflict theories (or research and practice) as well as guide the development of new ones.

In surveying the field, we are struck by the large number of theories that claim to provide explanations for conflict and conflict-resolving behavior. One grouping of the theories was suggested by the participants in a doctoral seminar at ICAR. This grouping divided them into equilibrium models (e.g., sociology of conflict, game theory, structural-functionalist theories), utility theories (e.g., social learning, behavioral reinforcement models), consistency theories (including relative deprivation, dissonance, entrapment, rank disequilibrium), cultural theories (such as identity, worldview and communication frameworks), and the more explicitly psychological theories of human needs, frustration-aggression, and psychoanalytic approaches. More recently, new theoretical frameworks have emerged which benefit from juxtaposing concepts from two or more of these traditions (e.g., Mitchell, 2000b), or from linking micro- to macro-level processes (e.g., Druckman, 2001b). However, with such variety it is difficult to distinguish among the theories in terms of their explanatory value or comprehensiveness.

We are also struck by the variety of methodologies used by researchers and approaches employed by practitioners. Methodologies cover both qualitative and quantitative approaches and include laboratory and field or quasi-experiments, sample surveys, ethnographic methods, focused comparisons of a small number of cases, and comparative studies of a large number of cases. At ICAR we are witnessing increased sophistication in the use of multi-method research designs by dissertation students. One strategy that is becoming quite popular is the combination of in-depth qualitative analyses of a small number of cases with comparative quantitative analyses of a large number of cases for evaluating hypotheses. Similarly, we are experiencing an expansion in approaches to resolving conflicts. In Part III of this volume, we surveyed both negotiation and a variety of third-party interventions including mediation, facilitation, consultation, arbitration, problem-solving workshops, peace-building, and structural transformation. As with researchers, practitioners are moving in the direction of the toolkit concept where several approaches can be used together or in tandem within the same intervention. The idea of combining methods and approaches is a step toward integrated knowledge. The above criteria can help to guide the process.

Evaluating Theories of Conflict

Focusing attention on theories for purposes of illustration, we apply the above criteria for judging the extent to which they integrate knowledge. Two well-known bodies of theoretical work are on the sociology of conflict and on exchange theory. These are good candidates for comparison. They are part of the same family of theories and emphasize many of the concepts discussed in this book. Both are equilibrium theories that focus on interaction processes as these are discussed in the chapters on dynamics, negotiation, and the various third-party interventions in Part III. They differ, however, on the primary source (or etiology) of conflict as this is discussed in the earlier chapters on types and sources. The conflict sociologists emphasize the importance of values and interests; the exchange theorists emphasize responsiveness in relation to the norm of reciprocity. Both provide clear definitions of their concepts, and this has facilitated empirical research intended to evaluate hypotheses derived from them. Each theory can be judged on the extent to which it is integrative and the two theories can then be compared on these criteria. Interestingly, the evaluation exercises lead to somewhat different judgments of integration. We begin with a brief overview of the sociology of conflict.

An attempt was made by Druckman and Zechmeister (1973) to systematize the ideas presented by Coser (1956, 1967) and Aubert (1963) on conflict of interest and value dissensus. Coser's (1956) reformulation of Simmel's theoretical writings on the way contrasting ideologies intensify conflict led to further development of the theory, first by Aubert and later by Druckman and Zechmeister. Varying levels of conflict intensity are a function of the way interests and values (or ideologies) affect each other through time and repeated interactions among groups. A propositional format was used to illuminate a process that alternates through time between exacerbating (interests derived explicitly from polarized values, within-group convergence on ideologies), and moderating (within-group differences on ideology, cross-cutting interests) influences on the conflict. These countervailing influences describe a process as a dynamic equilibrium which is summarized in terms of increasing polarization on the one hand, and mediating mechanisms (within-group cleavages, cross-cutting interests) on the other. This formulation has generated considerable research designed to evaluate the propositions.

We can now ask the question: How integrative is this theory? The answer comes from judgments made on each criterion. The theory is judged high on variety since it specifies seven interrelated concepts: conflict intensity, interests, values or ideologies, cleavages within groups, polarization, time or repeated encounters, and cross-cutting interests. The set of propositions highlights relationships among the concepts such that conflict intensity results from combinations of the variables. This suggests high complexity. Sources for the theory are limited, although it has generated a reasonably large number of experiments, leading to a judgment of moderate on the quantity criterion. With regard to abstraction, the theory is stated in a generic (rather than contextual) language and the propositional form depicts a model in the tradition of dynamic equilibria. These qualities render the theory abstract. It is also well harmonized in the sense that the set of interrelated propositions demonstrates a kind of harmony of social processes in operation. The validity of explanations based on the theory depends on how well the parts or concepts work together. The judgments made on these five criteria suggest that this is a highly integrated theory.

Turning to exchange theory, we can perform the same exercise for judging the extent to which the approach is integrative. The origins of this theory may be found in the writings of Thibaut and Kelley (1959), Gouldner (1960), Homans (1961), and Blau (1964) among others. A central idea is the importance of reciprocity in everyday social interactions. According to Thibaut and Kelley, "it is possible to describe much of the complex patterning in the interactions of an entire society in terms of a system of such reciprocal roles" (1959, p. 147). Reciprocity is seen by these theorists to function as a "mechanism" for achieving balanced social relations. Although the strength of the norm may vary from culture to culture, it has been shown to be quite pervasive in capturing interaction processes among people in both friendly and antagonistic relationships. The empirical work stimulated by this theory has elucidated the various forms in which exchanges occur and the factors that influence them. The dimensions of exchange include such considerations as timing, explicitness of obligation (to reciprocate), perceptions of equivalence, the strength of the norm of reciprocation, and perceptions of fairness. Influences on these dimensions include the relative power of the parties, culture (especially with regard to the strength of the norm), and incentives defined by the interactive situation. (See Larson (1998) for a review of the research on exchange processes in international relations.)

Judgments of integration turn on the criteria defined above. With regard to variety, the theory offers relatively few concepts. It focuses attention primarily on the form and conditions for reciprocal exchanges. Recent empirical work has moved the theory beyond earlier ideas of simple reciprocity (referred to as tit-for-tat). Various forms of delayed and comparative responding have been identified (e.g., Patchen, 1998). These developments render the approach as being moderately complex.

Although considerable research has been generated, the studies have concentrated on a small number of interaction-process variables. Since the theory deals with the form of response to offers or gestures (such as varying degrees of equivalence) rather than its content (such as the particular goods or values being exchanged), it is relatively abstract. (See Mitchell (2000b) for applications of the theory in international politics with special attention paid to Sadat's historic visit to Jerusalem in 1977.) Further, with regard to harmonization, the theory's emphasis on synchronous exchanges (toward an equilibrium) requires coordination among the parts of an interaction process. Harmony among the parts is also a feature of the sociology of conflict theory discussed above. Taken together, these judgments suggest that this is a moderately integrated theory. It is somewhat less integrated than the sociology of conflict framework, due largely to lower ratings on the variety, complexity, and quantity criteria.

These exercises were intended for illustrative purposes. Applying the criteria to other theories of conflict and conflict resolution would produce comparable judgments. For example, human needs theory may be judged as being moderately integrated (lower on the variety, complexity, and quantity than on the abstraction and harmonization criteria). A similar judgment results from an evaluation of game theory, leading to the observation that theories can be comparable in terms of integrating knowledge but differ on such other criteria as formalism, precision, scope of phenomena covered, and generation of research. Some theories are less integrated in earlier than in more recent versions. This is the case with exchange theory, as noted above. It also characterizes another popular theory of conflict processes referred to as ripeness theory. (See Zartman (2000) for the refinements that increased this theory's integration.) Increasing attention to a theory, due sometimes to current events, can lead to further development in the direction of enhanced integration. This has occurred with regard to identity theory discussed in Chapter 7 and elsewhere in this book.

A value of these exercises is that they provide a basis for comparison between various theories of conflict and conflict resolution. They also allow for a charting of progress toward integration by comparing earlier and later versions of particular theoretical frameworks. In addition, the criteria can perhaps serve as guidelines in the development of new theories for this young, dynamic field. At the very least, they can provoke debate about the meaning of integration and how it is to be judged. Nonetheless, however we define it, integration is a useful concept for evaluating the contributions of this book to the field, a task to which we now turn.

Toward an Integrated Field: Contributions Made by This Book

So far in this chapter we have looked back at the theories that have been dominant in teaching and research about conflict and conflict resolution, and provided a detailed evaluation of two of them. The contributors to this book have not dwelt on this set of theories; rather, they have provided new perspectives on the field. Variety and complexity are in evidence as the authors pave the way for emerging theories that can guide analysis and practice. These ideas and themes are highlighted in this final section as we begin to develop the contours of a larger framework for the field.

Above all, this book is an attempt to link conflict analysis, including theory and research, to the practical activities of interventions intended to resolve conflicts. The analyses of sources and influences, discussed in Parts I and II, inform the treatment of processes and interventions in Part III. They also show how research-based knowledge may have practical implications. The first chapter in Part I on *Typology* (Chapter 3) makes a connection between comprehensive frameworks and training of third parties. Effective intervention may well depend on an understanding of the multiple dimensions of any conflict. Chapter 4 on *Sources* distinguishes among personal, situational, and structural sources and develops implications for how conflict resolvers can help the disputing parties alter those structures that generate violent conflict.

Continuing along these lines, Chapter 5 on *Dynamics* illustrates how actions taken by individuals can influence escalatory processes and, by doing so, alter the structures that serve to perpetuate the conflict. The chapter on Narrative Analysis highlights the importance of contests over legitimacy. Diagnoses of conflict may be incomplete if they do not consider issues of social justice and marginality, particularly the way these issues surface in conflict narratives. These chapters enhance our awareness of complexity, both with regard to the way we think about conflicts and the kinds of action likely to be instrumental in altering the sources that sustain them.

The analyses in the chapters of Part II contribute further to integrated knowledge and may have practical implications. The discussion of *Situations* (Chapter 6) raises an interesting question concerning situation-personality influences on conflict behavior. In social interactions, one party's actions influence the other's actions leading the other to act in expected ways, as though these behaviors emanate from his or her "personality." Personality attributions for behavior persist because they are self-confirming and because we have an English vocabulary that is richer in trait-like than in situational or context terms (see Bem and Allen, 1974). This has implications also for group stereotypes, which are often attributions based on group characteristics rather than appraisals of the situations in which the group acts. Chapters 7 and 8 on *Identities* and *Culture* emphasize the way these influences are intertwined with conflict dynamics. Both are viewed as aggravating factors on conflict. Identities fuel conflict but are also affected by the outcomes of conflict. Culture is less a cause of conflict than a "lens" through which the conflict is "refracted." Culture influences communication, the way disputants define the situation, and the modalities for the way information about conflicts are processed. The way these factors influence (and are influenced by) conflict is similar to the interplay between interests and values discussed above in the integration exercise.

The analysis of *Structures* in Chapter 10 helps to broaden the scope of conflict analysis and resolution. It contributes such concepts as social action and function, power asymmetry between groups, and organizational dynamics. Structures also influence the way disputes are defined and handled. Chapter 10, on *Institutions*, shows that legal institutions are not equipped to deal with disputes that stem from disagreements over ethical and political norms. The increasing number of challenges to legitimate authority vested in established institutions calls for the kinds of approach to resolution discussed in Part III of this volume.

The chapters in Part II cover a variety of influences and illustrate a kind of recursive relationship between these influences and conflict. Situations, identities, cultures, and structures shape conflicts and the way they are resolved but are also shaped by those conflicts. As shaping influences (or independent variables), these factors play a causal role in conflict dynamics; as being shaped by conflict, the factors are seen as constructions linked to changing perceptions and definitions of situations. Both positivist and constructivist perspectives are relevant to analyses of influences. Two aspects of the context for conflict are discussed in the chapters on Globalization and Development. Although globalization may increase the intensity of conflicts in the short term, it is not clear whether it escalates (or de-escalates) old conflicts or creates new ones over the long term. Similarly, development influences the intensity of conflicts. Although most agree that lack of development exacerbates conflict, it is not at all clear how to generate the kind of sustainable and equitable development that would reduce violent conflict.

Turning to the chapters in Part III, we discover insights from each of several types of conflict intervention. In discussing the literature on *Negotiation*, Chapter 14 offers a counter-intuitive observation. The well-known strategy of preparing alternatives to negotiated agreements can backfire. Research has shown that while attractive alternatives reduce a negotiator's vulnerability, they also encourage negotiators to

focus primarily on their own interests and to perceive the other negotiator as having even more attractive alternatives. These are the
conditions for sub-optimal outcomes or impasses. When impasses occur,
it is often the case that third parties are called in to help resolve them.
The remainder of the chapters in Part III call attention to a variety of
types of third-party interventions and activities. The third-party roles
with the longest history are discussed in Chapter 13, *Mediation and
Arbitration*. This chapter raises two important issues. One is that the
effectiveness of mediation and arbitration is quite situation-specific
(when, where, over what, and with whom it occurs). The other issue is
that the techniques used are limited to nonviolent conflicts. These issues
suggest a need for new models of intervention or various combinations
of alternative approaches to address violent conflicts. Some new models
are discussed in Chapters 14 and 15.

Problem-solving workshops provide flexible environments for
addressing intractable conflicts. Even the most intransigent partisan
may discover the feasibility of revising his or her views about options,
alternatives, goals, and interests. However, it is also rarely the case that
the most extreme protagonists participate in these workshops. More
often, the workshops include moderates who are willing to take the
risks of exploring ideas for conflict termination or resolution. Further,
our experiences with these sorts of interventions caution us against
assuming that the changes we observe, however dramatic they may be,
transfer to changes in the larger conflict. Several variants on the theme
of problem-solving workshops are discussed in Chapter 15, *Facilitation
and Consultation*. A key distinction is made between a problem-
solving focus and an appreciative inquiry model. While the former
concentrates on fixing an existing problem, the latter attempts to
encourage a more positive learning frame so that such problems will not
recur. In the latter approach, a facilitator protects the process, allowing
the participants in the workshop to solve their own problems. This is
similar to the discussion of conceptual frameworks in Chapter 3,
Typology. Less is known, however, about the contingencies under
which one or other of these approaches is likely to be effective. Some
progress has been made in connecting the approaches to stages of
conflict (e.g., Fisher and Keashley, 1991). Less attention has been given
to the variety of *Informal Roles* that are practiced in many settings. The
discussion of these activities in Chapter 15 raises the issue of whether
they should be formalized by developing prescriptive guidelines.
Although professionalization has its advantages, it has been argued that
these roles are effective primarily because they are carried out more or
less spontaneously in the course of ongoing relationships between
disputants and mentors. However, some conflict situations are best

handled by trained professionals. This is particularly the case in attempts to manage violent conflicts between groups. The chapter on *Peace Operations* provides insight into the way peacekeepers contribute to the reduction of violence, usually following cease-fire agreements. The chapter also discusses the expanded activities performed by peacekeepers. They are increasingly taking on many of the third-party roles discussed in the other chapters of this part. A number of recent articles, reviewed in the chapter, have documented the link between the peacekeeping roles of managing and resolving conflicts.

The final two chapters in Part III deal with structural interventions. Both chapters remind us of the difficulties involved in trying to transform societal institutions. Yet it may well be the case that, without structural change, interventions are unlikely to be effective in sustaining peace over time. Although several of the other chapters in Part III call attention to transforming conflicts, the discussions in these chapters lodge the process in ongoing peace-building activities. To be effective, these activities may need to be "institutionalized" as part of everyday governance and decision-making processes. A similar observation was made earlier in Chapter 11, on *Institutions*. An optimistic chord is struck in Chapter 5 by providing a place for human actions in altering structures.

The chapters in Part III on interventions move from actions that can be taken by the disputants themselves (negotiation, appreciative inquiry) to actions that are suggested by either (or both) formal and informal third parties to actions that are part of ongoing societal peace-building programs. These may be regarded as complementary approaches contained in a "toolkit." We know little, however, about the conditions for effective application or how they may be used together in a particular situation. By defining the approaches, addressing the issues surrounding their use, and comparing them, we have taken a step in the direction of integrating research with practice.

Looking ahead, we ask how these concluding observations about the book's contributions may be used to further the goal of integrated knowledge. One way to do this is to unpack the categories corresponding to chapter titles in Figure 1.1 (p. 6). The key themes suggested by the chapters in each part provide direction for the framework-building task. The chapters in Part I suggest the theme of complexity in types, sources, and dynamics of conflict. When considering these aspects of conflict, the framework would depict variety but also show how different sources and types of conflict interact and change over time. The second part highlights a recursive relationship between influences, context, and conflict. This feature of the framework is represented by circular patterns where the situation (or identity, culture) leads to escalating or de-escalating paths which, in turn, influence the way the situation (identity, culture) is defined. Furthermore, the chapters in Part III call attention to layered third-party activities. The layering idea refers to sequencing or combining different kinds of intervention depending on the situation, which includes the type of conflict and the context for its development. This feature of the framework would specify some contingencies in the use of one or another third-party approach. By unpacking the framework shown in Figure 1.1 along these lines, we move closer to the goal of integrated knowledge. The new framework may go a long way toward satisfying the criteria for an integrated approach to the field, namely variety, complexity, quantity, abstraction, and harmony among its parts. Having defined the task, we can now take the next steps in the collaborative process of putting the framework together.

References

Aall, P. (1996) Nongovernmental organizations and peacemaking. In *Managing Global Chaos: Sources of and Responses to International Conflict*, edited by C. A. Crocker, F. O. Hampson, and P. Aall. Washington, DC: USIP Press.

Abercrombie, N., Hill, S., and Turner, B. S. (1994) *The Penguin Dictionary of Sociology*. London: Penguin.

Abreu Hernandez, V. M. (2002) The Mothers of La Plaza de Mayo: a peace movement. *Peace and Change*, 27(3), 385–411.

Abu-Lughod, L. (1991) Writing against culture. In *Recapturing Anthropology*, edited by R. G. Fox. Santa Fe, NM: School of American Research Press.

Abu-Nimer, M. (2003) *Nonviolence and Peace Building in Islam: Theory and Practice*. Gainesville: University Press of Florida.

Ackermann, A. (1999) *Making Peace Prevail: Preventing Violent Conflict in Macedonia*. Syracuse, NY: Syracuse University Press.

Adams, R. (1998) If pigs could fly. *Conciliation Quarterly*, 17(2), 9–10.

Adedeji, A. (1999) Which way forward? A panel discussion. In *Comprehending and Mastering African Conflicts*. London: Zed Books, pp. 41–52.

Adelman, H. and Suhrke, A. (1996) *Early Warning and Conflict Management*. Copenhagen: Steering Committee of the Joint Evaluation of Emergency Assistance to Rwanda.

Adler, P. (1981) *Momentum: A Theory of Social Action*. Newbury Park, CA: Sage.

African Rights (1994) *Humanitarianism Unbound? Current Dilemmas Facing Multi-mandate Relief Operations in Political Emergencies.* London: African Rights.

Agar, M. (1996) *The Professional Stranger: An Informal Introduction to Ethnography* (2nd edn). New York: Academic Press.

AIIS (2000) *Stability Pact Just Around the Corner.* Tirana: Albanian Institute for International Studies.

Akhtar, S. and Kramer, S. (1999) *Brothers and Sisters: Developmental, Dynamic, and Technical Aspects of the Sibling Relationship.* New York: Jason Aronson.

Alderfer, C. P. (1973) Improving organizational communication through long-term intergroup intervention. *Journal of Applied Behavioral Science*, 13, 193–210.

Alford, S. (1997) Professionals need not apply: South Carolina's juvenile arbitration program owes success to volunteers. *Corrections Today*, 59, 104+ il.

Allen Nan, S. (1999) *Complementarity and Coordination of Conflict Resolution Efforts in the Conflicts over Abkhazia, South Ossetia, and Transdniestria.* Unpublished doctoral dissertation, Institute for Conflict Analysis and Resolution, George Mason University.

Allport, G. (1954) *The Nature of Prejudice.* Cambridge, MA: Addison-Wesley.

Almond, G. (1960) *The Politics of the Developing Areas.* Princeton: Princeton University Press.

Amadiume, Abdullahi, A (eds) (2000) *The Politics of Memory: Truth, Healing and Social Justice.* New York: Zed Books.

American Anthropological Association (1997) Response to OMB Directive 15: Race and ethnic standards for federal statistics and administrative reporting. http://www.aaanet.org/gvt/ombdraft.htm.

American Anthropological Association (1998) AAA statement on "race". *Anthropology Newsletter*, 39(6), 3.

Amersfoort, H. V. (1982) *Immigration and the Formation of Minority Groups: The Dutch Experience 1945–1973*, translated from Dutch by R. Lyng. Cambridge: Cambridge University Press.

Anderson, B. (1991) *Imagined Communities: Reflections on the Origin and Spread of Nationalism.* Revised edn. London: Verso.

Anderson, J. R. (1983) *The Architecture of Cognition.* Cambridge, MA: Harvard University Press.

Anderson, J. R. and Bower, G. H. (1973) *Human Associative Memory.* Washington, DC: Winston & Sons.

Anderson, M. B. (1999) *Do No Harm: How Aid Can Support Peace or War.* Boulder, CO: Lynne Rienner.

Anderson, M. (2004, August) *Experiences with Impact Assessment: Can*

We Know What Good We Do? Berlin: Berghof Research Center for Constructive Conflict Management.

Anderson, M. (2001). Humanitarian NGOs in conflict intervention. In *Turbulent Peace: The Challenges of Managing International Conflict*, edited by C. A. Crocker, F. O. Hampson, and P. Aall. Washington, DC: USIP.

Anderson, M. (2004, August) *Experiences with Impact Assessment: Can We Know What Good We Do?* Berlin: Berghof Research Center for Constructive Conflict Management.

Anderson, R. C. and Pichert, J. W. (1978) Recall of previously unrecallable information following a shift in perspective. *Journal of Verbal Learning and Verbal Behavior*, 17, 1–12.

Annan, K. (1999) Address to the OSCE Permanent Council in Vienna, 20 July.

Arendt, H. (1970) *On Violence*. New York: Harcourt Brace.

Arendt, H. (1986) Communicative Power. In *Power*, edited by S. Lukes. New York: New York University Press.

Arnold, J. A. and Carnevale, P. J. (1997) Preferences for dispute resolution procedures as a function of intentionality, consequences, expected future interaction, and power. *Journal of Applied Social Psychology*, March 27(5), 371–99.

Arnold, J. A. and O'Connor, K. M. (1999) Ombudspersons or peers? The effect of third-party expertise and recommendations on negotiation. *Journal of Applied Psychology*, 84(5), 776–85.

Aron, R. (1981) *The Century of Total War*. Westport, CT: Greenwood Press.

Aronoff, M. (1989) *Israeli Visions and Divisions: Cultural Change and Political Conflict*. New Brunswick, NJ: Transaction Books.

Astarita, M. J. (1997–98) Overview of the arbitration process. *The Securities Law Home Page: The On-line Guide to the Law of the Securities Markets. http://www.seclaw.com*

Atkinson, P. and Hammersley, M. (1998) Ethnography and participant observation. In *Strategies of Qualitative Inquiry*, edited by N. K. Denzin and Y. S. Lincoln. Thousand Oaks, CA: Sage.

Aubert, V. (1963) Competition and dissensus: Two types of conflict and of conflict resolution. *Journal of Conflict Resolution*, 7, 26–42.

Auerbach, J. S. (1983) *Justice Without Law?* New York: Oxford University Press.

Augustine of Hippo (1963) *The Confessions of St. Augustine*. New York: Mentor.

Avruch, K. (1982) On the traditionalization of social identity. *Ethos*, 10(2), 95–116.

Avruch, K. (1992) Making culture and its costs. *Ethnic and Racial Studies*, 14(4), 614–26.

Avruch, K. (1998) *Culture and Conflict Resolution*. Washington, DC: U.S. Institute of Peace Press.

Avruch, K (2003) Type I and Type II Errors in Culturally Sensitive Conflict Resolution Practice. *Conflict Resolution Quarterly*, 20(3), 351-71.

Avruch, K. and Black, P. W. (1990) Ideas of human nature in contemporary conflict resolution theory. *Negotiation Journal*, 6(3), 222–8.

Avruch, K. and Black, P. W. (1991) The culture question and inter-cultural conflict resolution. *Peace and Change*, 16, 22–45.

Avruch, K. and Black, P. W. (1993) Conflict resolution in inter-cultural settings: Problems and prospects. In *Conflict Resolution Theory and Practice: Integration and Application*, edited by D. Sandole and H.van der Merwe. Manchester: Manchester University Press.

Avruch, K., Black, P. W., and Scimecca, J. (eds) (1998) *Conflict Resolution: Cross-cultural Perspectives*. New York: Praeger.

Axelrod, R. and Dion, D. (1988) The further evolution of cooperation. *Science*, 242, 1385–90.

Axelrod, R. M. (1990). *The Evolution of Cooperation*. London; New York: Penguin Books.

Ayres, J. M. (2004) Framing collective action against Neoliberalism: The case of the 'anti-globalization movement'. *Journal of World-Systems Research, 10* (1).

Azar, E. (1990) *The Management of Protracted Social Conflict: Theory and Cases*. Brookfield, VT: Gower.

Babbitt, E. and d'Estrée, T. P. (1996) An Israeli-Palestinian women's workshop: Application of the interactive problem-solving approach. In *Managing Global Chaos: Sources of and Responses to International Conflict*, edited by C. A. Crocker, F. O. Hampson, and P. Aall. Washington, DC: U.S. Institute of Peace Press.

Baca, L. R. (1988) The legal status of American Indians. In *Handbook of North American Indians*. Vol. 14. History of Indian–White Relations, edited by W. E. Washburn. Washington, DC: Smithsonian Institution.

Baker, A. C., Jensen, P. J., and Kolb, D. A. (1997) In conversation: Transforming experience into learning. *Simulation and Gaming*, 28(1), 6–7.

Baldwin, M. W. (1992) Relational schemas and the processing of social information. *Psychological Bulletin*, 112, 461–84.

Bamberg, M. G. W., & Andrews, M. (2004). *Considering Counter Narratives: Narrating, Resisting, Making Sense*. Amsterdam; Philadelphia: J. Benjamins.

Banard, C. (1968) Mind in everyday affairs. In *The Function of the Executive*. Cambridge, MA: Harvard University Press. First published in 1938.

Banks, M. (1996) *Ethnicity: Anthropological Constructions*. New York: Routledge.

Banks, Carrie Outhier (2004) *Finding Their Voice: Observation of the Surrogate Victim Offender Dialogue Project*. Unpublished doctoral dissertation, George Mason University.

Banton, M. (1965) *Roles: An Introduction to the Study of Social Relations*. New York: Basic Books.

Barber, B. (1992) Neofunctionalism and the theory of the social system. In *The Dynamics of Social Systems*, edited by P. Colomy. London: Sage.

Barber, B. (1992) Jihad Vs McWorld. *Atlantic Monthly*, (March).

Barker, R. G. (1968) *Ecological Psychology*. Stanford, CA: Stanford University Press.

Baron. R. A. (1990) Environmentally induced positive affect: Its impact on self-efficacy, task performance, negotiation, and conflict. *Journal of Applied Social Psychology*, 20, 368–84.

Barr, R. (2000) British court upholds surgery to split twins. Washington Post, (September 23) A20.

Barr, R. R. (2005) Bolivia: Another uncompleted revolution. *Latin American Politics and Society*, 47(3), 69–91.

Barsky, A. (1999) Community involvement through child protection mediation. *Child Welfare*, 78(4), 481–501.

Barsky, A. E. (2000) *Conflict Resolution for the Helping Professions*.Wadsworth: Brooks/Cole Thomson Learning.

Barsky, A., Este, D., and Collins, D. (1996) Cultural competence in family mediation. *Mediation Quarterly*, 13(3), 167–78.

Barth, F. (ed) (1969) *Ethnic Groups and Boundaries*. Boston: Little, Brown.

Bartlett, F. A. (1932) *A Study in Experimental and Social Psychology*. New York: Cambridge University Press.

Bartlett, R. (2000) *England Under the Norman and Angevin Kings, 1075–1225*. Oxford: Clarendon Press.

Bateman, T. S. (1980) Contingent concession strategies in dyadic bargaining. *Organizational Behavior and Human Performance*, 26, 212–21.

Bateson, G. (1972) *Steps to an Ecology of Mind; Collected Essays in Anthropology, Psychiatry, Evolution, and Epistemology*. San Francisco: Chandler Pub. Co.

Baumann, G. (1996) *Contesting Culture: Discourses of Identity in Multiethnic London*. London: Cambridge University Press.

Baumann, G. (1999) *The Multicultural Riddle: Rethinking National, Ethnic, and Religious Identities*. London: Routledge.

Bell, P. D. and Tousignant G. (2001) Getting beyond New York: Reforming peacekeeping in the field. *World Policy Journal*, VXIII (3), pp. 41–46.

Bell, R. L., Cleveland, S. E., Hanson, P. G., and O'Connell, W. E.(1969) Small group dialogue and discussion: An approach to police–community relationships. *Journal of Criminal Law, Criminology, and Police Science*, 103, 242–6.

Bem, D. J. and Allen, A. (1974) On predicting some of the people some of the time: The search for cross-situational consistencies in behavior. *Psychological Review*, 81, 306–20.

Benton, A. A. and Druckman, D. (1973) Salient solutions and the bargaining behavior of representatives and non-representatives. *International Journal of Group Tensions*, 3, 28–39.

Bentz, V. M. and Shapiro, J. J. (1998) *Mindful Inquiry in the Social Sciences*. Thousand Oaks, CA: Sage.

Berger, P. L. and Luckmann, T. (1967) *The Social Construction of Reality: A Treatise in the Sociology of Knowledge*. New York: Doubleday.

Beriker, N. and Druckman, D. (1996) Simulating the Lausanne peace negotiations 1922–1923: Power asymmetries in bargaining. *Simulation and Gaming*, 27, 162–83.

Berkeley, B. (2001) *The Graves Are Not Yet Full: Race, Tribe and Power in the Heart of Africa*. New York: Basic Books.

Berman, H. (1983) *Law and Revolution: The Formation of the Western Legal Tradition*. Cambridge, MA: Harvard University Press.

Berman, M. R. and Johnson, J. (1977) *Unofficial Diplomats*. New York: Columbia University Press.

Besteman, C. (1996) Representing violence and "othering" Somalia. *Cultural Anthropology*, 11, 120–33.

Besteman, C. (1998) Primordialist blinders: A reply to I. M. Lewis. *Cultural Anthropology*, 13, 109–20.

Bhagwati, J. (2004). *In Defense of Globalization*. New York: Oxford University Press.

Biddle, B. J. and Thomas, E. J. (eds) (1966) *Role Theory: Concepts and Research*. New York: John Wiley and Sons.

Billig, M. and Tajfel, H. (1973) Social categorization and similarity in intergroup behavior. *European Journal of Social Psychology*, 3, 27–52.

Binnendijk, H. (ed.) (1987) *National Negotiating Styles*. Washington, DC: Foreign Service Institute, U.S. Department of State.

Bion, W. (1959) *Experiences in Groups*. London: Tavistock Institute.

Birdsall, N., Graham, C., and Pettinato, S. (2000, August) *Stuck in the Tunnel: Is Globalization Muddling the Middle Class?* Working paper no. 14, The Brookings Institution, Center for Social and Economic Dynamics, Washington, DC.

Birkhoff, J. (2002) *Mediators' Perspectives on Power: A Window into a Profession?* Unpublished doctoral dissertation, Institute for Conflict Analysis and Resolution, George Mason University.

Black, C. E. (1969) *The Dynamics of Modernization: A Study In Comparative History*. Princeton, NJ: Princeton University Press.

Black, D. (1980) *The Manners and Customs of the Police*. New York: Academic Press.

Black, P. W. (1998) Surprised by common sense. In *Conflict Resolution: Cross-cultural Perspectives*, edited by K. Avruch, P. Black, and J. Scimecca. Westport: Praeger. First published in 1991 by Greenwood Press.

Black, P. W. (2000) *Planning for the future of Helen Reef: Sociocultural features of the Tubion community and their implications. http:// cas.gmu.edu/~tobi/misc/tobidocumentarchive.htm*.

Black, P. W. and Avruch, K. (1993) Culture, power and international negotiations: Understanding Palau–US status negotiations. *Millennium*, 22, 379–400. Reprinted in *Culture and World Politics*, edited by M. Verweij and D. Jacquir (1998). London: Macmillan.

Blake, R. R. (1959) Psychology and the crisis of statesmanship. *American Psychologist*, 14, 87–94.

Blake, R. R., Sephard, H. A., and Mouton, J. S. (1964) *Managing Intergroup Conflict in Industry*. Houston, TX: Gulf.

Blaker, M. (1977) *Japanese International Negotiating Style*. New York: Columbia University Press.

Blau, P. (1964) *Exchange and Power in Social Life*. New York: John Wiley & Sons.

Bloomfield, D. (1995) Towards complementarity in conflict management: Resolution and settlement in Northern Ireland. *Journal of Peace Research*, 32, May 2, 151–64.

Blumberg, A. and Weiner, W. (1971) One from two: Facilitating an organizational merger. *Journal of Applied Behavioral Science*, 7, 87–102.

Bodin, J. (1955) *Six Books of the Commonwealth*, translated by M. J. Tooley. Oxford: Blackwell.

Bohannon, R. (1970) The six stations of divorce. In *Divorce and After: An Analysis of the Emotional and Social Problems of Divorce*, edited by P. Bohaman. New York: Doubleday.

Bonham, G. M. (1971) Simulating international disarmament negotiations. *Journal of Conflict Resolution*, 15, 299–318.

Borton, J., Brusset, E., and Hallam, A. (1996) *Humanitarian Aid and Effects*. Copenhagen: Steering Committee of the Joint Evaluation of Emergency Assistance to Rwanda.

Boulden, J. (2001), *Peace Enforcement: The United Nations Experience in Congo, Somalia and Bosnia*. Westport: Praeger.

Boulding, K. E. (1956) *The Image: Knowledge in Life and Society*. Ann Arbor: University of Michigan Press.

Boulding, K. E. (1959) National images and international systems. *Journal of Conflict Resolution*, 3, 120–31.

Boulding, K. E. (1962) *Conflict and Defense: A General Theory*. New York: Harper & Row.

Boulding, K. E. (2000) *Cultures of Peace: The Hidden Side of History*. Syracuse, NY: Syracuse University Press.

Bourdieu, P. (1977) *Outline of a Theory of Practice*. Cambridge: Cambridge University Press.

Bourdieu, P. (1990) *The Logic of Practice*. Stanford, CA: Stanford University Press.

Bourdieu, P. (1991) *Language and Symbolic Power*, edited and introduced by J. Thompson and translated by G. Raymond and M. Adamson. Cambridge, MA: Harvard University Press.

Boutros-Ghali, B. (1995) *An Agenda for Peace: Preventive Diplomacy, Peacemaking and Peace-keeping*. New York: United Nations.

Boutros-Ghali, B. (1999) *Unvanquished: A US-UN Saga*. London: I.B. Tauris.

Bower, G. H., Black, J. B., and Turner, T. J. (1979) Scripts in memory for text. *Cognitive Psychology*, 11, 177–220.

Bowker, J. W. (1986) The burning fuse: The unacceptable face of religion. *Zygon*, 21, 415–28.

Bradford, L. P., Gibb, J. R., and Benne, K. D. (eds) (1964) *T-Group Theory and the Laboratory Method*. New York: John Wiley & Sons.

Brahimi, L. et al. (2000, August 21) *The Report of the Panel on United Nations Peace Operations* (A/55/305-S/2000/809).

Brams, S. J. (1994) Theory of moves. *American Scientist*, 81, 562–70.

Brand-Jacobsen, K. and Jacobsen, C. (2000) Beyond security: New approaches, new perspectives, new actors. In *Searching for Peace, the Road to TRANSCEND*, edited by J. Galtung and C. Jacobsen. Sterling, VA: Pluto Press.

Braun, J. (1998) Arbitration—promises made, promises broken. *Public Management*, November 8(11), 9–11.

Brewer, M. B. (1968) Determinants of social distance among East African tribal groups. *Journal of Personality and Social Psychology*, 10, 279–89.

Brewer, M. B. (1979) The role of ethnocentrism in intergroup conflict.

In *The Social Psychology of Intergroup Relations*, edited by W. G. Austin and S. Worchel. Monterey, CA: Brooks/Cole.

Brewer, M. B. and Campbell, D. T. (1976) *Ethnocentrism and Intergroup Attitudes: East African Evidence*. New York: John Wiley & Sons.

Brewer, M. B. and Kramer, R. M. (1985) The psychology of intergroup attitudes and behavior. *Annual Review of Psychology*, 36, 219–43.

Brison, K. (2002) The Pacific Islands. In *Race and Ethnicity: An Anthropological Focus on the U.S. and the World*, edited by R. Scupin. Englewood Cliffs, NJ: Prentice Hall.

Brodkin, K. (1998) *How Jews Became White Folks and What That Says About Race in America*. New Brunswick, NJ: Rutgers University Press.

Brooks, S. G. (2005) *Producing Security: Multinational Corporations, Globalization, and the Changing Calculus of Conflict*. Princeton: Princeton University Press.

Brown, B. R. (1977) Face-saving and face-restoration in negotiation. In *Negotiations: Social-Psychological Perspectives*, edited by D. Druckman. Beverly Hills, CA: Sage.

Brown, F. and Rogers, C. A. (1997) The role of arbitration in resolving transnational disputes: A survey of trends in the People's Republic of China. *Berkeley Journal of International Law*, 15(2), 329–51.

Brown, J. S. (1957) Principles of intrapersonal conflict. *Journal of Conflict Resolution*, 1(2), 135–53.

Brown, R. (1986) *Social Psychology: The Second Edition*. New York: The Free Press.

Brown, S. (1986) The superpowers' dilemma. *Negotiation Journal*, 2, 371–84.

Bruner, J. S. and Postman, L. (1949) On the perception of incongruity: A paradigm. *Journal of Personality*, 18, 206–23.

Brysk, A. (1996) Turning weakness into strength: The internationalization of Indian rights. *Latin American Perspectives, 23*(2).

Buller, P. F. and Bell, C. H. Jr. (1986) Effects of team building and goal setting on productivity: A field experiment. *Academy of Management Journal*, 29, 305–28.

Burgess, G. and Burgess, H. (1994) Justice without violence: Theoretical foundations. In *Justice Without Violence*, edited by P. Wehr, H. Burgess, and G. Burgess. Boulder, CO: Rienner.

Burgess, H. and Burgess, G. (1997) *Encyclopedia of Conflict Resolution*. Santa Barbara, CA: ABC-CLIO, Inc.

Burke, W.W. and Biggart, N.W. (1997). Interorganization relations. In *Enhancing Organizational Performance*, edited by D. Druckman, J. E. Singer, and H. Van Cott. Washington DC: National Academy Press.

Burn, M. (2006) *Loyalty and Order: Clan Identity and Political Preference in Kyrgyzstan and Kazakhstan, 2005*. Unpublished doctoral dissertation, George Mason University.

Burton, J. W. (1962) *Peace Theory*. New York: Knopf.

Burton, J. W. (1969) *Conflict and Communication: The Use of Controlled Communication in International Relations*. London: Macmillan.

Burton, J. W. (1979) *Deviance, Terrorism, and War: The Process of Solving Unsolved Social and Political Problems*. Oxford: Martin Robertson.

Burton, J. W. (1987) *Resolving Deep-rooted Conflict: A Handbook*. Lanham, MD: University Press of America.

Burton, J. W. (1988) *Conflict Resolution as a Political System*. Working paper no. 1, Center for Conflict Analysis and Resolution, George Mason University.

Burton, J. W. (1990b) *Conflict: Resolution and Provention*. London: Macmillan.

Burton, J. W. (1993) Conflict resolution as a political philosophy. In *Conflict Resolution Theory and Practice: Integration and Application*, edited by D. Sandole and H. van der Merwe. New York: Manchester University Press.

Burton, J. W. (1995) Conflict provention as a political system. In *Beyond Confrontation: Learning Conflict Resolution in the Post-Cold War Era*, edited by J. A. Vasquez, J. T. Johnson, S. Jaffe, and L. Stamato. Ann Arbor, MI: University of Michigan Press.

Burton, J. W. (1996a) Civilization in crisis: From adversarial to problem solving process. *International Journal of Peace Studies*, 1(1), 5–24.

Burton, J. W. (1996b) *Conflict Resolution: Its Language and Processes*. Lanham, MD: Scarecrow Press.

Burton, J. W. (1997, November) *Conflict Resolution: Toward Problem Solving*. Unpublished manuscript.

Burton, J. W. and Dukes, F. (1990) *Conflict: Practices in Management, Settlement and Resolution*. New York: St. Martin's Press.

Busek, E. (2006, February 16) *The Stability Pact for Southeastern Europe: Bringing Peace to the Balkans?* Presentation by the Special Coordinator of the Stability Pact for South Eastern Europe, Institute for Conflict Analysis and Resolution (ICAR), George Mason University.

Bush, Kenneth. (1998) *A Measure of Peace: Peace and Conflict Impact Assessment (PICA) of Development Projects in Conflict Zones*. Working paper no. 1, The Peacebuilding and Reconstruction Program Initiative and The Evaluation Unit.

Callan, E. and Sevastopulo, D. (2006) Middle East on verge of 'three civil wars', Jordan's king warns. *Financial Times*, (November 27), 6.

Callister, R. R. and Wall, J. A. Jr. (1997) Japanese community and organizational mediation. *Journal of Conflict Resolution*, 41(2), 311–28.

Caplan, R. (2005), *International Governance of War-Torn Territories: Rule and Reconstruction*. Oxford: Oxford University Press.

Cardoso, F. and Faletto, E. (1979) *Dependency and Development in Latin America*. Los Angeles: University of California Press.

Carnevale, P. and Henry, R. A. (1989) Determinants of mediator behavior: A test of the strategic choice model. *Journal of Applied Social Psychology*, 19, 481–98.

Carnevale, P. and Isen, A. M. (1985) The influence of positive affect and visual access on the discovery of integrative solutions in bilateral negotiation. *Organizational Behavior and Human Performance*, 37, 1–13.

Carnevale, P. and Lawler, E. J. (1986) Time pressure and the development of integrative agreements in bilateral negotiations. *Journal of Conflict Resolution*, 3(30), 636–59.

Carranza, M. E. (2005) Poster child or victim of imperialist globalization? Explaining Argentina's December 2001 political crisis and economic collapse. *Latin American Perspectives*, 32(6), 65–89.

Carter, C. C. (1999) *Cross-cultural conflict resolution: Obtaining just agreements*. Washington, DC: American Sociological Association, Sociological Abstracts.

Chaney, J. S. (1999) Mediation for the masses: Pioneer of low-cost services rolls out ADR on the cheap in Southern California. *ABA Journal*, July, 20.

Chapman, S. (1978) *Story and Discourse: Narrative Structure in Fiction and Film*. Ithaca: Cornell University Press.

Chasek, P. (1997) A comparative analysis of multilateral environmental negotiations. *Group Decision and Negotiation*, 6, 437–61.

Cheldelin, S. I. (2000) Handling resistance to change. In *Leading Academic Change: Essential Roles for Department Chairs*, edited by A. F. Lucas and Associates. San Francisco: Jossey-Bass.

Cheldelin, S. (2006) Engaging law, community, and victims in dialogue: From conflict to shared understanding. *Ohio State Journal on Dispute Resolution, 22*(1), 9–36.

Cheldelin, S., Jakobsen, M., and Yuille, D. (2007). *A Consensus Among Stakeholders: A Call for Change in Virginia's Involuntary Civil Commitment Process*. Unpublished white-paper available from author, 1–106.

Chigas, D., with McClintock, E. and Kamp, C. (1996) Preventive diplomacy and the Organization for Security and Cooperation in Europe: Creating incentives for dialogue and cooperation. In *Pre-

venting Conflict in the Post-Communist World: Mobilizing International and Regional Organizations, edited by A. Chayes and A. H. Chayes. Washington, DC: The Brookings Institution.

Chomsky, N. (1959) Verbal behavior. *Language*, 35, 26–58.

Christiansen, R. (1996) *Paris Babylon: The Story of the Paris Commune*. New York: Penguin.

Christie, D. J., Wagner, R. V., and Winter, D. (2001) Introduction to peace psychology. In *Peace, Conflict, and Violence: Peace Psychology for the 21st Century*. Upper Saddle River, NJ: Prentice Hall.

Clapham, C. (2002) Problems of peace enforcement: Lessons to be drawn from multinational peacekeeping operations in ongoing conflicts in Africa. In *Africa in Crisis*, edited by T. Zack-Williams et al. (pp. 196–215). London: Pluto Press.

Clegg, S. (1989) *Frameworks of Power*. London; Newbury Park: Sage Publications.

Clements, K. P. (1997) Peace building and conflict transformation. *Peace and Conflict Studies*, 4(1), 3–13.

Cleveland, S. E. (1971) Psychological intervention in a community crisis. In *Advances in Experimental Clinical Psychology*, edited by H. E. Admans and W. K. Boardman. New York: Pergamon.

Clifford, J. (1988) *The Predicament of Culture: Twentieth Century Ethnography, Literature and Art*. Cambridge: Cambridge University Press.

Clifford, J. and Marcus, G. E. (1986) *Writing Culture: The Poetics and Politics of Ethnography*. Berkeley: University of California Press.

CMG (1994) Methods and strategies in conflict prevention. Working Paper Series (Project on Preventive Diplomacy and Conflict Management in Europe). Cambridge, MA: Conflict Management Group.

Cobb, S. (1994a) A narrative perspective on mediation: Towards the materialization of the "storytelling" metaphor. In *New Directions in Mediation: Communication Research and Perspectives* edited by J. P. Folger and T. S. Jones (pp. 48–63). Thousand Oaks: Sage.

Cobb, S. (1994b) Theories of responsibility: The social construction of intentions in mediation. *Discourse Processes*, 18(2), 165–186.

Cobb, S. (1997) The domestication of violence in mediation. *Law and Society Review*, 31(3), 397–440.

Cobb, S. (2001). Creating sacred space: Toward a second-generation dispute resolution practice. *Dialogue on the Practice of Law and Spiritual Values*, 28(4), 1017–1033.

Cobb, S. (2003) Fostering coexistence in identity-based conflicts. In *Imagine Coexistence: Restoring Humanity after Violent Ethnic Conflict*, edited by A. H. Chayes and M. Minow (1st edn, pp. 294–310). San Francisco: Jossey-Bass.

Cobb, S. (2006) A developmental approach to turning points: "Irony" as an ethics for negotiation pragmatics. *Harvard Negotiation Law Review*, 11, 147–97.

Cobb, S. and Rifkin, J. (1991) Practice and paradox: Deconstructing neutrality in mediation. *Law and Social Inquiry*, 35–62.

Cohen, A. (1969) *Custom and Politics in Urban Africa*. Berkeley: University of California Press.

Cohen, A. (1974) *Two-Dimensional Man*. Berkeley: University of California Press.

Cohen, O., Luxenburg, A., Dattner, N., and Matz, D. (1999) Suitability of divorcing couples for mediation: A suggested typology. *American Journal of Family Therapy*, 27, 329–44.

Cohen, R. (1990) *Culture and Conflict in Egyptian–Israeli Relations: A Dialogue of the Deaf*. Bloomington: Indiana University Press.

Cohen, R. (1997) *Negotiating Across Cultures*, (revised edn). Washington, DC: U.S. Institute of Peace Press.

Cohen, S. P. and Azar, E. E. (1981) From war to peace: The transition between Egypt and Israel. *Journal of Conflict Resolution*, 25, 87–114.

Cohn, B. S. (1984) The census, social structure, and objectification in South Asia. *Folk*, 25, 25–49.

Coleman, J. S. (1957) *Community Conflict*. New York: The Free Press.

Collier, P., Elliott, V. L., Hegre, H., Hoeffler, A., Reynal-Querol, M., and Sambanis, N. (2003) *Breaking the Conflict Trap: Civil War and Development Policy*. Washington, DC: The World Bank; New York: Oxford University Press.

Collins, A. M. and Quillian, M. R. (1972) Experiments on semantic memory and language comprehension. In *Cognition and Learning*, edited by L. W. Gregg. New York: John Wiley & Sons.

Conlon, D. E., Carnevale, P., and Ross, W. H. (1994) The influence of third party power and suggestions on negotiation: The surface value of a compromise. *Journal of Applied Social Psychology*, 24, 1084–113.

Cook, S. W. (1984) The 1954 Social Science Statement and school desegregation: A reply to Gerard. *American Psychologist*, 39, 819–32.

Cook, T. D. and Campbell, D. T. (1979) *Quasi-Experimentation: Design and Analysis Issues for Social Research in Field Settings*. Boston: Houghton Mifflin.

Cook-Deegan, R. (2001) Hype and hope: A spate of new books seek to interpret quandries posed by our genomic future. *American Scientist*, January–February, 62–4.

Cooks, L. M. (1995) Putting mediation in context. *Negotiation Journal*, 11(2), 91–101.

Cooper, C. (1999) *Mediation and Arbitration by Patrol Police Officers*. New York: University Press of America.

Cooper, C. (2001) Mediation in black and white: Mediation center-police partnerships—a dignified police response. *Mediation Quarterly*, 18(3), 281–95.

Cooper, D. (1995) *Power in Struggle*. New York: New York University Press.

Cooperrider, D. L. (1990) Positive image, positive action: The affirmative basis of organizing. In *Appreciative Management and Leadership*, edited by S. Srivastva and D. L. Cooperrider. San Francisco: Jossey-Bass.

Cooperrider, D. L. and Srivastva, S. (1987) Appreciative inquiry in organizational life. In *Research in Organizational Change and Development*, edited by R. W. Woodman and W. A. Pasmore. Greenwich, CT: JAI Press.

Coser, L. A. (1956) *The Functions of Social Conflict*. New York: The Free Press.

Coser, L. A. (1964) *Sociological Theory*. New York: Random House.

Coser, L. A. (1967) *Continuities in the Study of Social Conflict*. New York: The Free Press.

Coser, L. A. (1968) Social aspects. In *International Encyclopedia of the Social Sciences*, edited by D. Sills. New York: Crowell Collier and Macmillan.

Cousens, E. M. (2001) Introduction. In *Peacebuilding as Politics: Cultivating Peace in Fragile Societies*, edited by E. M. Cousens and C. Kumar, with K. Wermester. London: Lynne Rienner.

Craver, C. B. (1999) Mediation: A trial lawyer's guide. *Trial: Negotiation and Settlement*, June, 37–45.

Creswell, J. W. (1998) *Qualitative Inquiry and Research Design: Choosing Among Five Traditions*. Thousand Oaks, CA: Sage.

Crocker, C. A. (1999) Central Africa needs a new momentum for peace. *International Herald Tribune*, August 7–8, p. 8.

Crookall, D. and Arai, K. (1995) *Simulation and Gaming Across Disciplines and Cultures*. Thousand Oaks, CA: Sage.

Cucolo, A. A. III. (1998) *Grunt Diplomacy: The Role of the Military as a Third Party Actor in Peacebuilding*. Carlisle Barracks, PA: U.S. Army War College.

Curle, A. (1971) *Making Peace*. London: Tavistock.

Czarniawska, B. (2004) *Narratives in Social Science Research*. London: Sage.

D'Andrade, R. (1992) Schemas and motivation. In *Human Motives and Cultural Models*, edited by R. D'Andrade and C. Strauss. Cambridge: Cambridge University Press.

D'Andrade, R. (1995) *The Development of Cognitive Anthropology*. Cambridge: Cambridge University Press.

Dahrendorf, R. A. (1958) Toward a theory of social conflict. *Journal of Conflict Resolution,* 2, 170–83.

Dahrendorf, R. A. (1959) *Class and Class Conflict in Industrial Society.* Stanford, CA: Stanford University Press.

Daly, J. P. (1991) The effects of anger on negotiations over mergers and acquisitions. *Negotiation Journal,* 7, 31–9.

Davidson, W. D. and Montville, J. V. (1981–82) Foreign policy according to Freud. *Foreign Policy,* 45, 145–57.

Davies, B., & Harré, R. (1990) *Positioning: The Discursive Production of Selves* [Electronic Version], 2007, 'Positioning' and its dynamics, para 2. from *http://www.massey.ac.nz/%7Ealock/position/posi-tion.htm*

Davies, J. C. (1997) *When Men Revolt and Why.* New Brunswick, NJ: Transaction Publications.

Davis, P. W. (1991) Stranger intervention into child punishment in public places. *Social Problems,* 38 (2), 227–46.

Davis, P. W. (2000) *Making it their Business: Public Intervention Work during Intimate Violence.* Unpublished paper, Department of Sociology, Georgia State University.

Deetz, S. (1994) The new politics of the workplace. In *After Postmodernism,* edited by H. Simons and M. Billing. London: Sage.

De La Rey, C. (2001) Reconciliation in divided societies. In *Peace, Conflict, and Violence: Peace Psychology for the 21st Century,* edited by D.J. Christie, R. V. Wagner, and D. D. Winter. Upper Saddle River, NJ: Prentice Hall.

Delgado, R. and Stefancic, J. (1997) *Critical White Studies: Looking Behind the Mirror.* Philadelphia: Temple University Press.

Denzin, N. K. (1992) *Symbolic Interactionism and Cultural Studies.* Oxford: Blackwell.

Denzin, N. K. and Lincoln, Y. S. (eds) (1998) *The Landscape of Qualitative Research: Theories and Issues.* Thousand Oaks, CA: Sage.

De Reuck, A. V. S. (1983) The theory of conflict resolution by problem solving. *Man, Environment, Space and Time,* 3(1), 53–69.

d'Estree, Tamra Pearson and Colby, Bonnie B.G. (2004) *Braving the Currents: Evaluating Environmental Conflict Resolution in the River Basins of the American West.* Norwell, MA: Kluwer Academic Publishers.

d'Estrée, T. P. and Colby, B. B.G. (2004) *Braving the Currents: Evaluating Environmental Conflict Resolution in the River Basins of the American West.* Norwell, MA: Kluwer Academic Publishers.

Derluguian, G. M. (n.d.) *Parades, Prayer, Patrol: Sources and Constraints of the Reinvented Kuban Cossacks.* Unpublished manuscript.

Derluguian, G. M. (2005) *Bourdieu's Secret Admirer in the Caucasus: A World-System Biography.* Chicago: University of Chicago Press.

Deutsch, K. W. (1954) *Political Community at the International Level.* Garden City, NY: Doubleday.

Deutsch, K. (1961) Social mobilization and political development. *American Political Science Review,* 55(3), 493–514.

Deutsch, M. (1973) *The Resolution of Conflict: Constructive and Destructive Processes.* New Haven: Yale University Press.

Deutsch, M. (1980) Fifty years of conflict. In *Retrospections on Social Psychology,* edited by L. Festinger. New York: Oxford University Press.

Deutsch, M. (1982) Conflict resolution: Theory and practice. *Political Psychology,* 4(3), 431–52.

Deutsch, M. (1983) The prevention of World War III: A psychological perspective. *Political Psychology,* 4(1), 3–31.

Deutsch, M. (1986) The malignant (spiral) process of hostile interaction. In *Psychology and the Prevention of Nuclear War,* edited by R. K. White. New York: New York University Press.

Deutsch, M. and Coleman, P. T. (eds) (2000) *The Handbook of Conflict Resolution.* San Francisco: Jossey-Bass.

Deutsch, M. and Krause, R. M. (1962) Studies of interpersonal bargaining. *Journal of Conflict Resolution,* 6, 52–76.

Diamond, L. and McDonald, L. (1996) *Multi-Track Diplomacy: A Systems Approach to Peace* (3rd edn). West Hartford, CT: Kumarian Press.

Diamond, S. (1970) The rule of law versus the order of custom. *Social Research* 38, 42–71.

Diehl, P. F., Druckman, D., and Wall, J. A. (1998) International peacekeeping and conflict resolution: A taxonomic analysis with implications. *Journal of Conflict Resolution,* 42(1), 33–55.

Dillon, P. A. and Emery, R. E. (1996) Divorce mediation and resolution of child custody disputes: Long term effects. *American Journal of Orthopsychiatry,* 66, 131–40.

Docherty, J. (1998) *When the Parties Bring their Gods to the Table: Learning Lessons from Waco.* Unpublished doctoral dissertation, George Mason University.

Dollar, D. and Kraay, A. (2000) Growth is good for the poor. *Journal of Economic Growth* (policy research working paper no. 2587).

Dollard, J., Doob, L. W., Miller, N. E., Mowrer, O. H., and Sears, R. R. (1939) *Frustration and Aggression.* New Haven, CT: Yale University Press. Abridged and reprinted in *The Dynamics of Aggression: Individual, Group, and International Analyses* (1970), edited by E. I. Megargee and J. E. Hokanson. New York; London: Harper and Row.

Dominguez, V. R. (1986) *White by Definition: Social Classification in Creole Louisiana.* New Brunswick, NJ: Rutgers University Press.

Doob, L. W. (ed) (1970) *Resolving Conflict in Africa: The Fermeda Workshop*. New Haven, CT: Yale University Press.

Doob, L. W. and Foltz, W. (1974) The Belfast workshop: An application of group techniques to a destructive conflict. *Journal of Conflict Resolution*, 18, 489–512.

Dougherty, J.M (2006) *The Critical Mass of Social Change: Northern Ireland Integrated Education*. Unpublished doctoral dissertation, George Mason University, Fairfax, Virginia.

Druckman, D. (1967) Dogmatism, prenegotiation experience, and simulated group representation as determinants of dyadic behavior in a bargaining situation. *Journal of Personality and Social Psychology*, 6, 279–90.

Druckman, D. (1968) Prenegotiation experience and dyadic conflict resolution in a bargaining situation. *Journal of Experimental Social Psychology*, 4, 367–83.

Druckman, D. (1971) The influence of the situation in inter-party conflict. *Journal of Conflict Resolution*, 15, 523–54.

Druckman, D. (1977) Boundary role conflict: Negotiation as dual responsiveness. *Journal of Conflict Resolution*, 21, 639–62.

Druckman, D. (ed) (1977) *Negotiations: Social-Psychological Perspectives*. Beverly Hills, CA: Sage.

Druckman, D. (1983) Social psychology and international negotiations: Processes and influences. In *Advances in Applied Social Psychology*, edited by R. F. Kidd and M. J. Saks (vol. 2). Hillsdale, NJ: Erlbaum.

Druckman, D. (1986) Stages, turning points, and crises: Negotiating military base rights, Spain and the United States. *Journal of Conflict Resolution*, 30, 327–60.

Druckman, D. (1990). The social psychology of arms control and reciprocation. *Political Psychology*, 11, 553–581.

Druckman, D. (1990a) Three cases of base-rights negotiations: Lessons learned. In *U.S. Bases Overseas*, edited by J. W. McDonald and D. B. Bendahmane. Boulder, CO: Westview.

Druckman, D. (1993) The situational levers of negotiating flexibility. *Journal of Conflict Resolution*, 37, 236–276.

Druckman, D. (1994) Compromising behavior in negotiation: A meta-analysis. *Journal of Conflict Resolution*, 38, 507–556.

Druckman, D. (1994a) Tools for discovery: Experimenting with simulations. *Simulation & Gaming*, 25, 446–55.

Druckman, D. (1995). Situational levers of position change: Further explorations. *The Annals of the American Academy of Political and Social Science*, 542, 61–80.

Druckman, D. (1996) Is there a U.S. negotiating style? *International Negotiation*, 1(2), 327–34.

Druckman, D. (1997). Dimensions of international negotiations: Structures, processes, and outcomes. *Group Decision and Negotiation*, 6, 395–420.

Druckman, D. (1997a) Negotiating in the international context. In *Peacemaking in International Conflict*, edited by I. W. Zartman and I. L. Ramussen. Washington, DC: United States Institution of Peace Press.

Druckman, D. (1999) *The Role of the Leader in International Relations: Challenging Person-Centered Analyses of Political Behavior*. Davis Occasional Papers No. 69, Hebrew University of Jerusalem.

Druckman, D. (2000) Frameworks, techniques, and theory: Contributions of research consulting in social science. *American Behavioral Scientist*, 43, 1635–66.

Druckman, D. (2000) *International Conflict Resolution: After the Cold War*. Washington, DC: National Academy Press.

Druckman, D. (2001). Turning points in international negotiation: A comparative analysis. *Journal of Conflict Resolution*, 45, 519–544.

Druckman, D. (2001a) Nationalism and war: A social-psychological perspective. In *Peace, Conflict, and Violence: Peace Psychology in the 21st Century*, edited by D. J. Christie, D. V. Wagner, and D. Du Nann Winter. Saddle River, NJ: Prentice Hall.

Druckman, D. (2001b) Negotiation and identity: Implications for negotiation theory. *International Negotiation*, 6, 281–91.

Druckman, D. (2004) Departures in negotiation: Extensions and new directions. *Negotiation Journal* 20(2), 185–204.

Druckman, D. (2005) *Doing Research: Methods of Inquiry for Conflict Analysis*. Thousand Oaks, CA: Sage.

Druckman, D. (2006) A marathon exercise. In *The Negotiator's Fieldbook: The Desk Reference for the Experienced Negotiator*, edited by A.K. Schneider and C. Honeyman. Washington DC: American Bar Association.

Druckman, D. and Bjork, R. A. (eds) (1994) *Learning, Remembering, Believing: Enhancing Human Performance*. Washington, DC: National Academy Press.

Druckman, D. and Bonoma, T. V. (1976) Determinants of bargaining behavior in a bilateral monopoly situation II: Opponent's concession rate and similarity. *Behavioral Science*, 21, 252–62.

Druckman, D. and Bonoma, T. V. (1977) A conflict resolution workshop for health service-delivery professionals: Design and appraisal. *International Journal of Group Tensions*, 7, 1–28.

Druckman, D. and Druckman, J. N. (1996) Visibility and negotiating flexibility. *Journal of Social Psychology*, 136, 117–20.

Druckman, D. and Harris, R. (1990) Alternative models of responsiveness in international negotiation. *Journal of Conflict Resolution*, 34, 234–51.

Druckman, D. and Hopmann, P. T. (1989) Behavioral aspects of negotiations on mutual security. In *Behavior, Society, and Nuclear War*, edited by P. E. Tetlock et al. New York: Oxford University Press.

Druckman, D. and Robinson, V. (1998) From research to application: Utilizing research findings in negotiation training programs. *International Negotiation*, 3, 7–38.

Druckman, D. and Stern, P. C. (1997) Evaluating peacekeeping missions. *Mershon International Studies Review*, 41, 151–65.

Druckman, D. and Zechmeister, K. (1973) Conflict of interest and value dissensus: Propositions in the sociology of conflict. *Human Relations*, 26, 449–66.

Druckman, D., Broome, B. J., and Korper, S. H. (1988) Value differences and conflict resolution: Facilitation or delinking? *Journal of Conflict Resolution*, 32, 489–510.

Druckman, D., Husbands, J. L., and Johnston, K. (1991) Turning points in the INF negotiations. *Negotiation Journal*, 7, 55–67.

Druckman, D., Martin, J. A., Nan, S., and Yagcioglu, D. (1999b) Dimensions of international negotiation: A test of Ikle's typology. *Group Decision and Negotiation*, 8, 89–108.

Druckman, D., Ramberg B., and Harris, R. (2002) Computer-assisted international negotiation: A tool for research and practice. *Group Decision and Negotiation*, 11, 231–56.

Druckman, D., Rozelle, R. M., and Zechmeister, K. (1977) Conflict of interest and value dissensus: Two perspectives. In *Negotiations: Social-Psychological Perspectives*, edited by D. Druckman. Beverly Hills, CA: Sage.

Druckman, D., Wall, J., and Diehl, P. (1999) Conflict resolution roles in international peacekeeping missions. In *The New Agenda for Peace Research*, edited by H.-W. Jeong. Aldershot: Ashgate.

DuBow, F. L. and Currie, E. (1993) Police and "nonstranger" conflicts in a San Francisco neighborhood: Notes on mediation and intimate violence. In *The Possibility of Popular Justice*, edited by S.E. Merry and N. Milner. Ann Arbor: University of Michigan Press.

Duffield, M. (2000) Globalization, transborder trade, and war economies. In *Greed and Grievance: Economic Agendas in Civil Wars*, edited by M. Berdal and D. M. Malone. Boulder, CO: Lynne Rienner.

Dugan, M. A. (1996) The nested theory of conflict. *A Leadership Journal: Women in Leadership*, 1, 10–19.

Dundes, A. and Falassi, A. (1975) *La Terra in Piazza: An Interpretation of the Palio of Siena*. Berkeley: University of California Press.

Dukes, F. (1996) *Resolving Public Conflict*. Manchester: Manchester University Press.

Dukes, F. (1999) Structural forces in conflict and conflict resolution in democratic society. In *Conflict Resolution: Dynamics, Process, and Structure*, edited by H. W. Jeong. Brookfield, VT: Ashgate.

Durch, W. J. (ed) (1996) *UN Peacekeeping, American Politics, and the Uncivil Wars of the 1990s*. New York: St. Martin's Press.

Durch, W. J. et al. (2003) *The Brahimi Report and the Future of UN Peace Operations*. Washington DC: Henry L. Stimson Center.

Eade, D. (1999) Preface. In *From Conflict to Peace in a Changing World: Social Reconstruction in Times of Transition*, edited by D. Eade. Oxford: Oxfam.

Elliott, J. (2005) Using narrative in social research: qualitative and quantitative approaches. London; Thousand Oaks: Sage.

Ember, C. R. (1995) Universal and variable patterns of gender difference. In *Cross-Cultural Research for Social Science*, edited by C. R. Ember and M. Ember. Englewood Cliffs, NJ: Prentice Hall.

Ember, C. R. (1996) Gender differences and roles. In *Encyclopedia of Cultural Anthropology*, edited by M. Ember. New York: Henry Holt.

Ember, C. R. and Ember, M. (1992) Resource unpredictability, mistrust, and war: A cross-cultural study. *Journal of Conflict Resolution*, 36, 242–62.

Ember, C.R. and Ember M, (eds) (1995) *Cross Cultural Research for Social Science*. Englewood Cliffs, NJ: Prentice Hall.

Emerson, R. and Messinger, S. (1977) The micro-politics of trouble. *Social Problems*, 25, 121–34.

Engels, F. (1968) Origins of the family, private property, and the state. In *Selected Works of Karl Marx and Friedrich Engels*. New York: International Publishers.

Ericsson, K. A. (1998) Basic capacities can be modified or circumvented by deliberate practice: A rejection of talent accounts of expert performance. *Behavioral and Brain Sciences*, 21, 413–14.

Ericsson, K. A. (1999) Creative expertise as superior reproducible performance: Innovative and flexible aspects of expert performance. *Psychological Inquiry*, 10, 329–61.

Ericsson, K. A., Krampe, R. T., and Tesch-Romer, C. (1993) The role of deliberate practice in the acquisition of expert performance. *Psychological Review*, 100, 363–406.

Erikson, E. (1959) The problem of ego identity. *Psychological Issues*, 1, 101–64.

Etzioni, A. (1962) *The Hard Way to Peace*. New York: Collier Books.

Ewart, D. M., Yaccino, T. G., and Yaccino, D. M. (1994) Cultural diversity and self-sustaining development: The effective facilitator. *Journal of the Community Development Society*, 225(1), 20–33.

Falk, R. A. (1994, August) Unpublished remarks at Conference on World Order, University of Malta.

Fairclough, N. (1995) *Critical Discourse Analysis: The Critical Study of Language*. London; New York: Longman.

Faure, A. M. (1994) Some methodological problems in comparative politics. *Journal of Theoretical Politics*, 6, 307–22.

Faure, G. O. and Rubin, J. Z. (eds) (1993) *Culture and Negotiation*. Newbury Park, CA: Sage.

Festinger, L. (1954) A theory of social comparison processes. *Human Relations*, 7, 117–40.

Festinger, L. (1962) *A Theory of Cognitive Dissonance*. Stanford, CA: Stanford University Press.

Festinger, L., Schacter, S., and Back, K. (1950) *Social Pressure in Informal Groups*. New York: Harper.

Fetherston, B. (1994) *Towards a Theory of United Nations Peace-keeping*. London: Macmillan.

Fisher, R.J. (1972) Third party consultation: A method for the study and resolution of conflict. *Journal of Conflict Resolution*, 16(1), 67–94.

Fisher, R.J. (1980) A third-party consultation workshop on the India-Pakistan conflict. *Journal of Social Psychology*, 112, 191–206.

Fisher, R.J. (1983) Third party consultation as a method of intergroup conflict resolution: A review of studies. *Journal of Conflict Resolution*, 27(2), 301–34.

Fisher, R. J. (1990) Social-psychological approaches for resolving intergroup and international conflict. In *The Social Psychology of Intergroup and International Conflict Resolution*, edited by R. J. Fisher. New York: Springer-Verlag.

Fisher, R. J. (1991) *Conflict Analysis Workshop on Cyprus: Final Workshop Report*. Ottawa: Canadian Institute for International Peace and Security.

Fisher, R. J. (1996) *Interactive Problem Solving*. Syracuse, NY: Syracuse University Press.

Fisher, R. J. (1997a) *Interactive Conflict Resolution*. Syracuse, NY: Syracuse University Press.

Fisher, R.J. (1997b) Interactive conflict resolution. In *Peacemaking in International Conflict: Methods and Techniques*, edited by I. W. Zartman and J. L. Rasmussen (p. 258). Washington, DC: U.S. Institute of Peace Press.

Fisher, R. J. (1999) Social-psychological processes in interactive conflict analysis and reconciliation. In *Conflict Resolution: Dynamics, Process and Structure*, edited by H.-W. Jeong. Aldershot: Ashgate.

Fisher, R. J. and Keashly, L. (1990) Toward a contingency approach of third party intervention in regional conflict: A Cyprus illustration. *International Journal*, 45, 424–53.

Fisher, R. J. (ed) (2005) *Paving the Way; Contributions of Interactive Conflict Resolution to Peacemaking*. Lanhan, MD: Lexington Books.

Fisher, R. J. and Keashly, L. (1991) The potential complementarity of mediation and consultation within a contingency model of third party intervention. *Journal of Peace Research*, 28(1), 29–42.

Fisher, S., Ibrahim Abdi, D., Ludin, J. L., Smith, R., Williams, S. and Williams, S. (2000) *Working with Conflict, Skills and Strategies for Action*. New York: St. Martin's Press.

Fisher, R. and Ury, W. with B. Patton (eds) (1991) *Getting to Yes: Negotiating Agreement Without Giving In* (2nd edn). New York: Penguin Books.

Fiske, S. T. and Taylor, S. E. (1984) *Social Cognition* (2nd edn) Reading, MA: Addison-Wesley Publishing. New York: McGraw-Hill, 1991.

Fitgerald, F. (1972) *Fire in the Lake: The Vietnamese and the Americans in Vietnam*. New York: Vintage Books.

Fleitz, F. H. Jr. (2002), *Peacekeeping Fiascos of the 1990s: Causes, Solutions and U.S. Interests*. Westport, CT: Praeger.

Follett, M. P. (1942) *Dynamic Administration: The Collected Papers of Mary Parker Follett*, edited by H. C. Whitbeck. Illinois: Moore Publishing.

Foster, R. F. (1997) *W. B. Yeats: A Life. Vol. 1, The Apprentice Mage*. New York: Oxford University Press.

Foucault, M. (1972) *The Archaeology of Knowledge*. New York: Pantheon Books.

Foucault, M. (1978) *Discipline and Punish*. New York: Pantheon Books.

Fox, R. G. (ed) (1990) *Nationalist Ideologies and the Production of National Cultures*. Washington, DC: American Anthropological Association.

Frankfort-Nachmias, C. and Nachmias, D. (1996) *Research Methods in the Social Sciences* (5th edn) New York: St. Martin's Press.

Frederiksen, N. (1971, September) *Toward a Taxonomy of Situations*. Paper presented at the annual meeting of the American Psychological Association, Washington, DC.

Freire, P. (1998) *Pedagogy of the Oppressed*. New York: Continuum.

French, M. (1994) Power/sex. In *Power/Gender: Social Relations Theory and Practice*, edited by H. Radtke, H. Lorraine, and J. Henderikus. London: Sage.

Freud, S. (1915/1957) Repression. In *The Standard Edition of the*

Complete Psychological Works of Sigmund Freud, edited by J. Strachey. London: Hogarth Press.

Fuller, L. L. (1958) Positivism and fidelity to law – a reply to Professor Hart. *Harvard Law Review,* 71, 630.

Fuller, L. L. (1978) The forms and limits of adjudication. *Harvard Law Review,* 92, 353.

Funk & Wagnells Standard Dictionary of the English Language: International Edition (1965) Chicago: Encyclopedia Britannica.

Gadlin, H. (1994) Conflict resolution, cultural differences, and the culture of racism. *Negotiation Journal,* 10(1), 33–47.

Galtung, J. (1964) A structural theory of aggression. *Journal of Peace Research,* 1, 95–119. Reprinted in *Conflict Resolution: Contributions of the Behavioral Sciences* (1971), edited by C. G. Smith. Notre Dame, IN; London: University of Notre Dame Press.

Galtung, J. (1969) Violence, peace and peace research. *Journal of Peace Research,* 6(3), 167–91.

Galtung, J. (1971) Structural theory of imperialism. *Journal of Peace Research,* 8(2), 81–117.

Galtung, J. (1975) Violence, peace, and peace research. In *Essays in Peace Research, Vol. 1. Peace: Research, Education, Action.* Copenhagen: Christian Ejlers.

Galtung, J. (1990) Cultural violence. *Journal of Peace Research,* 27(3), 291–305.

Galtung, J. (1996) *Peace By Peaceful Means: Peace and Conflict, Development and Civilization.* London; Thousand Oaks, CA: Sage.

Galtung, J. (2000) Leaving the twentieth century, entering the twenty first: Some basic conflict formations. In *Searching for Peace: The Road to TRANSCEND,* edited by J. Galtung and C. G. Jacobsen. London: Pluto Press.

Galtung, J. and Jacobsen, C. G. (2000) *Searching for Peace: The Road to TRANSCEND.* London: Pluto Press.

Galtung, J. and Tschudi, F. (2001) Crafting peace: On the psychology of the TRANSCEND approach. In *Peace, Conflict, and Violence: Peace Psychology for the 21st Century,* edited by D. J. Christie, R. V. Wagner, and D. D. Winter. Upper Saddle River, NJ: Prentice Hall.

Gamson, W. A. (1996) Rancorous conflict in community politics. *American Sociological Review,* 31, 71–81.

Gardiner, J. K. (ed) (1995) *Provoking Agents: Gender and Agency.* Champaign: University of Illinois Press.

Garver, R. (1997) *Restoration of Public Security: The Linchpin in Peacebuilding and Post-conflict Operations.* Carlisle Barracks, PA: U.S. Army War College.

Gastil, J. (1993) *Democracy in Small Groups*. Philadelphia: New Society Publishers.

Geertz, C. (1983) Thick description: Toward an interpretive theory of culture. In *Contemporary Field Research*, edited by R. Emerson. Boston: Little Brown Publishers.

Gelfand, M. and Realo, A. (1999) Individualism-collectivism and accountability in intergroup negotiations. *Journal of Applied Psychology*, 64, 721–36.

George, A. (1979) Case studies and theory development: The method of structured, focused comparison. In *Diplomacy: New Approaches in History, Theory and Policy*, edited by P. G. Lauren. New York: The Free Press.

Gerber, E. and de la Puente, M. (1996) The development and cognitive testing of race and ethnic origin questions for the year 2000 decennial census. *Proceedings of the Bureau of the Census' 1996 Annual Research Conference*, Rosslyn, Virginia.

Gergen, K. J. (1977) The social construction of self-knowledge. In *The Self: Psychological and Biological Issues*, edited by T. Mischel. Totowa, NJ: Rowman & Littlefield.

Gergen, K. J. (1985) The social constructionist movement in modern psychology. *American Psychologist*, 40(3), 266–75.

Gergen, K. J. and Gergen, M. M. (1986). Narrative form and the construction of psychological science. In T. R. Sarbin (ed.), *Narrative Psychology: The Storied Nature of Human Conduct* (pp. 22–44). New York: Praeger.

Gergen, K. J. and Gergen, M. M. (1988) Narrative and the self as relationship. In *Advances in Experimental Social Psychology*, edited by L. Berkowitz (vol. 21) New York: Academic Press.

Gibson, K., Thompson, L., and Bazerman, M. H. (1996) Shortcomings of neutrality in mediation: Solutions based on rationality. *Negotiation Journal*, 12 (January 1), 69–80.

Giddens, A. (1986) *The Constitution of Society*. Berkeley: University of California Press.

Giddens, A. (1990) *The Consequences of Modernity*. Stanford: Stanford University Press.

Gilles C. (1998) *Conflict, Postwar Rebuilding and the Economy: A Critical Review of the Literature*. War-Torn Societies Project Occasional Paper no. 2, UNRISD, Geneva.

Ginifer, J. (ed) (1997) *Beyond the Emergency: Development Within UN Peace Missions*. London: Frank Cass.

Gissinger, R. and Gleditsch, N. P. (1999) Globalization and conflict: Welfare, distribution and political unrest. *Journal of World-Systems Research*, 2.

Gladstein, D. L. (1984) Groups in context: A model of task group effectiveness. *Administrative Sciences Quarterly*, 29, 499–517.

Glaser, B. G. and Strauss, A. L. (1967) *The Discovery of Grounded Theory: Strategies for Qualitative Research*. New York: Aldine Publishing Company.

Gledistch, K. S. (2007) Transnational dimensions of civil wars. *Journal of Peace Research*.

Goffman, E. (1959) *The Presentation of Self in Everyday Life*. Garden City, NY: Doubleday.

Goffman, E. (1970) *Asylums*. Garden City, NY: Doubleday.

Goffman, E. (1971) *Relations in Public*. New York: Harper & Row.

Goldberg, S., Sander, F., and Rogers, N. (1999) *Dispute Resolution: Negotiation, Mediation, and Other Processes* (3rd edn). Gaithersburg, NY: Aspen Law and Business.

Goodhand, J. and Hulme, D. (1997) *NGOs and Peacebuilding in Complex Political Emergencies: An Introduction*. Working paper, Institute for Development Policy Management, University of Manchester.

Gopin, M. (2000) *Between Eden and Armageddon: The Future of World Religions, Violence, and Peacemaking*. New York: Oxford University Press.

Goulding, M. (1993) The evolution of UN peacekeeping. *International Affairs*, 69(3), 451–64.

Goulding, M. (2002) *Peacemonger*. London: John Murray.

Gouldner, A. W. (1960) The norm of reciprocity: A preliminary statement. *American Sociological Review*, 25, 161–78.

Gramsci, A. (1971) *Selections from the Prison Notebooks of Antonio Gramsci*, translated and edited by Q. Hoare and G. Nowell Smith. New York: International Publishers.

Gramsci, A. (1985) *Selections from Cultural Writings*. Oxford: Oxford University Press.

Gray, B. (1989). *Collaborating: Finding Common Ground for Multiparty Problems* (1st edn). San Francisco: Jossey-Bass.

Greenhouse, C. (1986) *Praying for Justice: Faith, Order, and Community in an American Town*. Ithaca, NY: Cornell University Press.

Greeno, J. G., Smith, D. R., and Moore, J. R. (1993) Transfer of situated learning. In *Transfer on Trial: Intelligence, Cognition, and Instruction*, edited by D. K. Detterman and R. J. Sternberg. Norwood, NJ: Ablex.

Griffiths, A. L. (ed) (1998) *Building Peace and Democracy in Post-Conflict Societies*. Halifax: Center for Foreign Policy Studies, Dalhousie University.

Grignon, F. (2003, October 23-24) *The Artemis Operation in the*

Democratic Republic of Congo: Lessons for the Future of EU peace-keeping in Africa. Paper presented at the Challenges of Europe-Africa Relations: An Agenda of Priorities conference, Lisbon.

Guba, E. G. and Lincoln, Y. S. (1998) Competing paradigms in qualitative research. In *The Landscape of Qualitative Research: Theories and Issues*, edited by N. K. Denzin and Y. S. Lincoln. Thousand Oaks, CA: Sage.

Guéhenno, J. M. (2003) Everybody's doing it. *The World Today*, 59(8/9), 35–36.

Guetzkow, H. and Valadez, J. J. (1981) *Simulated International Processes: Theories and Research in Global Modeling.* Beverly Hills, CA: Sage.

Guevara, E. (1988) Latin American Marxism. In *Marxism: Essential Writings*, edited by D. McLellan. Oxford: Oxford University Press.

Guidry, J. A., Kennedy, M. D., and Zald, M. N. (eds) (2000) *Globalizations and Social Movements: Culture, Power, and the Transnational Public Sphere.* Ann Arbor: Michigan University Press.

Gunder Frank, A. (1966) The development of underdevelopment. *Monthly Review*, 18(4), 17–31.

Gurr, T. R. (1970) *Why Men Rebel.* Princeton, NJ: Princeton University Press.

Gurr, T. R. (1993) *Minorities at Risk: A Global View of Ethnopolitical Conflicts.* Washington, DC: U.S. Institute of Peace Press.

Gurr, T. R. (2000) *Peoples Versus States: Minorities at Risk in the New Century.* Washington, DC: U.S. Institute of Peace Press.

Habermas, J. (1987) *The Theory of Communicative Action* (vol. 1), translated by Thomas McCarthy. London: Heinemann.

Hajer, M. A. (1995). *The Politics of Environmental Discourse: Ecological Modernization and the Policy Process.* Oxford; New York: Clarendon Press; Oxford University Press.

Haley, J. O. (1995) Victim–offender mediation: Lessons from the Japanese experience. *Mediation Quarterly*, 12(3), 233–48.

Hall, E. (1976) *Beyond Culture.* New York: Anchor Books.

Halpern, J. (1994) The effect of friendship on personal business transactions. *Journal of Conflict Resolution*, 38, 647–64.

Hampson, F. O. (1996) *Nurturing Peace: Why Peace Settlements Succeed or Fail.* Washington, DC: U.S. Institute of Peace Press.

Hampson, F. O. and Aall, P. (eds) (1996) *Managing Global Chaos: Sources of and Responses to International Conflict.* Washington, DC: U.S. Institute of Peace Press.

Handler, R. (1988) *Nationalism and the Politics of Culture in Quebec.* Madison: University of Wisconsin Press.

Harford, T. and Solomon, L. (1967) Reformed sinner and lapsed saint strategies in the prisoner's dilemma game. *Journal of Conflict Resolution*, 11, 104–9.

Harré, R. and Slocum, N. (2003) Disputes as complex social events: On the uses of positioning theory. In *Peace and Mind: Seriatim Symposium on Dispute, Conflict, and Enmity Part 4: Secret Accomplices*, edited by C. Knowledge (vol. 9, pp. 100–18).

Harris, M. (1999) *Theories of Culture in Postmodern Times*. Walnut Creek, CA: Alta Mira Press.

Harris, K. L. and Carnevale, P. J. (1990) Chilling and hastening: The influence of third-party power and interests in negotiation. *Organizational Behavior and Human Decision Processes*, 47, 138–60.

Harris, P. and Reilly, B. (1999) *Electoral Systems and Conflict in Divided Societies*. Washington, DC: National Academic Papers on International Conflict Resolution, No. 2.

Hart, H. L. A. (1958) Positivism and the separation of law and morals. *Harvard Law Review*, 71, 593.

Hartshorne, H., May, M. A., and Shuttleworth, F. K. (1930) *Studies in the Nature of Character*. Vol. 2, Studies in the Organization of Character. New York: Macmillan.

Hastings, A. (1998) *The Construction of Nationhood: Ethnicity, Religion and Nationalism*. Cambridge: Cambridge University Press.

Hegre, H. (2002, August 23) *Some Social Requisites of a Democratic Civil Peace: Democracy, Development, and Armed Conflict*. Washington, DC: The World Bank.

Hegre, H., Gissinger, R., and Gleditsch, N. P. (2003) Globalization and internal conflict. In *Globalization and Conflict*, edited by G. Schneider, K. Barbieri, and N. P. Gleditsch. Boulder, CO: Rowman and Littlefield.

Hermann, M. G. (1995) Leaders, leadership, and flexibility: Influences on heads of government as negotiators and mediators. *Annals of the American Academy of Political and Social Science*, 542, 148–67.

Hermann, M. G. and Kogan, N. (1977) Effects of negotiators' personalities on negotiating behavior. In *Negotiations: Social-Psychological Perspectives*, edited by D. Druckman. Beverly Hills, CA: Sage.

Herrnstein, B. H. (1996) Women and mediation: A chance to speak and to be heard. *Mediation Quarterly*, 13(3), 229–41.

Hilty, J. and Carnevale, P. (1992) Black-hat/white-hat strategy in bilateral bargaining. *Organizational Behavior and Human Performance*, 55, 444–69.

Himes, J. S. (1980) *Conflict and Conflict Management*. Athens, GA: University of Georgia Press.

Hirsch, S. F. (1994) Kadhi's courts as complex sites of resistance: The state, Islam, and gender in postcolonial Kenya. In *Contested States:*

Law, Hegemony and Resistance, edited by M. Lazarus-Black and S. F. Hirsch. New York: Routledge.

Hirschsohn, P. (1996) Negotiating a democratic order in South Africa: Learning from mediation and industrial relations. *Negotiation Journal*, 12(2), 139–50.

HMSO (1995) *Wider Peacekeeping*. London: Ministry of Defence.

HMSO (2004) *The Military Contribution to Peace Support Operations*. Joint Warfare Publication 3-50 (2nd edn).

Hobsbawn, E. J. (1990) *Nations and Nationalism since 1780*. New York: Cambridge University Press.

Hobsbawm, E. J. and Ranger, T. (eds) (1983) *The Invention of Tradition*. Cambridge: Cambridge University Press.

Hocker, J. L. and Wilmot, W. W. (1995) *Interpersonal Conflict* (4th edn). Madison, WI: Brown & Benchmark.

Hoddie, M. (2006) Peace as a process. *International Studies Review*, 8, 315–17.

Hofstadter, R. (1948) *The American Political Tradition and the Men Who Made It*. New York: Vintage Books.

Hofstede, G. (1980) *Culture's Consequences: International Differences in Work Related Values*. Beverly Hills, CA: Sage.

Holbrooke, R. (1998) *To End a War*. New York: Random House.

Hollis, M. (1994) *The Philosophy of Social Science: An Introduction*. Cambridge: Cambridge University Press.

Holt, V. K. (2006) The military and civilian protection: Developing roles and capacities. In *Resetting the Rules of Engagement: Trends and Issues in Military-Humanitarian Relations*, edited by V. Wheeler and A. Harmer (pp. 53–66). London: Overseas Development Institute (HPG Report 21).

Homans, G. C. (1974) *Social Behaviour: Its Elementary Forms*, New York: Harcourt Brace and Jovanovic.

Homer-Dixon, T. and Blitt, J. (eds) (1998) *Ecoviolence: Links Among Environment, Population, and Security*. Lanham, MD: Rowman & Littlefield.

Honig, J. W. and Both, N. (1996) *Srebrenica: Record of a War Crime*. London: Penguin.

Hopmann, P. T. (1999) Building security in post-Cold War Eurasia: The OSCE and U.S. foreign policy. *Peaceworks*, 31, (September). Washington, DC: U.S. Institute of Peace.

Hopmann, P. T. (2000) The Organization for Security and Cooperation in Europe: Its contribution to conflict prevention and resolution. In *International Conflict Resolution After the Cold War*, edited by P. C. Stern and D. Druckman. Washington, DC: National Academy Press.

Hopmann, P. T. (2005) The OSCE response to 9/11. In *European*

Security after September 11 and the War in Iraq, edited by I. Cuthbertson and H. Gärtner. London: Palgrave/Macmillan.

Hopmann, P. T. and King, T. D. (1976) Interactions and perceptions in the Test-Ban Negotiations. *International Studies Quarterly*, 20, 105–42.

Hopmann, P. T. and Smith, T. C. (1978) An application of a Richardson process model: Soviet–American interactions in the Test Ban Negotiations, 1962–1963. In *The Negotiation Process: Theories and Applications*, edited by I. W. Zartman. Beverly Hills, CA: Sage.

Horkheimer, M. and Adorno, T. (1979) *Dialectic of Enlightenment*. London: Verso.

Horowitz, D. L. (1985) *Ethnic Groups in Conflict*. Berkeley: University of California Press.

Hovey, J. (1999) A pledge designed to forestall Y2K lawsuits. *Nation's Business*, (May) 28.

Human Security Report. (2005) Vancouver: The University of British Columbia. *http://www.humansecurityreport.info/content/view/28/63/*

Human Security Center (2005) *Human Security Report 2005: War and Peace in the Twenty-First Century*. New York: Oxford University Press.

Hume, C. (1994) *Ending Mozambique's War: The Role of Mediation and Good Offices*. Washington, DC: U.S. Institute of Peace Press.

Hunter, J. D. (1992) *Culture Wars: The Struggle to Define America*. New York: Basic Books.

Huntington, S. F. (1969) *Political Order in Changing Societies*. New Haven, CT: Yale University Press.

Huntington, S. P. (1996) *The Clash of Civilizations and the Remaking of World Order*. New York: Simon & Schuster.

Husserl, E. (1931) *Ideas: A General Introduction to Pure Phenomenology*, translated by W. R. B. Gibson. New York: Humanities Press. Originally published 1913.

Huyse, L. (2001) Dealing with the past and imaging in the future: Amnesty, truth, or prosecution? In *Peacebuilding, A Field Guide*, edited by L. Reychler and T. Paffenholz. Boulder, CO: Lynne Reinner.

Ignatiev, N. (1995) *How the Irish Became White*. New York: Routledge.

Ignatiev, N. (1996) *Race Traitor*. New York: Routledge.

Ikle, F. C. (1964) *How Nations Negotiate*. New York: Harper & Row.

Insko, C. A., Hoyle, R. H., Pinkley, R. L., Hong, G. Y., and Slim, R. M. (1988) Individual-group discontinuity: The role of a consensus rule. *Journal of Experimental Social Psychology*, 24, 505–19.

International Alert (2004) *Conflict-Sensitive Approaches to Develop-*

ment, Humanitarian Assistance and Peacebuilding: A Resource Pack. London: International Alert.

International Crisis Group (2003) *Building Bridges in Mostar.* ICG *Europe report no. 150. Retrieved January 28, 2007, from http:// www.crisisgroup.org/library/documents/europe/150_building_bridges_ mostar.pdf*

International Election Observation Mission (2006, October 1) *Statement of Preliminary Findings, Bosnia and Herzegovina.* Retrieved January 28, 2007, from *http://www.osce.org/documents/odihr/2006/10/ 20826_en.pdf*

International Labor Organization, World Commission on the Social Dimensions of Globalization (2004) *A Fair Globalization: Creating Opportunities for All.* Geneva: International Labor Organization.

Irmer, C.G. (2003). *The Promise of Process: Evidence on Ending Violent International Conflict.* Unpublished doctoral dissertation, George Mason University.

Isaacs, H. (1975) *Idols of the Tribe: Group Identity and Political Change.* Cambridge, MA: Harvard University Press.

Isaacs, W. (1999) *Dialogue and the Art of Thinking Together.* Doubleday

Ishiyama, J. (2004) Does globalization breed ethnic conflict? In *Nationalism and Ethnic Conflict*, edited by Michael Brown. Cambridge, MA: MIT.

Jabri, V. (1990) *Mediating Conflict: Decision-making and Western Intervention in Namibia.* Manchester: Manchester University Press.

Janis, I. L. (1982) *Groupthink: Psychological Studies of Policy Decisions and Fiascos.* Boston: Houghton Mifflin.

Jantsch, E. (1980) *The Self-organizing Universe: Scientific and Human Implications of the Emerging Paradigm of Evolution.* New York: Pergamon Press.

Jehn, K. A. (1994) Enhancing effectiveness: An investigation of advantages and disadvantages of value-based intergroup conflict. *International Journal of Conflict Management*, 5, 223–38.

Jenkins, R. (1997) *Rethinking Ethnicity: Arguments and Explorations.* London: Sage.

Jeong, H.-W. (1999) Research on conflict resolution. In *Conflict Resolution: Dynamics, Process and Structure*, edited by H.-W. Jeong. Aldershot: Ashgate.

Jeong, H.-W. (2000a) *Peace and Conflict Studies.* Aldershot: Ashgate.

Jeong, H.-W. (2000b) *Peace Building in Post-Conflict Societies: Processes and Strategies.* Italy: Department of International Cooperation, Government of the Region Emilia-Romagna.

Jeong, H.-W. (2005) *Peacebuilding in Postconflict Societies.* Boulder, CO: Lynne Rienner.

Jeong, H.-W. and Kakonen, J. (1999) Linking conflict to environmental security. In *The New Agenda for Peace Research*, edited by H.-W. Jeong. Aldershot: Ashgate.

Jeong, H.-W. and Vayrynen, T. (1999) Identity formation and transformation. In *Conflict Resolution: Dynamics, Process and Structure*. Jeong. Aldershot: Ashgate.

Jervis, R. (1976) *Perception and Misperception in International Politics*. Princeton, NJ: Princeton University Press.

Johnson, A. G. (1995) *The Blackwell Dictionary of Sociology*. Cambridge, MA: Blackwell.

Johnson, D. W. (1971) Effects of warmth of interaction, accuracy of understanding, and the proposal of compromise on listener's behavior. *Journal of Counseling Psychology*, 18, 207–16.

Johnson, D. and Sampson, C. (1994) *Religion, the Missing Dimension of Statecraft*. New York: Oxford University Press.

Johnston, L. M. (2000) *The Tobacco Dispute: A Study in the Use of Discourse and Narrative Theory in the Understanding of Health Related Conflicts*. Unpublished doctoral dissertation, Institute for Conflict Analysis and Resolution, George Mason University.

Johnstone, I. (2006) Dilemmas of robust peace operations. In *Annual Review of Global Peace Operations*. Boulder, CO.: Lynne Rienner.

Jorgensen, D. L. (1989) *Participant Observation: A Methodology for Human Studies*, edited by L. Bickman and D. J. Rog. Vol. 15, Applied Social Research Methods Series. Newbury Park, CA: Sage.

Juergensmeyer, M. (2000) *Terror in the Mind of God: The Global Rise of Religious Violence*. Berkeley: University of California Press.

Junne, G. and Verkoren, W. (eds) (2005) *Postconflict Development: Meeting New Challenges*. Boulder, CO: Lynne Rienner.

Kahl, Colin H. (2006) *States, Scarcity, and Civil Strife in the Developing World*. Princeton: Princeton University Press.

Kahn, H. (1969) *On Thermonuclear War* (2nd edn). New York: The Free Press.

Kapferer, B. (1988) *Legends of People, Myths of State: Violence, Intolerance, and Political Culture in Sri Lanka and Australia*. Washington, DC: Smithsonian Institution Press.

Kaplan, R. D. (1994) The coming anarchy. *Atlantic Monthly*, (February).

Karambayya, R. and Brett, J. M. (1989) Managers handling disputes: Third-party roles and perceptions of fairness. *Academy of Management Journal*, 32(4), 687–704.

Karambayya, R. and Brett, J. M. (1994) Managerial third parties: Intervention strategies, process, and consequences. In *New Directions in Mediation: Communication Research and Perspectives*, edited by J. P. Folger and T. S. Jones. Thousand Oaks, CA: Sage.

Kaufman, S. and Duncan, G. T. (1989) Third party intervention: A theoretical framework. In *Managing Conflict, an Interdisciplinary Approach*, edited by M. A. Rahim. New York: Praeger.

Keashley, L. and Fisher, R. J. (1996) A contingency perspective on conflict interventions. In *Resolving International Conflicts*, edited by J. Bercovitch. Boulder, CO: Lynne Rienner.

Keck, M. E. and Sikkink, K. (1998) *Activists Beyond Borders: Advocacy Networks in International Politics*. Ithaca, NY: Cornell University Press.

Keeva, S. (1999) When mediation doesn't work: Landmark civil rights ruling illustrates cases that offer no alternative to court. *ABA Journal* (October).

Kehoe, A. (1998) Legitimating the study of peace. *Human Peace*, 4, 1–4.

Kelleher, C. (1976) *Predilections in negotiations*. Unpublished manuscript, University of Maryland, College Park.

Kelley, H. H. and Schenitzki, D. P. (1972) Bargaining. In *Experimental Social Psychology*, edited by C. G. McClintock. New York: Holt.

Kelley, H. H. and Stahelski, A. J. (1970) Social interaction basis of cooperators' and competitors' beliefs about others. *Journal of Personality and Social Psychology*, 16, 190–7.

Kelly, J. B. (1993) Developing and implementing post divorce parenting plans: Does the forum make a difference? In *Non-custodial Parenting: New Vistas in Family Living*, edited by C. E. Depner and J. H. Bray. Newbury Park, CA: Sage.

Kelly, J. B. (1995) Power imbalance in divorce and interpersonal mediation: assessment and intervention. *Mediation Quarterly*, 13(2), 85–98.

Kelly, J. B. (1996) A decade of divorce mediation research: Some answers and questions. *Family and Conciliation Courts Review*, 34, 373–85.

Kelman, H. C. (1968) *A Time to Speak: On Human Values and Social Research*. San Francisco: Jossey-Bass.

Kelman, H. C. (1972) The problem-solving workshop in conflict resolution. In *Communication in International Politics*, edited by R. L. Merritt. Champaign Urbana: University of Illinois Press.

Kelman, H. C. (1976) The problem-solving workshop: a social-psychological contribution to the resolution of international conflicts. *Journal of Peace Research*, 13, 79–90.

Kelman, H. C. (1992) Informal mediation by the scholar/practitioner. In *Mediation in International Relations*, edited by J Bercovitch and J. Z. Rubin (pp. 64–96). New York: St. Martin's Press.

Kelman, H. C. (1996) The interactive problem solving approach. In *Managing Global Chaos*, edited by C. Crocker, F. O. Hampson, and P. Aall. Washington, DC: U.S. Institute of Peace Press.

Kelman, H. C. and Cohen, S. P. (1979) Reduction of international conflict: An interactional approach. In *The Social Psychology of Intergroup Relations*, edited by W. G. Austin and S. Worchel. Monterey, CA: Brooks/Cole.

Kelman, H. C. and Hamilton, V. L. (1989) *Crimes of Obedience: Toward a Social Psychology of Authority and Responsibility*. New Haven, CT: Yale University Press.

Kelman, H. C. and Warwick, D. P. (1978) The ethics of social intervention: Goals, means, and consequences. In *The Ethics of Social Intervention*, edited by G. Bermant, H. C. Kelman, and D. P. Warwick (pp. 3–33). Washington, DC: Hemisphere Publishing.

Kemp, W., Olejarnik, M., Ghebali, V., and Androsov, A. (1999) OSCE *Handbook*. Vienna, Austria: OSCE Secretariat.

Keyes, C. (1984) Tribal ethnicity and the state in Vietnam. *American Ethnologist*, 11, 176–82.

Kirtley, J. E. (1999) Freedom of information. *Quill* (March/April).

Kiser, A. G. (1998) *Masterful Facilitation: Becoming a Catalyst for Meaningful Change*. New York: AMACOM.

Kleiboer, M. (1994) Ripeness of conflict: A fruitful notion? *Journal of Peace Research*, 31(1), 109–16.

Klieboer, M. (1995) What role to play? Intermediaries in international conflict as negotiators and facilitators. *Journal of Contingencies and Crisis Management*, 3(4), 247–53.

Kleiboer, M. (1996) Understanding success and failure of international mediation. *Journal of Conflict Resolution*, 40(2), 360–89.

Kochman, T. (1981) *Black and White Styles in Conflict*. Chicago: University of Chicago Press.

Kolb, D. M. (1983) *The Mediators*. Cambridge, MA: NUT Press.

Kolb, D. M. (1984) *Experiential Learning: Experience as the Source of Learning and Development*. Englewood Cliffs, NJ: Prentice Hall.

Kolb, D. M. (1986) Who are organizational third parties and what do they do? In *Research on Negotiation in Organizations, Volume 1*, edited by R. I. Lewicki and B. H. Sheppard. Greenwich, CT: JAI Press.

Kolb, D. M. (1989) Labor mediators, managers, and ombudsmen: Roles mediators play in different contexts. In *Mediation Research: The Process and Effectiveness of Third-Party Intervention*, edited by K. Kressel and D. G. Pruitt. San Francisco: Jossey-Bass.

Kolb, D. M. (1992) Women's work: Peacemaking in organizations. In

Hidden Conflicts in Organizations, edited by D. M. Kolb and J. M. Bartunek. London: Sage.

Kolb, D. M. and Associates (1994) Extending the reach of mediation. In *When Talk Works: Profiles of Mediators*, edited by D. M. Kolb and Associates. New York: Jossey-Bass.

Kolb, D. M. and Sheppard, B. H. (1985) Do managers mediate, or even arbitrate? *Negotiation Journal*, (October), 379–88.

Kothari, S. and Harcourt, W. (2004) Introduction: The violence of development. *Development*, 47(1), 3–7.

Kozan, K. (1998) Interpersonal conflict management styles of Jordanian managers. In *Conflict Resolution: Cross-cultural Perspectives*, edited by K. Avruch, P. Black, and J. Scimecca. Westport, CT: Praeger. First published 1991 by Greenwood Press.

Krause, M. S. (1970) Use of social situations for research purposes. *American Psychologist*, 25, 748–53.

Kraybill, R. (1995) *Development, Conflict and the RDP: A Handbook on Process-centred Development*. Cape Town, South Africa: Centre for Conflict Resolution.

Kraybill, R. and Price, A. M. (1995) Healing strategies: Working with feelings. In *Mediation and Facilitation Training Manual: Foundations and Skills for Constructive Conflict Transformation*, (3rd edn), edited by J. Stutzman and C. Schrock-Shenk. Akron, PA: Mennonite Conciliation Service.

Kressel, K. and Pruitt, D. (eds) (1989) *Mediation Research*. San Francisco: Jossey-Bass.

Kressel, K., Frontera, E. A., Forlenza, S., Butler, F., and Fish, L. (1994) The settlement orientation versus the problem-solving style in custody mediation. *Journal of Social Issues*, 50, 67–84.

Kriesberg, L. (1980) Interlocking conflicts in the Middle East. *Research in Social Movements, Conflicts and Change*, 3, 99–119.

Kriesberg, L. (1987) Timing and the initiation of de-escalation moves. *Negotiation Journal*, 3(5), 375–84.

Kriesberg, L. (1991) Formal and quasi-mediators in international disputes: An exploratory analysis. *Journal of Peace Research*, 28(1), 19–27.

Kriesberg, L. (1992) *International Conflict Resolution*. New Haven, CT: Yale University Press.

Kriesberg, L. (1995) Varieties of mediating activities and of mediation. In *Resolving International Conflicts*, edited by J. Bercovitch. Boulder, CO: Lynne Rienner.

Kriesberg, L. (1998) *Constructive Conflicts: From Escalation to Resolution*. Lanham, MD: Rowman & Littlefield.

Kroeber, A. and Kluckhohn, C. (1952) *Culture: A Critical Review of*

Concepts and Definitions. Papers of the Peabody Museum of American Archaeology and Ethnology, Vol. 47, Harvard University.

Kruk, E. (1998) Practice issues, strategies, and models: The current state of the art of family mediation. *Family and Conciliation Courts Review*, 36(2), 195–215.

Kumar, C. (2001) Conclusion. In *Peacebuilding as Politics: Cultivating Peace in Fragile Societies*, edited by E. M. Cousens and C. Kumar, with K. Wermester. London: Lynne Rienner.

Kumar, K. (ed) (1997) *Rebuilding Societies After Civil War: Critical Roles for International Assistance*. Boulder, CO: Lynne Rienner.

Laclau, E. and Zac, L. (1994) Minding the gap. In *The Making of Political Identities*, edited by E. Laclau. London: Verso.

Lamarchand, R. (1994) *Burundi: Ethnic Conflict and Genocide*. Cambridge: Cambridge University Press.

Larson, D. W. (1998) Exchange and reciprocity in international negotiations. *International Negotiation*, 3, 121–38.

Laue, J. H. (1987) The emergence and institutionalization of third party roles in conflict. In *Conflict Management and Problem-solving: Interpersonal to International Applications*, edited by D. J. D. Sandole and I. Sandole-Staroste. New York: New York University Press.

Laue, J. H. and Cormick, G. (1978) The ethics of intervention in community disputes. In *The Ethics of Social Intervention*, edited by G. Bermant, H. E. Kelman, and D. Warwick. New York: Halsted Press.

Lavin, J. H. and the Committee of Ministers to Member States on Family Mediation (1999) Family mediation in Europe. *Family and Conciliation Courts Review*, 37(2), 257–62.

Lax, D. A. and Sebenius, J. K. (1986) *The Manager as Negotiator: Bargaining for Cooperation and Competitive Gain*. New York: The Free Press.

Le Billon, P. (2001) The political ecology of armed conflict: Natural resources and armed conflict. *Political Geography*, 20.

Leary, K. (ed) (2004) Critical moments in negotiation. *Negotiation Journal*, 8(2).

Leatherman, J., Demars, W., Gaffney, P. D., and Vayrynen, R. (1999) *Breaking Cycles of Violence: Conflict Prevention in Intrastate Crises*.West Hartford, CT: Kumarian Press.

Lederach, J. P. (1986) The mediator's cultural assumptions. *Conciliation Quarterly Newsletter*, 5(1), 2–5.

Lederach, J. P. (1995a) Conflict transformation: A working definition. In *Mediation and Facilitation Training Manual: Foundations and Skills for Constructive Conflict Transformation* (3rd edn), edited by J. Stutzman and C. Schrock-Shenk. Akron, PA: Mennonite Conciliation Service.

Lederach, J. P. (1995b) *Preparing for Peace: Conflict Transformation Across Cultures*. Syracuse, NY: Syracuse University Press.

Lederach, J. P. (1995c) Conflict transformation in protracted internal conflicts: The case for a comprehensive network. In *Conflict Transformation*, edited by K. Rupesinghe. New York: St. Martin's Press.

Lederach, J. P. (1997) *Building Peace: Sustainable Reconciliation in Divided Societies*. Washington, DC: U.S. Institute of Peace Press.

Lederach, J. P. (1998) Beyond violence: Building sustainable peace. In *The Handbook of Interethnic Coexistence*, edited by E. Weiner. New York: Abraham Fund Publication.

Lederach, J. P. (2000) Journey from resolution to transformative peacebuilding. In *From the Ground Up: Mennonite Contributions to International Peacebuilding*, edited by C. Sampson and J. P. Lederach. Oxford: Oxford University Press.

Lederach, J. P. and Jenner, J. M. (eds) (2002) *Into the Eye of the Storm; A Handbook on International Peacebuilding*. San Francisco: Jossey-Bass.

Lee, M.-Y. (1998) See you in court—er, mediation. *Business Week*, October 12(Industrial/Technology edn, 3599), ENT22.

Lenin, V. I. (1917/1969) *Imperialism: The Highest Stage of Capitalism*. New York: International Publishers.

Leonard, B. (1999) EEOC officials praise new mediation program. *HR Magazine*, (November), 32.

Lepgold, J. and Shambaugh, G. (1998) Rethinking the notion of reciprocal exchange in international negotiation: Sino-Soviet relations, 1969–1982. *International Negotiation*, 3, 227–52.

Lerner, D. (1958) *The Passing of Traditional Society: Modernizing the Middle East*. Glencoe, IL: The Free Press of Glencoe.

Lerner, R. M. (1984) *On the Nature of Human Plastity*. Cambridge: Cambridge University Press.

Levin, M. (1997) The role of substantive law in business arbitration and the importance of volition. *American Business Law Journal*, 35(1), 105–80.

LeVine, R. A. and Campbell, D. T. (1972) *Ethnocentrism: Theories of Conflict, Ethnic Attitudes, and Group Behavior*. New York: John Wiley & Sons.

Lewicki, R. J., Saunders, D. M., and Minton, J. W. (1997) *Essentials of Negotiation*. Chicago: Irwin.

Lewin, K. (1936) *A Dynamic Theory of Personality*. New York: McGraw-Hill.

Lewin, K. (1951) *Field Theory in Social Science: Selected Theoretical Papers*. New York: Harper & Row.

Lewis, I. M. (1998) Doing violence to ethnography: A response to

Catherine Besteman's "Representing violence and 'othering' Somalia". *Cultural Anthropology*, 13, 100–8.

Lieberfeld, D. (2005) Contributions of a semi-official pre-negotiation in South Africa. In *Paving the Way; Contributions of Interactive Conflict Resolution to Peacemaking*, edited by Fisher, R. J. Lanhan, MD: Lexington Books.

Lincoln, Y. S. and Guba, E. (1985) *Naturalistic Inquiry*. Beverly Hills, CA: Sage.

Lindner, E. (2006). *Making Enemies: Humiliation and International Conflict*. Westport, Conn: Praeger Security International.

Lipset, S. M. (1959) Some social requisites of democracy: Economic development and political legitimacy. *The American Political Science Review*, 53(1).

Lissak, R. I. and Sheppard, B. H. (1983) Beyond fairness: The criterion problem in research on dispute intervention. *Journal of Applied Social Psychology*, 13(2), 45–65.

Locksley, A., Ortiz, V., and Hepburn, C. (1980) Social categorization and discriminatory behavior: Extinguishing the minimal intergroup discrimination effect. *Journal of Personality and Social Psychology*, 39, 773–83.

Lorenz, K. (1974) *On Aggression*. New York: Harcourt, Brace.

Lumsden, M. (1999) Breaking the cycle of violence. In *Conflict Resolution: Dynamics, Process and Structure*, edited by H.-W. Jeong. Aldershot: Ashgate.

Lund, M. E. (1999) A focus on emotion in mediation training. *Family and Conciliation Courts Review*, 38(1), 62–8.

Lund, M. E. (2001) A toolbox for responding to conflicts and building peace. In *Peacebuilding, A Field Guide*, edited by L. Reychler and T. Paffenholz. Boulder, CO: Lynne Rienner.

Lund, M. S. (1995) Underrating preventive diplomacy. *Foreign Affairs*, 74(4), 160–3.

Lund, M. S. (1996) *Preventing Violent Conflicts: A Strategy for Preventive Diplomacy*. Washington, DC: U.S. Institute of Peace Press.

Luxemberg, R. (1973) *Reform or Revolution*. New York: Pathfinder Books.

MacGinty, R. and Robinson, C. (2001) Peacekeeping and the violence in ethnic conflict. In *United Nations Peacekeeping Operations*, edited by R. Thakur and A. Schnabel. Tokyo: UNU Press.

MacKinley, J. (2000) Mission failure. *The World Today*, 56(11), 9–11.

MacKinley, J. and Chopra, J. (1992) Second generation multinational operations. *The Washington Quarterly*, 15(3), 113–31.

MacLean, P. (1975) On the evolution of three mentalities. In *New*

Dimensions in Psychiatry: A World View (vol. 2), edited by S. Arieti and G. Chrzanowski. New York: John Wiley & Sons.

MacLean, P. (1978) A mind of three minds: Educating the triune brain. In *Education and the Brain (77th Yearbook of the National Society for the Study of Education, Part 2)*. Chicago: University of Chicago Press.

Mahmood, C. K. (1996) *Fighting for Faith and Nation: Dialogues with Sikh Militants*. Philadelphia: University of Pennsylvania Press.

Malcom, T. (1998) No more mediation. *National Catholic Reporter*, (July 3), 12.

Maley, Y. (1995) From adjudication to mediation: Third party discourse in conflict resolution. *Journal of Pragmatics*, 23(1), 93–110.

Malkki, L. (1995) *Purity and Exile: Violence, Memory, and National Cosmology among Hutu Refugees in Tanzania*. Chicago: University of Chicago Press.

Mandel, E. (1999) *Late Capitalism* (2nd edn). London: Verso.

Månsson, K. (2005) The forgotten agenda: Human rights protection and promotion in Cold War peacekeeping. *Journal of Conflict and Security Law*, 10(3), 379–403.

Marcus, G. (1995) Mass toxic torts and the end of everyday life. In *Law in Everyday Life*, edited by A. Sarat and T. Kearns. Ann Arbor: University of Michigan Press.

Marshall, C. and Rossman, G. B. (1999) *Designing Qualitative Research* (3rd edn). Thousand Oaks, CA: Sage.

Marshall, M. G. and Gurr, T. R. (2005) *Peace and Conflict 2005: A Global Survey of Armed Conflicts, Self-Determination Movements, and Democracy*. College Park: Center for International Development and Conflict Management (CIDCM), University of Maryland. Retrieved from *www.cidcm.umd.edu/inscr/peace.htm*

Martel, G. (ed) (1999) *The Origins of the Second World War Reconsidered: A. J. P. Taylor and the Historians* (2nd edn). London: Routledge.

Martin, J. (1992) *Culture in Organizations: Three Perspectives*. Oxford: Oxford University Press.

Marx, K. (1848/1988) *The Communist Manifesto*. New York: W.W. Norton.

Marx, K. (1906) *Das Kapital*. New York: Random House.

Marx, K. and Engels, F. (1964) *The German Ideology*. New York: International Publishers.

Maslow, A. H. (1987) *Motivation and Personality* (3rd edn). New York; London: Harper & Row.

Mason, M. A. (1999) Mediation and custody disputes. *Dispute Resolution Journal*, (May), 88.

McCandless, E. (2000) Reconciling relationships while pursuing justice:

The case of land redistribution in Zimbabwe. *Peace and Change*, 25(2), 225–38.

McCormick, M. A. (1997) Confronting social injustice as a mediator. *Mediation Quarterly*, 14(4), 293–307.

McDonald, J. W. (ed) (1996) Defining a U.S. negotiating style. Special Issue of *International Negotiation*, 1(2).

McDonald, J. W. Jr. and Bendahmane, D. B. (eds) (1987) *Conflict Resolution: Track Two Diplomacy*. Washington, DC: U.S. Department of State, Foreign Service Institute, Center for the Study of Foreign Affairs.

Macdonald, L. (1997) *Supporting Civil Society: The Political Role of Non-governmental Organizations in Central America*. London: Macmillan.

McKay, S. (2002) Women and peace building. In *Approaches to Peace Building*, edited by H.-W. Jeong. London: Palgrave.

McLellan, D. (ed) (1988) *Marxism: Essential Writings*. Oxford: Oxford University Press.

Meade, G. H. (1934) *Mind, Self and Society*. Chicago: University of Chicago Press.

Mernitz, S. (1980) *Mediation of Environmental Disputes*. New York: Praeger.

Merry, S. E. (1990) *Getting Justice and Getting Even: Legal Consciousness among Working Class Americans*. Chicago: University of Chicago Press.

Merry, S. E. (1994) Courts as performances: Domestic violence hearings in a Hawaii family court. In *Contested States: Law, Hegemony and Resistance*, edited by M. Lazarus-Black and S. F. Hirsch. New York: Routledge.

Miall, H., Ramsbotham, O., and Woodhouse, T. (1999) *Contemporary Conflict Resolution: The Prevention, Management and Transformation of Deadly Conflicts*. Cambridge; Oxford: Polity Press; Blackwell.

Mikeladze, L. (2000) Georgia and the OSCE. In the *Institute for Peace Research and Security Policy at the University of Hamburg's OSCE Yearbook 1999*. Baden-Baden: Nomos Verlagsgesellschaft.

Milanovic, B. (2003) The two faces of globalization: Against globalization as we know it. *World Development*, 31(4); *Politics*, 9(4).

Milburn, T. W. (1996) What we can learn from comparing mediation across levels. *Peace and Conflict Studies*, 3(1), 39–52.

Milgram, S. (1963) Behavioral study of obedience. *Journal of Abnormal and Social Psychology*, 67, 371–8.

Milner, N. (1996) Mediation and political theory: A critique of Bush and Folger. *Law and Social Inquiry*, 21(3), 737–59.

Mischel, W. (1969) Continuity and change in personality. *American Psychologist*, 24, 1012–18.

Mischel, W. and Shoda, V. (1995) A cognitive-affective theory of personality: Reconceptualizing situations, dispositions, dynamics, and invariance in personality structure. *Psychological Review*, 102, 246–68.

Mishler, E. G. (1986) *Research Interviewing: Context and Narrative.* Cambridge, MA: Harvard University Press.

Mishler, E.G. (1995) Models of narrative analysis: A typology. *Journal of Narrative and Life History*, 5(2), 87–123.

Mitchell, C. R. (1981a) *Peacemaking and the Consultant's Role.* Basingstoke: Gower Press.

Mitchell, C. R. (1981b) *The Structure of International Conflict.* New York: St. Martin's Press.

Mitchell, C. R. (1993a) Problem solving exercises and theories of conflict resolution. In *Conflict Resolution Theory and Practice: Integration and Application*, edited by D. R. Sandole and H. van der Merwe. Manchester: Manchester University Press.

Mitchell, C. R. (1993b) The process and stages of mediation: Two Sudanese cases. In *Making War and Waging Peace: Foreign Intervention in Africa*, edited by D. R. Smock. Washington, DC: U.S. Institute of Peace Press.

Mitchell, C. R. (1999) The anatomy of de-escalation. In *Conflict Resolution: Dynamics, Process and Structure*, edited by H.-W. Jeong. Aldershot: Ashgate.

Mitchell, C. R. (2000a) Beyond Resolution: What Does Conflict Transformation Actually Transform? Unpublished paper, Institute for Conflict Analysis and Resolution, George Mason University.

Mitchell, C. R. (2000b) *Gestures of Conciliation: Factors Contributing to Successful Olive Branches.* London: Macmillan.

Mitchell, C. R. and Banks, M. (1996) *Handbook of Conflict Resolution: The Analytical Problem-solving Approach.* London: Pinter.

Mittelman, J. H. (2000) *The Globalization Syndrome: Transformation and Resistance.* Princeton: Princeton University Press.

Modelski, G. (1970) The world's foreign ministers: A political elite. *Journal of Conflict Resolution*, 14, 135–75.

Moghadam, Valentine. (2005) *Globalizing Women: Transnational Feminist Networks.* Baltimore: The Johns Hopkins University Press.

Monk, G., Winslade, J., Crocket, K., and Epston, D. (eds) (1997) *Narrative Therapy in Practice: The Archaeology of Hope.* San Francisco: Jossey-Bass.

Montiel, C. J. (2001) Toward a psychology of a structural peacebuilding. In *Peace, Conflict, and Violence: Peace Psychology for the 21st Cen-*

tury, edited by D. J. Christie, R. V. Wagner, and D. D. Winter. Upper Saddle River, NJ: Prentice Hall.

Montville, J. V. (n.d.) *Nationalism, Sectarianism and Political Separatist Minorities: Aggression and Defense Behaviors of Threatened and Separatist Minorities*. Washington, DC: Center for the Study of Foreign Affairs, Foreign Service Institute, U.S. Department of State.

Mooradian, M. and Druckman, D. (1999) Hurting stalemate or mediation? The conflict over Nagorno-Karabakh, 1990–1995. *Journal of Peace Research*, 36, 709–27.

Moore, B. (1993) *Social Origins of Dictatorship and Democracy: Lord and Peasant in the Making of the Modern World*. Boston: Beacon Press.

Moore, C. (1986) *The Mediation Process: Practical Strategies for Resolving Conflict*. San Francisco: Jossey-Bass.

Moore, David (2000) "Leveling the playing Fields and embedding Illusions: 'Post-Conflict' Discourse and neo-liberal 'development' in war-torn Africa," *Review of African Political Economy*, 83, March, 11–28

Morris, J. (1984) *The Matter of Wales: Epic Views of a Small Country*. New York: Oxford University Press.

Morris, M. W., Larrick, R., and Su, S. K. (1999) Misperceiving negotiation counterparts: When situationally determined bargaining behaviors are attributed to personality traits. *Journal of Personality and Social Psychology*, 77, 52–76.

Mosten, F. S. (2000) Mediation 2000: Training mediators for the 21st century. *Family and Conciliation Courts Review*, 38(1), 17–26.

Moyers, B. (1996) *Genesis: A Living Conversation*. Garden City, NY: Doubleday.

Mumby, D. K. (1993) *Narrative and Social Control: Critical Perspectives*. Newbury Park, CA: Sage.

Naim, M. (2003) The five wars of globalization. *Foreign Policy*, (January-February).

Nan, S. A. (2004, May 13) Intervention coordination. *Proceedings of the Intractable Conflict Knowledge Base Project, Conflict Resolution Consortium*, University of Colorado. Retrieved from *www.beyondintractability.org/m/intervention_coordination.jsp*

Nathan, L. (2000) 'The four horsemen of the apocalypse': The structural causes of crisis and violence in Africa. *Peace and Change*, 25(2), 188–24.

Neale, M. and Northcraft, G. B. (1986) Experts, amateurs and refrigerators: Comparing expert and amateur negotiators in a novel task. *Organizational Behavior and Human Performance*, 38, 305–17.

Nelson, M. C. and Sharp, W. R. (1995) Mediating conflicts of persons at risk of homelessness: The helping hand project. *Mediation Quarterly*, 12(4), 317–25.

Newcomb, T. M. (1929) *Consistency of Certain Extrovert-Introvert Behavior Patterns in 51 Problem Boys*. New York: Columbia University, Teacher's College, Bureau of Publications.

Niebuhr, R. (1996) *The Nature and Destiny of Man*. Upper Saddle River, NJ: Prentice Hall.

Nisbett, R. and Ross, L. (1980) *Human Inference: Strategies and Shortcomings of Social Judgment*. Englewood Cliffs, NJ: Prentice Hall.

Nordstrom, C. (1997) *A Different Kind of War Story*. Philadelphia: University of Pennsylvania Press.

Nordstrom, C. and Martin, J. A. (eds) (1992) *The Paths to Domination, Resistance and Terror*. Berkeley: University of California Press.

North, R. C. (1990) *War, Peace, Survival: Global Politics and Conceptual Synthesis*. Boulder, CO: Westview Press.

North, R. C., Brody, R. A., and Holsti, O. R. (1964) Some empirical data on the conflict spiral. *Peace Research Society (International) Papers*, 1, 1–14.

Nowak, A., Vallacher, R. R., Tesser, A., and Borkowski, W. (2000). Society of self: The emergence of collective properties in self-structure. *Psychological Review*, 107, 39–61.

Nowak, A. (2004) Dynamic minimalism: Why less is more in psychology. *Personality and Social Psychology Review*, 8, 183–192.

Nudler, O. (1990) On conflicts and metaphors: Towards an extended rationality. In *Conflict: Human Needs Theory*, edited by J. Burton. New York: St. Martin's Press.

Nudler, O. (1993). In search of a theory of conflict resolution: Taking a new look at world views analysis. *Institute of Conflict Analysis and Resolution Newsletter*, 5, 1–5.

O'Callaghan, J. (2000) Conjoined twins to be separated: Parents decline to appeal British court's order for surgery. *Washington Post*, (September 29), A29.

O'Donnell, G. (1979) *Modernization and Bureaucratic-Authoritarianism: Studies in South American Politics*. Berkeley: Institute for International Studies.

Ogay, T. (1998) Conflict mediation and resolution: The contribution of social psychology. *European Journal of Intercultural Studies*, 9(3), 269–77.

Olson, C. A. and Rau, B. L. (1997) Learning from interest arbitration: The next round. *Industrial and Labor Relations Review*, 50, 237–51.

Oneal, J. R. and Russett, B. (1999) The Kantian peace: The Pacific benefits of democracy, interdependence, and international organizations, 1885–1992. *World Politics*, 52(1).

Oplinger, J. (1990) *The Politics of Demonology: The European Witch-craze and the* Mass *Production of Deviance.* London: Associated University Presses.

Organization for Economic Co-operation and Development (OECD) (1998) *Conflict, Peace and Development Cooperation on the Threshold of the 21st Century.* Paris: OECD, Development Assistance Committee.

Orwell, G. (1990) *1984.* New York: New American Library.

OSCE Istanbul Summit (1999, November 19) *Charter for European Security.* Istanbul: Organization for Security and Cooperation in Europe.

OSCE Newsletter (2000) OSCE Secretariat undergoes restructuring: Changes aimed at significantly improving OSCE's reaction times. *OSCE Newsletter,* 7(9), 5–6.

Osgood, C. E. (1962) *An Alternative to War or Surrender.* Urbana: University of Illinois Press.

Osgood, C. E. (1966) *Perspective in Foreign Policy* (2nd edn). Palo Alto, CA: Pacific Books.

Osgood, C. E. (1986) Graduated and reciprocated initiatives in tension reduction: GRIT. In *Psychology and the Prevention of Nuclear War,* edited by R. K. White. New York: New York University Press.

O'Shea, B. (2002) The future of UN peacekeeping. *Conflict and Terrorism,* 25(2), 145–8.

Oxhorn, P. D. and Ducatenzeiler, G. (eds) (1998) *What Kind of Democracy?What Kind of Market? Latin America in the Age of Neoliberalism?* University Park, PA: The Pennsylvania State University Press.

Oxford English Dictionary (1979) *Compact Oxford English Dictionary.* Oxford: Oxford University Press.

Pacia, R. A. (1997) Arbitrating the uninsured motorist case. *Trial: Negotiation and Settlement,* 33, 26–8.

Padilla, L. A. (1994) Conflict transformation: Peace-making and peace building in Guatemala. *Peace Research,* 27(4), 17–24.

Pankhurst, D. (2000) Unraveling reconciliation and justice? Land and the potential for conflict in Namibia. *Peace and Change,* 25(2), 239–55.

Parkinson, F. (1977) *The Philosophy of International Relations: A Study in the History of Thought.* Beverly Hills, CA; London: Sage.

Parsons, T. (1951) *The Social System.* New York: The Free Press.

Parsons, T. (1961) *Theories of Society, Foundations of Modern Sociological Theory.* New York: Free Press.

Parsons, T. (1971) *The System of Modern Societies.* Englewood Cliffs, NJ: Prentice Hall.

Patchen, M. (1998) When does reciprocity in the actions of nations occur? *International Negotiation*, 3, 171–96.

Patchen, M. and Bogumil, D. D. (1995) Testing alternative models of interaction against interaction during the Cold War. *Conflict Management and Peace Science*, 14, 163–95.

Patten, T. H. Jr. (1989) Historical perspectives on organization development. In *The Emerging Practice of Organization Development*, edited by W. Sikes, A. Drexler, and J. Gant. Alexandria, VA: National Training Laboratories and University Associates, Inc.

Patton, M. Q. (1997) *Utilization-focused Evaluation: The New Century Text*. Thousand Oaks, CA: Sage.

Patton, M. Q. (2002). *Qualitative Research and Evaluation Methods* (3rd edn). Thousand Oaks, CA.: Sage.

Paul, J. A. (2000) NGOs and global policy-making. *Global Policy Forum*, (June). Retrieved from *http://www.globalpolicy.org/ngos/analysis/ana100.htm*

Pearce, W. B. and Littlejohn, S. W. (1997) *Moral Conflict: When Social Worlds Collide*. Thousand Oaks, CA: Sage.

Pearson, J. (1997) Mediating when domestic violence is a factor: Policies and practices in court-based divorce mediation programs. *Mediation Quarterly*, 14(4), 319–35.

Pearson, J. and Thoennes, N. (1984) Mediating and litigating custody disputes: A longitudinal evaluation. *Family Law Quarterly*, 17, 497–524.

Pearson, J. and Thoennes, N. (1985) Divorce mediation: An overview of research results. *Columbia Journal of Law and Sociological Problems*, 32, 451–67.

Pierre, A.J. (1999, September 20) *De-Balkanizing the Balkans: Security and Stability in Southeastern Europe*. Special report, U.S. Institute of Peace, Washington, DC.

Pinkley, R. L., Brittain, J., Neale, M. A., and Northcraft, G. B. (1995) Managerial third-party dispute intervention: An inductive analysis of intervenor strategy selection. *Journal of Applied Psychology*, 80(3), 386–402.

Pinkley, R. L., Neale, M. A., and Bennet, R. J. (1994) The impact of alternatives to settlement in dyadic negotiation. *Organizational Behavior and Human Performance*, 57, 97–116.

Pinzon, L. A. (1996) The production of power and knowledge in mediation. *Mediation Quarterly*, 14(1), 3–20.

Plous, S. W. (1987) Perceived illusions and military readiness: A computer simulated arms race. *Journal of Conflict Resolution*, 31, 5–33.

Polachek, S. W. (1980) Conflict and trade. *Journal of Conflict Resolution*, 24(1), 55–78.

Polyani, K. (1980) *The Great Transformation*. Boston: Beacon Books.

Polanyi, M. (1967) *The Tacit Dimension*. New York: Doubleday.

Potter, J. and Wetherell, M. (1987) *Discourse and Social Psychology: Beyond Attitudes and Behavior*. London: Sage.

Poulantzas, N. (1973) *Political Power and Social Classes*, translated and edited by T. O'Hagan. London: New Left Books and Sheed and Ward.

Pratto, F., Liu, J. H., Levin, S., Sidanius, J., Shih, M., Bachrach, H., and Hegarty, P. (2000) Social dominance orientation and the legitimization of inequality across cultures. *Journal of Cross-cultural Psychology*, 31, 369–409.

Princen, T. (1995) *Intermediaries in International Conflict*. Princeton, NJ: Princeton University Press.

Pruitt, D. (1981) *Negotiation Behavior*. New York: Academic Press.

Pruitt, D. G. and Carnevale, P. J. (1993) *Negotiation in Social Conflict*. Pacific Grove, CA: Brooks/Cole.

Pruitt, D. G. and Gahagan, J. P. (1974) Campus crisis: The search for power. In *Perspectives on Social Power*, edited by J. T. Tedeschi. Chicago: Aldine.

Pruitt, D. G. and Kim, S.H. (2004) *Social Conflict: Escalation, Stalemate, and Settlement*. Boston: McGraw-Hill.

Pruitt, D. and Rubin, J. Z. (1986) *Social Conflict: Escalation, Stalemate, and Settlement*. New York: Random House.

Przeworski, A. (1993) Economic reforms, public opinion, and political institutions: Poland in the Eastern European perspective. In *Economic Reforms in New Democracies: A Social Democratic Approach*, edited by L. C. Bresser Pereira, J. M. Maravall, and A. Przeworski. New York: Cambridge University Press.

Pugh, M. (1997) *The UN, Peace and Force*. London: Frank Cass.

Putnam, L. and Holmer, M. (1992) Framing, reframing, and issue development. In *Communication and Negotiation*, edited by L. Putnam and M. E. Roloff (pp. 128–55). Newbury Park, CA: Sage.

Putnam, R. D. (1988) Diplomacy and domestic politics: The logic of two-level games. *International Organization*, 43, 427–60.

Putnam, R. D. (1993) *Making Democracy Work: Civic Traditions in Modern Italy*. Princeton, NJ: Princeton University Press.

Rabie, M. (1994) *Conflict Resolution and Ethnicity*. Westport, CT: Praeger.

Raiffa, H. (1982) *The Art and Science of Negotiation*. Cambridge, MA: Harvard University Press.

Ramberg, B. (1977) Tactical advantages of opening positioning strategies: Lessons from the Seabeds Arms Control talks, 1967–1970. *Journal of Conflict Resolution*, 21, 685-700.

Ramsbotham, O. and Woodhouse, T. (eds) (2000) *Peacekeeping and Conflict Resolution*. London: Frank Cass.

Ramsbotham, O. and Woodhouse, T. (2005), Cosmopolitan peace-keeping and the globalization of security. *International Peacekeeping*, 12(2), 139-56.

Ramsbotham, O., Woodhouse, T., and Miall, H. (2005) *Contemporary Conflict Resolution* (2nd edn). Cambridge, MA: Polity Press.

Randolph, L. (1966) A suggested model of international negotiation. *Journal of Conflict Resolution*, 10, 344–53.

Random House (1997) *Random House Webster's College Dictionary* (2nd edn). New York: Random House.

Rapoport, A. (1974) *Conflict in Man-made Environment*. Harmondsworth: Penguin.

Rapoport, A. (1982) *The Meaning of the Built Environment: A Nonverbal Communication Approach*. Beverly Hills, CA: Sage.

Rapoport, A. (1960) *Fights, Games, and Debates*. Ann Arbor: University of Michigan Press.

Raspberry, W. (2000) The ultimate sacrifice. *Washington Post*, (September 25) A21.

Rawls, J. (1999) *A Theory of Justice* (rev. edn). Boston: Belknap Press.

Reich, C. (1995) *The Greening of America*. New York: Crown Books.

Reich, W. (1980) *The Mass Psychology of Fascism* (3rd edn). New York: Noonday Press.

Reimann, C. (2001) Towards conflict transformation: Assessing the state-of-the-art in conflict transformation. In *Berghof Handbook for Conflict Transformation* (Internet version). Retrieved from *www.berghof-center.org/handbook/cf.html*

Renner, M. (1993) *Critical Juncture: The Future of Peacekeeping*. Washington, DC: Worldwatch Institute.

Reychler, L. (1997) Field diplomacy: A new conflict prevention paradigm. *Peace and Conflict Studies*, 4(1), 35–47.

Reychler, L. (1999) *Democratic Peace-building and Conflict Prevention: The Devil Is in the Transition*. Leuven, Belgium: Leuven University Press.

Reychler, L. (2000, August) *Peace Architecture*. Paper presented to the International Peace Research Association, Tampare, Helsinki.

Reychler, L. (2001) From conflict to sustainable peacebuilding: Concepts and analytical tools, conceptual framework. In *Peacebuilding, a Field Guide*, edited by L. Reychler and T. Paffenholz. Boulder, CO: Lynne Rienner.

Rheinberger, H.-J. (2001) Limits of the genetic lexicon. *American Scientist*, 89, 65–6.

Rhoads, J. (1991) *Critical Issues in Social Theory*. Philadelphia: University of Pennsylvania Press.

Rice, A. K. (1963) *The Enterprise and Its Environment*. London: Tavistock Institute.

Rice, R. E. (1996) Making a place for the new American scholar. Working paper No.1, *New Pathways: Faculty Careers and Employment for the 21st Century*. Washington, DC: American Association for Higher Education.

Richardson, L. F. (1967) *Arms and Insecurity*. Chicago: Quadrangle.

Roberts, A. (1995) From San Francisco to Sarajevo: The UN and the use of force. *Survival*, 37(4), 7–28.

Roberts, J. and Hite, A. (2000) *From Modernization to Globalization: Perspectives on Development and Change*. Oxford: Blackwell.

Robinson, W. S. (1950) Ecological correlations and the behavior of individuals. *American Sociological Review*, 15, 351–7.

Robson, C. (1993) *Real-World Research*. Oxford: Blackwell.

Rogers, C. (1961) *On Becoming a Person*. Boston: Houghton Mifflin.

Rogers, C. (1977) *On Personal Power: Inner Strength and Its Revolutionary Impact*. New York: Delacorte Press.

Rohde, D. (1997) *Endgame: The Betrayal and Fall of Srebrenica, Europe's Worst Massacre Since World War II*. New York: Farrar, Straus & Giroux.

Romney, A. K. and Moore, C. (1998) Toward a theory of culture as shared cognitive structures. *Ethos*, 26(3), 314–37.

Ronen, D. (1998) Can there be a just resolution of conflict? *Peace and Conflict Studies*.

Rosch, E. H., Mervis, C. B., Gray, W., Johson, D., and Boyes-Braem, P. (1976) Basic objects in natural categories. *Cognitive Psychology*, 8, 382–439.

Rosch, E. H. (1978) Principles of categorization. In *Cognition and Categorization*, edited by E. H. Rosch and B. B. Lloyd. Hillsdale, NJ: Lawrence Erlbaum.

Rosen, L. (1984) *Bargaining for Reality: The Construction of Social Relations in a Muslim Community*. Chicago: University of Chicago Press.

Rosen, L. (1988) *The Anthropology of Justice: Law as Culture in Islamic Society*. Cambridge: Cambridge University Press.

Rosenau, J. N. (1990) *Turbulence in World Politics*. Princeton, NJ: Princeton University Press.

Rosencrance, R. (1996) The rise of the virtual state. *Foreign Affairs*, 75(4), 45–61.

Rosenthal, R. and Jacobson, L. (1968) *Pygmalion in the Classroom*. New York: Holt, Rinehart & Winston.

Ross, M. H. (1993) *The Management of Conflict: Interpretations and Interests in Comparative Perspective*. New Haven, CT: Yale University Press.

Ross, M. H. (1995) Psychocultural interpretation theory and peace-making in ethnic conflicts. *Political Psychology*, 16(3), 523–44.

Ross, M. H. (1997) Culture and identity in comparative political analysis. In *Comparative Politics: Rationality, Culture, and Structure*, edited by M. Lichback and A. Zuckerman. Cambridge: Cambridge University Press.

Rostow, W.W. (1960) *The Stages of Economic Growth: A Non-Communist Manifesto*. New York: Cambridge University Press.

Rothbart, M. (1981) Memory processes and social beliefs. In *Cognitive Processes in Stereotyping and Intergroup Behavior*, edited by D. Hamilton. Hillsdale, NJ: Lawrence Erlbaum.

Rothman, J. (1997) *Resolving Identity Based Conflicts*. San Francisco: Jossey-Bass.

Rouhana, N. N. (2000) Interactive conflict resolution: Issues in theory, methodology, and evaluation. In *International Conflict Resolution After the Cold War*, edited by P. Stern and D. Druckman. Washington, DC: National Academy Press.

Roy, B. (1994) *Some Trouble with Cows: Making Sense of Social Conflict*. Berkeley: University of California Press.

Rubenstein, R. E. (1985) *Alchemists of Revolution: Terrorism in the Modern World*. New York: Basic Books.

Rubenstein, R. E. (1990) Basic human needs: Beyond natural law. In *Conflict: Basic Human Needs*, edited by J. W. Burton. New York: St. Martin's Press.

Rubenstein, R. E. (1999) Conflict resolution and structural sources of conflict. In *Conflict Resolution: Dynamics, Process and Structure*, edited by H.-W. Jeong. Aldershot: Ashgate.

Rubenstein, R. E. and Crocker, J. (1993) Challenging Huntington. *Foreign Policy*, 96, 113–128.

Rubin, J. (1991) The timing of ripeness and the ripeness of timing. In *Timing the De-escalation of International Conflicts*, edited by L. Kriesberg and S. Thorson. New York: Syracuse University Press.

Rubin, J. Z. and Brown, B. R. (1975) *The Social Psychology of Bargaining and Negotiation*. New York: Academic Press.

Rubin, J. Z., Pruitt, D. G., and Kim, S. H. (1994) *Social Conflict: Escalation, Stalemate, and Settlement* (2nd edn). New York: McGraw-Hill.

Rupesinghe, K. (1995a) Conflict transformation. In *Conflict Transformation*, edited by K. Rupesinghe. London: Macmillan.

Rupesinghe, K. (ed) (1995b) *Conflict Transformation*. London: Macmillan.

Sacks, H., Schegloff, E. A., & Jefferson, G. (1974). A simple systematics for the organisation of turn-taking for conversation. *Language*, 50, 696–735.

Sadowski, Y. (1998) *The Myth of Global Chaos*. Washington, DC: The Brookings Institution.

Salacuse, J. (1998) Ten ways that culture affects negotiating style: Some survey results. *Negotiation Journal*, 14(July), 221–40.

Sampson, C. and Lederach, J. P. (2000) *From the Ground Up: Mennonite Contributions to International Peacebuilding*. New York: Oxford University Press.

Sandole, D. J. D. (1984) The subjectivity of theories and actions in world society. In *Conflict in World Society: A New Perspective on International Relations*, edited by M. Banks. New York: St. Martin's Press.

Sandole, D. J. D. (1987) Conflict management: Elements of generic theory and practice. In *Conflict Management and Problem Solving: Interpersonal to International Applications*, edited by D. J. D. Sandole and I. Sandole-Staroste. London: Pinter.

Sandole, D. J. D. (1993) Paradigms, theories, and metaphors in conflict and conflict resolution: Coherence or confusion? In *Conflict Resolution Theory and Practice: Integration and Application*, edited by D. J.D. Sandole and H. van der Merwe. Manchester: Manchester University Press.

Sandole, D. J. D. (1998a) A comprehensive mapping of conflict and conflict resolution: A three pillar approach. *IAPTC Newsletter* (International Association of Peacekeeping Training Centres), 1(5),7–8.

Sandole, D. J. D. (1998b) A comprehensive mapping of conflict and conflict resolution: A three pillar approach. *Peace and Conflict Studies*, 5(2), 1–30.

Sandole, D. J. D. (1998c) A peace and security system for post-Cold War Europe: Preventing future "Yugoslavias". In *Encyclopedia of the European Union*, edited by D. Dinan. Boulder, CO: Lynne Rienner.

Sandole, D. J. D. (1999a) A design for peace and security in post-Cold War Europe. *Ethnic Conflict Research Digest* (INCORE, University of Ulster, Northern Ireland), 2(1), 41–2.

Sandole, D. J. D. (1999b) *Capturing the Complexity of Conflict: Dealing with Violent Ethnic Conflicts of the Post-Cold War Era*. London: Pinter.

Sandole, D. J. D. (1999c) Kosovo: The straw that (finally!) broke the paradigm's back? *ICAR Newsletter* (Institute for Conflict Analysis and Resolution, George Mason University), 10(1), 1, 4.

Sandole, D. J. D. (2001) Preventing future Yugoslavias: The views of CSCE/OSCE negotiators, 1993 and 1997. In *Ten Years After: Democratization and Security Challenges in South Eastern Europe, Vol. 2*, edited by G. E. Gustanow. Vienna: National Defence Academy.

Sandole, D. J. D. (2002) Virulent ethnocentrism: A major challenge for transformational conflict resolution and peacebuilding in the post-Cold War era. *The Global Review of Ethnopolitics*, 1(4), 4–27.

Sandole, D. J.D. (2007) *Peace and Security in the Postmodern World: The OSCE and Conflict Resolution*. New York; London: Routledge.

Sarbin, T. R. and Allen, V. L. (1969) Role theory. In *The Handbook of Social Psychology: Second Edition*, edited by G. Lindzey and E. Aronson. Reading, MA: Addison-Wesley.

Saretzki, T. (1997) Mediation, social movements and democracy. *Forschungsjournal Neue Soziale Bewegungen*, 10(4), 27–42.

Saretzki, T., Klein, A., and Kulessa, P. (1997) Mediation—a fashionable theme? *Forschungsjournal Neue Soziale Bewegungen*, 10(4), 3–11.

Saunders, H. H. (1996) Prenegotiation and circum-negotiation: Arenas of the peace process. In *Managing Global Chaos*, edited by C. Crocker and F. O. Hampson, with P. Aall. Washington, DC: U.S. Institute of Peace Press.

Saunders, H. H. (1999) *A Public Peace Process: Sustained Dialogue to Transform Racial and Ethnic Conflicts*. New York: St. Martin's Press.

Sawyer, J. and Guetzkow, H. (1965) Bargaining and negotiation in international relations. In *International Behavior: A Social-Psychological Analysis*, edited by H. C. Kelman. New York: Holt.

Scarry, E. (1985). *The Body in Pain: The Making and Unmaking of the World*. New York: Oxford University Press.

Schecter, J. (1998) *Russian Negotiating Behavior*. Washington, DC: U.S. Institute of Peace Press.

Scheff, T. J. (1967) A theory of social coordination applicable to mixed-motive games. *Sociometry*, 30, 215–34.

Schein, E. E. (1987) *Process Consultation: Volume II. Lessons for Managers and Consultants*. Reading, MA: Addison-Wesley.

Schein, E. H. (1999) *Process Consultation Revisited: Building the Helping Relationship*. Reading, MA: Addison-Wesley.

Schellenberg, J. A. (1996) *Conflict Resolution: Theory, Research, and Practice*. Albany: State University of New York Press.

Schelling, T. C. (1963) *The Strategy of Conflict*. New York: Oxford University Press.

Schelling, T. C. (1966) *Arms and Influence*. New Haven, CT: Yale University Press.

Schmid, A. P. (2000) *Thesaurus and Glossary of Early Warning and Conflict Prevention Terms*. Erasmus, The Netherlands: Synthesis Foundation.

Schmitter, P. C. (1971) *Interest Conflict and Political Change in Brazil*. Stanford: Stanford University Press.

Schneider, A.K. and Honeyman, C. (eds) (2006) *The Negotiator's Fieldbook: The Desk Reference for the Experienced Negotiator*. Washington, DC: American Bar Association.

Scholte, J. A. (2004) *Democratizing the Global Economy: The Role of Civil Society*. Coventry: Center for the Study of Globalization and Regionalization.

Schön, D. A. (1983) *The Reflective Practitioner: How Professionals Think in Action*. New York: Basic Books.

Schön, D. A. (1995) The new scholarship requires a new epistemology. *Change*, (November/December), 27–34.

Schön, D. A., & Rein, M. (1994). *Frame Reflection: Toward the Resolution of Intractable Policy Controversies*. New York: Basic Books.

Schoorman, F. D. and Champagne, M. V. (1994) Managers as informal third parties: The impact of supervisor–subordinate relationships on interventions. *Employee Responsibilities and Rights Journal*, 7(1), 73–85.

Schumpeter, J. (1955) *The Sociology of Imperialism*. New York: Meridian Books. First published 1919.

Schwarz, R. M. (1994) *The Skilled Facilitator: Practical Wisdom for Developing Effective Groups*. San Francisco: Jossey-Bass.

Schwartz, T. (1982) Cultural totemism: Ethnic identity primitive and modern. In *Ethnic Identity: Cultural Continuities and Change* (2nd edn), edited by G. DeVos and L. Romanucci-Ross. Chicago: University of Chicago Press.

Schwartz, T. (1992) Anthropology and psychology: An unrequited relationship. In *New Directions in Psychological Anthropology*, edited by T. Schwartz, G. White, and C. Lutz. Cambridge: Cambridge University Press.

Scimecca, J. A. (1991) Conflict resolution in the United States: The emergence of a profession. In *Conflict Resolution: Cross Cultural Perspectives*, edited by K. Avruch, P. Black, and J. A. Scimecca. Westport, CT: Greenwood Press.

Sciolino, E. (1998) Iranian dismisses all hope for now of political thaw. *New York Times*, (September 28), A1.

Scott, J. P. (1958) *Aggression*. Chicago: University of Chicago Press.

Scott, J. C. (1990). *Domination and the Arts of Resistance: Hidden Transcripts*. New Haven: Yale University Press.

Seidman, S. (1994) Introduction. In *The Postmodern Turn*, edited by S. Seidman. Cambridge: Cambridge University Press.

Sells, S. B. (1966) A model for the social system for the multi-man extended duration space ship. *Aerospace Medicine*, 37, 1130–5.

SFCG (1997) *Search for Common Ground and European Center for Common Ground: Report*. Washington, DC: Search for Common Ground.

Shapiro, I. (1997) Beyond modernization: Conflict resolution in central and eastern Europe. *The Annals of the American Academy of Political and Social Science*, 552, 14–27.

Sharoni, S. (1995) *Gender and the Israeli–Palestinian Conflict*. Syracuse, NY: Syracuse University Press.

Sheppard, B. H. (1983) Managers as inquisitors: Some lessons from the law. In *Negotiating in Organizations*, edited by M. Bazerman and R. Lewicki. Beverley Hills, CA: Sage.

Sheppard, B. H. (1984) Third party conflict intervention: A procedural framework. *Research in Organizational Behavior*, 6, 141–90.

Sheppard, B. H., Blumenfeld-Jones, K., and Roth, J. (1989) Informal third partyship: Studies of everyday conflict intervention. In *Mediation Research: The Process and Effectiveness of Third-Party Intervention*, edited by K. Kressel, D. G. Pruitt and Associates. San Francisco: Jossey-Bass.

Sheppard, B. H., Roth, J., Blumenfeld-Jones, K., and Minton, J. (1991) *Third Party Dispute Interpretations: Simple Stories and Conflict Interventions*. Paper presented at the National Academy of Management Meetings, Miami Beach, FL.

Sherif, M. (1966) *Group Conflict and Cooperation; Their Social Psychology*. London: Routledge & Kegan Paul.

Sherif, M. and Sherif, C. W. (1956) *An Outline of Social Psychology*. New York: Harper.

Sherwyn, D. S. and Tracey, J. B. (1997) Mandatory arbitration of employment disputes: Implications for policy and practice. Cornell *Hotel and Restaurant Administration Quarterly*, 38(5), 58–9.

Shonholtz, R. and Linzer, J. (eds) (1997) Conflict management within transitioning societies. Special issue of *NIDR News* (National Institute for Dispute Resolution), 4(4).

Shonholtz, R. and Shapiro, I. (eds) (1997) Strengthening transitional democracies through conflict resolution. Special issue of *The Annals of the American Academy of Political and Social Science*, 552 (July).

Sidanius, J. and Pratto, F. (1999) *Social Dominance: An Intergroup*

Theory of Social Hierarchy and Oppression. Cambridge: Cambridge University Press.

Siegel, S. and Fouraker, L. F. (1960) *Bargaining and Group Decision Making.* New York: McGraw-Hill.

Simmel, G. (1955) *Conflict and the Web of Group-affiliations,* translated by K. H. Wolff and R. Bendix. Glencoe, IL: The Free Press.

Simon, H. (1972) *The Science of the Artificial.* Cambridge, MA: NUT Press.

Simpson, G. (1999) Reconstruction and reconciliation: Emerging from transition. In *From Conflict to Peace in a Changing World: Social Reconstruction in Times of Transition,* edited by D. Eade. Oxford: Oxfam.

Simpson, P. A. and Martocchio, J. J. (1997) The influence of work history factors on arbitration outcomes. *Industrial and Labor Relations Review,* 50(January), 252–67.

Singer, J. D. (1961) The level-of-analysis problem in international relations. In *The International System: Theoretical Essays,* edited by K. Knorr and S. Verba. Princeton, NJ: Princeton University Press.

Sipe, N. G. (1998) An empirical analysis of environmental mediation. *Journal of American Planning Association,* 64(3), 275–85.

Skocpol, T. (1979) *States and Social Revolutions: A Comparative Analysis of France, Russia, and China.* Cambridge: Cambridge University Press.

Skocpol, T. (1985) Bringing the state back in: Strategies of analysis in current research. In *Bringing the State Back In,* edited by P. Evans, D. Rueschemeyer, and T. Skocpol. Cambridge: Cambridge University Press.

Smith, R. J. (2000) West is tiring of struggle to rebuild Bosnia: Five years after war's end, efforts have largely failed. *Washington Post,* (November 25), A1, A14.

Smoke, R. (1977) *War: Controlling Escalation.* Cambridge, MA: Harvard University Press.

Snyder, G. H. and Diesing, P. (1977) *Conflict Among Nations.* Princeton, NJ: Princeton University Press.

Snyder, J. L. (2000) *From Voting to Violence: Democratization and Nationalistic Conflict.* New York: W. W. Norton.

So, A. (2005) *Social Change and Development: Modernization, Dependency and World Systems Theories.* Thousand Oaks, CA: Sage.

Sokalski, H. J. (2003) *An Ounce of Prevention: Macedonia and the UN Experience in Preventive Diplomacy.* Washington, DC: U.S. Institute of Peace Press.

Solomon, R. (1999) *Chinese Negotiating Behavior.* Washington, DC: U.S. Institute of Peace Press.

Somerville, P. and Steele, A. (1999) Making oneself at home: The mediation of residential action. *International Journal of Urban and Regional Research*, 23(1), 88–102.

Sommer, R. (1967) Small group ecology. *Psychological Bulletin*, 67, 145–52.

Sommer, R. (1968) Intimacy ratings in five countries. *International Journal of Psychology*, 3, 109–14.

Soros, G. (1999) Choose a set of concrete goals for the Balkan stability pact. *International Herald Tribune*, (July 30), 8.

Stability Pact for South Eastern Europe (1999, June 10) *Stability Pact for South Eastern Europe*. Adopted during the German Presidency of the European Union, in Cologne, Germany.

Spector, B. I. (1993) Decision analysis for practical negotiation applications. *Theory and Decision*, 34, 183–99.

Spence, D. (1986). Narrative smoothing and clinical wisdom. In *Narrative Psychology: The Storied Nature of Human Conduct*, edited by T.R. Sarbin. London: Praeger.

Spiro, M. (1987) Collective representations and mental representations in religious symbol systems. In *Culture and Human Nature*, edited by B. Kilborne and L. Langness. Chicago: University of Chicago Press.

Spitz, P. (1978) Silent violence: Famine and inequality. *International Social Science Journal*, 30(4), 867–92.

Starkey, B., Boyer, M. A., and Wilkenfeld, J. (1999) *Negotiating a Complex World: An Introduction to International Negotiation*. Lanham, MD: Rowman & Littlefield.

State of World Conflict Report (1995–1996) Atlanta, GA: The International Negotiation Network (INN), The Carter Center of Emory University.

Stedman, S. J. (1991) *Peacemaking in Civil Wars: International Mediation in Zimbabwe*. Boulder, CO: Lynne Rienner.

Stedman, S. J. (1995) Alchemy for a new world order. *Foreign Affairs*, 74(3), 14–20.

Stedman, S. J. (1997) Spoiler problems in peace processes. *International Security*, 22(2), 5–53.

Steger, M. B. (1997) *The Quest for Evolutionary Socialism: Eduard Bernstein and Social Democracy*. Cambridge: Cambridge University Press.

Stepansky, P. (1977) A History of Aggression in Freud. *Psychological Issues*, 39. Madison, CT: International Universities Press.

Stephan, W. G. and Brigham, J. C. (1985) Intergroup contact: Introduction. *Journal of Social Issues*, 41, 1–8.

Stern, P. C. and Druckman, D. (2000) Evaluating interventions in history: The case of international conflict resolution. In *International*

Conflict Resolution After the Cold War, edited by P. C. Stern and D. Druckman. Washington, DC: National Academy Press.

Stern, P. C., Young, O., and Druckman, D. (eds) (1992) *Global Environmental Change: Understanding the Human Dimensions*. Washington, DC: National Academy Press.

Stone, D., Patton, B., and Heen, S. (1999) *Difficult Conversations: How to Discuss What Matters Most*. New York: Viking.

Stone, J. (1985) *Racial Conflict in Contemporary Society*. London: Fontana Press.

Story, A.L. (2004) Self-esteem and self-certainty: A motivation analysis. *European Journal of Personality* 18, 115–125.

Strauss, A. and Corbin, J. (1990) *Basics of Qualitative Research: Grounded Theory Procedures and Techniques*. Newbury Park, CA: Sage.

Strauss, D. (1993) Facilitated collaborative problem solving. In *Negotiation: Strategies for Mutual Gain: The Basic Seminar of the Harvard Program on Negotiations*, edited by L. Hall. Newbury Park, CA: Sage.

Strong, P. T. and Van Winkle, B. (1996) "Indian blood": Reflections on the reckoning and refiguring of Native North American identity. *Cultural Anthropology*, 11, 547–76.

Stutzman, J. and Shrock-Shenk, C. (1994) *Mediation and Facilitation Training Manual* (3rd edn). Akron, PA: Mennonite Conciliation Service.

Styron, W. (1979) *Sophie's Choice*. New York: Random House.

Sumner, W. G. (1906) *Folkways*. Boston: Ginn.

Sundstrom, E., De Meuse, K. P., and Futrell, D. (1990) Work teams: Applications and effectiveness. *American Psychologist*, 45, 120–33.

Sunoo, J. J.-M. (1990) Some guidelines for mediators of intercultural disputes. *Negotiation Journal*, October, 6(4), 383–89.

Susskind, L. and Weinstein, A. (1980) Toward a theory of environmental dispute resolution. *Boston College Environmental Affairs Law Review*, 9, 311–57.

Tajfel, H. (1970) Experiments in intergroup discrimination. *Scientific American*, 223, 96–102.

Tajfel, H. (ed) (1978) *Differentiation Between Social Groups*. New York: Academic Press.

Tajfel, H. (1981) *Human Groups and Social Categories*. Cambridge: Cambridge University Press.

Tajfel, H. and Forgas, J. (1981) Social categories: Cognitions, values and groups. In *Social Cognition: Perspectives in Everyday Understanding*, edited by J. Forgas. London: Academic Press.

Tajfel, H. and Turner, J. (1986) The social identity theory of inter-group behavior. In *Psychology of Intergroup Relations*, edited by W. G. Austin and S. Worchel (2nd edn). Chicago: Nelson-Hall Publishers.

Tannen, D. (1994) *Gender and Discourse*. Oxford: Oxford University Press.

Terhune, K. W. (1970) The effects of personality on cooperation and conflict. In *The Structure of Conflict*, edited by P. G. Swingle. New York: Academic Press.

Thatchenkery, T. (1999, September 16-19) *Appreciative Inquiry as Shifting Conversation: A Case Study on the Power of Reframing*. Paper presented at the Social Construction and the Relational Practices International Conference, Durham, New Hampshire.

Thibaut, J. W. and Kelley, H. H. (1959) *The Social Psychology of Groups*. New York: John Wiley & Sons.

Thomas, K. (1975) Thomas–Kilmann conflict mode instrument. In *The Handbook of Industrial and Organizational Psychology*, edited by M. Dunnett. Chicago: Rand McNally.

Thompson, E. P. (1966) *The Making of the English Working Class*. New York: Random House.

Thompson, J. D. and Van Houten, D. R. (1970) *The Behavioral Sciences: An Interpretation*. Reading, MA; London: Addison-Wesley.

Thompson, L. (1990) An examination of naïve and experienced negotiators. *Journal of Personality and Social Psychology*, 59, 82–90.

Thompson, L. (1993) The influence of experience on negotiation performance. *Journal of Experimental Social Psychology*, 29, 304–25.

Tilly, C. (1985) State making and war making as organized crime. In *Bringing the State Back In*, edited by P. Evans, D. Rueschemeyer, and T. Skocpol. Cambridge: Cambridge University Press.

Tils, R. (1997) Beware: mediation! Opportunities and risks of environmental mediation from the perspective of environmental associations and citizens' initiatives. *Forschungsjournal Neue Soziale Bewegungen*, 10(4), 43–52.

Tomlin, B. W. (1989) The stages of prenegotiation: The decision to negotiate North American Free Trade. In *Getting to the Table*, edited by J. G. Stein. Baltimore: Johns Hopkins University Press.

Tomm, K. (1987) Interventive interviewing: Part I. *Strategizing as a Fourth Guideline for the Therapist*. Family Process, 26, 3–13.

Touval, S. (1995a) Ethical dilemmas in international mediation. *Negotiation Journal*, 11(4), 333–7.

Touval, S. (1995b), Mediator's Flexibility and the UN Security Council. *Annals of the American Academy of Political and Social Science*, 542, 202–212.

Trappl, R. (2006) (ed) *Programming for Peace: Computer-Aided*

Methods for International Conflict Resolution and Prevention. Dordrecht, The Netherlands: Springer.

Trice, H. and Beyer, J. (1993) *The Cultures of Work Organizations.* Englewood Cliffs, NJ: Prentice Hall.

Trotsky, L. (1969) *The Age of Permanent Revolution: A Trotsky Anthology,* edited by I. Deutscher. New York: Pathfinder Press.

Trotsky, L. (1971) *The Struggle Against Fascism in Germany.* New York: Pathfinder Press.

Trotsky, L. (1980) *History of the Russian Revolution.* New York: Pathfinder Press.

Tutzauer, F. (1990) Integrative potential and information exchange as antecedents of joint benefit in negotiation dyads. *International Journal of Conflict Management,* 1, 153–73.

Tyler, T., Linda, E. A., Ohbuchi, K.-I., Sugawara, I., and Huo, Y. J. (1998) Conflict with outsiders: Disputing within and across cultural boundaries. *Personality and Social Psychology Bulletin,* 24(2), 137–46

Ulvila, J. W. (1990) Turning points: An analysis. In *U.S. Bases Overseas,* edited by J. W. McDonald and D. B. Bendahmane. Boulder, CO: Westview Press.

Ulvila, J. W. and Snyder, W. D. (1980) Negotiation of international oil tanker standards: An application of multiattribute value theory. *Operations Research,* 28, 81–96.

UNDP (1994) *Human Development Report, 1994.* Oxford: Oxford University Press.

United Nations (2002), March 11) *Report of the Special Committee on Peacekeeping Operations, Comprehensive Review of the Whole Question of Peace-keeping Operations in all their Aspects* (A/56/863).

Uphoff, N. (2000) Understanding social capital: Learning from the analysis and experience of participation. In *Social Capital: A Multifaceted Perspective,* edited by P. Dasgupta and I. Serageldin. Washington, DC: The World Bank.

Urquhart, B. (1994) *Hammarskjold.* New York: Norton.

Ury, W. L. (1999) *Getting to Peace: Transforming Conflict at Home, at Work, and in the World.* New York: Viking.

Uvin, P. (1998) *Aiding Violence: The Development Enterprise in Rwanda.* West Hartford, CT: Kumarian Press.

Uvin, P. (2001) Difficult choices in the new post-conflict agenda: The international community in Rwanda after the genocide. *Third World Quarterly,* 22(2), 177–89.

Valenzuela, J. S. and Valenzuela, A. (1978) Modernization and dependency: Alternative perspectives in the study of Latin American underdevelopment. *Comparative Politics,* 10(4), 535–57.

Vallacher, R. R. and Nowak, A. (2007) Dynamical social psychology:

Finding order in the flow of human experience. In *Social Psychology: Handbook of Basic Principles*, edited by A. W. Kruglanski and E. T. Higgins. New York: Guilford Press.

Valley, K. L., Neale, M. A., and Mannix, E. (1995) Friends, lovers, colleagues, strangers: The effects of relationships on the process and outcomes of dyadic negotiations. *Research on Negotiation in Organizations*, 5, 65–93.

Van Creveld, M. (1991) *The Transformation of War*. New York: The Free Press.

Van der Merwe, H. (1989) *Pursuing Justice and Peace in South Africa*. London: Routledge.

Vasquez, J. A. (1993) *The War Puzzle*. Cambridge Studies in International Relations: 27). Cambridge: Cambridge University Press.

Väyrynen, R. (1991) To settle or to transform? Perspectives on the resolution of national and international conflicts. In *New Directions in Conflict Theory: Conflict Resolution and Conflict Transformation*, edited by R. Väyrynen. London: Sage.

Väyrynen, R. (1999) From conflict resolution to conflict transformation: A critical view. In *The New Agenda for Peace Research*, edited by H.-W. Jeong. Aldershot: Ashgate.

Verdery, K. (1991) Theorizing socialism: A prologue to the "transition". *American Ethnologist*, 18, 419–39.

Verdery, K. (1995) *National Ideology Under Socialism: Identity and Cultural Politics in Ceausescu's Romania*. Berkeley: University of California Press.

Volkan, V. D. (1985) The need to have enemies and allies: A developmental approach. *Political Psychology*, 6, 219–47.

Volkan, V. D. (1988) *The Need to Have Enemies and Allies: From Clinical Practice to International Relationships*. New York: Jason Aronson.

Volkan, V. D. (1997) *Bloodlines: From Ethnic Pride to Ethnic Terrorism*. Boulder, CO: Westview Press.

von Foerster, H. (1984) On constructing a reality. In *The Invented Reality: How Do We Know What We Believe We Know? Contributions to Constructivism*, edited by P. Watzlawick (1st edn, pp. 41–61). New York: Norton.

Von Neumann, J. and Morgenstern, O. (1944) *Theory of Games and Economic Behavior*. Princeton, NJ: Princeton University Press.

Wagner, L. M. (1998) *Problem-solving and Convergent Bargaining: An Analysis of Negotiation Processes and Their Outcomes*. Unpublished doctoral dissertation, The Johns Hopkins University.

Waldrop, M. M. (1992) *Complexity: The Emerging Science at the Edge of Order and Chaos*. New York; London: Simon & Schuster.

Walker, S. G. (2000, July) *Role Identities and the Operational Codes of Political Leaders*. Paper Presented at the Annual Meeting of the International Society of Political Psychology, Seattle.

Wall, J. A. Jr. and Callister, R. R. (1995) Ho'oponopono: Some lessons from Hawaiian mediation. *Negotiation Journal*, 11(1), 45–54.

Wall, J. A. Jr. and Callister, R. R. (1999) Malaysian community mediation. *Journal of Conflict Resolution*, 43(3), 343–65.

Wall, J. A. and Druckman, D. (2003) Mediating in peacekeeping missions. *Journal of Conflict Resolution*, 47(5), 693–705.

Wall, J. A. Jr., Sohn, D.-W., Cleeton, N., and Jin, D. J. (1995) Community and family mediation in the People's Republic of China. *International Journal of Conflict Management*, 6(1), 30–47.

Wallerstein, I. (1979) *The Capitalist World-Economy*. Cambridge, UK: Cambridge University Press.

Walton, J. and Ragin, C. (1990) Global and national sources of political protest: Third world responses to the debt crisis. *American Sociological Review*, 55(6), 876–890.

Walton, R. E. (1969) *Interpersonal Peacemaking: Confrontations and Third-Party Consultation*. Reading, MA: Addison-Wesley.

Walton, R. E. and McKersie, R. B. (1965) *A Behavioral Theory of Labor Negotiations: An Analysis of a Social Interaction System*. New York: McGraw-Hill.

Waltz, K. N. (1959) *Man, the State, and War: A Theoretical Analysis*. New York: Columbia University Press.

Washington Post (2002) Editorial: After the war. *Washington Post*, (November 12), A24.

Watson, G. (1945) Action for Unity. New York: Harper.

Watson-Gegeo, K. and White, G. (eds) (1990) Disentangling: Conflict Discourse in Pacific Societies. Stanford, CA: Stanford University Press.

Webb, K., Koutrakou, V., and Walters, M. (1996) The Yugoslavian conflict, European mediation, and the contingency model: A critical perspective. In *Resolving International Conflicts: The Theory and Practice of Mediation*, edited by J. Bercovitch. Boulder, CO: Lynne Rienner.

Weber, M. (1956) *Max Weber, Essays in Sociology*, translated by W. Gerth and C. Wright Mills. New York: Oxford University Press.

Weber, M. (1964) *Max Weber: The Theory of Social and Economic Organization*, edited by T. Parsons. New York: The Free Press.

Weber, M. (1977) *Theory of Social and Economic Organization*, Introduction by T. Parsons. New York: The Free Press.

Webne-Behrman, H. (1998) *The Practice of Facilitation: Managing Group Process and Solving Problems*. Westport, CT: Quorum Books.

Webster's New Collegiate Dictionary (1961) Springfield, MA: G. & C. Merriam.

Webster's New World Dictionary of the American Language (1978) New York: William Collins/World Publishing.

Wedge, B. (1970) A psychiatric model for intercession in intergroup conflict. *Journal of Applied Behavioral Science*, 6, 733–61.

Wedge, B. (1979) Reflections on a psychiatric model for intercession in intergroup conflict. In *Organizational Change Sourcebook II: Cases in Conflict Management*, edited by L. D. Goodstein, B. Lubin, and A. W. Lubin. LaJolla, CA: University Associates.

Wehr, P. (1979) Conflict Regulation. Boulder, CO: Westview Press.

Wehr, P. and Lederach, J. P. (1991) Mediating conflict in Central America. *Journal of Peace Research*, 28(1), 85–98.

Weinhold, B. K. and Weinhold, J. B. (2000) *Conflict Resolution: The Partnership Way*. Denver: Love Publishing.

Weiss, S. (1994a) Negotiating with Romans, part I. *Sloan Management Review*, 35(Winter), 51–61.

Weiss, S. (1994b) Negotiating With Romans, part II. *Sloan Management Review*, 35(Spring), 85–99.

Weiss, S. (1996) International negotiations: Bricks, mortar, and prospects. In *Handbook for International Management Research*, edited by B. J. Punnett and O. Shenkar. Cambridge, MA: Blackwell.

Wells, J. C. and Liebman, W. B. (1996) New models of negotiation, dispute resolution, and joint problem solving. *Negotiation Journal*, 12(2), 119–38.

Wendt, A. (1999) *Social Theory of International Politics*. Cambridge: Cambridge University Press.

White, G. and Kirkpatrick, J. (eds) (1985) *Person, Self and Experience: Exploring Pacific Ethnopsychologies*. Berkeley: University of California Press.

White, M. (1989) The externalizing of the problem and the reauthoring of lives and relationships. In *Selected Papers*, edited by M. White. Adelaide, Australia: Dulwich Center Publications.

White, M. and Epston, D. (1991) *Narrative Means to Therapeutic Ends*. New York: Norton.

White, N. D. (1997) *Keeping the Peace*. Manchester: Manchester University Press.

White, N. D. (2001) Commentary on the Report of the Panel on United Nations Peace Operations (the Brahimi report). *Journal of Conflict and Security Law*, 6(1), 127–46.

Whitman, J. (ed) (2000) *Peacekeeping and the UN Agencies*. Cambridge: Cambridge University Press.

Whitworth, S. (2004), *Men, Militarism and UN Peacekeeping: A Gendered Analysis.* Boulder, CO.: Lynne Rienner.

Williams, A. (2000) *Preventing War: The United Nations and Macedonia.* Lanham; Boulder; New York; Oxford: Rowman & Littlefield.

Williams, A. (2005) Second track conflict resolution processes in the Moldova conflict, 1993–2000. In *Paving the Way; Contributions of Interactive Conflict Resolution to Peacemaking,* edited by R. J. Fisher. Lanhan, MD: Lexington Books.

Williams, P.D. (2006) Military responses to mass killing: The African Union mission in Sudan. *International Peacekeeping,* 13(2), 168–83.

Williams, R. (1983) *Keywords.* New York: Oxford University Press.

Williams, R. M. Jr. (1947) *The Reduction of Intergroup Tensions: A Survey of Research on Ethnic, Racial, and Religious Group Tensions.* New York: Social Science Research Council, Bulletin 57.

Wilson, E. O. (1998a) Back from chaos. *The Atlantic Monthly,* 281(3), 41–4, 46–9, 52, 54–6, 58–9, 62.

Wilson, E. O. (1998b) *Consilience: The Unity of Knowledge.* New York: Knopf.

Wilson, W. W. (1971) Reciprocation and other techniques for inducing cooperation in the prisoner's dilemma game. *Journal of Conflict Resolution,* 15, 167–95.

Winham, G. R. (1979) Practitioners' views of international negotiation. *World Politics,* 32, 111–35.

Winslade, J. and Monk, G. (2000) *Narrative Mediation: A New Approach to Conflict Resolution.* San Francisco: Jossey-Bass.

Wolf, E. (1999) *Peasant Wars of the Twentieth Century.* Norman: University of Oklahoma Press.

Woodhouse, T. and Ramsbotham, O. (eds) (2000) *Peacekeeping and Conflict Resolution.* London: Frank Cass.

Woodward, S. L. (2005) *The Inequality of Violence: On the Discovery of Civil Wars as a Threat to 'the North' in the 1990s and the Debate over Causes and Solutions.* Washington, DC: American Political Science Association Taskforce on Difference and Inequality in the Developing World.

World Bank. (1998) *Post-Conflict Reconstruction: The Role of the World Bank.* Washington, DC: The World Bank.

Yin, J. (1984) *Government of Socialist China.* Lantham, MD: University Press of America.

Yngvesson, B. (1993) *Virtuous Citizens, Disruptive Subjects: Order and Complaint in a New England Court.* New York: Routledge.

Zaagman, R. and Thorburn, J. (1997) *The Role of the High Commissioner on National Minorities in OSCE Conflict Prevention: An Introduction.* The Hague: The Foundation on Inter-Ethnic Relations.

Zaher, S. (1998) The feminization of family mediation. *Dispute Resolution Journal*, 53(2), 36–43.

Zartman, I. W. (1989) *Ripe for Resolution: Conflict and Intervention in Africa* (2nd edn). New York: Oxford University Press.

Zartman, I. W. (1993) A skeptic's view. In *Culture and Negotiation*, edited by G. Faure and J. Rubin. Newbury Park, CA: Sage.

Zartman, I. W. (ed) (1994) *International Multilateral Negotiation*. San Francisco: Jossey-Bass.

Zartman, I. W. (2000) Ripeness: The hurting stalemate and beyond. In *International Conflict Resolution After the Cold War*, edited by P. C. Stern and D. Druckman (eds). Washington, DC: National Academy Press.

Zechmeister, K. and Druckman, D. (1973) Determinants of resolving a conflict of interest: A simulation of political decision making. *Journal of Conflict Resolution*, 17, 63–88.

Zetterburg, H. (1966) *On Theory and Verification in Sociology*. Totowa, NJ: Bedminster Press.

Zimbardo, P. G. (1970) The human choice: Individuation, reason, and order versus deindividuation, impulse and chaos. In *Nebraska Symposium on Motivation, 1969*, edited by W. J. Arnold and D. Levine (vol. 17, pp. 237–307). Lincoln: University of Nebraska Press.

Zimmerman, J. and Coyle, V. (1991) Council: Reviving the art of listening. *Utne Reader*, (March/April), 79–85.

INDEX